STARLIST
2000

STARLIST 2000

2000

A Quick Reference
Star Catalog for Astronomers

Richard Dibon-Smith

WILEY SCIENCE EDITIONS

John Wiley & Sons, Inc.
New York • Chichester • Brisbane • Toronto • Singapore

In recognition of the importance of preserving what has been written, it is a policy of John Wiley & Sons, Inc., to have books of enduring value published in the United States printed on acid-free paper, and we exert our best efforts to that end.

Copyright © 1992 by Richard Dibon-Smith

Published by John Wiley & Sons, Inc.

All rights reserved. Published simultaneously in Canada.

Reproduction or translation of any part of this work beyond that permitted by section 107 or 108 of the 1976 United States Copyright Act without the permission of the copyright owner is unlawful. Requests for permission or further information should be addressed to the Permissions Department, John Wiley & Sons, Inc.

This publication is designed to provide accurate and authoritative information in regard to the subject matter covered. It is sold with the understanding that the publisher is not engaged in rendering legal, accounting or other professional service. If legal advice or other expert assistance is required, the services of a competent professional person should be sought. FROM A DECLARATION OF PRINCIPLES JOINTLY ADOPTED BY A COMMITTEE OF THE AMERICAN BAR ASSOCIATION AND A COMMITTEE OF PUBLISHERS.

Library of Congress Cataloging in Publication Data
Dibon-Smith, Richard, 1939–
    StarList 2000: A Quick Reference Star Catalog for Astronomers/ Richard Dibon-Smith.
      p.   cm.
    Includes indexes.
    ISBN 0-471-55895-8 (paper : acid-free)
    1. Stars–Atlases. I. Title. II. Title: StarList 2000.
  III. Title: Starlist two thousand.
  QB65.D53 1992
  523.8'022'3–dc20
                                                   92-2907

Printed in the United States of America
10 9 8 7 6 5 4 3 2 1

To Deleine

Acknowledgments

I would like to thank Marlene Cummins, Librarian, and Rosemary Diamond, Library Assistant, who together constitute the Astronomy Library of the University of Toronto. Their continued assistance over the past two and a half years has made my own work much easier.

My appreciation to Bill Frucht and Fred Schaaf, whose kind support helped convince others that the manuscript showed some promise; to Kate Bradford of John Wiley & Sons, who expertly smoothed my path from writer to author; to Karen Hawk, Leslie Trimmer, Al Davis, and many more, whose hard work transformed my rough manuscript into the book you now see.

To my two boys, Eric and Christopher, who have long felt that I spent too much time at the computer, while Commander Keen anxiously awaited their attention.

And especially to my wife Marie-Madeleine. I don't know where she finds the patience.

Preface

Several years ago, having just finished a long and involved manuscript on other matters, I turned with some relief to enjoy a former pastime—stargazing. Purchasing a telescope, I set about to leisurely reexplore the skies. And to jostle my none-too-photographic memory, I collected a number of recently published reference books: Tirion's wonderful *Star Atlas*, Burnham's three-volume *Celestial Handbook*, and other, smaller works that helped make the reentry into an old hobby that much more enjoyable.

As I progressed, it became evident that something was missing from my library. What I really needed was one general guide to the stars that answered questions that popped up from time to time: Which was larger, Sirius or Vega? When are the red dwarfs of 70 Ophiuchi most easily resolved? What is the luminosity of Rigel? When will Mira come up to full brightness?

So I began taking notes, from one book and another, from one magazine and another. Gradually, note collection became a full-time occupation, and as the questions got more involved, I found myself spending much of my time at the Astronomy Library of the University of Toronto.

As the research continued, other ideas came to mind. It seemed a good idea to list the best binaries in one section and to group all the variable stars in another. Thus Parts Two and Three of this book were born. Finally, to help in my calculations, I wrote some programs for a small programmable calculator. This latter project turned out so well that it too found a permanent place, as the Appendix.

Having satisfied myself that I had filled that open spot on my shelves reserved for a general reference work, I thought that others might also find the book useful. So I offer it to you, whether you are a casual stargazer who has the occasional need for such a work or a more serious student of astronomy who becomes frustrated at having to thumb through a number of references to track down that elusive answer.

Although more and more books devoted to astronomy are incorporating the epoch 2000 figures into their data, there are still, surprisingly, many books that have stuck to the epoch 1950 data. I find this incomprehensible. The main stress throughout this guide is that the data are valid now, not four or five decades ago! You will thus find orbital paths of many rapid-motion binaries, completely redrawn for the year 2000 and beyond. And variable star enthusiasts will find the most favorable future dates to watch for maximum brightnesses.

Every effort has been made to be as accurate and error-free as possible. Even so, it is inevitable that errors will crop up. I would appreciate being notified if you find any errors—or suspected errors. And concerning the proposed dates of the maximum brightness of long-period variables, I would be interested to receive your observational data, giving the exact time (GMT or local, be sure to specify which!) and the date. This would make future estimates more accurate. Also, I wish to ask accomplished investigators of double stars for any pertinent information relating to the angle of separation and distance among the list of binaries in Part Two. (Much of the published data in this area is considerably out of date.) Again, please include the date and time of observation. I may be reached by E-mail through CompuServe (76437,177) or GEnie (R.DIBONSMITH), or you may write me in care of the publisher.

Richard Dibon-Smith
Toronto

Contents

STARLIST
2000

Introduction

StarList 2000 is divided into three parts: (1) the StarList, (2) a Binary Star section, and (3) a Variable Star section. There is also a special appendix containing a number of BASIC programs, written especially for this book, as well as a set of indexes.

Part 1: The StarList   This is the main body of the book: over 2400 stars, grouped by constellation, with a wealth of data pertaining to each entry. The main criterion for a star's selection was its apparent magnitude. Because of space considerations, three different categories of "bright stars" have been made. First, all stars that have a Greek letter ("Bayer letter") and visual magnitude equal to or brighter than 5.50 are included in *StarList 2000*. Second, all "Flamsteed stars" (numbered stars) equal to or brighter than 5.25 visual magnitude are included. Then there is a third category, including binary stars, variable stars, and a number of others that don't fit the first two categories. These additional stars may possess characteristics of particular interest, such as a very high proper motion; for example, Barnard's Star in Ophiuchus, which is very dim at magnitude 10.31. Or a star may be an interesting binary or variable, but be rather dim. Such stars have been added if it is thought they deserved particular recognition because of their inherent interest, despite their lower magnitude.

Following is a summary of the star designations that have been used in *StarList 2000:*

- The stars with *Bayer letters* rank first. In 1603, Johann Bayer assigned Greek letters to the brightest stars in each constellation, usually—but not always—in descending order of apparent brightness. These stars are listed first.

- The stars with *Flamsteed numbers* but no Bayer letters are given next. In the early 1700s John Flamsteed assigned numbers to the bright stars in each constellation, in order of right ascension. One eventually runs out of Greek letters, but there is no limit to the number of stars that can be given a Flamsteed number. Thus, this method of cataloguing stars has proven very useful.

- The *binary stars* are then listed. While many stars with Flamsteed numbers and Bayer letters are binaries, they are not usually known by their binary designation *except when treated as a binary*. In other words, if we speak of γ Virginis, we are dealing with this star in a general way. When we call this star Σ1670, we are dealing with the same star as a binary. Therefore, when a star has been included in the StarList because it is an interesting binary, it has been given its binary designation, even though it may have a Flamsteed number. An example of such a binary is Σ1909, found in Bootes. This star also goes under the Flamsteed number 44 Boo. It is found in the StarList as Σ1909 by virtue of its interesting characteristics as a binary.

  Binary stars have been catalogued over the years by their discoverer. Thus the designation of binaries has been fairly haphazard, with names like Σ186, β1111, OΣ514, h5014, and so on. There is, however, a better way to designate binaries. This is with the Aitken Double Star (ADS) catalogue number. The ADS number of each binary is found in the back of the book, in the index by right ascension.

- The variable stars are listed next. These stars have a confusing cataloguing system that reflects the chaotic method by which stars came to be designated. When the Bayer letters ran out (that is, the Greek alphabet had been exhausted), all remaining stars were given Roman letters, first a, b, c, and so on, then A, B, C, and so on. However, in the middle of the 19th century F. W. A. Argelander began using the letters R through Z to designate variable stars. After a while it was found that there were far too many variables for this system, and it was decided to double up. So after Z came RR through RZ, then SS through SZ, and so on through ZZ, and if there were still more variables to name, AA through QZ (but omitting J) were used. This ensured a total of 334 variables per constellation. But still that was not enough, and another system was introduced: the prefix V plus a number (starting at 335). Many faint stars that would otherwise go unnamed have been discovered to be variable and therefore acquired an official variable designation. For example, one fairly faint star in Ophiuchus would still be unnamed except that it was discovered some time ago to be a variable. So now it is listed as V2105 in that constellation.

- Last come the unnamed stars. Some constellations have a considerable number of bright stars that have never received any designation. Canis Major, for example, has nine bright stars listed that have no name; the Southern Hemisphere constellation Puppis has 22 bright stars that have never been named.

alpha	α	nu	ν
beta	β	xi	ξ
gamma	γ	omicron	o
delta	δ	pi	π
epsilon	ε	rho	ρ
zeta	ζ	sigma	σ
eta	η	tau	τ
theta	θ	upsilon	υ
iota	ι	phi	φ
kappa	κ	chi	χ
lambda	λ	psi	ψ
mu	μ	omega	ω

Convention has it that the constellations are given in Latin. When a star is identified, the genitive case of the constellation is used, for example, α Andromedæ.

Part 2: The Binary Star Section   This section deals in some detail with all stars designated in Part 1 as a binary. Please note that many stars that appear in Part 1 are binaries but are not so designated in the StarList. Many stars have very faint companions, unresolved except with very sophisticated equipment. The StarList includes only those binaries in which both components are bright enough to be observed by most amateur observers. For many of these, a small or medium telescope is all that is required to resolve the companions.

This section is composed of several parts. First comes the listing, by constellation, of all designated binaries. This listing gives the ADS catalogue number, the apparent magnitude of the primary (m_1) and the principal companion (m_2), then the combined visual magnitude ("comb."). This figure is the actual brightness as seen by an observer. It is the result of the combined brightnesses of both stars; the more distant the companion from its primary, or the weaker the companion, the less its influence to make the binary seem brighter than the primary taken by itself.

The remarks on page 229 explain the entries in this first part. Following this part comes the table of Orbital Elements of selected binaries, which is useful for those who wish to calculate the separation and position angle of the binary, given any epoch. The last column gives these values for specific years, such as 2000, 2010, and 2020. Thus, one will be able to judge whether a particular binary can be resolved or not.

The last part in the Binary Section is a collection of orbits, drawn especially for *StarList 2000* by the author. Many reference books give some of these stars' orbits, but often the data are out of date. The drawn orbits included here begin with the year 2000 (or a little earlier in some instances), so these orbits will remain useful references for a long time to come.

Part 3: The Variable Star Section   As with the binary stars, this section gives complete information on all aspects of the variable stars found in *StarList 2000*. Unlike the binary stars, however, every star in the StarList that is a variable is listed here. The data are correct at the time of publication. Thus, a number of stars recently discovered to be variable can be found here, updating older references.

The following data are given: the type of variable; maximum and minimum ranges; the epoch (Julian Date) of the establishment of the data; the variable's period in days, and—a unique feature of *StarList 2000*—the most favorable viewing date. This last feature gives the best estimate of when each Mira-type variable should reach its maximum brightness. For a non-Mira variable, the variable's period, converted to days, hours, minutes, and seconds, is given in square brackets [ ].

Appendix and Indexes   At the back of the book are a number of special features. First, there is an Appendix containing a number of programs written in BASIC, which the astronomy enthusiast may find useful. Then comes the right ascension index, in which all stars that appear in the StarList are listed by right ascension. In addition, the ADS number is given to all binaries, and all other official designations of the stars are given. Thus, α Ursæ Majoris is also listed as 50 UMa (the Flamsteed number) and β1077 (which is its binary designation). The last columns indicate, at each of three different latitudes, the rising and setting azimuths of each star or whether it is circumpolar at that latitude—either in the Northern Hemisphere, *cp,* or in the Southern Hemisphere, *(cp).* The notation *nv* indicates "not visible."

Following the right ascension index is a list of names of stars that are more often recognized by a name than by a letter or number. If in your readings you come across the name *Wesen,* for example, and are not sure which star this is, you can quickly identify it as δ CMa.

The final index is a complete list of all stars found in the *StarList 2000,* by constellation. This index is useful to consult if you wish to verify the inclusion of a particular star without taking the time to look up the constellation. All entries here are in the same order as found in the StarList.

The next several pages present a brief discussion of the approach taken in compiling this work, particularly concerning the discrepancies one encounters while comparing the data of various authorities. Then a number of useful formulas, tables, and graphs pertaining to the StarList are given.

A Note on the Discrepancies

A feature of the StarList is the comparison of such items as absolute magnitude, distance, and parallax among various authorities. At times the values are very far apart. The reader may be tempted to think that an error has been made by one of the authorities or that a printing error has been allowed to sneak through.

In most cases the discrepancies do not reflect errors, only points of view. Each authority has his or her source; the data collected by each source, the methods of analyzing these data, and the statistical parameters used to determine the "correct" values all help to create different results for quite a few of the stars on the StarList.

Many discrepancies result from slight differences over an accepted value. As an example, Burnham uses an absolute magnitude for the Sun of +4.8 (which is the value many authorities use). On the other hand, the *Observer's Handbook* uses +4.7. We have adopted the value +4.74 from Michael Stix's recent book, *The Sun* (Berlin, 1989). This difference of +0.06 between the StarList and Burnham creates a slight disparity in the calculated luminosities of all stars. For this reason, only widely disparate values are reported.

Our Use of the Figures

Some references tend to report certain figures to a precision that exceeds statistical reality. To say, for example, that a star is 2973 light years away and has a luminosity of 23,768 Suns, a radius of 183.1 Suns, and a temperature of 5322 K is to mislead the reader into accepting accuracies that do not exist.

Like all other scientific data, the physical characteristics of the stars are deduced from an accumulation of observations and calculations. The resulting averages are always accompanied, in scientific literature, by an appended figure that tells the reader just how accurate the values really are. This figure is the *standard deviation,* and it is an invaluable tool in statistical analysis.

To give an example of the use of the standard deviation, let us take the fairly precise parallax of the nearby Barnard's Star, in Ophiuchus. As cited by W. Gliese, this star has a parallax of 0.552″ with what is called a "probable error" of ±0.01″. It is assumed here that by this the writer is referring to the standard deviation (SD).

Without dwelling at length on statistical methods, let us accept that ±2 SD gives us the maximum and minimum range for 95 percent of all observed data. In other words, only 5 percent of the observed parallaxes of this star fall outside this range. If we were to take our maximum and minimum limits out to three times the standard deviation, we would have 99 percent of the observed data (theoretically 99.7 percent). This measure is the generally accepted norm for statistical analysis. That is to say, if we know the standard deviation of any statistical average, we can find the expected limits of any future observation, with only a 1 percent failure rate.

Taking Barnard's Star, Gliese gives us a standard deviation of ±0.01″. Three times this value added and subtracted from 0.552″ gives us the range of 0.549″ to 0.555″. Converting these to distance, we obtain 5.874–5.938 light years, and it is impossible to establish a more precise value. If these two extremes are averaged, we get a distance of 5.906 light years. For distances of less than 15 light years, we report to the nearest one-hundredth. Thus, in the StarList we give the distance of Barnard's Star as 5.91 l.y.

Added to the difficulty of measuring the properties of the stars are the errors built into the general mathematical formulas used to find the relationships between one property and another. Let us take, as an example, the simple calculation of the luminosity of a star, given the absolute magnitude (see page 7 for the formula). If a star is reported to have an absolute magnitude of +4.0, it will then have a luminosity of 2.0 (exactly twice the brightness of the Sun if seen from the same distance). If the absolute magnitude is +4.1, the luminosity then drops off to 1.8. And if the star instead should have an absolute magnitude of +5.5, then the luminosity drops to 0.5. Often the choice between an absolute magnitude of +4 and +5.5 (to give an example) is not easy to make, and you will notice that a number of stars have even a wider range of possibilities.

Star distances have been rounded to two significant figures. Thus a computer-generated distance of 371 light years is reported as 370, and a distance of 2771 light years is given as 2800.

The StarList, then, is not to be taken as always providing the "right" answer; it is a conscientious effort to supply the interested reader with as much information as possible, information that is always subject to further refinement. In many cases, we present only what can be described as the best guess (although many in the field might take umbrage at the thought that their hard work was seen in such a light). Of course, I do not wish to belittle their efforts. Rather, I would wish that the user of this reference book might accept the figures found on these pages as only the latest results in an ongoing effort to understand the makeup of our Universe and of all its marvelous occupants.

Radial Velocities

A particularly troublesome property of stars is their radial velocity (RV). Many stars have variable RVs. Disparate results happen when one's observations are made at different times from those of another observer. Several authorities have published catalogs of the radial velocities of stars, and it is not surprising that not all their results agree. Below is a table of the most widely disparate RVs (for stars cited on the StarList).

The two main star catalogs (*Yale Bright Star Catalogue* and the *Sky Catalogue*) use different sources for the radial velocities. The *Sky Catalogue* relies on Ralph E. Wilson, *General Catalogue of Stellar Radial Velocities* (Washington, D.C., 1953). The *Yale Catalogue* uses a number of sources, more recent than Wilson. The main source is David S. Evans, *Catalogue of Stellar Radial Velocities* (Strasbourg, 1967). Also cited is M. Barbier and M. Petit, *Bibliographic Catalogue of Stellar Radial Velocities* (Strasbourg, 1976).

We have relied on the Yale data throughout, and on Evans and others (noted) if the star is not in the *Bright Star Catalogue*. Whenever gross differences (that is, of about 20 percent or more) appear between the Yale and *Sky* catalogues, then the *Sky Catalogue* values are mentioned in the notes. The most flagrant differences are given in the following list. Note the degree of reliability (graded A through E, as noted by both Evans and Wilson).

Star	Evans	Wilson	Star	Evans	Wilson
ε Cen	+3 C	+5.6 B	χ Lup	+5 E	−18 C
λ Cen	−1.4 D	+7.9 B	Σ2470A Lyr	−17.3 C	−8 C
μ Cen	+9.1 C	+12.6 B	S Mus	+11.4 B	0 B
π Cen	+9.4 C	+16 C	ψ Per	−1.1 A	+0.3 A
ζ Cha	−42 C	−52 D	SX Phe	−29 −	15 C
θ Cir	+3 C	−4 C	δ Pic	+30.6 A	−2 D
ζ Crv	−6.4 C	+2 D	ρ Sco	−0.4 C	+2.8 B
κ Cru	−3.5 C	−1.3 B	τ Sco	+2.0 A	−0.7 A
16 Del	+2 C	−1 C	υ Sco	+8 −	+18 C
ω Eri	−6 C	−9 C	γ TrA	−3 C	0 C
δ Hyi	+6 D	11 C	R TrA	−13.8 C	−18.9 B
γ Lup	+2.3 C	+6 C	S TrA	+4.9 B	+2.0 B
δ Lup	+0.2 C	+2 C	δ¹ Vel	+7 C	+2.2 B
ε Lup	+7.9 C	+4 C	ψ Vel	+8.8 B	+12.0 B
κ¹ Lup	−6 C	+3 C			

Definitions and Formulas

The magnitude of a star is the measure of its brightness. While there are various ways by which a star's magnitude can be expressed, we will deal here with only the two most common. These are the apparent magnitude (m) and the absolute magnitude (M).

The law of light propagation tells us that the brightness of a star drops with the square of its distance. That is, if a star at distance x has brightness y, its brightness would become $(\frac{1}{2})^2 y$, or $\frac{1}{4}y$, if it were moved to $2x$ distance. If moved to $3x$ distance, its brightness would diminish to $(\frac{1}{3})^2$, or one-ninth the original brightness.

The apparent magnitude of a star depends not only on the distance of that star but also on its absolute brightness. A more distant, but inherently brighter, star may appear brighter to us than a closer but inherently dimmer star.

The *apparent magnitude* (m) of a star is a measure of its brightness as seen from Earth. The magnitude scale is logarithmic, because vision (like other senses) responds to ratios rather than differences. A star with apparent magnitude m is 100 times as bright as a star with magnitude $m+5$. In other words, a difference of one magnitude means a brightness ratio of $100^{1/5} = 2.512$. Therefore, one can compare the apparent brightness l of any two stars:

$$\frac{l_1}{l_2} = 2.512^{(m_2 - m_1)}$$

where m_1 and m_2 are the visual magnitudes of stars 1 and 2.

Example: Given Arcturus ($m = -0.04$) and Deneb ($m = 1.25$): Then Arcturus/Deneb $= 2.512^{(1.25+0.04)} = 3.05$. That is, Arcturus appears three times as bright as Deneb.

To place each star on an equal comparison and thus establish its *absolute magnitude* (M), it is now conventional to state its brightness as if seen 10 parsecs (33 light-years) away, where its parallax would be 0.100″. For instance, if the Sun were placed at 33 light-years distance, it would have a 4.74 magnitude as seen on Earth, about the same as ρ Orionis or φ Virginis or ζ Ursæ Majoris appears to us.

Given the parallax of a star (π) and its apparent magnitude, the absolute magnitude can be computed:

$$M = m + 5 + 5 \log \pi$$

Example: Given α CMi: $m = 0.38$, $\pi = 0.285″$. Then $M = 0.38 + 5 + 5(\log 0.285)$; $M = 2.65$.

Given the distance of a star (D) in light-years and its apparent magnitude, then:

$$M = m + 5 - 5 \log(D/3.26)$$

Example: Given 41 And: $m = 5.03$, $D = 105$ l.y. Then $M = 5.03 + 5 - 5 (\log 32.21)$; $M = 2.5$.

Luminosity($\mathcal{L}$)   This term refers to the absolute brightness of a star, measuring the total outflow of radiation in ergs per second. The Sun's luminosity($\mathcal{L}_0$) is taken as the standard reference, to which other stars are compared.

The Sun has a luminosity of 3.90×10^{33} ergs/sec. To find the luminosity of another star:

$$\log \frac{\mathcal{L}}{\mathcal{L}_0} = 0.4(M_0 - M)$$

where M_0 is the absolute magnitude of the Sun ($= 4.74$), and M is the absolute magnitude of another star.

Example: Given Sirius: $M = 1.4$. Then $\log \mathscr{L}/\mathscr{L}_0 = 0.4(4.74 - 1.4) = 1.34$. Inverse $\log = 21.68$. Thus, the luminosity of Sirius is almost 22 times that of the Sun, or about 8.6×10^{34} ergs per sec.

Formulas Pertaining to the StarList

To find	Given	Formula
M	m, distance in parsecs (d)	$M = m + 5 - 5(\log d)$
M	m, π (parallax)	$M = m + 5 + 5(\log \pi)$
l.y.	π	$D = \text{(l.y.)} = 3.26/\pi$
l.y.	distance in parsecs (d)	$D = \text{(l.y.)} = 3.26d$
D (distance)	m, M	$\log D = (m + 5 - M)/5$ (in pc) $\log D = (m + 5 - M)(.652)$ (in l.y.)
μ (proper motion)	proper motion in right ascension, $\mu(\alpha)''$ and proper motion in declination, $\mu(\delta)''$	$\mu = \sqrt{\mu(\alpha)^2 + \mu(\delta)^2}$
$\mu(\alpha)''$	$\mu(\alpha)^s$ and δ of star	$\mu(\alpha)'' = 15\mu(\alpha)^s(\cos \delta)$
θ (direction of movement)	$\mu(\alpha)''$, $\mu(\delta)''$	$\theta^* = \tan^{-1}\left(\dfrac{\mu(\alpha)}{\mu(\delta)}\right)$ (*see note below)
V (velocity in space)	π, μ, RV	$V = \sqrt{\left[\dfrac{4.74\mu}{\pi}\right]^2 + RV^2}$
D_s (star's diameter, compared to Sun's)	T (temp. in K), $\mathscr{L}$ (Luminosity)	$D_s = \sqrt{\mathscr{L}}\left(\dfrac{5800}{T}\right)^2$
$\mathscr{L}/\mathscr{L}_0$ (Luminosity of star, compared to Sun's)	M	$\log \mathscr{L}/\mathscr{L}_0 = 0.4(4.74 - M)$

Formulas Pertaining to the Binary Section

The mass of a binary system, compared to the Sun	Separation in arcsec (s) and the period P	$M + M^1 = s^3/\pi^3 P^2$
Combined magnitude of two (binary) stars	m_1 and m_2	$m_{comb} = m_2 - 2.5 \log [\text{inv log } 0.4(m_2 - m_1) + 1]$

*Add the appropriate amount, depending on the sign of both $\mu(\alpha)$ and $\mu(\delta)$:

$\dfrac{\mu(\alpha)+}{\mu(\delta)+}$: use the result as is $\dfrac{\mu(\alpha)+}{\mu(\delta)-}$: $+ 180°$ $\dfrac{\mu(\alpha)-}{\mu(\delta)-}$: $+ 180°$ $\dfrac{\mu(\alpha)-}{\mu(\delta)+}$: $+ 360°$

Table I.1   Spectral types and corresponding temperatures

Spectral type		Temperature (K)	Star example
WR	rare, very luminous	~50,000	γ² Vel
O	extremely hot; blue	28,000–50,000	Alnitak (ζ Ori)
B	hot, blue stars	10,000–28,000	Regulus (α Leo)
A	blue-white stars	7500–10,000	Vega (α Lyr)
F	white stars	6000–7500	Procyon (α CMi)
G	yellow stars	5000–6000	Capella (α Aur)
K	orange stars	3500–5000	Aldebaran (α Tau)
M	red giants	2000–3500	Ras Algethi (α Her)
S	red giants (zirconium)	2000–3500	R Andromedæ
C	red giants (carbon stars)	<2,000	X Cancri

Tables and Figures

The three tables and six figures that appear on the following pages are presented to help visualize some of the interrelationships among the physical properties of the stars. Several of the figures are useful in estimating unknown properties given certain data, as pointed out subsequently. For more details concerning the properties of stars, consult Valerie Illingworth's *Dictionary of Astronomy* (see Bibliography).

Table I.1 gives the spectral types and the corresponding temperature. The spectral types are arranged, according to custom, in the following manner: WR O B A F G K M S C. The first group, WR, is the extremely luminous and rare Wolf-Rayet group of stars. The bulk of the list, in decreasing order of temperature, can be remembered by the traditional mnemonic, "Oh Be A Fine Girl (Guy) Kiss Me." The last two types are a recent change. The S stars are a special kind of red giant similar to M stars. Formerly, the rare carbon stars R and N closed out the series. These have been newly designated as C stars, which are deep red giants, the coolest type of star known.

Table I.2 presents the luminosity class, which always accompanies the spectral type. The table is straightforward.

Table I.3 shows the relationship between the average period of a Mira-type variable and its absolute magnitude at maximum.

Figure I.1 is the celebrated Hertzsprung-Russell diagram, one of the most useful relationships ever discovered between stars. The absolute magnitude (*M*) is on the left vertical axis, the spectral type on the bottom, the luminosity at the right vertical axis, and the star's temperature (in kelvin) at the top.

Table I.2   Luminosity classes

0	very luminous supergiants
Ia	bright supergiants
Ib	supergiants
II	bright giants
III	giants (normal giants)
IV	subgiants
V	main sequence (dwarfs)
VI	subdwarfs
VII	white dwarfs

Table I.3   Long-period (Mira) variables

Average period (in days)	Absolute magnitude at maximum
150	−3.2
200	−2.9
250	−2.1
300	−1.6
350	−1.1
400	−0.5

Figure I.2 shows the relationship between the absolute magnitude, the spectral type, and the luminosity class. This figure is useful to estimate the absolute magnitude, given the luminosity class of a star and its spectral type.

Figure I.3 is another useful figure to estimate unknown values. Here the relationship is between the color index $(B − V)$, the luminosity class, and the star size. Color index is the difference between a star's magnitude as recorded by a blue-sensitive photometer (B) and as recorded by the eye $(V$, for visual). The bluer the star, the greater a percentage of its light will affect the blue-sensitive instrument and the lower its color index will be.

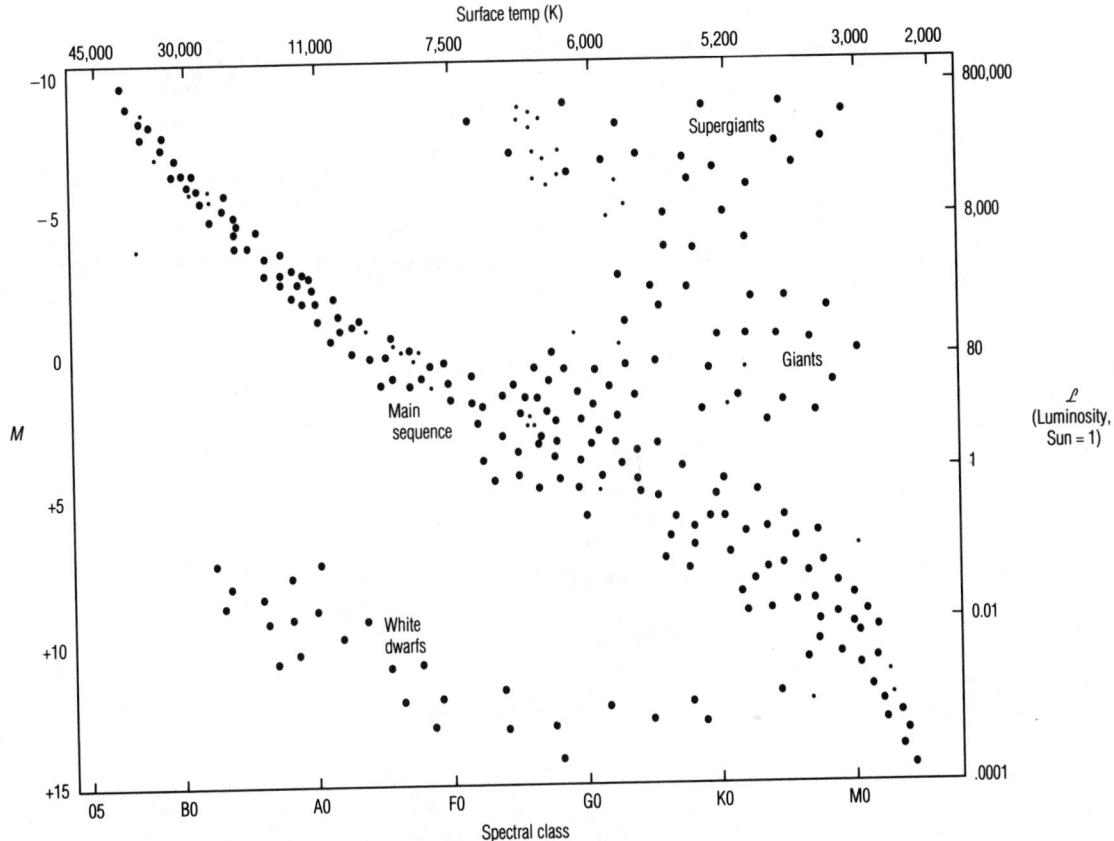

Figure I.1   The Hertzsprung-Russell Diagram, showing the spectral type, absolute magnitude, temperature, and luminosity of the various star groups.

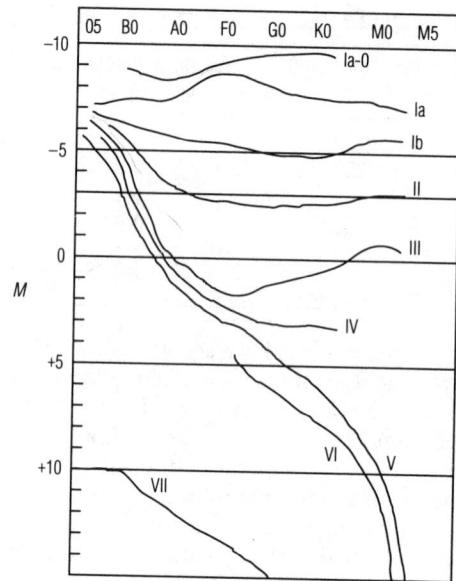

Figure I.2   Luminosity classes.

Figure I.4 gives a representation between the luminosity of a star and its mass. The star's luminosity is on the left vertical axis, the absolute magnitude on the right vertical axis, the solar mass on the bottom, and the life expectancy (in years) across the top.

Figure I.5 is useful for estimating the absolute magnitude of Cepheid variables, given the color index and the star's period.

Figure I.6 shows the relationship between the color index and a star's surface temperature. This relationship forms the basis of my method for computing the star's size (D_s), given the formula as found on page 7.

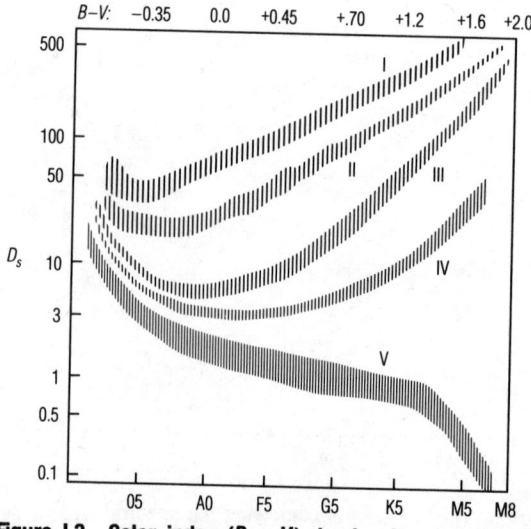

Figure I.3   Color index ($B - V$), luminosity class, and size of star (relative to the Sun).

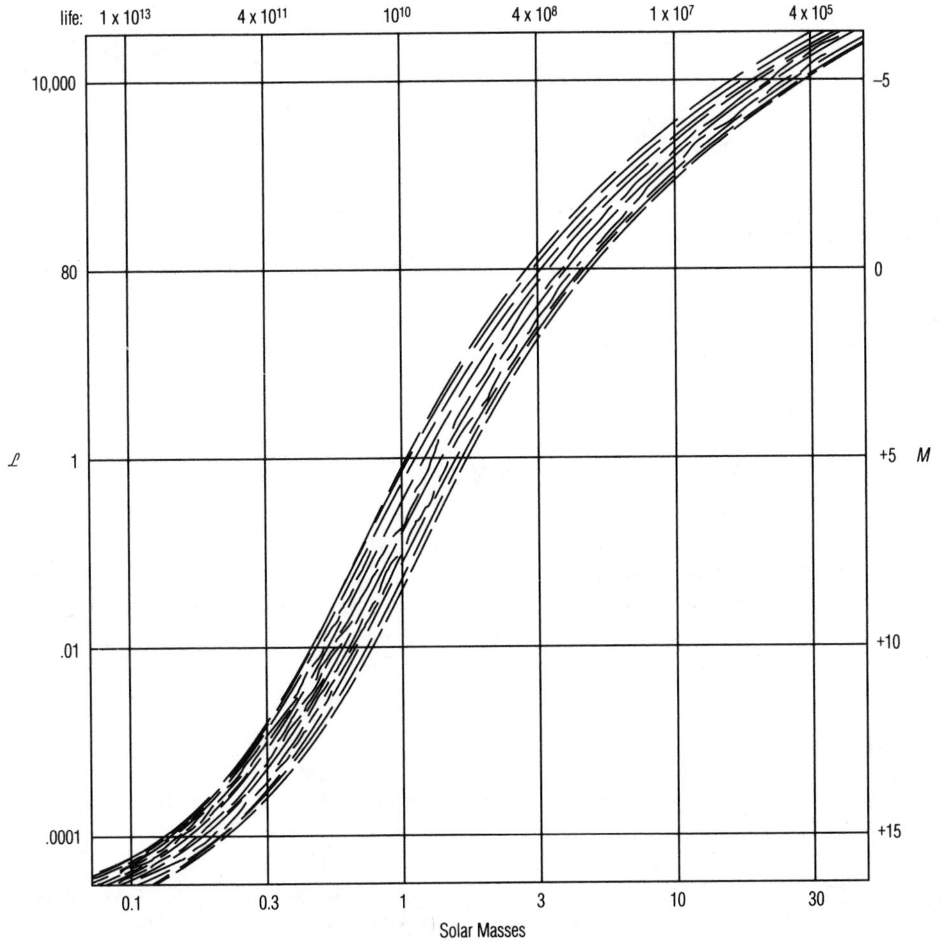

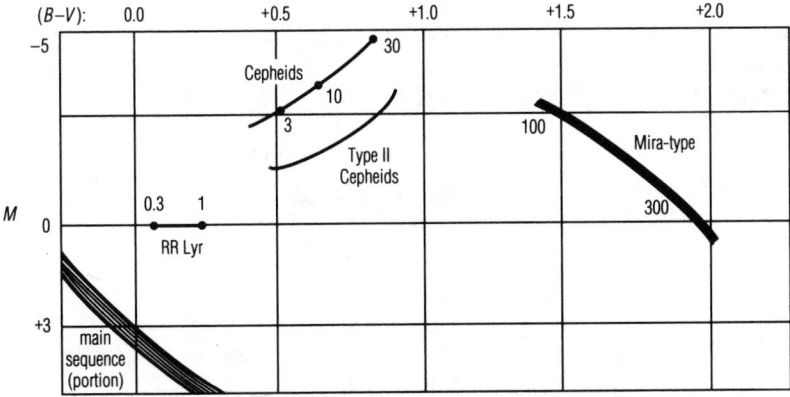

Figure I.4   Relationship between the luminosity of a star and its mass (excluding white dwarfs). Also the life-expectancy of stars (in years), based on their initial mass.

Figure I.5   Pulsating variables (numbers inside figure are periods).

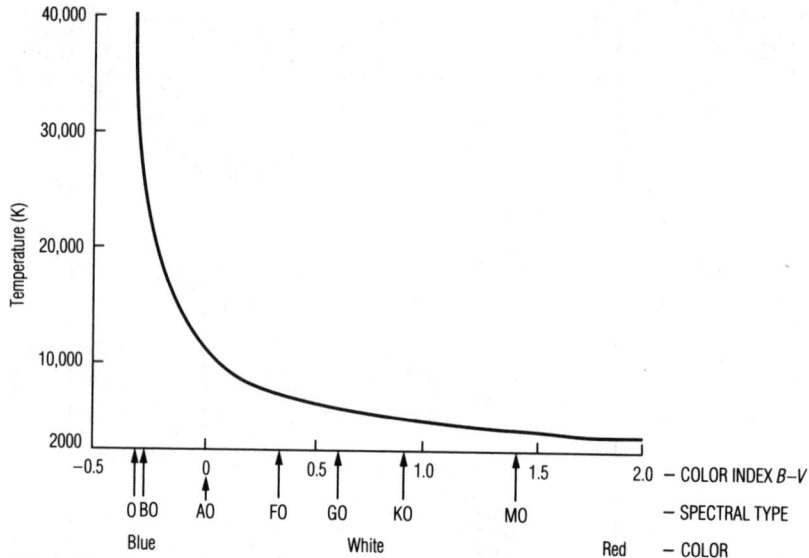

Figure I.6   The relationship between the color index ($B - V$) of a star and its surface temperature (K). This relationship has been used to determine the star size (D_s) in StarList 2000.

Transit Dates

This table lists the transit dates for α of every constellation (or for the principal star of a constellation that has no α), at midnight local time (daylight savings time not considered). To find the transit date of other stars, use the following procedure.

As 24 hours pass through the meridian line over one year (365.25 days), each day sees an advance in R.A. of $3^m56.55^s$. Converted to a fraction, this becomes .06570842 of an hour R.A. per day.

If we use Sirius (α CMa) as a known value, we can compute the number of days from Sirius to any other star. Sirius (R.A. $= 6^h45^m$) lines up on the meridian at midnight on the second of January. When is Vega (18^h37^m) found on the meridian at midnight? The difference ($18^h37^m - 6^h45^m$) is 11^h52^m or, as a decimal, 11.87^h. Divide this by the foregoing fraction: $11.87/.06570842 = 180.6$ days, round off to 181. Some may find it more convenient to multiply the reciprocal of .06570842 by the hour difference.

Since 18^h comes after 6^h, we add 181 days to 2 January. Referring to the following table we see that the 181st day of the year is 30 June. Add one more day to this and we have the 181st day since 2 January. Thus, our answer is 1 July.

Total days at month's end
(leap year, add one day after Feb.)

31 Jan:	31	31 Jul:	212
28 Feb:	59	31 Aug:	243
31 Mar:	90	30 Sep:	273
30 Apr:	120	31 Oct:	304
31 May:	151	30 Nov:	334
30 Jun:	181	31 Dec:	365

Written as a formula, and using the reciprocal of .06570842, we have

$$\Delta(15.22) = \text{days between events}$$

where Δ is the difference in R.A.

The transit times may not suit your locale; due south may be obstructed by trees or buildings. Choose the best viewing direction and with the following procedure you can find when any constellation will be at that point.

Suppose you determine that your best viewing angle is to the southeast, that is, at 135°. This is 45° before transit; call this angle θ (theta). One hour of the celestial sphere covers 15°. Thus, our given difference in azimuth (45°) equals three hours of the celestial sphere. Now, since there are 24^h per year in the celestial sphere, each month sees an advance of 2^h. Therefore, one can see that the answer is 3/2 or 1.5 months prior to transit time. If the transit date is 15 June, for example, then the day to observe the star at 135° azimuth at midnight is 1 May.

$$M = \theta/30$$

where M is the number of months prior (or after) transit and θ is the angle between the desired direction and due south.

TRANSIT DATES (Midnight Local)

Const.	Date	Const.	Date	Const.	Date	Const.	Date
And	23 Sept	Cir	3 May	Lac	29 Aug	PsA	5 Sep
Ant	27 Feb	Col	16 Dec	Leo	22 Feb	Pup	22 Jan
Aps	4 May	Com	9 Apr	LMi	27 Feb	Pyx	31 Jan
Aqr	23 Aug	CrA	9 Jul	Lep	14 Dec	Ret	24 Nov
Aql	20 Jul	CrB	16 May	Lib	5 May	Sge	17 Jul
Ara	14 Jun	Crv	24 Mar	Lup	2 May	Sgr	13 Jul
Ari	23 Oct	Crt	7 Mar	Lyn	10 Feb	Sco	29 May
Aur	10 Dec	Cru	29 Mar	Lyr	1 Jul	Scl	6 Oct
Boo	26 Apr	Cyg	1 Aug	Men	24 Dec	Sct	30 Jun
Cae	1 Dec	Del	31 Jul	Mic	3 Aug	Ser	18 May
Cam	4 Dec	Dor	29 Nov	Mon	16 Jan	Sex	22 Feb
Cnc	4 Feb	Dra	23 Apr	Mus	31 Mar	Tau	30 Nov
CVn	5 Apr	Equ	10 Aug	Nor	26 May	Tel	28 Jun
CMa	2 Jan	Eri	16 Oct	Oct	7 Aug	Tri	20 Oct
CMi	15 Jan	For	9 Nov	Oph	15 Jun	TrA	3 Jun
Cap	26 Jul	Gem	14 Jan	Ori	20 Dec	Tuc	26 Aug
Car	27 Dec	Gru	23 Aug	Pav	28 Jul	UMa	8 Mar
Cas	1 Oct	Her	10 Jun	Peg	7 Sep	UMi	29 Oct
Cen	2 May	Hor	24 Nov	Per	12 Nov	Vel	23 Jan
Cep	11 Aug	Hya	12 Feb	Phe	28 Sep	Vir	13 Apr
Cet	6 Nov	Hyi	21 Oct	Pic	2 Jan	Vol	5 Feb
Cha	25 Jan	Ind	31 Jul	Psc	22 Oct	Vul	14 Jul

Primary Sources

The Bright Star Catalogue (New Haven, CT, 1982); and its Supplement (1983). Dorrit Hoffleit and Carlos Jaschek. For right ascension, declination, visual magnitude, spectral type for declinations above −12°, and, indirectly, proper motion, radial velocity, and parallax.

Catalogue of Nearby Stars (Karlsruhe, 1969 ed.). W. Gliese. For absolute magnitude and parallax for stars with a parallax equal to or greater than .045″. [Stars on the StarList are marked with a dagger (†) when this source has been cited.]

Catalogue of Stellar Radial Velocities (Strasbourg, 1967). David S. Evans. For radial velocities of stars not found in the *Bright Star Catalogue*.

General Catalogue of Trigonometric Stellar Parallaxes (New Haven, CT, 1963). Louise F. Jenkins. For parallax values of stars other than those found in the *Catalogue of Nearby Stars*. [Also the source for the *Bright Star Catalogue*.]

General Catalogue of Variable Stars, Fourth Edition (Moscow, 1985–87) 3v. ed: P. N. Kholopov. For all values related to variable stars except when later epochs have been supplied by other sources (such as the *Sky Catalogue*).

Lick Observatory Index Catalogue of Visual Binary Stars, 1961.0. (Mount Hamilton, CA, 1963) 2v. H. M. Jeffers and W. H. van den Bos. For visual binary information, supplemented by the *Sky Catalogue*.

Michigan Catalogue of Two-Dimensional Spectral Type for the HD Stars (Ann Arbor, MI, 1988) 4v. Spectral type for stars of declination −12° and below.

Sky Catalogue 2000.0 (Cambridge, MA, 1982) 2v. Alan Hirshfeld and R. W. Sinnott. For the absolute magnitude of all stars not found in the *Catalogue of Nearby Stars*.

Smithsonian Astrophysical Observatory Catalogue (Washington DC, 1966). For the right ascension, declination, and proper motion of all stars not included in the *Bright Star Catalogue*. The star positions have been updated by the present author for Epoch 2000. [This is also the source for the *Bright Star Catalogue*.]

The Sun (Berlin, 1989). Michael Stix. For the Sun's absolute magnitude of 4.74.

Third Catalogue of Orbits of Visual Binary Stars (*Republic Observatory Johannesburg Circulars*. Volume 7, no. 129, 1970, pp. 203–54). W. S. Finsen and C. E. Worley. For information pertaining to visual binaries, occasionally updated by the *Sky Catalogue*, vol. 2.

Abbreviations of Sources Referred to in StarList Notes

See Bibliography for full publishing information of these titles.

B:	Robert Burnham, *Celestial Handbook*
B&P:	M. Barbier and M. Petit, *Catalogue bibliographique de vitesses radiales stellaires*
Boss:	Benjamin Boss, *General Catalogue of 33342 Stars for the Epoch 1950.0.*
DA:	Valerie Illingworth (ed.), *The Facts on File Dictionary of Astronomy*
Eicher:	David J. Eicher, *Deep-Sky Observing with Small Telescopes*
Evans:	David S. Evans, *Catalogue of Stellar Radial Velocities*
G:	W. Gliese, *Catalogue of Nearby Stars*
IBVS:	*Information Bulletin of Variable Stars* (followed by bulletin number)
Kholopov:	P. N. Kholopov, *General Catalogue of Variable Stars*, 4th ed.
Levy:	David H. Levy, *Observing Variable Stars*
N/M:	Iain Nicolson and Patrick Moore, *The Universe*
OH:	Roy L. Bishop (ed.), *Observer's Handbook* (1989 ed.)
Petit:	Michel Petit, *Variable Stars*
SAO:	*The Smithsonian Astrophysical Observatory Catalogue*
SC:	Alan Hirshfeld and R. W. Sinnott, *The Sky Catalogue 2000.0*
Y:	Dorrit Hoffleit and Carlos Jaschek, *The Bright Star Catalogue*

All the data on the StarList not found in parentheses are either published data or values directly related to published data, such as the proper motion. If the absolute magnitude (M) is found in parentheses, it has been generated by the distance modulus formula, given the parallax and the visual magnitude. If the parallax is in square brackets, it has been generated by the distance modulus formula, given the visual and absolute magnitudes. As this property is highly speculative (due mainly to the difficulty in obtaining accurate absolute magnitude values), its use here has only been to estimate the star's space velocity (V), which in this case also appears in brackets. (If the radial velocity is missing, the space velocity cannot be calculated, and the parallax in this case has been left blank.)

As an example, look at the StarList for Andromeda. γ^2 And has an absolute magnitude in parentheses; this value has been generated by the known values for the parallax and the visual magnitude. Now look at ν And; the parallax and velocity are in brackets, indicating they are only estimations based on published values for the visual and absolute magnitudes. Finally, look at R Andromedæ. Here all the values marked by an asterisk have been estimated and can be found in the Notes.

All other special symbols that you find on the StarList are explained in the following list.

Abbreviations and Explanation of Symbols in StarList 2000

Column	Symbol	Explanation
2	HD	The star reference as found in the *Henry Draper Catalogue*.
2	∞	This symbol indicates a binary star; for details consult the Visual Binaries Section.
3	R.A.	The right ascension of the star, at epoch 2000.0
3	Declin.	The declination of the star, at epoch 2000.0
4	m	The apparent magnitude. The subscript v (m_v) indicates a variable star; consult the Variable Star Section.
5	M	The absolute magnitude of the star. Stars noted with a dagger (†) come from Gliese, *Catalogue of Nearby Stars*.
6	Spectra	The spectral classification of the star.
7	l.y.	The distance of the star in light-years. If the parallax is equal to or greater than .025″, it has been used to calculate this distance. Otherwise, the distance has been calculated from the distance modulus formula, given the visual and absolute magnitudes. The computer-generated distance has been rounded in most cases to two significant digits.
8	μ	The proper motion of the star, in arc seconds.
9	Dir.	The direction of the star's apparent motion through space over time, disregarding precession, as viewed from Earth. North: 360°; East: 90°.
10	V	The space velocity of the star. This is a function of both the radial velocity and the transverse velocity of the star. If the radial velocity is unknown, the space velocity cannot be calculated, and the column is left blank.
11	RV	The radial velocity, in km/sec. This is the speed of the star along the sight of an observer on Earth. If positive, the star is receding; if negative, the star is approaching the Solar System.
12	π	The parallax of the star, in arc seconds.
13	D_s	The diameter of the star, as a multiple of the Sun's diameter.

(Continued)

Column	Symbol	Explanation
14	$\mathcal{L}$	The luminosity of the star, compared to the Sun.
15	Rmk	Refer to the accompanying note for the item indicated. Attention is called to the following special symbol: $\mathcal{O}$ which indicates that the star's orbital elements are listed in the Orbital Elements part of the Binary Star Section.

An example of a typical entry in the Notes:

$B:M+4.1, D_s3, \mathcal{L}2.$ $SC:M+2.9, RV-7.$ $Y:\pi.041.$

This entry indicates that Burnham gives an absolute magnitude for this star of +4.1, a size of 3 Sun-diameters, and a luminosity of 2 Suns. It then points out that the *Sky Catalogue* gives an absolute magnitude of +2.9 and a radial velocity of −7. Finally, it gives a parallax of .041″, as indicated in the Yale *Bright Star Catalogue*. (This last entry will only be found when the star's absolute magnitude and parallax have been taken from Gliese, shown on the StarList with a dagger alongside the absolute magnitude entry.)

A notation such as m12 means apparent magnitude 12. Occasionally two components of a binary are cited like this: m4.5, m8.9. This means the primary has an apparent magnitude of 4.5 and the companion has an apparent magnitude of 8.9.

The StarList

Andromeda
(Andromedae)

a) *Alpheratz, Sirrah.* Spect. class from OH. Once part of Pegasus (and still sometimes known as δ Pegasi), it forms the northeast corner of the Great Square of Pegasus.

b) *Mirach.* B:$M+0.2$, $\mathscr{L}75$. OH:$M-1.6$, giving a luminosity of 345. SC:$M-0.4$, hence $\mathscr{L}115$. The diffuse light-ball NW is the galaxy NGC 404.

c) *Almach.* A noted binary, with color contrast (gold and blue). The blue companion is also a close binary. While the distance modulus yields 95 light-years for γ^1 and 250 light-years for γ^2, the parallax of the two is identical. Indeed, disagreement over vital statistics of γ^1 yields widely disparate results: B:$M-2.4$; $\mathscr{L}650$, 260 l.y.; OH:$M+1.8$, 42 l.y.

   Three degrees E of γ And is an excellent edge-on spiral galaxy, NGC 891, for medium or large telescopes, and SSW 5° is NGC 752, a large bright cluster suitable for binoculars.

d) The parallax indicates that the star may be closer, about 115 l.y. It has a faint (m12) companion, a red dwarf 28.7″ away.

e) The distance modulus gives 210 l.y.

f) The distance modulus gives 580 l.y. The low M (-2.2) may be questioned; Burnham cites studies that assign a value of $M+0.8$, which would yield a luminosity of about 40, and a distance of 145 l.y.

g) WSW 2.5° is NGC 7662 ("Blue Snowball"), a planetary nebula with a blue-green central star (m12).

h) Located just east of the Andromeda Galaxy (M31).

i) The parallax indicates the distance may be more than double the cited value, which is based on the distance modulus formula.

j) SC:$M+4.0$, for a luminosity of 2. Y:$\pi.066$.

k) The parallax yields a distance of about 800 l.y.

l) The parallax indicates a distance of about 1600 l.y.

m) The parallax would suggest the star is about 150 l.y. away.

n) One of the closest stars, although quite dim. See Burnham for a finder's chart. M, Spec., μ, Dir., RV, and π: all from Gliese.

o) If the absolute magnitude is estimated to be 1.5, then: 280 l.y., $\pi.012$, $V20$ km/s, $D_s1.7$, and $\mathscr{L}20$.

   In the same field is 26 And, a fixed binary (6.5, 10; PA 238°, 6.2″).

p) Red giant, Mira variable. Burnham, who has a finder's chart, estimates the distance at about 800–1000 light-years. If we estimate M at 0.0, then: 1000 l.y., $\pi.003$, $V31$, D_s37, and $\mathscr{L}80$.

ANDROMEDA	HD	R.A.			Declin.			m	M	Spectra	l.y.	μ	Dir.	V	RV	π	D_s	$\mathscr{L}$	Rmk
						2000.0													
α And	358	00^h 08^m 23.2^s			+29° 05' 26''			2.06$_v$	−0.7	B9 IV	100	0.209''	139°	33	−12	.032''	1.6	150	(a)
β And	6860	01 09	43.9		+35 37	14		2.06	0.0†	M0 III	84	0.210	121	25	0	.039	26	78	(b)
γ¹ And ∞	12533	02 03	53.9		+42 19	47		2.18	−0.1	K3 III	93	0.066	136	27	−12	.013	23	86	(c)
γ² And ∞	12534	02 03	54.7		+42 19	51		4.84	(0.4)	B8 V	250	0.063	144	27	−14	.013	2.6	54	𝒪
δ And	3627	00 39	19.6		+30 51	40		3.27	−0.2	K3 III	160	0.161	122	28	−7	.028	22	95	(d)
ε And	3546	00 38	33.3		+29 18	43		4.37	0.3	G8 III	88	0.338	222	94	−84	.037	11	60	(e)
ζ And	4502	00 47	20.3		+24 16	02		4.06$_v$	−2.2	K1 IIIe	88	0.127	232	29	−24	.037	46	597	(f)
η And	5516	00 57	12.4		+23 25	04		4.42	1.8	G8 IIIb	110	0.050	223	28	−10	.009	5.8	15	
θ And	1280	00 17	05.4		+38 40	54		4.61	1.4	A2 V	140	0.054	254	12	1	.022	1.8	22	
ι And	222173	23 38	08.1		+43 16	05		4.29	−0.2	B8 V	260	0.029	82	13	−1	.011	1.4	95	(g)
κ And	22439	23 40	24.4		+44 20	02		4.14	−0.2	B9 IVn	240	0.082	100	23	−9	.018	1.6	95	
λ And	222107	23 37	33.8		+46 27	30		3.82$_v$	1.8	G8 III/IV	65	0.446	159	43	7	.050	6.3	15	
μ And	5448	00 56	45.1		+38 29	58		3.87	2.1	A5 V	84	0.156	76	21	8	.039	1.5	11	
ν And	4727	00 49	48.8		+41 04	44		4.53	−1.1	B5 V	440	0.026	129	[29]	−24	[.007]	5.0	217	(h)
ξ And	8207	01 22	20.3		+45 31	44		4.88	1.7	K0 IIIb	140	0.034	69	14	−13	.026	7.2	16	
o And	217675	23 01	55.2		+42 19	34		3.62$_v$	1.4	B6 IIIe	91	0.021	90	15	−14	.015	0.7	22	(i)
π And ∞	3369	00 36	52.8		+33 43	10		4.36	−1.1	B5 V	400	0.016	90	27	9	.003	1.6	217	
ρ And	1671	00 21	07.2		+37 58	07		5.18	2.1	F5 III	140	0.070	119	21	9	.017	2.2	11	
σ And	1404	00 18	19.6		+36 47	07		4.52	1.4	A2 V	140	0.072	241	17	−8	.023	1.8	22	
τ And	10205	01 40	34.7		+40 34	37		4.94	−0.6	B8 III	420	0.025	148	[21]	−14	[.008]	1.8	137	
υ And	9826	01 36	47.8		+41 24	20		4.09	3.06†	F8 V	53	0.417	205	42	−28	.062	1.8	4.7	(j)
φ And	6811	01 09	30.1		+47 14	31		4.25	−1.2	B7 Ve	400	0.010	114	16	0	.003	2.8	238	
χ And	10072	01 39	20.9		+44 23	10		4.98	0.3	G8 III	280	0.027	306	[16]	7	[.009]	11	60	
ψ And	223047	23 46	02.0		+46 25	13		4.95	−4.5	G5 Ib+	2500	0.009	90	49	−25	.001	130	5000	
ω And	8799	01 27	39.2		+45 24	25		4.83	2.0	F5 IV	110	0.361	106	58	11	.030	2.3	12	
2 And ∞	217782	23 02	36.2		+42 45	28		5.10	3.7†	A3 Vn	63	0.053	90	5	2	.052	0.7	2.6	
3 And	218031	23 04	10.9		+50 03	08		4.65	0.2	K0 IIIb+	250	0.236	43	282	−35	.004	14	65	(k)
7 And	219080	23 12	32.9		+49 24	23		4.52	2.8†	F0 V	71	0.136	41	19	13	.046	1.2	6.0	
8 And	219734	23 17	44.6		+49 00	55		4.85	−0.5	M2 III	380	0.037	70	18	−8	.011	36	125	
14 And	221345	23 31	17.3		+39 14	11		5.22	0.2	K0 III	330	0.297	105	111	−59	.015	13	65	
22 And	571	00 10	19.2		+46 04	20		5.03	−2.0	F2 II	830	0.008	50	19	−5	.002	14	497	(l)
28 And	2628	00 30	07.3		+29 45	06		5.23$_v$	−4.8	A7 III	3300	0.063	141	300	−10	.001	36	6368	
36 And ∞	5286	00 54	58.0		+23 37	42		5.47	0.0	K1 IV	410	0.134	101	29	2	.022	14	79	(m)𝒪
41 And	6658	01 08	00.8		+43 56	32		5.03	(2.5)	A3 m	110	0.174	108	28	9	.031	1.2	8.0	
58 And	13041	02 08	29.2		+37 51	33		4.82	1.9	A5 IV/V	130	0.162	103	128	8	.006	1.7	14	
60 And	13520	02 13	13.2		+44 13	55		4.83	−0.3	K3.5 III	350	0.024	251	[48]	−46	[.009]	28	104	
64 And	14770	02 24	24.8		+50 00	24		5.19	0.3	G8 III	310	0.042	146	202	−13	.001	12	60	
65 And	14872	02 25	37.3		+50 16	43		4.71	−0.3	K4 III	330	0.026	113	12	−5	.011	29	104	
Grb 34 ∞	1326	00 18	12.9		+44 01	22		8.07	10.32†	M1 V	11.56	2.903	82	51	13	.282	0.2	0.006	(n)𝒪
h1947 ∞	1185	00 16	21.5		+43 35	42		6.15	*	A2 V	*	0.048	121	*	3	*	*	*	(o)
OΣ514 ∞	225218	00 04	36.6		+42 05	32		6.10	1.4	A2	280	0.017	170	[11]	−8	[.011]	1.6	22	
R And	1967	00 24	01.9		+38 34	38		7.40$_v$	*	S6 III	*	0.021	203	*	−11	*	*	*	(p)
- And	2421	00 28	13.7		+44 23	40		5.17	0.7	A2 V	250	0.095	94	35	2	.013	2.3	40	
- And	3346	00 36	46.5		+44 29	19		5.13	−0.3	K5/M0 III	400	0.045	327	45	−33	.007	31	104	
- And	10307	01 41	47.1		+42 36	49		4.95	4.66†	G1.5 V	38	0.822	100	45	4	.087	1.0	1.1	

Antlia
(Antliae)

a) The parallax indicates a distance roughly half that determined by the distance modulus formula. In the same field, NE, is δ Ant—a fixed binary (m6, m9.5; PA 226°, 11″).

b) Given m and π, the distance modulus gives $M-3.7$. This yields a distance of 3000 l.y., $\mathscr{L}2400$.

c) SC:m5.77, $M+0.6$. This catalog does not distinguish between ζ^{1A} and ζ^{1B}, giving the HD of A, the R.A. and declination of B, a visual magnitude of 5.77 (which is the combined magnitude of A and B), and an absolute magnitude of $+0.6$.

   The distance modulus of ζ^{1B} gives $M-2.8$, using $\pi.001$. This in turn yields a distance of 3000 l.y. Also, at $M-2.8$, the luminosity exceeds 1000. If we estimate M at $+1$ (Fig. 2), then: 570 l.y., $D_s2.4$, and $\mathscr{L}31$.

d) If M is estimated to be 2.7, then: 144 l.y., $\pi.023$, $D_s1.2$, and $\mathscr{L}6.5$.

e) Y:$\pi.053$.

f) The parallax yields a distance of 130 l.y.

ANTLIA	HD	2000.0 R.A.	Declin.	m	M	Spectra	l.y.	μ	Dir.	V	RV	π	D_s	$\mathscr{L}$	Rmk
α Ant	90610	$10^h\,27^m\,09.1^s$	$-31°\,04'\,04''$	4.25	−0.4	K4 III	280	0.077″	277°	19	12	.024″	28	114	(a)
ε Ant	82150	09 29 14.7	−35 57 06	4.51	−0.4	K3 IIIa	310	0.025	254	32	22	.005	28	114	
ζ¹ᴬ Ant	82384	09 30 46.1	−31 53 22	6.35	0.6	A1 V	460	0.039	142	—	—	.001	2.5	45	(b)
ζ¹ᴮ Ant	82383	09 30 45.4	−31 53 29	7.21	*	A1 V	*	0.034	210	—	—	.001	*	*	(c)
ζ² Ant	82513	09 31 32.2	−31 52 18	5.93	*	A9 IV	*	0.043	267	—	—	*	*	*	(d)
η Ant	86629	09 58 52.2	−35 53 28	5.23	2.6	A8 IV	110	0.102	256	34	30	.029	1.4	7.2	
θ Ant	84367	09 44 12.1	−27 46 10	4.79	3.9†	A7 V	68	0.057	301	25	24	.048	1.1	2.2	(e)
ι Ant	94890	10 56 43.0	−37 08 16	4.60	0.3	K1 III	240	0.154	150	29	0	.025	13	60	(f)
U Ant	91793	10 35 12.8	−39 33 45	5.38ᵥ	—	C5	—	0.032	261	—	37	—	—	—	

Apus
(Apodis)

a) The parallax gives a distance of about half that of the distance modulus formula.

b) The distance modulus formula gives a distance of about 210 l.y.

c) SC:M+3.2, $\mathcal{L}$4. Y:π.056.

d) The parallax indicates a distance about half of the distance modulus value. This star and δ^2 form a wide binary, fixed at PA 12°, 103″, with a slight color contrast, red and orange.

e) The parallax yields a distance of 150–170 l.y.

f) If the absolute magnitude is estimated at +1, then: 250 l.y., π.013, V7, D_s1.3, and $\mathcal{L}$31.

g) There is some discrepancy in catalogs over the luminosity class of this star. SC gives IV, that is, a "subdwarf," rather than a supergiant (Ib). If we estimate the absolute magnitude from Fig. 2 to be −7, then: 10,000 l.y., π.003, V370, D_s25, and $\mathcal{L}$50,000. Using the SC luminosity class instead yields the following: M−2.3, 1180 l.y., 2.4 Suns, $\mathcal{L}$655. SC:RV+96.

h) If M is estimated from Fig. 2 to be −3, this would yield: 1750 l.y., π.002, V74, D_s5.7, and $\mathcal{L}$1200.

i) This star was mistakenly regarded as a variable, and therefore given the name R Apodis. It has since been eliminated from variable catalogs (or redesignated in catalogs as CST, the term reserved for stars wrongly cataloged originally as variables).

APUS	HD	R.A. 2000.0			Declin.			m	M	Spectra	l.y.	μ	Dir.	V	RV	π	D_s	$\mathcal{L}$	Rmk
α Aps	129078	14^h 47^m	51.6^s		−79°	02′	41″	3.83	−0.3	K3 III	220	0.018″	189°	3	−1	.029″	26	104	(a)
β Aps	149324	16 43	04.4		−77	31	03	4.24	0.2	K0 III	96	0.447	219	69	−30	.034	14	65	(b)
γ Aps	147675	16 33	27.1		−78	53	49	3.89	2.7†	K0 III	55	0.137	240	12	5	.059	3.7	6.5	(c)
δ¹ Aps	145366	16 20	20.7		−78	41	45	4.68$_v$	−0.5	M4 III	350	0.037	188	15	−12	.020	37	125	(d)
δ² Aps	145388	16 20	26.7		−78	40	02	5.27	−0.3	K3 III	420	0.024	178	12	−10	.020	26	104	(e)
ε Aps	124771	14 22	22.7		−80	06	32	5.06	−2.0	B3 V	840	0.021	235	[26]	5	[.004]	3.2	497	
ζ Aps	156277	17 21	59.5		−67	46	13	4.78	−0.3	K1 III	340	0.026	274	16	13	.014	21	104	
η Aps	123998	14 18	13.6		−81	00	27	4.91	—	A2 m	—	0.065	205	—	−9	—	—	—	
θ Aps	122250	14 05	19.8		−76	47	48	5.50$_v$	−0.5	M7 III	520	0.094	248	[71]	10	[.006]	33	125	
ι Aps	156190	17 22	05.8		−70	07	24	5.41	*	B9 V+	*	0.016	165	*	−4	*	*	*	(f)
κ¹ Aps	137387	15 31	30.8		−73	23	22	5.49$_v$	*	B3 Ib	*	0.019	171	*	62	*	*	*	(g)
κ² Aps	138800	15 40	21.2		−73	26	48	5.65	*	B7 III/IV	*	0.030	201	*	−19	*	*	*	(h)
R Aps	131109	14 57	52.8		−76	39	45	5.34	−0.1	K4 III	400	0.073	258	53	−31	.008	25	86	(i)

Aquarius
(Aquarii)

a) *Sadal Melik* (Lucky One of the King). This star and β Aqr are twin giants, having the same size and luminosity, and traveling in the same direction at about the same speed. The parallax indicates the star may be much closer.

b) *Sadal Suud* (Luckiest of the Lucky). N 5° is M2, a bright globular star cluster.

c) *Sadachbia* (Lucky Star of Hidden Things). The distance modulus yields a distance of 150 l.y. B:$M+1.5$, $\mathscr{L}20$.

d) *Skat* (Shinbone). The distance modulus indicates a distance of 160 l.y. B:$M+1.2$, $\mathscr{L}28$.

e) *Al Bali* (The Good Fortune of the Swallower).

f) The parallax indicates a slightly closer star, about 150 l.y. This star forms, with ζ^2, a noted binary (see Visual Binary Section and Orbital Elements Section). Burnham gives ζ^1 an absolute magnitude of +2.6, $\mathscr{L}8$.

g) A third companion, a red dwarf, is suspected. Burnham gives ζ^2 an absolute magnitude of +2.8, $\mathscr{L}7$.

h) The parallax suggests a distance of 130 l.y.

i) *Ancha*.

j) W 1.5° is the planetary nebula NGC 7009 ("Saturn Nebula"), which takes a large telescope to fully appreciate.

k) W 1.5° is the Helix Nebula (NGC 7293), considered the largest and closest of planetary nebulae, about 500 l.y.—although the distance is still a matter of some dispute.

l) Y:π.049.

m) Not your usual Mira variable. This one resembles the Z Andromedae "symbiotic stars." R Aqr is a red giant with a small blue—and very hot—companion, which is encircled by a gas cloud. When this small star eclipses the red giant, the visual magnitude of the primary drops several magnitudes.

   If M is estimated from Fig. 2 at −1, then: 1000 l.y., parallax .003, V61 km/s, 60 Suns, and $\mathscr{L}200$. Burnham estimated the size to be "at least" 100 Suns.

AQUARIUS	HD	R.A. (2000.0)			Declin.			m	M	Spectra	l.y.	μ	Dir.	V	RV	π	D_s	ℒ	Rmk
α Aqr	209750	22h	05m	46.9s	−00°	19'	11"	2.96	−4.5	G2 Ib	1000	0.016"	104°	10	8	.012"	111	5000	(a)
β Aqr	204867	21	31	33.3	−05	34	16	2.91	−4.5	G0 Ib	990	0.020	105	17	7	.006	91	5000	(b)
γ Aqr	212061	22	21	39.3	−01	23	14	3.84	0.6	A0 V	71	0.130	85	20	−15	.046	1.4	45	(c)
δ Aqr	216627	22	54	38.9	−15	49	15	3.27	−0.2	A2 III	86	0.047	242	19	18	.038	3.7	95	(d)
ε Aqr	198001	20	47	40.5	−09	29	45	3.77	1.2	A1 V	110	0.046	134	19	−16	.021	1.7	26	(e)
ζ¹ Aqr ∞	213051	22	28	49.6	−00	01	13	4.53	0.6	F2 III	200	0.179	86	48	29	.022	4.2	45	(f)
ζ² Aqr	213052	22	28	50.0	−00	01	12	4.31	(1.0)	F2 IV	150	0.212	77	52	25	.022	3.4	31	(g)
η Aqr	213998	22	35	21.3	−00	07	03	4.02	−0.2	B8 V	230	0.102	120	21	−8	.025	1.5	95	(h)
θ Aqr	211391	22	16	49.9	−07	47	00	4.16	1.8	G8 III/IV	97	0.119	99	31	−15	.021	6.1	15	(i)
ι Aqr	209819	22	06	26.1	−13	52	11	4.27	−0.2	B8 V	250	0.066	144	[26]	−10	[.013]	1.7	95	
κ Aqr	214376	22	37	45.3	−04	13	41	5.03	−0.1	K2 III	350	0.134	212	34	8	.019	18	86	
λ Aqr	216386	22	52	36.8	−07	34	47	3.74	−0.5	M2 III	230	0.040	10	14	−9	.017	35	125	
μ Aqr	198743	20	52	39.1	−08	59	00	4.73	(1.1)	A3 m	170	0.050	124	15	−9	.019	2.8	28	
ν Aqr	201381	21	09	35.5	−11	22	18	4.51	0.3	G8 III	230	0.092	99	28	−12	.017	12	60	(j)
ξ Aqr	205767	21	37	45.0	−07	51	15	4.69	2.4	A7 V	94	0.115	102	50	−21	.012	1.5	8.6	
o Aqr	209409	22	03	18.7	−02	09	19	4.69v	−0.2	B7 IVe	310	0.019	122	[15]	12	[.011]	1.9	95	
π Aqr	212571	22	25	16.5	+01	22	39	4.66v	−4.1	B1 Ve	1800	0.019	74	[50]	4	[.002]	15	3436	
ρ Aqr	211838	22	20	11.8	−07	49	16	5.37	−0.2	B8 III	420	0.013	81	[12]	−9	[.008]	1.9	95	
σ Aqr	213320	22	30	38.7	−10	40	41	4.82	0.0	A0 IV	300	0.027	180	13	11	.021	1.7	79	
τ² Aqr	216032	22	49	35.4	−13	35	33	4.01	−0.4	M0 III	250	0.036	204	8	1	.021	32	114	
υ Aqr	213845	22	34	41.6	−20	42	30	5.20	3.4†	F4 IV	76	0.263	123	29	−2	.043	1.3	3.4	(k)
φ Aqr	219215	23	14	19.3	−06	02	56	4.22	−0.5	M2 III	290	0.196	169	93	0	.010	33	125	
χ Aqr	219576	23	16	50.8	−07	43	36	5.06v	(0.0)	M3 III	330	0.022	240	19	−15	.009	27	79	
ψ¹ Aqr	219449	23	15	53.4	−09	05	16	4.21	1.8†	K0 III	99	0.369	92	59	−26	.033	7.1	15	(l)
ψ² Aqr	219688	23	17	54.1	−09	10	57	4.39	−1.1	B5 V	410	0.020	114	[13]	−6	[.008]	5.0	217	
ψ³ Aqr	219832	23	18	57.6	−09	36	38	4.98	0.6	A0 V	240	0.044	86	20	−10	.012	1.9	45	
ω¹ Aqr	222345	23	39	47.0	−14	13	18	5.00	(1.0)	F0 IV	200	0.064	122	19	−2	.016	2.5	31	
ω² Aqr	222661	23	42	43.2	−14	32	42	4.49	0.4	B9.5 V	80	0.115	123	14	3	.041	1.7	54	
1 Aqr	196758	20	39	24.8	+00	29	11	5.16	0.0	K1 III	350	0.098	98	63	−43	.010	15	79	
3 Aqr	198026	20	47	44.1	−05	01	40	4.42v	−0.5	M3 III	310	0.037	182	31	−22	.008	36	125	
66 Aqr	215167	22	43	35.2	−18	49	50	4.69	−0.3	K4 III	320	0.037	229	26	22	.013	25	104	
86 Aqr	218240	23	06	40.8	−23	44	35	4.47	0.2	G9 III	230	0.066	89	19	15	.028	11	65	
88 Aqr	218594	23	09	26.7	−21	10	21	3.66	0.2	K1 III	160	0.064	56	37	21	.010	17	65	
89 Aqr	218640	23	09	54.7	−22	27	27	4.69	4.4	G2 IV+	82	0.025	101	6	−5	.040	1.2	1.4	
94 Aqr	219834	23	19	06.6	−13	27	32	5.08	3.2	G6/8 IV	81	0.310	108	38	10	.040	2.5	4	
97 Aqr	220278	23	22	39.1	−15	02	21	5.20	(1.9)	A5 Vn	150	0.111	79	27	−12	.022	1.5	14	
98 Aqr	220321	23	22	58.1	−20	06	02	3.97	0.2	K0 III	91	0.152	234	21	−7	.036	15	65	
99 Aqr	220704	23	26	02.7	−20	38	31	4.39	−0.3	K5 III	280	0.076	224	54	16	.007	28	104	
101 Aqr	221565	23	33	16.5	−20	54	52	4.71	—	A1 n	—	0.019	335	—	15	—	—	—	
104 Aqr	222574	23	41	45.7	−17	48	59	4.82	−2.0	G0 Ib/II	750	0.015	58	9	3	.009	28	497	
108 Aqr	223640	23	51	21.2	−18	54	33	5.18v	(2.0)	B9 pSi+	140	0.018	77	14	13	.023	0.4	13	
R Aqr	222800	23	43	49.4	−15	17	04	6.36v	*	M7 IIIpec	*	0.036	126	*	−22	*	*	*	(m)

Aquila
(Aquilae)

a)   *Altair* (Flying Eagle). This star spins very rapidly, completing one revolution about every 6.5 hours. This high speed is thought to have deformed the star, with its equatorial diameter almost twice its polar diameter.

b)   *Alshain*. Yale indicates this to be a variable (type unspecified), with an amplitude of .05 visual magnitude. Its companion (B) is a red dwarf.

c)   *Tarazed*. The parallax suggests a closer distance, just over 200 l.y.

d)   SC:$M+2.1$, which gives a luminosity of 11.

e)   *Deneb el Okab* (a name shared with ζ Aql). The parallax suggests a distance of 115 l.y.

f)   *Deneb el Okab* (a name shared with ϵ Aql). The parallax gives a distance of 118 l.y. B:$M+0.8$ ($= \mathscr{L}40$).

g)   A Cepheid variable whose variation (m3.5–4.4) is easily discernible with the naked eye. A period of 7^d4^h. The rise takes about two days of this period; the balance of time is taken up by the star slowly diminishing in magnitude.

   The parallax suggests a much closer star (326 l.y.). But the most reliable means of estimating the distance of Cepheid variables is the period-luminosity relation, which, given the data found on the StarList, indicates a distance of 1555 l.y. Also using the period-luminosity relationship, Burnham calculates a distance of 870 l.y.

h)   B:$M-1.7$.

i)   If M is estimated from Fig. 2 to be -3, then: 1300 l.y., $\pi.003$, $V20$, $D_s11.9$, and $\mathscr{L}1250$.

j)   *Althalimain*. The distance modulus gives a distance of 160 l.y. B:$M-0.1$ ($= \mathscr{L}90$).

k)   The distance modulus gives a much greater distance (280 l.y.).

l)   Y:$\pi.048$.

m)   Y:$\pi.056$.

n)   A red giant, Mira variable, with naked-eye visibility at its peak. It becomes more deeply red as the magnitude decreases. At its faintest, its spectral type is M8, corresponding to a drop of temperature from 3100 to 2600 K. Burnham indicates a drop from 2350 to 1890 K, and calls it "one of the coolest stars known."

   If M is estimated to be -1.5, then: 800 l.y., $\pi.004$, $V85$, D_s54, and $\mathscr{L}313$.

AQUILA	HD	R.A. 2000.0		Declin.			*m*	*M*	Spectra	l.y.	μ	Dir.	V	RV	π	D_s	$\mathscr{L}$	Rmk
α Aql	187642	19^h 50^m 46.9^s		+08° 52′	06″		0.77	2.24†	A7 IV/V	16.5	0.662″	54°	30	−26	.198″	1.3	10	(a)
β Aql ∞	188512	19 55	18.7	+06 24	24		3.71	3.0†	G8 IV	46.6	0.481	175	52	−40	.070	3.0	5.0	(b)
γ Aql	186791	19 46	15.5	+10 36	48		2.72	−2.3	K3 II	330	0.016	83	5	−2	.016	73	655	(c)
δ Aql	182640	19 25	29.8	+03 06	53		3.36	2.6†	F0 IV/V	46.6	0.266	72	35	−30	.070	1.4	7.2	(d)
ε Aql	176411	18 59	37.3	+15 04	06		4.02	−0.1	K1 III+	220	0.090	215	50	−48	.028	17	86	(e)
ζ Aql	177724	19 05	24.5	+13 51	48		2.99	0.2	A0 Vn	72	0.095	184	27	−25	.045	2.8	65	(f)
η Aql	187929	19 52	28.3	+01 00	20		3.90$_v$	−4.5	G0 Ib	1600	0.009	131	16	−15	.010	99	5000	(g)
θ Aql	191692	20 11	18.2	−00 49	17		3.23	−0.8	B9.5 III	210	0.037	79	31	−27	.012	2.3	164	(h)
ι Aql	184930	19 36	43.2	−01 17	11		4.36	−2.2	B5 III	670	0.016	176	28	−21	.004	4.1	597	
κ Aql	184915	19 36	53.4	−07 01	39		4.95	*	B0.5 III	*	0.004	180	*	−19	*	*	*	(i)
λ Aql	177756	19 06	14.8	−04 52	57		3.44	0.0	B9 Vn	100	0.090	193	18	−12	.032	1.4	79	(j)
μ Aql	184406	19 34	05.3	+07 22	44		4.45	−0.2	K3 IIIb	72	0.265	126	37	−24	.045	19	95	(k)
ν Aql	182835	19 26	31.0	+00 20	19		4.66	−4.6	F2 Ib	2300	0.004	315	3	−1	.008	67	5500	
ξ Aql	188310	19 54	14.8	+08 27	41		4.71	0.2	K0 IIIb	260	0.126	129	49	−42	.023	14	65	
o Aql	187691	19 51	01.5	+10 24	56		5.11	3.8†	F8 V	62	0.276	120	25	0	.053	1.3	2.4	(l)
ρ Aql	192425	20 14	16.5	+15 11	51		4.95	1.4	A2 V	170	0.081	45	28	−23	.023	1.9	22	
σ Aql	185507	19 39	11.5	+05 23	52		5.17$_v$	−1.7	B3 V+	770	0.001	315	[5]	−5	[.004]	7.0	377	
φ Aql	188728	19 56	14.1	+11 25	25		5.28	1.2	A1 IV	210	0.032	74	28	−27	.023	1.5	26	
χ Aql ∞	186203	19 42	33.9	+11 49	36		5.27	3.4	G2+B8	77	0.006	211	22	−22	.006	1.6	3.4	
ω^1 Aql	180868	19 17	48.9	+11 35	44		5.28	(1.0)	F0 IV	230	0.016	360	15	−14	.014	2.3	31	
4 Aql	173370	18 44	49.8	+02 03	36		5.02	0.2	B9 V	300	0.018	161	21	−13	.005	1.6	65	
11 Aql	176303	18 59	05.6	+13 37	21		5.23	1.5	F8 V	84	0.123	174	22	16	.039	3.6	20	
12 Aql	176678	19 01	40.7	−05 44	20		4.02	0.0	K1 III	210	0.040	214	45	−44	.021	16	79	
18 Aql	178125	19 06	58.5	+11 04	17		5.09$_v$	−0.6	B8 III	450	0.028	186	21	−19	.016	2.1	137	
19 Aql	178596	19 08	59.8	+06 04	24		5.22	−6.6	F0 III/IV	100	0.076	189	48	−47	.032	106	35000	
21 Aql	179761	19 13	42.6	+02 17	38		5.15$_v$	(−0.1)	B8 II/III	360	0.008	67	6	−5	.009	1.6	85	
23 Aql	180972	19 18	32.4	+01 05	07		5.10	−1.1	K2 II/III	570	0.021	19	41	−24	.003	28	217	
26 Aql	181391	19 20	32.8	−05 24	57		5.01	1.8	G8 III/IV	110	0.122	67	27	−19	.030	5.6	15	
31 Aql	182572	19 24	58.1	+11 56	40		5.16	4.0†	G8 IV+	54	0.965	48	126	−100	.060	1.7	2.0	(m)
36 Aql	183630	19 30	39.7	−02 47	20		5.03	−0.5	M1 III	420	0.019	108	11	−11	.029	39	125	
37 Aql	184492	19 35	07.2	−10 33	38		5.12	0.3	G9 IIIa	300	0.008	113	31	−31	.007	15	60	
41 Aql	184930	19 36	43.2	−01 17	11		4.36	−2.2	B5 III	670	0.016	176	28	−21	.004	4.1	597	
69 Aql	195135	20 29	38.9	−02 53	08		4.91	−0.1	K2 III	330	0.071	104	28	−23	.021	18	86	
70 Aql	196321	20 36	43.5	−02 32	59		4.89	−2.3	K5 II	890	0.004	104	10	−10	.016.	78	655	
71 Aql	196574	20 38	20.2	−01 06	19		4.32	0.3	G8 III	210	0.022	148	12	−6	.010	12	60	
R Aql	177940	19 06	22.0	+08 13	48		5.40$_v$	*	M5 III	*	0.069	178	*	32	*	*	*	(n)
FF Aql	176155	18 58	14.6	+17 21	39		5.38$_v$	−6.5	F8 Ib	7700	0.008	210	23	−22	.007	219	30000	

Ara
(Arae)

a) The parallax suggests a distance of about 465 l.y. B:$M-2.4$, 390 l.y., $\mathscr{L}760$. SC:$RV-2$.

b) The given parallax differs from others. Burnham cites an estimated distance of about 1030 l.y., which would mean a parallax of about .003; he also gives an absolute magnitude of -4.6.

c) Burnham gives a luminosity class of III (and $M-3.3$, $\mathscr{L}1700$, 680 l.y.). However, the luminosity class has been revised; both OH and Yale indicate a class of Ib.
    If we estimate M to be -6 (from Fig. 2), then: 2400 l.y., parallax .0014, velocity 38 km/s, 47 Suns, and $\mathscr{L}20,000$.
    OH has nearly the same values: $M-5.8$, 2000 l.y.

d) The parallax gives a distance of over 500 l.y.

e) The distance modulus formula gives a distance of 160 l.y. B:$M+1.0$, $\mathscr{L}35$, 90 l.y.

f) The large parallax suggests a distance of around 130 l.y.

g) If M is estimated at -3, then: 1450 l.y., parallax .002, velocity 41 km/s, diameter 5 Suns, and $\mathscr{L}1250$. The large parallax suggests a distance of around 130 l.y.

ARA	HD	R.A.	Declin.	m	M	Spectra	l.y.	μ	Dir.	V	RV	π	D_s	$\mathscr{L}$	Rmk
		| 2000.0 |													
α Ara	158427	17^h 31^m 50.4^s	−49° 52′ 34″	2.95	−1.7	B2 Vne	280	0.075″	199°	51	0	.007″	3.3	377	(a)
β Ara	157244	17 25 17.9	−55 31 47	2.85	−4.4	K0/1 Ib	96	0.024	182	3	0	.034	180	4500	(b)
γ Ara	157246	17 25 23.5	−56 22 39	3.34	*	B1 Ib	*	0.011	170	*	−3	*	*	*	(c)
δ Ara	158094	17 31 05.9	−60 41 01	3.62	−0.2	B8 Vn	190	0.106	207	[31]	10	[.017]	1.4	95	
ε¹ Ara	152980	16 59 35.0	−53 09 38	4.06	−0.5	K3 III	270	0.017	25	28	23	.005	30	125	(d)
ε² Ara	153580	17 03 08.6	−53 14 13	5.29	4.0	F5 V	84	0.143	180	19	7	.039	1.0	2.0	
ζ Ara	152786	16 58 37.1	−55 59 24	3.13	−0.3	K3 III	74	0.037	200	7	−6	.044	31	104	(e)
η Ara	151249	16 49 47.0	−59 02 29	3.76	−0.3	K5 III	210	0.051	127	13	9	.025	30	104	(f)
θ Ara	165024	18 06 37.7	−50 05 30	3.66	−5.1	B2 Ib	1800	0.020	213	[54]	3	[.002]	15	8630	
ι Ara	157042	17 23 16.0	−47 28 05	5.25	*	B2 IIIne	*	0.017	208	*	−19	*	*	*	(g)
κ Ara	157457	17 25 59.9	−50 38 01	5.23	0.0	G8 III	110	0.010	79	17	17	.030	15	79	
λ Ara	160032	17 40 23.4	−49 24 56	4.77	3.1†	F3 IV	71	0.192	156	20	4	.046	1.3	4.5	
μ Ara	160691	17 44 08.6	−51 50 03	5.15	4.9†	G3 IV/V	37	0.193	184	14	−9	.089	1.0	0.9	
π Ara	159492	17 38 05.5	−54 30 01	5.25	3.1†	A5 IV/V	88	0.152	194	20	−3	.037	0.9	4.5	
σ Ara	159217	17 35 39.4	−46 30 20	4.59	(0.3)	A0 V	230	0.044	219	15	4	.014	1.9	59	

Aries
(Arietis)

a) *Hamal* (Head of the Sheep). Also known as *Arietis, El Nath,* and *Ras Hammel.* B:M+0.2 (= $\mathcal{L}$70). OH: M+0.1, 78 l.y. SC:M−0.1 (= $\mathcal{L}$86).

b) *Sheratan* (The Sign). SC:M+2.1; Y:π.074.

c) *Mesarthim.* Note that the primary of this noted binary is γ^2. This is one of the first binary systems to be discovered (in 1664 by Robert Hooke). Burnham gives a distance of 160 l.y.

d) The distance modulus gives a distance of 250 l.y. However, in order for it to agree with its companion, we have given it a distance of 125 l.y.

e) *Botein.*

f) The Yale *Bright Star Catalogue* gives identical data for ϵ^A and ϵ^B, except that B has an RV of −6, and therefore a calculated space velocity of 7 km/s. Given m and π, the distance modulus calculation of M is then −1.9, at considerable variance with the published value of 1.4.

g) The parallax indicates a distance of 165 l.y.

h) Note the large parallax, generated from the distance modulus formula. Indeed, the Yale *Bright Star Catalogue* notes that this is "possibly [a] nearby star on basis of spectroscopic parallax."

i) If M is estimated at +5 from Fig. 2, then the distance is a mere 34 l.y.! The luminosity would then be about 0.8, and the size about that of our Sun. But as this short distance would generate a very large parallax (about .100″), we must conclude that the absolute magnitude is not that dim.

j) In the same field is T Arietis, a Mira variable (7.4–11, period 314 days).

k) This is an easily resolved binary with 30B Ari (see Visual Binary Section). B:M+2.8.

l) The distance modulus gives a distance of 325 l.y., compared to 120 l.y. for 30A, despite the fact that the two stars have the same parallax. B:M+3.6 (= $\mathcal{L}$3).

m) The published absolute magnitude yields a distance of 171 l.y.; however, the parallax suggests a much greater distance, over 1500 l.y.

ARIES	HD	R.A.	Declin.	m	M	Spectra	l.y.	μ	Dir.	V	RV	π	D_s	𝓛	Rmk
		2000.0													
α Ari	12929	02^h 07^m 10.3^s	+23° 27' 45''	2.00	0.6†	K2 III	63	0.238''	127°	26	−14	.052''	13	45	(a)
β Ari	11636	01 54 38.3	+20 48 29	2.64	1.7†	A5 V	50	0.145	138	11	−2	.065	1.9	16	(b)
γ² Ari	11502	01 53 31.8	+19 17 37	4.75$_v$	0.2	A1 pSi	270	0.127	142	23	−1	.026	1.9	65	(c)
γ¹ Ari ∞	11503	01 53 31.7	+19 17 45	4.83	(1.9)	B9 V	130	0.133	144	25	4	.026	1.2	14	(d)
δ Ari	19787	03 11 37.7	+19 43 36	4.35	−0.1	K2 III	250	0.151	93	36	25	.027	16	86	(e)
ε Ari ∞	18520	02 59 12.6	+21 20 25	4.63	1.4	A2 V	140	0.017	263	18	−8	.005	1.7	22	(f)
ζ Ari	20150	03 14 54.0	+21 02 40	4.89	0.0	A1 V	310	0.076	201	19	7	.020	2.7	79	(g)
η Ari	13555	02 12 48.0	+21 12 39	5.27	3.4	F5 V	77	0.161	88	[19]	6	[.042]	1.2	3.4	(h)
ι Ari	11909	01 57 21.0	+17 49 03	5.10	*	K1 Vp	*	0.039	114	—	−5	—	—	—	(i)
κ Ari	12869	02 06 33.8	+22 38 54	5.03	—	A2 m	—	0.036	150	—	12	—	—	—	
λ Ari ∞	11973	01 57 55.7	+23 35 46	4.79	1.7	F0 IV	140	0.090	264	15	−1	.028	2.0	16	
ν Ari	16432	02 38 48.9	+21 57 41	5.30	2.4	A7 V	120	0.016	210	10	8	.013	1.5	8.6	
ξ Ari	14951	02 24 49.0	+10 36 38	5.47	−1.0	B7 IV	640	0.021	115	[20]	4	[.005]	2.0	198	
π Ari	17543	02 49 17.5	+17 27 51	5.22	−1.3	B6 IV	660	0.012	185	[15]	9	[.005]	3.1	261	(j)
σ Ari	17769	02 51 29.5	+15 04 55	5.49	−0.6	B7 V	540	0.040	127	[36]	17	[.006]	1.8	137	
τ¹ Ari	20756	03 21 13.6	+21 08 49	5.28	−1.1	B5 IV	620	0.035	130	[35]	14	[.005]	2.6	217	
τ² Ari	20893	03 22 45.2	+20 44 31	5.09	−0.4	K3 III	410	0.048	246	29	2	.008	23	114	
14 Ari	13174	02 09 25.3	+25 56 24	4.98	0.6	F2 III	250	0.083	114	[30]	1	[.013]	3.7	45	
30A Ari ∞	16246	02 37 00.4	+24 38 51	6.50	3.7	F6 V	120	0.137	91	39	15	.018	1.0	2.6	(k)
30B Ari	16232	02 36 57.7	+24 38 54	7.09	2.1	F5 IV	330	0.143	88	41	17	.018	2.6	11	(l)
33 Ari ∞	16628	02 40 41.0	+27 03 39	5.30	1.7	A3 V	170	0.072	112	172	17	.002	1.7	16	(m)
35 Ari	16908	02 43 27.0	+27 42 26	4.66	−1.7	B3 V	610	0.011	131	[16]	13	[.005]	2.3	377	
38 Ari	17093	02 44 57.5	+12 26 45	5.18$_v$	1.5	A7 III/IV	180	0.144	124	25	−2	.027	2.0	20	
39 Ari	17361	02 47 54.5	+29 14 50	4.51	0.0	K1 III	260	0.191	128	37	−15	.027	16	79	
41 Ari	17573	02 49 59.0	+27 15 38	3.63	−0.2	B8 Vn	96	0.131	149	19	4	.034	1.4	95	
SX Ari	19832	03 12 14.2	+27 15 26	5.79$_v$	—	B9 pSi	—	0.017	140	—	11	—	—	—	
- Ari	20644	03 20 20.3	+29 02 55	4.47	−1.1	K2 II/III	420	0.012	180	7	−2	.008	43	217	

Auriga
(Aurigae)

a) *Capella* (Little She-goat). Also known as the Goat Star. It has an m10 companion, a red dwarf, which is itself a close binary.
SC:M+0.3. Y:π.080. B:M−0.6, $\mathcal{L}$60. OH:M+0.4.

b) *Menkalinan* (Shoulder of the Charioteer). An Algol-type eclipsing binary of very small amplitude over 3^d23^h. B:M−0.3, which results in a luminosity of 110. OH:55 l.y.

c) *Almaaz, Al Anz.* A supergiant Algol-type eclipsing variable of very high luminosity and exceptionally long period (9892 days, i.e., over 27 years). The eclipse phase lasts about a year, and the next eclipse is due in the year 2010.
B:M−7.1 (= $\mathcal{L}$60,000), D_s180, estimated distance of 3300 l.y. OH:M−7.8; 2800 l.y.

d) *Hoedus I, Sadatoni.* An Algol-type eclipsing variable with a period of 972 days. B:M−3.5, $\mathcal{L}$2100, D_s160, 1200 l.y. Burnham cites others who put the absolute magnitude at −4.4, and who give a diameter of 300 Suns.

e) *Hoedus II.* The parallax suggests a distance under 200 l.y. B:M−2.1, $\mathcal{L}$580. Yale indicates this may be a βC variable.

f) B:M+0.1, $\mathcal{L}$85.

g) *Hassaleh.*

h) The small parallax suggests a much larger distance, over 1000 l.y.

i) The *Bright Star Catalogue* shows this as a variable; it is not. East 4° is M37, the best of the three open clusters in this constellation which bear Messier numbers.

j) The parallax suggests a distance of about 650 l.y.

k) The parallax indicates a distance of about 500 l.y.

l) A Mira-type variable. If M is estimated from Fig. 2 at −1, then: 1031 l.y., π.003, V41 km/s, D_s43, and $\mathcal{L}$198.

AURIGA	HD	R.A.	Declin.	m	M	Spectra	l.y.	μ	Dir.	V	RV	π	D_s	ℒ	Rmk
		2000.0													
α Aur	34029	$05^h\,16^m\,41.3^s$	+45° 59′ 53″	0.08	0.09†	G8 III	44	0.430″	169°	40	30	.075″	11	72	(a)
β Aur	40183	05 59 31.7	+44 56 51	1.90$_v$	0.6	A2 IV	80	0.055	269	19	−18	.041	2.4	45	(b)
δ Aur	40035	05 59 31.6	+54 17 05	3.72	0.2	K0 III	170	0.151	147	33	8	.022	13	65	
ε Aur	31964	05 01 58.1	+43 49 24	2.99$_v$	−8.5	F0 Ia	6500	0.004	166	4	−3	.007	365	200000	(c)
ζ Aur	32068	05 02 28.6	+41 04 33	3.75$_v$	−2.3	K4 II	530	0.024	158	26	13	.005	53	655	(d)
η Aur	32630	05 06 30.8	+41 14 04	3.17	−1.7	B3 V	310	0.073	157	17	7	.022	2.6	377	(e)
θ Aur ∞	40312	05 59 43.2	+37 12 45	2.62$_v$	(−0.7)	A0 pec	150	0.096	149	36	29	.022	2.0	146	(f)
ι Aur	31398	04 56 59.6	+33 09 58	2.69	−2.3	K3 II	330	0.018	167	18	18	.021	73	655	(g)
κ Aur	43039	06 15 22.6	+29 29 53	4.35	0.3	G8.5 IIIb	210	0.274	195	75	20	.018	13	60	
λ Aur	34411	05 19 08.4	+40 05 57	4.71	3.84†	G2 IV/V	49	0.844	142	89	66	.067	1.4	2.3	
μ Aur	33641	05 13 25.6	+38 29 04	4.86	(1.7)	A4 Vm	140	0.078	194	26	21	.023	2.2	16.9	
ν Aur	39003	05 51 29.3	+39 08 55	3.97	0.2	K0 III	190	0.009	324	10	10	.017	15	65	
ξ Aur	39283	05 54 50.7	+55 42 25	4.99	(0.4)	A2 V	270	0.025	331	16	−12	.012	2.8	55	
π Aur	40239	05 59 56.1	+45 56 13	4.26$_v$	−2.4	M3 II	700	0.005	169	8	1	.003	91	718	
ρ Aur	34759	05 21 48.4	+41 48 17	5.23	−1.1	B3 V	600	0.036	152	[34]	13	[.005]	5.0	217	
σ Aur	35186	05 24 39.1	+37 23 08	4.99	−0.3	K4 III	370	0.008	173	23	−19	.003	26	104	(h)
τ Aur	38656	05 49 10.4	+39 10 52	4.52	0.3	G8 III	230	0.033	226	30	−20	.007	12	60	
υ Aur	38944	05 51 02.4	+37 18 20	4.74	−0.5	M0 III	360	0.059	136	144	38	.002	35	125	
φ Aur	35620	05 27 38.8	+34 28 33	5.07	(−0.2)	K3 III	360	0.047	182	40	31	.009	24	91	
χ Aur	36371	05 32 43.6	+32 11 31	4.76	−6.3	B5 Iab	5300	0.002	180	[15]	0	[.001]	90	25000	(i)
ψ¹ Aur	44537	06 24 53.8	+49 17 17	4.91$_v$	−5.7	M0 Iab*	4300	0.001	225	5	5	.007	511	15000	
ψ² Aur	47174	06 39 19.8	+42 29 20	4.79	−0.2	K3 III	330	0.059	173	72	17	.004	21	95	
ψ³ Aur	47100	06 38 49.1	+39 54 09	5.20	−1.2	B8 III	620	0.016	210	[17]	9	[.005]	2.8	238	
ψ⁴ Aur	47914	06 43 04.9	+44 31 28	5.02	−0.3	K5 III	380	0.053	237	74	−73	.019	28	104	
ψ⁵ Aur	48682	06 46 44.3	+43 34 39	5.25	4.37†	G0 V	49	0.164	359	27	−24	.067	1.0	1.4	
ψ⁶ Aur	48781	06 47 39.5	+48 47 22	5.22	0.0	K0 III	360	0.007	344	[9]	−8	[.009]	17	79	
ψ⁷ Aur	49520	06 50 45.9	+41 46 53	5.02	−0.2	K3 III	360	0.134	190	220	61	.003	21	95	
1 Aur	30504	04 49 54.6	+37 29 18	4.88	−2.3	K3.5 III	890	0.054	317	25	−23	.025	67	655	
2 Aur	30834	04 52 37.9	+36 42 11	4.78	−0.2	K2.5 IIIb	320	0.027	255	[21]	−17	[.010]	25	95	
4 Aur ∞	31647	04 59 15.3	+37 53 24	4.94	0.6	A0 V	240	0.108	158	103	5	.005	2.5	45	(j)
9 Aur	32537	05 06 40.6	+51 35 52	5.00	3.4†	F0 V	70	0.174	189	18	−5	.049	1.0	3.4	
14 Aur ∞	33959	05 15 24.3	+32 41 16	5.02$_v$	2.5	A9 V	100	0.028	300	21	−10	.007	1.2	8	(k)
16 Aur	34334	05 18 10.6	+33 22 18	4.54	−0.2	K3 III	290	0.166	164	63	−28	.014	21	95	
19 Aur	34578	05 20 00.8	+33 57 28	5.03	−2.1	A5 II	870	0.010	191	[14]	−5	[.004]	11	545	
63 Aur	54716	07 11 39.3	+39 19 14	4.90	−1.3	K4 III/a	570	0.044	89	28	−27	.023	43	261	
65 Aur	57264	07 22 02.6	+36 45 38	5.13	0.2	K0 III	320	0.093	254	30	23	.022	14	65	
66 Aur	57669	07 24 08.4	+40 40 20	5.19	0.2	K0 IIIa+	330	0.028	193	28	21	.007	17	65	
Σ872 ∞	43017	06 15 39.0	+36 08 55	6.92	3.3	dF4	170	0.065	274	[18]	7	[.019]	1.4	3.8	
R Aur ∞	34019	05 17 17.8	+53 35 10	6.5$_v$	*	M7 IIIe	*	0.027	138	*	8	*	*	*	(l)

Bootes
(Bootis)

a) *Arcturus* (Guardian of the Bear). B:$M-0.3$, $\mathscr{L}115$, D_s25. Y:$\pi.097$.

This is the fourth brightest star and is capable of being seen in daylight with a carefully aligned telescope. The star's high space velocity will carry it past the solar system in a few thousand years. Burnham points out that in half a million years this bright giant will have disappeared from naked-eye visibility.

b) *Nekkar* (Herdsman).

c) *Seginus, Haris.*

d) *Izar.* Noted binary with contrasting colors (yellow and blue). B:$M-1.9$, based on the Yale (1964 ed.) parallax of .013″. This would yield a luminosity of 500.

SC lists an HD of 129988 as the only ε Boo, with the same data that Yale lists for 129989. According to Boss, 129989 is the primary, and 129988 is the companion (which Yale has adopted). Note that ε^B has the same parallax, although the distance modulus formula—given m and M—results in a greater distance.

e) ζ^B is given identical values in BC, except: HD 129246, m4.83, $B-V$ unknown.

f) *Muphrid, Saak.* Y:$\pi.102$.

g) *Asellus Primus* (The First Little Donkey). SC:$M+3.8$.

h) *Asellus Secundus* (The Second Little Donkey). Designated a variable in 1984 [IBVS #2681].

i) *Asellus Tertius* (The Third Little Donkey). The parallax suggests 300 l.y.

Note that the primary is κ^2. Along with κ^1 (m6.7) it forms a wide, fixed binary: PA 236°, 13.3″.

SC gives one entry, with the right ascension and declination of κ^1 [$14^h13^m27.6^s$, $+51°47'15''$]; the remaining values are of κ^2.

j) *Alkalurops.* B:$M+2.0$.

k) B:$M+4.2$.

l) The parallax indicates a distance of 165 l.y., agreeing with that of ν^2.

m) Y:$\pi.156$.

n) SC:$M+8.2$.

o) B:$M+4.4$.

p) Mira variable. If M is estimated at -1, then: 747 l.y., $\pi.004$, $V59$ km/s, D_s43, and $\mathscr{L}198$.

BOOTES	HD	R.A.	Declin.	m	M	Spectra	l.y.	μ	Dir.	V	RV	π	D_s	ℒ	Rmk
		2000.0													
α Boo	124897	$14^h 15^m 39.6^s$	+19° 10′ 57″	−0.04	−0.24†	K2 III	35	2.281″	209°	118	−5	.092″	21	98	(a)
β Boo	133208	15 01 56.6	+40 23 26	3.50	0.3	G8 III	88	0.056	235	21	−20	.037	12	60	(b)
γ Boo	127762	14 32 04.6	+38 18 29	3.03$_v$	0.5	A7 III	110	0.189	322	51	−36	.025	2.8	50	(c)
δ Boo	135722	15 15 30.1	+33 18 53	3.47	0.3	G8 III	110	0.143	144	26	−12	.030	12	60	
ε^A Boo ∞	129989	14 44 59.1	+27 04 27	2.37	−0.9	K0 II	150	0.054	289	23	−17	.016	21	180	(d)
ε^B Boo	129988	14 44 59.1	+27 04 30	5.12	−0.9	A2 V	520	0.054	289	28	−23	.016	1.9	180	
ζ Boo ∞	129247	14 41 08.8	+13 43 42	4.43	−0.2	A2 III	280	0.056	111	30	−5	.009	3.7	95	(e)⊘
η Boo	121370	13 54 41.0	+18 23 52	2.68	2.72†	G0 IV	32	0.369	190	17	0	.102	2.2	6.4	(f)
θ Boo	126660	14 25 11.7	+51 51 03	4.05	3.22†	F7 V	48	0.468	211	34	−11	.068	1.5	4.1	(g)
ι Boo ∞	125161	14 16 09.8	+51 22 02	4.75$_v$	2.4	A7 V	68	0.177	300	24	−17	.048	1.2	8.6	(h)
κ^2 Boo ∞	124675	14 13 28.9	+51 47 24	4.54$_v$	1.5	A8 IV	130	0.058	97	32	−17	.010	1.8	20	(i)
λ Boo	125162	14 16 22.9	+46 05 18	4.18	(2.4)	A0 pec	72	0.247	310	27	−8	.045	1.2	8.3	
μ^1 Boo ∞	137391	15 24 29.3	+37 22 38	4.31	2.6	F0 V	84	0.169	300	23	−10	.039	1.4	7.2	(j)
μ^2 Boo ∞	137392	15 24 30.8	+37 20 51	6.50	5.9	G1 V	84	0.174	302	23	−9	.039	0.5	0.3	(k)⊘
ν^1 Boo	138481	15 30 55.7	+40 49 59	5.02	−0.3	K5 III	380	0.012	145	10	−10	.020	31	104	(l)
ν^2 Boo	138629	15 31 46.9	+40 53 58	5.02	(1.5)	A2 n	160	0.024	240	17	−16	.020	1.7	19	
ξ Boo ∞	131156	14 51 23.2	+19 06 04	4.55$_v$	5.53†	G8 V	22	0.171	127	7	4	.148	0.8	0.5	(m)⊘
ο Boo	129972	14 45 14.4	+16 57 52	4.60	0.2	G8.5 III	72	0.079	228	12	−9	.045	13	65	
π^1 Boo ∞	129174	14 40 43.5	+16 25 06	4.93	(−3.6)	B9 pec	1600	0.018	52	42	−1	.002	11	2099	
π^2 Boo	129175	14 40 43.8	+16 25 04	5.81	(−2.7)	A6 V	1600	0.006	360	16	−7	.002	13	933	
ρ Boo	127665	14 31 49.7	+30 22 17	3.58	−0.2	K3 III	190	0.155	319	29	−14	.029	22	95	
σ Boo	128167	14 34 40.7	+29 44 42	4.46	3.2†	F2 V	57	0.228	56	19	0	.057	1.2	4.1	
τ Boo ∞	120136	13 47 15.7	+17 27 24	4.50	3.5†	F7 V	53	0.484	274	40	−16	.062	1.3	3.1	
υ Boo	120477	13 49 28.5	+15 47 52	4.07	−0.3	K5 III	240	0.102	291	44	−6	.011	29	104	
φ Boo	139641	15 37 49.5	+40 21 12	5.24	3.2	G8 III/IV	83	0.083	45	21	−10	.021	2.8	4.1	
χ Boo	135502	15 14 29.1	+29 09 51	5.26	1.4	A2 V	190	0.074	291	21	−16	.026	1.7	22	
ψ Boo	133582	15 04 26.7	+26 56 51	4.54	−0.1	K2 III	280	0.176	267	53	−26	.018	20	86	
ω Boo	133124	15 02 06.4	+25 00 29	4.81	4.8	K4 III+	33	0.050	186	17	14	.025	2.7	0.9	
6 Boo	120539	13 49 42.7	+21 15 51	4.91	−0.3	K4 III	360	0.021	53	12	−3	.009	26	104	
9 Boo	121710	13 56 34.1	+27 29 31	5.01	−0.2	K3 III	360	0.059	153	53	−40	.008	25	95	
12 Boo	123999	14 10 23.9	+25 05 30	4.83	2.4	F9 IV	78	0.068	200	13	11	.042	2.4	8.6	
20 Boo	125560	14 19 45.1	+16 18 25	4.86	−0.2	K3 III	340	0.155	291	[76]	−8	[.010]	21	95	
31 Boo	129312	14 41 38.7	+08 09 42	4.86	0.3	G8 III+	270	0.004	270	22	−22	.011	12	60	
34 Boo	129712	14 43 25.3	+26 31 40	4.81$_v$	(−3.7)	M3 III	1600	0.025	217	60	6	.002	156	2344	
45 Boo	134083	15 07 18.0	+24 52 09	4.93	3.7†	F5 V	58	0.252	133	22	−7	.056	1.1	2.6	
β1111	126129	14 23 22.6	+08 26 48	5.12	(1.1)	F0 V+	200	0.078	262	29	−18	.016	3.5	28	
Σ1785 ∞	120476	13 49 05.0	+26 58 46	7.04	7.26†	dK6	38	0.447	258	32	−21	.086	0.6	0.1	(n)⊘
Σ1835 ∞	126128	14 23 22.5	+08 26 42	6.86	2.5	A0 V	240	0.078	262	33	−23	.016	0.8	7.9	
Σ1909 ∞	133640	15 03 47.3	+47 39 16	4.76	4.87†	F9-G1 Vn	39	0.413	274	34	−25	.084	0.9	0.9	(o)⊘
R Boo	128609	14 37 11.7	+26 44 11	5.80$_v$	*	M5 III	*	0.010	315	*	−58	*	*	*	(p)
- Boo	125351	14 17 59.7	+35 30 34	4.81	0.0	K0 III	300	0.011	350	[26]	−26	[.011]	15	79	

Caelum
(Caeli)

a) Y:π.045.

b) Y:π.058. SC:M+4.0.

c) If M is estimated at +2, then: 241 l.y., π.014, V17 km/s, D_s1.8, $\mathscr{L}$12.

CAELUM	HD	2000.0 R.A.	Declin.	m	M	Spectra	l.y.	μ	Dir.	V	RV	π	D_s	$\mathscr{L}$	Rmk
α Cae	29875	$04^h 40^m 33.6^s$	$-41° 51' 50''$	4.45	2.9†	F1 V	65	0.170″	243°	16	−1	.050″	1.3	5.4	(a)
β Cae	29992	04 42 03.4	−37 08 40	5.05	3.5†	F3 V	67	0.198	11	33	27	.049	1.1	3.1	(b)
γ¹ Cae	32831	05 04 24.3	−35 29 00	4.55	0.2	K2 III	240	0.132	112	49	10	.013	17	65	
γ² Cae	32846	05 04 26.0	−35 42 19	6.34	*	F2 IV/V	*	0.044	28	*	6	*	*	*	(c)
δ Cae	28873	04 30 50.1	−44 57 14	5.07	−1.7	B2 IV/V	740	0.003	108	[14]	14	[.004]	2.0	377	

Camelopardalis
(Camelopardalis)

a) The parallax indicates a distance of perhaps 400–500 l.y.

b) The parallax indicates a distance of about 275–300 l.y.

c) This is a splendid multiple binary (see Visual Binary Section).

d) A pleasant binary with fixed separation of 21.6″ (see Visual Binary Section).

e) The distance modulus formula indicates a distance of 3800 l.y. Since its parallax appears to be equal to that of the primary, the same distance has been given to this star.

CAMELO-PARDALIS	HD	R.A. 2000.0		Declin.			_m_	_M_	Spectra	l.y.	μ	Dir.	_V_	_RV_	π	_Ds_	_L_	Rmk
α Cam	30614	04^h 54^m 03.0^s	+66° 20' 34"				4.29	−6.2	O9.5 Ia	4100	0.009"	27°	22	6	.002"	55	25000	
β Cam ∞	31910	05 03 25.1	+60 26 32				4.03	−4.5	G0 Ib	1700	0.015	196	8	−2	.009	103	5000	(a)
γ Cam	23401	03 50 21.5	+71 19 57				4.63	0.9	A2 IVn	180	0.043	150	17	−1	.012	2.1	34	(b)
3 Cam	29317	04 39 54.7	+53 04 47				5.05	0.2	K0 III	300	0.012	185	42	−41	.008	14	65	
7 Cam	31278	04 57 17.1	+53 45 08				4.47	1.2	A1 V	150	0.024	289	[10]	−8	[.022]	1.4	26	
11 Cam	32343	05 06 08.4	+58 58 21				5.08	−1.7	B2.5 Ve	740	0.007	207	[13]	−11	[.004]	3.2	377	
16 Cam	34787	05 23 27.6	+57 32 40				5.23	0.6	A0 Vn	280	0.062	208	18	12	.023	1.7	45	
31 Cam	39220	05 54 57.7	+59 53 18				5.2$_v$	0.6	A2 V	270	0.019	177	10	−3	.009	2.4	45	
42 Cam	48879	06 50 57.1	+67 34 19				5.14	−2.3	B4 IV	1000	0.008	67	6	5	.010	4.4	655	
43 Cam	49340	06 53 42.2	+68 53 18				5.12	−1.0	B7 III	550	0.008	45	29	−21	.002	1.7	198	
OΣ67 ∞	24480	03 57 08.2	+61 06 32				5.00	−0.3	K3 I/II	370	0.011	190	4	−2	.015	27	104	
Σ385 ∞	21291	03 29 04.1	+59 56 25				4.21	−7.1	B9 Ia	6000	0.001	135	[14]	−7	[.001]	150	55000	
Σ390 ∞	21447	03 30 00.2	+55 27 07				5.09	1.2	A1 V	200	0.044	262	8	0	.025	1.9	26	
Σ1051 ∞	57044	07 26 35.1	+73 04 57				6.79	1.9	F2 IV	310	0.028	64	[36]	−34	[.011]	1.9	14	(c)
Σ1694A ∞	112028	12 49 13.5	+83 24 46				5.28	(−4.7)	A1 III	3300	0.034	297	159	2	.001	20	6081	(d)
Σ1694B	112014	12 49 06.5	+83 25 04				5.85	(−4.2)	A0 V	3300	0.032	302	151	1	.001	12	3597	(e)
L Cam	42818	06 18 50.8	+69 19 12				4.80	0.6	A0 Vn	230	0.105	176	63	−7	.008	2.4	45	
R Cam	127226	14 17 51.2	+83 49 56				6.97$_v$	—	S2-S8	—	0.084	78	—	—	—	—	—	
VZ Cam	55966	07 31 04.5	+82 24 42				4.96$_v$	(−5.0)	M4 IIIa	3300	0.041	181	195	14	.001	291	8166	
BD Cam	22649	03 42 09.3	+63 13 01				5.10$_v$	(−3.4)	S3.5/2	1600	0.027	318	67	−22	.002	133	1794	
BE Cam	23475	03 49 31.2	+65 31 34				4.47$_v$	−4.8	M2 IIab	2300	0.010	204	4	−3	.014	314	6500	
BK Cam	20336	03 19 59.3	+65 39 09				4.84$_v$	−2.5	B2.5 V	960	0.019	115	10	−3	.009	9.4	787	
- Cam	21389	03 29 54.8	+58 52 44				4.54	−7.1	A0 Ia	6900	0.007	74	[74]	−6	[.0005]	198	55000	
- Cam	23089	03 46 02.3	+63 20 42				4.80	0.6	G0 III	230	0.009	193	[4]	−2	[.014]	8.3	45	
- Cam	24479	03 57 25.3	+63 04 20				5.03	−0.8	B9.5 Ve	480	0.007	27	[7]	5	[.007]	2.0	164	
- Cam	25291	04 04 27.1	+59 09 20				5.06	−2.0	F0 II	840	0.004	326	[20]	−20	[.004]	17	497	
- Cam	26764	04 16 43.1	+53 36 43				5.19	(0.4)	A2 Vn	300	0.012	275	6	−3	.011	2.8	55	
- Cam	33564	05 22 33.5	+79 13 52				5.05	3.7†	F6 V	62	0.179	333	19	−10	.053	1.2	2.6	
- Cam	49878	07 00 04.0	+76 58 39				4.55	−0.3	K4 III	300	0.076	100	30	−26	.023	25	104	
- Cam	106112	12 12 11.8	+77 36 58				5.14	(2.6)	A5 m	110	0.020	24	3	0	.031	1.5	7.2	

Cancer
(Cancri)

a) *Acubens* (Claw). Sometimes known as *Sartan*.

b) *Altarf.*

c) *Asellus Borealis* (The Northern Donkey). Smack in the middle of the triangle formed by γ, δ, and η Cnc is M44 ("Beehive" or "Praesepe"), a splendid open cluster so large and bright it can be seen with the naked eye on a good night.

d) *Asellus Australis* (The Southern Donkey). The parallax suggests a distance of about 130 l.y. The double is only optical.

e) *Tegmine.* With ζ^B and ζ^C forms an interesting multiple system (see Visual Binary and Orbital Elements Sections).

   Burnham gives ζ^A an absolute magnitude of 3.9, luminosity 2, and parallax .047, but these values have been superseded by more recent studies.

f) A long-period binary, circling ζ^{AB} about every 1150 years (see Orbital Elements Section).

g) The parallaxes of ι^A and ι^B suggest that these stars are considerably closer, perhaps about 200 l.y. away. These stars form a fixed visual binary easily resolved (see Visual Binary Section).

h) If the absolute magnitude is estimated at -1.0, then: 580 l.y., π.006, V31, D_s1.9, and $\mathcal{L}$198.

i) If the absolute magnitude is estimated to be $+0.5$, then: 285 l.y., π.011, V24, D_s3.4, and $\mathcal{L}$50.

j) Note the high parallax, generated from the distance modulus formula, which may indicate that the given value of M is too dim.

k) SC:$M+3.7$. Y:π.067.

l) A Mira-type variable with period 361.6 days, so it will not be until the mid-2000s that the best viewing of the maximum will occur (see Variable Section).

   M may be estimated at -1 from Fig. 2 (the $B-V$ index of 1.56 reinforces this estimate). Then: 1400 l.y., D_s41, and $\mathcal{L}$198. However, the reported parallax yields a distance of only 160 l.y., which in turn would mean an absolute magnitude of $M+3.7$, a size of 7 Suns and $\mathcal{L}$3.

   Petit indicates that this star at maximum only reaches m6.2.

CANCER	HD	R.A. 2000.0		Declin.		m	M	Spectra	l.y.	μ	Dir.	V	RV	π	D_s	$\mathscr{L}$	Rmk
α Cnc	76756	08^h 58^m 29.2^s		+11° 51′ 28″		4.25	(1.2)	A5 m	140	0.049″	134°	17	−14	.024″	2.5	27	(a)
β Cnc	69267	08 16 30.9		+09 11 08		3.52	−0.3	K4 III	190	0.068	220	35	22	.012	28	104	(b)
γ Cnc	74198	08 43 17.1		+21 28 06		4.66	1.2	A1 V	160	0.112	247	44	29	.016	1.8	26	(c)
δ Cnc	74442	08 44 41.0		+18 09 15		3.94	0.2	K0 III	180	0.234	184	47	17	.025	14	65	(d)
ζ^{1A} Cnc ∞	68257	08 12 12.6		+17 38 52		4.67	(2.6)	F8 V	84	0.154	154	20	−8	.039	2.2	7.0	(e)⌀
ζ^{1C} Cnc	68255	08 12 12.6		+17 38 52		6.20	(4.2)	F9 V	84	0.154	154	20	−6	.039	1.2	1.7	(f)⌀
ζ^{2B} Cnc	68256	08 12 13.2		+17 38 51		6.01	(4.0)	G5 V	84	0.149	139	21	−11	.039	1.2	2.0	
η Cnc	72292	08 32 42.4		+20 26 28		5.33	−0.2	K3 III	420	0.066	223	34	24	.013	21	95	
θ Cnc	72094	08 31 35.7		+18 05 40		5.35	−0.3	K5 III	440	0.083	224	[69]	45	[.007]	30	104	
ι^A Cnc ∞	74739	08 46 41.8		+28 45 36		4.02	−2.1	G8 II	550	0.051	208	21	16	.017	38	545	(g)
ι^B Cnc	74738	08 46 40.0		+28 45 55		6.57	1.7	A3 V	310	0.047	201	15	8	.017	1.5	16	
κ Cnc	78316	09 07 44.8		+10 40 06		5.24$_v$	*	B8 IIIp+	*	0.024	240	*	24	*	*	*	(h)
μ^1 Cnc	66875	08 06 18.3		+22 38 08		5.99$_v$	−0.5	M3 III	650	0.011	221	[28]	26	[.005]	36	125	
μ^2 Cnc	67228	08 07 45.8		+21 34 54		5.30	3.0	G1 Vb	96	0.077	164	38	−36	.034	2.1	5.0	
ν Cnc	77350	09 02 44.2		+24 27 11		5.45	(−2.2)	A0 pSi	1100	0.008	203	19	−15	.003	5.5	578	
ξ Cnc	78515	09 09 21.5		+22 02 43		5.14	0.2	K0 III	320	0.003	90	[7]	−7	[.010]	13	65	
o^1 Cnc	76543	08 57 14.9		+15 19 21		5.20	*	A5 III	*	0.057	77	*	−5	*	*	*	(i)
π^2 Cnc	79554	09 15 13.8		+14 56 29		5.34	0.2	K1 III	350	0.043	252	[34]	26	[.009]	19	65	
ρ^2 Cnc	76219	08 55 39.6		+27 55 39		5.22	−0.9	G8 II/III	550	0.039	198	41	17	.005	22	180	
σ^2 Cnc	76398	08 56 56.6		+32 54 37		5.45	(0.7)	A7 IV	300	0.087	214	38	5	.011	2.9	43	
σ^3 Cnc	76813	08 59 32.6		+32 25 07		5.20	3.2	G8 III	82	0.060	229	[24]	23	[.040]	3.0	4.1	(j)
τ Cnc	78235	09 08 00.0		+29 39 15		5.43	0.3	G8 III	350	0.030	262	[20]	−13	[.009]	11	60	
χ Cnc	69897	08 20 03.8		+27 13 03		5.14	4.1†	F6 V	52	0.382	182	44	33	.063	1.0	1.8	(k)
8 Cnc	66664	08 05 04.4		+13 07 05		5.12	0.0	A1 V	350	0.077	207	26	21	.023	3.1	79	
27 Cnc	71250	08 26 43.8		+12 39 17		5.50$_v$	−0.5	M3 IIIab	110	0.106	194	18	−7	.030	34	125	
h 785	71115	08 25 54.7		+07 33 53		5.13	−2.1	G8 II	910	0.037	259	19	15	.016	35	545	
R Cnc	69243	08 16 33.9		+11 43 35		7.13$_v$	*	M7 IIIe	*	0.018	137	32	32	.021	*	*	(l)

Canes Venatici
(Canum Venaticorum)

a) With α^2, a celebrated fixed binary with—perhaps—a color contrast. (Observers vary on this point.)

b) *Cor Caroli*. The primary is known as α^2 since its position is east of its companion. It is a curious variable, being the prototype of a rare class known as "spectrum variables." That is, the spectral lines vary in their intensity over a number of days—in Cor Caroli's case, 5.469 days. Its visual magnitude is not affected.

c) Y:π.117. East three degrees is the spiral galaxy M94, bright and round.

d) 2.5° S is NGC 4244, an edge-on galaxy, quite bright.

e) If the absolute magnitude is estimated at -1, then: 590 l.y., π.010, V10 km/s, D,50, $\mathcal{L}$198.

f) 1.5° N is M63, a spiral galaxy somewhat less spectacular than the Whirlpool Galaxy, which is NE 5.5°.

g) The superb Whirlpool Galaxy (M51) is SSE 2°; this was the first discovered to have the classic spiral pattern (1773).

h) *La Superba*. A noted semiregular variable of unusually vivid red. Burnham gives the spectral type as C5 and notes evidence that the absolute magnitude may be only between -1.5 and -2.4.

   The period of Y CVn has been recently reassessed at 251.8 days [IBVS #2271].

i) Neither this star nor AW CVn is indicated as a variable by Tirion.

CANES VENATICI	HD	2000.0 R.A.	Declin.	m	M	Spectra	l.y.	μ	Dir.	V	RV	π	D_s	$\mathscr{L}$	Rmk
α^1 CVn ∞	112412	12^h 56^m 00.3^s	+38° 18′ 53″	5.60	(2.8)	F0 V	120	0.245″	283°	43	−3	.027″	1.4	6.2	(a)
α^2 CVn	112413	12 56 01.6	+38 19 06	2.9$_v$	0.0	A0 III	120	0.242	282	43	−3	.027	1.1	79	(b)
β CVn	109358	12 33 44.5	+41 21 27	4.26	4.46†	G0 V	30	0.763	292	34	7	.109	1.0	1.3	(c)
2 CVn	106690	12 16 07.5	+40 39 36	5.66	−0.5	M1 III+	560	0.040	158	50	−16	.004	33	125	(d)
3 CVn	107274	12 19 48.7	+48 59 03	5.29	*	M0 III	*	0.012	279	*	8	*	*	*	(e)
5 CVn	107950	12 24 01.4	+51 33 44	4.80	0.3	G6 III+	86	0.013	39	12	−12	.038	11	60	
6 CVn	108225	12 25 50.9	+39 01 07	5.02	1.8	G9 III	110	0.089	245	15	−4	.030	5.9	15	
14 CVn	113797	13 05 44.4	+35 47 56	5.25	0.2	B9 V	330	0.037	297	21	−13	.011	1.3	65	
20 CVn	115604	13 17 32.5	+40 34 21	4.73$_v$	−0.7	F3 III	400	0.128	278	33	8	.019	6.3	150	(f)
21 CVn	115735	13 18 14.5	+49 40 55	5.15	(1.7)	A0 V	160	0.036	294	9	−3	.020	0.7	17	
24 CVn	118232	13 34 27.2	+49 00 57	4.70	1.9	A5 V	96	0.131	280	26	−18	.034	1.6	14	(g)
25 CVn ∞	118623	13 37 27.5	+36 17 41	4.82	0.5	A7 III	110	0.103	282	17	−6	.030	3.1	50	⊘
Y CVn	110914	12 45 07.8	+45 26 25	4.99$_v$	(−3.5)	C7	1600	0.012	351	31	12	.002	277	1986	(h)
AW CVn	120933	13 51 47.4	+34 26 39	4.74$_v$	(1.8)	K5 III	130	0.042	213	45	−44	.026	12	15	
BH CVn	118216	13 34 47.7	+37 10 57	4.98$_v$	1.9	F2 IV	140	0.083	99	19	7	.022	2.3	14	(i)
- CVn	115004	13 13 42.9	+40 09 10	4.92	0.2	K0 III	290	0.052	281	65	−21	.004	14	65	

Canis Major
(Canis Majoris)

a) *Sirius* (Sparkling). Also known as the Dog Star. DA: Spect. A9 IV, D_s1.7.

   The brightest star in the heavens, and the fifth closest. Its high proper motion led Halley to find differences in its eighteenth-century position whem compared to Ptolemy's catalog, thus revealing for the first time that the stars were not permanent fixtures.

   Sirius has a close companion, very difficult but not impossible to discern with a large enough telescope (see Orbital Elements Section). Sirius B is a white dwarf: m8.7, M11.5, A5, D_s0.022 (that is, a diameter of only 20,000 km—just over twice that of the Earth). Its mass is nearly equal to the Sun's.

   Four degrees south is M41, a spendid globular cluster for binoculars.

b) *Murzim* (The Announcer). A prototype of the variable class that now usually goes under the name of β Cephei stars. The slight variation in magnitude (from 1.93 to 2.00), every 6^h2^s, is not large enough to be visible to the naked eye. The parallax gives a distance of only 170 l.y.

c) *Muliphein*. This star is exceeded in brightness by ten other members of this constellation, including ω. B:$M-3.8$, $\mathcal{L}2700$.

d) *Wesen* (Weight). One of the most luminous stars. Burnham gives a distance of 2100 l.y., also $M-7.0$ (= $\mathcal{L}60,000$). The parallax gives a distance of about 300 l.y.

   Between δ and τ (see note (l)) lies NGC 2354, an open cluster of about 100 stars.

e) *Adhara* (Virgins). B:$M-5.0$, $\mathcal{L}9000$, 680 l.y. The parallax gives a distance of over 3000 l.y.

f) *Phurud*. The RV is extremely variable. During an observation period in 1980–81, the RV went from 50.3 km/s to 0.7 km/s in five days; the maximum observed speed then occurred sixteen days later, at 78.2 km/s [IBVS #2330].

   B:$M-2.4$, $\mathcal{L}750$, 390 l.y.

g) *Aludra*.

h) If the absolute magnitude is estimated at -5.5, then: 3000 l.y., $\mathcal{L}12,500$, and D_s20. However, given m and π, the distance modulus formula yields: 650 l.y., $M-2.1$, D_s4, and $\mathcal{L}545$. SC:$M-3.9$, $\mathcal{L}2900$, D_s5.1, 1500 l.y.

i) SC:M0.0.

j) The parallax suggests a distance of about 130 l.y.

k) This star, with o^1, forms one of the most luminous pairs in the heavens. Burnham gives o^2 an absolute magnitude of -7.1.

l) The star is encircled by a spectacular open cluster (NGC 2362), at one million years old, still a baby. B: Lum. class III. SC:III also, D_s about 5, $\mathcal{L}20,000$, $M-6.0$, 3900 l.y. If we estimate M at -7, then: 6200 l.y., π.0005, V151, D_s75, and $\mathcal{L}50,000$.

m) Estimating M at 0.0, then: 375 l.y., π.009, V17, D_s2, and $\mathcal{L}79$.

n) A beautiful binary, gold and blue.

o) If the absolute magnitude is estimated at -3, then: 1550 l.y., π.002, V54 km/s, D_s13, $\mathcal{L}1250$.

p) If the absolute magnitude is estimated at 0.0, then: 320 l.y., π.010, V27 km/s, D_s2, $\mathcal{L}80$.

CANIS MAJOR	HD	R.A.			Declin.			m	M	Spectra	l.y.	μ	Dir.	V	RV	π	D_s	ℒ	Rmk
			2000.0																
α CMa ∞	48915	06^h	45^m	08.9^s	−16°	42′	58″	−1.46	1.42†	A1 V	8.65	1.328″	204°	19	−8	.377″	1.6	21	(a)
β CMa	44743	06	22	41.9	−17	57	22	1.98$_v$	−4.8	B1 II/III	740	0.014	253	34	34	.019	4.0	6500	(b)
γ CMa	53244	07	03	45.4	−15	38	00	4.11	−3.4	B8 II	1000	0.011	214	[34]	30	[.003]	5.3	1803	(c)
δ CMa	54605	07	08	23.4	−26	23	35	1.86	−8.0	F8 Ia	3100	0.009	291	34	34	.011	365	125000	(d)
ε CMa	52089	06	58	37.5	−28	58	20	1.50	−4.4	B2 II	490	0.002	27	29	27	.001	4.7	4500	(e)
ζ CMa	44402	06	20	18.7	−30	03	48	3.02	−1.7	B2.5 V	290	0.006	59	33	32	.004	2.0	377	(f)
η CMa	58350	07	24	05.6	−29	18	11	2.44	−7.0	B5 Ia	2500	0.008	284	[51]	41	[.001]	37	50000	(g)
θ CMa	50778	06	54	11.3	−12	02	19	4.07	−0.3	K4 III	240	0.145	263	102	97	.022	26	104	
ι CMa	51309	06	56	08.1	−17	03	15	4.37$_v$	*	B3 Ib/II	*	0.013	309	43	41	.005	*	*	(h)
κ CMa	50013	06	49	50.4	−32	30	31	3.96$_v$	−2.5	B1.5 IV	640	0.011	280	[17]	14	[.005]	1.4	787	
λ CMa	45813	06	28	10.1	−32	34	49	4.48	(0.05)	B4 V	250	0.033	314	43	41	.013	1.5	75	
μ CMa ∞	51250	06	56	06.6	−14	02	37	5.00	(−3.5)	K2/3 III	1600	0.007	286	26	20	.002	89	1968	
ν² CMa	47205	06	36	41.0	−19	15	22	3.95	2.6†	K1 III	59	0.096	143	9	3	.055	4.7	7.2	(i)
ν³ CMa	47442	06	37	53.3	−18	14	15	4.43	0.0	K1 III	250	0.018	241	7	−2	.013	17	79	
ξ¹ CMa	46328	06	31	51.3	−23	25	06	4.33$_v$	−3.9	B1 III	1400	0.015	312	[41]	27	[.002]	2.3	2858	
ξ² CMa	46933	06	35	03.3	−22	57	53	4.54	0.6	A0 V	200	0.014	17	26	26	.025	1.4	45	(j)
o¹ CMa	50877	06	54	07.8	−24	11	02	3.87$_v$	−6.0	K3 Iab	3100	0.016	313	53	36	.002	482	20000	
o² CMa	53138	07	03	01.4	−23	50	00	3.02	−6.8	B3 Ia	3000	0.007	262	[57]	48	[.001]	34	40000	(k)
π CMa	51199	06	55	37.3	−20	08	11	4.68	0.6	gF2	96	0.058	45	11	8	.034	4.0	45	
σ CMa	52877	07	01	43.1	−27	56	06	3.47$_v$	−5.7	K4 III	2200	0.008	284	22	22	.024	420	15000	
τ CMa	57061	07	18	42.4	−24	57	15	4.40	*	O9 Ib	*	0.016	300	*	40	*	*	*	(l)
ω CMa	56139	07	14	48.6	−26	46	22	3.85$_v$	−2.3	B2 IV/V	550	0.013	288	[28]	26	[.006]	4.4	655	
10 CMa	48917	06	44	28.3	−31	04	14	5.20$_v$	−1.6	B2 IIIe	750	0.022	286	[41]	34	[.004]	2.3	344	
11 CMa	49229	06	46	51.0	−14	25	34	5.29	*	B9 III	*	0.013	315	*	15	*	*	*	(m)
15 CMa	50707	06	53	32.8	−20	13	27	4.83$_v$	−3.9	B1 IV	1800	0.013	283	[45]	28	[.002]	3.7	2858	
27 CMa	56014	07	14	15.1	−26	21	09	4.66$_v$	−2.9	B3 IIIe	1100	0.014	291	[22]	0	[.003]	3.5	1138	
29 CMa	57060	07	18	40.3	−24	33	32	4.98$_v$	—	O7 e+	—	0.011	260	—	−11	—	—	—	
h3945 ∞	56577	07	16	36.7	−23	18	56	4.51	−0.4	K4 III	310	0.015	270	28	28	.019	36	114	(n)
R CMa	57167	07	19	28.1	−16	23	43	5.70$_v$	3.7	F1 V	81	0.202	132	46	−39	.040	0.9	2.6	
FN CMa	53974	07	06	40.6	−11	17	39	5.39$_v$	*	B0.5 IV	*	0.020	246	*	31	*	*	*	(o)
- CMa	43445	06	15	44.8	−13	43	06	5.01	−0.2	B9 Vn	360	0.012	160	[38]	38	[.009]	1.6	95	
- CMa	43827	06	17	41.7	−16	48	57	5.14	−0.2	K3 III	380	0.018	289	9	−8	.017	22	95	
- CMa	44951	06	24	10.2	−11	31	49	5.22	−0.2	K3 III	400	0.072	236	34	−26	.016	21	95	
- CMa	46184	06	31	22.9	−12	23	30	5.15	−0.2	K3 III	380	0.038	118	19	17	.022	21	95	
- CMa	47536	06	37	47.5	−32	20	23	5.27	−0.1	K2 III	390	0.120	56	86	79	.017	19	86	
- CMa	47667	06	39	16.6	−14	08	45	4.82	−2.2	K2 II	830	0.004	180	30	29	.003	68	597	
- CMa	56618	07	16	34.9	−27	52	52	4.64	−0.5	M3 III	350	0.043	336	45	42	.012	34	125	
- CMa	57821	07	22	13.5	−19	01	00	4.96	*	B7 IV	*	0.007	172	*	27	*	*	*	(p)
- CMa	60532	07	34	03.1	−22	17	46	4.45	3.3†	F6 IV	55	0.060	310	61	61	.059	1.5	3.8	

Canis Minor
(Canis Minoris)

a) *Procyon* (Before the Dog). The close companion—Procyon B—is a white dwarf, and extremely difficult to see (m10.8, M13.1). Y:π.292.

b) *Gomeisa.* B:M−1.1, $\mathcal{L}$230, 210 l.y. OH:M+0.1.

c) This multiple binary is extremely close to α CMi—less than one minute of right ascension east of Procyon.

d) This rather bright star has no name. It is one degree east of the much dimmer 14 CMi.

CANIS MINOR	HD	2000.0 R.A.		Declin.			m	M	Spectra	l.y.	μ	Dir.	V	RV	π	D_s	$\mathcal{L}$	Rmk
α CMi	61421	07^h 39^m 18.1^s	+05°	13′	30″		0.38	2.64†	F5 IV	11.44	1.248″	214°	21	−3	.285″	1.7	6.9	(a)
β CMi	58715	07 27 09.0	+08	17	21		2.90$_v$	−0.2	B8 Ve	140	0.066	233	28	22	.019	1.5	95	(b)
γ CMi	58972	07 28 09.7	+08	55	32		4.32	(0.7)	K3 III	170	0.066	283	50	47	.019	17	41	
δ^1 CMi	59881	07 32 05.8	+01	54	52		5.25	(1.3)	F0 III	200	0.016	256	29	29	.016	2.1	24	
ε CMi	58367	07 25 38.8	+09	16	34		4.99	0.3	G6.5 IIb	280	0.015	208	12	−8	.008	13	60	
ζ CMi	63975	07 51 41.9	+01	46	01		5.14	(0.5)	B8 II	270	0.020	255	33	32	.012	0.9	48	
η CMi	58923	07 28 02.0	+06	56	31		5.25	0.6	F0 III	280	0.046	187	28	18	.010	2.9	45	
Σ1126	61563	07 40 06.9	+05	13	51		6.02	(1.8)	A0 III	230	0.027	202	19	17	.014	0.9	16	(c)
6 CMi	59294	07 29 47.7	+12	00	24		4.54	−0.1	K1 III+	280	0.021	180	15	−15	.029	21	86	
- CMi	66141	08 02 15.9	+02	20	04		4.39	−0.1	K2 III	260	0.106	342	74	71	.024	20	86	(d)

Capricornus
(Capricorni)

a) With α^2, forms an optical double; however, each star is a visual binary as well. Burnham gives the distance of α^1 at about 500 l.y., based apparently on the parallax. The StarList distance (based on the distance modulus formula, given the visual and the absolute magnitudes) seems rather large for a parallax of .006".

b) *Al Giedi* (The Goat). The brighter of the two Alpha stars. Like its neighbor, it has three visible companions, the brightest of which is m9.3.

c) *Dabih* (Lucky One of the Slaughterers). B: Luminosity class V, distance 150 l.y., $\mathscr{L}$100. SC: Lum. class V ($=M+4.0$, $\mathscr{L}$2, D_s1.7). But the luminosity class of II now seems the accepted value.

   If M is estimated at -1, then: 213 l.y., π.010, V27 km/s, D_s17, $\mathscr{L}$200. OH:$M-2.2$, 560 l.y.

d) *Deneb Algiedi* (The Tail of the Goat). Eclipsing Algol-type variable, with a period slightly over one day. B:50 l.y., $\mathscr{L}$25. OH:$M+1.5$, π.087.

   One investigator has suggested that since it satisfies the photometric properties of RS CVn-type variables, this star should be considered a candidate for reclassification [IBVS #3008].

e) This is a γC variable. In the same field, southeast, is the binary 41 Cap (5.5, 12; PA 205°, 5.5"), and one-half degree west of this is the globular cluster M30 (NGC 7099).

f) If M is estimated at -1.5, then: 730 l.y., π.004, V22 km/s, D_s3.2, and $\mathscr{L}$313.

g) SC:$M+0.6$.

h) The distance modulus formula—using m and M—indicates a distance of 1070 l.y., suggesting that M may be too low.

i) The visual magnitude is the combined magnitude of a primary and its close companion (5.8, 6.3). This is a rapid-motion binary (Hu 200), with a period of 200 days; at Epoch 2000.0: 123°, 0.2".

j) The parallax suggests a much greater distance, at least ten times that given on the StarList, which is derived from the distance modulus formula.

CAPRI-CORNUS	HD	R.A.		Declin.		m	M	Spectra	l.y.	μ	Dir.	V	RV	π	D_s	$\mathscr{L}$	Rmk
		2000.0															
α¹ Cap ∞	192876	20ʰ 17ᵐ 38.8ˢ	−12° 30′ 30″			4.24	−4.5	G3 Ib	1800	0.019″	84°	30	−26	.006″	124	50000	(a)
α² Cap ∞	192947	20 18 03.2	−12 32 42			3.57	0.2	G9 III	96	0.061	85	9	0	.034	12	65	(b)
β Cap	193495	20 21 00.5	−14 46 53			3.08	*	K0 II	*	0.039	86	*	−19	*	*	*	(c)
γ Cap	206088	21 40 05.4	−16 39 45			3.68	(1.0)	F0 pec	110	0.189	97	44	−31	.029	3.0	32	
δ Cap	207098	21 47 02.3	−16 07 38			2.87ᵥ	2.0†	Amv	47	0.394	138	28	−6	.069	1.8	12	(d)
ε Cap	205637	21 37 04.7	−19 27 58			4.68ᵥ	−2.3	B3 V	810	0.012	59	[28]	−24	[.004]	4.4	655	(e)
ζ Cap	204075	21 26 39.9	−22 24 41			3.74	−4.5	G4 Ib	1400	0.027	2	13	3	.010	114	5000	
η Cap	200499	21 04 24.2	−19 51 18			4.84	3.6†	A5 V	65	0.049	225	24	24	.050	0.9	2.9	
θ Cap	200761	21 05 56.7	−17 13 58			4.07	0.6	A1 V	160	0.100	124	30	−11	.017	2.0	45	
ι Cap	203387	21 22 14.7	−16 50 05			4.28	0.3	G7 III+	99	0.033	79	13	12	.033	11	60	
κ Cap	206453	21 42 39.4	−18 51 59			4.73	0.3	G8 III	250	0.146	92	25	−3	.028	11	60	
λ Cap	207052	21 46 32.0	−11 21 58			5.58	1.4	A1 V	220	0.029	104	9	1	.015	1.4	22	
μ Cap	207958	21 53 17.7	−13 33 07			5.08	3.2†	F1 III	78	0.309	87	41	−22	.042	1.2	4.1	
ν Cap	193432	20 20 39.7	−12 45 33			4.76	−0.3	B9.5 V	340	0.024	138	6	−2	.021	2.1	104	
π Cap	194636	20 27 19.1	−18 12 42			5.25	*	B3/5 V	*	0.016	128	*	−13	*	*	*	(f)
ρ Cap	194943	20 28 51.5	−17 48 49			4.78	2.8†	F3 V	84	0.026	219	18	18	.039	1.5	6.0	(g)
σ Cap	193150	20 19 23.5	−19 07 07			5.28	−2.3	K2 III	1100	0.008	135	11	−11	.025	65	655	(h)
τ Cap	196662	20 39 16.3	−14 57 17			5.22	−1.9	B6 III	870	0.021	169	21	−5	.005	2.7	453	(i)
υ Cap	196777	20 40 02.9	−18 08 19			5.10	−0.5	M2 III	430	0.028	229	15	−13	.019	36	125	
φ Cap	202320	21 15 37.8	−20 39 06			5.24	0.2	gG9	330	0.014	73	6	−5	.020	16	65	
ψ Cap	197692	20 46 05.6	−25 16 16			4.14	3.7	F5 V	33	0.164	197	27	26	.098	1.1	2.6	
ω Cap	198542	20 51 49.2	−26 55 09			4.11	−0.3	K4 III	250	0.005	270	25	9	.001	32	104	(j)
24 Cap	200914	21 07 07.6	−25 00 21			4.50	−0.5	M0.5 III	330	0.047	209	34	32	.022	34	125	
36 Cap	204381	21 28 43.3	−21 48 26			4.51	0.3	G5 III	230	0.138	92	36	−22	.023	11	60	
42 Cap	206301	21 41 32.8	−14 02 51			5.18	3.0	G1 V+	96	0.328	202	46	−1	.034	2.2	5.0	
46 Cap	206834	21 45 00.2	−09 04 57			5.09	−0.9	G8 II/III	510	0.018	96	43	−5	.002	25	180	

Carina
(Carinae)

a) *Canopus* (Pilot of King Menelaos's Fleet). Second brightest star, after Sirius. The absolute magnitude has in this instance been taken from the OH. Burnham cites conflicting views on the distance of this star, giving 100–120 l.y. as a reasonable estimate, with an absolute magnitude of −3.4, $\mathscr{L}1400$, and 30 diameters.

b) *Miaplacidus.*

c) *Avior.* Perhaps a variable: the Yale *Bright Star Catalogue* states "E? 3.1–3.4p, 785?d." The *Bibliographic Catalogue of Variable Stars* (H. Huth and W. Wenzel, 1983) notes one reference to this star as a variable (*RAS Mem.* 73, 153). However, the present writer could find no reference to ε Car in this article by L. R. Wackerling. B:340 l.y., $\mathscr{L}1400$. SC:HD 71130, $RV+12$. WSW 3° is the bright open cluster NGC 2516.

d) One of the most curious stars in the heavens, η Car is thought to be either a very young star not yet on the main sequence, or a very old star, nearing death. At the present time the latter seems more probable. When it finally does die, it will create one of the brightest supernovae ever seen.

   The star is found in the region of one of the largest and most complex of all diffuse nebulae—the so-called Keyhole Nebula (NGC 3372), which has a northern branch (NGC 3324) nearly as large and just as bright.

   The classification of this variable has been difficult to ascertain. Some put the star in the S Dor group; others call it a "nebular variable," a " nova-like variable," or an "ejection variable."

   If we take the distance to be 2000 parsecs (as listed in DA), then: $M-5.3$, 6500 l.y., $\pi.0005$ (by definition), $V65$ km/s, D_s95, and $\mathscr{L}10,400$. Burnham gives a distance of only 3700 l.y., and a variation in absolute magnitude from about −9 to perhaps as much as −19 in its 1843 flare-up, which would put its luminosity at that time at 3 billion Suns! Burnham claims its present luminosity is about 1600 Suns, which would yield $M-3.3$, 2600 l.y. Others maintain that the star is several million times the Sun's luminosity.

   Three degrees east of η Car is the splendid open cluster NGC 3532.

e) This bright star is in the center of a large galactic cluster IC 2602.

f) The absolute magnitude comes from the OH, and the $B-V$ index (+.27) and luminosity class indicate a size of about fifty Suns, which would agree with the OH's value for M. However, the very high parallax suggests the star is considerably closer. SC:$M-2.0$, 320 l.y., D_s12, $\mathscr{L}500$.

g) B:430 l.y., $\mathscr{L}600$.

h) If the absolute magnitude is estimated from Fig. 2 to be +1, then: 205 l.y., $\pi.016$, $V14$, $D_s0.7$, and $\mathscr{L}31$.

i) A Mira-type variable. If the absolute magnitude is estimated to be −1, then: 850 l.y., $\pi.004$, $V55$ km/s, D_s37, $\mathscr{L}198$.

   Close by, at about 1.5° E, is the bright variable known as l ("ell," not "one"), or ZZ Car. (See note (j).)

CARINA	HD	R.A. 2000.0			Declin.			m	M	Spectra	l.y.	μ	Dir.	V	RV	π	D_s	$\mathscr{L}$	Rmk
α Car	45348	06^h	23^m	57.2^s	−52°	41′	44″	−0.72	−2.4	F0 II	71	0.034″	50°	22	21	.028″	13	718	(a)
β Car	80007	09	13	12.1	−69	43	02	1.68	−0.6	A1 III	93	0.182	304	41	−5	.021	3.9	137	(b)
ε Car	71129	08	22	30.8	−59	30	34	1.86	−2.1	K3 III	200	0.029	301	[9]	2	[.016]	52	545	(c)
η Car	93308	10	45	03.6	−59	41	03	6.21$_v$	*	Pec	*	0.006	342	*	−25	*	*	*	(d)
θ Car	93030	10	42	57.4	−64	23	40	2.76	−4.1	B0.5 Vp	770	0.022	291	[35]	24	[.004]	3.4	3436	(e)
ι Car	80404	09	47	05.4	−59	16	31	2.25	−4.7	A9 Ib	800	0.020	285	14	13	.017	40	6000	
υ^A Car	85123	09	47	06.1	−65	04	18	2.96	(−5.0)	A8 Ib	1300	0.012	305	14	14	.027	42	7870	(f)
υ^B Car	85124	09	47	06.7	−65	04	21	6.03	(−2.0)	A8 Ib	1300	0.021	337	—	—	.027	11	497	
χ Car	65575	07	56	46.7	−52	58	56	3.47$_v$	(−3.5)	B3IV pec	820	0.042	306	53	19	.004	5.9	2013	(g)
ω Car	89080	10	13	44.3	−70	02	16	3.32	−1.0	B8 IIIe	240	0.032	275	[13]	7	[.014]	2.3	198	
A Car	50337	06	49	51.3	−53	37	20	4.40$_v$	0.4	G6 II	210	0.030	352	27	26	.025	11	54	
B Car	68456	08	09	00.7	−61	18	07	4.76	3.5†	F5 V	58	0.325	209	37	25	.056	1.2	3.1	
C Car	69863	08	15	15.9	−62	54	57	5.16	2.6	A2 V	110	0.033	220	6	4	.031	1.1	7.1	
D^1 Car	66591	08	00	20.0	−63	34	03	4.82	−2.3	B3 V	870	0.019	3	[33]	22	[.004]	4.4	655	
E Car	78764	09	05	38.4	−70	32	19	4.71$_v$	−2.5	B2 IVe	900	0.010	204	[23]	19	[.004]	9.4	787	
G Car	78791	09	05	09.3	−72	36	10	4.48	−0.6	F9 II	340	0.014	129	22	22	.024	11	137	
I Car	90589	10	24	23.7	−74	01	54	4.00	0.6†	F2 IV	45	0.036	210	5	−4	.072	3.8	45	
K Car	91375	10	30	20.0	−71	59	34	4.74	0.5	A1 V	230	0.039	150	16	8	.014	2.6	51	
L Car	90264	10	22	58.1	−66	54	06	4.99	*	B8 V	*	0.024	268	*	12	*	*	*	(h)
M Car	88981	10	13	30.6	−66	22	22	5.16	(0.6)	A m	270	0.035	270	20	−15	.012	2.8	47	
N Car	47306	06	34	58.5	−52	58	32	4.39	−0.8	A0 II	360	0.018	308	[25]	23	[.009]	3.5	164	
Q Car	61248	07	35	39.7	−52	32	02	4.94	−0.4	K3 III	380	0.025	138	63	62	.012	27	114	
b^1 Car	77002	08	56	58.3	−59	13	46	4.92$_v$	−2.3	B2 IV/V	910	0.016	288	[34]	27	[.004]	2.7	655	
b^2 Car	77370	08	59	24.1	−59	05	01	5.16	3.6†	F3 V	68	0.328	328	34	11	.048	1.1	2.9	
c Car	76728	08	55	02.8	−60	38	40	3.84	−1.0	B8/9 II	300	0.044	327	[32]	25	[.011]	2.0	198	
d Car	74375	08	40	37.0	−59	45	40	4.33$_v$	−8.4	B1.5 III	11000	0.006	225	[95]	13	[.0003]	57	180000	
e^2 Car	73389	08	35	19.6	−58	00	33	4.86	0.3	K0 III	270	0.046	63	27	24	.017	12	60	
g Car	80230	09	16	12.2	−57	32	28	4.34	−0.3	M1 III	280	0.017	239	6	−5	.025	32	104	
h Car	83183	09	34	26.6	−59	13	46	4.08	−3.7	B5 II	1200	0.017	315	[36]	22	[.003]	17	2377	
i Car	79447	09	11	16.7	−62	19	02	3.97	−2.3	B3 III	590	0.041	278	[40]	18	[.006]	3.4	655	
k Car	81101	09	20	57.1	−62	24	17	4.81	0.3	G6 III	260	0.011	139	51	51	.017	12	60	
m Car	83944	09	39	21.0	−61	19	41	4.52	0.2	B9 IV/V	240	0.044	294	[25]	20	[.014]	1.4	65	
r Car	91942	10	35	35.2	−57	33	27	4.45	−0.4	K3/4 II	300	0.022	262	11	10	.026	33	114	
s Car	90853	10	27	52.7	−58	44	22	3.82	−2.0	F2 II	480	0.015	247	12	9	.010	12	497	
u Car	94510	10	53	29.6	−58	51	12	3.78	1.7	K1 III	78	0.074	69	12	8	.042	6.1	16	
y Car	97534	11	12	36.0	−60	19	03	4.60	−8.5†	A6 Iae	14000	0.004	270	9	−8	.005	371	200000	
z^1 Car	96566	11	06	32.4	−62	25	26	4.61	−6.2†	G8 III	60	0.040	283	4	−2	.054	259	25000	
R Car	82901	09	32	14.7	−62	47	19	6.10$_v$	*	M6/7 III	*	0.038	297	*	28	*	*	*	(i)
GM Car	92397	10	38	45.1	−59	10	59	4.66$_v$	−5.9	K4/5 III	4200	0.010	259	11	11	.016	367	18000	
PP Car	91465	10	32	01.4	−61	41	07	3.32$_v$	−1.7	B4 Vne	330	0.021	287	[28]	26	[.010]	3.0	377	

(Continued)

j) A pulsating Cepheid variable with an exceptionally long period (35.56 days). The $B-V$ index and luminosity class suggest a size between twenty and fifty Suns. This in turn yields an estimated absolute magnitude of about –3, hence: 710 l.y., D_s75, $\mathscr{L}$1250.

   Burnham says it is thought to be a very distant supergiant (200 diameters) with a maximum luminosity of 12,000 and a distance of 3000 l.y. The *Sky Catalogue,* however, reports an absolute magnitude of +4.4, which would make it about the same size as the Sun, and the same luminosity. The Yale *Bright Star Catalogue* gives a parallax of .027″, which would mean a distance of somewhat over 120 l.y., M+0.8, $\mathscr{L}$38, D_s6.

k) If the absolute magnitude is estimated at 0.0, then: 360 l.y., π.009, V13, D_s1.6, and $\mathscr{L}$79.

CARINA (CONT.)	HD	R.A.			Declin.			m	M	Spectra	l.y.	μ	Dir.	V	RV	π	D_s	$\mathcal{L}$	Rmk
							2000.0												
ZZ Car	84810	09^h 45^m	14.8^s	−62°	30′	28″	3.69$_v$	*	G5 lab	*	0.016″	281°	4	3	.027″	*	*	(j)
V337 Car	89388	10 17	04.9	−61	19	56	3.40$_v$	−4.4	K3 lla	1200	0.027	276	9	8	.027	195	4500	
V344 Car	75311	08 46	42.7	−56	46	11	4.49$_v$	−2.5	B3 Vne	820	0.009	6	[29]	27	[.004]	4.8	787	
V357 Car	79351	09 10	57.9	−58	58	01	3.44$_v$	−3.0	B2 IV/V	630	0.027	283	[34]	23	[.005]	3.7	1247	
V371 Car	96919	11 08	33.8	−61	56	49	5.13$_v$	−7.1	B9 la	9100	0.023	288	25	−22	.009	99	55000	
V382 Car	96918	11 08	35.3	−58	58	30	3.91$_v$	−8.0	G4 0/la	7900	0.007	254	35	7	.001	747	125000	
- Car	50223	06 49	54.5	−46	36	52	5.14	3.5†	F5 V	69	0.373	359	43	20	.047	1.2	3.1	
- Car	51799	06 56	16.0	−48	43	16	4.95	−0.5	M1 III	400	0.010	360	27	22	.003	37	125	
- Car	53047	07 00	51.5	−51	24	09	5.14	−0.5	M1 III	440	0.028	312	11	5	.014	34	125	
- Car	54118	07 04	18.3	−56	44	59	5.17	(1.1)	A0 pSi	220	0.003	135	30	30	.015	1.3	30	
- Car	66342	07 59	37.6	−60	35	13	5.17	−2.4	M1.5 lla	1100	0.009	18	51	23	.001	93	718	
- Car	90772	10 27	24.4	−57	38	20	4.66	−8.5	A9 la	14000	0.012	261	5	−1	.012	346	200000	
- Car	91496	10 31	02.0	−73	13	18	4.93	−0.5	K4/5 III	400	0.013	247	[13]	11	[.008]	37	125	
- Car	92063	10 36	20.3	−59	33	53	5.08	0.2	K1 III	86	0.080	226	16	−13	.038	16	65	
- Car	92938	10 42	14.0	−64	27	58	4.82	−1.7	B4 V	660	0.027	301	[35]	24	[.005]	2.2	377	
- Car	93070	10 43	32.1	−60	33	59	4.57	−0.3	K4 III	310	0.030	276	11	9	.020	34	104	
- Car	93194	10 44	06.9	−63	57	40	4.82	−1.7	B5 Vn	660	0.017	301	[31]	26	[.005]	2.3	377	
- Car	93549	10 46	29.7	−64	15	47	5.23	*	B7 IV	*	0.009	328	*	12	*	*	*	(k)
- Car	93607	10 46	51.2	−64	23	00	4.85	−2.0	B3 IV	760	0.022	292	[29]	16	[.004]	7.5	497	
- Car	97583	11 12	45.3	−64	10	12	5.23	0.2	B8 V	330	0.040	261	[29]	21	[.010]	1.6	65	

Cassiopeia
(Cassiopeiae)

a) *Shedir, Schedar* (Breast). A bluish optical neighbor (m9, PA 280°, 64″) offers a nice color contrast to this orange giant (or is it yellow?).

b) *Caph*. A pulsating variable with very small amplitude and period of 2.5 hours. SC:$M+1.9$; OH:$M+2.0$.

c) Prototype of a class of variables; rotating B stars, usually of small amplitude. B: estimates 100 l.y., $\mathcal{L}100$.

 SE 4° is NGC 457, the "Owl Cluster," a fine open star cluster.

d) *Ruchbah*. B:45 l.y., $\mathcal{L}12$.

e) *Segin*. OH:$M-2.4$, 440 l.y.

f) A well-known binary with contrasting colors, yellow and red, although some see other colors, such as gold and purple.

g) The parallax indicates a greater distance, about 250 l.y.

h) Marvelous triple-star system, with a yellow primary and blue companions. B:160 l.y., $\mathcal{L}35$.

i) If the absolute magnitude is estimated at -0.5, then: 390 l.y., $\pi.008$, $V21$, $D_s1.5$, and $\mathcal{L}125$.

j) There is some question about the absolute magnitude; Burnham cites various studies that give a range from $+0.4$ to -8. Also in question is the distance; the parallax suggests a distance of perhaps 150 l.y., while the distance modulus formula gives a much higher figure, over 10,000 l.y.

 Classified as a semiregular variable, it could perhaps also be termed an irregular, for its period is uncertain.

 Between ρ and σ Cas can be found NGC 7789, a fine open cluster of over a thousand stars.

k) If M is estimated at -2, then: 815 l.y., $\pi.004$, $V29$, $D_s3.2$, and $\mathcal{L}500$.

l) Splendid binary with color contrast, gold and blue.

m) If M is estimated at $+0.5$, then: 300 l.y., $\pi.011$, $V16$, $D_s2.4$, and $\mathcal{L}50$.

n) This is a rapid binary currently at its widest separation, 1.6″. The companion is a G8 star, m7.2, $M5.6$, $RV-16$ (from Gliese). Gliese gives the primary a visual magnitude of 6.43. The primary may be a variable, type unkown, with a period of 1.08 days [IBVS #2389].

 In the same field, west of Σ3062, is Σ3057 (7, 9; PA 298°, 3.9″ fixed).

o) A Mira-type variable with wide range (4.7−13.5). B:$M-1$ (at maximum); 800 l.y. If the absolute magnitude is estimated at -0.5, then: 375 l.y., $\pi.009$, $V48$ km/s, D_s42, $\mathcal{L}125$.

CAS-SIOPEIA	HD	R.A.	Declin.	m	M	Spectra	l.y.	μ	Dir.	V	RV	π	D_s	$\mathscr{L}$	Rmk
														2000.0	
α Cas	3712	$00^h\,40^m\,30.4^s$	$+56°\,32'\,15''$	2.23	−0.9	K0 III	140	0.059''	117°	18	−4	.016''	27	180	(a)
β Cas ∞	432	00 09 10.6	+59 08 59	2.27$_v$	1.37†	F2 III	49	0.555	109	42	12	.066	2.6	22	(b)
γ Cas	5394	00 56 42.4	+60 43 00	2.47$_v$	−4.6	B0 IVe	850	0.025	90	10	−7	.016	25	5500	(c)
δ Cas	8538	01 25 48.9	+60 14 07	2.68$_v$	2.1	A5 V	88	0.303	99	39	7	.037	1.5	11	(d)
ε Cas	11415	01 54 23.6	+63 40 13	3.38	−2.9	B3 III	590	0.036	114	19	−8	.010	11	1138	(e)
ζ Cas	3360	00 36 58.2	+53 53 49	3.66	−2.5	B2 IV	560	0.020	105	23	2	.004	2.4	787	
η Cas ∞	4614	00 49 06.0	+57 48 58	3.44	4.6†	G0 V	19	1.218	115	35	9	.170	0.9	1.1	(f)⊘
θ Cas	6961	01 11 06.1	+55 09 00	4.33	2.4	A7 V	79	0.230	94	78	9	.014	1.5	8.6	(g)
ι Cas ∞	15089	02 29 03.9	+67 24 09	4.52$_v$	(1.3)	A5 p	140	0.022	317	4.6	1	.023	2.1	23	(h)⊘
κ Cas	2905	00 32 59.9	+62 55 55	4.16$_v$	−6.6	B1 Iae	4600	0.003	18	[21]	−2	[.001]	87	35000	
λ Cas	2772	00 31 46.3	+54 31 20	4.73	(2.1)	B8 Vn	110	0.044	96	14	−12	.030	0.5	11	
μ Cas	6582	01 08 16.3	+54 55 14	5.17	5.75†	G5 Vp	25	3.768	115	168	−97	.130	0.7	0.4	
ν Cas	4636	00 48 50.0	+50 58 06	4.89	*	B9 III	*	0.034	92	*	9	*	*	*	(i)
ξ Cas	3901	00 42 03.8	+50 30 45	4.80	−2.5	B2 V	940	0.013	94	[20]	−10	[.003]	3.8	787	
o Cas	4180	00 44 43.5	+48 17 04	4.54$_v$	−2.5	B5 IIIe	830	0.019	99	[29]	−17	[.004]	5.0	787	
π Cas	4058	00 43 28.0	+47 01 29	4.94	(1.7)	A5 V	140	0.036	217	15	13	.023	2.1	16	
ρ Cas	224014	23 54 23.0	+57 29 58	4.54$_v$	−8.0	F8 Ia	11000	0.006	329	43	−43	.023	738	125000	(j)
σ Cas ∞	224572	23 59 00.4	+55 45 18	4.88	−3.5	B1 V	1500	0.008	83	14	−13	.006	8.0	1977	
τ Cas	223165	23 47 03.4	+58 39 07	4.87	0.0	K1 IIIa	310	0.086	46	36	−21	.014	16	79	
υ¹ Cas	5234	00 55 00.0	+58 58 22	4.83	−0.1	K2 III	320	0.050	221	46	−23	.006	19	86	
υ² Cas	5395	00 56 39.7	+59 10 52	4.63	1.8	G8.5 II	64	0.101	246	48	−47	.051	5.9	15	
φ Cas	7927	01 20 04.8	+58 13 54	4.98	−8.5	F0 Ia	16000	0.003	360	24	−24	.003	460	200000	
χ Cas	9408	01 33 55.9	+59 13 56	4.71	0.2	G9 IIIb	260	0.040	247	11	6	.021	13	65	
ψ Cas	8491	01 25 56.0	+68 07 48	4.74	0.2	K0 III	260	0.082	67	32	−12	.013	14	65	
ω Cas	11529	01 55 59.9	+68 41 07	4.99	*	B8 III	*	0.014	126	*	−24	*	*	*	(k)
1 Cas	218376	23 06 36.8	+59 25 12	4.85	−4.4	B0.5 IV	2300	0.010	53	[35]	−9	[.001]	17	4500	
4 Cas	220652	23 24 50.2	+62 16 59	4.98	−0.3	M1 III	370	0.011	124	38	−37	.007	33	104	(l)
6 Cas	223385	23 48 50.1	+62 12 53	5.43$_v$	−7.6	A3 Iae	13000	0.008	310	59	−46	.001	299	85000	
42 Cas	10250	01 42 55.8	+70 37 22	5.18	−1.8	B9 V	820	0.079	94	94	6	.004	4.7	417	
48 Cas	12111	02 01 57.3	+70 54 26	4.54	2.3	A3 IV	93	0.066	279	10	−5	.035	1.5	9.5	
49 Cas	12339	02 05 31.2	+76 06 55	5.22	1.9	G8 III	150	0.024	232	5	0	.022	5.6	14	
50 Cas	12216	02 03 26.0	+72 25 17	3.98	1.2	A2 V	120	0.051	305	[16]	−14	[.028]	1.5	26	
h 1100	11946	01 59 37.9	+64 37 18	5.26	*	A0 Vn	*	0.037	112	*	5	*	*	*	(m)
β497	5015	00 53 04.1	+61 07 27	4.82	4.1†	F8 V	48	0.192	338	25	21	.068	1.1	1.8	
OΣ 16	3574	00 39 09.8	+49 21 16	5.43	−0.1	K7 III	420	0.009	131	[10]	−8	[.008]	29	86	
Σ3053 ∞	225009	00 02 36.0	+66 05 57	5.86	0.3	G8 III	420	0.011	63	19	−18	.010	14	60	(n)
Σ3062 ∞	123	00 06 15.9	+58 26 12	5.96	4.8†	G5 V	68	0.264	82	29	−12	.048	1.0	0.9	(o)⊘
R Cas	224490	23 58 24.7	+51 23 19	4.8$_v$	*	M7 IIIe	*	0.079	80	*	21	*	*	*	(p)
AR Cas	221253	23 30 01.9	+58 32 57	4.91$_v$	−1.7	B3 IV	680	0.021	62	21	−13	.006	2.4	377	
V509 Cas	217476	23 00 05.0	+56 56 44	5.00$_v$	−8.0	G4 0	13000	0.012	336	65	−58	.002	910	125000	
- Cas	3240	00 36 08.2	+54 10 07	5.08	−0.2	B7 III	370	0.021	76	[11]	1	[.009]	1.3	95	
- Cas	15920	02 38 01.9	+72 49 06	5.16	0.3	G8 III	310	0.037	308	16	−2	.011	11	60	
- Cas	19275	03 11 56.3	+74 23 37	4.87	0.6	A2 Vn	100	0.087	168	16	10	.032	2.4	45	

Centaurus
(Centauri)

a) *Rigel Kentaurus* (Foot of the Centaur), but better known as Alpha Centauri. Third brightest star, with the largest proper motion of any bright star. Y:π.750.

b) A noted binary with α^A. B:D_s1.22. All catalog references except SC give the same right ascension and declination for α^A and α^B. SC gives for α^B these differences: 35.4^s in R.A. and 13″ in declination. Y:period 81.18y.

c) *Proxima Centauri.* This very faint red dwarf is the closest star to our Solar System. It is a flare star, of quite frequent bursts, with a maximum amplitude of about one magnitude.
   Burnham gives a diameter of 0.05 Suns, parallax .762, M+10.7, and a luminosity of about 7.7×10^{-5} Suns (that is, 1/13,000 that of the Sun).

d) *Hadar.* OH:M−4.4, 320 l.y.

e) A close binary. A and B are nearly identical twins; OH gives the following: A:m2.87, M−0.3; B:m2.9, M0.0. Burnham only mentions the primary: M−1.3, $\mathcal{L}$275, 160 l.y. The parallax indicates a distance of around 200 l.y.

f) The parallax suggests a closer distance, 125–150 l.y.

g) SC:RV+6.

h) B:M−3.4, $\mathcal{L}$1900, 520 l.y. West 4.5° is found what Burnham calls the finest globular cluster in the heavens, so bright it goes under the name ωCentauri. This is NGC 5139, which contains over seven thousand close-packed stars, including hundreds of RR Lyrae variables.

i) OH:M−3.5, 450 l.y.

j) *Menkent.* B:M+0.9, $\mathcal{L}$40, 55 l.y. OH:M+0.7. SC:M+1.7.

k) B:M+1.1. Y:π.062. In the same field, NW, is NGC 5102.

l) The star lies in the center of a diffuse nebula (I 2944), and in the same field is the open cluster I 2948.
   B:M−2.1, $\mathcal{L}$630, 370 l.y. OH:M−0.6. SC:RV+8.

m) B:M−2.7, $\mathcal{L}$1000, 470 l.y. OH:M−2.5. SC:RV+13.

n) This star was designated an Ell.-type variable in 1984 [IBVS #2681].

o) SC:RV+16.

p) B:M−3.4, $\mathcal{L}$1900, 750 l.y.

q) SC:M+0.6, R.A. 43.0^s, decl. 30″.

r) Possible variable: the *Bright Star Catalogue* notes "αCV?"; Kholopov does not include the star in his catalog. If M is estimated at −1, then: 450 l.y., π.007, V42, D_s2.3, $\mathcal{L}$198.

s) An atypical Mira, as it alternates between two maxima (5.3 and 6.0), and it has an exceptionally long period (546.2 d). Levy states that it has two minima: m11.8 and m8.3. Burnham has a finder's chart.
   If we estimate the absolute magnitude to be −2, then: 1550 l.y., π.002, V62, D_s100, and $\mathcal{L}$500.

CENTAURUS	HD	R.A.		Declin.			m	M	Spectra	l.y.	μ	Dir.	V	RV	π	D_s	ℒ	Rmk
α^A Cen ∞	128620	14^h 39^m 36.2^s		−60° 50′	07″		−0.01	4.35†	G2 V	4.39	3.678″	281°	34	−25	.743″	1.3	1.4	(a)
α^B Cen	128621	14 39 36.2		−60 50	07		1.33	5.69†	K1 V	4.39	3.678	281	31	−21	.743	0.9	0.4	(b)
α^C Cen	—	14 29 42.0		−62 41	07		11.05	15.45†	M5.5 Ve	4.28	3.850	282	29	−16	.761	0.03	.00005	(c)
β Cen	122451	14 03 49.4		−60 22	22		0.61_v	−5.1	B1 III	450	0.030	221	17	6	.009	4.6	8630	(d)
γ Cen ∞	110304	12 41 30.9		−48 57	34		2.17	−0.6	A0 IV	120	0.190	268	57	−6	.016	3.5	137	(e)
δ Cen	105435	12 08 21.5		−50 43	20		2.60_v	−2.5	B2 IVne	340	0.034	249	13	11	.026	3.5	787	(f)
ε Cen	118716	13 39 53.2		−53 27	59		2.30_v	−3.5	B1 III	470	0.028	232	[19]	3	[.007]	2.6	1977	(g)
ζ Cen	121263	13 55 32.3		−47 17	18		2.55	−3.0	B2.5 IV	420	0.072	232	[45]	7	[.008]	2.1	1247	(h)
η Cen	127972	14 35 30.3		−42 09	28		2.31_v	−2.9	B1.5 Vn	360	0.050	226	[26]	0	[.009]	3.5	1138	(i)
θ Cen	123139	14 06 40.8		−36 22	12		2.06	1.2†	K0 IIIb	49	0.738	225	52	1	.067	8.4	26	(j)
ι Cen	115892	13 20 35.7		−36 42	44		2.75	1.3†	A2 V	64	0.351	255	33	0	.051	1.8	24	(k)
κ Cen	132200	14 59 09.6		−42 06	15		3.13	−2.5	B2 IV	440	0.033	215	[22]	8	[.007]	2.4	787	
λ Cen	100841	11 35 46.8		−63 01	11		3.13	−0.8	B9 III	200	0.040	258	[12]	−1	[.016]	2.9	164	(l)
μ Cen	120324	13 49 36.9		−42 28	26		3.04_v	−1.7	B2 IV/V	290	0.034	220	[17]	9	[.011]	3.3	377	(m)
ν Cen	120307	13 49 30.2		−41 41	16		3.41_v	−2.5	B2 IV	500	0.035	224	[27]	9	[.007]	1.6	787	(n)
ξ¹ Cen	113314	13 03 33.1		−49 31	38		4.85	0.6	A0 V	230	0.062	254	25	0	.012	2.4	45	
o¹ Cen	100261	11 31 46.1		−59 26	32		5.13_v	−8.0	G3 0/Ia	14000	0.009	193	20	−20	.024	629	125000	
o² Cen	100262	11 31 48.6		−59 30	56		5.15_v	−7.5	A2 Ia	11000	0.018	264	18	−17	.014	210	80000	
π Cen	98718	11 21 00.4		−54 29	27		3.89	−1.1	B5 Vn	330	0.032	259	16	9	.011	5.0	217	(o)
ρ Cen	105937	12 11 39.1		−52 22	06		3.96	−1.4	B3 V	100	0.040	242	16	15	.032	5.7	286	
σ Cen	108483	12 28 02.3		−50 13	51		3.96	−1.7	B2 V	440	0.036	232	[24]	8	[.007]	2.0	377	
τ Cen	109787	12 37 42.1		−48 32	28		3.86	1.4	A2 V	100	0.186	268	37	5	.024	1.8	22	
υ¹ Cen	121790	13 58 40.7		−44 48	13		3.87	−2.3	B2 IV/V	560	0.035	227	[29]	5	[.006]	2.2	655	
υ² Cen	122223	14 01 43.3		−45 36	12		4.34	−2.0	F6 II	600	0.023	178	8	−1	.013	20	497	(p)
φ Cen	121743	13 58 16.2		−42 06	03		3.83	−2.5	B2 IV	600	0.036	226	[32]	6	[.005]	1.9	787	
χ Cen	122980	14 06 02.7		−41 10	46		4.36_v	−2.5	B2 V	770	0.031	218	[36]	12	[.004]	2.9	787	
ψ Cen	125473	14 20 33.3		−37 53	07		4.05	0.0	A0 IV	200	0.070	257	110	−5	.003	2.2	79	
1 Cen	119756	13 45 41.2		−33 02	37		4.23	2.7†	F3 V	65	0.484	252	51	−22	.050	1.6	6.5	(q)
2 Cen	120323	13 49 26.6		−34 27	02		4.19_v	−0.5	M5 III	110	0.075	215	43	41	.031	31	125	
3A Cen	120709	13 51 49.5		−32 59	40		4.56	−1.6	B4 III	560	0.054	219	18	10	.017	2.2	344	
3B Cen	120710	13 51 50.0		−32 59	41		6.06	2.2	B9 V	190	0.065	241	18	0	.017	0.7	10	
4 Cen	120955	13 53 12.4		−31 55	39		4.73	−1.6	B4 IV	600	0.022	223	[20]	5	[.005]	2.1	344	
j Cen	102776	11 49 41.0		−63 47	18		4.32	−1.1	B3 Vne	400	0.021	265	[31]	29	[.008]	5.0	217	
I Cen	110073	12 39 52.4		−39 59	15		4.64_v	*	B8 II/III	*	0.062	236	*	15	*	*	*	(r)
m Cen	116243	13 24 00.5		−64 32	09		4.53	1.8	G6 II	120	0.048	132	115	12	.002	5.1	15	
F Cen	107079	12 18 59.7		−55 08	35		5.00	−0.5	M1 III	410	0.076	254	37	−7	.010	34	125	
R Cen	124601	14 16 34.2		−59 54	50		6.39_v	*	M5 IIe	*	0.026	212	*	−20	*	*	*	(s)
V761 Cen	125823	14 23 02.1		−39 30	44		4.42_v	−1.9	B7 IIIp	600	0.046	219	[41]	8	[.005]	2.8	453	
V795 Cen	124367	14 14 56.9		−57 05	09		5.07_v	−1.7	B4 Vne	740	0.036	249	[40]	7	[.004]	3.2	377	
V810 Cen	101947	11 43 31.2		−62 29	21		5.03_v	−8.0	G0 0/Ia+	88	0.004	243	10	10	.037	437	125000	

(Continued)

t)   αCV-type variable, amplitude m0.03, period of 2.433 d. The star is not indicated in Tirion's *Sky Atlas* as variable.

u)   The parallax suggests a distance of about 130–150 l.y.

CENTAURUS (CONT.)	HD	R.A.	2000.0 Declin.	m	M	Spectra	l.y.	μ	Dir.	V	RV	π	D_s	$\mathscr{L}$	Rmk
V815 Cen	96616	11^h 07^m 16.5^s	−42° 38′ 19″	5.15$_v$	(−4.8)	A3 p	3300	0.108″	291°	513	2	.001″	30	6855	(t)
- Cen	98993	11 23 12.5	−36 09 54	5.00	−0.3	K6 III	370	0.042	248	9	−5	.025	27	104	(u)
- Cen	99322	11 25 29.3	−36 03 47	5.22	0.3	K0 III	100	0.118	278	18	4	.032	12	60	
- Cen	99453	11 25 43.2	−63 58 22	5.17	3.1	F7 V	81	0.320	255	38	−5	.040	1.6	4.5	
- Cen	99803	11 28 35.0	−42 40 27	5.08	(−0.7)	B9 V	470	0.044	275	30	3	.007	3.1	149	
- Cen	100673	11 34 45.6	−54 15 51	4.62	0.0	B9 Ve	270	0.061	284	[24]	3	[.012]	1.5	79	
- Cen	101021	11 37 00.6	−61 17 00	5.15	0.0	K0 III	350	0.220	271	521	3	.002	17	79	
- Cen	101189	11 38 07.3	−61 49 35	5.15	−0.3	A p+	400	0.068	281	14	4	.024	2.8	104	
- Cen	101570	11 40 53.6	−62 05 23	4.94	−6.2	G3 Ib	5500	0.016	281	14	14	.025	298	25000	
- Cen	102350	11 46 30.7	−61 10 42	4.11	−2.0	G5 Ib/II	540	0.035	233	15	−3	.011	32	497	
- Cen	102365	11 46 31.0	−40 30 01	4.91	5.2†	G5 V	33	1.586	284	78	15	.098	0.8	0.7	
- Cen	102964	11 51 08.1	−45 10 26	4.46	−0.3	K3 III	290	0.084	258	18	2	.022	23	104	
- Cen	104731	12 03 39.5	−42 26 03	5.15	3.3	F6 V	84	0.348	111	56	36	.039	1.2	3.8	
- Cen	105382	12 08 05.1	−50 39 40	4.47	−1.6	B6 IIIe	530	0.038	250	[34]	17	[.006]	6.2	344	
- Cen	108257	12 26 31.5	−51 27 02	4.82	−1.1	B3 Vn	500	0.048	246	[35]	5	[.007]	1.6	217	
- Cen	109536	12 35 45.4	−41 01 19	5.13	(2.0)	A7 III	140	0.109	265	24	−11	.024	1.5	12	
- Cen	110458	12 42 35.3	−48 48 47	4.66	0.0	K0 III	280	0.133	255	28	−12	.025	16	79	
- Cen	111597	12 50 41.1	−33 59 57	4.91	0.0	A0 IV	310	0.035	230	9	4	.020	2.0	79	
- Cen	111915	12 53 06.8	−48 56 35	4.33	−0.1	K3/4 III	250	0.088	255	21	−2	.020	23	86	
- Cen	111968	12 53 26.1	−40 10 44	4.27	0.5†	A7 III	60	0.069	113	7	−3	.054	2.9	50	
- Cen	112409	12 57 04.3	−51 11 55	5.16	−0.2	B8/9 V	390	0.032	234	[31]	25	[.008]	1.9	95	
- Cen	113703	13 06 16.6	−48 27 48	4.71	−2.0	B5 V	720	0.040	230	[43]	6	[.005]	2.5	497	
- Cen	114529	13 12 17.4	−59 55 15	4.60	−0.2	B8 V	300	0.053	237	22	12	.014	1.6	95	
- Cen	114613	13 12 03.1	−37 48 11	4.85	4.6†	G3 V	37	0.387	276	25	−15	.089	1.1	1.1	
- Cen	114837	13 14 14.7	−59 06 12	4.92	3.7†	F7 IV	57	0.307	238	70	−65	.057	1.2	2.6	
- Cen	115310	13 16 53.1	−31 30 23	5.10	0.0	K1 III	340	0.066	147	23	13	.016	14	79	
- Cen	116087	13 22 37.9	−60 59 18	4.53	−1.1	B3 V	440	0.038	243	[25]	6	[.007]	1.7	217	
- Cen	116713	13 26 07.7	−39 45 19	5.09	(0.5)	K0.5 III+	270	0.194	109	102	67	.012	15	50	
- Cen	117150	13 29 25.2	−51 09 55	5.06	(0.3)	A1 V	300	0.021	183	9	−2	.011	3.1	62	
- Cen	117440	13 31 02.6	−39 24 26	3.88	0.3	G9 Ib	170	0.024	216	10	−2	.012	15	60	
- Cen	118991	13 41 44.6	−54 33 36	5.01	−0.2	B8 Vn	360	0.068	223	108	10	.003	2.0	95	
- Cen	119834	13 46 39.3	−51 25 58	4.65	0.2	K0 III	250	0.037	167	11	−6	.018	12	65	
- Cen	119921	13 46 56.3	−36 15 08	5.15	1.5	A0 V	170	0.026	208	12	−10	.019	1.2	19	
- Cen	121474	13 57 38.9	−63 41 12	4.71	−0.3	K0 III	99	0.047	227	23	22	.033	19	104	
- Cen	123569	14 09 54.7	−53 26 20	4.75	0.3	G8 III	250	0.175	235	51	−16	.017	12	60	
- Cen	125158	14 19 51.4	−61 16 23	5.23	(2.9)	A m	96	0.191	240	34	21	.034	1.2	5.5	
- Cen	125288	14 20 19.4	−56 23 12	4.33	−3.7	B6 Ib	1300	0.023	218	[44]	4	[.002]	22	2377	
- Cen	125628	14 22 36.9	−58 27 34	4.92	0.3	G8 III+	270	0.048	281	18	15	.024	10	60	
- Cen	129116	14 41 57.5	−37 47 37	4.00	−1.7	B3 V	450	0.043	214	[28]	1	[.007]	3.3	377	
- Cen	129456	14 43 39.3	−35 10 26	4.05	−0.3	K5 III	240	0.198	199	77	−38	.014	24	104	
- Cen	129685	14 44 59.1	−35 11 31	4.92	(1.3)	A0 V	170	0.008	166	5	−5	.019	1.7	23	
- Cen	131120	14 52 50.9	−37 48 11	5.03	−0.9	B7 IIIp	500	0.038	241	[28]	6	[.007]	3.1	180	

Cepheus
(Cephei)

a) *Alderamin* (Right Shoulder). B:$M+1.4$, $\mathcal{L}23$. SC:$M+1.9$. This will become the Pole Star in 5500 years.

b) *Alfirk*. It belongs to a rare class of variable of the β CMa type, with a period of nearly 4^h35^m, and an amplitude of m0.11. The parallax suggests a distance of less than 300 l.y. B:$M-4.2$, $\mathcal{L}4000$, 980 l.y. OH:$M-4.4$, 1000 l.y.

c) *Er Rai* (Shepherd). OH:$M+1.5$.

d) The prototypical star of a class of short-period pulsating variables known as Cepheids. δ Cephei was the first of this type discovered, in 1784, and it remains one of the easiest stars with which to begin one's study of variables, due to the presence of ζ Cep and η Cep in the same field, allowing a good estimation of the brightness of δ Cep. (If using Levy's fine book (1989) to introduce yourself to variables, note that in his Fig. 6.1, ζ Cep is mislabeled "ξ Cep.")

   The stars in this group are known for their high luminosity. Burnham gives a maximum luminosity of 3300 for δ Cep, and a distance of about 1000 l.y. Petit gives an absolute magnitude of -3.4, which yields 880 l.y., D_s37, and a luminosity of 1800.

e) B:$M+2.2$. The period has recently been revised, with five minutes shaved off its time (i.e., P$=.038$ d) [IBVS #2278].

f) B:$M-4.6$, $\mathcal{L}5800$. OH:$M-4.0$, 750 l.y.

g) B:$M+2.6$, $\mathcal{L}7$, 46 l.y. SC:$M+3.2$. Despite its ADS number, this is only an optical double.

h) *Erakis*. A giant which Burnham calls "perhaps the reddest star visible to the naked eye" in the Northern Hemisphere. A semiregular variable of about 730 days; because it is irregular, this star bears watching on a consistent basis.

   The distance, derived from the distance modulus formula, may be too great: B:$M-5$, 800–1200 l.y., D_s "at least several hundred suns."

   From its unusual shade of red, Herschel named this the "Garnet Star."

i) A nice double, with a small color contrast.

j) The parallax suggests a distance of around 135–150 l.y.

k) The *Bright Star Catalogue* gives the same right ascension and declination for Σ2840A and Σ2840B, although SAO distinguishes between the two, as does SC. The listed R.A. and declination values were computed by the present writer from the SAO (and agree with SC to within one second). Note that Σ2840B is not so identified in SC, and that the visual magnitude of Σ2840A in SC is given as 5.34 (which is the combined visual magnitude of A and B).

   For the companion, Σ2840B, if the absolute magnitude is estimated at $+0.3$, then: 600 l.y., $\pi.005$, $V23$, $D_s1.9$, and $\mathcal{L}60$.

l) A well-known binary, famous as one of the closest of visual binaries. Both stars are red dwarfs.

   The right ascension and declination have been calculated from Gliese's 1950 values, and this same reference was used for m, M, μ, RV, and the parallax. Burnham gives for Kr60B:m11.4, $M+13.4$, $\mathcal{L}0.0004$, $D_s0.19$. He gives a size of one-third the Sun's diameter for the primary. See Burnham, p. 600, for a finder's chart.

m) Mira-type long-period variable. This is a deep red carbon star, making it easy to find. The absolute magnitude comes from Burnham.

n) This star is designated on some charts as 2 UMi.

CEPHEUS	HD	R.A.	Declin.	m	M	Spectra	l.y.	μ	Dir.	V	RV	π	D_s	ℒ	Rmk
		2000.0													
α Cep	203280	21ʰ 18ᵐ 34.7ˢ	+62° 35′ 08″	2.44	1.5†	A7 IV/V	51	0.159″	71°	15	−10	.064″	1.9	20	(a)
β Cep	205021	21 28 39.5	+70 33 39	3.23ᵥ	−3.6	B2 III	760	0.016	38	9.7	−8	.014	2.7	2168	(b)
γ Cep	222404	23 39 20.8	+77 37 57	3.21	2.27†	K1 IV	50	0.169	337	44	−42	.065	5.2	10	(c)
δ Cep ∞	213306	22 29 10.2	+58 24 55	3.75ᵥ	−4.6	F8 Ib	1500	0.013	67	18	−17	.011	67	5500	(d)
ε Cep	211336	22 15 01.9	+57 02 37	4.19ᵥ	1.7	F0 IV	80	0.447	83	52	−1	.041	2.0	16	(e)
ζ Cep	210745	22 10 51.2	+58 12 05	3.35	−4.4	K1.5 Ib	1200	0.015	58	18	−18	.017	200	4500	(f)
η Cep	198149	20 45 17.3	+61 50 20	3.43	2.72†	K0 IV	45	0.827	6	103	−87	.072	3.7	6.4	(g)
θ Cep	195725	20 29 34.8	+62 59 39	4.22	(2.1)	A7 III	86	0.042	105	8.8	−7	.038	1.4	11	
ι Cep	216228	22 49 40.7	+66 12 02	3.52	0.0	K0 III	80	0.137	209	20	−12	.041	15	79	
κ Cep	192907	20 08 53.2	+77 42 41	4.39	−0.8	B9 III	360	0.029	20	138	−23	.001	2.7	164	
λ Cep	210839	22 11 30.6	+59 24 53	5.04	(−1.1)	O6 I	540	0.006	171	74	−74	.006	6.6	211	
μ Cep	206936	21 43 30.3	+58 46 48	4.08ᵥ	−7.0	M2 Ia	5400	0.001	360	19	19	.003	1224	50000	(h)
ν Cep	207260	21 45 26.8	+61 07 15	4.29	−7.5	A2 Ia	7400	0.004	284	21	−21	.013	222	80000	
ξ Cep ∞	209790	22 03 47.3	+64 37 41	4.29	(1.8)	A3/6 V	100	0.226	67	34	−7	.032	2.1	15	(i)⊘
o Cep	219916	23 18 37.4	+68 06 42	4.75	0.2	K0 III	270	0.062	69	22	−18	.024	11	65	(j)
π Cep	218658	23 07 53.8	+75 23 16	4.41	0.4	G2 III	210	0.026	152	28	−19	.006	9.1	54	
6 Cep	203467	21 19 22.1	+64 52 19	5.18	−1.7	B3 IVe	780	0.008	30	18	−18	.015	4.4	377	
9 Cep	206165	21 37 55.1	+62 04 55	4.73ᵥ	−5.7	B2 Ib	4000	0.004	284	13	−13	.008	63	15000	
11 Cep	206952	21 41 55.2	+71 18 42	4.56	0.2	K0 III	240	0.156	48	100	−37	.008	15	65	
16 Cep	209369	21 59 14.8	+73 10 48	5.03	3.4	F5 V	99	0.170	205	32	−21	.033	1.3	3.4	
19 Cep	209975	22 05 08.8	+62 16 48	5.11	−5.9	O9 Ib	5200	0.005	11	[41]	−13	[.001]	54	18000	
24 Cep	210807	22 09 48.3	+72 20 29	4.79	0.3	G7 II/III	260	0.033	72	18	−15	.017	11	60	
30 Cep	214734	22 38 38.9	+63 35 04	5.19	(−0.3)	A3 IV	410	0.021	194	16	11	.008	3.9	103	
31 Cep	214470	22 35 46.0	+73 38 36	5.08	−0.6	F3 III/IV	450	0.173	80	102	0	.008	7.2	137	
OΣ482 ∞	216446	22 47 28.8	+83 09 14	4.74	−0.2	K3 III	320	0.058	22	35	−31	.018	21	95	
Σ460	25007	04 10 02.8	+80 41 55	5.10	1.40	G8 III	180	0.012	270	12	4	.005	4.0	22	
Σ2840A ∞	208095	21 52 00.9	+55 47 49	5.71	−0.6	B6 IV/V	600	0.026	21	25	−7	.005	1.4	137	(k)
Σ2840B	208063	21 52 00.3	+55 47 32	6.62	*	A1 p	*	0.026	21	*	−6	*	*	*	
Σ2883	210884	22 10 38.8	+70 07 58	5.50	3.0	F2 V	86	0.070	300	9	1	.038	1.4	5.0	
Kr 60A ∞	239960	22 28 04.0	+57 41 52	9.85	11.87†	M3 V	12.89	0.864	246	31	−26	.253	(0.11)	.0014	(l)⊘
S Cep	206362	21 35 12.6	+78 37 29	7.9ᵥ	−1.5	C7 e	2500	0.008	23	[44]	−34	[.001]	76	313	(m)
T Cep	202012	21 09 31.8	+68 29 25	7.33ᵥ	(−1)	M5 IIIe	1500	0.071	209	169	−12	.002	39	198	
VV Cep	208816	21 56 39.1	+63 37 33	4.91ᵥ	(−2.1)	M2 Iaep+	820	0.007	333	21	−19	.004	82	534	
OV Cep	51802	07 40 31.1	+87 01 12	5.07ᵥ	−0.5	M2 IIIab	420	0.050	227	82	−25	.003	35	125	
- Cep	5848	01 08 44.9	+86 15 26	4.25	−0.1	K2 II/III	240	0.081	94	[30]	9	[.013]	19	86	(n)
- Cep	30338	05 00 20.6	+81 11 39	5.07	−0.2	K3 III	370	0.029	356	11	−8	.020	22	95	
- Cep	198084	20 45 21.0	+57 34 47	4.51	2.4	F8 IV/V	71	0.242	197	40	−31	.046	2.4	8.6	
- Cep	207130	21 43 03.9	+72 19 13	5.17	0.0	K0 III	350	0.056	235	43	−39	.015	15	79	
- Cep	210855	22 11 48.5	+56 50 22	5.24	4.0	F8 V	58	0.263	61	55	−19	.024	1.1	2.0	
- Cep	217382	22 54 24.6	+84 20 47	4.71	−0.3	K4 III	330	0.098	71	466	3	.001	26	104	
- Cep	218029	23 03 32.8	+67 12 34	5.24	−0.2	K3 III	400	0.028	51	68	−7	.002	21	95	
- Cep	223274	23 47 54.7	+67 48 25	5.04	(0.9)	A1 Vn	220	0.014	69	11	10	.015	1.8	34	

Cetus
(Ceti)

a) *Menkar* (Nose). B:$M-0.8$, $\mathcal{L}175$. OH:$M-1.5$, 200 l.y.

b) *Deneb Kaitos* (Tail of the Whale); also known as *Diphda*. SC:$M+0.2$. OH:$M+0.3$, 53 l.y. Y:$\pi.061$.

c) *Kaffaljidhma*. SC:$M+1.4$. Y:$\pi.052$.

d) Two spiral galaxies of interest are in the vicinity. NGC 1055 (east 0.5°) is an edge-on Sombrero-type, and NGC 1068 ($=$M77) is SE 1°. This is a so-called "Seyfert galaxy," which means that its nucleus is extraordinarily bright and that it emits some kind of radiation.

e) In the same field, SW, is χ Ceti. Due west 0.5° is the spiral galaxy NGC 681, while due north 0.5° is the spiral galaxy NGC 701.

f) B:$\mathcal{L}35$. OH:$M+0.1$, 140 l.y.

g) To the northwest, from two to three degrees, is a string of four galaxies, of which NGC 584 is the brightest (m11.5). The only spiral galaxy of the group, NGC 615, has been officially described as "pretty bright and pretty large."

h) The parallax suggests a greater distance, about 250 l.y.

i) The parallax suggests a much closer distance, between 130 and 175 l.y.

j) *Mira* (Wonderful). The best known of all variables, and the first discovered, in 1596. Prototype of the long-period pulsating variables.

   The absolute magnitude is from the *Observer's Handbook,* which, however, gives a distance of 200 l.y. Burnham's estimate is in the same range, 220 l.y., and he gives a maximum diameter of 550 Suns, with a density of only 2×10^{-7} (0.0000002) of the Sun's— a "virtual vacuum," as that author describes it. As the star expands, its temperature drops from 2500 to about 1900 K. For a finder's chart, see Burnham, p. 636.

k) B:$D_s0.9$. Y:$\pi.287$.

   This is one of the closest stars, and subject of a (fruitless, so far) study for the existence of a planetary system similar to our own.

l) Y:$\pi.056$.

m) SC:$M+5.2$.

n) A semiregular variable. If the absolute magnitude is estimated from Fig. 2 to be -6, then: 5500 l.y., $\pi.0006$, $V550$ km/s, D_s520, and $\mathcal{L}20,000$.

CETUS	HD	R.A.	Declin.	m	M	Spectra	l.y.	μ	Dir.	V	RV	π	D_s	$\mathscr{L}$	Rmk
		2000.0													
α Cet	18884	03^h 02^m 16.7^s	+04° 05′ 23″	2.53$_v$	−0.5	M2 III	130	0.075″	189°	47	−26	.009″	35	125	(a)
β Cet	4128	00 43 35.3	−17 59 12	2.04	0.7†	K0 III	59	0.235	81	24	13	.055	11	41	(b)
γ Cet ∞	16970	02 43 18.0	+03 14 09	3.47	1.9†	A2 V	71	0.207	224	22	−5	.046	1.5	14	(c)
δ Cet	16582	02 39 28.9	+00 19 43	4.07$_v$	−3.0	B2 IV	850	0.009	84	45	13	.001	2.1	1247	(d)
ε Cet	16620	02 39 33.7	−11 52 20	5.58	2.8	F8 V	47	0.273	149	24	15	.069	1.7	6.0	
ζ Cet	11353	01 51 27.5	−10 20 06	3.73	−0.1	K0 III	110	0.050	136	12	9	.031	18	86	(e)
η Cet	6805	01 08 35.3	−10 10 56	3.45	−0.1	K1.5 III	80	0.252	122	32	12	.041	18	86	(f)
θ Cet	8512	01 24 01.3	−08 11 01	3.60	0.2	K0 IIIb	80	0.233	201	32	17	.041	14	65	(g)
ι Cet	1522	00 19 25.6	−08 49 26	3.56	−0.1	K1.5 III	180	0.036	212	23	19	.013	19	86	(h)
κ^1 Cet	20630	03 19 21.6	+03 22 13	4.83	4.99†	G5 V	31	0.284	70	24	20	.107	0.9	0.8	
λ Cet	18604	02 59 42.8	+08 54 27	4.70	−2.2	B6 III	780	0.010	163	[16]	10	[.004]	3.1	597	
μ Cet	17094	02 44 56.5	+10 06 51	4.27	1.7	F0 IV	71	0.283	96	42	30	.046	2.1	16	
ν Cet	16161	02 35 52.4	+05 35 36	4.86	0.3	G8 III	270	0.037	236	89	5	.002	11	60	
ξ^1 Cet	13611	02 12 59.9	+08 50 48	4.37	−2.1	G6 II/III	640	0.025	263	7	−4	.022	33	545	(i)
ξ^2 Cet	15318	02 28 09.5	+08 27 36	4.28	−0.8	B9 III	110	0.037	96	12	11	.030	2.5	164	
o Cet	14386	02 19 20.7	−02 58 39	3.04$_v$	(−0.5)	M7 IIIe	170	0.233	183	79	64	.024	29	125	(j)
π Cet	17081	02 44 07.3	−13 51 32	4.25	−0.6	B7 IV	300	0.018	223	[17]	15	[.011]	1.3	137	
ρ Cet	15130	02 25 56.9	−12 17 26	4.89	0.2	B9.5 Vn	280	0.019	249	10	10	.029	2.0	65	
σ Cet	15798	02 32 05.1	−15 14 41	4.75	2.1	F4 IV	93	0.193	204	39	−29	.035	2.3	11	
τ Cet	10700	01 44 04.0	−15 56 15	3.50	5.72†	G8 Vp	11.77	1.922	297	37	−16	.277	0.7	0.4	(k)
υ Cet	12274	02 00 00.2	−21 04 40	4.00	−0.5	M0.5 III	260	0.133	99	92	18	.007	33	125	
φ^1 Cet	4188	00 44 11.3	−10 36 34	4.76	0.2	K0 III	270	0.109	187	23	1	.022	13	65	
φ^2 Cet	4813	00 50 07.5	−10 38 40	5.19	4.23†	F7 IV/V	51	0.320	226	25	8	.064	1.0	1.6	
φ^3 Cet	5437	00 56 01.4	−11 16 00	5.31	−0.3	K4 III	430	0.025	259	29	−26	.009	29	104	
χ Cet	11171	01 49 35.0	−10 41 11	4.67	1.9	F3 III	71	0.177	239	18	−1	.046	2.0	14	
2 Cet	225132	00 03 44.3	−17 20 10	4.55	−0.3	B9.5 Vn	300	0.024	99	17	−5	.007	2.1	104	
3 Cet	225212	00 04 30.0	−10 30 35	4.94	−4.4	K3 Ib	2400	0.011	232	42	−42	.016	211	4500	
6 Cet	693	00 11 15.8	−15 28 05	4.89	3.8†	F7 V	53	0.276	197	26	14	.061	1.2	2.4	
7 Cet	1038	00 14 38.3	−18 55 58	4.44$_v$	−0.5	M3 III	320	0.069	203	26	−23	.029	36	125	
13 Cet	3196	00 35 14.8	−03 35 34	5.20	4.69†	F8 V	52	0.411	93	32	9	.063	0.9	1.0	
20 Cet	5112	00 53 00.4	−01 08 40	4.77	−0.4	M0 III	350	0.014	155	28	16	.003	32	114	
37 Cet ∞	7439	01 14 24.0	−07 55 23	5.13	3.5†	F2	69	0.303	24	38	22	.047	1.3	3.1	(l)
46 Cet	8705	01 25 37.1	−14 35 56	4.90	−0.2	K2.5 IIIb	340	0.038	113	35	−23	.007	21	95	
48 Cet	9132	01 29 36.1	−21 37 46	5.12	1.2	AI V	200	0.054	79	9	1	.028	1.8	26	
56 Cet	11930	01 56 40.1	−22 31 36	4.85	−0.3	K4 III	350	0.062	109	37	27	.012	26	104	
94 Cet	19994	03 12 46.4	−01 11 46	5.06	3.8†	F8 V	59	0.203	108	25	18	.055	1.3	2.4	
β395 ∞	3443	00 37 20.6	−24 46 02	5.57	5.7	K1 V	44	1.389	90	91	17	.074	0.7	0.4	(m)⊘
Σ186 ∞	11803	01 55 53.7	+01 50 59	6.01	(3.0)	G0	130	0.244	39	55	30	.025	1.9	5	⊘
T Cet	1760	00 21 46.3	−20 03 28	5.12$_v$	*	M5/6 Ib	*	0.069	91	*	29	*	*	*	(n)
AD Cet	1014	00 14 27.5	−07 46 50	5.12$_v$	−0.5	M3 III	430	0.056	82	88	−2	.003	35	125	
- Cet	2696	00 30 22.6	−23 47 16	5.19	1.7	A5 Vn	160	0.031	307	8	0	.018	1.8	16	
- Cet	4247	00 44 44.3	−22 00 22	5.24	3.3†	F1 III/IV	80	0.110	322	18	12	.041	1.1	3.8	
- Cet	10550	01 42 43.4	−03 41 25	4.99	−1.3	K3 II/III	590	0.032	196	38	−34	.009	40	261	

Chamaeleon
(Chamaeleontis)

a)   Y:π.053.

b)   The parallax suggests a distance of over 1000 l.y.

c)   SC:$RV-52$. In the same field NW is the equally bright ι Cha.

CHA-MAELEON	HD	2000.0 R.A.	Declin.	m	M	Spectra	l.y.	μ	Dir.	V	RV	π	D_s	𝓛	Rmk
α Cha	71243	08^h 18^m 31.7^s	−76° 55′ 11″	4.07	2.5†	F5 V	67	0.156″	46°	21	−14	.049″	1.7	8	(a)
β Cha	106911	12 18 20.7	−79 18 43	4.26	−0.9	B4 V	350	0.046	289	[33]	23	[.009]	1.7	180	
γ Cha	92305	10 35 28.1	−78 36 27	4.11	−0.4	K5 III	260	0.042	292	31	−22	.009	32	114	
δ^1 Cha	93779	10 45 15.8	−80 28 10	5.47	0.2	K0 III	370	0.048	225	77	11	.003	12	65	(b)
δ^2 Cha	93845	10 45 46.6	−80 32 24	4.45	−1.7	B3 V	550	0.053	274	[49]	23	[.006]	2.0	377	
ε Cha	104174	11 59 37.3	−78 13 18	4.91	0.2	B9 Vn	290	0.050	264	24	13	.012	1.6	65	(c)
ζ Cha	83979	09 33 53.4	−80 56 29	5.11	−1.6	B4 IV	720	0.042	280	[60]	−42	[.005]	2.1	344	
η Cha	75416	08 41 19.9	−78 57 48	5.47	−6.3	B8 V	7400	0.031	312	[334]	14	.004	23	25000	
θ Cha	71701	08 20 38.7	−77 29 04	4.35	1.7	K1 III	91	0.134	286	28	22	.036	7.9	16	
ι Cha	82554	09 24 09.2	−80 47 13	5.36	0.6	F3/5 IV	290	0.193	311	[82]	7	[.011]	4.7	45	
κ Cha	104902	12 04 46.5	−76 31 08	5.04	−0.3	K4 III	380	0.087	300	137	−2	.003	28	104	
ν Cha	85396	09 46 21.3	−76 46 33	5.45	(1.8)	G8 III	170	0.116	116	31	11	.019	5.3	14	

Circinus
(Circini)

a) B:M+1.7, $\mathcal{L}$17. SC:M+2.6; this catalog also gives an R.A. of $14^h42^m28.0^s$ and declination of $-64°58'43''$.

This is a binary of fixed separation (15.7″) and decreasing PA (1951: 232°). α Circini was determined in 1985 to be an α CVNO-type variable, of very small amplitude [IBVS #2681].

b) SC:M+1.7. Y:π.053.

c) The parallax suggests a slightly closer star.

CIRCINUS	HD	R.A.		Declin.			m	M	Spectra	l.y.	μ	Dir.	V	RV	π	D_s	$\mathscr{L}$	Rmk
				2000.0														
α Cir	128898	$14^h 42^m$	30.3^s	−65° 58′	31″		3.19_v	2.0†	ApSrEu	56	0.302″	218°	26	7	.058″	1.6	12	(a)
β Cir	135379	15 17	30.8	−58 48	04		4.07	2.1†	A3 V	80	0.169	214	22	10	.041	1.4	11	(b)
γ Cir	136415	15 23	22.6	−59 19	15		4.51	−1.0	B3/4 V	410	0.042	195	26	−17	.010	5.5	198	(c)
δ Cir	135240	15 16	56.7	−60 57	27		5.09	−4.8	O8.5 V	3100	0.017	225	[77]	9	[.001]	16	6500	
ε Cir	135291	15 17	38.8	−63 36	38		4.86	−0.3	K2 III	350	0.008	45	11	−5	.004	22	104	
η Cir	132905	15 04	48.1	−64 01	54		5.17	3.2	G8 III	100	0.106	91	48	45	.032	3.0	4.1	
θ Cir	131492	14 56	44.0	−62 46	51		5.11_v	−1.7	B2 IV/V	750	0.006	225	[7]	3	[.004]	6.5	377	
- Cir	131342	14 55	34.4	−60 06	50		5.20	0.0	K2 III	110	0.167	230	29	−14	.031	17	79	

Columba
(Columbae)

a) *Phaet.* B:$M-0.6$, $\mathcal{L}145$. OH:$M-1.1$, 180 l.y. Tirion indicates a binary; Burnham believes it to be optical only.

   Just over 1° E is NGC 2090, a bright spiral galaxy.

b) *Wezn.* B:$M0.0$. OH:$M+0.1$.

c) If the absolute magnitude is estimated to be $+0.5$, then: 260 l.y., $\pi.012$, $V45$, $D_s0.9$, $\mathcal{L}50$.

d) The parallax suggests a closer star, perhaps 130–150 l.y.

e) Note the high velocity. This is one of three "runaway stars," along with 53 Arietis and AE Aurigae. They are believed to be leaving the nebulous area of Orion, perhaps due to a supernova explosion sometime in the past.

f) If the absolute magnitude is estimated at -1, then: 1130 l.y., $\pi.003$, $V120$ km/s, D_s43, and $\mathcal{L}198$.

COLUMBA	HD	R.A.			Declin.			m	M	Spectra	l.y.	μ	Dir.	V	RV	π	D_s	$\mathscr{L}$	Rmk
		2000.0																	
α Col	37795	05^h 39^m 38.9^s			$-34°$ $04'$ $27''$			2.64	-0.2	B7 IVe	120	0.027″	178°	133	35	.001″	1.2	95	(a)
β Col	39425	05	50	57.5	-35	46	06	3.12	-0.1	K1.5 III	140	0.405	7	112	89	.028	18	86	(b)
γ Col	40494	05	57	32.2	-35	17	00	4.36	-2.3	B2.5 IV	700	0.009	333	(26)	24	[.005]	3.4	655	
δ Col	44762	06	22	06.7	-33	26	11	3.85	0.5	G7 II	150	0.064	208	16	-3	.019	9.7	50	
ε Col	36597	05	31	12.7	-35	28	14	3.87	0.2	KI IIIa	180	0.043	146	26	-5	.008	15	65	
η Col	40808	05	59	08.7	-42	48	55	3.96	0.2	G8/K1 II	180	0.022	137	18	17	.019	15	65	
θ Col	42167	06	07	31.6	-37	15	10	5.02	*	B9 IV	*	0.004	270	*	45	*	*	*	(c)
κ Col	43785	06	16	33.0	-35	08	26	4.37	0.3	G8 II	210	0.085	351	29	24	.025	12	60	(d)
λ Col	39764	05	53	06.8	-33	48	05	4.87_v	-1.1	B5 V	93	0.034	343	30	30	.035	5.0	217	
μ Col	38666	05	45	59.9	-32	18	23	5.17	-4.4	B1 IV/V	2700	0.025	171	[147]	109	[.001]	1.7	4500	(e)
ν^2 Col	37495	05	37	44.6	-28	41	22	5.31	3.6†	F4 V	72	0.064	323	37	36	.045	1.2	2.9	
ξ Col	40176	05	55	29.8	-37	07	15	4.97	0.0	K1 III	320	0.036	136	62	60	.011	16	79	
o Col	34642	05	17	29.0	-34	53	43	4.83	3.2	K0 IV	69	0.349	166	94	21	.018	3.3	4.1	
π^2 Col	42303	06	07	52.9	-42	09	14	5.50	0.6	A0 V	310	0.016	207	31	31	.016	2.3	45	
σ Col	40248	05	56	20.9	-31	22	57	5.50	2.6	F2 III	120	0.008	353	[19]	19	[.026]	1.7	7.2	
T Col	34897	05	19	17.5	-33	42	27	6.7_v	*	M5/6 e	*	0.060	56	*	67	*	*	*	(f)
- Col	46568	06	32	21.3	-37	41	48	5.24	3.2	G8 III	83	0.097	143	48	39	.016	3.3	4.1	

Coma Berenices
(Comae Berenicis)

a) *Diadem.* SC:*M*+5.22. The Yale *Bright Star Catalogue* notes that the star has some variability, due possibly to eclipsing with its companion star.

  The binary is seen edge-on; the two stars form a straight-line orbit, and the companion never gets farther away than 1″, with a period of nearly 26 years.

  NE 1° is M53, a highly condensed globular cluster. In the same field is NGC 5053, a fainter cluster.

b) SC:*M*+6.33. The spectacular star cluster M3 (NGC 5272) is 7° E (in CVn). It has thousands of stars, including over two hundred RR Lyrae variables.

c) If the absolute magnitude is estimated at 0.0, then: 245 l.y., D_s12, $\mathscr{L}$80. If the parallax is used instead, we have M−3.3, D_s55, $\mathscr{L}$1600.

  From γ Com, south 2.5° and east 2° is NGC 4565 (the binary 17 Com is 1.5° west of it). This is a superb edge-on spiral galaxy, even for small telescopes. It is thought to be about 20 million light years away.

d) A member of the Coma Star Cluster, best seen with binoculars. Besides a half-dozen bright stars, there are another thirty or so dimmer stars associated with this open cluster.

e) NE 1° is M64, the Black-Eye Galaxy, a spiral galaxy of some interest. While rather bright, it is nevertheless thought to be over 20 million light years away.

f) This star offers two entirely different sorts of data, depending on one's starting point. Using the visual magnitude and the parallax (the distance modulus formula), the cited values have been automatically generated by computer.

  If, instead, we use the $B - V$ index (+1.17), Fig. 3 gives an estimated diameter of about 50 Suns, and the luminosity becomes about 1200, giving an absolute magnitude of −3 and a distance of 1200 l.y.

g) SC:m6.3.

h) A Mira-type variable with period of nearly one year. Thus, it takes many years to change its maximum-magnitude date. In 2000 the maximum is calculated to arrive on 5 December, but one must see it in the very early morning hours at that time of year. The best time of view, in the summer, will not be favorable until well past 2050! (See Variable Section.)

  In the same field, 0.5° south, is the bright spiral galaxy NGC 4064, and 1.5° east of this is the globular cluster NGC 4147.

  Just SE of R Com is the richest field of galaxies in the heavens, including many Messier objects. This field extends far south, into Virgo.

i) The parallax suggests a distance of about 150 l.y.

COMA BERENICES	HD	R.A. 2000.0		Declin.			m	M	Spectra	l.y.	μ	Dir.	V	RV	π	D_s	$\mathscr{L}$	Rmk
α Com	114378	13^h 09^m 59.2^s	+17°	31'	46"	4.32	3.69†	F5 V	62	0.450"	287°	44	−18	.053"	1.1	2.6	(a)
β Com	114710	13 11 52.3	+27	52	41	4.26	4.66†	G0 V	27	1.189	318	47	6	.120	0.9	1.1	(b)
γ Com	108381	12 26 56.2	+28	16	06	4.36	*	K1 III	*	0.121	224	191	4	.003	*	*	(c)
6 Com	106661	12 16 00.1	+14	53	57	5.10	1.4	A3 V	180	0.090	249	19	10	.026	1.8	22	
7 Com	106714	12 16 20.5	+23	56	43	4.95	0.2	G8 III+	290	0.032	248	38	−28	.006	13	65	
11 Com	107383	12 20 42.9	+17	47	34	4.74	0.3	G8 III	250	0.141	307	[67]	42	[.013]	13	60	
12 Com	107700	12 22 30.2	+25	50	46	4.81	(0.5)	G0 III/IV	230	0.018	221	6	1	.014	5.2	48	(d)
13 Com	107966	12 24 18.4	+26	05	55	5.18$_v$	(0.0)	A3 V	360	0.022	227	12	1	.009	3.7	82	
14 Com	108283	12 26 24.0	+27	16	05	4.95	(0.7)	F0 p	230	0.020	229	8	−4	.014	3.1	42	
16 Com	108382	12 26 59.3	+26	49	32	5.00	1.9	A4 V	140	0.017	205	4	2	.024	1.5	14	
23 Com	109485	12 34 51.0	+22	37	45	4.81	−0.6	A0 IV	390	0.070	283	84	−16	.004	3.9	137	
24 Com ∞	109511	12 35 07.7	+18	22	37	5.02	−0.1	K2 III	350	0.019	342	45	4	.002	18	86	
27 Com	111067	12 46 38.7	+16	34	39	5.12	−0.2	K3 III	380	0.009	77	[53]	53	[.009]	23	95	
31 Com	111812	12 51 41.8	+27	32	26	4.94	0.6	G0 IIIp	240	0.018	225	8	−1	.011	6.9	45	
35 Com	112033	12 53 19.3	+21	14	25	4.90	0.3	G8 III	270	0.067	250	17	−7	.021	11	60	(e)
36 Com	112769	12 58 55.4	+17	24	33	4.78	−0.5	M1 IIIb	370	0.042	305	[23]	−2	[.009]	33	125	
37 Com	112989	13 00 16.4	+30	47	06	4.90	(0.9)	G9 III	200	0.024	240	15	−13	.016	11	34	(f)
41 Com	113996	13 07 10.6	+27	37	29	4.80	−0.3	K5 III	340	0.083	159	52	−16	.008	28	104	
Σ1633 ∞	107398	12 20 41.3	+27	03	17	7.13	3.0	F3 V	220	0.118	180	72	−15	.008	1.3	5.0	(g)
Σ1639 ∞	108007	12 24 26.7	+25	34	58	6.40	2.6	A7 V	190	0.017	242	11	−8	.011	1.3	7.2	(i)
R Com	104785	12 04 00.9	+18	48	53	7.7$_v$	−0.1	K2 III	1200	0.094	197	—	—	[.003]	17	86	(h)
- Com	106760	12 16 30.1	+33	03	41	5.00	0.0	K0.5 IIIb	330	0.130	203	50	−42	.022	17	79	(i)

Corona Australis
(Coronae Australis)

a) SC:m4.21, $M+4.0$. This is a rapid binary of two equally bright stars, with a period of about 120 years. Last report (1944): PA 54°, 2.7″, but the PA is said to be decreasing.

   While the Yale *Bright Star Catalogue* lists both γ^A and γ^B, it gives to the companion the identical values as γ^A. Gliese gives these differences: γ^A a visual magnitude of 4.91, γ^B a visual magnitude of 5.01, absolute magnitude 3.7.

   Three diffuse nebulae of some interest are about 0.8° to the west of γ CrA. NGC 6726–27 form a tiny figure eight, tipped to the NE. In the middle of NGC 6729 (SE 4.6°) lies the irregular variable R CrA.

   Directly west of γ, about 1.4°, is the W UMa variable ε CrA (see note b).

b) In the same field are a couple of notable items: one-half degree north is the fairly bright but small globular cluster NGC 6723 (in Sagittarius), and 2.4° east of ε CrA can be found the pleasant binary Brs 14 (6.5, 7) fixed at 281°, 12.7″.

c) SC:$M+5.90$. Note that while this star is designated κ^1, it is the companion to the primary κ^2.

d) SC:$M+5.90$. The two stars form a very attractive fixed binary.

e) SC lists only HD 165189, m4.95 (which is the combined visual magnitude).

CORONA AUSTRALIS	HD	2000.0 R.A.	Declin.	m	M	Spectra	l.y.	μ	Dir.	V	RV	π	D_s	$\mathscr{L}$	Rmk
α CrA	178253	19^h 09^m 28.2^s	−37° 54′ 16″	4.11	(1.9)	A0/1 V	91	0.130″	140°	25	−18	.036″	1.4	14	
β CrA	178345	19 10 01.6	−39 20 27	4.11	0.3	K0 III	190	0.037	177	11	3	.016	16	60	
γ CrA	177474	19 06 25.0	−37 03 48	5.01	3.7†	F8 V	56	0.289	161	57	−52	.058	1.3	2.6	(a)
δ CrA	177873	19 08 20.8	−40 29 48	4.59	0.2	K1 III	250	0.044	125	24	20	.016	15	65	
ε CrA	175813	18 58 43.3	−37 06 26	4.87$_v$	2.6	F2 V	100	0.161	233	59	54	.032	1.7	7.2	(b)
ζ CrA	176638	19 03 06.7	−42 05 43	4.75	0.6	B9.5 V	100	0.074	133	17	−13	.031	1.9	45	
η^1 CrA	173715	18 48 50.4	−43 40 48	5.49	1.4	A3 V	210	0.029	125	[10]	−4	[.015]	2.1	22	
θ CrA	170845	18 33 30.1	−42 18 45	4.64	0.3	G8 III	240	0.037	124	177	−2	.001	13	60	
κ^1 CrA	170868	18 33 23.2	−38 43 13	6.32	0.4	B8	500	0.034	142	[29]	−16	[.007]	2.5	54	(c)
κ^2 CrA ∞	170867	18 33 23.0	−38 43 34	5.65	0.0	B8/A1	440	0.029	188	[27]	−20	[.007]	1.7	79	(d)
λ CrA	172777	18 43 46.8	−38 19 25	5.13	1.2	A0/1 V	200	0.056	178	28	−26	.024	2.1	26	
μ CrA	173540	18 47 44.4	−40 24 22	5.24	2.0	G5/6 III	140	0.016	150	18	−18	.023	4.2	12	
h 5014 ∞	165189	18 06 49.7	−43 25 29	5.77	2.1	A5 V	180	0.098	181	23	−6	.021	1.4	11	(e)⊘
- CrA	168592	18 22 18.5	−38 39 25	5.10	0.2	K4/5 III	310	0.043	231	26	18	.011	22	65	
- CrA	170642	18 32 21.2	−39 42 15	5.16	1.4	A3 Vn	180	0.053	137	13	−6	.022	1.9	22	

Corona Borealis
(Coronae Borealis)

a) *Gemma, Alphecca.* B:D_s2.9.

b) *Nusakan.* 2° SW is the splendid Corona Borealis Galaxy Cluster, containing perhaps 500 galaxies in a space the size of the Moon. It is estimated to be over a thousand million light years away.

c) B:140 l.y., $\mathcal{L}$40.

d) The parallax suggests a distance of 135–150 l.y. A quite close binary with faint (m12) companion.

e) This is a rapid binary; by 1993 it will be at its maximum separation of 1″, then will close to 0.3″ by 2020.

f) The parallax suggests a distance of 120–150 l.y.

g) Eicher calls this star and ν^2 a "wide pair" (4.8, 5.1, PA 166°, 371.9″). It may, however, be optical; neither Burnham nor Tirion lists it as a true binary.

h) Very nice binary, easily resolved. It is slowly widening, and by 2000 will be 7.1″ apart. SC:m5.22, which is the combined visual magnitudes, and M+4.4.

i) An interesting irregular variable, prototype of the RCB type, in that it is usually seen at maximum brightness, but will undergo a sudden drop in magnitude which lasts several weeks or months—on occasion, a year or more. Eicher calls it a "recurrent nova in reverse," a wonderfully descriptive phrase, but few authorities actually consider the star to be a nova. Burnham, p.705, has a finder's chart.

   The luminosity class indicates a supergiant, with an absolute magnitude of around −4.5 (which agrees with Burnham). However, SC has M+4.4, G0 V. If we accept M−4.5, then: 3800 l.y., D_s83, and $\mathcal{L}$5000. Note that the listed parallax would give a distance of only 325 l.y. and thus cannot be relied upon.

CORONA BOREALIS	HD	2000.0 R.A.	Declin.	m	M	Spectra	l.y.	μ	Dir.	V	RV	π	D_s	$\mathcal{L}$	Rmk
α CrB	139006	15^h 34^m 41.2^s	+26° 42' 53''	2.23$_v$	0.6	A0 V	72	0.151''	127°	16	2	.045''	1.9	45	(a)
β CrB	137909	15 27 49.7	+29 06 20	3.68$_v$	(1.2)	F0 p	100	0.197	295	35	−19	.032	2.5	26	(b)
γ CrB	140436	15 42 44.5	+26 17 44	3.84$_v$	−0.3	B9 IV	99	0.114	292	20	−11	.033	3.4	104	(c)
δ CrB	141714	15 49 35.6	+26 04 06	4.63$_v$	1.8	G3.5 III/IV	120	0.105	228	40	−19	.014	4.8	15	
ε CrB	143107	15 57 35.2	+26 52 40	4.15	−0.2	K2 IIIab	240	0.100	231	37	−31	.024	21	95	(d)
ζ^2 CrB ∞	139892	15 39 22.6	+36 38 09	5.00	−0.6	B9 V	430	0.019	242	25	−24	.015	1.5	137	
η CrB ∞	137107	15 23 12.2	+30 17 16	4.98	4.5†	G0 V	54	0.233	145	20	−7	.060	1.0	1.2	(e)⊘
θ CrB	138749	15 32 55.7	+31 21 32	4.14	−1.1	B6 Vne	360	0.027	236	25	−25	.027	1.7	217	(f)
ι CrB	143807	16 01 26.6	+29 51 04	4.99	−0.6	A0 p+	430	0.032	252	24	−19	.010	2.1	137	
κ CrB	142091	15 51 13.8	+35 39 26	4.82	1.7	K1 IVa	96	0.351	182	55	−24	.034	6.6	16	
λ CrB	142908	15 55 47.6	+37 56 49	5.45	(3.7)	F0 IV	74	0.086	23	15	−12	.044	0.9	2.7	
μ CrB	139153	15 35 14.8	+39 00 36	5.11	−0.5	M2 IIIab	430	0.024	83	43	−19	.003	35	125	
ν^1 CrB	147749	16 22 21.3	+33 47 56	5.20	−0.5	M2 IIIab	450	0.040	174	65	−13	.003	34	125	(g)
ν^2 CrB	147767	16 22 29.1	+33 42 13	5.39	−0.3	K5 III	450	0.057	350	42	−40	.021	29	104	
ξ CrB	147677	16 22 05.7	+30 53 32	4.85	0.2	K0 III	280	0.148	319	53	−29	.016	13	65	
ρ CrB	143761	16 01 02.6	+33 18 13	5.41	4.1†	G2 V	59	0.793	195	71	18	.055	1.2	1.8	
σ(A) CrB ∞	146361	16 14 40.7	+33 51 30	5.64$_v$	4.0†	G0 V+	72	0.286	254	32	−11	.045	1.1	2.0	(h)⊘
σ(B) CrB	146362	16 14 40.7	+33 51 30	6.66	5.0†	G1 V	72	0.286	254	35	−17	.045	1.0	0.8	
τ CrB	145328	16 08 58.2	+36 29 27	4.76	0.2	K0 III/IV	110	0.333	350	54	−19	.031	13	65	
R CrB	141527	15 48 34.3	+28 09 24	5.85$_v$	(−4.5)	G0 Iep	3800	0.017	193	26	25	.010	83	5000	(i)

Corvus
(Corvi)

a) *Al Chiba*. SC:M +1.9. Y:π.070. Curiously, this star, although designated α, is dimmer than four others in this constellation.

b) *Kraz*. B:$\mathscr{L}$85. OH:310 l.y.

c) *Gienah* (Wing). B:M −3.1, $\mathscr{L}$1200, 450 l.y. OH gives a proper motion of 0.163″, and 190 l.y.

    3.7° WSW is NGC 4038, the "Ringtail Galaxy," one of the oddest-shaped galaxies known. In the same field, the star SSW of the galaxy is 31 Crv.

d) *Algorab*. An attractive binary with contrasting colors, said by some to be yellow and lilac. OH:M −0.3, 150 l.y.

e) *Minkar*. OH:M −0.8.

f) If the absolute magnitude is estimated to be 0.0, then: 360 l.y., π.009, V54 km/s, D_s1.3, and $\mathscr{L}$79.

g) SC:M +1.7.

h) A typical Mira-type variable. Kholopov gives a maximum visual magnitude for this star of only 6.7.

    If the absolute magnitude is estimated to be −1, then: 750 l.y., π.004, V23 km/s, D_s43, and $\mathscr{L}$198. NE 1° is the planetary nebula 4361, large and bright with a m13 central star.

CORVUS	HD	2000.0 R.A.	Declin.	m	M	Spectra	l.y.	μ	Dir.	V	RV	π	D_s	$\mathscr{L}$	Rmk
α Crv	105452	12ʰ 08ᵐ 24.7ˢ	−24° 43′ 44″	4.02	3.1†	F0 IV/V	49	0.096″	118°	8	4	.066″	1.1	4.5	(a)
β Crv	109379	12 34 23.2	−23 23 48	2.65	−2.1	G5 II	96	0.058	179	11	−8	.034	33	545	(b)
γ Crv	106625	12 15 48.3	−17 32 31	2.59	−1.2	B8 III	190	0.164	276	45	−4	.017	2.1	238	(c)
δ Crv ∞	108767	12 29 51.8	−16 30 56	2.95	0.2	B9.5 V	120	0.257	236	51	9	.024	1.7	65	(d)
ε Crv	105707	12 10 07.4	−22 37 11	3.00	−0.1	K2 III	140	0.073	278	14	5	.027	22	86	(e)
ζ Crv	107348	12 20 33.6	−22 12 57	5.21	*	B8 Vne	*	0.102	251	*	−6	*	*	*	(f)
η Crv	109085	12 32 04.1	−16 11 46	4.31	2.9†	F2 V	63	0.435	261	40	−4	.052	1.4	5.4	(g)
R Crv	107199	12 19 37.9	−19 15 21	5.80ᵥ	*	M5 III	*	0.007	63	*	−22	*	*	*	(h)
- Crv	107418	12 20 55.7	−13 33 56	5.14	0.0	K1 III	350	0.013	360	13	13	.020	15	79	

Crater
(Crateris)

a) *Alkes*. On its eastern edge is found R Crt, 1″ away. This is a Mira-type variable, 6.7–14.4, 317d.

b) SC:$M+0.2$, which gives a luminosity of 65 and a size of three Suns.

c) The parallax suggests a distance of about 115 l.y.

d) The parallax yields a distance of about 135 l.y.

e) The parallax indicates a distance of 150 l.y.

f) The estimated parallax—derived from the computed distance (given m and M)—seems quite large. There is reason, therefore, to suppose that the absolute magnitude is less than that given.

CRATER	HD	2000.0 R.A.	Declin.	m	M	Spectra	l.y.	μ	Dir.	V	RV	π	D_s	$\mathscr{L}$	Rmk
α Crt	95272	$10^h 59^m 46.4^s$ $-18°$	$17'$ $56''$	4.08	0.2	K1 III	110	0.481″	285°	87	47	.031″	15	65	(a)
β Crt	97277	11 11 39.4 -22	49 33	4.48	3.0†	A1 V	64	0.102	180	11	6	.051	0.8	5.0	(b)
γ Crt ∞	99211	11 24 52.8 -17	41 03	4.08	2.1	A9 V	81	0.103	269	17	1	.028	1.4	11	(c)
δ Crt	98430	11 19 20.4 -14	46 43	3.56	1.8	K0 III	73	0.238	328	47	-5	.024	7.2	15	(d)
ε Crt	99167	11 24 36.5 -10	51 34	4.83	-0.3	K5 III	350	0.038	303	[19]	3	[.009]	30	104	
ζ Crt	102070	11 44 45.7 -18	21 03	4.73	0.3	G8 IIIa	110	0.046	141	9	-5	.030	12	60	
η Crt	103632	11 56 00.9 -17	09 03	5.18	0.6	A0 V	270	0.057	259	19	15	.023	1.9	45	(e)
θ Crt	100889	11 36 40.8 -09	48 08	4.70	0.2	B9.5 Vn	260	0.067	273	[25]	1	[.013]	1.3	65	
ι Crt	101198	11 38 40.0 -13	12 07	5.48	3.4	F7 V	85	0.144	38	[30]	-24	[.038]	1.5	3.4	(f)
λ Crt	98991	11 23 21.8 -18	46 48	5.09	2.1	F3 IV	130	0.318	263	67	11	.023	2.2	11	

Crux
(Crucis)

a) *Acrux,* but usually known as *Alpha Crucis.* Forms the foot of the Southern Cross, and a marvelous binary. To the east lies the so-called "Coal Sack," a large dark nebula thought to be only 500 l.y. away.

   The combined brightness of α^1 and α^2 results in a magnitude of m1.1. Burnham gives a visual magnitude of 1.39 for α^1, and 1.86 for α^2, with a combined magnitude of 0.87. OH:α^1 m1.33. SC:α^1 m1.41.

b) Forms a splendid double with α^1. SC has a visual magnitude of 1.88; OH:m1.72.

c) *Mimosa; Becrux.* B:$M-4.6$, $\mathscr{L}5800$, 490 l.y. SC:$RV+20$.

   The eastern point of the Southern Cross. In the same field, SE 1°, is the famed "Jewel Box" cluster (NGC 4755).

d) *Gacrux.* The top of the Southern Cross. The reported distance, generated from the distance modulus formula, may be too little; the resulting estimated parallax is quite large.

   B:$M-2.5$, $\mathscr{L}900$, 220 l.y. He points out that γ^A and γ^B do not form a binary system, since they are traveling in different directions. OH:$M-1.2$.

e) If the absolute magnitude is estimated to be $+2$, then: 250 l.y., D_s2, and $\mathscr{L}12$.

f) If the absolute magnitude is estimated to be -0.5, then: 215 l.y., D_s30, $\mathscr{L}125$. However, the large parallax would suggest a distance of 125 l.y., which would mean the following: $M+0.7$, D_s15, $\mathscr{L}40$.

g) SC:$RV+19$.

h) SC:$M+0.6$, $D_s4.7$, $\mathscr{L}45$.

i) If M is estimated at -1.2, then: 615 l.y., $\pi.005$, $V35$, $D_s1.9$, and $\mathscr{L}238$.

j) SC:m6.6. In the same field, SE 0.5°, is the open cluster NGC 4349, comprised of a hundred or so stars.

CRUX	HD	R.A.		2000.0 Declin.		m	M	Spectra	l.y.	μ	Dir.	V	RV	π	D_s	$\mathscr{L}$	Rmk
α^1 Cru	108248	$12^h\,26^m\,35.9^s$	$-63°\,05'\,56''$			1.58	-3.9	B0.5 IV	410	$0.030''$	$236°$	21	-11	$.008''$	1.8	2858	(a)
α^2 Cru	108249	12 26 36.5	-63 05 58			2.09	(-3.4)	B1 V	410	0.031	248	19	-1	.008	1.6	1794	(b)
β Cru	111123	12 47 43.3	-59 41 19			1.25_v	-5.0	B0.5 III	580	0.042	246	[39]	16	[.006]	4.4	7870	(c)
γ^A Cru	108903	12 31 09.9	-57 06 47			1.63	-0.5	M4 III	87	0.269	174	[40]	21	[.037]	34	125	(d)
γ^B Cru	108925	12 31 16.7	-57 04 51			6.42	*	A3 V	*	0.006	129	—	—	*	*	*	(e)
δ Cru	106490	12 15 08.6	-58 44 56			2.80_v	-3.0	B2 IV	470	0.039	255	66	22	.003	1.8	1247	
ε Cru	107446	12 21 21.5	-60 24 04			3.59	*	K3/4 III	*	0.194	295	*	-5	*	*	*	(f)
ζ Cru	106983	12 18 26.1	-64 00 11			4.04	-2.3	B2.5 V	600	0.047	250	[44]	16	[.005]	4.4	655	(g)
η Cru	105211	12 06 52.8	-64 36 49			4.15	2.7	F0 IV	63	0.052	139	10	9	.052	1.4	6.5	(h)
θ^1 Cru	104671	12 03 01.5	-63 18 46			4.33	(0.9)	A3mA8	160	0.146	271	33	-2	.021	2.7	33	
θ^2 Cru	104841	12 04 19.2	-63 09 56			4.72_v	-3.0	B3 V	1100	0.016	281	[31]	16	[.003]	5.9	1247	
ι Cru	110829	12 45 37.8	-60 58 52			4.69	0.0	K0 III	91	0.123	123	18	7	.036	15	79	
λ Cru	112078	12 54 39.1	-59 08 47			4.62_v	-1.1	B4 Vne	450	0.035	246	[26]	12	[.007]	5.0	217	
μ^1 Cru	112092	12 54 35.6	-57 10 40			4.03	-2.3	B2 IV/V	600	0.031	251	[30]	14	[.005]	4.4	655	
μ^2 Cru	112091	12 54 36.8	-57 10 05			5.17_v	*	B5 Vne	*	0.032	261	*	19	*	*	*	(i)
R Cru	107805	12 23 37.9	-61 37 44			6.42_v	3.4	F7 Ib	130	0.019	141	[14]	-14	[.025]	1.6	3.4	(j)
- Cru	108250	12 26 30.9	-63 07 21			4.86	-2.0	B4 IV	770	0.046	229	[58]	27	[.004]	2.8	497	
- Cru	110335	12 41 56.6	-59 41 08			4.93	-1.0	B6 IVe	500	0.022	254	[21]	13	[.007]	3.2	198	
- Cru	110956	12 46 22.6	-56 29 30			4.65	-1.7	B3 V	610	0.051	233	[48]	17	[.005]	4.5	377	

Cygnus
(Cygni)

a) *Deneb* (Tail). Pale-blue supergiant, which has recently become known as the prototype of a class of pulsating variables. B:$M-7.1$, 1600 l.y., D_s60, and $\mathscr{L}$60,000.

   Three degrees east is the curious North American Nebula (NGC 7000).

b) *Albireo*. A splendid double of contrasting colors, gold and blue. Burnham apparently gives a proper motion of 0.01″ for both stars, whereas this is true only for the companion, β^2.

c) *Sadr* (Breast). Both Burnham and the OH cite a proper motion of 0.001″, half that indicated by the Yale *Bright Star Catalogue* values for $\mu(\alpha)$″ and $\mu(\delta)$″ (+0.001; +0.002).

d) A slow and difficult binary. B:$M-1.7$, 270 l.y., $\mathscr{L}$400. OH:$M-0.3$.

e) *Gienah* (Wing). B:75 l.y., $\mathscr{L}$40. OH and SC:$M+0.2$. Y:π.057.

   In the same field, NE, is T Cygni.

f) OH:$M-0.8$, 200 l.y. The Veil Nebula (east) (NGC 6992/5) is 3° W, in the middle of the triangle formed by ϵ, ζ, and 52 Cygni.

g) Nearby is Cygnus X-1, thought to be a black hole. See Burnham, 793ff., and the *Observer's Handbook,* 1989 ed., p. 195.

h) In the same field is R Cyg (see below), and east 1° is the planetary nebula NGC 6826.

i) With μ^2, a slow and close binary.

j) SC:$M+3.7$.

k) In the same field, SE 0.5° is the variable W Cygni, and directly north of ρ, 3°, is the open cluster M39 (NGC 7092), best seen with binoculars.

l) B:$\mathscr{L}$15, P.A. 15°. SC:$M+1.7$.

m) A noted variable of the Mira type, with a period of 406.93 days, easily visible to the naked eye at maximum (see Variable Star Section).

   Burnham believes its size to be "at least several hundred times" that of the Sun. He estimates M at from -1 to -2.

n) B:π.002.

o) B: Size of about 200 Suns, and distance 500–600 l.y.

CYGNUS	HD	R.A.			Declin.			m	M	Spectra	l.y.	μ	Dir.	V	RV	π	D_s	$\mathscr{L}$	Rmk
		2000.0																	
α Cyg	197345	20^h 41^m	25.8^s	+45°	16′	49″	1.25$_v$	−7.5	A2 Ia	1800	0.005″	11°	6	−5	.006″	116	80000	(a)
β¹ Cyg ∞	183912	19 30	43.1	+27	57	35	3.08	−2.3	K3 II	390	0.002	153	23	−23	.017	48	655	(b)
β² Cyg	183914	19 30	45.2	+27	57	55	5.11	−0.2	B8 Ve	380	0.011	280	18	−18	.017	1.4	95	
γ Cyg	194093	20 22	13.6	+40	15	24	2.20	−4.6	F8 Ib	750	0.002	27	9	−8	.003	76	5500	(c)
δ Cyg ∞	186882	19 44	58.4	+45	07	51	2.87	−0.6	A0 III	110	0.069	45	24	−21	.030	2.9	137	(d)⊘
ε Cyg	197989	20 46	12.6	+33	58	13	2.46	0.8†	K0 III	71	0.484	47	51	−10	.046	10	38	(e)
ζ Cyg	202109	21 12	56.1	+30	13	37	3.20	−2.1	G8 III	370	0.052	181	19	17	.027	37	545	(f)
η Cyg	188947	19 56	18.3	+35	05	00	3.89	0.2	K0 III	180	0.042	232	30	−27	.015	13	65	(g)
θ Cyg	185395	19 36	26.4	+50	13	16	4.48	3.2†	F4 V	58	0.257	355	35	−28	.056	1.2	4.1	(h)
ι² Cyg	184006	19 29	42.2	+51	43	47	3.79	2.1	A5 Vn	71	0.131	8	126	−20	.005	1.6	11	
κ Cyg	181276	19 17	06.0	+53	22	07	3.77	0.2	G9 III	170	0.137	24	40	−29	.024	12	65	
λ Cyg	198183	20 47	24.4	+36	29	27	4.53	−1.1	B5 Ve	440	0.007	117	23	−23	.008	2.0	217	
μ¹ Cyg ∞	206826	21 44	08.5	+28	44	34	4.77	3.1†	F6 V	71	0.375	129	42	17	.046	1.6	4.5	(i)⊘
μ² Cyg	206827	21 44	08.2	+28	44	35	6.20	4.5†	G2 V	71	0.314	133	37	17	.046	0.9	1.2	(j)
ν Cyg	199629	20 57	10.3	+41	10	02	3.94	0.6	A1 Vn	150	0.014	146	29	−28	.010	2.4	45	
ξ Cyg	200905	21 04	55.8	+43	55	40	3.72	−4.4	K4/5 Ib	1400	0.006	51	20	−20	.007	215	4500	
π¹ Cyg	206672	21 42	05.6	+51	11	23	4.67	−1.7	B3 IV	610	0.004	14	[9]	−8	[.005]	2.4	377	
π² Cyg	207330	21 46	47.5	+49	18	35	4.23	−2.9	B3 III	870	0.004	34	21	−12	.001	4.2	1138	
ρ Cyg	205435	21 33	58.8	+45	35	31	4.02	0.3	G8 III	180	0.095	196	224	7	.002	11	60	(k)
σ Cyg	202850	21 17	24.9	+39	23	41	4.23	−7.1	B9 Iab	6000	0.002	270	4	−4	.011	104	55000	
τ Cyg ∞	202444	21 14	47.4	+38	02	44	3.72$_v$	2.32†	F0 IV	65	0.465	20	49	−21	.050	1.9	9.3	(l)⊘
υ Cyg	202904	21 17	55.0	+34	53	49	4.43$_v$	−2.5	B2 Vne	790	0.011	90	5	4	.019	3.8	787	
φ Cyg	185734	19 39	22.5	+30	09	12	4.69	1.8	G8 III/IV	120	0.042	360	29	6	.007	6.0	15	
χ Cyg	187796	19 50	33.8	+32	54	51	4.23$_v$	0.2	K0 III	210	0.048	218	19	−2	.012	30	65	(m)
ψ Cyg ∞	189037	19 55	37.7	+52	26	20	4.92	1.3	A3 IV/V	170	0.050	236	48	−11	.005	2.2	24	
2 Cyg	182568	19 24	07.5	+29	37	17	4.97	−2.3	B3 IV	930	0.020	45	[34]	−21	[.004]	3.7	655	
4 Cyg	183056	19 26	09.0	+36	19	04	5.15$_v$	(−0.6)	B9 pSi	470	0.011	5	23	−22	.007	1.5	140	
8 Cyg	184171	19 31	46.2	+34	27	11	4.74	−2.3	B3 IV	830	0.002	270	[22]	−22	[.004]	2.8	655	
15 Cyg	186675	19 44	16.5	+37	21	16	4.89	0.3	G7 III	270	0.078	63	30	−24	.021	12	60	
17 Cyg	187013	19 46	25.5	+33	43	40	4.99	3.35†	F7 V	69	0.445	178	45	5	.047	1.4	3.6	
19 Cyg	187849	19 50	33.9	+38	43	21	5.12$_v$	−0.5	M2 IIIa	430	0.108	4	[79]	−39	[.008]	37	125	
20 Cyg	188056	19 50	37.6	+52	59	17	5.03	−0.2	K3 III+	360	0.067	192	30	−20	.014	22	95	
22 Cyg	188892	19 55	51.6	+38	29	12	4.94	−1.9	B5 V	760	0.005	307	31	−30	.004	3.5	453	
23 Cyg	188665	19 53	17.3	+57	31	25	5.14	−1.1	B5 V	580	0.016	18	[28]	−25	[.006]	1.7	217	
25 Cyg	189687	19 59	55.1	+37	02	35	5.19	−1.7	B3 IVe	780	0.006	351	[8]	−4	[.004]	3.3	377	
26 Cyg	190147	20 01	21.5	+50	06	17	5.05	−1.1	K1 II/III	550	0.015	67	5	1	.014	27	217	
28 Cyg	191610	20 09	25.5	+36	50	23	4.93$_v$	−1.7	B2.5 Ve	690	0.016	4	[21]	−14	[.005]	2.3	377	
29 Cyg	192640	20 14	31.9	+36	48	23	4.97$_v$	(2.8)	A2 V	91	0.096	42	21	−17	.036	1.2	6.2	
30 Cyg	192514	20 13	17.9	+46	48	57	4.83	(0.2)	A5 III	270	0.008	83	26	−26	.012	3.3	64	(n)
31 Cyg	192577	20 13	37.8	+46	44	29	3.79$_v$	−2.2	K2 II	510	0.005	360	9	−8	.007	55	597	
32 Cyg	192909	20 15	28.2	+47	42	52	3.98$_v$	−3.4	K3 Ib	980	0.010	343	14	−14	.014	120	1803	(o)
33 Cyg	192696	20 13	23.8	+56	34	04	4.30	1.3	A3 IV/Vn	130	0.105	36	30	−18	.021	2.1	24	
35 Cyg	193370	20 18	39.0	+34	58	58	5.17	−4.6	F5 Ib	2900	0.005	158	14	−14	.007	73	5500	
39 Cyg	194317	20 23	51.5	+32	11	25	4.43	−0.2	K3 III	280	0.039	87	20	−15	.014	23	95	
41 Cyg	195295	20 29	23.6	+30	22	07	4.01	−2.0	F5 II	520	0.005	68	18	−18	.014	14	497	

(Continued)

p) The star is on the western edge of the Bridal Veil Nebula (NGC 6960, along with NGC 6992).

q) A well-known binary, currently slowly increasing its separation.

r) An enigmatic variable, and apparently the most luminous star known (although the figures are questionable). Burnham gives an estimated absolute magnitude of −6.8 to −8.9. If we use the latter figure, then: 18,000 l.y., £300,000, and a velocity of nearly 200 km/sec. The parallax is not to be trusted; it yields a distance of only 815 l.y.

s) A Mira-type variable with a fairly long period (426 days). In the same field, 1° NE, is the pleasant binary 16 Cyg; 1955: m5, m5; PA 134°, 39″.

t) If the absolute magnitude is estimated to be −1, then: 900 l.y., π.004, V119, D_s43, £198.

u) If the absolute magnitude is estimated to be −2, then: 900 l.y., π.004, V9, D_s3.8, £500.

CYGNUS (CONT.)	HD	R.A.	Declin.	m	M	Spectra	l.y.	μ	Dir.	V	RV	π	D_s	$\mathscr{L}$	Rmk
45 Cyg	195556	$20^h\,30^m\,03.4^s$ +48° 57′ 06″		4.95	−2.5	B2.5 IV	1000	0.014″	39°	[30]	−22	[.003]″	4.3	787	
47 Cyg	196093	20 33 54.1 +35 15 03		4.61	−4.4	K2 Ib+	2100	0.004	194	11	−4	.002	206	4500	
52 Cyg	197912	20 45 39.6 +30 43 11		4.22	0.2	K0 III	210	0.033	339	11	−1	.015	14	65	(p)
55 Cyg	198478	20 48 56.2 +46 06 51		4.84$_v$	−6.8	B3 Iae	6900	0.003	18	7	−7	.017	131	40000	
56 Cyg	198639	20 50 04.8 +44 03 34		5.04	(2.0)	A4 m+	130	0.183	42	41	−21	.025	1.4	12	
57 Cyg	199081	20 53 14.7 +44 23 14		4.78	−1.1	B5 V	490	0.007	56	[21]	−20	[.007]	1.6	217	
59 Cyg	200120	20 59 49.5 +47 31 16		4.74$_v$	−3.9	B1 ne	1700	0.006	31	[15]	1	[.002]	11	2858	
60 Cyg	200310	21 01 10.8 +46 09 21		5.37	−3.5	B1 Ve	1900	0.011	15	[34]	−12	[.002]	3.1	1977	
61A Cyg ∞	201091	21 06 53.7 +38 44 57		5.22	7.58†	K5 V	11.01	5.259	52	106	−64	.296	0.5	0.07	(q)⌀
61B Cyg	201092	21 06 55.2 +38 44 30		6.03	8.39†	K7 V	11.01	5.165	53	105	−64	.296	0.5	0.03	
63 Cyg	201251	21 06 36.0 +47 38 54		4.55	−2.3	K4 Ib/IIa	760	0.006	59	26	−26	.008	76	655	
68 Cyg	203064	21 18 27.0 +43 56 46		5.00	—	O8 e	—	0.006	189	—	1	—	—	—	
70 Cyg	204403	21 27 21.3 +37 07 01		5.31	−2.3	B3 V	1100	0.006	9	[22]	−20	[.003]	2.8	655	
71 Cyg	204771	21 29 26.9 +46 32 26		5.24	0.2	K0 III	330	0.115	21	30	−19	.023	13	65	
72 Cyg	205512	21 34 46.5 +38 32 03		4.90	0.0	K0.5 III	310	0.157	50	91	−66	.012	16	79	
74 Cyg	205835	21 36 56.9 +40 24 49		5.01	(1.5)	A5 V	160	0.018	341	8	7	.020	2.3	19	
75 Cyg	206330	21 40 11.0 +43 16 26		5.11	−0.5	M1 IIIab	430	0.058	68	75	−28	.004	34	125	
P Cyg	193237	20 17 47.0 +38 01 59		4.81$_v$	*	B2 pec	*	0.008	256	*	−9	.004	*	*	(r)
R Cyg	185456	19 36 49.2 +50 11 59		6.5$_v$	—	S7.7 e	—	0.009	221	—	−25	—	35	79	(s)
T Cyg	198134	20 47 10.7 +34 22 27		4.92$_v$	−0.2	K3 III	—	0.045	82	50	−25	.005	23	95	
U Cyg	193680	20 19 36.3 +47 53 42		7.87$_v$	4.4	G0 V	160	0.058	301	—	—	[.020]	1.4	1.4	
RT Cyg	186686	19 43 37.7 +48 46 42		6.2$_v$	*	M5 III	*	0.020	345	*	−116	*	*	*	(t)
V1746 Cyg	189687	19 59 55.1 +37 02 35		5.19$_v$	*	B3 IVe	*	0.006	351	*	−4	*	*	*	(u)
- Cyg	185351	19 36 37.8 +44 41 42		5.17	−0.4	G9 IIIb+	420	0.146	227	37	−5	.019	16	114	
- Cyg	186155	19 40 50.1 +45 31 29		5.06	0.6	F5 II/III	250	0.145	37	38	−20	.021	4.2	45	
- Cyg	189276	19 55 55.2 +58 50 46		4.96	−1.3	K5 II/III	580	0.022	216	27	5	.004	49	261	
- Cyg	193092	20 16 55.2 +40 21 54		5.24	−2.3	K3.5 IIab	1100	0.001	180	20	−20	.004	82	655	

Delphinus
(Delphini)

a) *Sualocin.* Tirion indicates a binary; the double is only optical, according to Yale.

b) *Rotanev.* A close and rapid binary, increasing its separation to a maximum of 0.64″ midway through 2003 (see Orbital Elements Section).

   In the same field, W 0.5° is ζ Del, and nestled between these two, slightly north, is the attractive fixed binary Σ2703 (7.6, 7.6; PA 290°, 25.3″).

c) A pleasant binary with—according to some—a slight color contrast, yellow and blue.

d) SC:RV−18.

e) If we estimate the absolute magnitude to be −1, then: 1600 l.y., π.002, V83, D_s43, and $\mathcal{L}$198.

DEL-PHINUS	HD	R.A. 2000.0	Declin.	m	M	Spectra	l.y.	μ	Dir.	V	RV	π	D_s	$\mathscr{L}$	Rmk
α Del	196867	$20^h\,39^m\,38.1^s$	$+15°\,54'\,43''$	3.77	0.2	B9 V	170	0.065″	90°	39	−6	.008″	1.6	65	(a)
β Del ∞	196524	20 37 32.9	+14 35 43	3.63	0.7	F5 IV	130	0.116	105	30	−23	.028	4.4	41	(b)
γ^1 Del ∞	197963	20 46 38.6	+16 07 27	5.22	(2.3)	F8 IV/V	130	0.191	190	36	−8	.026	2.3	10	(c)
γ^2 Del	197964	20 46 39.3	+16 07 27	4.27	3.2	G5 IV	53	0.198	190	37	−7	.026	3.5	4.1	
δ Del	197461	20 43 27.3	+15 04 28	4.43$_v$	0.5	A7 III	200	0.046	206	19	9	.013	3.8	50	
ε Del	195810	20 33 12.7	+11 18 12	4.03	−1.9	B6 III	500	0.021	151	19	−19	.025	2.5	453	
ζ Del	196180	20 35 18.4	+14 40 27	4.68	1.7	A3 V	130	0.047	72	29	−25	.015	1.8	16	
η Del	195943	20 33 56.9	+13 01 38	5.38	1.4	A3 IV	200	0.076	67	44	−25	.010	1.8	22	(d)
ι Del	196544	20 37 49.0	+11 22 40	5.43	1.4	A2 V	210	0.038	96	9	−4	.024	1.8	22	
κ Del	196755	20 39 07.7	+10 05 10	5.05	3.2	G5 IV/V	76	0.319	86	78	−52	.026	2.2	4.1	
17 Del	199253	20 55 36.6	+13 43 18	5.17	0.2	K0 III	320	0.016	125	11	−10	.017	15	65	
R Del	192502	20 14 54.9	+09 05 20	7.5$_v$	*	M5 III	*	0.029	211	*	−46	*	*	*	(e)
S Del	197420	20 43 04.8	+17 05 20	8.3$_v$	—	M5e–M8e	—	0.039	35	—	—	—	—	—	

Dorado
(Doradus)

a)   Located three degrees north of the Large Magellanic Cloud; one of the brightest of Cepheid variables. The absolute magnitude, from the *Sky Catalogue*, gives a huge luminosity and size. Burnham gives a distance of 1700 l.y. and a luminosity of 7000, which would mean an absolute magnitude of about −4.8.

b)   SC:M+2.6.

c)   If the absolute magnitude is estimated at +0.5, then: 360 l.y., π.009, V24, D_s1.8, $\mathcal{L}$50.

d)   If the absolute magnitude is estimated at −1, then: 620 l.y., π.005, V98, D_s42, $\mathcal{L}$198.

DORADO	HD	R.A. 2000.0			Declin.			m	M	Spectra	l.y.	μ	Dir.	V	RV	π	D_s	$\mathscr{L}$	Rmk
α Dor	29305	04^h 33^m 59.8^s			−55° 02′ 42″			3.27_v	−0.6	A0 III	190	0.052″	89°	29	26	.018″	1.7	137	
β Dor	37350	05 33	37.5		−62 29	24		3.76_v	−8.0	F8/G0 Ib	7300	0.007	8	8	7	.012	450	125000	(a)
γ Dor	27290	04 16	01.6		−51 29	12		4.25_v	3.1†	F0 V	55	0.216	29	30	25	.059	1.1	4.5	(b)
δ Dor	39014	05 44	46.5		−65 44	08		4.35	2.4	A7 V	80	0.027	285	6	−3	.027	1.2	8.6	
ε Dor	39844	05 49	53.7		−66 54	05		5.11	(0.5)	B6 V	270	0.021	313	18	16	.012	0.8	49	
ζ Dor	33262	05 05	30.6		−57 28	22		4.72	4.1†	F7 V	44	0.121	343	8	−2	.075	1.1	1.8	
η¹ Dor	42525	06 06	09.5		−66 02	23		5.71	*	A0 V	*	0.031	36	*	18	*	*	*	(c)
η² Dor	43455	06 11	15.0		−65 35	22		5.01	(−0.2)	M2 III	360	0.116	348	70	35	.009	31	96	
θ Dor	34649	05 13	45.4		−67 11	08		4.83	−0.1	K2.5 IIIa	320	0.037	24	31	11	.006	21	86	
κ Dor	30478	04 44	21.2		−59 43	58		5.27	(2.2)	A8 III/IV	140	0.055	41	11	0	.024	1.3	11	
λ Dor	36189	05 26	19.2		−58 54	46		5.14	(0.5)	G6 III	270	0.030	334	15	10	.012	11	48	
ν Dor	43107	06 08	44.3		−68 50	36		5.06	−0.2	B8 V	370	0.053	291	[34]	18	[.009]	1.6	95	
π² Dor	46116	06 25	28.7		−69 41	25		5.38	0.3	G8 III	340	0.199	356	135	9	.007	12	60	
R Dor	29712	04 36	45.6		−62 04	39		5.40_v	*	M8 III	*	0.105	218	*	26	*	*	*	(d)
WZ Dor	33684	05 07	34.1		−63 23	59		5.2_v	−0.5	M3 III	450	0.045	153	22	19	.018	36	125	
- Dor	40409	05 54	06.1		−63 05	23		4.65	3.0†	K1 III/IV	71	0.561	14	63	25	.046	3.8	5.0	

Draco
(Draconis)

a) *Thuban.* This was the Pole Star about 2800 B.C.

b) *Rastaban.* OH:$M-3.5$, 490 l.y.

c) *Eltanin* (Dragon's Head).

d) *Nodus I.* B:$M-3.2$, 600 l.y., $\mathcal{L}$1500.

e) *Aldhibain.* OH:$M+0.3$, π.051.

f) SC:$M+3.2$.

g) *Ed Asich.* B:$M+0.8$, $\mathcal{L}$45. OH:140 l.y.

h) B:100 l.y., $\mathcal{L}$8. The reported visual magnitude is the combined of μ^A and μ^B. The primary is m5.80; the secondary is m5.83. The companion μ^B otherwise is given the same values as the primary in the Yale *Bright Star Catalogue,* except HD 154905 and RV-18.

i) A fine double for small telescopes, or even binoculars, with equal magnitude stars 61.6″ apart. Burnham gives a luminosity of 11 for both ν^1 and ν^2.

j) This is an optical double with nice color contrast, orange and blue. The star was designated an RS CVn-type variable in 1989 [IBVS #3323].

k) An interesting triple of nearly equal magnitudes; the component C is 16 Dra. SC:m5.08, which is the combined visual magnitude.

l) Another triple system: AB is a rapid binary and C is considerably fainter.

DRACO	HD	R.A.		Declin.		*m*	*M*	Spectra	l.y.	μ	Dir.	*V*	*RV*	π	D_s	$\mathscr{L}$	Rmk
					2000.0												
α Dra	123299	$14^h\,04^m\,23.2^s$	+64° 22′ 33″			3.65	−0.6	A0 III	230	0.060″	285°	22	−16	.018″	2.5	137	(a)
β Dra	159181	17 30 25.8	+52 18 05			2.79	−2.1	G2 II	310	0.026	301	22	−20	.013	37	545	(b)
γ Dra	164058	17 56 36.2	+51 29 20			2.23	−0.3	K5 III	110	0.024	213	28	−28	.025	29	104	(c)
δ Dra	180711	19 12 33.1	+67 39 42			3.07	0.2	G9 III	100	0.129	44	32	25	.032	13	65	
ε Dra ∞	188119	19 48 10.3	+70 16 04			3.83	0.3	G8 III	170	0.087	63	26	3	.016	11	60	
ζ Dra	155763	17 08 47.1	+65 42 53			3.17	−1.9	B6 III	340	0.033	310	18	−17	.023	2.7	453	(d)
η Dra	148387	16 23 59.3	+61 30 51			2.74	1.0†	G8 IIIab	71	0.064	338	15	−14	.046	8.1	31	(e)
θ Dra	144284	16 01 53.2	+58 33 55			4.01	2.3†	F8 IV	71	0.467	316	49	−9	.046	2.4	9.5	(f)
ι Dra	137759	15 24 55.6	+58 57 57			3.29	−0.1	K2 III	81	0.020	311	11	−11	.040	18	86	(g)
κ Dra	109387	12 33 28.9	+69 47 17			3.87ᵥ	(−0.6)	B6 IIIp	250	0.060	279	24	−11	.013	1.4	132	
λ Dra	100029	11 31 24.2	+69 19 52			3.84	−0.4	M0 III	230	0.044	243	11	7	.026	33	114	
μ Dra ∞	154906	17 05 19.5	+54 28 13			4.92	(3.2)	F5	71	0.115	317	19	−15	.046	1.5	4.0	(h)∅
ν¹ Dra ∞	159541	17 32 10.4	+55 11 03			4.88	(2.6)	A6 V	93	0.149	68	25	−15	.035	1.3	7.2	(i)
ν² Dra	159560	17 32 15.9	+55 10 22			4.87	(2.6)	A4 m	93	0.151	69	26	−16	.035	1.3	7.2	
ξ Dra	163588	17 53 31.6	+56 52 21			3.75	−0.1	K2 III	93	0.117	48	30	−26	.035	19	86	
o Dra ∞	175306	18 51 11.9	+59 23 18			4.66ᵥ	−0.9	K0 II	420	0.078	70	65	−20	.006	27	180	(j)
π Dra	182564	19 20 40.0	+65 42 52			4.59	0.6	A2 III	210	0.043	15	31	−29	.020	2.4	45	
ρ Dra	190940	20 02 48.9	+67 52 25			4.51	−0.2	K3 III	290	0.051	12	17	−9	.017	23	95	
σ Dra	185144	19 32 21.5	+69 39 40			4.68	5.92†	K0 V	18.5	1.836	162	56	27	.176	0.7	0.3	
τ Dra	181984	19 15 32.8	+73 21 20			4.45	−0.2	K3 III+	280	0.181	308	65	−30	.015	21	95	
υ Dra	176524	18 54 23.7	+71 17 50			4.82	0.2	K0 III	270	0.064	45	23	−7	.014	16	65	
φ Dra	170000	18 20 45.3	+71 20 16			4.22ᵥ	−0.4	A0 pSi	270	0.042	346	23	−16	.012	1.5	112	
χ Dra	170153	18 21 03.2	+72 43 58			3.57	4.13†	F7 V	25	0.631	124	40	33	.129	1.0	1.8	
ψ¹ᴬ Dra ∞	162003	17 41 56.1	+72 08 56			4.58	3.0†	F5 IV/V	69	0.267	177	29	−10	.047	1.5	5.0	
ψ¹ᴮ Dra	162004	17 41 57.8	+72 09 25			5.79	4.2†	G0 V	69	0.279	176	30	−10	.047	1.0	1.6	
ψ² Dra	164613	17 55 10.9	+72 00 19			5.45	3.0	F2/3 II/III	100	0.003	18	[2]	−2	[.032]	1.1	5.0	
ω Dra	160922	17 36 56.9	+68 45 29			4.80	3.4	F5 V	72	0.322	360	37	−14	.045	1.2	3.4	
2 Dra	100696	11 36 02.7	+69 19 22			5.20	0.2	K0 III	330	0.170	140	32	−2	.025	13	65	
4 Dra	108907	12 30 06.6	+69 12 04			4.95ᵥ	−0.5	M3 IIIa	400	0.083	228	28	−13	.016	35	125	
6 Dra	109551	12 34 43.9	+70 01 18			4.94	−0.1	K2 III	330	0.034	265	[17]	5	[.010]	21	86	
8 Dra	112429	12 55 28.4	+65 26 18			5.24	(2.8)	A5 n	100	0.035	195	10	9	.032	1.2	6.2	
10 Dra	121130	13 51 25.8	+64 43 23			4.65ᵥ	−0.5	M3.5 III	350	0.007	214	11	−11	.014	34	125	
15 Dra	149212	16 27 58.8	+68 46 05			5.00	−0.3	A0 III	370	0.046	318	17	−7	.014	2.0	104	
16 Dra ∞	150100	16 36 11.3	+52 54 00			5.53	0.4	B9.5 V	350	0.034	334	19	−9	.010	1.3	54	
17ᴬ Dra ∞	150117	16 36 13.6	+52 55 28			5.08	0.2	B9 V	310	0.029	329	18	−11	.010	1.9	65	(k)
17ᴮ Dra	150118	16 36 14.0	+52 55 27			6.58	(1.6)	A1 Vn	330	0.029	329	23	−18	.010	0.4	18	
18 Dra	151101	16 40 55.0	+64 35 20			4.83	(−0.4)	K1 p	360	0.017	193	9	0	.009	22	114	
19 Dra	153597	16 56 01.6	+65 08 05			4.89	3.7†	F6 V	55	0.237	79	30	−23	.059	1.2	2.6	
20 Dra ∞	153697	16 56 25.1	+65 02 20			6.90	2.6	F0 V	240	0.057	303	23	−21	.029	1.7	7.2	∅
26 Dra ∞	160269	17 34 59.4	+61 52 30			5.23	4.46†	G1 V	49	0.568	154	42	−13	.067	1.1	1.3	(l)∅
27 Dra	159966	17 31 57.7	+68 08 06			5.05	0.2	K0 III	300	0.135	353	80	−73	.020	14	65	
30 Dra	162579	17 49 04.1	+50 46 52			5.02	(−3.5)	A2 V	1600	0.216	345	515	−55	.002	15	1932	
35 Dra	163989	17 49 26.8	+76 57 46			5.04	2.2	F6 IV/V	100	0.249	8	43	−23	.032	2.4	10	
36 Dra	168151	18 13 53.6	+64 23 50			5.03	3.4†	F5 V	69	0.342	85	49	−35	.047	1.1	3.4	
39 Dra ∞	170073	18 23 54.4	+58 48 02			4.98	1.2	A1 V	93	0.075	324	17	−13	.035	2.1	26	

(Continued)

m) The parallax indicates a distance of 130–150 l.y. This star forms a binary with 41 Dra (see note (n)).

n) This companion to 40 Draconis has the same parallax, but the distance modulus formula yields a distance of only 24.5 light-years. Thus, we have ignored this value and gone with the same distance as 40 Draconis.

o) A Mira-type variable with a 245.5-day period. If we estimate the absolute magnitude at 0.0, then: 780 l.y., D_s17, and $\mathcal{L}80$.

DRACO (CONT.)	HD	2000.0 R.A.	Declin.	*m*	*M*	Spectra	l.y.	μ	Dir.	*V*	*RV*	π	*D$_s$*	$\mathcal{L}$	Rmk
40 Dra ∞	166865	18^h 00^m 03.1^s	+80° 00′ 03″	6.04	3.7	F6 V	96	0.134″	19°	26	4	.025″	1.3	2.6	(m)
41 Dra	166866	18 00 09.0	+80 00 14	5.68	6.3	K2 V	96	0.126	18	26	10	.025	0.4	0.2	(n)
42 Dra	170693	18 25 58.9	+65 33 49	4.82	−0.1	K2 III	310	0.100	105	39	32	.021	19	86	
45 Dra	171635	18 32 34.3	+57 02 44	4.77	−4.6	F7 Ib	2400	0.012	250	13	−12	.013	68	5500	
46 Dra	173524	18 42 37.8	+55 32 22	5.04	−6.8	B9.5 p+	7600	0.025	342	32	−30	.011	31	40000	
53 Dra	180006	19 11 40.4	+56 51 33	5.12	0.3	G8 III	300	0.058	36	28	−16	.012	13	60	
54 Dra	180610	19 13 55.1	+57 42 18	4.99	−0.1	K2 III	340	0.071	193	30	−27	.025	18	86	
59 Dra	180777	19 09 09.7	+76 33 38	5.13	3.2†	A9 V	80	0.129	160	15	−4	.041	1.1	4.1	
73 Dra	196502	20 31 30.3	+74 57 17	5.20$_v$	(0.6)	A0 pSr+	270	0.012	166	10	9	.012	2.7	45	
R Dra	149880	16 32 40.0	+66 45 13	6.9$_v$	*	M5 IIIe	*	0.058	217	—	—	*	*	*	(o)
CL Dra	143466	15 57 47.3	+54 44 59	4.95$_v$	1.7	F0 IV	150	0.191	305	43	−11	.022	1.9	16	
- Dra	81817	09 37 05.2	+81 19 35	4.29	−0.2	K3 III	260	0.025	223	9	−5	.017	27	95	
- Dra	91190	10 35 05.5	+75 42 46	4.84	0.2	G8.5 III	280	0.032	259	18	17	.027	12	65	
- Dra	141653	15 46 39.8	+62 35 58	5.19	(1.5)	A2 IV	180	0.067	152	19	−6	.018	1.7	20	
- Dra	151613	16 45 17.7	+56 46 55	4.85	3.0	F2 V	71	0.065	10	8	−4	.046	1.4	5.0	
- Dra	169305	18 21 32.5	+49 07 18	5.05	−0.5	M2 IIIab	420	0.064	330	[41]	14	[.008]	36	125	
- Dra	175535	18 53 13.5	+50 42 29	4.92	0.3	G8 III	270	0.025	182	9	8	.024	11	60	

Equuleus
(Equulei)

a) The star is usually given a period of 314 days, but Kholopov notes that "data on the periodicity of the rotational variability of light, spectrum, and magnetic field are contradictory" and gives four periods: 17.492d, 314d, 1785d, and 72 years.

b) An extremely close binary and one of the fastest known, with a period of 5.7 years. The maximum separation (about 0.37″) occurs nearly midway through 2001 and then again in 2007 (see Visual Binary Section).

c) SC:$RV-10$.

d) Not always named on sky atlases (e.g., Tirion), this star also goes under the designation 2 Equulei.

EQUULEUS	HD	2000.0 R.A.	Declin.	m	M	Spectra	l.y.	μ	Dir.	V	RV	π	D_s	$\mathscr{L}$	Rmk
α Equ	202447	$21^h 15^m 49.3^s$	$+05°\ 14'\ 52''$	3.92	0.6	G0 III	150	0.102″	146°	28	-16	.021″	5.4	45	
β Equ	203562	21 22 53.5	$+06\ 48\ 40$	5.16	(2.4)	A3 V	120	0.056	75	14	-11	.028	1.1	8.7	
γ Equ	201601	21 10 20.5	$+10\ 07\ 53$	4.69$_v$	(1.9)	F0 p	120	0.163	159	32	-17	.028	1.7	13	(a)
δ Equ ∞	202275	21 14 28.8	$+10\ 00\ 25$	4.49	3.93†	F5 V	59	0.304	171	30	-15	.055	1.1	2.1	(b)
ε Equ	199766	20 59 04.3	$+04\ 17\ 37$	5.23	2.1	F6 IV	140	0.182	218	45	18	.021	2.4	11	(c)
λ Equ ∞	200256	21 02 12.2	$+07\ 10\ 47$	7.4	4.0	F8 V	160	0.012	228	[6]	-5	[.021]	1.1	2.0	(d)

Eridanus
(Eridani)

a) *Achernar* (End of the River). B:120 l.y., $\mathcal{L}$650. OH:M−1.3, 69 l.y.

    The Yale *Bright Star Catalogue* considers this to be a variable, noting that the star is either an EB or E-type variable, with amplitude of m0.02. It is not listed in Kholopov as a variable.

b) *Kursa,* or *Cursa*. B:M+0.8, 80 l.y., $\mathcal{L}$40. OH:M+0.5.

c) *Zaurak*. B:M−1.5, 260 l.y., $\mathcal{L}$330. OH:M−0.7, 170 l.y.

d) Designated a variable in 1987 [IBVS #3058].

e) At 10.79 light-years away, this star ranks third closest, after Proxima Centauri and Sirius. It apparently has a very small companion (see Burnham).

f) *Acamar*. OH:m3.42, M+1.3, μ.065.

    This is a fixed binary with 8.2″ separation. Burnham gives θ^1 a luminosity of 50 and M+0.6.

g) *Keid*. A very close star at 15.9 light-years, with a quite high space velocity. This is an interesting triple system; the principal companion star (B) is a white dwarf which has its own companion (C), a red dwarf revolving around the white dwarf. Currently (1992–95) the orbit is at maximum separation of 9″.

h) If we estimate the absolute magnitude to be −1, then: 400 l.y., π.008, V62, D_s44, and $\mathcal{L}$198.

i) SC:RV−9.

ERIDANUS	HD	R.A.	Declin.	m	M	Spectra	l.y.	μ	Dir.	V	RV	π	D_s	$\mathscr{L}$	Rmk
			2000.0												
α Eri	10144	01^h 37^m 42.9^s	−57° 14′ 12″	0.46	−1.6	B3 Vpe	84	0.108″	105°	25	16	.026″	4.3	344	(a)
β Eri	33111	05 07 50.9	−05 05 11	2.79	0.0	A3 III	65	0.128	231	15	−9	.050	4.1	79	(b)
γ Eri	25025	03 58 01.7	−13 30 31	2.95$_v$	(−2.0)	M1 IIIe	330	0.124	153	85	62	.010	69	520	(c)
δ Eri	23249	03 43 14.8	−09 45 48	3.54$_v$	3.77†	K0 IV	29	0.753	352	33	−6	.111	2.3	2.4	(d)
ε Eri	22049	03 32 55.8	−09 27 30	3.73	6.13†	K2 V	10.79	0.979	271	22	16	.302	0.7	0.3	(e)
ζ Eri	20320	03 15 49.9	−08 49 11	4.80	(1.8)	A5 m	130	0.050	350	10	−4	.025	1.7	15	
η Eri	18322	02 56 25.6	−08 53 53	3.89	(1.5)	K1 IIIb	99	0.229	161	39	−20	.033	8.3	20	
θ¹ Eri ∞	18622	02 58 15.6	−40 18 17	3.24	1.7	A5 III	93	0.056	294	14	12	.035	1.8	16	(f)
θ² Eri	18623	02 58 16.2	−40 18 16	4.42	(2.1)	A1 V	93	0.074	287	22	19	.035	0.5	11	
ι Eri	16815	02 40 40.0	−39 51 19	4.11	0.2	K0 III	86	0.136	101	19	−9	.038	13	65	
κ Eri	15371	02 26 59.1	−47 42 14	4.25	−2.2	B5 IV	640	0.023	103	[35]	28	[.005]	2.7	597	
λ Eri	33328	05 09 08.7	−08 45 15	4.27$_v$	−3.0	B2 IVe	930	0.006	225	9	3	.003	3.7	1247	
μ Eri	30211	04 45 30.1	−03 15 17	4.02	−1.6	B5 IV	430	0.015	138	[13]	9	[.008]	6.2	344	
ν Eri	29248	04 36 19.1	−03 21 09	3.93$_v$	−3.6	B2 III	1000	0.003	198	[16]	15	[.003]	3.2	2168	
ξ Eri	27861	04 23 40.8	−03 44 44	5.17	1.2	A2 V	200	0.076	225	30	−11	.013	2.1	26	
o¹ Eri	26574	04 11 51.9	−06 50 16	4.04$_v$	−0.7	F2 II/III	99	0.083	3	16	11	.033	6.7	150	
o² Eri ∞	26965	04 15 16.3	−07 39 10	4.43	5.99†	K1 V	15.9	4.083	213	103	−42	.205	0.7	0.3	(g)⊘
π Eri	23614	03 46 08.4	−12 06 06	4.42$_v$	*	M2 III	*	0.072	35	*	46	*	*	*	(h)
ρ² Eri	18953	03 02 42.2	−07 41 07	5.32	0.3	K0 II/III	330	0.042	89	[32]	25	[.010]	12	60	
ρ³ Eri	19107	03 04 16.3	−07 36 03	5.26	(2.3)	A8 V	130	0.053	74	18	15	.026	1.2	9.2	
τ¹ Eri	17206	02 45 06.1	−18 34 21	4.47	3.7†	F6 V	47	0.328	83	34	26	.070	1.2	2.6	
τ² Eri	17824	02 51 02.2	−21 00 15	4.75	0.2	K0 III	110	0.056	251	12	−9	.031	12	65	
τ³ Eri	18978	03 02 23.5	−23 37 28	4.09	2.4†	A4 IV	69	0.156	251	19	−10	.047	1.5	8.6	
τ⁴ Eri	20720	03 19 30.9	−21 45 28	3.69$_v$	−0.5	M3/4 III	230	0.059	53	47	42	.013	35	125	
τ⁵ Eri	22203	03 33 47.2	−21 37 59	4.27	−0.2	B8 V	260	0.047	121	[22]	14	[.013]	1.3	95	
τ⁶ Eri	23754	03 46 50.8	−23 14 59	4.23	3.1†	F3 III	54	0.551	197	44	7	.060	1.4	4.5	
τ⁷ Eri	23878	03 47 39.6	−23 52 29	5.24	(1.0)	A2	230	0.063	37	36	29	.014	2.2	32	
τ⁸ Eri	24587	03 53 42.6	−24 36 45	4.65$_v$	−1.1	B6 V	460	0.024	126	[28]	23	[.007]	1.7	217	
τ⁹ Eri	25267	03 59 55.4	−24 00 59	4.66$_v$	−0.6	B6 V	370	0.012	24	24	24	.015	1.4	137	
υ¹ Eri	29085	04 33 30.6	−29 46 00	4.51	0.3	K0 III	230	0.293	201	54	21	.028	12	60	
φ Eri	14228	02 16 30.6	−51 30 44	3.56	−0.2	B8 V	180	0.098	103	[28]	10	[.018]	1.2	95	
χ Eri	11937	01 55 57.5	−51 36 32	3.70	2.7†	G8 IIIb	52	0.742	66	56	−6	.063	3.4	6.5	
ψ Eri	32249	05 01 26.3	−07 10 26	4.81	−2.5	B3 V	950	0.009	339	[28]	25	[.003]	2.9	787	
ω Eri	31109	04 52 53.6	−05 27 10	4.39	1.6	F4 III	120	0.033	313	13	−6	.013	1.9	18	(i)
15 Eri	20610	03 18 22.1	−22 30 41	4.88	0.3	G6 III	270	0.020	45	24	24	.028	11	60	
17 Eri	21790	03 30 37.0	−05 04 31	4.73	−0.2	B9 V	320	0.013	42	[16]	15	[.010]	1.5	95	
20 Eri	22470	03 36 17.3	−17 28 02	5.23$_v$	1.4	B9 p	190	0.021	109	16	14	.014	0.5	22	
32A Eri ∞	24555	03 54 17.4	−02 57 17	4.46	0.3	G8 III	220	0.025	78	40	27	.004	12	60	
32B Eri	24554	03 54 17.3	−02 57 10	6.14	(−0.8)	A2 V	820	0.026	67	36	18	.004	5.4	172	
39 Eri	26846	04 14 23.6	−10 15 23	4.87	−0.2	K3 III	340	0.163	185	52	7	.015	19	95	
41 Eri	27376	04 17 53.6	−33 47 54	3.56	0.0	B9 V	170	0.061	96	[23]	18	[.019]	1.1	79	
43 Eri	28028	04 24 02.1	−34 01 01	3.96	−0.5	K4 III	250	0.080	51	53	24	.008	31	125	
45 Eri	28749	04 31 52.6	−00 02 39	4.91	−1.3	K3 II/III	570	0.007	188	17	17	.009	38	261	
47 Eri	29064	04 34 11.5	−08 13 53	5.11$_v$	−0.5	M3 III	430	0.033	279	29	−12	.006	37	125	
51 Eri	29391	04 37 36.0	−02 28 25	5.23	(2.9)	F0 V	96	0.070	148	23	21	.034	1.1	5.5	

(Continued)

j) The cited distance has been generated by the distance modulus formula. However, since this is a companion of f^A, and since it has the same parallax, one might conclude that it has the same distance, viz. about 135 l.y.

k) R Eridani is no longer considered a variable.

ERIDANUS (CONT.)	HD	R.A.			Declin.			m	M	Spectra	l.y.	μ	Dir.	V	RV	π	D_s	$\mathscr{L}$	Rmk
52 Eri	29291	04^h 35^m	33.0^s	−30°	33′	45″	3.82	0.2	G8 III	170	0.049″	256°	17	−4	.014″	13	65	
53 Eri	29503	04 38	10.7	−14	18	15	3.87	−0.1	K2 IIIb	74	0.180	206	46	42	.044	17	86	
54 Eri	29755	04 40	26.4	−19	40	18	4.32$_v$	−0.5	M3/4 III	300	0.097	171	66	−33	.008	34	125	
60 Eri	30814	04 50	11.5	−16	13	02	5.03	0.2	K0 IIIv	300	0.064	33	39	37	.023	13	65	
64 Eri	32045	04 59	55.7	−12	32	15	4.79$_v$	1.7	F0 IV	140	0.099	157	23	−9	.022	1.9	16	
66 Eri	32964	05 06	45.6	−04	39	18	5.12$_v$	(2.0)	B9 V	140	0.013	48	31	31	.024	0.7	12	
68 Eri	33256	05 08	43.6	−04	27	22	5.12	3.5†	F2 V	69	0.043	65	10	9	.047	1.2	3.1	
82 Eri	20794	03 19	55.6	−43	04	11	4.27	5.29†	G8 III	20	3.131	76	127	87	.161	0.8	0.6	
f(A) Eri ∞	24072	03 48	35.8	−37	37	14	4.86	(1.8)	B9/A0 V	140	0.075	107	22	16	.024	1.2	16	
f(B) Eri	24071	03 48	35.3	−37	37	20	5.42	0.6	A1 V	300	0.053	101	19	16	.024	2.0	45	(j)
g Eri	24160	03 49	27.2	−36	12	01	4.17	0.3	G9 II/III	190	0.071	227	14	2	.025	12	60	
i Eri	24626	03 53	38.9	−34	43	57	5.11	−1.3	B6 V	620	0.035	108	[38]	21	[.005]	1.9	261	
p(A) Eri ∞	10361	01 39	47.7	−56	11	41	5.82	6.67†	K5 V	21	0.280	84	22	20	.153	0.4	0.2	𝒪
p(B) Eri	10360	01 39	47.4	−56	11	53	5.86	6.83†	K0 V	21	0.313	92	25	23	.153	0.5	0.1	
q^2 Eri	10939	01 46	06.3	−53	31	19	5.04	(1.8)	A1 V	140	0.152	61	33	10	.023	1.4	14	
y Eri	22663	03 37	05.6	−40	16	29	4.58	0.2	KI III	250	0.030	210	18	12	.011	14	65	
R Eri	31444	04 55	18.5	−16	25	04	5.72	0.3	gG4	400	0.045	180	[41]	32	[.008]	11	60	(k)
- Eri	16754	02 39	47.9	−42	53	30	4.75	1.4	A2 V	150	0.097	102	24	18	.028	1.8	22	
- Eri	18331	02 56	37.4	−03	42	44	5.17	1.2	A1 Vn	200	0.054	222	18	−15	.026	2.1	26	
- Eri	18543	02 58	42.0	−02	46	57	5.23	(1.3)	A2 IV	200	0.063	213	20	−7	.016	1.7	25	
- Eri	23319	03 42	50.0	−37	18	49	4.59	−0.3	K2.5 III	310	0.117	233	22	10	.028	21	104	
- Eri	29573	04 38	53.5	−12	07	23	5.01	(2.2)	A2 IV	120	0.061	260	12	7	.028	1.2	10	

2000.0

Fornax
(Fornacis)

a)   An easy binary, with nearly 4″ separation, and gradually widening. SE 8° is the Fornax Galaxy Cluster, eighteen bright galaxies, of which NGC 1316 is brightest at m10.

b)   The parallax indicates a distance of about 125–130 l.y.

c)   If the absolute magnitude is estimated to be −1, then: 520 l.y., π.006, V30, D_s1.5, and $\mathcal{L}$200.

d)   If M is estimated to be 0.0, then: 500 l.y., π.007, V47, D_s12, and $\mathcal{L}$80.

e)   Y:π.056, 60 l.y.

f)   If the absolute magnitude is estimated to be −0.5, then: 395 l.y., π.008, V17, D_s2.3, and $\mathcal{L}$125.

FORNAX	HD	R.A. 2000.0		Declin.		m	M	Spectra	l.y.	μ	Dir.	V	RV	π	D_s	$\mathscr{L}$	Rmk
α For ∞	20010	$03^h\,12^m\,04.2^s$		$-28°\,59'\,14''$		3.87	3.3	F8 V	44	0.725″	27°	51	−21	.074″	1.5	3.8	(a)
β For	17652	02 49 05.4		−32 24 22		4.46	0.3	G8 III	220	0.183	30	37	17	.026	12	60	(b)
γ¹ For	17713	02 49 50.9		−24 33 37		6.14	0.3	K1 III	480	0.132	200	[92]	−6	[.007]	14	60	
γ² For	17729	02 49 54.1		−27 56 31		5.39	2.4	A0 V	130	0.054	54	26	24	.025	1.0	8.8	
δ For	23227	03 42 14.9		−31 56 18		5.00	*	B5 IV	*	0.018	16	*	26	*	*	*	(c)
η² For	17793	02 50 14.7		−35 50 37		5.92	*	K0 III	*	0.058	64	*	22	*	*	*	(d)
η³ For	17829	02 50 40.3		−35 40 34		5.47	0.2	K5 III	370	0.057	179	20	12	.017	17	65	
κ For	14802	02 22 32.5		−23 48 59		5.20	4.6†	G1 V	42	0.205	106	22	18	.077	1.0	1.1	
λ² For	16417	02 36 58.5		−34 34 42		5.79	4.0†	G5 IV	76	0.267	184	31	10	.043	1.4	2.0	(e)
μ For	13709	02 12 54.4		−30 43 26		5.28	4.3†	B9 V	51	0.021	62	10	10	.064	0.3	1.5	
ν For	12767	02 04 29.4		−29 17 49		4.69ᵥ	−0.6	B9.5 p	370	0.014	45	[20]	19	[.009]	2.0	137	
π For	12438	02 01 14.7		−30 00 07		5.35	0.3	G5 III	330	0.149	225	48	24	.017	11	60	
φ For	15427	02 28 01.6		−33 48 40		5.14	0.6	A2 V	260	0.017	54	20	19	.015	2.9	45	
ω For ∞	16046	02 33 50.6		−28 13 57		4.90	*	B9 V	*	0.024	248	*	10	*	*	*	(f)

Gemini
(Geminorum)

a) *Castor* (Horseman). B:M+1.99, $\mathcal{L}$30. OH:M+1.94. SC:M+1.2, RV−1.

The star is slightly less bright than its brother Pollux. One of the finest doubles, its reported visual magnitude is actually the combined magnitudes of the two components (1.9 and 2.9). There are several orbital possibilities, based mainly on different periods (see Orbital Elements Section). It is clear, however, that the two stars are now drifting slowly apart, for a separation by the year 2000 of about 4°.

The *Sky Catalogue* designates α^A as HD 60178 and gives a radial velocity of −1 (which is actually the RV for α^B). SC does not give an entry for α^B. The *Bright Star Catalogue* gives identical values (including R.A. and declination) for α^A and α^B, with these exceptions for α^B:HD 60178, spectral type A2 V, and RV−1.

A third component (Castor C, m9.1) is in very slow orbit around the other two, PA 164°, 72.5″. This is a red dwarf and an eclipsing binary, found in the variable star catalogs as YY Gem. It has a period of 0.8143 days (= 19^h33^m). While gravitationally held to Castor, it is over 1000 AU (160 thousand million kilometers) from its primary.

West 1° is the binary ρ Gem and another double (OΣ 175) is 1° south of Castor. SW 3° from Castor is the bright planetary nebula NGC 2371-72.

b) *Pollux* (Boxer). B:D_s11. OH:M+0.7. SC:M+0.2. The star NW 1° is σ Gem.

c) *Alhena.* B:M−0.7, $\mathcal{L}$160. OH:M+0.7, 57 l.y. (although a parallax of .037 is given).

d) *Wasat.* OH:μ.029″. SC:M+1.9. This is a very slow binary (see Visual Binary Section).

SE 2° is the bright planetary nebula NGC 2392, which in large telescopes reveals a bluish tint and "facelike" features, which gave it the name "Eskimo Nebula."

e) *Mebsuta.* Burnham doubts this is a true binary. OH:M−1.2, 940 l.y.

f) *Mekbuda.* A very bright Cepheid variable with period 10.15 days.

g) *Propus, Tejat Prior.* Semiregular variable, slow binary (B:η^B:m6.5 (1962), P.A. 266°, 1.5″). NW 2° is the large star cluster M35 (NGC 2168).

h) *Tejat Posterior.* OH:M−1.1.

i) *Alzirr.* OH:M−4.0. SC:M+0.7. The Yale *Bright Star Catalogue* asks whether the star might be a variable: "δ Sct?"

j) SC:M+7.1. Petit gives a spectrum of S3e–S7e. As this Mira-type variable has a period of 369 days, it will not have a local midnight transit at maximum brightness until the third or fourth decade of the 21st century.

GEMINI	HD	R.A. 2000.0		Declin.	m	M	Spectra	l.y.	μ	Dir.	V	RV	π	D_s	ℒ	Rmk
α Gem ∞	60179	07ʰ 34ᵐ 35.9ˢ	+31° 53′ 18″		1.58	1.14†	A1 V	47	0.198″	239°	15	6	.069″	1.9	28	(a)⊘
β Gem	62509	07 45 18.9	+28 01 34		1.14	0.98†	K0 IIIb	35	0.629	265	32	3	.093	9.1	32	(b)
γ Gem	47105	06 37 42.7	+16 23 57		1.93	0.0	A0 IV	88	0.062	136	15	−13	.037	3.0	79	(c)
δ Gem ∞	56986	07 20 07.3	+21 58 56		3.53	2.46†	F2 IV	53	0.029	241	4	3	.061	1.6	8.2	(d)⊘
ε Gem	48329	06 43 55.9	+25 07 52		2.98	−4.5	G8 Ib	1000	0.016	195	11	10	.017	178	5000	(e)
ζ Gem	52973	07 04 06.5	+20 34 13		3.79ᵥ	−4.5	G0 Ib	1500	0.009	249	10	7	.006	86	5000	(f)
η Gem ∞	42995	06 14 52.6	+22 30 24		3.28ᵥ	−0.5	M3 III	190	0.068	259	30	19	.014	34	125	(g)
θ Gem	50019	06 52 47.3	+33 57 40		3.60	0.0	A3 III	170	0.051	181	24	21	.021	3.8	79	
ι Gem	58207	07 25 43.5	+27 47 53		3.79	0.2	G9 IIIb+	100	0.150	234	24	8	.032	14	65	
κ Gem	62345	07 44 26.8	+24 23 53		3.57	0.3	G8 III	150	0.063	209	24	21	.026	11	60	
λ Gem ∞	56537	07 18 05.5	+16 32 25		3.58	1.7	A3 V	69	0.063	231	11	−9	.047	1.8	16	
μ Gem	44478	06 22 57.6	+22 30 49		2.88ᵥ	−0.5	M3 IIIa	160	0.125	154	62	55	.020	35	125	(h)
ν Gem	45542	06 28 57.7	+20 12 43		4.15	−1.0	B7 IV	350	0.018	199	40	39	.009	1.7	198	
ξ Gem	48737	06 45 17.3	+12 53 44		3.36	2.1†	F5 III	59	0.226	211	32	25	.055	2.3	11	(i)
o Gem	61110	07 39 09.9	+34 35 04		4.90	0.6	F3 III	240	0.118	196	28	7	.021	4.2	45	
π Gem	62898	07 47 30.3	+33 24 56		5.14	−0.4	M1 IIIa	420	0.034	206	18	−12	.012	33	114	
ρ Gem ∞	58946	07 29 06.6	+31 47 04		4.18	2.84†	F0 V	53	0.227	41	18	−4	.062	1.3	5.8	
σ Gem	62044	07 43 18.7	+28 53 00		4.28ᵥ	0.0	K1 III	230	0.243	164	79	46	.018	17	79	
τ Gem	54719	07 11 08.3	+30 14 43		4.41	−0.1	K2 III	260	0.055	211	43	22	.007	20	86	
υ Gem	60522	07 35 55.3	+26 53 44		4.06	−0.4	M0 III(b)	250	0.114	197	44	−21	.014	31	114	
φ Gem	64145	07 53 29.7	+26 45 57		4.97	1.7	A3 V	150	0.049	226	[13]	8	[.022]	1.7	16	
χ Gem	66216	08 03 31.0	+27 47 39		4.94	−0.1	K2 III	330	0.051	210	19	−11	.016	17	86	
ω Gem	52497	07 02 24.7	+24 12 56		5.18ᵥ	−2.1	G5 IIa/Ib	930	0.007	254	9	−9	.012	35	545	
1 Gem	41116	06 04 07.2	+23 15 48		4.16	0.3	G7 III	110	0.102	183	25	20	.031	10	60	
26 Gem	48097	06 42 24.3	+17 38 43		5.21	1.4	A2 V	190	0.089	176	[29]	15	[.017]	1.8	22	
30 Gem	48433	06 43 59.2	+13 13 40		4.49	0.0	K0 III	260	0.060	183	43	14	.007	17	79	
38 Gem ∞	50635	06 54 38.6	+13 10 40		4.65	2.6	F0 Vp	76	0.114	137	25	22	.043	1.4	7.2	⊘
51 Gem	55383	07 13 22.2	+16 09 32		5.00ᵥ	−0.5	M4 IIIab	410	0.046	162	22	−9	.011	36	125	
56 Gem	57423	07 21 56.8	+20 26 37		5.10	−0.4	M0 IIIab	410	0.072	245	170	4	.002	30	114	
57 Gem	57727	07 23 28.4	+25 03 02		5.03	0.3	G8 III	290	0.072	250	17	6	.022	11	60	
63 Gem	58728	07 27 44.3	+21 26 42		5.22	2.8	F5 V	80	0.136	204	30	25	.041	1.5	6.0	
64 Gem	59037	07 29 20.3	+28 07 05		5.05	2.2	A4 V	120	0.070	215	54	35	.008	1.4	10	
65 Gem	59148	07 29 48.7	+27 54 58		5.01	−0.1	K2 III	340	0.042	232	38	36	.018	17	86	
74 Gem	61338	07 39 28.6	+17 40 29		5.05	−0.4	K5 III+	400	0.006	81	28	28	.009	31	114	
81 Gem	62721	07 46 07.4	+18 30 36		4.88	−0.3	K5 III	350	0.095	229	87	81	.014	27	104	
R Gem	53791	07 07 21.3	+22 42 13		7.68ᵥ	—	C	—	0.006	135	—	−41	—	—	—	(j)
- Gem	52960	07 03 38.0	+10 57 06		5.13	−0.2	K3 III	380	0.023	203	23	21	.011	24	95	
- Gem	59686	07 31 48.3	+17 05 09		5.42	0.2	gK2	360	0.094	151	447	−40	.001	15	65	

Grus
(Gruis)

a) *Al Nair.* B:M+0.2, 65 l.y., $\mathcal{L}$70. SC:M−1.1, 60 l.y., π.057.

b) OH:M−1.0, 140 l.y.

c) *Gacrux.* B:M−3.1, 540 l.y., $\mathcal{L}$1450.

d) The two stars δ^1 and δ^2 do not form a true binary—note the difference in their distance.

GRUS	HD	2000.0 R.A.	Declin.	m	M	Spectra	l.y.	μ	Dir.	V	RV	π	D_s	$\mathcal{L}$	Rmk
α Gru	209952	$22^h\,08^m\,13.9^s$	$-46°\,57'\,40''$	1.74	-0.2†	B7 IV	78	0.198''	139°	25	12	.042''	1.1	95	(a)
β Gru	214952	22 42 40.0	-46 53 05	2.10_v	-2.4	M5 III	260	0.138	92	82	2	.008	82	718	(b)
γ Gru	207971	21 53 55.6	-37 21 54	3.01	-1.2	B8 III	230	0.104	99	38	-2	.013	1.9	238	(c)
δ^1 Gru	213009	22 29 16.1	-43 29 45	3.97	0.3	G6 III	180	0.028	96	7	5	.024	13	60	
δ^2 Gru	213080	22 29 45.4	-43 44 58	4.11_v	(-2.4)	M5 IIIa	650	0.009	302	9	2	.005	79	715	(d)
ε Gru	215789	22 48 33.2	-51 19 01	3.49	1.4	A3 V	74	0.126	120	14	0	.044	1.9	22	
ζ Gru	217364	23 00 52.8	-52 45 15	4.12	0.3	K0 III	84	0.063	263	8	-1	.039	12	60	
η Gru	215369	22 45 37.8	-53 30 00	4.85	0.2	K2 III+	280	0.042	56	49	28	.005	16	65	
θ Gru ∞	218227	23 06 52.7	-43 31 14	4.28	2.2	F5 mδDel	85	0.045	246	16	10	.017	2.1	10	
ι Gru	218670	23 10 21.5	-45 14 48	3.90	0.2	K1 III	110	0.139	99	22	-4	.030	13	65	
κ Gru	217902	23 04 39.5	-53 57 55	5.37	-0.3	K5 III	440	0.057	100	29	18	.012	27	104	
λ Gru	209688	22 06 06.8	-39 32 36	4.46	-0.4	K3 III	310	0.119	190	58	39	.013	26	114	
μ^1 Gru	211088	22 15 36.9	-41 20 48	4.79	0.3	G8 III	260	0.058	59	31	-7	.009	9.6	60	
μ^2 Gru	211202	22 16 26.5	-41 37 39	5.10	0.3	G8 III	300	0.011	218	14	13	.010	11	60	
ν Gru	212953	22 28 39.1	-39 07 55	5.47	-0.4	G9 III	490	0.168	168	54	11	.015	16	114	
ξ Gru	204783	21 32 05.7	-41 10 46	5.29	-0.3	K0 III	430	0.019	65	11	-8	.012	19	104	
ρ Gru	215104	22 43 30.0	-41 24 52	4.85	0.2	K0 III	110	0.092	166	32	29	.030	14	65	

Hercules
(Herculis)

a) *Ras Algethi* (Kneeler's Head). A fine double, of an orange supergiant and blue-green giant. The parallax yields a distance of over 1500 l.y. B:$M-2.5$, 430 l.y., $\mathcal{L}$830.

   If the absolute magnitude of α^2 is estimated to be -1, then: 625 l.y., π.005, V55, D_s15, and $\mathcal{L}$198. The cited parallax (with the visual magnitude) would yield an absolute magnitude of -3.1, 1630 l.y., V109, D_s35, and $\mathcal{L}$1350.

b) *Kornephoros, Rutilicus.* OH:$M-0.8$.

c) The binary is only optical. In the same field, 0.7° ESE, is U Herculis, a Mira-type variable (m6.5–13; 406 days).

d) *Sarin.* This optical double is gradually widening. The colors are variously described as green or pale yellow and a soft violet or blue; the spectral types would point to yellow and orange. OH:94 l.y.

e) A close binary which is rapidly approaching its closest separation of 0.5″ in 2002; thereafter it gradually increases to a maximum of 1.6″ in 2024 (see Orbital Elements Section).

f) B:$M+2.1$, 60 l.y., $\mathcal{L}$11. OH:$M+0.7$.

   Due south 2.5° is the splendid globular cluster M13 (NGC 6205), a very compact and bright cluster perhaps 25,000 light-years away. It contains some 300,000 stars and is the best example of a globular cluster in the Northern Hemisphere.

g) This is an optical double only.

h) In the same field, SW 1°, is 30 Herculis (note j). 7° east, 1° north, is the globular cluster M92, only slightly less striking than M13 (see note f).

i) If we estimate the absolute magnitude to be 0.0, then: 290 l.y., π.011, V34, D_s1.2, and $\mathcal{L}$80.

j) Also known as g Herculis, a semiregular variable with a wide variation (m4.3–6.3) every 89.2 days.

   If we estimate the absolute magnitude at -1, then: 525 l.y., π.006, D_s40, and $\mathcal{L}$200. The parallax gives a distance of 180 l.y., which would produce the following: $M+1.3$, D_s18, and $\mathcal{L}$24.

HERCULES	HD	R.A. 2000.0	Declin.	m	M	Spectra	l.y.	μ	Dir.	V	RV	π	D_s	ℒ	Rmk
α¹ Her ∞	156014	17ʰ 14ᵐ 38.8ˢ	+14° 23′ 25″	3.20ᵥ	−3.2	M5 II	620	0.035″	348°	89	−33	.002″	102	1500	(a)✐
α² Her	156105	17 14 39.1	+14 23 24	5.41	*	G5 III	*	0.043	355	*	−37	.002	*	*	(a)
β Her	148856	16 30 13.1	+21 29 22	2.77	0.3	G8 III	100	0.100	260	33	−26	.024	12	60	(b)
γ Her	147547	16 21 55.1	+19 09 11	3.75	0.6	A9 III	140	0.063	312	37	−35	.024	3.2	45	(c)
δ Her ∞	156164	17 15 01.8	+24 50 21	3.14	0.9	A3 IV	74	0.159	188	44	−41	.044	2.4	34	(d)
ε Her	153808	17 00 17.3	+30 55 35	3.92	0.6	A0 V	150	0.056	300	27	−25	.028	2.0	45	
ζ Her ∞	150680	16 41 17.1	+31 36 10	2.89	2.97†	G0 IV	31	0.614	310	75	−70	.104	2.2	5.1	(e)✐
η Her	150997	16 42 53.7	+38 55 20	3.53	1.8	G8 IIIb	96	0.089	158	15	8	.034	5.6	15	(f)
θ Her	163770	17 56 15.1	+37 15 02	3.86	−2.2	K1 IIIa	530	0.006	9	31	−27	.002	59	597	
ι Her	160762	17 39 27.8	+46 00 23	3.80ᵥ	−1.7	B3 IV	410	0.011	292	22	−20	.005	2.6	377	
κᴬ Her ∞	145001	16 08 04.4	+17 02 49	5.00	0.3	G8 III	280	0.034	251	81	−9	.002	12	60	(g)
κᴮ Her	145000	16 08 04.8	+17 03 16	6.25	−0.1	K2 III	610	0.045	226	112	38	.002	18	86	
λ Her	158899	17 30 44.2	+26 06 38	4.41	−0.3	K3.5 III+	290	0.026	43	27	−26	.016	27	104	
μ Her	161797	17 46 27.5	+27 43 15	3.42	3.89†	G5 IV	26	0.808	202	37	−16	.124	1.7	2.2	
ν Her	164136	17 58 30.1	+30 11 22	4.41ᵥ	−2.0	F2 II	620	0.008	337	23	−22	.007	14	497	
ξ Her	163993	17 57 45.8	+29 14 52	3.70	0.2	G8 III	160	0.086	101	19	−2	.021	12	65	
o Her	166014	18 07 32.5	+28 45 45	3.83ᵥ	0.2	B9.5 V	170	0.010	354	31	−30	.005	2.0	65	
π Her	156283	17 15 02.7	+36 48 33	3.16	−2.3	K3 IIab	400	0.030	276	27	−26	.025	67	655	
ρᴮ Her	157778	17 23 40.6	+37 08 48	5.47	0.6	A0 Vn	310	0.045	274	109	−19	.002	2.3	45	
ρᴬ Her ∞	157779	17 23 40.9	+37 08 45	4.17	0.6	A0 V	170	0.042	277	102	−19	.002	1.7	45	
σ Her	149630	16 34 06.1	+42 26 13	4.20	0.2	B9 V	210	0.046	342	24	−11	.010	2.5	65	(h)
τ Her	147394	16 19 44.3	+46 18 48	3.89	−1.6	B5 IV	110	0.041	335	15	−14	.030	6.2	344	
υ Her	144206	16 02 47.8	+46 02 12	4.76	*	B9 III	*	0.080	141	*	3	*	*	*	(i)
φ Her	145389	16 08 46.1	+44 56 06	4.26	(0.8)	B9 p	160	0.046	319	19	−16	.020	1.1	39	
χ Her	142373	15 52 40.4	+42 27 06	4.62	4.2†	F8 V+	58	0.765	35	85	−55	.056	1.1	1.6	
ω Her	148112	16 25 24.9	+14 02 00	4.57ᵥ	(2.6)	B9 pCr	80	0.077	145	11	−6	.041	0.9	7.2	
5 Her	143666	16 01 14.2	+17 49 06	5.12	0.2	G8 III	310	0.158	341	109	−19	.007	13	65	
29 Her	149161	16 32 36.2	+11 29 17	4.84	−0.3	K7 III	350	0.195	246	77	3	.012	28	104	
30 Her	148783	16 28 38.4	+41 52 54	5.04ᵥ	*	M6 III	*	0.023	97	7	3	.018	*	*	(j)
42 Her	150450	16 38 44.7	+48 55 42	4.90	−0.5	M2.5 IIIa	390	0.059	302	57	−55	.017	33	125	
43 Her	151217	16 45 49.8	+08 34 57	5.15	−0.3	K5 III	400	0.014	356	22	−21	.010	29	104	
51 Her	152326	16 51 45.2	+24 39 23	5.04	−1.1	K0.5 IIIa	550	0.013	67	17	−16	.010	32	217	
52 Her	152107	16 49 14.1	+45 59 00	4.82ᵥ	(−0.2)	A2 Vp+	330	0.060	161	29	−1	.010	4.0	93	
60 Her	154494	17 05 22.6	+12 44 27	4.91	0.9	A4 IV	210	0.051	102	12	−4	.022	2.6	34	
68 Her	156633	17 17 19.4	+33 06 00	4.82ᵥ	−2.9	B1.5 Vp+	1100	0.012	246	22	−21	.009	5.8	1138	
69 Her	156729	17 17 40.2	+37 17 29	4.65	1.4	A2 V	150	0.073	328	22	−10	.018	1.8	22	
70 Her	157198	17 20 54.1	+24 29 58	5.12	1.2	A2 V	200	0.023	272	21	−18	.010	1.3	26	
72 Her	157214	17 20 39.5	+32 28 04	5.39	4.71†	G0 V	45	1.051	173	104	−79	.073	1.0	1.0	
87 Her	162211	17 48 49.0	+25 37 22	5.12	−0.1	K2 III	360	0.040	187	29	−26	.016	18	86	
90 Her	163217	17 53 17.9	+40 00 29	5.16	−0.2	K1 IIIb	390	0.052	8	39	−35	.014	19	95	

(Continued)

k) A well-known and very attractive binary of equal stars with—perhaps—a subtle color contrast. B:$M-0.4$, 400 l.y., $\mathcal{L}$120.

l) A rapid binary at its closest in May of 1997. It moves out to its greatest separation of 1.6″ in 2020.

m) Very nice double of equal-magnitude stars.

n) Not much is known about this star, but it is a stunning binary.

o) If the absolute magnitude is estimated at -1, then: 750 l.y., π.004, V13, D_s43, and $\mathcal{L}$198.

HERCULES (CONT.)	HD	R.A.	2000.0	Declin.	m	M	Spectra	l.y.	μ	Dir.	V	RV	π	D_s	$\mathcal{L}$	Rmk
93 Her	164349	18^{h}00^{m}03.3^s	+16° 45′ 03″		4.67	−0.9	K0.5 IIb	420	0.014″	210°	29	−24	.004″	29	180	
95B Her	164668	18 01 29.8	+21 35 43		5.18	0.5	G8 III	280	0.033	18	[34]	−31	[.012]	11	50	
95A Her ∞	164669	18 01 30.3	+21 35 44		4.96	0.5	A5 IIIn	250	0.036	18	[33]	−30	[.013]	3.1	50	(k)
98 Her	165625	18 06 01.8	+22 13 08		5.06	−0.5	M3 III+	420	0.014	234	21	−20	.014	34	125	
99 Her ∞	165908	18 07 01.3	+30 33 43		5.04	3.8	F7 V	54	0.120	306	10	1	.060	1.2	2.4	(l)𝒪
100A Her ∞	166045	18 07 49.4	+26 05 51		5.86	(1.3)	A3	270	0.033	353	20	−15	.012	2.2	25	(m)
100B Her	166046	18 07 49.4	+26 06 05		5.90	(1.3)	A3	270	0.034	346	22	−17	.012	2.3	24	
102 Her	166182	18 08 45.4	+20 48 52		4.36	−2.5	B2 IV	770	0.009	162	16	−15	.010	6.6	787	
104 Her	167006	18 11 54.1	+31 24 19		4.97$_v$	(−0.8)	M3 III	470	0.026	332	18	0	.007	41	165	
106 Her	168720	18 20 17.8	+21 57 41		4.95	−0.4	M1 III	380	0.058	165	37	−33	.016	32	114	
107 Her	168914	18 21 00.9	+28 52 12		5.12	(1.7)	A7 V	160	0.050	3	32	−30	.021	1.6	16	
109 Her	169414	18 23 41.8	+21 46 11		3.84	−0.1	K2.5 IIIa	200	0.312	142	83	−58	.025	19	86	
110 Her	173667	18 45 39.6	+20 32 47		4.19	3.7	F6 V	63	0.334	182	39	24	.052	1.1	2.6	
111 Her	173880	18 47 01.2	+18 10 53		4.36	1.7	A5 III	100	0.136	32	49	−45	.032	1.9	16	
113 Her	175492	18 54 44.8	+22 38 43		4.59	1.7	G4 III+	120	0.009	54	24	−24	.013	4.9	16	
Hu 1176	155103	17 08 01.9	+35 56 07		5.39	(1.3)	A5-F1 III+	220	0.030	247	32	−30	.015	2.6	24	
Σ2319 ∞	170267	18 27 43.8	+19 17 45		8.2	—	F5	—	0.041	54	—	—	—	5.6	79	(n)
S Her	152276	16 51 53.7	+14 56 29		5.8$_v$	*	M5 III	*	0.007	146	*	−10	*	*	*	(o)
V656 Her	157049	17 20 18.8	+18 03 25		5.00$_v$	−0.5	M2 IIIab	410	0.056	173	64	−46	.006	35	125	
- Her	154143	17 03 07.8	+14 05 31		4.98	−0.5	M3 III	410	0.070	162	79	43	.005	34	125	
- Her	155410	17 09 33.1	+40 46 37		5.08	−0.2	K3 III	370	0.057	279	58	−56	.019	22	95	
- Her	166208	18 07 28.7	+43 27 42		5.00	0.4	G8 III+	270	0.060	183	[29]	−16	[.012]	11	55	

Horologium
(Horologii)

a)   SC:M+3.0.

b)   In the same field, N 1°, is V Horologii, a semiregular variable, fluctuating from m7.8 to m8.9.

HORO-LOGIUM	HD	2000.0 R.A.	Declin.	m	M	Spectra	l.y.	μ	Dir.	V	RV	π	D_s	$\mathscr{L}$	Rmk
α Hor	26967	04^h 14^m 00.1^s	−42° 17′ 40″	3.86	0.0	K2 III	190	0.212″	169°	44	22	.026″	16	79	
β Hor	18866	02 58 47.8	−64 04 16	4.99	0.3	A3 III	280	0.026	53	[26]	24	[.012]	3.5	60	
δ Hor	26612	04 10 50.5	−41 59 37	4.93	2.6	F2 IV/V	95	0.200	70	87	37	.012	1.5	7.2	
ζ Hor	16920	02 40 39.6	−54 33 00	5.21	3.0	F3 IV/V	110	0.040	81	6	−1	.031	1.4	5.0	
η Hor	16555	02 37 24.2	−52 32 36	5.31	(2.3)	A6 V	130	0.085	99	16	−3	.025	1.5	9.5	
ι Hor	17051	02 42 33.4	−50 48 01	5.41	4.63†	G0 V	47	0.401	55	32	16	.070	0.9	1.1	(a)
λ Hor	15233	02 24 53.9	−60 18 43	5.35	0.6	F2 III	290	0.144	207	30	6	.023	4.2	45	
μ Hor	19319	03 03 36.8	−59 44 16	5.11	2.6	F0 IV	100	0.093	229	24	17	.025	1.5	7.2	(b)
ν Hor	17848	02 49 01.5	−62 48 24	5.26	(−4.7)	A2 V	3300	0.099	71	472	31	.001	33	6194	
R Hor	18242	02 53 52.8	−49 53 25	4.0$_v$	(−0.4)	M7 IIIe	250	0.134	81	77	60	.013	50	117	

Hydra
(Hydrae)

a) *Alphard* (Solitary One). OH:M -1.0.

b) OH:M -0.8, 190 l.y.

c) A multiple binary with five companions. The first of these has a rapid period of 15.05 years; it is extremely close (0.26″–0.06″). The third component is easier to resolve, with a 2.7″ separation, slowly widening after 2000 (see Orbital Elements Section).
   B:140 l.y. The star was designated a BY Dra-type variable in 1989 [IBVS #3323].

d) B:M -1.1, 220 l.y., $\mathcal{L}$230. OH:M -1.0, 220 l.y. despite its agreement with the StarList on a parallax of .035″.

e) SC:RV $+21$.

f) SC:RV -8.

g) OH:M $+0.1$, 110 l.y.

h) If the absolute magnitude is estimated to be $+1$, then: 180 l.y., π.018, V13, D_s1.0, and $\mathcal{L}$31.

i) SC:M -0.1, π.049. OH:M $+0.7$, 67 l.y.

j) A very fast and close binary, with a period of 7.4 years. B:90 l.y.

k) If the absolute magnitude is estimated to be 0.0, then: 450 l.y., π.007, V39, D_s1.7, and $\mathcal{L}$79.

l) If the absolute magnitude is estimated to be $+1$, then: 220 l.y., π.015, V19, D_s0.8, and $\mathcal{L}$31.

m) SC:M $+0.6$, π.049. SW 2° is the globular cluster NGC 5694. At over 100,000 l.y. away, it is one of the most distant clusters known.

n) A rapid binary, with separation of 1.4″ in 2000.

o) A lovely triple (see Binary Star Section). North just 20° is Σ1473 (8, 8.9; 10°, 31″).

p) Also known as 30 Monocerotis. SE 3° is the open cluster M48 (NGC 2548).

HYDRA	HD	R.A. (2000.0)			Declin.			m	M	Spectra	l.y.	μ	Dir.	V	RV	π	D_S	$\mathcal{L}$	Rmk
α Hya	81797	09ʰ	27ᵐ	35.2ˢ	−08°	39′	31″	1.98	−0.2	K3 III	89	0.033″	327°	8	−4	.022″	26	95	(a)
β Hya ∞	103192	11	52	54.5	−33	54	28	4.28ᵥ	−0.3	B9 IV	270	0.052	271	25	−1	.010	1.5	104	
γ Hya	115659	13	18	55.2	−23	10	18	3.00	0.3	G5 III	110	0.081	127	15	−5	.027	11	60	(b)
δ Hya	73262	08	37	39.3	+05	42	13	4.16	0.6	A0 V	99	0.068	260	15	11	.033	2.3	45	
ε Hya ∞	74874	08	46	46.5	+06	25	08	3.38ᵥ	0.6	G0 III	120	0.199	254	50	36	.027	7.0	45	(c)⌀
ζ Hya	76294	08	55	23.6	+05	56	44	3.11	0.2	G9 II/III	93	0.101	276	27	23	.035	13	65	(d)
η Hya	74280	08	43	13.4	+03	23	55	4.30ᵥ	−1.7	B9 V	520	0.020	255	[23]	17	[.006]	1.6	377	(e)
θ Hya	79469	09	14	21.8	+02	18	51	3.88	0.6	B9.5 V	150	0.339	158	60	−10	.027	1.3	45	(f)
ι Hya	83618	09	39	51.3	−01	08	34	3.91	−0.2	K2.5 IIIb	220	0.083	146	28	23	.026	23	95	
κ Hya	83754	09	40	18.3	−14	19	56	5.06	−1.1	B5 V	560	0.040	233	[37]	18	[.006]	5.0	217	
λ Hya	88284	10	10	35.2	−12	21	15	3.61	0.2	K0 III	160	0.228	245	44	19	.027	13	65	
μ Hya	90432	10	26	05.4	−16	50	11	3.81	−0.3	K4 III	220	0.156	238	57	40	.018	28	104	
ν Hya	93813	10	49	37.4	−16	11	37	3.11	−0.1	K0/1 III	140	0.215	24	36	−1	.028	20	86	(g)
ξ Hya	100407	11	33	00.1	−31	51	27	3.54	0.3	G8 III	150	0.211	259	37	−5	.027	12	60	
o Hya	101431	11	40	12.7	−34	44	41	4.70	∗	B9 V	∗	0.045	266	∗	6	∗	∗	∗	(h)
π Hya	123123	14	06	22.2	−26	40	56	3.27	1.2	K2 III	86	0.150	163	33	27	.038	9.5	26	(i)
ρ Hya	75137	08	48	25.9	+05	50	16	4.36	0.6	A0 Vn	180	0.042	207	36	33	.014	1.5	45	
σ Hya	73471	08	38	45.4	+03	20	29	4.44	−0.1	K2 III	93	0.028	222	25	25	.035	19	86	
τ¹ Hya	81997	09	29	08.8	−02	46	08	4.60	3.9†	F6 V	46	0.127	98	13	10	.071	1.0	2.2	
τ² Hya	82446	09	31	58.9	−01	11	05	4.57	0.0	A3 V	270	0.021	225	7	6	.027	3.8	79	
υ¹ Hya	85444	09	51	28.6	−14	50	48	4.12	0.3	G7 III(b)	190	0.035	153	17	−15	.021	11	60	
υ² Hya	87504	10	05	07.4	−13	03	53	4.60	−1.2	B9 III/IV	470	0.043	283	[41]	28	[.007]	2.4	238	
φ³ Hya	92214	10	38	34.9	−16	52	36	4.91	0.2	G7.5 III+	290	0.107	281	40	18	.014	12	65	
χ¹ Hya ∞	96202	11	05	19.9	−27	17	36	4.94	3.3	F4 V	76	0.190	268	27	17	.043	1.1	3.8	(j)⌀
χ² Hya	96314	11	05	57.5	−27	17	16	5.71	∗	B8 III/IV+	∗	0.037	119	∗	30	∗	∗	∗	(k)
ψ Hya	114149	13	09	03.2	−23	07	05	4.95	0.2	K1 III	290	0.049	208	27	−19	.012	14	65	
ω Hya	77996	09	05	58.3	+05	05	32	4.97	−1.1	K2 II/III	530	0.021	241	27	25	.011	31	217	
6 Hya	73840	08	40	01.4	−12	28	32	4.98	−0.1	K4 III	340	0.089	266	21	−11	.023	24	86	
9 Hya	74137	08	41	43.2	−15	56	36	4.88	0.0	K0 III	100	0.096	185	14	−2	.032	15	79	
12 Hya	74918	08	46	22.5	−13	32	52	4.32	0.3	G8 III	210	0.019	148	11	−8	.013	11	60	
23 Hya	79910	09	16	41.6	−06	21	11	5.24	−0.1	K2 III	380	0.016	83	12	−8	.008	18	86	
26 Hya	80499	09	19	46.3	−11	58	30	4.79	0.3	G8 III	260	0.029	280	6	−2	.023	11	60	
27 Hya	80586	09	20	28.9	−09	33	21	4.80	1.8	G8 III/IV	130	0.039	209	26	25	.022	5.7	15	
44 Hya	91550	10	34	00.8	−23	44	32	5.08	−0.3	K4 III	390	0.021	325	7	−4	.017	31	104	
47 Hya	121847	13	58	31.1	−24	58	20	5.15	∗	B8 VpShell	∗	0.058	238	∗	5	∗	∗	∗	(l)
50 Hya	124206	14	12	45.9	−27	15	40	5.08	3.4	K3 III	71	0.040	198	27	27	.046	3.6	3.4	
51 Hya	125932	14	23	05.7	−27	45	14	4.77	−0.3	K4 III	82	0.225	239	33	20	.040	23	104	
52 Hya	126769	14	28	10.3	−29	29	30	4.97	−0.6	B8 V	420	0.036	224	[27]	16	[.008]	2.1	137	
54 Hya	129926	14	46	00.0	−25	26	35	4.94	2.8	F0 III	91	0.185	235	28	−13	.036	1.4	6.0	(m)
56 Hya	130259	14	47	44.7	−26	05	15	5.24	0.3	G5 III	96	0.043	102	6	−1	.034	12	60	
58 Hya	130694	14	50	17.2	−27	57	37	4.41	−0.3	K4 III	290	0.248	256	107	−10	.011	26	104	
β411 ∞	91881	10	36	04.5	−26	40	30	6.29	3.7	F5 V	110	0.066	174	28	−23	.020	1.2	2.6	(n)⌀
Σ1474 ∞	93526	10	47	37.9	−15	15	44	6.67	(2.1)	A0 III	270	0.019	189	23	22	.012	1.0	12	(o)
C Hya	71155	08	25	39.6	−03	54	23	3.90	0.6	A0 V	150	0.075	249	17	10	.026	1.9	45	(p)
F Hya	74395	08	43	40.4	−07	14	01	4.62	−4.1	G1 Ib	1800	0.007	262	31	31	.007	77	3436	

(Continued)

q) An interesting variable, and one of the first discovered. Burnham notes that it often attains a maximum of 4. The period of 388.9 days means that it is not always visible when the constellation makes its annual visit; it can only be enjoyed for two or three years in a row each decade.

Burnham gives an estimated distance of 325 l.y. This would yield an absolute magnitude of about 0.0, π.010, V30, D_s30, and $\mathcal{L}$80. SC: maximum visual magnitude of 3.

r) If the absolute magnitude is estimated to be -1, then: 1400 l.y., π.002, V41, D_s43, $\mathcal{L}$198.

s) Y:π.080. This nameless star is quite bright and close. In the same field, NW 0.5°, is I Hya (see StarList).

HYDRA (CONT.)	HD	2000.0			M	Spectra	l.y.	μ	Dir.	V	RV	π	D_s	$\mathscr{L}$	Rmk
		R.A.	Declin.	m											
G Hya	81799	09^h 27^m 18.3^s	−22° 20′ 38″	4.69	−0.2	K3 III	110	0.241″	133°	48	29	.030″	19	95	
I Hya	83953	09 41 16.9	−23 35 30	4.77	−1.1	B5 V	490	0.033	256	[35]	26	[.007]	1.9	217	
b^3 Hya	94388	10 53 29.4	−20 08 20	5.24	3.7†	F6 V	67	0.255	163	25	−5	.049	1.2	2.6	
R Hya	117287	13 29 42.7	−23 16 52	4.97$_v$	*	M6/7 e	*	0.058	281	*	−10	*	*	*	(q)
T Hya	76400	08 55 39.7	−09 08 29	7.2$_v$	*	M5 III	*	0.020	282	*	−3	*	*	*	(r)
U Hya	92055	10 37 33.1	—13 23 04	4.82$_v$	—	C	—	0.047	142	—	−25	—	—	—	
II Hya	102620	11 48 45.0	−26 44 59	5.11$_v$	−0.5	M4 III	430	0.037	246	12	7	.019	34	125	
- Hya	82734	09 33 12.4	−21 06 57	5.01	3.2†	K0 IV	72	0.030	290	13	13	.045	3.4	4.1	
- Hya	83425	09 38 27.2	+04 38 57	4.68	−0.2	K3 III	310	0.173	251	87	45	.011	23	95	
- Hya	84117	09 42 14.4	−23 54 56	4.94	4.2†	F9 IV	45	0.474	303	46	34	.072	1.0	1.6	(s)
- Hya	85859	09 54 12.2	−25 55 55	4.88	−0.2	K3 III	110	0.198	289	59	51	.031	21	95	
- Hya	85951	09 54 52.1	−19 00 34	4.94	−0.5	M1 III	400	0.066	231	58	50	.011	33	125	
- Hya	92036	10 37 13.7	−27 24 46	4.89	−0.3	M2 III	360	0.108	277	54	17	.010	32	104	
- Hya	100393	11 32 54.0	−31 05 14	5.04	−0.5	M2 IIIb	420	0.032	274	21	19	.019	34	125	
- Hya	101666	11 41 43.9	−32 29 59	5.22	−0.3	K5 III+	410	0.046	179	37	34	.015	28	104	

Hydrus
(Hydri)

a)   B:$M+2.9$, 30 l.y., $\mathcal{L}6$. SC:$M+2.6$.

b)   B:$M-1.5$, 300 l.y., $\mathcal{L}330$.

c)   SC:$RV+11$.

HYDRUS	HD	R.A. 2000.0		Declin.		m	M	Spectra	l.y.	μ	Dir.	V	RV	π	D_s	$\mathscr{L}$	Rmk
α Hyi	12311	01^h 58^m 46.2^s		−61° 34′ 12″		2.86	2.1†	F0 V	47	0.271″	83°	19	1	.069″	1.6	11	(a)
β Hyi	2151	00 25 45.3		−77 15 16		2.80	3.8†	G1 IV	21	2.253	82	71	23	.159	1.4	2.4	
γ Hyi	24512	03 47 14.5		−74 14 21		3.24	−0.4	M2 III	170	0.128	24	122	16	.005	33	114	(b)
δ Hyi	15008	02 21 45.1		−68 39 34		4.09	1.8†	A3 V	93	0.044	281	8	6	.035	1.4	15	(c)
ε Hyi	16978	02 39 35.5		−68 16 01		4.11	−0.8	B9 V	310	0.094	85	[43]	6	[.010]	2.5	164	
ζ Hyi	17566	02 45 32.6		−67 37 00		4.84	(−0.4)	A2 IV/V	360	0.083	59	44	4	.009	4.1	113	
η^1 Hyi	11733	01 52 34.8		−67 56 40		6.7	0.6	B9 V	540	0.026	97	[25]	15	[.006]	2.3	45	
η^2 Hyi	11977	01 54 56.1		−67 38 51		4.69	0.3	G8 III/IV	250	0.109	44	[42]	−16	[.013]	12	60	
κ Hyi	15248	02 22 52.3		−73 38 45		5.01	0.2	K1 III	300	0.081	279	[42]	22	[.011]	15	65	
λ Hyi	4815	00 48 35.4		−74 55 25		5.07	−0.5	K5 III	420	0.139	101	28	−9	.025	27	125	
μ Hyi	16522	02 31 40.7		−79 06 34		5.28	0.3	G8 III	320	0.135	109	640	−15	.001	12	60	
ν Hyi	18293	02 50 28.7		−75 04 01		4.75	−0.3	K3 III	330	0.032	236	15	5	.011	24	104	
π^1 Hyi	14141	02 14 14.8		−67 50 31		5.55	(1.1)	M1 III	250	0.057	46	33	26	.013	15	28	
π^2 Hyi	14287	02 15 28.6		−67 44 48		5.69	−0.3	K2 III	510	0.041	108	[35]	17	[.006]	23	104	

Indus
(Indi)

a) B:M+1.1, 85 l.y., $\mathcal{L}$33. SC:M+0.2. Y:π.046.

b) One of the closest stars, at 11.2 l.y. Burnham gives a size of 0.8 Suns, and he points out that this star is "one of the few" that might be close enough to reveal planets, but that probes for radio signals have so far been negative. SC gives a slightly different R.A. ($22^h03^m21.5^s$).

c) A nice binary, yellow and red. SC: R.A. $21^h19^m51.1^s$.

INDUS	HD	2000.0 R.A.	Declin.	m	M	Spectra	l.y.	μ	Dir.	V	RV	π	D_s	$\mathscr{L}$	Rmk
α Ind	196171	20^h 37^m 34.0^s	−47° 17′ 29″	3.11	1.1†	K0 III	81	0.090″	39°	11	−1	.040″	8.6	29	(a)
β Ind	198700	20 54 48.5	−58 27 15	3.65	0.2	K1 II	160	0.033	133	31	−5	.005	17	65	
δ Ind	208450	21 57 55.0	−54 59 34	4.40	1.7	F0 IV	110	0.055	95	20	15	.020	2.0	16	
ε Ind	209100	22 03 21.3	−56 47 10	4.69	7.0†	K4/5 V	11.20	4.696	123	86	−40	.291	0.6	0.12	(b)
ζ Ind	198048	20 49 28.9	−46 13 37	4.89	−0.5	K5 III	390	0.056	61	23	−5	.012	32	125	
η Ind	197157	20 44 02.2	−51 55 16	4.51	2.4	A7 III/IV	67	0.170	109	17	−2	.049	1.4	8.6	
θ Ind	202730	21 19 51.9	−53 26 59	4.39	2.1	A5 IV/V	76	0.128	122	21	−15	.043	1.3	11	(c)
ι Ind	198308	20 51 30.0	−51 36 30	5.05	0.2	K1 II/III	300	0.013	138	67	21	.001	15	65	
μ Ind	200365	21 05 14.1	−54 43 37	5.16	0.2	K2 III	320	0.035	162	14	12	.023	17	65	
ν Ind	211998	22 24 36.7	−72 15 20	5.29	4.4	A3 V+	110	1.473	118	226	21	.031	1.2	1.4	

Lacerta
(Lacertae)

a) WSW 3° is the open cluster NGC 7243, and 1.5° NW of α is the planetary nebula I 5217, with a m14 central star.

b) If the absolute magnitude is estimated at 0.5, then: 175 l.y., D_s19, and $\mathcal{L}$50. If the parallax were used, we would then have: $M-3.5$, 1100 l.y., and $\mathcal{L}$2000.

c) W 3° is the open cluster NGC 7209.

d) The *Sky Catalogue* lists only one star, HD 214167, and appears to give the visual magnitude of the companion, 8B.

e) If we use the same parallax as the primary, and the given visual magnitude, we then obtain an absolute magnitude of -2.9, and then: 2300 l.y., V85, D_s5.2, and $\mathcal{L}$1150.

f) In the same field is RX Lac, a semiregular variable (8.0–9.8) with a period of 174 days.

LACERTA	HD	2000.0 R.A.	Declin.	m	M	Spectra	l.y.	μ	Dir.	V	RV	π	D_s	$\mathscr{L}$	Rmk
α Lac	213558	22^{h}31^{m}17.4^s	+50° 16′ 57″	3.77	1.4	A2 V	81	0.137″	80°	17	−4	.040″	1.6	22	(a)
β Lac	212496	22 23 33.5	+52 13 45	4.43	0.2	G9 III	230	0.184	185	43	−10	.021	13	65	
1 Lac	211388	22 15 58.1	+37 44 56	4.13	*	K3 II/III	*	0.014	54	23	−8	.003	*	*	(b)
2 Lac	212120	22 21 01.5	+46 32 12	4.57	−1.3	B6 V	81	0.023	67	10	−10	.040	2.3	261	(c)
4 Lac	212593	22 24 30.9	+49 28 35	4.57	−6.5	B9 Iab	5300	0.010	276	30	−26	.003	73	30000	
5 Lac	213310	22 29 31.8	+47 42 25	4.36	−2.4	M0 II+	730	0.003	90	5	−4	.006	88	718	
6 Lac	213420	22 30 29.1	+43 07 25	4.51	−3.0	B2 IV	1000	0.008	284	[15]	−8	[.003]	5.4	1247	
8A Lac ∞	214168	22 35 52.2	+39 38 04	5.73	−3.5	B2 Ve	2300	0.003	135	[14]	−10	[.001]	15	1977	(d)
8B Lac	214167	22 35 51.9	+39 37 43	6.35	*	B2 V	*	0.025	307	*	−14	*	*	*	(e)
9 Lac	214454	22 37 22.3	+51 32 43	4.63	1.5	A8 IV	140	0.113	210	27	12	.022	2.0	20	
10 Lac	214680	22 39 15.6	+39 03 01	4.88	−4.8	O9 V	2800	0.000	0	[10]	−10	[.001]	6.8	6500	
11 Lac	214868	22 40 30.8	+44 16 35	4.46	−0.2	K3 III	280	0.093	80	45	−10	.010	23	95	
12 Lac	214993	22 41 28.5	+40 13 32	5.25$_v$	−3.6	B2 III	1900	0.008	293	[26]	−15	[.002]	5.2	2168	
13 Lac	215373	22 44 05.4	+41 49 09	5.08	0.2	K0 III	310	0.012	312	14	13	.010	12	65	
15 Lac	216397	22 52 02.0	+43 18 45	4.94	−0.4	M0 III	380	0.112	73	30	−17	.021	31	114	
Σ2902 ∞	212468	22 23 33.8	+45 21 00	7.60	3.2	G5 IV	250	0.036	79	—	—	[.013]	2.5	4.1	
h1823 ∞	216369	22 51 49.3	+41 18 46	7.07	0.6	A0	640	0.015	113	[23]	−18	[.005]	2.3	45	(f)
- Lac	209945	22 06 01.9	+45 00 52	5.14	−0.3	K5 III	400	0.012	215	25	−23	.006	30	104	
- Lac	211073	22 13 52.6	+39 42 54	4.49	−0.2	K3 III	280	0.040	69	14	−11	.020	24	95	
- Lac	214665	22 38 37.8	+56 47 45	5.21	−0.5	M4 III	450	0.056	117	22	8	.013	34	125	
- Lac	216946	22 56 25.9	+49 44 01	4.95	−4.4	K5 Ib	2400	0.002	27	15	−10	.001	241	4500	

Leo
(Leonis)

a) *Regulus* (The Little King). Burnham gives an estimated diameter of five times the Sun. OH:$M-0.3$.

    Regulus has a companion (m8) at P.A. 307°, 177″ away. East 10° are three galaxies: M95, M96, and M105. 5° west is the bright red variable R Leonis (see note k).

b) *Denebola* (Lion's Tail). Y:π.082. This star was designated a variable in 1985.

c) *Algieba,* or *Algeiba* (Lion's Mane). A renowned binary, sometimes described as having slightly different colors. Most will find that the stars are both orange-yellowish. Given the same parallax as the primary, γ^2 would have an absolute magnitude of $+1.4$, the same distance of 87 l.y., D_s4.5, and $\mathscr{L}$22. The distance modulus formula (given m and π) yields an absolute magnitude of $+0.2$ and a distance of 150 l.y. (at some variance from the parallax). B:$\gamma^1 M-0.1$, $\mathscr{L}$90 and $\gamma^2 M+1.2$, $\mathscr{L}$30 (with both stars then having a distance of 95–100 l.y.).

d) *Zosma* (Girdle). B:$M+0.6$, 80 l.y., $\mathscr{L}$50. Y:π.048.

e) *Ras Elased Australis* (Southern Star of the Lion's Head).

f) *Aldhafera.* OH:$M+1.5$, 77 l.y. Between ζ and γ are several galaxies lying in the same field: NGC 3185, 3187, 3190, and 3193, although they are best seen in large telescopes.

g) A supergiant that, because of its great distance, is far from impressive. Burnham notes that if η Leonis had the same distance as Regulus, it would be six times brighter than Sirius.

h) *Chort.* OH:$M+1.4$. SSE 2.7° are the twin spiral galaxies M65 and M66, well seen in binoculars.

i) South 1.5° is the fine spiral galaxy NGC 2903.

j) South 7° is the spiral galaxy NGC 3521, about half the size as NGC 2903 (above), but nearly as bright.

k) An unusually bright Mira-type variable, making it a favorite subject for many amateurs. The absolute magnitude—derived from m and π—would be around $+2.5$ (with a luminosity of about 10). However, the luminosity class suggests an estimated absolute magnitude of -1 (which agrees with Burnham). This would yield a distance of around 500 l.y. The parallax suggests a much closer distance, around 150–175 l.y. Given M of -1, then the size of R Leo is about 30 Suns, with a luminosity of around 200 Suns. SC:m4.9. The *Observer's Handbook* notes a maximum brightness of m5.8.

LEO	HD	R.A.		Declin.			m	M	Spectra	l.y.	μ	Dir.	V	RV	π	D_s	$\mathscr{L}$	Rmk
				2000.0														
α Leo	87901	$10^h 08^m 22.2^s$	+11° 58′ 02″				1.35	−0.6	B7 V	72	0.249″	271°	27	4	.045″	1.6	137	(a)
β Leo	102647	11 49 03.5	+14 34 19				2.14$_v$	1.54†	A3 V	43	0.511	257	32	0	.076	1.8	19	(b)
γ¹ Leo ∞	89484	10 19 58.3	+19 50 30				2.28	0.2	K0 III	85	0.342	116	82	−37	.022	16	65	(c)⦰
γ² Leo	89485	10 19 58.6	+19 50 25				3.53	*	G7 III	*	0.358	119	85	−36	.022	*	*	
δ Leo	97603	11 14 06.4	+20 31 25				2.56	1.4†	A4 V	55	0.197	133	26	−21	.059	2.1	22	(d)
ε Leo	84441	09 45 51.0	+23 46 27				2.98	−2.0	G0 II	320	0.047	252	23	5	.010	28	497	(e)
ζ Leo	89025	10 16 41.4	+23 25 02				3.44	0.6	F0 III	120	0.022	124	16	−15	.017	3.5	45	(f)
η Leo	87737	10 07 19.9	+16 45 45				3.52	−5.2	A0 Ib	1800	0.006	189	10	3	.003	24	9500	(g)
θ Leo	97633	11 14 14.3	+15 25 46				3.34	1.4	A2 V	80	0.103	216	20	8	.026	1.4	22	(h)
ι Leo ∞	99028	11 23 55.4	+10 31 45				3.94	2.1	F9 IV	78	0.184	115	23	−10	.042	2.2	11	⦰
κ Leo	81146	09 24 39.2	+26 10 56				4.46	−0.1	K2 III	270	0.059	213	98	28	.003	20	86	
λ Leo	82308	09 31 43.1	+22 58 04				4.31	−0.3	K5 III	270	0.049	211	29	27	.020	29	104	(i)
μ Leo	85503	09 52 45.8	+26 00 25				3.88	−0.1	K2 IIIb+	200	0.223	254	45	14	.025	19	86	
ν Leo	86360	09 58 13.3	+12 26 41				5.26	0.4	B9 IV	310	0.032	231	16	14	.018	1.7	54	
ξ Leo	82395	09 31 56.7	+11 17 59				4.97	0.2	K0 III(b)	290	0.127	227	36	29	.028	14	65	
o Leo	83808	09 41 09.0	+09 53 32				3.52	2.1	A5 V	96	0.149	254	34	27	.034	2.5	11	
π Leo	86663	10 00 12.7	+08 02 39				4.70	−0.5	M2 IIab	360	0.042	232	26	23	.017	34	125	
ρ Leo	91316	10 32 48.6	+09 18 24				3.85$_v$	−5.7	B1 Ib	2700	0.011	236	42	42	.011	14	15000	
σ Leo	98664	11 21 08.1	+06 01 46				4.05	0.2	B9.5 V	190	0.096	261	456	−5	.001	1.6	65	
τ Leo	99648	11 27 56.2	+02 51 22				4.95	−0.9	G8 II	96	0.023	137	10	−9	.034	22	180	
φ Leo	98058	11 16 39.6	−03 39 06				4.47	1.5	A7 IVn	130	0.119	250	30	−3	.019	1.8	20	
χ Leo	96097	11 05 01.0	+07 20 10				4.63	1.3	F2 III/IV	150	0.346	262	57	5	.029	2.7	24	(j)
ψ Leo	84194	09 43 43.8	+14 01 18				5.35	−0.5	M2 IIIab	480	0.008	157	[10]	8	[.007]	35	125	
ω Leo	81858	09 28 27.4	+09 03 24				5.41	4.0	F8	96	0.053	98	10	−6	.034	1.3	2.0	
6 Leo	82381	09 31 57.5	+09 42 57				5.07	−0.2	K3 III	370	0.016	194	[21]	19	[.009]	24	95	
10 Leo	83240	09 37 12.6	+06 50 09				5.00	0.0	K1 III	330	0.061	268	25	20	.019	15	79	
31 Leo	87837	10 07 54.2	+09 59 51				4.37	−0.3	K3.5 IIIb	280	0.104	231	[59]	41	[.012]	27	104	
40 Leo	89449	10 19 44.1	+19 28 15				4.79	2.2†	F6 IV	64	0.320	227	31	7	.051	2.2	10	
48 Leo	91612	10 34 47.9	+06 57 14				5.08	−0.9	G9 III+	96	0.121	298	18	5	.034	20	180	
54A Leo ∞	94601	10 55 36.7	+24 44 59				4.50	1.2	A1 V	150	0.074	257	24	5	.015	1.8	26	
54B Leo	94602	10 55 37.2	+24 44 46				6.30	(2.2)	A2 V	220	0.079	248	25	−1	.015	1.1	11	
58 Leo	95345	11 00 33.6	+03 37 03				4.84	0.0	K1 III+	300	0.023	149	17	6	.007	17	79	
59 Leo	95382	11 00 44.7	+06 06 05				4.99	2.1	A5 III	93	0.059	240	14	−12	.035	1.7	11	
60 Leo	95608	11 02 19.7	+20 10 47				4.42	(0.6)	A1 m	190	0.034	341	14	−10	.017	2.6	46	
61 Leo	95578	11 01 49.6	−02 29 04				4.74	−0.3	M0 III	100	0.040	161	15	−14	.032	32	104	
72 Leo	97778	11 15 12.2	+23 05 44				4.63	−0.5	M3 IIb	350	0.024	246	20	16	.010	36	125	
75 Leo	98118	11 17 17.3	+02 00 38				5.18	−0.4	M0 III(b)	430	0.157	161	95	−59	.010	30	114	
87 Leo	99998	11 30 18.8	−03 00 13				4.77	−0.3	K3.5 III(b)	340	0.026	141	21	19	.015	29	104	
91 Leo	100920	11 36 56.9	−00 49 26				4.30	0.2	G8.5 III	220	0.038	2	10	1	.019	13	65	
93 Leo	102509	11 47 59.1	+20 13 08				4.53	(1.2)	A7 V	150	0.150	267	32	0	.022	4.2	25	
R Leo	84748	09 47 33.4	+11 25 43				6.02$_v$	*	M8IIIe	*	0.046	179	17	13	.020	*	*	(k)

Leo Minor
(Leonis Minoris)

a) Leo Minor is one of four constellations with no Alpha—the others being Norma, Puppis, and Vela (all in the Southern Hemisphere).

There is a brighter member of this constellation than β, and that one doesn't even have a letter: 46 LMi. The parallax of β yields a distance of 150 l.y., which in turn gives an absolute magnitude of 0.9, a size of 8 Suns, and a luminosity of 34.

b) Y:π.050.

c) If the absolute magnitude is estimated to be -1, then: 900 l.y., π.004, V25, D_s43, and $\mathcal{L}$198.

LEO MINOR	HD	R.A. 2000.0		Declin.		m	M	Spectra	l.y.	μ	Dir.	V	RV	π	D_s	$\mathscr{L}$	Rmk
β LMi	90537	10^h 27^m 52.9^s		+36° 42′ 26″		4.21	*	G9 III	*	0.159″	229°	35	6	.022″	*	*	(a)
8 LMi	82198	09 31	32.3	+35 06	11	5.37	−0.3	M1 IIIab	440	0.121	208	[87]	38	[.007]	29	104	
10 LMi	82635	09 34	13.3	+36 23	51	4.55$_v$	0.3	G8.5 III	230	0.027	167	[15]	−12	[.014]	11	60	
19 LMi	86146	09 57	41.0	+41 03	20	5.14	3.4	F6 V	81	0.122	256	18	−10	.040	1.3	3.4	
21 LMi	87696	10 07	25.7	+35 14	41	4.48	2.5	A7 V	80	0.050	89	19	−18	.041	1.5	7.9	(b)
30 LMi	90277	10 25	54.8	+33 47	46	4.74	2.6	F0 V	87	0.097	227	[19]	14	[.037]	1.2	7.2	
37 LMi	92125	10 38	43.2	+31 58	34	4.71	−2.1	G2 IIa	750	0.002	27	7	−7	.021	29	545	
41 LMi	92825	10 43	24.9	+23 11	18	5.08	1.4	A3 Vn	180	0.117	272	40	19	.016	1.7	22	
42 LMi	93152	10 45	51.8	+30 40	56	5.24	0.2	A1 Vn	330	0.048	210	[26]	12	[.010]	1.6	65	
46 LMi	94264	10 53	18.6	+34 12	53	3.83	(0.7)	K0 III	140	0.295	163	61	16	.024	11	40	
R LMi	84346	09 45	34.1	+34 30	44	6.2$_v$	*	M5 III	*	0.017	301	*	10	*	*	*	(c)

Lepus
(Leporis)

a) *Arneb.* OH:$M-5.1$, 1090 l.y. East 1.8° is the open cluster NGC 2017, which also includes the multiple star h 3780 (see note j).

b) *Nihal.* B:$M+0.1$, 115 l.y., $\mathcal{L}$70. SSW 4° is the globular cluster M79.

c) B:29 l.y. A nice double with color contrast, yellow and orange.

d) B:170 l.y., $\mathcal{L}$120. In the same field, north 0.8°, is T Leporis, a rather faint Mira-type variable (m7.4–m13.5, 368-day period).

e) SC:$M+1.7$.

f) Fig. 2 would suggest an absolute magnitude of about –3. This gives the following: 1000 l.y., D_s1, and $\mathcal{L}$1250. However, if the $B-V$ color index is considered (–0.26), we get the following: Fig. 3 shows a size of 3–5 Suns, and Fig. 6 gives us a rough estimate of 25,000 K surface temperature. Putting these together, we can estimate a luminosity of about 400. This means an absolulte magnitude of -1.8, and a distance of 500–600 light-years.

g) B:390 l.y., $\mathcal{L}$580.

h) A pleasant binary system, which Herschel called "most beautiful."

i) ENE just 35′ from this binary is M79, a globular star cluster that requires a large telescope to appreciate.

j) A striking multiple system 2° east of α Leporis that goes under the name NGC 2017.
    If the absolute magnitude is estimated at -0.7, then: 850 l.y., π.004, V22, D_s1.5, $\mathcal{L}$150.

k) If the absolute magnitude is estimated to be -1.5, then: 2300 l.y., π.001, V87, D_s450, and $\mathcal{L}$313.

l) If the absolute magnitude is estimated to be $+1$, then: 212 l.y., π.015, V30, D_s0.8, $\mathcal{L}$31.

LEPUS	HD	R.A.			Declin.			m	M	Spectra	l.y.	μ	Dir.	V	RV	π	D_s	$\mathscr{L}$	Rmk
						2000.0													
α Lep	36673	05^h	32^m	43.7^s	$-17°$	$49'$	$20''$	2.58	−4.7	F0 Ib	930	0.006″	279°	24	24	.007″	32	6000	(a)
β Lep	36079	05	28	14.7	−20	45	34	2.84	−2.1	G5 II	320	0.091	185	26	−14	.020	30	545	(b)
γ^A Lep ∞	38393	05	44	27.8	−22	26	54	3.60	4.05†	F7 V	27	0.475	218	21	−10	.123	1.0	1.9	(c)
γ^B Lep	38392	05	44	26.4	−22	25	19	6.15	6.6	K2 V	26	0.473	221	20	−10	.128	0.6	0.2	
δ Lep	39364	05	51	19.2	−20	52	45	3.81	0.3	G8 III/IV	160	0.688	161	160	99	.026	12	60	
ε Lep	32887	05	05	27.6	−22	22	16	3.19	0.3	K4 III	120	0.073	166	32	1	.011	21	60	(d)
ζ Lep	38678	05	46	57.3	−14	49	19	3.55	1.8†	A3 V	72	0.023	263	20	20	.045	1.6	15	
η Lep	40136	05	56	24.2	−14	10	04	3.71	2.8†	F1 V	49	0.145	340	11	−2	.066	1.3	6.0	(e)
θ Lep	41695	06	06	09.3	−14	56	07	4.67	(0.1)	A1 Vn	270	0.026	309	34	32	.012	3.2	74	
ι Lep	33802	05	12	17.8	−11	52	09	4.45	−0.2	B8 V	280	0.026	127	[27]	25	[.012]	1.4	95	
κ Lep ∞	33949	05	13	13.8	−12	56	30	4.36	−1.2	B7 V	96	0.022	243	18	18	.034	2.2	238	
λ Lep	34816	05	19	34.4	−13	10	37	4.29	*	B0.5 IV	*	0.010	253	*	20	*	*	*	(f)
μ Lep	33904	05	12	55.8	−16	12	20	3.31_v	−0.8	B9 IV	220	0.043	129	29	28	.023	1.7	164	(g)
ν Lep	34863	05	19	59.0	−12	18	56	5.30	−0.6	B7 IV	490	0.015	302	[19]	16	[.007]	1.5	137	
17 Lep	41511	06	04	59.0	−16	29	04	4.93_v	(2.5)	A2 eShell	100	0.013	257	20	20	.032	1.3	8.2	
h 3750 ∞	34968	05	20	26.8	−21	14	23	4.71	0.6	A0 V	220	0.000	45	30	30	.002	1.4	45	(h)
h 3752	35162	05	21	46.2	−24	46	23	5.06	1.3	G7 II/III	180	0.032	246	38	5	.004	5.0	24	(i)
h 3780 ∞	37643	05	39	16.2	−17	50	58	6.38	*	B7 V	*	0.006	288	*	21	*	*	*	(j)
R Lep	31996	04	59	36.4	−14	48	21	7.71_v	*	C7	*	0.024	35	*	32	*	*	*	(k)
- Lep	32309	05	01	25.5	−20	03	07	4.91	0.2	B9.5 Vn	290	0.032	118	[27]	24	[.011]	1.7	65	
- Lep	32436	05	02	09.8	−26	16	31	5.02	0.2	K1 III	300	0.115	134	82	27	.007	14	65	
- Lep	34310	05	15	24.3	−26	56	36	5.07	*	B9 V	*	0.019	164	*	29	*	*	*	(l)
- Lep	41312	06	03	15.5	−26	17	04	5.04	−0.2	K3 III	360	0.104	29	[190]	182	[.009]	23	95	

Libra
(Librae)

a) *Zubenelgenubi* (Southern Claw). B:M+1.2, 65 l.y., $\mathcal{L}$25. An easily resolved pair, yellowish and pale blue.

b) *Zubeneschamali* (Northern Claw). B:140 l.y., $\mathcal{L}$145.

c) *Zubenelakrab*.

d) If the absolute magnitude is estimated to be +3, then: 100 l.y., π.033, V33, D_s1, and $\mathcal{L}$5.

e) The cited visual magnitude is the combined magnitude of two stars (ι^{1A}: 5.1, and ι^{1a}: 5.6). This is a very rapid binary: the period is but 22.35 years. The companion travels in a retrograde motion, i.e., 1 Jan 1991 it had a PA of 268°, and two years later a PA of 219°. The distance in both cases was 0.1″.

   The more easily resolved fixed companion, ι^{1B}, is nearly 60″ away, at 111° (see Visual Binary Section).

f) *Brachium, Zubenalgubi*. B:M+1.9, 60 l.y., $\mathcal{L}$15. SC:M−0.5. Y:π.064 (which yields a distance of 51 l.y., an absolute magnitude of +2.3, and a luminosity of about 10 Suns).

g) If we estimate the absolute magnitude to be −1, then: 760 l.y., π.004, V138, D_s30, $\mathcal{L}$200.

h) The star is encircled by an outer shell of gas, which rapidly expands, causing the RV to vary.

   If the absolute magnitude is estimated to be −2, then: 775 l.y., π.004, V28, D_s3.2, $\mathcal{L}$500.

i) A nice looking pair of equal brightness, both pale blue-green. Contrary to the *Bright Star Catalogue*, the *Sky Catalogue* has this star the companion (B) rather than the primary, at a visual magnitude of 6.48.

j) The *Sky Catalogue* shows this to be the primary (m5.79).

k) If we estimate the absolute magnitude to be −1, then: 1965 l.y., π.002, V332, D_s43, $\mathcal{L}$198.

LIBRA	HD	R.A.			Declin.			m	M	Spectra	l.y.	μ	Dir.	V	RV	π	D_s	$\mathscr{L}$	Rmk
																		2000.0	
α^1 Lib ∞	130819	14^h 50^m	41.1^s	$-15°$	$59'$	$50''$	5.16	3.9†	F4 IV	57	0.124″	235°	25	−23	.057″	0.9	2.2	(a)
α^2 Lib ∞	130841	14 50	52.6	−16	02	31	2.75	1.5†	A3 III/IV	57	0.129	237	15	−10	.057	2.1	20	
β Lib	135742	15 17	00.3	−09	22	58	2.61	−0.2	B8 V	120	0.101	257	163	−35	.003	63	95	(b)
γ Lib	138905	15 35	31.5	−14	47	22	3.91	1.8	K0 III	80	0.062	87	29	−28	.041	6.3	15	
δ Lib	132742	15 00	58.3	−08	31	08	4.9$_v$	0.6	A0 V	240	0.068	262	42	−39	.020	2.3	45	(c)
ε Lib	137052	15 24	11.8	−10	19	20	4.94	3.4	F5 IV	93	0.173	204	26	−10	.035	1.3	3.4	
ζ^4 Lib	138485	15 32	55.1	−16	51	11	5.50	−2.5	B2 Vn	1300	0.022	216	[43]	9	[.003]	3.1	787	
η Lib	140417	15 44	04.3	−15	40	22	5.41	*	F0 IV	*	0.076	208	*	−31	*	*	*	(d)
θ Lib	142198	15 53	49.4	−16	43	46	4.15	1.8	K0 III	91	0.162	37	22	3	.036	6.4	15	
ι^1 Lib ∞	134759	15 12	13.2	−19	47	30	4.54	−0.3	A0 pSi	110	0.057	221	15	−12	.030	1.7	104	(e)
κ Lib	139997	15 41	56.7	−19	40	44	4.74	−0.3	M0 IIIb	82	0.114	200	14	−4	.040	30	104	
λ Lib	142096	15 53	20.0	−20	10	02	5.03	−1.7	B2.5 V	720	0.029	202	[31]	6	[.005]	5.9	377	
μ Lib ∞	130559	14 49	19.0	−14	08	56	5.31	(−0.7)	ApSr.	540	0.067	253	53	−4	.006	4.9	151	
ν Lib	133774	15 06	37.5	−16	15	24	5.20	−0.3	K5 III	410	0.051	241	19	−15	.020	31	104	
ξ^2 Lib	131918	14 56	46.0	−11	24	35	5.46	−0.3	K4 III	460	0.007	56	[16]	15	[.007]	28	104	
ρ Lib	139365	15 38	39.3	−29	46	40	3.66	−1.4	B2.5 V	340	0.036	203	[18]	3	[.010]	2.9	286	
σ Lib	133216	15 04	04.1	−25	16	55	3.29$_v$	0.7†	M3/4 III	110	0.087	237	8	−4	.030	37	125	(f)
υ Lib	139063	15 37	01.4	−28	08	06	3.58	−0.3	K3 III	74	0.008	256	25	−25	.044	25	104	
11 Lib	130952	14 51	00.9	−02	17	57	4.94	1.8	G8 III/IV	140	0.151	147	94	83	.016	6.1	15	
12 Lib	131430	14 54	20.0	−24	38	32	5.30	0.2	K2 III	80	0.033	198	10	9	.041	19	65	
16 Lib	132052	14 57	10.9	−04	20	47	4.49	1.7	F0 V	69	0.189	213	29	22	.047	2.2	16	
18 Lib ∞	132345	14 58	53.5	−11	08	39	5.84	*	K3 III	*	0.124	238	*	−12	*	*	*	(g)
36 Lib	138688	15 34	37.2	−28	02	49	5.15	0.2	K4 III	320	0.039	157	21	12	.011	18	65	
37 Lib	138716	15 34	10.6	−10	03	53	4.62	0.0	K1 III/IV	270	0.387	128	83	48	.027	15	79	
42 Lib	139663	15 40	16.8	−23	49	05	4.96	−0.3†	K3 III+	68	0.025	225	22	−22	.048	24	104	
48 Lib	142983	15 58	11.3	−14	16	46	4.88$_v$	*	B5 IIIpe	*	0.024	218	*	−6	*	*	*	(h)
Σ1962A ∞	139461	15 38	40.0	−08	47	28	6.48	3.8	F7 V	110	0.033	131	[12]	0	[.011]	1.2	2.4	(i)
Σ1962B	139460	15 38	39.9	−08	47	40	6.50	3.8	F6 IV/V	110	0.026	133	12	4	.011	1.2	2.4	(j)
S Lib	136458	15 21	23.6	−20	23	16	7.9$_v$	*	M1/3	*	0.054	282	*	294	*	*	*	(k)
- Lib	138764	15 34	26.5	−09	11	00	5.17	−1.3	B6 IV	640	0.033	215	[31]	−2	[.005]	2.5	261	

Lupus
(Lupi)

a) B:430 l.y., $\mathcal{L}$1700.

b) B:540 l.y., $\mathcal{L}$1900.

c) B:570 l.y., $\mathcal{L}$1900.

d) B:300 l.y., $\mathcal{L}$240.

e) B:90 l.y., $\mathcal{L}$28.

f) If the absolute magnitude is estimated to be -0.5, then: 360 l.y., π.009, V16, D_s1.0, and $\mathcal{L}$114.

g) SC:$RV-18$.

h) SC:m5.30.

LUPUS	HD	R.A.	Declin.	m	M	Spectra	l.y.	μ	Dir.	V	RV	π	D_s	ℒ	Rmk
			2000.0												
α Lup	129056	14^h 41^m 55.7^s	$-47°$ $23'$ $17''$	2.30_v	−4.4	B1.5 Vn	710	0.026''	220°	[28]	5	[.005]''	5.7	4500	(a)
β Lup	132058	14 58 31.8	−43 08 02	2.68	−2.5	B2 IV	350	0.057	221	[29]	0	[.009]	1.6	787	(b)
γ Lup ∞	138690	15 35 08.3	−41 10 00	2.78	−1.7	B2 IV	260	0.035	207	21	2	.008	1.6	377	(c)⊘
δ Lup	136298	15 21 22.2	−40 38 52	3.22_v	−3.0	B1.5 IV	570	0.036	207	[30]	0	[.006]	2.1	1247	
ε Lup ∞	136504	15 22 40.8	−44 41 22	3.37	−2.3	B2 IV/V	440	0.024	232	15	8	.009	3.4	655	(d)
ζ Lup	134505	15 12 17.0	−52 05 57	3.41	0.3	G8 III	76	0.128	237	17	−10	.043	11	60	(e)
η Lup ∞	143118	16 00 07.2	−38 23 49	3.41	−2.5	B2.5 IV	500	0.040	213	25	8	.008	1.6	787	
θ Lup	144294	16 06 35.4	−36 48 08	4.23	−2.3	B2.5 Vn	660	0.038	210	[39]	15	[.005]	4.4	655	
ι Lup	125238	14 19 24.1	−46 03 28	3.55	−1.7	B2.5 IV	370	0.014	266	[23]	22	[.009]	2.6	377	
κ¹ Lup ∞	134481	15 11 56.0	−48 44 16	3.87	0.2	B9.5 Vne	180	0.108	243	[28]	−6	[.018]	1.7	65	
κ² Lup	134482	15 11 57.5	−48 44 37	5.69	0.6	A3/5 V	340	0.110	248	[54]	0	[.010]	3.2	45	
λ Lup	133955	15 08 50.5	−45 16 47	4.05	−2.3	B3 V	610	0.027	216	15	10	.012	3.4	655	
μ Lup ∞	135734	15 18 31.9	−47 52 30	4.27	−0.2	B8 Ve	260	0.047	212	23	15	.013	1.6	95	
ν¹ Lup	136351	15 22 08.2	−47 55 40	5.00	3.4	F8 V	100	0.194	224	31	−11	.032	1.4	3.4	
ξ¹ Lup ∞	142629	15 56 53.4	−33 57 59	5.37	(2.4)	A3 V	130	0.049	157	14	−10	.025	1.2	9.0	
ξ² Lup	142630	15 56 54.1	−33 57 51	5.73	(2.7)	B9 V	130	0.047	155	15	−12	.025	1.1	6.4	
o Lup	130807	14 51 38.3	−43 34 31	4.32	−1.9	B5 IV	570	0.037	215	[31]	7	[.006]	7.2	453	
π¹ Lup	133242	15 05 07.1	−47 03 04	4.72	(−0.5)	B5 V	360	0.028	222	16	5	.009	1.2	126	
π² Lup	133243	15 05 07.1	−47 03 04	4.82	*	B5 IV	*	0.028	222	*	5	*	*	*	(f)
ρ Lup	128345	14 37 53.1	−49 25 32	4.05	−1.1	B3/4 V	350	0.037	234	[21]	8	[.009]	5.0	217	
σ Lup	127381	14 32 36.8	−50 27 25	4.42	−2.5	B2 III	790	0.043	252	[49]	−2	[.004]	2.9	787	
τ¹ Lup	126341	14 26 08.1	−45 13 17	4.56_v	−3.0	B2 IV	1100	0.020	221	[38]	−22	[.003]	12	1247	
τ² Lup	126354	14 26 10.7	−45 22 46	4.35	4.0	F7	38	0.019	126	44	−1	.002	0.9	2.0	
υ Lup	136933	15 24 44.8	−39 42 37	5.37	(−0.1)	A0 pSi	410	0.063	217	38	−8	.008	1.3	87	
φ¹ Lup	136422	15 21 48.3	−36 15 41	3.56	−0.3	K5 III	190	0.126	226	52	−29	.014	29	104	
φ² Lup	136664	15 23 09.2	−36 51 30	4.54	−2.3	B4 V	760	0.031	216	[34]	2	[.004]	8.6	655	
χ Lup	141556	15 50 57.4	−33 37 38	3.95	−0.3	B9.5 III/IV	230	0.033	196	[12]	5	[.014]	2.3	104	(g)
ψ¹ Lup	139521	15 39 45.9	−34 24 42	4.67	0.3	G8 III	100	0.016	104	23	−23	.032	12	60	
ψ² Lup	140008	15 42 40.9	−34 42 38	4.75	−0.9	B5 V	440	0.038	213	[25]	4	[.007]	0.1	180	
ω Lup	139127	15 38 03.1	−42 34 02	4.33	−0.4	K4.5 III	290	0.156	292	44	−7	.017	27	114	
1 Lup	135153	15 14 37.2	−31 31 09	4.91	−6.6	F1 II	6500	0.006	239	23	−23	.014	110	35000	
2 Lup	135758	15 17 49.7	−30 08 55	4.34	0.2	G9 IIIa+	220	0.013	222	5	−4	.018	15	65	
h Lup	139980	15 42 38.2	−37 25 30	5.24	0.2	K0 III	330	0.055	248	36	−16	.008	13	65	
- Lup	125442	14 20 42.4	−45 11 14	4.77	2.6	F0 IV	89	0.090	159	21	0	.020	1.4	7.2	
- Lup	129893	14 47 01.2	−52 23 01	5.21	0.3	G8 III	310	0.090	191	29	−21	.021	12	60	
- Lup	133340	15 05 19.0	−41 04 02	5.15	0.2	G8 III	320	0.020	110	6	−3	.019	13	65	(h)
- Lup	134687	15 12 49.4	−44 30 02	4.82	−2.9	B3 IV	1100	0.046	228	[78]	14	[.003]	5.8	1138	
- Lup	135345	15 16 03.9	−41 29 28	5.16	−8.0	G5 Ia+	14000	0.011	214	32	−27	.003	310	125000	
- Lup	137058	15 25 20.1	−38 44 01	4.60	0.0	A0 IV	270	0.056	250	22	−3	.012	3.0	79	
- Lup	137709	15 29 24.2	−46 43 58	5.24	−4.4	K4 III	2800	0.015	222	31	−28	.005	233	4500	
- Lup	138769	15 35 53.1	−44 57 31	4.54	−2.3	B3 IVp	760	0.041	219	16	7	.014	3.4	655	
- Lup	139664	15 41 11.2	−44 39 40	4.64	2.8†	F5 IV/V	58	0.318	214	27	−5	.056	1.5	6.0	
- Lup	143009	15 59 30.2	−41 44 39	4.99	0.3	K0 II/III	280	0.040	248	29	−27	.019	12	60	
- Lup	143699	16 03 24.0	−38 36 09	4.89	−1.7	B6 IV	680	0.046	222	[45]	−2	[.005]	2.2	377	

Lynx
(Lyncis)

a)   SC:m5.2.

b)   This companion star has an interesting color—a kind of lilac blue, or perhaps green; observers disagree.

c)   Also known as 10 UMa.

d)   SC:m5.3.

LYNX	HD	R.A.	2000.0 Declin.	m	M	Spectra	l.y.	μ	Dir.	V	RV	π	D_s	$\mathscr{L}$	Rmk
α Lyn	80493	09^h 21^m 03.2^s	+34° 23' 33''	3.13	−0.4	K7 III	170	0.223''	273°	57	38	.025''	31	114	
1 Lyn	42973	06 17 54.9	+61 30 55	4.98$_v$	−0.5	M3 IIIab	410	0.004	207	12	11	.006	42	125	(a)
2 Lyn	43378	06 19 37.3	+59 00 39	4.48$_v$	1.4	A2 V	93	0.025	349	5	−4	.035	1.6	22	
5 Lyn	44708	06 26 48.8	+58 25 02	5.21	−0.3	K4 III	410	0.009	198	9	−3	.005	29	104	
12 Lyn ∞	48250	06 46 14.1	+59 26 30	4.87	0.8	A3 V	210	0.021	262	10	−3	.011	2.5	38	⊘
15 Lyn	50522	06 57 16.5	+58 25 21	4.35	1.8	G5III/IV	110	0.136	181	47	9	.014	5.1	15	
16 Lyn	50973	06 57 37.0	+45 05 39	4.90	1.4	A2 Vn	160	0.022	267	19	−8	.006	1.7	22	
18 Lyn	55280	07 15 54.8	+59 38 15	5.20	−0.1	K2 III	78	0.275	200	39	24	.042	16	86	
19A Lyn ∞	57103	07 22 52.0	+55 16 53	5.45	0.0	B8 V	400	0.031	184	14	5	.011	3.0	79	
19B Lyn	57102	07 22 50.8	+55 17 04	6.53	1.7	B9 V	300	0.026	171	15	10	.011	1.4	16	(b)
21 Lyn	58142	07 26 42.8	+49 12 42	4.64	0.3	A1 V	240	0.048	195	33	27	.012	2.1	60	
24 Lyn	61497	07 43 00.4	+58 42 37	4.99	0.0	A3 IVn	330	0.063	215	19	9	.018	3.6	79	
27 Lyn	67006	08 08 27.4	+51 30 24	4.84	1.4	A2 V	160	0.060	263	34	11	.009	1.8	22	
31 Lyn	70272	08 22 50.1	+43 11 17	4.25	−0.3	K4.5III	270	0.101	190	32	24	.023	30	104	
35 Lyn	75506	08 51 56.8	+43 43 36	5.15	0.2	K0 III	320	0.046	342	19	15	.018	13	65	
38 Lyn ∞	80081	09 18 50.6	+36 48 09	3.82	1.7	A3 V	78	0.130	193	15	4	.042	1.6	16	
Kui 37 ∞	76943	09 00 38.3	+41 46 58	3.97	3.50†	F5 V	44	0.507	240	42	26	.074	1.2	3.1	(c)⊘
Σ1338 ∞	80441	09 20 59.2	+38 11 18	6.12	3.1	F2 V	130	0.048	249	13	1	.018	1.3	4.5	⊘
R Lyn	51610	07 01 17.9	+55 19 51	7.80$_v$	—	C	—	0.006	321	—	28	—	—	—	
RR Lyn	44691	06 26 25.8	+56 17 06	5.64$_v$	(2.4)	A3 Vm	140	0.030	312	12	−10	.023	1.3	8.3	
- Lyn	56169	07 18 31.9	+49 27 54	5.05	0.4	A4 IIIn	280	0.013	342	14	−12	.008	3.0	54	
- Lyn	61931	07 44 04.1	+50 26 01	5.27	(1.2)	A0 IIIn	220	0.034	199	11	0	.015	1.8	27	
- Lyn	62647	07 46 39.2	+37 31 03	5.18	−0.5	M2 IIIb	450	0.029	65	[40]	−35	[.007]	34	125	(d)
- Lyn	77912	09 06 31.7	+38 27 08	4.56	−3.3	G7 Ib/II	1200	0.035	237	19	17	.021	69	1644	
- Lyn	82741	09 35 03.8	+39 37 17	4.81	0.2	K0 III	270	0.028	297	[16]	−12	[.012]	13	65	

Lyra
(Lyrae)

a) *Vega* (Falling Eagle; Harp Star). Fifth brightest star, the Pole Star some 12,000 years ago, and destined to be again in another 12,000. SW 1.3° is the very red T Lyrae, an irregular variable (m7.5–m9.3).

b) *Sheliak* (Tortoise). B:$M-4.0$, 860 l.y., D_s19, and $\mathcal{L}3000$. The splendid Ring Nebula (M57) is 1° ESE, almost midway between β and γ Lyr. It takes a medium-sized telescope to bring out the ring; the larger the scope the better.

c) *Sulafat.* B:370 l.y., $\mathcal{L}525$.

d) Binary with a nice color contrast, orange and blue. δ^2 is the primary.

e) B: the absolute magnitude is "about -3," with a luminosity of 1300.

f) The famous Double-Double. Use high power to see all four components. The Orbital Elements Section has orbital information on both pair.

g) *RV* from Evans.

h) If the absolute magnitude is estimated to be -1, then: 330 l.y., $\pi.010$, $V50$, D_s43, $\mathcal{L}198$.

i) *RV* from *B&P.*

j) Prototype of a class of pulsating variable; its period changes. B:$M+0.3$, 900 l.y.

LYRA	HD	R.A.	Declin.	m	M	Spectra	l.y.	μ	Dir.	V	RV	π	D_s	$\mathscr{L}$	Rmk
α Lyr	172167	$18^h\,36^m\,56.2^s$	$+38°\,47'\,01''$	0.03_v	0.50†	A0 V	26	0.348''	35°	19	−14	.124''	2.4	50	(a)
β Lyr ∞	174638	18 50 04.7	+33 21 46	3.45_v	−0.6	B7 V	210	0.002	180	20	−19	.002	3.9	137	(b)
γ Lyr	176437	18 58 56.5	+32 41 22	3.24	−0.8	B9 III	210	0.006	288	22	−22	.021	2.7	164	(c)
δ^1 Lyr	175426	18 53 43.5	+36 58 18	5.58	−1.6	B3.5 V	890	0.003	198	26	−26	.004	6.2	344	(d)
δ^2 Lyr	175588	18 54 30.1	+36 53 56	4.30_v	−2.4	M4 II	710	0.016	308	82	−26	.001	88	718	(e)
ε^{1A} Lyr ∞	173582	18 44 20.3	+39 40 12	5.06	1.7	A3 V	130	0.060	12	34	−31	.021	2.0	16	(f)∅
ε^{1B} Lyr	173583	18 44 20.2	+39 40 15	6.02	(2.6)	F1 V	160	0.059	359	36	−33	.021	.9	7.0	
ε^{2C} Lyr ∞	173607	18 44 22.8	+39 36 46	5.14	2.1	A5 V	130	0.064	3	28	−24	.021	1.3	11	∅
ε^{2D} Lyr	173608	18 44 22.8	+39 36 46	5.37	(2.0)	F0 Vn	160	0.064	3	32	−28	.021	1.2	13	
ζ^1 Lyr ∞	173648	18 44 46.3	+37 36 18	4.36	(1.8)	A m	110	0.034	45	27	−26	.031	1.5	15	
ζ^2 Lyr	173649	18 44 48.1	+37 35 40	5.73	1.7	F0 IV	110	0.026	43	24	−24	.031	2.0	16	
η Lyr	180163	19 13 45.4	+39 08 46	4.39	−3.0	B2 IV	980	0.003	360	11	−8	.002	12	1247	
θ Lyr	180809	19 16 22.0	+38 08 01	4.36	−2.1	K0 III	640	0.007	304	31	−31	.013	51	545	
ι Lyr	178475	19 07 18.0	+36 06 01	5.28	−1.0	B6 IV	590	0.004	256	[18]	−18	[.006]	1.9	198	
κ Lyr	168775	18 19 51.6	+36 03 52	4.33	−0.1	K2 IIIab	250	0.047	336	30	−22	.011	18	86	
λ Lyr	176670	19 00 00.8	+32 08 44	4.93	−2.3	K2.5 III	910	0.016	38	30	−16	.003	69	655	
μ Lyr	169702	18 24 13.7	+39 30 26	5.12	0.0	A3 IVn	350	0.023	252	36	−24	.004	3.2	79	
ν^2 Lyr	174602	18 49 52.8	+32 33 03	5.25	1.7	A3 V	170	0.019	223	11	10	.020	1.6	16	
16 Lyr	177196	19 01 26.3	+46 56 05	5.01	(2.8)	A7 V	91	0.084	170	14	8	.036	1.0	6.0	
17 Lyr	178449	19 07 25.5	+32 30 06	5.23	2.6	F0 V	110	0.129	80	36	4	.017	1.5	7.2	
β 648 ∞	176051	18 57 01.5	+32 54 05	5.22	4.00†	F9 V	60	0.230	133	51	−47	.054	1.3	2.0	∅
Σ2333 ∞	171026	18 31 06.9	+32 14 44	7.80	0.6	A0 V	900	0.013	90	[30]	−25	[.004]	2.3	45	(g)
Σ2470 ∞	178849	19 08 45.1	+34 45 37	7.0	−1.6	B3 V	1700	0.005	143	[21]	−17	[.002]	2.3	344	
Σ2474 ∞	178911	19 09 04.3	+34 36 02	6.74	4.5	G1 V	91	0.202	15	56	−41	.025	1.1	1.2	
R Lyr	175865	18 55 20.0	+43 56 46	4.04_v	*	M5 III	*	0.087	14	*	−28	*	*	*	(h)
W Lyr	167740	18 14 55.8	+36 40 13	7.3_v	—	M0	—	0.015	152	—	−172	.003	—	—	(i)
RR Lyr	182989	19 25 27.7	+42 47 05	7.2_v	3.4	F5 V	190	0.220	213	119	−72	.011	.9	3.4	(j)
- Lyr	173780	18 46 04.4	+26 39 43	4.83	−0.2	K3 III	330	0.027	36	18	−17	.023	20	95	

Mensa
(Mensae)

a) On the southern edge of the Large Magellanic Cloud.

b) If the absolute magnitude is estimated at +0.5, then: 350 l.y., $\pi.010$, $V37$, D_s10, and $\mathscr{L}50$.

c) If the absolute magnitude is estimated to be +2, then: 160 l.y., $\pi.020$, $V6$, $D_s1.3$, and $\mathscr{L}12$.

d) If the absolute magnitude is estimated to be +2, then: 160 l.y., $\pi.020$, $V19$, $D_s0.6$, and $\mathscr{L}12$.

MENSA	HD	R.A.			Declin.			m	M	Spectra	l.y.	μ	Dir.	V	RV	π	D_s	$\mathscr{L}$	Rmk
					2000.0														
α Men	43834	06^h 10^m 14.6^s			−74° 45′ 11″			5.09	5.39†	G6 V	28	0.244″	150°	36	35	.115″	0.8	0.5	
β Men	33285	05	02	43.2	−71	18	50	5.31	0.9	G8 III	250	0.025	7	14	−11	.013	9.6	35	
γ Men	37763	05	31	53.0	−76	20	28	5.19	−0.3	K2 III	410	0.306	21	92	57	.020	19	104	(a)
δ Men	28525	04	17	59.2	−80	12	51	5.69	∗	K2/3 III	∗	0.066	14	∗	−20	∗	∗	∗	(b)
η Men	32440	04	55	11.3	−74	56	13	5.47	−0.3	K4 III	470	0.064	26	29	26	.026	29	104	
θ Men	54239	06	56	34.5	−79	25	13	5.45	∗	B9.5 V	∗	0.009	257	∗	6	∗	∗	∗	(c)
κ Men	40953	05	50	16.5	−79	21	41	5.47	∗	B9 V	∗	0.069	343	∗	10	∗	∗	∗	(d)

Microscopium
(Microscopii)

a)   SC:$RV-7$.

b)   Also known as 1 Piscis Austrini.

MICRO-SCOPIUM	HD	2000.0 R.A.	Declin.	m	M	Spectra	l.y.	μ	Dir.	V	RV	π	D_s	$\mathscr{L}$	Rmk
α Mic ∞	198232	20ʰ 49ᵐ 58.0ˢ	−33° 46′ 48″	4.90	0.3	G8 III	270	0.024″	156°	18	−15	.012″	12	60	
β Mic	198529	20 51 58.7	−33 10 38	6.04	1.4	A1 IV	280	0.023	41	[15]	−12	[.012]	1.7	22	(a)
γ Mic	199951	21 01 17.4	−32 15 28	4.67	0.3	G8 III	96	0.008	360	18	18	.034	11	60	(b)
ε Mic	202627	21 17 56.2	−32 10 21	4.71	(2.3)	A0 V	99	0.062	113	9	−1	.033	1.2	9.4	
ζ Mic	200163	21 02 57.8	−38 37 54	5.30	2.6	F3 V	110	0.114	194	23	5	.024	1.7	7.2	
θ¹ Mic	203006	21 20 45.5	−40 48 35	4.82ᵥ	(0.2)	A2 p	270	0.068	93	27	2	.012	2.8	65	
θ² Mic ∞	203585	21 24 24.7	−41 00 24	5.77	(−0.3)	ApSi	540	0.030	84	26	11	.006	2.2	108	
ι Mic	197937	20 48 29.0	−43 59 19	5.11	3.3†	F1 IV	76	0.213	119	28	−15	.043	1.1	3.8	
ν Mic	195569	20 33 55.0	−44 30 58	5.11	0.2	K0 III	310	0.038	155	28	9	.007	13	65	
- Mic	200763	21 06 24.6	−32 20 30	5.18	0.2	K2 III	320	0.013	360	6	3	.012	15	65	

Monoceros
(Monocerotis)

a) Splendid triple—one of the best for small telescopes—forming a fixed (?) triangle (see Visual Binary Section).

   The distance has been generated from the distance modulus formula, given the visual and absolute magnitudes; the parallax would give a distance of only 135 l.y. Burnham, relying on the parallax, suggests an absolute magnitude of +1.0.

   About 8.5° east and 1.5° south is the pleasant open cluster M50 (NGC 2323). Near its center is a faint red giant.

b) The distance comes from the distance modulus formula, given m and M. The parallax indicates a distance of about 155 l.y. Burnham, relying on the parallax, offers a suggested absolute magnitude of +1.6.

c) East 2.5° is the bright open cluster NGC 2244 (which includes 12 Mon). Encircling the cluster is the Rosetta Nebula, which requires a large telescope to fully appreciate.

d) A visual binary and variable (S Mon), located in the large open cluster NGC 2264. Surrounding the cluster is a large and faint diffuse nebula. Just south of 15 Mon, 1°, is the Cone Nebula, a beautiful sight in large telescopes. See Burnham, p. 1206ff., for finder's chart and discussion.

   SW 1.5° of 15 Mon is Hubble's Variable Nebula, quite faint, with R Mon at its tip.

e) One of the most massive spectroscopic binary systems known, estimated at 120 Suns. B:$M-4.0$, 2700 l.y. (assuming it to be part of NGC 2244), £3000. Burnham includes a photograph, which makes locating this star quite easy.

   If the absolute magnitude is estimated to be -4.5, then: 4220 l.y., π.001, V33, D_s27, £5000.

MONOCEROS	HD	R.A.			Declin.			m	M	Spectra	l.y.	μ	Dir.	V	RV	π	D_s	$\mathscr{L}$	Rmk
			2000.0																
α Mon	61935	07^h	41^m	14.8^s	−09°	33′	04″	3.93	0.2	K0 III	180	0.081″	253°	19	11	.024″	13	65	
β^A Mon ∞	45725	06	28	48.9	−07	01	59	4.60	−1.7	B3 Ve	590	0.022	265	21	20	.021	2.8	377	(a)
β^B Mon	45726	06	28	49.4	−07	02	04	5.40	−2.6	B3 ne	1300	0.022	278	19	18	.021	5.3	863	(b)
γ Mon	43232	06	14	51.3	−06	16	29	3.98	−0.2	K3 III	220	0.021	205	9	−5	.013	23	95	
δ Mon	55185	07	11	51.8	−00	29	34	4.15	0.0	A2 V	220	0.006	321	15	15	.016	2.7	79	
ε^A Mon ∞	44769	06	23	46.0	+04	35	34	4.44	0.3	A5 IV	220	0.021	298	16	15	.025	4.0	60	(c)
ε^B Mon	44770	06	23	46.9	+04	35	44	6.72	3.3	F5 V	160	0.026	245	17	16	.025	1.4	3.8	
ζ Mon	67594	08	08	35.6	−02	59	02	4.34	−4.5	G2 Ib	1900	0.022	249	46	30	.003	110	5000	
2 Mon	40536	05	59	04.3	−09	33	30	5.03	(0.0)	A6 m	330	0.055	170	34	22	.010	3.4	77	
3 Mon	40967	06	01	50.3	−10	35	53	4.95	−1.6	B5 III	670	0.013	261	44	39	.003	2.3	344	
10 Mon	45546	06	27	57.5	−04	45	44	5.06	−2.5	B2 V	1100	0.010	270	[29]	25	[.003]	4.8	787	
13 Mon	46300	06	32	54.2	+07	19	58	4.50	−5.2	A0 Ib	2800	0.009	201	13	12	.007	33	9500	
15 Mon ∞	47839	06	40	58.6	+09	53	44	4.66$_v$	(−2.3)	O7 Ve	820	0.007	172	34	33	.004	1.0	673	(d)
17 Mon	49161	06	47	19.8	+08	02	14	4.77	−0.3	K4 III	340	0.031	243	48	47	.013	26	104	
18 Mon	49293	06	47	51.6	+02	24	44	4.47	0.2	K0 III	230	0.025	238	13	11	.017	15	65	
19 Mon	52918	07	02	54.6	−04	14	21	4.99$_v$	−3.5	B1 V	1600	0.016	266	45	25	.002	3.7	1977	
20 Mon	54810	07	10	13.6	−04	14	14	4.92	0.2	K0 III	110	0.214	358	86	79	.030	14	65	
25 Mon	61064	07	37	16.6	−04	06	40	5.13	0.7	F6 III	250	0.074	281	48	46	.028	4.4	41	
27 Mon	65695	07	59	44.1	−03	40	47	4.93	−0.1	K2 III	330	0.059	262	45	−29	.008	19	86	
28 Mon	65953	08	01	13.2	−01	23	33	4.68$_v$	−0.3	K4 III	320	0.096	143	57	27	.009	28	104	
Plaskett's	47129	06	37	24.0	+06	08	07	6.06	*	O8 V	*	0.004	124	*	25	*	*	*	(e)
U Mon	59693	07	30	47.3	−09	46	37	5.82$_v$	−4.5	F8 Ibe	3800	0.024	261	67	35	.002	141	5000	
- Mon	41335	06	04	13.4	−06	42	33	5.21	−2.8	B2 Ve	1300	0.011	248	[32]	25	[.003]	6.2	1038	
- Mon	42690	06	11	51.7	−06	33	02	5.05	−2.5	B2 V	1100	0.012	239	[34]	29	[.003]	2.4	787	
- Mon	46089	06	31	48.2	+11	32	40	5.23	1.9	A3 V	150	0.033	21	16	−3	.010	1.8	14	
- Mon	46487	06	33	37.8	−01	13	13	5.10	−0.9	B5 Vn	520	0.024	202	[31]	25	[.006]	1.5	180	
- Mon	48217	06	41	56.4	−09	10	03	5.19	−0.4	M0 III	110	0.056	139	9	1	.031	31	114	
- Mon	49331	06	47	37.1	−08	59	54	5.07	−2.4	M1 Ib/II	1000	0.022	275	58	24	.002	97	718	
- Mon	52666	07	01	56.3	−05	43	20	5.20	−0.5	M2 III	450	0.021	267	33	3	.003	37	125	

Musca
(Muscae)

a) B:430 l.y, $\mathcal{L}$1200. SC:RV+18. In the same field, 0.5° SE, is R Muscae, a Cepheid variable (5.93–6.73, with a period of 7.5 days).

b) B:470 l.y., $\mathcal{L}$580.

c) SC:RV+14. SW one degree is the globular cluster NGC 4372.

d) In the same field, north one degree, is the bright globular cluster NGC 4833.

e) If the absolute magnitude is estimated at −7.5, then: 13,000 l.y., D_s78, $\mathcal{L}$80,000. The *Sky Catalogue* gives a completely different picture, with a spectral type of O9.8 (and no luminosity class): M+3.0, 105 l.y., D_s0.8, and $\mathcal{L}$5.

f) The cited absolute magnitude may be too dim, for it yields a distance of only 66 l.y. and a parallax of .049″. The range of the luminosity class (II/III) prohibits all but the most general estimations. One can say only that the brightest possible absolute magnitude should be about −3, yielding a distance of 700 l.y. and luminosity of 1250. Most likely, the star is much closer, and therefore considerably less luminous.

MUSCA	HD	R.A.			Declin.			m	M	Spectra	l.y.	μ	Dir.	V	RV	π	D_s	$\mathscr{L}$	Rmk
				2000.0															
α Mus	109668	12^h 37^m	11.0^s	$-$69°	08′	08″	2.69$_v$	$-$2.3	B2 IV	330	0.043″	248°	[24]	13	[.010]″	2.2	655	(a)
β Mus ∞	110879	12 46	16.9	$-$68	06	29	3.05	$-$1.7	B2 V	290	0.040	233	44	42	.015	2.6	377	(b)✏
γ Mus	109026	12 32	28.0	$-$72	07	58	3.87	$-$1.1	B5 V	320	0.049	259	[23]	3	[.010]	5.0	217	(c)
δ Mus	112985	13 02	16.3	$-$71	32	56	3.62	$-$0.1	K2 III	110	0.272	97	57	37	.030	19	86	(d)
ε Mus	106849	12 17	34.2	$-$67	57	38	4.11$_v$	(2.4)	M4 III	71	0.240	263	26	7	.046	8.7	8.4	
ζ^1 Mus	107567	12 22	11.9	$-$68	18	27	5.74	0.2	K0 III	420	0.065	189	[45]	22	[.008]	14	65	
ζ^2 Mus	107566	12 22	07.4	$-$67	31	20	5.15	($-$0.6)	A5 V	470	0.026	239	24	$-$17	.007	4.7	140	
η Mus	114911	13 15	14.9	$-$67	53	41	4.80$_v$	$-$0.2	B8 V	330	0.037	243	[19]	$-$8	[.010]	1.6	95	
θ Mus	113904	13 08	07.0	$-$65	18	22	5.51$_v$	*	B0 Ia	*	0.017	211	*	$-$28	*	*	*	(e)
ι Mus	116244	13 25	07.2	$-$74	53	16	5.05	0.3	K0 III	290	0.169	218	57	28	.016	14	60	
λ Mus	102249	11 45	36.4	$-$66	43	43	3.64	2.1	A7II/III	*	0.102	289	*	16	*	*	*	(f)
μ Mus	102584	11 48	14.4	$-$66	48	53	4.72$_v$	$-$0.5	K4 III	360	0.028	138	38	37	.013	32	125	
GT Mus	101379	11 39	29.5	$-$65	23	52	5.17$_v$	0.3	G2 III+	310	0.039	252	34	14	.006	9.6	60	
- Mus	99104	11 23	21.8	$-$64	57	18	5.11	$-$1.0	B5 V	540	0.010	163	20	19	.010	2.3	198	
- Mus	102839	11 49	56.3	$-$70	13	32	4.97	$-$5.9	G6 Ib	4900	0.021	262	21	18	.009	339	180000	
- Mus	103079	11 51	51.2	$-$65	12	22	4.90	$-$2.0	B4 V	780	0.038	245	[48]	21	[.004]	3.0	497	
- Mus	105340	12 07	49.9	$-$75	22	00	5.18	$-$0.4	K2 II/III	430	0.094	285	50	$-$45	.020	24	114	
- Mus	115211	13 17	13.0	$-$66	47	01	4.87	$-$0.3	K2 Ib/II	350	0.024	210	19	$-$10	.007	28	104	

Norma
(Normae)

a) Between γ^2 and ι^1 (SSW 5° of γ^2) is the attractive open cluster NGC 6067, with more than 100 stars, and 3.5° SE of γ^2 is the large open cluster NGC 6152.

b) SC:m5.3.

c) East 2.5° is the open cluster NGC 6087, which contains S Normae, a Cepheid variable (6.1–6.8, with a period of 9.8 days).

NORMA	HD	R.A.			Declin.			m	M	Spectra	l.y.	μ	Dir.	V	RV	π	D_s	$\mathscr{L}$	Rmk
			2000.0																
γ^1 Nor	146143	16^h 17^m	00.8^s	$-50°$	$04'$	$05''$		4.99	−6.3	F7 Ib	5900	0.006″	211°	32	−17	.001″	200	25000	
γ^2 Nor	146686	16 19	50.3	−50	09	20		4.02	0.3	K0 III	74	0.165	251	34	−29	.044	14	60	(a)
δ Nor	144197	16 06	29.3	−45	10	23		4.72	(2.4)	A1 m	93	0.027	4	16	−16	.035	1.3	8.3	
ε Nor ∞	147971	16 27	11.0	−47	33	18		4.47	−1.7	B2 V	560	0.030	188	[27]	−12	[.006]	3.5	377	
η Nor	143546	16 03	12.7	−49	13	47		4.65	0.3	G8 III	240	0.030	82	7	0	.022	11	60	
θ Nor	145842	16 15	15.2	−47	22	20		5.14	0.0	B8 V	350	0.061	212	[31]	1	[.009]	1.0	79	(b)
ι^1 Nor ∞	143474	16 03	31.9	−57	46	31		4.63	2.1	A7 IV	110	0.146	234	33	−14	.023	1.5	11	(c)
κ Nor	145397	16 13	28.6	−54	37	50		4.94	0.3	G8 III	280	0.027	176	15	−14	.022	13	60	
λ Nor	146667	16 19	17.6	−42	40	26		5.45	1.7	A3 Vn	180	0.020	131	[16]	−15	[.018]	1.7	16	
μ Nor	149038	16 34	04.8	−44	02	43		4.94_v	−6.2	B0 Ia	5500	0.011	243	[90]	9	[.001]	58	25000	
R Nor	138743	15 35	57.5	−49	30	29		6.3_v	−0.5	M3 e	750	0.032	108	—	—	—	3.8	125	

Octans
(Octantis)

a) SC:$RV+60$.

b) The distance (generated from the distance modulus formula) may be too close. The absolute magnitude, if estimated from Fig. 2, would be about $+2$, which yields 88 l.y., $\pi.037$, $D_s1.5$, and $\mathscr{L}13$ which is still rather a large parallax to go undetected.

c) If the absolute magnitude is estimated to be -1, then: 540 l.y., $\pi.006$, $V50$, D_s38, $\mathscr{L}198$.

d) If the absolute magnitude is estimated to be $+2$, then: 160 l.y., $\pi.020$, $V28$, $D_s1.9$, and $\mathscr{L}12$.

e) The parallax gives a much greater distance, at least 300 l.y.

f) If the absolute magnitude is estimated to be 0.0, then: 385 l.y., $\pi.009$, $V22$, $D_s0.9$, and $\mathscr{L}79$.

g) If the absolute magnitude is estimated at -5, then: 4400 l.y., $\pi.0007$, $V102$, D_s200, and $\mathscr{L}8000$.

h) This is the Southern Pole Star, presently (2000) $1°03'$ from true south.
   If the absolute magnitude is estimated to be $+1$, then: 255 l.y., $\pi.013$, $V15$, $D_s2.7$, and $\mathscr{L}31$.

i) This star is erroneously named λ Oct in the *Bright Star Catalogue*.

OCTANS	HD	R.A.		Declin.			m	M	Spectra	l.y.	μ	Dir.	V	RV	π	D_s	$\mathscr{L}$	Rmk
				2000.0														
α Oct	199532	21ʰ 04ᵐ 42.8ˢ		−77° 01′ 26″			5.15	0.7	F6 m pec	250	0.364″	179°	82	45	.025″	4.8	41	(a)
β Oct	214846	22 46 03.3		−81 22 54			4.15	2.6	A9 IV/V	67	0.062	276	[25]	24	[.049]	1.1	7.2	(b)
γ¹ Oct	223647	23 52 06.8		−82 01 08			5.11	0.3	G6/8 III	300	0.042	252	[24]	15	[.011]	11	60	
γ³ Oct	636	00 10 02.3		−82 13 27			5.28	0.3	K1/2 III	320	0.024	235	[19]	15	[.010]	13	60	
δ Oct	124882	14 26 54.8		−83 40 04			4.32	−0.1	K2 III	250	0.100	265	[37]	5	[.013]	21	86	
ε Oct	210967	22 20 01.4		−80 26 23			5.10ᵥ	*	M5 III	*	0.062	129	*	12	*	*	*	(c)
ζ Oct	79837	08 56 41.9		−85 39 47			5.42	*	A8/9 IV	*	0.118	286	*	−4	*	*	*	(d)
θ Oct	224889	00 01 35.8		−77 03 57			4.78	−0.1	K3 III	310	0.178	197	55	24	.017	21	86	
ι Oct	111482	12 54 58.9		−85 07 24			5.46	0.2	K0 III	370	0.072	70	66	53	.009	13	65	
λ Oct ∞	206240	21 50 54.2		−82 43 09			5.29	4.4	G8 III	49	0.072	117	33	−11	.011	1.3	1.4	(e)
ν Oct	205478	21 41 28.6		−77 23 24			3.76	2.3	K0 III	64	0.246	167	41	34	.051	5.0	9.5	
ξ Oct	215573	22 50 22.9		−80 07 27			5.35	*	B5/7 V	*	0.029	125	*	16	*	*	*	(f)
π² Oct	131246	15 04 46.6		−83 02 17			5.65	*	G8 Ib	*	0.016	220	*	−21	*	*	*	(g)
σ Oct	177482	21 08 44.8		−88 57 24			5.47ᵥ	*	F0 III	*	0.026	92	*	12	*	*	*	(h)
τ Oct	219765	23 28 03.9		−87 28 57			5.49	−0.1	K2 III	430	0.022	60	[34]	31	[.008]	21	86	
φ Oct	167468	18 23 36.0		−75 02 39			5.47	0.6	A0 V	310	0.032	9	[15]	5	[.011]	2.4	45	(i)
χ Oct	164461	18 54 44.3		−87 36 21			5.28	−2.3	K3 III	1100	0.140	200	[220]	34	[.003]	57	655	

Ophiuchus
(Ophiuchi)

a) *Ras Alhague* (Head of the Snake-Charmer). Y:π.067. An unseen companion may be present, according to oscillations in the proper motion.

b) *Cebalrai, Cheleb* (Shepherd's Dog). OH:$M+0.1$. NE 1.5° is the very large but sparse open cluster I. 4665, and 3.5° E of β Oph is Barnard's Star (note n).

c) *Yed Prior.*

d) *Yed Posterior.* B:90 l.y., $\mathcal{L}$35.

e) *Han.* B:520 l.y. SSW 2.8° is the globular cluster NGC 6171, also known as M107.

f) *Sabik.* B:$\mathcal{L}$40. A close and difficult binary. In the same field, SW 0.5°, is the Mira-type variable R Oph (7–14, 302 d).

g) B:$\mathcal{L}$1900.

h) OH:$M+0.1$.

i) SE 5.5° is the globular cluster M12 (NGC 6218), and 3° SE of M12 is M10 (NGC 6254), a brighter, more compact globular cluster.

j) North 2.5° between ξ and η, is the small but bright globular cluster M9 (NGC 6333).

k) West 2.5° is the small, bright globular cluster M19 (NGC 6273).

l) SE 5.5° is the large and bright globular cluster M14 (NGC 6402), resolved only in large telescopes.

m) A well-known binary with color contrast (yellow, red?). Both are red dwarfs, whose total luminosity, Burnham notes, is about half that of the Sun.

n) Red dwarf, and the second nearest star (if the α Centauri system is taken in the singular). It has the largest proper motion of any known star. Burnham points out that it takes 351 years for the star to move 1° in the sky. The proper motion is in fact gradually increasing, as the star approaches us. See Burnham for a finder's chart.

o) A short-period eclipsing binary. B:$M-1.9$, D,3.2, $\mathcal{L}$480.

p) A Mira-type variable. B:$M-0.3$, 780 l.y. Burnham has a finder's chart.

OPHIUCHUS	HD	R.A.	Declin.	m	M	Spectra	l.y.	μ	Dir.	V	RV	π	D_s	ℒ	Rmk
		2000.0													
α Oph	159561	17ʰ 34ᵐ 55.9ˢ	+12° 33′ 36″	2.08	0.96†	A5 III	54	0.255″	153°	24	13	.060″	2.8	33	(a)
β Oph	161096	17 43 28.3	+04 34 02	2.77	−0.1	K2 III	99	0.164	345	26	−12	.033	18	86	(b)
γ Oph	161868	17 47 53.5	+02 42 26	3.75	0.6	A0 V	84	0.078	198	12	−7	.039	2.5	45	
δ Oph	146051	16 14 20.6	−03 41 39	2.74	−0.5	M1 III	96	0.153	198	29	−20	.034	34	125	(c)
ε Oph	146791	16 18 19.1	−04 41 33	3.24	0.3	G3 III	76	0.090	64	14	−10	.043	12	60	(d)
ζ Oph	149757	16 37 09.4	−10 34 02	2.56ᵥ	−4.4	O9.5 V	800	0.026	28	44	−15	.003	24	4500	(e)
η Oph ∞	155125	17 10 22.6	−15 43 29	2.43	1.4†	A2 V	67	0.102	22	10	−1	.049	1.8	22	(f)⦶
θ Oph	157056	17 22 00.5	−24 59 58	3.27ᵥ	−3.0	B2 IV	590	0.021	188	[18]	−2	[.006]	2.1	1247	(g)
ι Oph	152614	16 54 00.4	+10 09 55	4.38	−0.6	B8 V	320	0.065	234	24	−21	.029	1.9	137	
κ Oph	153210	16 57 40.0	+09 22 30	3.20ᵥ	−0.1	K2 III	110	0.294	268	72	−56	.031	18	86	(h)
λ Oph ∞	148857	16 30 54.7	+01 59 02	3.82	1.2	A1 V	110	0.081	202	41	−14	.010	1.8	26	(i)⦶
μ Oph	159975	17 37 50.6	−08 07 08	4.62	−0.2	B8 II/IIIp	300	0.028	208	[23]	−19	[.011]	4.2	95	
ν Oph	163917	17 59 01.5	−09 46 25	3.34	0.2	K0 IIIa+	140	0.119	184	30	13	.021	13	65	
ξ Oph ∞	156897	17 21 00.1	−21 06 46	4.39	3.3	F2/3 V	54	0.312	132	26	−9	.060	1.2	3.8	(j)
oᴬ Oph	156349	17 18 00.6	−24 17 13	5.20	0.0	K0 II/III	360	0.054	259	35	−29	.013	16	79	
oᴮ Oph	156350	17 18 00.4	−24 17 03	6.80	(2.4)	F6 IV/V	250	0.073	262	39	−28	.013	2.3	8.9	
ρ Oph ∞	147933	16 25 34.9	−23 26 46	4.59	−2.5	B2 V	850	0.021	172	13	−10	.013	12	787	
σ Oph	157999	17 26 30.8	+04 08 25	4.34	−2.3	K2 II	690	0.005	11	27	−27	.008	71	655	
τᴬ Oph ∞	164765	18 03 04.8	−08 10 50	5.24	3.5†	F0 V	72	0.046	147	40	−40	.045	1.6	7.2	⦶
τᴮ Oph	164764	18 03 04.8	−08 10 50	5.94	4.2†	F5 V	72	0.046	147	38	−38	.045	0.8	1.6	
υ Oph	148367	16 27 48.1	−08 22 18	4.63	(1.9)	A3 m	120	0.077	275	34	−31	.028	1.9	14	
φ Oph	148786	16 31 08.2	−16 36 46	4.28	0.3	G8 III	200	0.065	234	41	−34	.014	11	60	
χ Oph	148184	16 27 01.3	−18 27 23	4.42ᵥ	−2.5	B2 IVpe	790	0.031	201	[36]	−3	[.004]	14	787	
ψ Oph	147700	16 24 06.1	−20 02 15	4.50	0.2	K0 II/III	240	0.057	209	136	0	.002	13	65	
ω Oph	148898	16 32 08.0	−21 27 59	4.45ᵥ	(1.7)	A7 p	120	0.036	21	7	3	.028	1.9	17	
20 Oph	151769	16 49 49.9	−10 46 59	4.65	0.7	F7 IV	200	0.134	136	40	−1	.016	4.6	41	
30 Oph	153687	17 01 03.5	−04 13 21	4.82	−0.3	K4 III	350	0.089	211	29	−7	.015	28	104	
36 Oph ∞	155886	17 15 20.7	−23 36 05	4.31	6.38†	K0 V	17	1.235	204	32	−1	.184	0.6	0.2	(k)⦶
41 Oph	156266	17 16 36.6	−00 26 43	4.73	−0.1	K2 III	300	0.072	200	34	−2	.010	18	86	(l)
44 Oph	157792	17 26 22.1	−24 10 31	4.17	2.6†	A3 m	68	0.116	180	39	−37	.048	1.3	7.2	
45 Oph	157919	17 27 21.2	−29 52 01	4.29	2.1	F5 IV+	89	0.142	171	49	37	.021	2.1	11	
51 Oph	158643	17 31 24.8	−23 57 46	4.81	(2.8)	B9.5 Ve	82	0.028	172	12	−12	.040	0.8	5.9	
58 Oph	160915	17 43 25.7	−21 41 00	4.87	4.2†	F6 V	69	0.106	244	15	11	.047	0.9	1.6	
66 Oph	164284	18 00 15.7	+04 22 07	4.64ᵥ	−2.5	B2 Ve	870	0.013	180	[21]	−13	[.004]	7.0	787	
67 Oph	164353	18 00 38.6	+02 55 53	3.97	−5.7	B5 Ib	2800	0.010	186	24	−4	.002	43	15000	
68 Oph	164577	18 01 45.1	+01 18 19	4.45	1.2	A2 Vn	150	0.017	135	7	6	.021	1.8	26	
70 Oph ∞	165341	18 05 27.2	+02 29 58	4.03	5.67†	K0 V	16.7	1.124	167	28	−7	.195	0.9	0.4	(m)⦶
71 Oph	165760	18 07 18.3	+08 44 02	4.64	1.8	G8 III	120	0.033	16	8	−3	.021	5.9	15	
72 Oph	165777	18 07 20.9	+09 33 50	3.73	1.9	A4 IV	69	0.102	323	26	−24	.047	1.7	14	
74 Oph	168656	18 20 52.0	+03 22 38	4.86	0.3	G8 III	270	0.010	354	6	5	.019	11	60	
Σ2178	158614	17 30 23.7	−01 03 45	5.31	4.58†	G9 IV/V+	63	0.208	215	79	−77	.052	1.2	1.2	
Σ2276 ∞	165475	18 05 43.2	+12 00 14	7.04	1.2	A7 IV	480	0.010	276	14	13	.009	2.6	26	
Barnard's	—	17 57 50.4	+04 38 19	9.54	13.25†	M3.8 V	5.91	10.31	360	140	−108	.552	0.06	0.0004	(n)
U Oph	156247	17 16 31.6	+01 12 38	5.88ᵥ	−1.1	B5 V	810	0.012	194	31	−11	.002	5.7	217	(o)
X Oph	172171	18 38 20.9	+08 50 02	6.4ᵥ	0.0	K1 III	620	0.017	294	71	−71	.011	21	79	(p)
V2105 Oph	148349	16 27 43.4	−07 35 53	5.23ᵥ	−0.5	M2.5 III	460	0.158	176	136	99	.008	38	125	
- Oph	150416	16 41 34.3	−17 44 32	4.96	−2.1	G7.5 II+	69	0.023	260	25	−25	.047	43	545	
- Oph	156681	17 18 36.9	+10 51 53	5.03	−1.3	K4 II/III	600	0.092	178	222	40	.002	47	261	
- Oph	157950	17 26 37.8	−05 05 12	4.54	3.1	F3 V	100	0.106	245	16	0	.032	1.3	4.5	

Orion
(Orionis)

a) *Betelgeuse* (Arm of the Central One). A giant red variable, and a very low-density star. Burnham notes that while over 160 million times the Sun's volume, Betelgeuse has only about 20 solar masses, or a density between 2×10^{-8} and 9×10^{-8} of the Sun's density. OH:$M-7.2$, 1400 l. y. DA:$M-5.7$, 650 l. y.

b) *Rigel* (Left Leg of the Giant). This white supergiant is actually brighter than α Ori. It has a faint, fixed companion (see Visual Binary Section). B:540–900 l. y. OH:$M-8.1$, 1400 l. y.

c) *Bellatrix* (Female Warrior). B:470 l. y., $\mathcal{L}$4000. OH:1400 l. y.

d) *Mintaka* (Belt). An eclipsing binary and multiple system, with B a very faint companion and C an easily seen pale blue companion. The parallax gives a distance of only 230 l. y. If instead we use the same distance as the companion C, then we have: $M-7$, 2300 l. y. (by definition), D_s13, and $\mathcal{L}$50,000. B:1500 l. y., $\mathcal{L}$20,000. OH:$M-5.8$, 1400 l. y., $\mathcal{L}$15,000.

e) *Alnilam* (String of Pearls). B:$M-6.8$, 1600 l. y., $\mathcal{L}$40,000. OH:$M-7.0$.

f) *Alnitak* (The Girdle). A very nice triple; AB are quite close, C is nearly 60″ away. (Burnham questions whether C is part of the system.) For ζ^A Burnham gives: $M-6.6$, 1600 l. y., $\mathcal{L}$35,000. The ζ^A and ζ^B parallaxes are deceptive!

   If we give ζ^B the same distance as the primary, then: $M-3.7$, D_s1.8, and $\mathcal{L}$2500.

   NE 2.3° of ζ is M78, a bright diffuse nebula, actually a portion of the nebulosity that covers much of this constellation. 0.5° south of ζ is the famed "Horsehead Nebula," a dark nebula that is disappointing except in the largest telescopes, under the best conditions. The many photographs of this famous object (as in Burnham) lead the amateur observer to expect the same sight. On an exceptional night one might catch a hint of its splendor.

   Boss shows the proper motion in right ascension at +0.0003″, which would result in a proper motion of 0.0045″ and direction of 117°. Burnham gives a proper motion of 0.005″, which appears to be based on Boss.

g) *Algiebba*. A close and difficult binary. B:940 l. y., $\mathcal{L}$4000. OH:1400 l. y.

h) The most famous multiple star system in the heavens: the Trapezium. The very young stars that make up this quartet are generally considered by authorities to be about 1300–1900 l. y. away, although the distance modulus gives us 3300 l. y.

   The system lies in the Great Orion Nebula (M42 and M43). Much of Orion is covered by a vast shell of ionized hydrogen—the Great Orion Nebula is perhaps the brightest emission nebula in the heavens. See Burnham, p. 1317ff. The bright star at the bottom of the nebula is ι Orionis (note j), and SW of this is Σ 747 (note p).

   The θ^{1A} spectra is from Kholopov: the star is also an Algol-type variable (V1016).

i) Also an attractive binary, often overlooked because of its famous neighbor.

j) *Nair al Saif*. A very attractive triple (white, blue, red). Companion C: m11, PA 103°, 49.7″. OH:1400 l. y.

k) *Saiph* (Sword). SC:$M-2.0$, which is apparently derived from the parallax; the resulting values contradict the supergiant status of the star: 210 l. y., D_s1, and $\mathcal{L}$500. We have taken the absolute magnitude instead from the OH.

l) *Meissa*. OH:$M-5.8$, 2200 l. y., luminosity class III.

m) If the absolute magnitude is estimated at +0.5, then: 220 l. y., π.015, V46, D_s2.9, $\mathcal{L}$50.

n) Spectacular multiple system, with five visible components (see Visual Binary section).

o) If the absolute magnitude is estimated to be +1, then: 225 l. y., π.015, V12, D_s2.5, $\mathcal{L}$31.

ORION	HD	2000.0 R.A.	Declin.	m	M	Spectra	l.y.	μ	Dir.	V	RV	π	D_s	ℒ	Rmk
α Ori	39801	05ʰ 55ᵐ 10.3ˢ	+07° 24′ 25″	0.50ᵥ	−5.6	MI Iab	540	0.027″	68°	33	21	.005″	800	13500	(a)
β Ori ∞	34085	05 14 32.2	−08 12 06	0.12	−7.1	B8 Iac	910	0.004	236	21	21	.013	58	55000	(b)
γ Ori	35468	05 25 07.8	+06 20 59	1.64	−3.6	B2 III	360	0.018	221	18	18	.029	2.7	2168	(c)
δᴬ Ori ∞	36486	05 32 00.3	−00 17 57	2.23ᵥ	*	B0 III	*	0.003	252	16	16	.014	*	*	(d)
δᶜ Ori	36485	05 32 00.4	−00 17 04	6.85	−2.5	B2 V	2400	0.005	127	21	21	.014	6.6	787	
ε Ori	37128	05 36 12.7	−01 12 07	1.70ᵥ	−6.2	B0 Iae	1200	0.004	236	27	26	.002	16	25000	(e)
ζᴬ Ori ∞	37742	05 40 45.5	−01 56 34	2.05	−5.9	O9.5 Ib	1300	0.002	207	18	18	.024	9.3	18000	(f)⬚
ζᴮ Ori	37743	05 40 45.5	−01 56 34	4.21	−3.7	B0 III	1300	0.002	207	13	13	.024	1.8	2500	
η Ori ∞	35411	05 24 28.6	−02 23 49	3.36ᵥ	−3.5	B1 V	770	0.003	288	20	20	.007	7.6	1977	(g)
θ¹ᴬ Ori ∞	37020	05 34 15.8	−05 23 14	6.73ᵥ	(−3.3)	B0.5 V	1600	0.002	333	34	32	.001	14	1600	(h)
θ¹ᴮ Ori	37021	05 35 16.0	−05 23 07	7.96	(−2.0)	B0 V	1600	0.002	333	26	24	.001	10	515	
θ¹ᶜ Ori	37022	05 35 16.4	−05 23 23	5.13	(−4.9)	O6	1600	0.002	333	35	33	.001	29	6982	
θ¹ᴰ Ori	37023	05 35 17.2	−05 23 16	6.70	(−3.3)	B0.5 Vp	1600	0.002	333	33	31	.001	17	1644	
θ²ᴬ Ori	37041	05 35 22.8	−05 24 58	5.08	−4.4	O9.5 Vep	2600	0.006	321	47	36	.001	10	4500	(i)
ι Ori ∞	37043	05 35 25.9	−05 54 36	2.77	−6.0	O9 III	1900	0.004	284	22	22	.025	6.0	20000	(j)
κ Ori	38771	05 47 45.3	−09 40 11	2.06	−7.0	B0.5 Ia	2100	0.006	211	21	21	.015	38.2	50000	(k)
λᴬ Ori ∞	36861	05 35 08.2	+09 56 03	3.66	(−2.2)	O8 e	470	0.005	191	34	34	.007	3.1	552	(l)
λᴮ Ori	36862	05 35 08.4	+09 56 06	5.56	(−0.2)	B0.5 V	470	0.005	191	36	36	.007	0.1	96	
μ Ori	40932	06 02 23.0	+09 38 51	4.12	1.4	A2 V	120	0.031	155	45	45	.028	2.4	23	
ν Ori	41753	06 07 34.3	+14 46 06	4.42	−1.7	B3 V	100	0.023	165	24	24	.032	3.3	377	
ξ Ori	42560	06 11 56.4	+14 12 31	4.48	−1.7	B3 IV	560	0.021	172	103	24	.001	2.6	377	
o¹ Ori	30959	04 52 31.9	+14 15 02	4.74ᵥ	−2.2	S3.5	820	0.057	181	68	−8	.004	94	625	
π¹ Ori	31295	04 54 53.7	+10 09 03	4.65	*	A0 V	*	0.137	161	*	13	*	*	*	(m)
π² Ori	30739	04 50 36.7	+08 54 01	4.36	0.6	A1 Vn	91	0.030	178	24	24	.036	2.3	45	
π³ Ori	30652	04 49 50.3	+06 57 41	3.19	3.8	F6 V	24	0.463	88	29	24	.137	1.1	2.4	
π⁴ Ori	30836	04 51 12.3	+05 36 18	3.69	−3.6	B2 III	940	0.004	284	30	23	.001	8.0	2168	
π⁵ Ori	31237	04 54 15.0	+02 26 26	3.72ᵥ	−3.6	B8 III	950	0.004	270	24	23	.003	6.1	2168	
π⁶ Ori	31767	04 58 32.8	+01 42 51	4.47	−2.2	K2 II	700	0.006	252	14	14	.018	62	597	
ρ Ori ∞	33856	05 13 17.4	+02 51 40	4.46	−0.2	K3 III	280	0.006	211	41	41	.010	20	95	
σᴬ Ori ∞	37468	05 38 44.7	−02 36 00	3.81	−4.4	O9.5 V	1400	0.003	288	29	29	.003	2.9	4500	(n)
σᴱ Ori ∞	37479	05 38 47.0	−02 35 39	6.65	−2.5	B2 Vp	2200	0.025	299	34	29	.007	2.9	787	
τ Ori	34503	05 17 36.3	−06 50 40	3.60	−2.2	B5 III	470	0.022	249	27	20	.006	3.3	597	
υ Ori	36512	05 31 55.8	−07 18 06	4.62	−4.1	B0 V	1800	0.009	229	30	17	.002	1.9	3436	
φ¹ Ori	36822	05 34 49.2	+09 29 22	4.41	−4.6	B0 III	2100	0.003	180	[34]	33	[.002]	17	5500	
φ² Ori	37160	05 36 54.3	+09 17 26	4.09	0.2	K0 IIIb	110	0.317	164	111	99	.030	12	65	
χ¹ Ori	39587	05 54 22.9	+20 16 34	4.41	4.43†	G0 V	32	0.206	245	17	−14	.101	1.0	1.3	
χ² Ori	41117	06 03 55.2	+20 08 18	4.63	−6.8	B2 Iave	6300	0.008	157	17	17	.025	99	40000	
ψ¹ Ori	35439	05 24 44.8	+01 50 47	4.95	−3.5	B1 Vp	1600	0.004	270	21	19	.002	3.7	1977	
ψ² Ori	35715	05 26 50.2	+03 05 44	4.59	−3.0	B2 IV	1100	0.003	198	12	12	.016	2.5	1247	
ω Ori	37490	05 39 11.1	+04 07 17	4.57ᵥ	−2.9	B3 IIIe	1000	0.006	279	24	22	.003	4.5	1138	
6 Ori	31283	04 54 46.8	+11 25 34	5.19	*	A3 V	*	0.026	324	*	9	*	*	*	(o)
9 Ori	31421	04 56 22.2	+13 30 52	4.07	−0.1	K2 III	220	0.087	238	22	1	.019	18	86	
11 Ori	32549	05 04 34.1	+15 24 14	4.68ᵥ	(1.0)	A0 pSi	180	0.038	155	20	17	.018	1.1	33	
15 Ori	33276	05 09 41.9	+15 35 50	4.82	1.9	F2 IV	130	0.013	176	34	30	.004	2.0	14	
22 Ori	35039	05 21 45.7	−00 22 57	4.73	−3.0	B2 IV/V	1100	0.004	256	[30]	29	[.003]	6.1	1247	

(Continued)

p) Just SW of ι Orionis, near the edge of the Great Orion Nebula. This is a fine fixed binary of two bright stars.

q) If the absolute magnitude is estimated at -1, then: 620 l.y., π.005, $V25$, D_s22, $\mathcal{L}198$. B:$M-1.3$, 800–900 l.y., $\mathcal{L}250$.

ORION (CONT.)	HD	2000.0 R.A.	Declin.	m	M	Spectra	l.y.	μ	Dir.	V	RV	π	D_s	$\mathscr{L}$	Rmk
23 Ori	35149	05^h 22^m 49.9^s	+03° 32' 40"	5.00	−3.5	B1 V	1600	0.007"	262°	[25]	18	[.002]"	15	1977	
27 Ori	35410	05 24 28.9	−00 53 29	5.08	0.2	G9 III	310	0.133	356	36	20	.021	12	65	
29 Ori	35369	05 23 56.8	−07 48 29	4.14	0.3	G8 III	190	0.049	206	28	−18	.011	12	60	
31 Ori	36167	05 29 43.9	−01 05 32	4.71	−0.3	K5 III	330	0.022	180	19	8	.006	30	104	
32 Ori	36267	05 30 47.0	+05 56 53	4.20	−1.6	B5 V	470	0.034	165	38	19	.005	2.1	344	
42 Ori	37018	05 35 23.1	−04 50 18	4.59	−3.6	B1 V	1400	0.001	270	30	30	.006	4.8	2168	
49 Ori	37507	05 38 53.0	−07 12 47	4.80	1.0	A4 V	78	0.057	198	7	−1	.042	2.6	31	
51 Ori	37984	05 42 28.6	+01 28 29	4.91	0.0	K1 III	310	0.059	256	90	88	.015	18	79	
56 Ori	39400	05 52 26.4	+01 51 19	4.78	−2.2	K1.5 IIb	810	0.011	232	15	10	.005	60	597	
60 Ori	40446	05 58 49.5	+00 33 11	5.22	(−1.8)	A1 V	820	0.015	274	39	35	.004	6.9	402	
64 Ori	41040	06 03 27.3	+19 41 26	5.14	−1.2	B8 III	600	0.018	180	[20]	12	[.005]	2.1	238	
69 Ori	42545	06 12 03.3	+16 07 50	4.95	−1.1	B5 Vn	530	0.017	149	[26]	22	[.006]	1.6	217	
71 Ori	43042	06 14 50.8	+19 09 23	5.20	3.7	F6 V	80	0.213	207	44	36	.041	1.1	2.6	
74 Ori	43386	06 16 26.6	+12 16 20	5.04	2.8	F5 IV/V	80	0.202	24	25	9	.041	1.6	6.0	
77 Ori	45416	06 27 13.7	+00 17 57	5.20	−2.2	K1 II	990	0.009	162	34	33	.005	49	597	
Σ747A ∞	36960	05 35 02.6	−06 00 07	4.78	−4.1	B0.5 V	1900	0.002	333	28	28	.005	2.2	3436	(p)
Σ747B	36959	05 35 00.8	−06 00 34	5.67	−3.5	B1 V	2200	0.016	270	34	30	.005	2.2	1977	
U Ori	39816	05 55 49.2	+20 10 30	5.4$_v$	*	M6.5 III	*	0.015	176	*	−21	*	*	*	(q)
- Ori	33554	05 11 41.5	+16 02 44	5.18	−0.3	K5 III	410	0.012	48	[9]	−6	[.008]	28	104	
- Ori	37756	05 40 50.6	−01 07 44	4.95	−3.0	B2 IV/V	1300	0.017	249	[41]	26	[.003]	2.5	1247	
- Ori	40657	06 00 03.3	−03 04 27	4.53	−0.1	K2 III	280	0.071	177	30	26	.022	19	86	
- Ori	44131	06 19 59.5	−02 56 40	4.90	−0.5	M1 III	400	0.018	279	98	47	.001	34	125	

Pavo
(Pavonis)

a) *Peacock Star.* B:310 l.y., $\mathscr{L}$1200. OH:M−1.6, 150 l.y. WSW 10° is the splendid globular cluster NGC 6752.

b) B:160 l.y., $\mathscr{L}$90. OH:M+1.5.

c) Classified a supergiant by Yale, but subgiant (V) by the *Sky Catalogue.* The cited values for absolute magnitude, distance, size, and luminosity derive from the Yale classification. If classified V, and M+3.4 (as given by SC), then: D_s2 and $\mathscr{L}$3. However the distance modulus formula gives a subsequent distance of only 56.6 l.y., much too close for the parallax.

d) SC:RV+20.

PAVO	HD	2000.0			m	M	Spectra	l.y.	μ	Dir.	V	RV	π	D_s	$\mathscr{L}$	Rmk
		R.A.		Declin.												
α Pav	193924	$20^h\ 25^m\ 38.8^s$	$-56°\ 44'\ 07''$		1.94	−2.3	B2.5	230	0.086″	169°	[29]	2	[.014]″	2.2	655	(a)
β Pav	197051	20 44 57.4	−66 12 11		3.42	1.2	A7 III	93	0.041	295	11	10	.035	2.5	26	(b)
γ Pav	203608	21 26 26.7	−65 21 59		4.22	4.53†	F7 V	28	0.803	7	44	−30	.116	0.8	1.2	
δ Pav	190248	20 08 43.2	−66 10 56		3.56	4.76†	G7 IV	19	1.654	134	50	−22	.175	1.2	1.0	
ε Pav	188228	20 00 35.4	−72 54 38		3.96	0.6	A0 V	150	0.155	148	46	−2	.016	1.7	45	
ζ Pav	171759	18 43 02.1	−71 25 42		4.01	−0.1	K0 III	93	0.158	177	27	−16	.035	18	86	
η Pav	160635	17 45 43.9	−64 43 26		3.62	0.0	K2 II	170	0.052	183	13	−8	.025	18	79	
ι Pav	165499	18 10 26.1	−62 00 08		5.49	4.1†	G0 V	63	0.238	341	37	30	.052	1.2	1.8	
κ Pav	174694	18 56 57.0	−67 14 01		4.44_v	(−3.5)	G5 Iab	1300	0.013	360	38	38	.010	48	1977	(c)
λ Pav	173948	18 52 12.9	−62 11 16		4.22_v	−3.5	B2 IIe	1100	0.018	180	[31]	9	[.003]	4.9	1977	(d)
$μ^2$ Pav	188887	20 01 52.3	−66 56 39		5.31	0.2	K2 IV+	340	0.082	152	45	42	.025	17	65	
ν Pav	169978	18 31 22.3	−62 16 42		4.64	−1.2	B7/8 III	480	0.043	175	[66]	59	[.007]	2.1	238	
ξ Pav	168339	18 23 13.5	−61 29 38		4.36	−0.5	K4 III	310	0.006	45	12	12	.016	31	125	
o Pav	201371	21 13 20.4	−70 07 36		5.02	−0.5	M1/2 III	410	0.052	121	36	−19	.008	34	125	
π Pav	165040	18 08 34.7	−63 40 06		4.35	(2.1)	A7 pSr	91	0.186	174	29	−16	.036	1.4	11	
ρ Pav	195961	20 37 35.2	−61 31 48		4.88_v	3.4	F5+	64	0.088	137	140	8	.003	1.2	3.4	
σ Pav	197635	20 49 18.0	−68 46 36		5.41	0.2	K0 III	360	0.084	232	[48]	19	[.009]	15	65	
υ Pav	196519	20 41 57.1	−66 45 39		5.15	−0.2	B9 III	380	0.030	143	[18]	7	[.009]	1.9	95	
$φ^1$ Pav	195627	20 35 34.7	−60 34 54		4.76	(1.8)	F1 III	130	0.194	158	41	−20	.026	1.9	15	
$φ^2$ Pav	196378	20 40 02.4	−60 32 56		5.12	3.7†	F8 V	62	0.647	151	66	−32	.053	1.3	2.6	
ω Pav	175329	18 58 36.3	−60 12 02		5.14	(1.5)	K2 III+	170	0.126	286	183	180	.019	11	19	
NU Pav	189124	20 01 44.5	−59 22 34		5.13	−0.5	M6 III	440	0.033	151	33	−10	.005	32	125	
- Pav	172555	18 45 26.6	−64 52 17		4.79	2.4	A5 IV/V	93	0.158	172	21	2	.035	1.2	8.6	

Pegasus
(Pegasi)

a) *Markab* (Saddle). The SW corner of the Great Square of Pegasus. B:$M-0.1$, 110 l.y., $\mathcal{L}$95. OH:$M+0.7$, 74 l.y., Spec A0 III/IV. South three degrees is the spiral galaxy NGC 7479.

b) *Scheat* (Upper Arm). An irregular variable which forms the NW corner of the Great Square. B:210 l.y., $\mathcal{L}$240–500, and a maximum size of 160 Suns. OH:$M-2.0$.

c) *Algenib* (The Side or The Wing). A β CMa variable; forms the SE corner of the Great Square. B:$M-3.4$, 570 l.y., $\mathcal{L}$1900.

d) *Enif* (The Nose). OH: 470 l.y. NW 4° is the compact globular cluster M15 (NGC 7078).

e) *Homam* (Lucky Star of the Hero). B:210 l.y., $\mathcal{L}$145.

f) *Matar* (Fortunate Rain). B:$M-2.2$, 360 l.y., $\mathcal{L}$630. OH:$M-2.1$, 330 l.y.
   NNW 4.5° is NGC 7331, a fairly bright spiral galaxy.

g) *Baham*. OH:82 l.y.

h) A very close binary and extremely difficult to resolve. B:$M+2.7$.

i) B: $\mathcal{L}$30. OH:140 l.y.

j) B:$M+2.0$, 165 l.y., $\mathcal{L}$10.

k) A close, rapid, and very difficult binary. There are two orbital possibilities. At 2000.0 the companion will be either exactly due south of the primary or slightly west of this point (184°): see the Orbital Elements Section and the drawn orbits.

PEGASUS	HD	R.A.		Declin.		m	M	Spectra	l.y.	μ	Dir.	V	RV	π	D_s	$\mathcal{L}$	Rmk
					2000.0												
α Peg	218045	$23^h 04^m 45.6^s$		+15° 12′	19″	2.49	0.2	B9 V	86	0.073″	122°	10	−4	.038″	1.9	65	(a)
β Peg	217906	23 03 46.4		+28 04	58	2.42$_v$	−1.4	M2 II/III	190	0.236	53	52	9	.022	55	286	(b)
γ Peg	886	00 13 14.1		+15 11	01	2.83$_v$	−3.0	B2 IV	480	0.008	157	18	4	.002	1.8	1247	(c)
ε Peg	206778	21 44 11.0		+09 52	30	2.38$_v$	−4.4	K2 Ib	740	0.030	81	25	5	.006	193	4500	(d)
ζ Peg	214923	22 41 27.6		+10 49	53	3.40	0.0	B8.5 V	160	0.080	96	18	7	.023	1.4	79	(e)
η Peg	215182	22 43 00.1		+30 13	17	2.94	−0.9	G2 II/III	190	0.025	148	8	4	.017	18	180	(f)
θ Peg	210418	22 10 11.9		+06 11	52	3.53	1.4	A2 V	67	0.277	83	27	−6	.049	1.9	22	(g)
ι Peg	210027	22 07 00.6		+25 20	42	3.76	3.14†	F5 V	44	0.300	85	19	−4	.075	1.4	4.4	
κ Peg ∞	206901	21 44 38.5		+25 38	42	4.13	2.1	F5 IV	93	0.037	66	9	−8	.035	2.3	11	(h)
λ Peg	215665	22 46 31.8		+23 33	56	3.95	−0.9	G8 III	78	0.058	96	8	−4	.042	24	180	
μ Peg	216131	22 50 00.1		+24 36	06	3.48	0.2	G8 III	81	0.152	104	23	14	.040	12	65	(i)
ν Peg	209747	22 05 40.7		+05 03	31	4.84	−0.3	K4 III	350	0.151	46	54	−16	.014	27	104	
ξ Peg	215648	22 46 41.5		+12 10	22	4.19	2.6†	F6 III/IV	68	0.545	155	54	−5	.048	2.0	7.2	
o Peg	214994	22 41 45.3		+29 18	27	4.79	1.2	A1 IV	170	0.023	193	10	9	.024	1.5	26	
π² Peg	210459	22 09 59.1		+33 10	42	4.29	−0.6	F5 II/III	310	0.023	221	15	2	.007	8.3	137	
ρ Peg	216735	22 55 13.6		+08 48	58	4.90	1.2	A1 V	180	0.079	76	63	−10	.006	1.7	26	
σ Peg	216385	22 52 24.0		+09 50	09	5.16	2.3	F7 IV	76	0.524	85	59	12	.043	2.3	9.5	
τ Peg	220061	23 20 38.2		+23 44	25	4.60$_v$	1.2	A5 V	88	0.033	93	17	16	.037	2.6	26	
υ Peg	220657	23 25 22.7		+23 24	15	4.40	2.4	F8 III	91	0.198	77	28	−11	.036	2.7	8.6	
φ Peg	223768	23 52 29.2		+19 07	13	5.08	−0.5	M2.5 IIIb	430	0.030	188	15	−8	.011	34	125	
χ Peg	1013	00 14 36.1		+20 12	24	4.80	−0.5	M2+III	370	0.094	87	55	−46	.015	33	125	
ψ Peg	224427	23 57 45.5		+25 08	29	4.66	−0.5	M3 III	350	0.043	231	41	−4	.005	34	125	
1 Peg	203504	21 22 05.1		+19 48	16	4.08	0.0	K1 III	210	0.124	58	87	−76	.014	16	79	
2 Peg	204724	21 29 56.8		+23 38	20	4.57	−0.5	M1 III	340	0.024	73	21	−19	.013	35	125	
9 Peg	206859	21 44 30.6		+17 21	00	4.34	−4.5	G5 Ib	1900	0.015	132	24	−22	.008	139	4966	
14 Peg	207650	21 49 50.6		+30 10	27	5.04	0.6	A1 V	250	0.029	145	33	−23	.006	1.7	45	
16 Peg	208057	21 53 03.7		+25 55	31	5.08	−1.7	B3 Ve	740	0.008	76	18	−12	.003	3.3	377	
31 Peg	212076	22 21 31.0		+12 12	19	5.01	−2.5	B2 IV/Ve	1000	0.015	37	[25]	10	[.003]	3.3	787	
32 Peg	212097	22 21 19.2		+28 19	50	4.81	−0.2	B9 III	330	0.018	68	9	8	.023	3.3	95	
35 Peg	212943	22 27 51.5		+04 41	44	4.79	0.2	K0 III	270	0.317	165	81	54	.025	14	65	
37 Peg ∞	213235	22 29 57.9		+04 25	54	5.48	0.7	F2 V	100	0.141	190	21	1	.032	3.9	41	(j)𝒪
55 Peg	218329	23 07 00.2		+09 24	34	4.52	−0.5	M1 IIIab	330	0.013	138	6	−5	.016	33	125	
56 Peg	218356	23 07 06.6		+25 28	06	4.76	−2.1	G8 Ib	770	0.026	189	34	−27	.006	55	545	
57 Peg	218634	23 09 31.4		+08 40	38	5.12$_v$	(−0.7)	M4 III+	470	0.009	21	15	14	.007	32	144	
59 Peg	218918	23 11 44.1		+08 43	12	5.16	1.4	A5 Vn	180	0.007	270	10	10	.029	2.1	22	
66 Peg	220363	23 23 04.5		+12 18	50	5.08	−0.2	K3 III	370	0.029	115	136	−4	.001	22	95	
70 Peg	221115	23 29 09.2		+12 45	38	4.55	0.3	G7 III	230	0.072	62	26	−15	.016	12	60	
72 Peg	221673	23 33 57.1		+31 19	32	4.98	−0.3	K4 IIIb	370	0.052	102	28	−24	.018	25	104	
77 Peg	222764	23 43 22.3		+10 19	54	5.06	(0.1)	M2 III	330	0.018	19	35	−34	.010	28	74	
78 Peg	222842	23 43 59.4		+29 21	42	4.93	0.2	K0 III	290	0.078	114	22	−7	.018	12	65	
85 Peg ∞	224930	00 02 10.1		+27 04	56	5.75	5.38†	G2 V	39	1.295	140	81	−36	.084	0.8	0.6	(k)𝒪

Perseus
(Persei)

a) *Mirfak* (Elbow) or *Algenib* (The Side). In a rich star field—actually a widely dispersed open cluster, as pointed out by Burnham, but unnamed and not recognized as such on atlases. δ and ε are also members of this cluster. B:570 l.y., $\mathscr{L}$4000.

b) *Algol* (Demon). Famous prototype of an eclipsing variable class (see Variable Section). The variable of this star may have been known in antiquity, if its name is any indication. OH:M+0.1.

c) B:M−0.4, $\mathscr{L}$100.

d) B:M−3.3, 590 l.y., $\mathscr{L}$1700.

e) A rather difficult pair to resolve; color contrast (yellow?/bluish). The star has recently been determined to be a variable [IBVS #3058, 1987]. B:M−3.7, 680 l.y., $\mathscr{L}$2500.

f) B:M−4.7, 1000 l.y., $\mathscr{L}$6300.

g) An easily resolved double, with color contrast (yellow, blue). Slightly over 4° NW is the outstanding pair of open clusters, the Double Cluster (NGC 869, NGC 884). See Burnham, pp. 1438–47.

h) SC:M+3.8. South 7° is the bright open cluster M34. At its center is h1123, an easily resolved fixed binary (8.5, 8.5; PA 248°, 20″).

i) NE 2° is the large bright open cluster NGC 1528, and SSE 1° is the smaller cluster NGC 1513. Due east 2° from λ Per is the bright variable b^1 Per (see note s).

j) *Menkib*. The spectra come from Kholopov. Y: spec. O 7e. Neither Yale nor Kholopov indicates the type of variable this star may be.

k) A semiregular variable. B:M−1.0, 260–300 l.y. OH:M−2.6, 500 l.y.

l) A recently-established Algol-type eclipsing variable [IBVS #3058].

m) NNW 1° is the unusually shaped planetary nebula M76, quite faint.

n) If the absolute magnitude is estimated to be −1, then: 360 l.y., π.009, V18, D_s2.7, $\mathscr{L}$198.

o) A very nice fixed binary, which forms the lower point of a triangle with γ and τ.

p) If the absolute magnitude is estimated to be 0.0, then: 725 l.y., π.005, V25, D_s3, and $\mathscr{L}$80.

q) If the absolute magnitude is estimated to be −4, then: 2030 l.y., π.002, V32, D_s17, and $\mathscr{L}$150.

r) SC:M+7.0.

s) If the absolute magnitude is estimated to be +1, then: 170 l.y., π.019, V27, D_s2.1, and $\mathscr{L}$31.

t) If the absolute magnitude is estimated to be −1, then: 1900 l.y., π.002, V83, D_s43, $\mathscr{L}$198.

u) A semiregular variable in a remarkable field, just north of the Double Cluster. This red supergiant is thought to grow to about 1000 Sun diameters. The spectra come from Kholopov and the *RV* from *B&P*.

   If the absolute magnitude is estimated to be −7, then: 23,000 l.y., π.0001, V673, D_s800, and $\mathscr{L}$50,000.

   Other semiregular supergiants in the region are T, RS, SU, and YZ Persei.

PERSEUS	HD	R.A.			Declin.			m	M	Spectra	l.y.	μ	Dir.	V	RV	π	D_s	$\mathscr{L}$	Rmk
			2000.0																
α Per	20902	03ʰ 24ᵐ	19.3ˢ	+49° 51′	41″			1.79	−4.6	F5 Ib	620	0.033″	131°	10	−2	.016″	54	5500	(a)
β Per	19356	03 08	10.1	+40 57	21			2.12$_v$	−0.2	B8 V	72	0.004	56	4	4	.045	2.0	95	(b)
γ Per	18925	03 04	47.7	+53 30	23			2.93	0.3	G8 III	110	0.002	180	3	3	.016	8.2	60	(c)
δ Per	22928	03 42	55.4	+47 47	15			3.01$_v$	−2.2	B5 III	360	0.043	139	13	4	.016	2.9	597	(d)
ε Per ∞	24760	03 57	51.2	+40 00	37			2.89$_v$	(−2.3)	B0.5 V	360	0.029	145	16	1	.009	3.4	678	(e)
ζ Per ∞	24398	03 54	07.9	+31 53	01			2.85	−5.7	B1 Ib	1700	0.011	146	21	20	.010	55	15000	(f)
η Per ∞	17506	02 50	41.8	+55 53	44			3.76	−4.4	M3 Ib	1400	0.022	120	17	−1	.006	221	4500	(g)
θ Per	16895	02 44	11.9	+49 13	43			4.12	3.62†	F8 V	41	0.346	104	32	25	.079	1.3	2.8	(h)
ι Per	19373	03 09	04.0	+49 36	48			4.05	3.72†	G0 V	38	1.266	94	86	50	.086	1.4	2.6	
κ Per	19476	03 09	29.7	+44 51	27			3.80	0.2	K0 III	99	0.235	131	44	29	.033	13	65	
λ Per	25642	04 06	35.0	+50 21	05			4.29	0.2	A0 IVn	210	0.037	202	[13]	6	[.015]	2.8	65	(i)
μ Per	26630	04 14	53.8	+48 24	34			4.14	−4.5	G0 Ib	1700	0.017	159	9	8	.017	107	5000	
ν Per	23230	03 45	11.6	+42 34	43			3.77	−2.0	F5 II	470	0.013	270	13	−13	.020	15	497	
ξ Per	24912	03 58	57.8	+35 47	28			4.04$_v$	(−2.9)	O7.5 III	820	0.004	76	70	70	.004	12	1191	(j)
o Per	23180	03 44	19.1	+32 17	18			3.83$_v$	−4.4	B1 III	1400	0.012	138	19	19	.023	25	4500	
π Per	18411	02 58	45.6	+39 39	46			4.70	1.4	A2 Vn	150	0.047	142	28	14	.009	1.8	22	
ρ Per	19058	03 05	10.5	+38 50	25			3.39$_v$	−0.5	M4 III	200	0.165	128	77	28	.011	40	125	(k)
σ Per	21552	03 30	34.4	+47 59	43			4.36	−0.2	K3 III	270	0.023	10	32	16	.004	23	95	
τ Per	17878	02 54	15.4	+52 45	45			3.95$_v$	0.3	G4 III	180	0.001	180	2	2	.019	8.8	60	(l)
φ Per	10516	01 43	39.6	+50 41	20			4.07$_v$	−3.9	B2 Vep	1300	0.028	113	5	1	.025	12	2858	(m)
ψ Per	22192	03 36	29.3	+48 11	34			4.23$_v$	*	B5 Ve	*	0.034	133	*	−1	*	*	*	(n)
ω Per	19656	03 11	17.3	+39 36	42			4.63	0.0	K1 III	280	0.024	289	9	7	.023	16	79	
4 Per	12303	02 02	18.0	+54 29	16			5.04	−0.2	B8 III	360	0.035	85	[19]	−2	[.009]	1.6	95	
9 Per	14489	02 22	21.3	+55 50	45			5.17	−7.5	A2 Ia	11000	0.004	346	68	−15	.000	167	80000	
12 Per	16739	02 42	14.9	+40 11	38			4.91	4.2	F9 V	68	0.185	185	29	−23	.048	1.1	1.6	
16 Per	17584	02 50	34.9	+38 19	07			4.23	0.6	F2 III	170	0.216	119	45	14	.024	3.8	45	
17 Per	17709	02 51	30.8	+35 03	35			4.53	−0.3	K7 III	300	0.064	166	77	14	.004	30	104	
21 Per	18296	02 57	17.2	+31 56	03			5.11$_v$	(−2.5)	B9pSi	1100	0.029	182	47	8	.003	8.5	790	
24 Per	18449	02 59	03.6	+35 10	59			4.93	−0.1	K2 III	330	0.049	282	[43]	−36	[.010]	20	86	
29 Per	20365	03 18	37.7	+50 13	20			5.15	−1.7	B3 V	760	0.038	127	[42]	−4	[.004]	3.8	377	
31 Per	20418	03 19	07.6	+50 05	42			5.03	−1.1	B5 V	550	0.032	134	[26]	3	[.006]	2.9	217	
32 Per	20677	03 21	26.5	+43 19	47			4.95	1.4	A3 V	170	0.059	271	13	−7	.026	1.7	22	
34 Per	21428	03 29	22.0	+49 30	32			4.67	−2.3	B3 V	810	0.035	133	10	−2	.018	3.9	655	
42 Per	23848	03 49	32.6	+33 05	29			5.11$_v$	1.4	A3 V	180	0.029	272	48	−14	.003	1.8	22	
48 Per	25940	04 08	39.6	+47 42	45			4.04$_v$	−1.7	B3 Ve	460	0.035	143	8	1	.020	4.9	377	
52 Per	26673	04 14	53.3	+40 29	02			4.71	−4.5	G5 Ib	2300	0.027	149	32	−2	.004	115	5000	
53 Per	27396	04 21	33.1	+46 29	56			4.85$_v$	−1.7	B4 IV	670	0.041	151	[40]	1	[.005]	4.9	377	
54 Per	27348	04 20	24.6	+34 34	00			4.93	0.3	G8 III	280	0.024	263	[29]	−27	[.012]	12	60	
58 Per	29094	04 36	41.3	+41 15	53			4.25	−2.1	K4 III	610	0.022	223	8	5	.016	49	545	
Σ331A ∞	18537	03 00	52.1	+52 21	06			5.28	−1.0	B7 V	590	0.037	128	[32]	−5	[.006]	3.0	198	(o)
Σ331B	18538	03 00	53.3	+52 21	08			6.74	*	B9 V	*	0.023	140	*	−2	*	*	*	(p)
Σ431 ∞	22951	03 42	22.5	+33 57	54			4.97	*	B0.5 V	*	0.009	216	*	20	*	*	*	(q)
Σ552 ∞	28503	04 31	24.0	+40 00	37			6.26	0.0	B8 V	580	0.014	205	[17]	−12	[.006]	3.3	79	(r)
b¹ Per	26961	04 18	14.6	+50 17	44			4.61$_v$	*	A2 V	*	0.071	137	*	20	*	*	*	(s)
k Per	18970	03 05	32.4	+56 42	21			4.76	−0.9	G9.5 III	440	0.079	348	87	−45	.005	22	180	
R Per	21567	03 30	03.2	+35 40	17			7.80$_v$	*	M5 III	*	0.009	148	*	−79	*	*	*	(t)
S Per	14528	02 22	51.7	+58 35	13			7.21$_v$	*	M3 Iae	*	0.020	42	—	−37	—	*	*	(u)
X Per	24534	03 55	22.9	+31 02	45			6.10$_v$	(−2.4)	O9.5 ep	1600	0.014	249	36	15	.002	13	714	
- Per	20123	03 16	12.1	+50 56	16			5.03	−2.1	G6Ib/IIa	870	0.015	208	7	2	.010	45	545	
- Per	20468	03 18	43.7	+34 13	21			4.82	−2.2	K2 III+	830	0.010	174	4	2	.012	67	597	
- Per	21278	03 28	03.0	+49 03	46			4.98	−1.7	B5 V	710	0.035	135	[36]	2	[.005]	3.0	377	

Phoenix
(Phoenicis)

a) SC:$M+0.2$.

b) This star has a faint (m11.5) companion.

c) The spectral type comes from Kholopov. If the absolute magnitude is estimated to be $+1$, then: 180 l.y., $\pi.018$, $V22$, $D_s1.5$, $\mathcal{L}31$. However, the resultant distance seems much too close. The star probably has an absolute magnitude of 0.0 or brighter.

d) SC:$M+1.7$. Y:$\pi.072$.

e) If the absolute magnitude is estimated to be -1, then: 560 l.y., $\pi.006$, $V15$, $D_s1.5$, and $\mathcal{L}198$.

f) One of the best-known dwarf Cepheids. B:$M+4.1$, $D_s0.8$. SC:m7.21, $RV-15$, declination $-41°34'54''$.

PHOENIX	HD	2000.0 R.A.	Declin.	m	M	Spectra	l.y.	μ	Dir.	V	RV	π	D_s	$\mathscr{L}$	Rmk
α Phe	2261	$00^h\,26^m\,17.0^s$ $-42°\,18'\,22''$		2.39	0.2	K0 IIIb	84	0.442''	152°	92	75	.039''	15	65	
β Phe	6595	01 06 05.0 -46 43 08		3.31	0.3	G8 III	130	0.030	279	7	-1	.021	11	60	
γ Phe	9053	01 28 21.9 -43 19 06		3.41_v	-4.4	K4/5 III	1200	0.204	185	[353]	26	[.003]	200	4500	
δ Phe	9362	01 31 15.0 -49 04 22		3.95	1.7	K0 IIIb	110	0.210	41	33	-7	.031	6.5	16	
ε Phe	496	00 09 24.6 -45 44 51		3.88	2.9†	K0 III	50	0.219	144	18	-9	.065	3.9	5.4	(a)
ζ Phe	6882	01 08 23.0 -55 14 45		3.92_v	-0.2	B7 V	220	0.037	33	20	15	.013	1.6	95	
η Phe	4150	00 43 21.2 -57 27 47		4.36	2.6†	A0 IV	72	0.016	353	3	2	.045	0.9	7.2	(b)
ι Phe	221760	23 35 04.5 -42 36 55		4.71_v	*	A2 V	*	0.044	84	*	19	*	*	*	(c)
κ Phe	2262	00 26 12.1 -43 40 48		3.94	2.8†	A6 Vn	56	0.112	72	14	11	.058	1.2	6.0	(d)
λ^1 Phe	2834	00 31 24.9 -48 48 13		4.77	0.6	A0 V	220	0.142	79	25	-2	.027	2.4	45	
μ Phe	3919	00 41 19.5 -46 05 06		4.59	0.3	G8 III	240	0.019	286	29	19	.004	12	60	
ν Phe	7570	01 15 11.1 -45 31 54		4.96	4.2†	F8 V	45	0.692	74	47	12	.072	1.1	1.6	
π Phe	224554	23 58 55.7 -52 44 45		5.13	0.0	K0 III	350	0.085	39	29	-14	.016	17	79	
ρ Phe	4919	00 50 41.0 -50 59 13		5.22_v	2.6	F2 III	110	0.072	51	72	22	.005	1.6	7.2	
σ Phe	223145	23 47 15.9 -50 13 35		5.18	*	B3 V	*	0.013	148	*	11	*	*	*	(e)
υ Phe	6767	01 07 47.8 -41 29 14		5.21	1.7	A3 IV	160	0.038	76	19	14	.014	2.0	16	
φ Phe	11753	01 54 21.9 -42 29 50		5.11	1.7	A3 V	160	0.046	233	[16]	12	[.021]	0.8	16	
χ Phe	12524	02 01 42.3 -44 42 48		5.14	-0.3	K5 III	400	0.051	216	33	-31	.019	28	104	
ψ Phe	11695	01 53 38.7 -46 18 10		4.41_v	-0.5	M4 III	310	0.118	227	51	2	.011	34	125	
SX Phe	223065	23 46 32.9 -41 33 29		6.78_v	1.4	A3 V	390	0.892	163	149	-29	.029	1.8	22	(f)
- Phe	12055	01 57 10.0 -47 23 06		4.83	1.4	G8 III	160	0.101	77	26	12	.021	6.3	21	
- Phe	222095	23 37 50.9 -45 29 33		4.74	1.4	A2 V	150	0.070	97	23	10	.016	1.9	22	

Pictor
(Pictoris)

a) Y:π.052.

b) SC:M+0.3. Y:π.061.

c) SC:RV−2. An eclipsing binary. If the absolute magnitude is estimated to be −5, then: 3000 l.y., π.001, V58, D_s4.4, and £8000.

d) This faint red dwarf is known for its very large proper motion, second only to Barnard's Star. Burnham points out that it takes 414 years for the star to move 1°. See Burnham for a finder's chart.

PICTOR	HD	2000.0 R.A.			Declin.			m	M	Spectra	l.y.	μ	Dir.	V	RV	π	D_s	$\mathcal{L}$	Rmk
α Pic	50241	06^h 48^m	11.4^s		−61° 56′	29″		3.27	2.1†	A6 III/IV	56	0.275″	345°	31	21	.058″	1.4	11	(a)
β Pic	39060	05 47	17.1		−51 03	59		3.85	2.5†	A5 V	62	0.087	3	21	20	.053	1.4	7.9	(b)
γ Pic	39523	05 49	49.6		−56 10	00		4.51	0.0	K1 III	260	0.107	134	32	16	.018	16	79	
δ Pic	42933	06 10	17.9		−54 58	07		4.81$_v$	*	B1/2 III	*	0.011	315	*	31	*	*	*	(c)
ζ Pic	35072	05 19	22.0		−50 36	22		5.45	0.6	F6 IV	300	0.229	4	65	45	.023	5.2	45	
η^1 Pic	32743	05 02	48.6		−49 09	05		5.38	3.3	F3/5 V	59	0.056	297	22	21	.055	1.3	3.8	
η^2 Pic	33042	05 04	57.9		−49 34	41		5.03	−0.5	K5 III	420	0.062	91	49	36	.009	31	125	
λ Pic	30185	04 42	46.3		−50 28	52		5.31	0.3	K0 III	330	0.058	312	[28]	5	[.010]	12	60	
Kapteyn's	33793	05 11	17.8		−44 59	04		8.84	10.85†	M0 V	12.73	8.718	131	163	24	.256	0.2	0.004	(d)
- Pic	39640	05 50	53.3		−52 06	32		5.17	0.3	G8 III	310	0.078	174	16	1	.023	12	60	
- Pic	42540	06 07	03.4		−62 09	17		5.05	0.2	K2/3 III	300	0.079	165	36	22	.013	17	65	
- Pic	46355	06 29	28.4		−56 51	11		5.22	0.3	K0 III	310	0.046	299	25	13	.010	14	60	

Pisces
(Piscium)

a) *Al Rischa* (The Cord). A pleasant binary with—perhaps—a slight color contrast (yellow, blue?).

b) If the absolute magnitude is estimated to be −1, then: 415 l.y., $\pi.008$, $V6$, $D_s1.9$, $\mathcal{L}198$.

c) South 2° is the barely discernible white dwarf, van Maanen's star (m12.4). It is only about 12,500 kilometers in diameter (slightly smaller than Earth) with a luminosity of .0002 Suns. See Burnham for a finder's chart.

d) Easily resolved binary with contrast (pale yellow, pale rose, or grey).

e) ENE 1.5° is M74, a large but faint spiral galaxy, seen face-on.

f) B:140 l.y., $\mathcal{L}8$–10. Y:$\pi.075$.

g) A rarity: a carbon star bright enough for naked-eye viewing.

h) If the absolute magnitude is estimated to be +2, then: 140 l.y., $\pi.023$, $V4$, $D_s1.5$, and $\mathcal{L}12$.

PISCES	HD	R.A. 2000.0			Declin.			m	M	Spectra	l.y.	μ	Dir.	V	RV	π	D_s	$\mathscr{L}$	Rmk
α^A Psc ∞	12447	02^h	02^m	02.7^s	+02°	45'	49''	4.33	1.4	A0 p	130	0.030''	90°	30	9	.005''	1.7	22	(a) 🖉
α^B Psc	12446	02	02	02.7	+02	45	49	5.23	(−1.3)	A3 m	650	0.030	90	30	9	.005	2.3	255	
β Psc	217891	23	03	52.5	+03	49	12	4.53	*	B6 Ve	*	0.011	112	*	0	*	*	*	(b)
γ Psc	219615	23	17	09.9	+03	16	56	3.69	0.3	K0 III	91	0.759	88	101	−14	.036	11	60	
δ Psc	4656	00	48	40.9	+07	35	06	4.43	−0.3	K5 III	290	0.095	119	40	32	.019	28	104	(c)
ε Psc	6186	01	02	56.5	+07	53	24	4.28	0.2	K0 III	210	0.085	289	16	7	.027	12	65	
ζ^A Psc ∞	7344	01	13	43.8	+07	34	31	5.24	2.1	A7 IV	140	0.150	110	29	9	.026	1.8	11	(d)
ζ^B Psc	7345	01	13	45.2	+07	34	42	6.30	3.7	F7 V	110	0.151	108	30	11	.026	1.2	2.6	
η Psc	9270	01	31	28.9	+15	20	45	3.62	0.3	G7 IIIa	150	0.028	94	17	15	.015	12	60	(e)
θ Psc	220954	23	27	58.0	+06	22	44	4.28	0.0	K1 III	230	0.129	251	39	6	.016	16	79	
ι Psc	222368	23	39	57.0	+05	37	35	4.13	3.39†	F7 V	46	0.572	139	39	5	.071	1.4	3.5	(f)
κ Psc	220825	23	26	55.9	+01	15	20	4.94_v	(3.0)	A0pCr	81	0.125	137	15	−3	.040	0.8	5.2	
λ Psc	222603	23	42	02.7	+01	46	48	4.50	2.4	A7 V	86	0.196	221	35	12	.028	1.2	8.6	
μ Psc	9138	01	30	11.1	+06	08	38	4.84	−0.3	K4 III	350	0.297	98	85	34	.018	25	104	
ν Psc	10380	01	41	25.8	+05	29	15	4.44	−0.2	K3 IIIb	80	0.025	284	3	0	.041	24	95	
ξ Psc	11559	01	53	33.3	+03	11	15	4.62	0.2	K0 III	250	0.034	34	44	30	.005	12	65	
o Psc	10761	01	45	23.6	+09	09	28	4.26	0.2	G8 III	210	0.088	54	23	14	.023	12	65	
ρ Psc	8723	01	26	15.2	+19	10	20	5.38	3.0	F2 V	86	0.028	300	10	−9	.038	1.4	5.0	
σ Psc	6118	01	02	49.0	+31	48	16	5.50	0.2	B9.5 V	370	0.027	149	[18]	10	[.009]	1.7	65	
τ Psc	7106	01	11	39.6	+30	05	23	4.51	1.7	K0 IIIb	120	0.080	114	34	30	.023	7.3	16	
υ Psc	7964	01	19	27.9	+27	15	51	4.76	1.4	A3 V	150	0.026	103	10	8	.019	1.7	22	
φ Psc	7318	01	13	44.8	+24	35	01	4.65	0.2	K0 III	250	0.031	151	22	6	.007	14	65	
χ Psc	7087	01	11	27.1	+21	02	05	4.66	0.2	G8.5 III	250	0.038	99	20	16	.015	14	65	
ψ^1 Psc	6456	01	05	40.9	+21	28	24	5.34	−0.1	A1 Vn	400	0.051	102	15	−3	.016	2.3	86	
ω Psc	224617	23	59	18.6	+06	51	48	4.01	0.3	F4 IV	180	0.187	126	49	2	.018	5.1	60	
7 Psc	220009	23	20	20.5	+05	22	53	5.05	−0.1	K2 III	350	0.098	125	236	38	.002	19	86	
19 Psc	223075	23	46	23.4	+03	29	13	5.04_v	(−1.9)	C5 II	820	0.039	247	48	11	.004	141	474	(g)
27 Psc	224533	23	58	40.3	−03	33	22	4.86	0.2	G9 III	280	0.084	216	14	0	.029	12	65	
29 Psc	224926	00	01	49.3	−03	01	39	5.10	−1.2	B7 III/IV	590	0.014	107	[26]	23	[.005]	1.9	238	
30 Psc	224935	00	01	57.5	−06	00	51	4.41_v	(−1.7)	M3 III	540	0.061	126	50	−12	.006	61	376	
33 Psc	28	00	05	20.1	+05	42	27	4.61_v	0.0	K0 IIIb+	270	0.095	353	33	−6	.014	15	79	
47 Psc	2411	00	28	02.9	+17	53	36	5.06_v	−0.5	M3 IIIv	420	0.120	78	36	6	.016	36	125	
64 Psc	4676	00	48	58.6	+16	56	26	5.07	3.4†	F8 V	71	0.200	180	21	2	.046	1.4	3.4	
65A Psc ∞	4758	00	49	53.5	+27	42	35	7.1	2.6	F5 III	260	0.091	93	40	7	.011	1.7	7.2	
65B Psc	4757	00	49	53.1	+27	42	37	7.0	(2.2)	F4 III	300	0.084	93	37	5	.011	1.6	10	
82 Psc	7034	01	11	06.7	+31	25	29	5.16	*	F0 V	*	0.015	233	*	2	*	*	*	(h)
89 Psc	7804	01	17	47.9	+03	36	52	5.16	1.7	A3 V	160	0.055	250	21	5	.013	1.6	16	
91 Psc	8126	01	21	07.3	+28	44	18	5.23	0.2	K5	330	0.073	157	[50]	−36	[.010]	20	65	
107 Psc	10476	01	42	29.7	+20	16	07	5.24	5.88†	K1 V	24	0.730	204	43	−34	.134	0.8	0.3	

Piscis Austrinus
(Piscis Austrini)

a) *Fomalhaut* (Mouth of the Fish). A white main-sequence star that often appears reddish to observers in the Northern Hemisphere because of atmospheric pollution.

b) A red dwarf, with the fourth fastest proper motion, after Barnard's Star (Oph), Kapteyn's Star (Pic), and Groombridge 1830 (UMa). See Burnham for a finder's chart.

| PISCIS AUSTRINUS | HD | 2000.0 | | | | | | | | | | | | | | | Rmk |
		R.A.			Declin.			m	M	Spectra	l.y.	μ	Dir.	V	RV	π	D_s	$\mathscr{L}$	
α PsA	216956	22^h 57^m	39.0^s	$-29°$	$37'$	$20''$	1.16	2.03†	A3 V	22	0.373''	116°	14	7	.149''	1.4	12	(a)
β PsA	213398	22 31	30.3	-32	20	46	4.29	0.6	A0 V	180	0.068	100	16	6	.021	2.3	45	
γ PsA	216336	22 52	31.5	-32	52	32	4.46	0.6	A0 V	76	0.037	235	17	17	.043	1.5	45	
δ PsA	216763	22 55	56.8	-32	32	23	4.21	0.3	G8 III	200	0.039	27	15	-12	.021	12	60	
ε PsA	214748	22 40	39.3	-27	02	37	4.17	-0.2	B8 Ve	240	0.029	80	[11]	3	[.013]	1.3	95	
η PsA ∞	209014	22 00	50.1	-28	27	13	5.42	-0.2	B8 V	430	0.020	60	10	-5	.011	1.5	95	
θ PsA	207155	21 47	44.1	-30	53	54	5.01	-0.2	A2 V	360	0.023	272	23	14	.006	3.6	95	
ι PsA	206742	21 44	56.7	-33	01	33	4.34	0.6	A0 V	80	0.097	159	11	2	.041	1.4	45	
λ PsA	210934	22 14	18.7	-27	46	01	5.43	-1.2	B8 III	690	0.028	86	13	-6	.012	3.6	238	
μ PsA	210049	22 08	22.9	-32	59	19	4.50	1.4	A2 V	110	0.084	113	18	12	.030	1.8	22	
π PsA	217792	23 03	29.7	-34	44	58	5.11	3.6†	F0 V+	65	0.111	40	12	-6	.050	0.8	2.9	
τ PsA	210302	22 10	08.7	-32	32	55	4.92	3.6†	F6 V	60	0.434	88	41	-15	.054	1.2	2.9	
υ PsA	210066	22 08	25.9	-34	02	38	4.99	-0.3	M1 III	370	0.046	171	31	20	.009	28	104	
Lacaille 9352	217987	23 05	32.2	-35	51	52	7.44	9.59†	M1 Ve	11.68	6.901	79	118	9	.279	0.29	0.01	(b)

Puppis
(Puppis)

a) *Naos.* B:M−7.1, $\mathscr{L}$60,000. NW 2.5° is the globular cluster NGC 2477, very rich and compact.

b) B:M−3.2, $\mathscr{L}$1600, 600 l.y.

c) *Asmidiske.* NE 1.5° is M93, a bright open star cluster (NGC 2447). To the NNE 9° are the two open clusters M46 and M47 (the latter larger and brighter).

d) One of the best-known δ Sct variables, with a very fast period (3^h23^m). B:M+0.3.

e) SC only lists k^1, but gives this star the R.A. and decl. of k^2.

f) If the absolute magnitude is estimated to be 0.0, then: 275 l.y., π.012, V33, D_s1.2, $\mathscr{L}$79.

g) If the absolute magnitude is estimated to be −1, then: 530 l.y., π.006, V27, D_s3.3, $\mathscr{L}$198.

h) If the absolute magnitude is estimated to be −2.5, then: 1050 l.y., π.003, V14, D_s4.8, $\mathscr{L}$787.

i) A bright semiregular variable mostly naked-eye (see Variable Star Section). B:M−3.1, 600–650 l.y., $\mathscr{L}$1400. Levy mentions that this star can attain a brightness of m2.6.

j) If the absolute magnitude is estimated to be −2, then: 855 l.y., π.004, V18, D_s3.8, $\mathscr{L}$500.

k) A spectroscopic binary and eclipsing variable. The reported apparent magnitude is the combined magnitudes of components *A* and *B*. Yale gives no breakdown on individual brightnesses; Burnham gives these figures for the two components: V^A:M−2.8, D_s6.1, $\mathscr{L}$1100; V^B:M−2.15, D_s5.3, $\mathscr{L}$580; and both a distance of 1300 l.y. Burnham questions whether the star is a true visual binary (h4025) or only optical.

l) If the absolute magnitude is estimated to be −4, then: 1860 l.y., π.002, V38, D_s7.5, $\mathscr{L}$3150.

PUPPIS	HD	R.A. 2000.0			Declin.			m	M	Spectra	l.y.	μ	Dir.	V	RV	π	D_s	ℒ	Rmk
ζ Pup	66811	08^h	03^m	35.0^s	−40°	00′	11″	2.25	−6.8	O5 Ia	2100	0.033″	290°	[103]	−24	[.002]″	6.7	4000	(a)
ν Pup	47670	06	37	45.6	−43	11	45	3.17	−1.2	B8 III	240	0.009	234	[28]	28	[.013]	2.1	238	(b)
ξ Pup	63700	07	49	17.6	−24	51	35	3.34	−4.5	G6 Ia	1200	0.008	240	13	3	.003	151	5000	(c)
o Pup	63462	07	48	05.1	−25	56	14	4.50	−3.5	B0 Vpe	1300	0.014	282	[31]	15	[.003]	9.3	1977	
π Pup	56855	07	17	08.5	−37	05	51	2.70	−0.3	K3 Ib	100	0.012	284	16	16	.032	32	104	
ρ Pup	67523	08	07	32.6	−24	18	15	2.81$_v$	−2.0	F6 II	93	0.100	299	48	46	.035	15	497	(d)
σ Pup	59717	07	29	13.8	−43	18	05	3.25	−0.3	K5 III	170	0.195	342	99	88	.020	29	104	
τ Pup	50310	06	49	56.1	−50	36	53	2.93	0.2	K1 III	120	0.080	157	[38]	36	[.028]	17	65	
1 Pup	62576	07	43	32.3	−28	24	40	4.59	−0.3	K3 Ib	310	0.028	321	34	33	.018	32	104	
3 Pup	62623	07	43	48.4	−28	57	18	3.96	−7.5	A2 Iabe	6400	0.012	246	[115]	25	[.001]	147	80000	
4 Pup	62952	07	45	56.8	−14	33	50	5.04	(2.5)	F0 V	110	0.020	279	4	−2	.031	1.5	7.9	
6 Pup	63697	07	49	41.1	−17	13	43	5.18	−0.2	K3 III	390	0.129	159	[85]	44	[.008]	22	95	
9 Pup ∞	64096	07	51	46.2	−13	53	53	5.17	4.91†	G0 V	47	0.350	191	30	−18	.069	0.8	0.9	⊘
11 Pup	65228	07	56	51.5	−22	52	49	4.20	−2.0	F7 II	570	0.033	279	16	14	.023	25	497	
12 Pup	65699	07	59	05.6	−23	18	38	5.11	−6.0	cK2	5400	0.017	263	29	11	.003	263	20000	
16 Pup	67797	08	09	01.5	−19	14	42	4.40	−1.1	B5 V	410	0.023	245	[24]	19	[.008]	5.0	217	
19 Pup	68290	08	11	16.2	−12	55	37	4.72	0.2	G9 III(b)	110	0.032	284	36	36	.031	12	65	
20 Pup	68752	08	13	19.9	−15	47	18	4.99	−2.1	G5 II	110	0.021	251	17	17	.030	41	545	
a Pup	64440	07	52	13.0	−40	34	33	3.73	0.3	K1/2II(a)	110	0.016	270	24	24	.031	13	60	
b Pup	64503	07	52	38.6	−38	51	47	4.49	−2.3	B2.5 V	740	0.012	228	31	−31	.012	2.7	655	
c Pup	53704	07	04	02.7	−42	20	15	5.20	(2.2)	A m	130	0.069	345	31	28	.025	1.3	10	
f Pup	61330	07	37	22.0	−34	58	06	4.53	−0.2	B8 III	290	0.031	295	[27]	24	[.011]	1.5	95	
h^2 Pup	69142	08	14	02.8	−40	20	53	4.44	−0.1	K1II/III	260	0.081	150	41	14	.010	18	86	
k^1 Pup ∞	61555	07	38	49.3	−26	48	07	4.50	(−0.5)	B6 V	330	0.026	307	27	24	.010	1.9	125	
k^2 Pup	61556	07	38	49.7	−26	48	13	4.62	−0.4	B5 IVa	330	0.042	306	39	33	.010	0.2	112	(e)
p Pup	60863	07	35	22.8	−28	22	10	4.64	*	B8 V	*	0.081	254	*	3	*	*	*	(f)
q Pup	70060	08	18	33.3	−36	39	34	4.45	0.5	A7 III	57	0.146	310	13	5	.057	3.0	50	
t Pup	52092	06	58	25.0	−34	06	42	5.06	*	B3 V	*	0.025	304	*	19	*	*	*	(g)
v^1 Pup	56779	07	16	49.4	−36	35	34	5.03	*	B2 IV/V	*	0.007	236	*	9	*	*	*	(h)
y Pup	47973	06	38	37.6	−48	13	13	4.93	(0.3)	G8 III	270	0.012	9	28	28	.012	10	58	
A Pup	54893	07	08	51.0	−39	39	21	4.83	−1.7	B2 IV/V	660	0.013	288	[23]	20	[.005]	2.6	377	
H Pup	53811	07	03	53.7	−49	35	02	4.93	(1.4)	A4 IV	160	0.155	340	46	27	.020	2.1	21	
I Pup	55892	07	12	33.6	−46	45	34	4.49	2.8	F0 IV	71	0.172	306	18	−1	.046	1.3	6.0	
J Pup	64760	07	53	18.2	−48	06	11	4.24	−5.7	B0.5 Ib	3200	0.001	270	[41]	41	[.001]	14	15000	
L$_2$ Pup	56096	07	13	32.3	−44	38	23	5.10$_v$	(1.8)	M5 IIIe	150	0.346	18	92	53	.022	11	15	(i)
N Pup	65551	07	57	18.5	−44	06	35	5.09	*	B2.5 IV	*	0.007	344	*	16	*	*	*	(j)
O Pup	65685	07	57	51.7	−45	34	40	5.17	−0.4	K2 III	420	0.023	326	52	51	.009	24	114	
P Pup	63922	07	49	14.3	−46	22	24	4.11	−5.6	B0 III	2900	0.008	310	[40]	24	[.001]	15	13500	
Q Pup	63744	07	48	20.2	−47	04	40	4.71	0.2	K0 III	260	0.122	230	96	−1	.006	14	65	
V Pup	65818	07	58	14.3	−49	14	42	4.41$_v$	−4.0	B2II/III	1600	0.017	294	[44]	19	[.002]	9.6	3133	(k)
W Pup	70555	08	21	23.0	−33	03	16	4.83$_v$	−0.4	K3 II	110	0.015	290	33	33	.030	28	114	
KQ Pup	60414	07	33	47.8	−14	31	26	4.97$_v$	−5.6	M2 Iab+	4200	0.019	270	37	22	.003	298	13500	
MX Pup	68980	08	13	29.5	−35	53	59	4.78$_v$	*	B1.5 IIIe	*	0.006	225	*	35	*	*	*	(l)
NS Pup	68553	08	11	21.5	−39	37	07	4.45$_v$	−5.9	K3 Ib	3800	0.009	229	18	16	.006	418	18000	
NV Pup	57150	07	18	18.4	−36	44	03	4.66$_v$	−1.7	B2 V+	610	0.010	264	[21]	19	[.005]	2.8	377	

(Continued)

m) If the absolute magnitude is estimated to be 0.0, then: 285 l.y., π.011, V41, D_s1.2, $\mathscr{L}$79.

n) If the absolute magnitude is estimated to be 0.0, then: 290 l.y., π.011, V39, D_s1.3, $\mathscr{L}$79.

o) If the absolute magnitude is estimated to be -2, then: 760 l.y., π.004, V35, D_s2.3, $\mathscr{L}$500.

p) If the absolute magnitude is estimated to be -2, then: 900 l.y., π.004, V23, D_s2.3, $\mathscr{L}$500.

PUPPIS (CONT.)	HD	R.A. 2000.0		Declin.		m	M	Spectra	l.y.	μ	Dir.	V	RV	π	D_s	$\mathcal{L}$	Rmk
NW Pup	57219	$07^h\,18^m\,38.2^s$		$-36°\,44'\,34''$		5.11_v	-1.7	B2 IVne	750	$0.008''$	$277°$	[20]	18	$[.004]''$	4.5	377	
OS Pup	69081	08 13 58.3		-36 19 21		5.08_v	-1.7	B1.5 IV	740	0.006	141	[19]	18	[.004]	2.0	377	
OU Pup	56022	07 13 13.3		-45 10 59		4.89_v	(-0.1)	A0 pSi	330	0.103	194	49	4	.010	2.6	87	
PU Pup	61429	07 38 17.9		-25 21 54		4.70_v	$*$	B8 IV	$*$	0.015	228	$*$	41	$*$	$*$	$*$	(m)
- Pup	50235	06 50 52.3		-34 22 02		4.99	(0.6)	K5 III	250	0.004	14	30	30	.013	17	47	
- (A) Pup	53705	07 03 57.2		-43 36 29		5.54	4.3	G3 V	57	0.402	343	92	86	.057	1.2	1.5	
- (B) Pup	53706	07 03 58.8		-43 36 42		6.79	5.6	K0 V	63	0.389	342	97	90	.052	0.8	0.5	
- Pup	55526	07 10 47.4		-48 55 55		5.14	-0.3	K2 III	110	0.207	354	71	64	.031	22	104	
- Pup	56456	07 14 38.1		-48 16 18		4.76	$*$	B8/9 V	$*$	0.004	333	$*$	39	$*$	$*$	$*$	(n)
- Pup	59219	07 26 21.8		-51 01 07		5.10	-0.3	K0 III	390	0.004	304	8	8	.007	18	104	
- Pup	59612	07 29 51.4		-23 01 28		4.85	-4.8	A5 Ib	2800	0.012	222	42	37	.003	35	6500	
- Pup	59890	07 30 42.5		-30 57 44		4.65	-4.5	G3 Ib	2200	0.026	266	15	14	.023	104	5000	
- Pup	61772	07 40 23.1		-15 15 49		4.94	-2.3	K3 II	920	0.031	212	29	0	.005	75	655	
- Pup	61831	07 39 27.3		-38 18 30		4.84	$*$	B2.5 V	$*$	0.021	275	$*$	26	$*$	$*$	$*$	(o)
- Pup	62644	07 42 57.2		-45 10 24		5.06	3.8†	G6 IV	59	0.563	187	56	28	.055	1.9	2.4	
- Pup	62713	07 43 41.9		-40 56 03		5.17	-0.2	K1 III	390	0.229	146	67	53	.026	18	95	
- Pup	63032	07 45 15.2		-37 58 07		3.61	-5.9	K2.5Ib/II	2600	0.014	266	20	17	.006	460	18000	
- Pup	63465	07 47 24.9		-38 30 40		5.08	(-1.9)	B2.5 III	820	0.013	261	20	12	.004	3.1	457	
- Pup	63578	07 47 31.5		-46 36 31		5.23	-3.5	B2 III	1800	0.009	297	[41]	34	[.002]	4.9	1977	
- Pup	64379	07 52 15.6		-34 42 19		5.01	4.4†	F5 V	45	0.313	320	34	27	.073	0.8	1.4	
- Pup	64740	07 53 03.7		-49 36 47		4.63	-3.6	B1.5 Vp	1400	0.015	349	[33]	8	[.002]	2.3	2168	
- Pup	65456	07 57 40.1		-30 20 04		4.79	1.4	A2 V	160	0.012	305	28	28	.025	2.2	22	
- Pup	65810	07 59 52.0		-18 23 58		4.61	1.7	A2 Vn	130	0.047	191	16	-12	.021	1.6	16	
- Pup	65925	07 59 28.3		-39 17 50		5.24	2.6	F5 III	86	0.099	242	15	-8	.038	1.7	7.2	
- Pup	68601	08 11 25.9		-42 59 14		4.75	(-2.2)	A5 Ib	820	0.003	315	19	19	.004	13	619	
- Pup	70556	08 21 21.0		-36 29 04		5.20	$*$	B2 IV/V	$*$	0.013	241	$*$	16	$*$	$*$	$*$	(p)

Pyxis
(Pyxidis)

a) This is probably a βC variable, but has not been officially recognized as such. The *RV* is extremely variable. Measurements in December 1980 and early 1981 revealed a maximum velocity of 52.1 km/s, and a minimum of 5.9 km/s. In a span of just 34 minutes, on March 20, 1981 the velocity went from 7.3 km/s to 45.5 km/s [IBVS #2330].

PYXIS	HD	R.A.			Declin.			*m*	*M*	Spectra	l.y.	μ	Dir.	*V*	*RV*	π	D_s	$\mathscr{L}$	Rmk
				2000.0															
α Pyx	74575	08^h 43^m 35.5^s			−33° 11′ 11″			3.68	−4.4	B1.5 III	1300	0.020″	297°	[42]	15	[.002]″	8.8	4500	(a)
β Pyx	74006	08	40	06.2	−35	18	29	3.97	0.3	G5II/III	180	0.023	140	14	−13	.018	12	60	
γ Pyx	75691	08	50	31.9	−27	42	36	4.01	−0.3	K3 III	99	0.156	302	34	25	.033	22	104	
δ Pyx	76483	08	55	31.5	−27	40	55	4.89	1.7	A3 IV	88	0.130	144	17	5	.037	1.8	16	
ζ Pyx	73898	08	39	42.5	−29	33	40	4.89	0.3	G5 III	270	0.102	190	39	−32	.021	11	60	
η Pyx	73495	08	37	52.1	−26	15	18	5.27	(3.2)	A0 V	86	0.027	236	31	31	.038	0.5	4.3	
θ Pyx	80874	09	21	29.6	−25	57	56	4.72	−0.5	M0 III	360	0.016	227	21	20	.010	35	125	
κ Pyx	78541	09	08	02.8	−25	51	30	4.58	−0.4	K4 III	320	0.038	83	47	−45	.013	32	114	
λ Pyx	81169	09	23	12.1	−28	50	02	4.69	0.3	G8 III	86	0.141	277	20	10	.038	11	60	
- Pyx	75605	08	49	51.5	−32	46	50	5.21	0.4	G5 III	300	0.050	174	12	−8	.028	10	54	
- Pyx	73752	08	39	07.9	−22	39	43	5.05	4.2†	G6 IV	53	0.495	331	57	43	.062	1.4	1.6	

Reticulum
(Reticuli)

a) The same field contains the optical double h3641, and SW 1° is θ Ret (discussed in note e). Between α and θ is NGC 1559, a large and bright spiral galaxy.

b) SC:$M+3.2$.

c) If the absolute magnitude is estimated to be -1, then: 410 l.y., π.008, V18, D_s45, $\mathcal{L}$198. The Yale *Bright Star Catalogue* indicates that the star is possibly an Lb variable. Kholopov has the star as a semiregular variable.

d) With ζ^2, it forms a very wide binary (Y:310″) of nearly equal-magnitude stars.

e) In the same field, NW 0.5°, is θ Ret, a visual double (1941: 6, 8; PA 4°, 4.1″).

RETICULUM	HD	2000.0 R.A.	Declin.	m	M	Spectra	l.y.	μ	Dir.	V	RV	π	D_s	$\mathscr{L}$	Rmk
α Ret	27256	$04^h\,14^m\,25.5^s$	$-62°\,28'\,26''$	3.35	-2.1	G6 II/III	400	0.068″	43°	44	36	.013″	34	545	(a)
β Ret	23817	03 44 12.0	-64 48 26	3.84	2.3†	K1/2 III	65	0.324	76	60	51	.050	5.8	9.5	(b)
γ Ret	25705	04 00 53.8	-62 09 34	4.51$_v$	$*$	M4 III	$*$	0.028	4	$*$	-7	$*$	$*$	$*$	(c)
δ Ret	25422	03 58 44.7	-61 24 01	4.56	-0.5	M0 III	340	0.020	150	93	-1	.001	35	125	
ε Ret	27442	04 16 28.9	-59 18 07	4.44	3.5†	K1/2 III	50	0.170	197	32	29	.065	3.2	3.1	
ζ^1 Ret	20766	03 17 46.1	-62 34 32	5.54	5.28†	G3/5 V	37	1.491	64	80	12	.089	0.3	0.6	(d)
ζ^2 Ret	20807	03 18 12.8	-62 30 23	5.24	4.98†	G2 V	37	1.486	64	80	12	.089	0.8	0.8	
η Ret	28093	04 21 53.4	-63 23 11	5.24	0.3	G8 III	320	0.195	27	73	45	.016	12	60	(e)
ι Ret	25728	04 01 18.2	-61 04 44	4.97	-0.4	K4 III	390	0.116	35	72	61	.014	27	114	
κ Ret	22001	03 29 22.6	-62 56 16	4.72	3.4†	F5 IV/V	59	0.535	45	48	12	.055	1.2	3.4	

Sagitta
(Sagittae)

a) SE 1.5° (between γ and δ) is M71, usually described as a globular cluster, but nearly scattered enough to be considered open.

b) A slight discrepancy exists in the major catalog over the exact location of this star. If one uses the Epoch 1900 position from the *Bright Star Catalogue*, one gets the BC result (which we have used). If one relies on the Epoch 1950 position, as found in Boss, one gets the same result found in the *Sky Catalogue:* $20^h09^m56.4^s$; $+20°54'50''$. (SC does not indicate that this star is either 17 Sge or θ Sge.)

c) An Algol-type eclipsing binary. B:$M-0.4$, $D_s2.5$, $\mathscr{L}120$. Burnham has a finder's chart.

SAGITTA	HD	2000.0 R.A.	Declin.	m	M	Spectra	l.y.	μ	Dir.	V	RV	π	D_s	$\mathscr{L}$	Rmk
α Sge	185758	19ʰ 40ᵐ 05.7ˢ	+18° 00′ 50″	4.37	−2.0	G0 II	610	0.024″	147°	[21]	2	[.005]″	27	497	
β Sge	185958	19 41 02.9	+17 28 33	4.37	−2.1	G8 II	640	0.034	165	26	−22	.011	40	545	
γ Sge	189319	19 58 45.3	+19 29 32	3.47	−0.3	K5 III	190	0.070	69	42	−33	.013	30	104	
δ Sge	187076	19 47 23.2	+18 32 02	3.82ᵥ	−2.4	M2 II	570	0.012	35	58	3	.001	68	718	
ε Sge ∞	185194	19 37 17.3	+16 27 46	5.66	0.3	G8 III	390	0.025	50	[36]	−33	[.008]	13	60	
ζ Sge	187362	19 48 58.6	+19 08 31	5.00	1.7	A3 V	150	0.037	33	19	−7	.010	1.7	16	(a)
η Sge	190608	20 05 09.4	+19 59 28	5.10	−0.1	K2 III	100	0.088	19	42	−40	.032	16	86	
θ Sge ∞	191570	20 09 52.2	+20 53 48	6.48	3.0	F5 IV	160	0.010	336	40	−40	.029	1.4	5.0	(b)
U Sge	181182	19 18 48.4	+19 36 38	6.58ᵥ	−1.6	B8 III	1400	0.021	82	[47]	−17	[.002]	6.7	344	(c)

Sagittarius
(Sagittarii)

a) *Rukbat* (Knee) or *Al Rami* (The Archer). Curiously called α, for there are more than a half-dozen brighter stars.

   If the absolute magnitude is estimated to be +0.5, then: 160 l.y., π.020, V30, D_s1.1, and $\mathscr{L}$50.

b) *Arkab Prior* (Front of the Leg). A fixed binary (1953: m4, m8; 77°, 28.4″).

   If the absolute magnitude is estimated to be +1, then: 130 l.y., π.025, V12, D_s0.8, and $\mathscr{L}$31.

c) *Arkab Posterior* (Back of the Leg). Not associated with β^1.

d) *Al Nasl* (The Point; i.e., the tip of the arrow) or *Nash*. In the same field, NW 1°, is NGC 6522, a bright globular cluster. This is near the center of a triangle formed by γ, W Sgr (1° N of γ), and the m5 binary h5003 (1.5° W of γ).

e) *Kaus Meridianalis* (Middle of the Bow). B:M+0.7, 85 l.y., $\mathscr{L}$60. OH:M−0.8, 140 l.y., π.047.

f) *Kaus Australis* (Southern Part of the Bow). B:M−1.1, 125 l.y., $\mathscr{L}$250. OH:M0.0, 76 l.y., RV−15. NE 2.5° is M69, a globular cluster; and NE 4° is M70, a larger and brighter globular cluster.

g) *Ascella* (Arm of the Centaur). A close and difficult binary. B:M+0.1 (comb), 140 l.y., $\mathscr{L}$145. ESE 7° is M55, a large scattered globular cluster; WSW 1.5° is M54, a very bright and large globular cluster.

h) *Arkab*. B:M+1.1, 90 l.y., $\mathscr{L}$40. OH:M−1.0, 210 l.y. This star has a fairly faint companion: m9; 104°, 3.6″ (1959).

i) *Kaus Borealis* (Northern Part of the Bow). OH:M+0.7, 62 l.y., π.053.

   WNW 4.7° is the "Lagoon Nebula" (M8), a superb diffuse nebula. NNW 1.5° from M8 is the diffuse nebula M20—the "Trifid Nebula"—which is less impressive than one might expect. In the same field is M21, a bright globular cluster, and NE 2.3° is M22, a fine globular cluster, while NW 0.8° of λ is the large globular cluster M28. In fact, if you are a Messier follower, there are more of his objects in Sagittarius than in any other constellation—perhaps due in part at least to the fact that this is a fine-weather constellation, highest in the skies in mid-July about 11 P.M.

j) This star is not associated with ν^1.

k) With the dimmer ξ^1, forms a wide optical pair, with contrasting colors.

l) *Albaldah*. A triple system; all three are quite bright (m4, m4, m6) but both companions are very close to the primary (0.1″ and 0.6″). B:M−0.7, 250 l.y., $\mathscr{L}$360. OH:480 l.y.

m) *Nunki*. B:M−2.7, 300 l.y., $\mathscr{L}$1100.

n) B:85 l.y., $\mathscr{L}$30.

o) A β Lyrae type variable with bizarre spectrum. If the absolute magnitude is estimated to be −2, then: 700 l.y., π.005, V11, D_s1.2, $\mathscr{L}$500.

p) B:M−3.1, 590 l.y., $\mathscr{L}$1600.

q) NE 2.2° is the planetary nebula NGC 6818; south 1° of this is the faint galaxy NGC 6822.

SAGIT-TARIUS	HD	R.A. (2000.0)	Declin. (2000.0)	m	M	Spectra	l.y.	μ	Dir.	V	RV	π	Ds	L	Rmk
α Sgr	181869	19ʰ 23ᵐ 53.0ˢ	−40° 36′ 58″	3.97	*	B8 V	*	0.125″	166°	*	−1	* ″	*	*	(a)
β¹ Sgr	181454	19 22 38.2	−44 27 32	4.01	*	B9 V	*	0.019	162	*	−11	*	*	*	(b)
β² Sgr	181623	19 23 13.1	−44 47 59	4.29	1.7	F2 III	110	0.110	118	26	19	.030	2.3	17	(c)
γ¹ Sgr	164975	18 05 01.2	−29 34 48	5.09ᵥ	—	F8	—	0.014	94	—	−29	—	11	79	
γ² Sgr	165135	18 05 48.4	−30 25 27	2.99	0.2	K0 III	120	0.192	196	43	22	.025	13	65	(d)
δ Sgr	168454	18 20 59.6	−29 49 41	2.70	0.9†	K2 III	76	0.049	127	21	−20	.043	15	34	(e)
ε Sgr	169022	18 24 10.3	−34 23 05	1.85	−0.3	B9 IV	88	0.129	194	29	−11	.023	2.6	104	(f)
ζ Sgr	176687	19 02 36.6	−29 52 49	2.60	0.6	A3 IV	82	0.014	266	22	22	.025	2.7	45	(g)
η Sgr	167618	18 17 37.5	−36 45 42	3.11ᵥ	−2.4	M2 III	72	0.210	218	22	1	.045	79	718	(h)
θ¹ Sgr	189103	19 59 44.1	−35 16 35	4.37	−2.3	B2.5IV	700	0.025	164	[26]	1	[.005]	8.6	655	
θ² Sgr	189118	19 59 51.2	−34 41 53	5.30	1.7	A4/5 V	99	0.124	127	25	−18	.033	2.1	16	
ι Sgr	188114	19 55 15.5	−41 52 06	4.13	0.2	K0 II/III	93	0.058	14	37	36	.035	14	65	
λ Sgr	169916	18 27 58.1	−25 25 18	2.81	1.0†	K2 III	74	0.190	193	48	−43	.044	9.5	31	(i)
μ Sgr	166937	18 13 45.7	−21 03 32	3.86ᵥ	−7.1	B2 III	5100	0.003	72	6	−6	.012	101	55000	
ν¹ Sgr ∞	174974	18 54 10.1	−22 44 42	4.82	−6.0	K2 I	110	0.014	135	12	−12	.030	359	20000	
ν² Sgr	175190	18 55 07.0	−22 40 17	4.99	(3.1)	K3 II	78	0.105	104	111	−110	.042	5.0	5	(j)
ξ¹ Sgr	175687	18 57 20.4	−20 39 23	5.08	0.6	A0 II	260	0.007	188	6	2	.006	3.1	45	
ξ² Sgr	175775	18 57 43.7	−21 06 24	3.51	0.0	G5 II	160	0.034	111	25	−20	.011	18	79	(k)
o Sgr	177241	19 04 40.9	−21 44 30	3.77	0.3	G9 III	74	0.099	127	27	25	.044	13	60	
π Sgr	178524	19 09 45.7	−21 01 25	2.89	−2.0	F2 II	310	0.035	180	12	−10	.026	13	497	(l)
ρ¹ Sgr	181577	19 21 40.3	−17 50 50	3.93ᵥ	1.7	F0 III/IV	78	0.035	313	4	1	.042	1.7	16	
σ Sgr	175191	18 55 15.8	−26 17 48	2.02	−2.0	B2.5 V	210	0.056	166	[20]	−11	[.016]	1.3	497	(m)
τ Sgr	177716	19 06 56.3	−27 40 14	3.32	0.0	K1/2 III	74	0.255	192	53	45	.044	18	79	(n)
υ Sgr	181615	19 21 43.5	−15 57 18	4.61ᵥ	*	B2 Vpe	*	0.006	180	*	9	*	*	*	(o)
φ Sgr	173300	18 45 39.3	−26 59 27	3.17	−1.2	B8.5 III	240	0.053	89	[29]	22	[.013]	2.1	238	(p)
χ¹ Sgr	182369	19 25 16.4	−24 30 31	5.03	2.1	A m	93	0.078	134	43	−42	.035	1.5	11	
χ³ Sgr	182416	19 25 29.6	−23 57 44	5.43	−0.3	K4 III	460	0.015	254	[41]	40	[.007]	26	104	
ψ Sgr	179950	19 15 32.3	−25 15 24	4.85	3.4	F2+	64	0.052	119	60	−33	.005	1.6	3.4	
ω Sgr	188376	19 55 50.3	−26 17 58	4.70	3.6†	G5 V	53	0.224	68	27	−21	.061	1.9	2.9	
4 Sgr	163955	17 59 47.5	−23 48 58	4.76	(−0.2)	B9 V	330	0.043	176	27	−18	.010	2.3	98	
11 Sgr	166464	18 11 43.3	−23 42 04	4.98	0.2	K0 III	300	0.027	138	10	4	.014	14	65	
21 Sgr	169420	18 25 20.9	−20 32 30	4.81	0.2	K2 II	270	0.027	167	15	−12	.013	19	65	
29 Sgr	174116	18 49 40.0	−20 19 29	5.24	0.2	K4 III	96	0.036	6	19	−18	.034	21	65	
43 Sgr	180540	19 17 38.0	−18 57 11	4.96	−2.1	G8 II	840	0.019	216	21	15	.006	39	545	
52 Sgr	184707	19 36 42.3	−24 53 01	4.60	(−3.9)	B9	1600	0.073	104	175	−19	.002	9.5	2844	
54 Sgr ∞	185644	19 40 43.3	−16 17 36	6.2	(4.0)	K1 III	88	0.082	123	59	−58	.037	2.6	2	(q)
55 Sgr	186005	19 42 31.0	−16 07 27	5.06	0.6	F1 III	82	0.064	99	28	−27	.040	3.7	45	
56 Sgr	186648	19 46 21.6	−19 45 40	4.86	0.0	K1 III	310	0.157	236	36	20	.025	13	79	
59 Sgr	188603	19 56 56.7	−27 10 12	4.52	−0.2	K3 II+	290	0.015	143	17	−16	.014	26	95	
60 Sgr	189005	19 58 57.1	−26 11 44	4.83	0.3	G6 III+	260	0.050	47	52	−49	.014	11	60	

(Continued)

r) If the absolute magnitude is estimated to be -1, then: 1080 l.y., π.003, V55, D_s43, and $\mathcal{L}$198.

s) The absolute magnitude comes from Burnham, as the SC value (-8.2) seems very high. The star is a member of the bright open cluster M25.

t) This Mira-type variable is not in the *Bright Star Catalogue*. As there is no luminosity class, one cannot use either Fig. 2 or 3 to estimate the absolute magnitude or other properties.

u) An unusual variable (RCB type) in that it may have a brightness of about m5.8 for years, then quickly drop out of sight. It slowly climbs back to its normal brightness. B:$M-4$ or -5. SC:$M+4.4$. Burnham has a finder's chart.

SAGIT-TARIUS (CONT.)	HD	2000.0 R.A.	Declin.	*m*	*M*	Spectra	l.y.	μ	Dir.	*V*	*RV*	π	D_s	$\mathscr{L}$	Rmk
61 Sgr	188899	19^h 57^m 56.9^s	−15° 29′ 29″	5.02	3.6†	A3 IV	63	0.099″	172°	9	3	.052″	0.6	2.9	
62 Sgr	189763	20 02 39.4	−27 42 36	4.58$_v$	−0.5	M4 III	340	0.042	63	12	10	.028	36	125	
Kui 89	176162	18 59 23.6	−12 50 26	5.53	−1.1	B5 IV	49	0.019	183	13	−13	.066	3.4	217	
R Sgr	180275	19 16 41.6	−19 18 25	6.6$_v$	*	M5 III	*	0.020	20	*	−45	*	*	*	(r)
U Sgr	170764	18 31 53.0	−19 07 30	6.5$_v$	−3.6	F5 I	3400	0.010	270	[50]	−2	[.001]	88	2168	(s)
X Sgr	161592	17 47 33.5	−27 49 51	4.54$_v$	−2.0	F7 II	93	0.009	174	13	−13	.035	28	497	
Y Sgr	168608	18 21 22.9	−18 51 36	5.4$_v$	−6.3	F8 I	7100	0.014	135	12	−3	.006	242	25000	
RU Sgr	188813	19 58 42.8	−41 51 04	6.7$_v$	*	M4 e	*	0.122	185	*	−68	*	*	*	(t)
RY Sgr	180093	19 16 32.6	−33 31 18	6.1$_v$	−4.0	G0 V	3400	0.028	26	[140]	−23	[.001]	20	3133	(u)
- Sgr	165634	18 08 04.9	−28 27 25	4.57	(1.4)	G8 IIIp+	140	0.041	135	10	−5	.023	7.0	22	
- Sgr	167818	18 18 03.1	−27 02 33	4.65	−0.3	K3 II	99	0.010	61	17	−17	.033	33	104	
- Sgr	170680	18 31 26.2	−18 24 10	5.14	0.6	A0 Vn	260	0.026	189	38	−37	.017	2.3	45	
- Sgr	172910	18 44 19.3	−35 38 32	4.87	−2.5	B2.5 V	970	0.036	177	[51]	4	[.003]	3.7	787	
- Sgr	189831	20 03 33.4	−37 56 27	4.77	−0.4	K5 III	350	0.108	142	46	−38	.020	27	114	
- Sgr	190056	20 04 19.5	−32 03 22	4.99	0.2	K1 III	300	0.043	93	32	−12	.007	17	65	

Scorpius
(Scorpii)

a) *Antares* (Rival of Mars). One of the four Royal Stars of the ancients, along with Aldebaran, Regulus, and Fomalhaut. It has an m5 companion (see Visual Binary Section).

    NNW 4.2° is M80, a bright globular cluster, and in the same field is R Sco. West of Antares 1.2° is M4, also a bright globular cluster; about midway between Antares and M7 is M62, a very bright and dense globular cluster. In the same field as M62 is the bright variable RR Sco, noted for its ruddy appearance (see note u).

    B:$M-5.1$, 520 l.y., D_s700, $\mathscr{L}$9000. OH:$M-5.2$, 522 l.y.

b) *Graffias* (Crab). OH:$RV-1$.

c) *Dschubba* (Forehead). OH:$RV-7$.

d) *Wei.* B:$M+0.7$, $\mathscr{L}$45. OH:$M+0.1$.

e) A wide, naked-eye, optical double of two supergiants, with color contrast (blue and orange). B:$\zeta^1 M-8$, $\mathscr{L}$100,000; ζ^2 155 l.y., PA 208°.

f) OH:$M+2.7$. SC:$M+0.6$. Y:π.062.

g) *Sargas.* B:$M-4.6$, 650 l.y., $\mathscr{L}$5800. OH:$M-2.4$.

h) B:$M-7.1$, 3400 l.y., $\mathscr{L}$60,000. OH:3500 l.y.

i) Supergiant (as is ι^1), but this one is much less luminous; it is not associated with ι^1 — note the different proper motion and direction.

j) *Girtab.* OH:$M-4.2$, 650 l.y.

k) *Shaula* (Sting). A bright βC variable. NW 2.5° is the large nebula NGC 6334; NE 4° is the open cluster M7, large and bright. NW 3.5° of M7 is M6, also large and bright.

l) A wide, naked-eye pair with μ^2. B:$\mu^1 M-2.7$, D_s5.6, $\mathscr{L}$1000; $\mu^2 M-2.3$, D_s6.2, $\mathscr{L}$700.

m) *Jabbah.* A fine quadruple, as nice as the Double-Double in Lyra. B:$>$400 l.y.

n) *Elacrab.* An interesting multiple system: AB is a close pair, and C an orange dwarf (see Visual Binary Section). Also, the two stars which form the binary Σ1999 (see note s) are members of this group, having similar proper motions.

o) *Al Niyat* (The Shield of the Heart?). Sometimes reported to have a color contrast (white and blue).

p) *Lesuth, Lesath* (The Sting). B:$M-3.4$, 540 l.y., $\mathscr{L}$1900. OH:$M-3.1$, 460 l.y., SC:$RV+18$.

q) B:$M+0.7$, $\mathscr{L}$45. OH:$M+0.1$, 130 l.y., μ.064.

r) The $B-V$ index ($+1.57$) combined with the luminosity class (III) indicates a size of about fifty Suns (see Fig. 3).

s) The BC gives the combined visual magnitude for AB (6.96). Σ1999B has a visual magnitude of 8.02. This is a multiple star system, a "sextuple" comprised of Σ1999, its two companions, ζ Sco (see note n), and its two companions.

t) A multiple system in the very bright large open cluster NGC 6231. If we estimate the absolute magnitude to be -8, then: 16,000 l.y., π.0002, V280, D_s139, $\mathscr{L}$125,000.

u) Mira-type variable, which reaches naked-eye visibility about every 281 days. It is WSW 1° from M62; Burnham has a finder's chart.

v) This star has recently been designated a variable [IBVS #3530, Oct. 1990].

SCORPIUS	HD	R.A. 2000.0	Declin.	m	M	Spectra	l.y.	μ	Dir.	V	RV	π	D_s	$\mathcal{L}$	Rmk
α Sco ∞	148478	16^h 29^m 24.4^s	−26° 25′ 55″	0.96$_v$	−4.7	M1 I	440	0.024″	197°	6	−3	.024″	600	6000	(a)
β^1 Sco ∞	144217	16 05 26.1	−19 48 19	2.64	−3.5	B0.5 V	550	0.022	196	13	−7	.009	8.0	1977	(b)
β^2 Sco	144218	16 05 26.4	−19 48 07	4.92	−2.5	B2 V	990	0.030	221	[44]	−4	[.003]	7.7	787	
δ Sco	143275	16 00 19.9	−22 37 18	2.32	−4.1	B0 V	630	0.027	202	[28]	−14	[.005]	7.4	3436	(c)
ε Sco	151680	16 50 09.7	−34 17 36	2.29	−0.1	K2 III	98	0.661	247	142	−3	.022	18	86	(d)
ζ^1 Sco	152236	16 53 59.6	−42 21 43	4.73$_v$	−6.7	B1 Iape	6300	0.006	149	[59]	−26	[.001]	146	37670	(e)
ζ^2 Sco	152334	16 54 34.9	−42 21 41	3.62	−0.3	K4 III	200	0.267	208	49	−19	.028	25	104	
η Sco	155203	17 12 09.1	−43 14 21	3.33	2.1†	F2 V	58	0.286	175	37	−28	.056	2.2	11	(f)
θ Sco	159532	17 37 19.0	−42 59 52	1.87	−5.6	F0 I/II	1000	0.016	90	3	1	.027	74	13500	(g)
ι^1 Sco	161471	17 47 35.0	−40 07 37	3.03	−8.4	F2 Iae	6300	0.006	171	28	−28	.019	330	180000	(h)
ι^2 Sco	161912	17 50 11.0	−40 05 26	4.81	(−5.2)	A2 Ib	3300	0.011	139	51	−10	.001	45.2	9376	(i)
κ Sco	160578	17 42 29.1	−39 01 48	2.41$_v$	−3.0	B1.5 III	390	0.030	194	[22]	−14	[.008]	2.1	1247	(j)
λ Sco	158926	17 33 36.4	−37 06 13	1.63$_v$	−3.0	B2 IV	280	0.029	178	[12]	0	[.012]	2.1	1247	(k)
μ^1 Sco	151890	16 51 52.1	−38 02 51	3.04$_v$	−3.0	B1.5 V	530	0.031	202	[35]	−25	[.006]	3.0	1247	(l)
μ^2 Sco	151985	16 52 20.0	−38 01 03	3.57	−3.0	B2 IV	670	0.027	204	[27]	2	[.005]	2.5	1247	
ν^{AB} Sco ∞	145502	16 11 59.6	−19 27 38	4.00	−2.8	B2 IV/V	110	0.028	203	5	2	.030	11.9	1038	(m)
ν^C Sco	145501	16 11 58.5	−19 26 59	6.30	0.0	B8 V	110	0.016	223	14	−14	.030	4.1	79	
ξ^A Sco ∞	144070	16 04 22.0	−11 22 23	4.77	2.2	F5 IV	68	0.071	242	30	−29	.048	2.3	10	(n)
ξ^B Sco	144069	16 04 22.0	−11 22 23	5.07	2.2	F5 IV	68	0.071	242	30	−29	.048	2.0	10	
o Sco	147084	16 20 38.1	−24 10 10	4.55	−2.1	A5 II	700	0.026	187	26	−8	.005	31	545	
π Sco	143018	15 58 51.0	−26 06 51	2.89	−3.5	B1 V	620	0.028	198	14	−3	.010	4.6	1977	
ρ Sco	142669	15 56 53.0	−29 12 50	3.88	−2.5	B2 IV/V	620	0.022	201	[20]	0	[.005]	2.4	787	
σ Sco ∞	147165	16 21 11.2	−25 35 34	2.89$_v$	−4.4	B2 III	940	0.025	201	[34]	3	[.003]	31	4500	(o)
τ Sco	149438	16 35 52.9	−28 12 58	2.82	−4.1	B0 V	790	0.026	198	7	2	.020	2.2	3436	
υ Sco	158408	17 30 45.7	−37 17 45	2.69	−5.7	B2 IV	1600	0.032	182	[73]	8	[.002]	7.2	15000	(p)
χ Sco	145897	16 13 50.7	−11 50 16	5.22	−0.2	K3 III	400	0.016	232	25	−25	.029	25	95	
ψ Sco	145570	16 11 59.9	−10 03 51	4.94	(1.4)	A3 IV	160	0.019	208	8	−6	.020	1.9	21	
ω^1 Sco	144470	16 06 48.3	−20 40 09	3.96	−3.5	B1 V	1000	0.026	203	[38]	−3	[.003]	10	1977	
ω^2 Sco	144608	16 07 24.2	−20 52 07	4.32	0.4	G3 II/II	200	0.058	135	14	−5	.021	9.7	54	
1 Sco	141637	15 50 58.6	−25 45 05	4.64	−1.7	B3 V	600	0.032	214	[29]	3	[.005]	4.1	377	
2 Sco ∞	142114	15 53 36.6	−25 19 38	4.59	−2.1	B2.5 Vn	710	0.032	208	27	−10	.006	4.2	545	
13 Sco	145482	16 12 18.1	−27 55 35	4.59	−2.1	B2 V	710	0.030	203	[33]	10	[.005]	5.5	545	
22 Sco	148605	16 30 12.4	−25 06 54	4.79	−2.5	B2 V	940	0.025	196	[34]	4	[.003]	3.8	787	
G Sco	161892	17 49 51.4	−37 02 36	3.21	1.2	K0/1 III	81	0.064	58	26	25	.040	10	26	(q)
H Sco	149447	16 36 22.4	−35 15 20	4.16	(0.9)	K5 III	150	0.022	95	5	−2	.022	18	35	(r)
N Sco	148703	16 31 22.8	−34 42 16	4.23	−2.5	B2 III/IV	720	0.020	210	[21]	1	[.005]	6.6	787	
Σ1999 ∞	144087	16 04 25.7	−11 26 56	7.46	5.6	G8 V	67	0.076	249	34	−33	.049	0.9	0.5	(s)
B1833	152234	16 54 01.7	−41 48 23	5.45	*	B0.5 Ia	*	0.012	222	*	−6	*	*	*	(t)
RR Sco	152783	16 56 37.9	−30 34 47	5.4$_v$	*	M5 III	*	0.025	159	*	−36	*	*	*	(u)
V973 Sco	151804	16 51 33.6	−41 13 50	5.22$_v$	0.0	O8 Ip	360	0.002	153	[65]	−65	[.009]	3.5	79	(v)
- Sco	143787	16 03 20.5	−25 51 55	5.00	0.2	K5 III	100	0.081	240	41	−39	.032	17	65	
- Sco	145250	16 11 01.9	−29 24 59	5.13	0.2	K3 III	320	0.128	226	36	−27	.025	15	65	
- Sco	146624	16 18 17.8	−28 36 51	4.78	1.4	A0 V	110	0.110	195	21	−13	.031	1.6	22	
- Sco	153613	17 01 52.6	−32 08 37	5.03	−0.2	B8 V	360	0.050	185	[27]	5	[.009]	1.4	95	
- Sco	154090	17 04 49.3	−34 07 23	4.87	−6.2	B1 Iae	5300	0.009	108	[74]	4	[.001]	72	25000	
- Sco	154948	17 10 42.2	−44 33 27	5.08	0.4	G8+	280	0.065	211	19	−7	.017	9.9	54	
- Sco	157243	17 24 12.9	−44 09 45	5.12	−0.9	B7 III	520	0.030	201	[26]	13	[.006]	2.6	180	
- Sco	159433	17 36 32.7	−38 38 07	4.29	0.2	K0 IIIb	210	0.201	184	72	−49	.018	15	65	
- Sco	161840	17 49 10.4	−31 42 12	4.83	−0.2	B8 V	330	0.021	141	[16]	−13	[.010]	2.2	95	
- Sco	163145	17 56 47.3	−44 20 32	4.86	−0.3	K2 III	350	0.015	228	45	45	.017	21	104	
- Sco	163376	17 57 47.6	−41 42 58	4.88	−0.5	M0 III	390	0.019	238	18	4	.005	36	125	

Sculptor
(Sculptoris)

a) NW 4.5° is the spiral galaxy NGC 253. NW 3° of α is the South Galactic Pole.

b) SC:m7.20.

c) ESE 5° is NGC 55. Of all the galaxies outside our Local Group, this is one of the closest, at about 8 million light-years.

d) A red giant, and a carbon star. These are "cool" stars, somewhere around 2000 K, and are usually too dim to be included in the StarList.

e) If the absolute magnitude is estimated to be −1, then: 570 l.y., π.006, V36, D_s27, and $\mathcal{L}$79.

SCULPTOR	HD	R.A.			Declin.			m	M	Spectra	l.y.	μ	Dir.	V	RV	π	D_s	$\mathscr{L}$	Rmk
						2000.0													
α Scl	5737	00^h 58^m 36.3^s			$-29°$ 21$'$ 28$''$			4.31	-1.2	B7 III	410	0.018$''$	74°	[15]	10	[.008]$''$	3.6	238	(a)
β Scl	221507	23	32	58.2	-37	49	07	4.37	0.0	B9.5 IV	240	0.088	77	[31]	2	[.013]	1.4	79	
γ Scl	219784	23	18	49.4	-32	31	55	4.41	0.3	K1 III	76	0.067	162	18	16	.043	15	60	
δ Scl	223352	23	48	55.5	-28	07	49	4.57	0.6	A0 V	84	0.146	134	23	14	.039	2.3	45	
ε Scl ∞	10830	01	45	38.7	-25	03	10	5.31	2.8	F1 V	88	0.169	109	26	15	.037	1.5	6.0	$\mathcal{O}$
ζ Scl	224990	00	02	19.9	-29	43	15	5.01	-1.1	B3/5 V	540	0.016	68	[13]	0	[.006]	5.0	217	
η Scl	2429	00	27	55.7	-33	00	26	4.81$_v$	0.5	M4 III	230	0.048	202	20	11	.014	22	48	
θ Scl	739	00	11	43.9	-35	07	59	5.25	3.3	F4 V	96	0.208	53	29	-2	.034	1.3	3.8	
ι Scl	1737	00	21	31.2	-28	58	54	5.18	0.3	G5 III	310	0.079	151	25	21	.027	12	60	
κ^1 Scl ∞	493	00	09	20.9	-27	59	16	5.42	3.0	F2 V	99	0.071	89	17	9	.023	1.5	5.0	
κ^2 Scl	720	00	11	34.4	-27	47	59	5.41	-0.3	K5 III	450	0.023	31	[16]	-6	[.007]	24	104	(b)
λ^1 Scl	4065	00	42	42.8	-38	27	48	6.06	0.6	B9.5 V	400	0.000	0	[10]	10	[.008]	1.7	45	(c)
μ Scl	222433	23	40	38.1	-32	04	24	5.31	0.2	K1 III	340	0.106	242	23	14	.027	13	65	
π Scl	10537	01	42	08.5	-32	19	37	5.25	0.3	K0 III	320	0.078	254	75	10	.005	13	60	
σ Scl	6178	01	02	26.3	-31	33	07	5.50	1.4	A2 V	220	0.078	77	[26]	-8	[.015]	1.9	22	
τ Scl ∞	9906	01	36	08.3	-29	54	27	5.69	3.3	F2 V	98	0.107	65	21	5	.025	1.1	3.8	$\mathcal{O}$
R Scl	8879	01	26	58.0	-32	32	36	5.79$_v$	—	C6 II	—	0.030	208	—	-8	—	—	—	(d)
S Scl	1115	00	15	22.6	-32	02	41	6.20$_v$	*	M7 III	*	0.009	297	*	35	*	*	*	(e)

Scutum
(Scuti)

a)   In the same field, 0.5° east, is the large open cluster NGC 6664.

b)   Prototype of a class of short-period pulsating variables. B:$M+0.3$. Southeast 1° is M26, a large and bright open cluster.

c)   A semiregular pulsating variable. B:$M-4.5$ to -5, 2500–3000 l.y., $\mathcal{L}$8000.
        SE 1.2° is M11 (NGC 6705), a magnificent open cluster—very large and bright.

SCUTUM	HD	2000.0 R.A.	Declin.	m	M	Spectra	l.y.	μ	Dir.	V	RV	π	D_s	$\mathcal{L}$	Rmk
α Sct	171443	$18^h 35^m 12.3^s$	$-08° 14' 39''$	3.85	−0.2	K3 III	210	0.313''	183°	99	36	.016''	23	95	(a)
β Sct	173764	18 47 10.4	−04 44 53	4.22	−2.1	G5 II	600	0.018	202	22	−22	.019	43	545	
γ Sct	170296	18 29 11.7	−14 33 57	4.70	1.4	A3 Vn	150	0.005	169	41	−41	.025	1.8	22	
δ Sct	172748	18 42 16.3	−09 03 09	4.72$_v$	1.3	F3 III	160	0.006	81	45	−45	.025	2.8	24	(b)
ε Sct	173009	18 43 31.2	−08 16 31	4.90	−2.1	G8 II	820	0.022	72	13	−11	.016	44	545	
ζ Sct	169156	18 23 39.4	−08 56 04	4.68	0.2	G9 IIIb+	260	0.060	43	20	−6	.015	12	65	
η Sct	175751	18 57 03.6	−05 50 46	4.83	−0.1	K2 III	84	0.073	120	93	−93	.039	17	86	
R Sct	173819	18 47 28.9	−05 42 18	5.2$_v$	−5.4	G5 I	4300	0.053	238	255	44	.001	288	11500	(c)
- Sct	171391	18 35 02.3	−10 58 38	5.14	0.3	G8 III	300	0.047	94	20	7	.012	11	60	
- Sct	175156	18 54 43.0	−15 36 11	5.1	−2.9	B5 II	1300	0.012	239	[22]	−3	[.003]	17	1138	

Serpens
(Serpentis)

a) *Unukalhai* (Neck of the Snake). OH:M+0.7. Y:π.053.

b) Although nameless, this star marks the head of the serpent. The companion to this primary is difficult to resolve, due to its relatively faint magnitude. B:95 l.y., $\mathscr{L}$23.

c) B:$\mathscr{L}$6. Y:π.058. South 11° is M16 (NGC 6611), a large nebula with loose cluster of about 60 stars.

d) *Alya* (Serpent). A very attractive binary. B:130 l.y., $\mathscr{L}$19.

e) Northwest 0.5° is M5 (NGC 5904), a splendid globular cluster.

f) SC erroneously gives HD 169986.

g) A striking binary, just east 1.5° of the very large open cluster I. 4756.

h) A Mira-type variable which at maximum may just be visible to the naked eye.
   If the absolute magnitude is estimated to be −1, then: 570 l.y., π.006, V44, D_s51, and $\mathscr{L}$198.

SERPENS	HD	2000.0 R.A.	Declin.	m	M	Spectra	l.y.	μ	Dir.	V	RV	π	D_s	$\mathscr{L}$	Rmk
α Ser	140573	15^h 44^m 16.0^s	+06° 25′ 32″	2.65	1.1†	K2 III	67	0.143″	72°	14	3	.049″	11	29	(a)
β Ser ∞	141003	15 46 11.2	+15 25 18	3.67	0.6	A2 IV	80	0.084	126	10	−1	.041	2.6	45	(b)
γ Ser	142860	15 56 27.1	+15 39 42	3.85	3.4†	F6 V	40	1.321	167	78	7	.081	1.4	3.4	
δ^A Ser ∞	138918	15 34 48.1	+10 32 21	3.80$_v$	1.7	F0 IV	86	0.076	278	45	−42	.021	1.9	16	$\mathcal{O}$
δ^B Ser	138917	15 34 48.0	+10 32 15	3.80	1.7	F0 IV	86	0.075	265	42	−38	.021	1.9	16	
ε Ser	141795	15 50 48.9	+04 28 40	3.71	1.8	A2 m	80	0.140	64	19	−9	.041	1.9	15	
ζ Ser	164259	18 00 28.8	−03 41 25	4.62	4.1†	F2 IV	67	0.151	108	45	−43	.049	0.9	2.0	
η Ser	168723	18 21 18.5	−02 53 56	3.26	1.8†	K2 IIIab	64	0.890	218	83	9	.051	5.8	15	(c)
θ^{1A} Ser ∞	175638	18 56 13.1	+04 12 13	4.06	2.1	A5 V	110	0.056	55	46	−45	.030	1.7	11	(d)
θ^{1B} Ser	175639	18 56 14.5	+04 12 07	4.98	2.1	A5 Vn	110	0.053	60	54	−53	.030	1.4	11	
ι Ser	140159	15 41 33.0	+19 40 13	4.52	1.2	A1 V	150	0.076	230	37	−17	.011	1.9	26	
κ Ser	141477	15 48 44.3	+18 08 29	4.09	−0.5	M0.5 III	270	0.104	209	46	−39	.021	35	125	
λ Ser	141004	15 46 26.5	+07 21 11	4.43	4.3†	G0 V	35	0.235	253	67	−66	.094	1.1	1.5	
μ Ser	141513	15 49 37.1	−03 25 49	3.53	0.6	A0 V	130	0.094	253	64	−9	.007	1.5	45	
ν Ser ∞	156928	17 20 49.5	−12 50 48	4.33	1.2	A1 V	140	0.042	85	9	5	.028	1.8	26	
ξ Ser	159876	17 37 35.1	−15 23 55	3.54	1.7	F0 IV	110	0.076	216	45	−43	.030	1.9	16	
o Ser	160613	17 41 24.8	−12 52 31	4.26$_v$	1.4	A2 V	120	0.091	233	78	−30	.006	1.9	22	
π Ser	143894	16 02 17.7	+22 48 16	4.83	1.7	A3 V	140	0.023	31	29	−28	.012	1.6	16	
ρ Ser	141992	15 51 15.8	+20 58 40	4.76	−0.3	K4/5 III	340	0.055	287	64	−62	.015	29	104	
σ Ser	147449	16 22 04.3	+01 01 45	4.82	2.6	F0 V	76	0.164	287	53	−50	.043	1.5	7.2	
τ^1 Ser	137471	15 25 47.3	+15 25 41	5.17	−0.5	M1 III	440	0.018	229	21	−20	.013	36	125	
τ^4 Ser	139216	15 36 28.1	+15 06 05	6.25$_v$	−0.5	M5 IIb+	730	0.010	315	[28]	−26	[.004]	28	125	
χ Ser	140160	15 41 47.3	+12 50 50	5.33$_v$	(2.9)	A0 pSr	100	0.042	111	7	2	.032	0.9	5.7	
ω Ser	141680	15 50 17.5	+02 11 47	5.23	0.3	G8 III	320	0.060	152	11	−4	.027	13	60	
3 Ser	135482	15 15 11.3	+04 56 22	5.33	1.9	K0 III	160	0.018	273	34	−34	.021	6.7	14	
5 Ser ∞	136202	15 19 18.7	+01 45 55	5.05	3.2	F8 IV	88	0.637	144	98	54	.037	1.7	4.1	(e)
10 Ser	137898	15 28 38.1	+01 50 31	5.17	(2.6)	A8 IV	110	0.097	244	18	−10	.031	1.2	7.0	
36 Ser	141851	15 51 15.5	−03 05 26	5.11	(0.1)	A3 Vn	330	0.095	252	46	−8	.010	3.8	71	
59 Ser	169985	18 27 12.3	+00 11 46	5.21	0.6	G0 III+	270	0.010	259	23	−23	.016	5.1	45	(f)
Σ2375 ∞	173495	18 45 28.3	+05 29 59	5.83	−0.3	A1 V	550	0.016	130	17	−11	.006	3.7	104	(g)
R Ser	141850	15 50 41.6	+15 08 00	5.2$_v$	*	M7 IIIe	*	0.044	188	*	24	*	*	*	(h)

Sextans
(Sextantis)

a) East 3° is the large, bright elliptical galaxy NGC 3115, seen edge-on.

b) If the absolute magnitude is estimated to be 0.0, then: 360 l.y., π.009, V34, D_s1.7, and $\mathcal{L}$79.

SEXTANS	HD	R.A. 2000.0		Declin.		m	M	Spectra	l.y.	μ	Dir.	V	RV	π	D_s	$\mathscr{L}$	Rmk
α Sex	87887	$10^h\,07^m\,56.2^s$		$-00°\,22'\,18''$		4.49	-1.1	A0 III	430	$0.023''$	232°	10	7	$.015''$	3.4	217	
β Sex	90994	10 30	17.4	-00 38	13	5.09$_v$	-0.9	B9 V	510	0.049	238	[39]	12	[.006]	1.5	180	
γ Sex	85558	09 52	30.4	-08 06	18	5.05	(0.6)	A1 V	250	0.074	233	30	12	.013	2.5	44	(a)
δ Sex	90882	10 29	28.6	-02 44	21	5.21	*	B9.5 V	*	0.054	251	*	19	*	*	*	(b)
ε Sex	89254	10 17	37.7	-08 04	08	5.24	0.6	F2 III	280	0.163	270	31	15	.028	3.5	45	
SS Sex	90044	10 23	26.4	-04 04	27	5.97$_v$	—	B9 pSi+	—	0.052	270	—	23	—	—	—	

Taurus
(Tauri)

a) *Aldebaran* (The Follower—after the Pleiades?). One of the four Royal Stars of the ancients, with Antares, Regulus, and Fomalhaut. It is found in the star cluster Hyades, but is not a member. OH:M−0.3. Y:π.054.

b) *El Nath* (The Butting One). On the border with Auriga and sometimes called γ Aurigae. OH:π.028.

c) An outer member of the Hyades cluster (see note h). Just as the Pleiades carry names from antiquity, so once did the principal stars of this group, but they have now disappeared from use.

d) North is Hind's Variable Nebula (NGC 1555), exceedingly difficult. Associated with Hind's Variable Nebula is the irregular variable T Tauri (9.6–13.5), which is the prototype of a special kind of irregular variable associated with a gaseous nebula. It is generally considered now that such stars are in the last stages of a protostar, just before the onset of nuclear reactions which will produce a full-blown star.

e) It is this part of the sky that delivers the Taurid meteor shower, which occurs annually around 3 November.

f) A shell star, sometimes called Be stars because they have spectral type B with conspicuous emission lines of hydrogen. These stars rotate very rapidly, causing a loss of mass to an ever-expanding shell.

   NW 1° is the Crab Nebula (M1; NGC 1952), the famous remnant of the supernova of the summer of 1054. The nebula is still rapidly expanding, about 1000 km/s, or about 80 million kilometers per day.

g) *Alcyone.* Brightest star of the Pleiades. The variable BU Tau (see note r) is just to the north. OH:450 l.y.

h) A fixed binary of two bright stars, in the Hyades open cluster. Use low power. This cluster is one of the closest to us, at about 100 l.y. away (and it's receding). A number of visual binaries can be found here; see Burnham, pp. 1817–27. OH:M+1.1.

i) BC asks if this is a variable ("δ Sct?"). It is not listed as such by Kholopov.

j) A bright, naked-eye, eclipsing variable with a period of 3.95 days.

k) *Celaeno* in the Pleiades.

l) *Electra* in the Pleiades.

m) *Taygeta* in the Pleiades.

n) *Maia* in the Pleiades.

o) *Asterope* in the Pleiades; forms an easily resolved binary with 22 Tau. Sometimes these two go under the names Asterope I and II.

p) *Merope* in the Pleiades.

q) *Atlas* in the Pleiades, an attractive, very wide (300″) visual binary.

r) *Pleione* in the Pleiades, also known as BU Tau. This is a shell star whose activities cause it to vary its visual magnitude at irregular intervals.

TAURUS	HD	R.A. (2000.0)		Declin.		m	M	Spectra	l.y.	μ	Dir.	V	RV	π	D_s	ℒ	Rmk
α Tau	29139	04^h 35^m 55.2^s	+16° 30' 33''			0.85$_v$	−0.6	K5 III	65	0.200''	161°	57	54	.050''	34	137	(a)
β Tau	35497	05 26 17.5	+28 36 27			1.65	−1.6	B7 III	150	0.177	172	[38]	8	[.022]	2.2	344	(b)
γ Tau	27371	04 19 47.5	+15 37 39			3.65	0.2	K0 IIIab	160	0.118	102	44	39	.028	13	65	(c)
δ^1 Tau	27697	04 22 56.0	+17 32 33			3.76	0.2	K0 III	170	0.111	105	46	39	.021	13	65	(d)
δ^2 Tau	27819	04 24 05.7	+17 26 38			4.80	2.4	A7 V	98	0.116	109	51	39	.017	1.4	8.6	
δ^3 Tau	27962	04 25 29.3	+17 55 41			4.29$_v$	1.4	A2 IV	120	0.112	104	45	35	.019	1.8	22	
ε Tau	28305	04 28 36.9	+19 10 49			3.53	0.2	G9.5 III	150	0.114	108	47	39	.020	13	65	(e)
ζ Tau	37202	05 37 38.6	+21 08 33			3.00$_v$	−3.0	B4 III	520	0.022	177	24	20	.008	3.7	1247	(f)
η Tau	23630	03 47 29.0	+24 06 18			2.87	−1.6	B7 III	260	0.048	157	30	10	.008	2.9	344	(g)
θ^1 Tau	28307	04 28 34.4	+15 57 44			3.84	0.2	K0 IIIb	86	0.105	104	42	40	.038	12	65	
θ^2 Tau ∞	28319	04 28 39.7	+15 52 15			3.40$_v$	0.5	A7 III	120	0.105	103	44	40	.029	3.7	50	(h)
ι Tau	32301	05 03 05.7	+21 35 24			4.64	2.4	A7 V	91	0.078	122	45	41	.019	1.5	8.6	
κ^1 Tau ∞	27934	04 25 22.1	+22 17 38			4.22	2.4	A7 IV/V	75	0.107	115	45	40	.025	1.3	8.6	
κ^2 Tau	27946	04 25 24.9	+22 11 59			5.28	2.4	A7 V	120	0.122	115	[39]	32	[.027]	1.3	8.6	(i)
λ Tau	25204	04 00 40.8	+12 29 25			3.47$_v$	(−5.0)	B3 v	1600	0.011	218	32	18	.002	11.3	8053	(j)
μ Tau	26912	04 15 32.0	+08 53 32			4.29	−1.7	B3 IV	510	0.030	136	[28]	17	[.006]	3.8	377	
ν Tau	25490	04 03 09.3	+05 59 22			3.91	1.2	A1 V	110	0.001	90	6	−6	.030	1.8	26	
ξ Tau	21364	03 27 10.1	+09 43 58			3.74	(−0.1)	B9 Vn	190	0.068	121	19	−2	.017	1.4	87	
o Tau	21120	03 24 48.7	+09 01 44			3.60	0.3	G6 III	150	0.101	222	37	−21	.016	11	60	
π Tau	28100	04 26 36.4	+14 42 49			4.69	0.3	G7 IIIa	250	0.032	185	34	32	.014	12	60	
ρ Tau	28910	04 33 50.8	+14 50 40			4.65$_v$	2.6	A8 V	84	0.103	104	44	40	.026	1.2	7.2	
σ^1 Tau ∞	29479	04 39 09.2	+15 47 59			5.07	(1.7)	A4 m	160	0.081	151	26	19	.021	2.0	17	
σ^2 Tau	29488	04 39 16.4	+15 55 05			4.69	2.1	A5 Vn	110	0.083	101	41	36	.020	1.6	11	
τ Tau	30780	04 51 22.4	+18 50 23			5.10$_v$	2.6	A7 IV/V	100	0.089	113	42	37	.022	1.1	7.2	
υ Tau	28024	04 26 18.4	+22 48 49			4.29$_v$	1.1	A8 Vn	91	0.114	113	38	35	.036	2.5	29	
φ Tau	27382	04 20 21.2	+27 21 03			4.95	0.0	K1 III	320	0.082	197	[38]	3	[.010]	17	79	
χ Tau	27638	04 22 34.9	+25 37 45			5.37	0.4	B9 V	320	0.028	139	[21]	17	[.010]	1.6	54	
ψ Tau	25867	04 07 00.4	+29 00 05			5.23	2.6	F1 V	110	0.088	275	[17]	9	[.030]	1.5	7.2	
ω^1 Tau	26162	04 09 09.9	+19 36 33			5.50	3.2	K2 III	94	0.111	106	34	25	.023	3.6	4.1	
ω^2 Tau	27045	04 17 15.6	+20 34 43			4.94	—	A3 m	—	0.072	218	—	16	—	—	—	
4 Tau	21686	03 30 24.4	+11 20 11			5.14	0.4	A0 Vn	290	0.018	214	43	0	.002	1.8	54	
5 Tau	21754	03 30 52.3	+12 56 12			4.11	−0.9	K0 II/III	330	0.019	84	17	15	.012	25	180	
10 Tau	22484	03 36 52.3	+00 24 06			4.28	3.2	G9 V	53	0.535	206	50	28	.061	1.8	4.1	
16 Tau	23288	03 44 48.1	+24 17 22			5.46	−1.0	B7 IV	640	0.045	164	18	3	.012	3.2	198	(k)
17 Tau	23302	03 44 52.5	+24 06 48			3.70	−1.9	B6 IIIe	430	0.046	156	16	12	.020	2.9	453	(l)
19 Tau	23338	03 45 12.4	+24 28 02			4.30	−0.9	B6 IV	360	0.046	156	[25]	6	[.009]	1.8	180	(m)
20 Tau	23408	03 45 49.5	+24 22 04			3.87	−1.6	B8 III	410	0.048	154	19	−1	.012	3.3	344	(n)
21 Tau	23432	03 45 54.3	+24 33 17			5.76	−0.2	B8 V	510	0.041	163	[31]	9	[.006]	2.2	95	(o)
23 Tau	23480	03 46 19.5	+23 56 54			4.18$_v$	−1.3	B6 IVe	410	0.047	152	[29]	6	[.008]	3.1	261	(p)
27 Tau	23850	03 49 09.7	+24 03 12			3.63	−1.2	B8 III	300	0.047	157	12	9	.026	2.4	238	(q)
28 Tau	23862	03 49 11.1	+24 08 12			5.09$_v$	(0.5)	B8 Vpe	270	0.049	163	20	4	.012	1.2	50	(r)
30 Tau	23793	03 48 16.2	+11 08 36			5.07	−1.7	B3 V	740	0.033	125	21	16	.011	2.3	377	
37 Tau	25604	04 04 41.7	+22 04 55			4.36	0.2	K0 III	220	0.108	121	40	9	.013	14	65	
41 Tau	25823	04 06 36.3	+27 36 00			5.20$_v$	—	B9 p	—	0.055	159	—	−2	—	—	—	
47 Tau	26722	04 13 56.3	+09 15 49			4.84	0.3	G5 III	260	0.038	198	9	−7	.029	9.6	60	

(Continued)

s) SC:m4.92, $M+5.0$.

t) A very attractive binary (see Visual Binary Section). SC:$M+7.3$.

u) An eclipsing variable of some distinction in that a hydrogen ring rotates about the primary, eclipsing the star, B:$M-0.5$, $D_i 2.3$, $\mathscr{L}130$.

v) If the absolute magnitude is estimated to be $+1$, then: 230 l.y., $\pi.014$, $V10$, $D_s 0.8$, $\mathscr{L}31$.

TAURUS (CONT.)	HD	R.A.	Declin.	2000.0												
				m	*M*	Spectra	l.y.	μ	Dir.	V	RV	π	D_s	$\mathcal{L}$	Rmk
66 Tau	27820	04^h 23^m 51.8^s	+09° 27′ 39″	5.12	(−4.9)	A3 V	3300	0.019″	252°	90	−4	.001″	33	7047	
71 Tau	28052	04 26 20.7	+15 37 06	4.49$_v$	2.6	F0 V	78	0.113	101	85	38	.007	1.2	7.2	
75 Tau	28292	04 28 26.3	+16 21 35	4.97	−0.1	K2 IIIv	340	0.030	12	[23]	18	[.010]	18	86	
79 Tau	28355	04 28 50.2	+13 02 52	5.03	2.4	A7 V	110	0.109	96	[37]	33	[.030]	1.3	8.6	
80 Tau ∞	28485	04 30 08.3	+15 38 17	5.58	2.6	F0 V	110	0.104	103	34	30	.031	1.4	7.2	⊘
88 Tau	29140	04 35 39.2	+10 09 39	4.25	2.4	A5 Vm	91	0.069	130	30	29	.036	1.5	8.6	
90 Tau	29388	04 38 09.4	+12 30 39	4.27	2.1	A6 V	89	0.099	96	49	45	.024	1.5	11	
94 Tau	29763	04 42 14.6	+22 57 25	4.28	−1.7	B3 V	510	0.016	184	16	15	.017	2.3	377	
104 Tau	32923	05 07 27.0	+18 38 42	5.00	4.5†	G4 V	55	0.537	88	48	20	.059	1.1	1.2	(s)
109 Tau	34559	05 19 16.5	+22 05 47	4.94	0.3	G8 III	280	0.082	172	43	19	.010	11	60	
111 Tau	35296	05 24 25.4	+17 23 00	4.99	4.00†	F8 V	52	0.246	92	41	37	.063	1.1	2.0	
114 Tau	35708	05 27 38.0	+21 56 13	4.88	−1.7	B2.5 IV	680	0.008	157	[15]	13	[.005]	6.5	377	
119 Tau	36389	05 32 12.7	+18 35 39	4.38$_v$	−4.8	M2 Iab	2200	0.004	124	25	23	.002	364	6500	
125 Tau	37438	05 39 44.2	+25 53 50	5.18	−2.5	B3 IV	1100	0.030	138	[51]	15	[.003]	9.4	787	
126 Tau	37711	05 41 17.7	+16 32 02	4.86	−2.3	B3 IV	880	0.021	155	22	21	.014	3.0	655	
132 Tau	38751	05 49 00.9	+24 34 03	4.86	0.3	G8 IIIv	270	0.027	180	30	16	.005	13	60	
134 Tau	38899	05 49 32.9	+12 39 04	4.91	−0.3	B9 IV	360	0.031	220	[24]	18	[.009]	1.8	104	
136 Tau	39357	05 53 19.6	+27 36 44	4.58	0.4	A0 V	220	0.015	160	16	−16	.021	2.0	54	
139 Tau	40111	05 57 59.6	+25 57 14	4.82	−5.7	B0.5 II	4100	0.002	153	[16]	8	[.001]	24	15000	
Σ422 ∞	22468	03 36 47.2	+00 35 16	5.71	5.7	G9 V	100	0.164	191	33	−23	.032	0.9	0.4	⊘
Σ572 ∞	29364	04 38 29.5	+26 56 24	6.47	2.6	F2 V	190	0.074	139	17	4	.021	1.7	7.2	(t)
R Tau	28309	04 28 18.1	+10 09 45	7.3$_v$	−1.0	M5 III	1500	0.016	94	[50]	32	[.002]	43	198	
RW Tau	25487	04 03 54.4	+28 07 33	8.0$_v$	−0.2	B8 Ve	1400	0.039	125	[95]	−20	[.002]	3.3	95	(u)
- Tau	26793	04 14 36.2	+10 00 40	5.22	*	B9 Vn	*	0.023	180	*	7	*	*	*	(v)
- Tau	28527	04 30 33.6	+16 11 38	4.78	2.6†	A6 IV	91	0.110	104	41	38	.036	1.4	7.2	

Telescopium
(Telescopii)

a)   SW 3.5° is the large and fairly bright globular cluster NGC 6584.

b)   If the absolute magnitude is estimated to be +1, then: 240 l.y., π.013, V59, D_s2.3, $\mathscr{L}$31.

TELE-SCOPIUM	HD	R.A. 2000.0		Declin.		m	M	Spectra	l.y.	μ	Dir.	V	RV	π	D_s	$\mathscr{L}$	Rmk
α Tel	169467	$18^h\,26^m\,58.3^s$		−45° 58′ 06″		3.51	−2.9	B3 IV	620	0.048″	198°	[44]	0	[.005]″	5.8	1138	
δ¹ Tel	170465	18 31 45.3		−45 54 54		4.96	−1.3	B6	580	0.031	193	[27]	7	[.006]	2.2	261	
δ² Tel	170523	18 32 01.9		−45 45 26		5.07	−1.6	B3 IV/V	700	0.007	146	[11]	8	[.005]	2.1	344	
ε Tel	166063	18 11 13.7		−45 57 15		4.53	0.3	K0 III	230	0.034	206	27	−26	.023	13	60	
ζ Tel	169767	18 28 49.8		−49 04 15		4.13	0.3	K0 III	190	0.281	149	[84]	−31	[.017]	13	60	(a)
η Tel	181296	19 22 51.0		−54 25 25		5.05	(1.6)	A0 Vn	160	0.071	165	21	13	.020	1.5	19	
ι Tel	184127	19 35 12.8		−48 05 57		4.90	0.2	K0 III	280	0.038	200	93	22	.002	15	65	
κ Tel	174295	18 52 39.5		−52 06 27		5.17	0.2	K0 III	320	0.109	160	58	−44	.014	12	65	
λ Tel	175510	18 58 27.6		−52 56 18		4.87	−0.8	A0 V	440	0.013	90	[9]	−2	[.007]	2.7	164	
ν Tel	186543	19 48 01.1		−56 21 46		5.35	*	A7 III/IV	*	0.165	145	*	−12	*	*	*	(b)
ξ Tel	190421	20 07 23.1		−52 52 51		4.94	−0.5	M1 IIab	400	0.012	325	36	36	.014	35	125	
ρ Tel	177171	19 06 19.8		−52 20 27		5.16	3.0	F7 V	88	0.119	164	26	2	.022	1.8	5.0	

Triangulum
(Trianguli)

a) *Caput Trianguli, Rasalmothallah, Metallah.* OH:M+2.6, 53 l.y. Y:π.057.

WNW 4° is M33 (NGC 598), the "Pinwheel Galaxy," a very nice spiral, fairly bright and very large.

b) B:M−0.1, 140 l.y., $\mathscr{L}$90. OH:M+1.3, 71 l.y.

c) An attractive double with color contrast (yellow, blue?). B:200 l.y., $\mathscr{L}$30.

TRIAN-GULUM	HD	2000.0			m	M	Spectra	l.y.	μ	Dir.	V	RV	π	D_s	𝓛	Rmk
		R.A.	Declin.													
α Tri	11443	01^h 53^m 04.8^s	+29° 34′ 44″		3.41	1.9	F6 IV	65	0.229″	177°	25	−13	.050″	2.8	14	(a)
β Tri	13161	02 09 32.5	+34 59 14		3.00	0.3	A5 III	110	0.153	104	34	10	.022	3.6	60	(b)
γ Tri	14055	02 17 18.8	+33 50 50		4.01	0.6	A1 Vn	84	0.065	135	16	14	.039	2.4	45	
δ Tri	13974	02 17 03.2	+34 13 28		4.87	4.8	G0 V	34	1.178	102	58	−6	.097	0.9	0.9	
ε Tri	12471	02 02 57.9	+33 17 03		5.50	−0.2	A2 V	450	0.018	241	9	3	.010	3.5	95	
6 Tri ∞	13480	02 12 22.2	+30 18 11		4.94$_v$	0.3	G5 III	280	0.087	227	105	−18	.004	9.3	60	(c)
10 Tri	14252	02 18 57.0	+28 38 33		5.03	1.4	A2 V	170	0.011	100	[4]	3	[.019]	1.7	22	
14 Tri	15656	02 32 06.1	+36 08 50		5.15	−0.3	K5 III	400	0.049	70	[46]	−36	[.008]	28	104	
R Tri	16210	02 37 02.4	+34 15 50		5.3$_v$	(−0.2)	M4 IIIe	410	0.063	115	77	67	.008	35	95	

Triangulum Australe
(Trianguli Australis)

a)   *Atria.* OH:$M-1.0$.

b)   NNE 3° is the fairly bright open cluster NGC 6025.

c)   B:$M+0.2$, $\mathscr{L}70$. OH:$M+0.2$.

d)   The very high $B-V$ index ($+1.11$) would suggest a size of over 200 Suns, yet this would mean an absolute magnitude of -6.7, a luminosity of 38,000, and 4200 l.y. The parallax suggests a distance of about 120 l.y.

TRIANGULUM AUSTRALE	HD	2000.0 R.A.	Declin.	m	M	Spectra	l.y.	μ	Dir.	V	RV	π	D_s	$\mathscr{L}$	Rmk
α TrA	150798	16^h 48^m 39.9^s	−69° 01′ 40″	1.92	−0.1	K2 II	110	0.044″	141°	7	−3	.031″	24	86	(a)
β TrA	141891	15 55 08.4	−63 25 40	2.85	2.4	F0 III/IV	39	0.438	205	25	0	.083	1.5	8.6	(b)
γ TrA	135382	15 18 54.6	−68 40 46	2.89	0.6	A0 IV	94	0.068	243	32	−3	.010	2.3	45	(c)
δ TrA	145544	16 15 26.2	−63 41 08	3.85	−2.1	G5 Ib	510	0.017	144	6	−5	.029	43	545	(d)
ε TrA	138538	15 36 43.1	−66 19 02	4.11	0.2	K1/2 III	86	0.071	156	18	−16	.038	16	65	
ζ TrA	147584	16 28 28.1	−70 05 04	4.91	4.4†	F9 V	35	0.231	64	15	9	.093	1.0	1.4	
θ TrA	148890	16 35 44.7	−65 29 44	5.52	0.3	G8 III	360	0.055	139	21	10	.014	11	60	
ι TrA	147787	16 27 57.2	−64 03 29	5.27	2.6	F0 IV	110	0.060	66	11	−5	.029	1.6	7.2	
κ TrA	141767	15 55 29.5	−68 36 11	5.09	−6.2	G5 IIa	5900	0.015	200	12	6	.007	291	25000	
LP TrA	150549	16 46 40.0	−67 06 35	5.13$_v$	−1.4	A pSi	650	0.018	196	17	−2	.005	2.8	279	
- TrA	148291	16 30 49.3	−61 38 00	5.20	−0.1	K0 II/III	370	0.007	207	7	4	.006	20	86	
- TrA	150549	16 46 40.0	−67 06 35	5.13	−1.4	A0 pSi	650	0.018	196	17	−2	.005	2.8	279	

Tucana
(Tucanae)

a)   B:62 l.y., $\mathscr{L}$20.

b)   If the absolute magnitude is estimated to be +2, then: 230 l.y., π.016, V39, D_s3.3, $\mathscr{L}$13.
     SE 1.5° is the large, bright globular cluster NGC 362, just north of the Small Magel-
lanic Cloud. SW 4° of λ Tuc is NGC 104, a magnificent globular cluster, bright and large
(also known as 47 Tuc).

TUCANA	HD	2000.0 R.A.	Declin.	m	M	Spectra	l.y.	μ	Dir.	V	RV	π	D_s	$\mathcal{L}$	Rmk
α Tuc	211416	22ʰ 18ᵐ 30.1ˢ	−60° 15′ 35″	2.86	−0.2	K3 III	130	0.071″	237°	44	42	.026″	24	95	(a)
β¹ Tuc ∞	2884	00 31 32.7	−62 57 30	4.37	−0.2	B8/A0	110	0.107	118	22	14	.030	1.7	95	
β² Tuc	2885	00 31 33.6	−62 57 57	4.54	(1.9)	A2 V	110	0.117	116	21	10	.030	1.8	13	
β³ Tuc	3003	00 32 43.8	−63 01 53	5.09	(3.5)	A0 V	67	0.092	112	10	5	.049	0.6	3.0	
γ Tuc	219571	23 17 25.7	−58 14 08	3.99	0.6	F3 IV/V	76	0.092	344	21	18	.043	4.2	45	
δ Tuc ∞	212581	22 27 20.0	−64 58 00	4.48	−0.2	B9/A0 V	280	0.078	86	[34]	12	[.012]	2.4	95	
ε Tuc	224686	23 59 55.0	−65 34 38	4.50	0.0	B9 IV	260	0.059	110	[25]	11	[.013]	1.5	79	
ζ Tuc	1581	00 20 04.2	−64 52 30	4.23	4.96†	G0 V	23	2.070	56	71	9	.140	0.8	0.8	
η Tuc	224392	23 57 35.2	−64 17 55	5.00	(2.8)	A1 V	91	0.112	126	36	33	.036	1.0	6.1	
ι Tuc	6793	01 07 18.7	−61 46 31	5.37	0.3	G5 III	99	0.078	94	14	−8	.033	11	60	
κ Tuc ∞	7788	01 15 46.2	−68 52 34	4.99	3.3†	F5 V	72	0.420	75	45	9	.045	1.4	3.8	
λ¹ Tuc ∞	5190	00 52 24.4	−69 30 16	6.22	*	F7 IV/V	*	0.083	179	*	30	*	*	*	(b)
λ² Tuc	5457	00 55 00.3	−69 31 38	5.45	0.3	K2 III	93	0.042	165	8	5	.035	14	60	
ν Tuc	213442	22 33 00.0	−61 58 57	4.81ᵥ	(−1.0)	M4 III	470	0.048	120	33	−3	.007	43	191	
ρ Tuc	4089	00 42 28.4	−65 28 05	5.39	3.3	F6 V	86	0.075	50	17	14	.038	1.5	3.8	

Ursa Major
(Ursae Majoris)

a) *Dubhe* (Back of the Great Bear). The "lip" of the Big Dipper (North America) or The Plough (UK), and pointer to the North Star. This star and the end-star η are not members of the group of stars that make up the rest of the Dipper/Plough, and as time goes by, the constellation will become distorted. OH:m1.79, $M-0.8$.

   Dubhe has an m7 companion, PA 104°, 6.3″.

b) *Merak* (Loin). SE 2.4° is M97 (NGC 3587), the faint Owl Nebula—large telescope needed. In the same field is NGC 3356, an almost edge-on spiral galaxy, large and bright.

c) *Phecda,* or *Phad* (The Thigh). SE 1° is M109, a fairly bright barred spiral galaxy.

d) *Megrez* (Root of the Tail). OH:$M+1.2$, 53 l.y. Y:π.061.

e) *Alioth.* The absolute magnitude comes from OH. B:$M+0.2$, $\mathscr{L}$85.

f) *Mizar* (Girdle, or Apron). A well-known double (with Mizar B); considered the first binary ever discovered, in 1650. At 14″ separation, it is easily resolved, even by small telescopes. B:$\mathscr{L}$70. OH:$M+0.7$, $RV-6$.

   Mizar has a more noted companion, Alcor (see note s), which is also most likely gravitationally bound to the system. East 5.5° is M101, one of the largest spiral galaxies, seen face-on.

g) *Benetnasch, Alkaid* (Leader of the Mourners).

h) OH:$M+2.6$. In the same field is the visual binary OΣ 199, also known as 37 Lyncis. WSW 1.5° is NGC 2841, a nice oval spiral galaxy.

i) *Talitha;* has an m10 companion, which is itself a rapid binary, 39 years. Both faint stars are red dwarfs. OH:$M+1.7$, 43 l.y. Y:π.075.

j) *Al Kaprah.*

k) *Tania Borealis.* This star is considered a distant member of the Hyades Cluster, in Taurus. It has an interesting color contrast with μ UMa. OH:$M+1.0$.

l) *Tania Australis,* OH:$M-0.7$, 170 l.y.

m) *Alula Borealis.* Has an m9.5 companion 7″ away. OH:M0.0, 130 l.y. In 1990 this star was designated an RS CVn-type variable of very small amplitude [IBVS #3530].

n) *Alula Australis.* A visual binary presently (1990–95) at its closest, and gradually widening.

o) *Muscida* (Muzzle). OH:$M+0.5$, 120 l.y.

p) A close binary, with disputed period, placed at about 700 years by some and over 1000 by others (see Visual Binary Section). Burnham gives a drawn orbit.

   ENE 4° is one of the finest spiral galaxies, M81 (NGC 3031), and in the same field is the smaller and dimmer galaxy, M82 (NGC 3034).

q) A close binary, 107-year period. See Burnham for orbit.

r) If the absolute magnitude is estimated to be +2, then: 135 l.y., π.024, V16, D_s1.6, $\mathscr{L}$13.

URSA MAJOR	HD	R.A. 2000.0	Declin.	m	M	Spectra	l.y.	μ	Dir.	V	RV	π	D_s	𝓛	Rmk
α UMa	95689	11ʰ 03ᵐ 43.6ˢ	+61° 45′ 03″	1.49	0.2	K0 III	86	0.138″	239°	19	−9	.038″	14	65	(a)
β UMa	95418	11 01 50.4	+56 22 56	2.37	(1.0)	A1 V	62	0.086	70	14	−12	.053	1.5	32	(b)
γ UMa	103287	11 53 49.8	+53 41 41	2.44	0.6	A0 V	76	0.093	86	20	−13	.028	2.3	45	(c)
δ UMa	106591	12 15 25.5	+57 01 57	3.31	1.9†	A3 V	62	0.102	88	16	−13	.053	1.5	14	(d)
ε UMa	112185	12 54 01.7	+55 57 35	1.77ᵥ	0.3	A0 IV	64	0.109	95	58	−9	.009	2.1	60	(e)
ζᴬ UMa ∞	116656	13 23 55.5	+54 55 31	2.27	1.4	A2 Va	69	0.122	102	15	−9	.047	1.6	22	(f)
ζᴮ UMa	116657	13 23 56.3	+54 55 18	3.95	(2.3)	A1 m	69	0.120	106	15	−9	.047	1.4	9.4	
η UMa	120315	13 47 32.3	+49 18 48	1.86	−1.7	B3 V	93	0.127	264	20	−11	.035	2.0	377	(g)
θ UMa	82328	09 32 51.3	+51 40 38	3.17	2.0†	F6 IV	55	1.094	240	89	15	.059	2.5	12	(h)
ι UMa	76644	08 59 12.4	+48 02 30	3.14	2.2†	A7 IV	49	0.501	242	37	9	.066	1.3	10	(i)
κ UMa	77327	09 03 37.5	+47 09 24	3.60	(−0.4)	A1 Vn	200	0.066	211	20	4	.016	3.6	112	(j)
λ UMa	89021	10 17 05.7	+42 54 52	3.45	0.6	A2 IV	110	0.171	255	32	18	.030	2.4	45	(k)
μ UMa	89758	10 22 19.7	+41 29 58	3.05	−0.4	M0 III	93	0.088	290	24	−21	.035	32	114	(l)
ν UMa	98262	11 18 28.7	+33 05 39	3.48	−0.2	K3 III	180	0.036	309	12	−9	.020	25	95	(m)
ξᴬ UMa ∞	98231	11 18 10.9	+31 31 45	4.41	4.9†	G0 V	25	0.732	216	31	−16	.130	0.8	0.9	(n)
ξᴮ UMa	98230	11 18 10.9	+31 31 45	4.87	5.4	G0 V	25	0.732	216	31	−16	.130	0.6	0.6	
o UMa	71369	08 30 15.8	+60 43 05	3.36	−0.9	G5 III	230	0.171	230	92	20	.009	18	180	(o)
π² UMa	73108	08 40 12.9	+64 19 41	4.60	0.2	K1 IIIb+	250	0.057	295	23	15	.016	16	65	
ρ UMa	76827	09 02 32.7	+67 37 47	4.76	(0.5)	M3III(b)+	230	0.026	309	10	5	.014	20	50	
σ¹ UMa	77800	09 08 23.5	+66 52 24	5.14	−0.3	K5 III	400	0.045	204	24	15	.011	29	104	
σ² UMa ∞	78154	09 10 23.1	+67 08 04	4.8	3.4†	F7 IV/V	63	0.080	195	8	−2	.052	1.4	3.4	(p)
τ UMa	78362	09 10 55.0	+63 30 49	4.67	—	A m	—	0.118	123	—	−9	—	—	—	
υ UMa	84999	09 50 59.3	+59 02 19	3.80ᵥ	1.9	F2 IV	80	0.332	242	47	27	.041	1.8	14	
φ UMa	85235	09 52 06.3	+54 03 51	4.59	(2.1)	A3 IV	100	0.018	344	12	−12	.032	1.2	11	(q)
χ UMa	102224	11 46 03.0	+47 46 46	3.71	0.2	K2 III	160	0.140	280	36	−9	.019	16	65	
ψ UMa	96833	11 09 39.7	+44 29 54	3.01	0.0	K1 III	130	0.075	245	[15]	−4	[.025]	17	79	
ω UMa	94334	10 53 58.7	+43 11 24	4.71	1.2	A1 V	160	0.053	122	25	−17	.014	1.1	26	
15 UMa	78209	09 08 52.2	+51 36 16	4.48	—	A m	—	0.141	254	—	0	—	—	—	
16 UMa	79028	09 14 20.6	+61 25 24	5.13	3.5†	F9 V	71	0.034	178	14	−14	.046	1.6	3.1	
18 UMa	79439	09 16 11.3	+54 01 18	4.83ᵥ	2.1	A5 V	78	0.079	42	21	−19	.042	1.3	11	
23 UMa	81937	09 31 31.7	+63 03 43	3.67	1.7	F0 IV	80	0.112	77	16	−10	.041	2.2	16	
24 UMa	82210	09 34 28.8	+69 49 49	4.56ᵥ	2.9†	G4 III/IV	71	0.099	320	29	−27	.046	2.8	5.4	
26 UMa	82621	09 34 49.4	+52 03 05	4.50	1.4	A2 V	140	0.077	239	27	23	.025	1.6	22	
27 UMa	83506	09 42 57.1	+72 15 09	5.17	0.2	K0 III	320	0.040	219	[25]	−17	[.010]	14	65	
31 UMa	85795	09 55 42.9	+49 49 12	5.27	(2.3)	A3 III	130	0.021	341	7	−6	.025	1.2	10	
36 UMa	90839	10 30 37.5	+55 58 50	4.84	4.0†	F8 V	40	0.181	259	14	9	.083	1.1	2.0	
37 UMa	91480	10 35 09.6	+57 04 57	5.16	2.8	F1 V	91	0.075	62	14	−10	.036	1.4	6.0	
38 UMa	92424	10 41 56.5	+65 42 58	5.12	−0.1	K2 III	361	0.181	245	35	−11	.026	19	86	
44 UMa	94247	10 53 34.3	+54 35 06	5.10	−0.2	K3 III	370	0.072	260	21	1	.016	24	95	
46 UMa	94600	10 55 44.3	+33 30 25	5.03	0.0	K1 III	330	0.115	254	[59]	−22	[.010]	16	79	
47 UMa	95128	10 59 27.9	+40 25 49	5.05	4.4†	G0 V	44	0.324	279°	24	13	.074	1.1	1.4	
49 UMa	95310	11 00 50.3	+39 12 43	5.08	*	F0 V	*	0.078	252	*	3	*	*	*	(r)
55 UMa	98353	11 19 07.8	+38 11 08	4.78	1.4	A2 V	160	0.094	218	18	−3	.025	2.1	22	
56 UMa	98839	11 22 49.5	+45 28 58	4.99	−2.1	G7.5 IIIa	850	0.038	250	91	3	.002	37	545	
67 UMa	104513	12 02 06.8	+43 02 44	5.21ᵥ	(1.6)	A7 m	170	0.331	282	83	6	.019	2.0	18	

(Continued)

s) *Alcor* (The Rider?). While many authorities believe Alcor to be gravitationally bound to Mizar, some references (e.g. DA) consider this an optical double. The proper motion and direction of the two stars is quite similar despite the great distance, about a quarter of a light-year.

t) A subdwarf with one-fifth the Sun's luminosity, famous for its large proper motion. B:$M+6.8$, $\mathcal{L}0.14$ (= one-seventh the Sun's). Burnham points out that this star will continue to approach the solar system until around 9900, then will slowly begin to recede. He provides a finder's chart.

u) A visual binary of nearly equal magnitudes, fixed at 16.7″. The distance is deduced from the distance modulus formula (given m and M); the parallax yields a distance of about 125 l.y.

v) A Mira-type variable. If the absolute magnitude is estimated to be -1, then: 750 l.y., $\pi.004$, $V66$, D_s43, $\mathcal{L}198$. B:1350 l.y., $\mathcal{L}250$ ($=M-1.2$).

  From R UMa to ε UMa—on the handle of the Dipper/Plough—lie a number of Mira variables: RY, Z, T, S, RS—all worth investigating. See Levy, 28f., 129f.

w) One of the nearest stars, faint because it is a red dwarf. See Burnham for a finder's chart.

x) SC:$M+4.7$.

URSA MAJOR (CONT.)	HD	R.A.			Declin.			m	M	Spectra	l.y.	μ	Dir.	V	RV	π	D_s	$\mathscr{L}$	Rmk
				2000.0															
78 UMa ∞	113139	13^{h}00^m	43.7^s	+56°	21'	59''	4.93	3.0	F2 V	96	0.112''	97°	19	−10	.034''	1.3	5.0	⊘
80 UMa	116842	13 25	13.4	+54	59	17	4.01	2.1	A5 V	72	0.117	100	15	−9	.045	1.7	11	(s)
83 UMa	119228	13 40	44.1	+54	40	54	4.66	−0.5	M2 IIIab+	350	0.029	248	20	−17	.014	35	125	
Grb 1830	103095	11 52	58.7	+37	43	07	6.45	6.71†	G8 V	29	7.050	145	312	−98	.113	0.5	0.2	(t)
Σ1415 ∞	88849	10 17	51.3	+71	03	22	6.66	0.5	A8	560	0.060	212	16	11	.026	3.8	50	(u)
R UMa	92763	10 44	38.3	+68	46	32	5.8$_v$	*	M5 III	*	0.052	240	*	34	*	*	*	(v)
T UMa	109729	12 36	23.2	+59	29	12	5.5$_v$	−1.2	M4 III	710	0.032	242	[97]	−91	[.005]	47	238	
CS UMa	84335	09 46	31.6	+57	07	41	5.2$_v$	−0.5	M3 IIIab	450	0.030	4	[21]	8	[.007]	35	125	
Lalande 21185	95735	11 03	20.2	+35	58	13	7.49	10.49†	M2 V	8.21	4.777	187	102	−84	.397	0.2	0.01	(w)
- UMa	84737	09 48	35.3	+46	01	15	5.09	4.20†	G0.5 Va	49	0.243	113	18	5	.066	1.2	1.6	(x)
- UMa	89822	10 24	07.8	+65	33	59	4.97	(3.1)	A0 pSi+	76	0.027	200	3	0	.043	0.4	4.4	
- UMa	91312	10 33	13.8	+40	25	31	4.75	1.5	A7 IV	110	0.138	268	23	9	.031	1.9	20	
- UMa	92523	10 43	04.0	+69	04	34	5.00	−0.2	K3 III(b)	360	0.016	176	15	0	.005	24	95	
- UMa	92787	10 43	32.8	+46	12	14	5.18	(1.8)	F5 III	160	0.279	255	63	4	.021	2.1	15	

Ursa Minor
(Ursae Minoris)

a) *Polaris; North Star.* Currently drawing even closer to the Pole, with its closest at 2102 A.D. (27′31″). A binary, it is considered a nice test for small telescopes. It is also a Cepheid variable.

b) *Kochab.*

c) *Pherkad.* OH:M+0.4, 110 l.y.

URSA MINOR	HD	2000.0 R.A.	Declin.	m	M	Spectra	l.y.	μ	Dir.	V	RV	π	D_s	$\mathscr{L}$	Rmk
α UMi ∞	8890	02^h 31^m 50.5^s	+89° 15′ 51″	2.02$_v$	−4.6	F7 lb	690	0.046″	95°	36	−17	.007″	67	5500	(a)
β UMi	131873	14 50 42.2	+74 09 20	2.08	−0.3	K4 III	84	0.036	286	18	17	.039	28	104	(b)
γ UMi	137422	15 20 43.6	+71 50 02	3.05$_v$	−1.1	A3 II/III	220	0.031	308	49	−4	.003	5.5	217	(c)
δ UMi	166205	17 32 12.5	+86 35 11	4.36	1.2	A1 Vn	140	0.055	9	65	−8	.004	1.8	26	
ε UMi	153751	16 45 57.8	+82 02 14	4.23$_v$	0.3	G5 III	200	0.011	75	12	−11	.010	11	60	
ζ UMi	142105	15 44 03.3	+77 47 40	4.32	1.7	A3 Vn	110	0.014	102	14	−13	.016	1.5	16	
η UMi	148048	16 17 30.2	+75 45 19	4.95	2.6	F5 V	76	0.264	341	31	−10	.043	1.1	7.2	
θ UMi	139669	15 31 24.7	+77 20 57	4.96	−0.3	K5 III	370	0.054	280	28	−25	.021	31	104	
λ UMi	183030	17 16 56.0	+89 02 15	6.38	−0.5	M1 III	780	0.027	272	[31]	2	[.004]	33	125	
4 UMi	124547	14 08 50.8	+77 32 51	4.82	−0.2	K3 III	330	0.045	311	22	6	.010	24	95	
5 UMi	127700	14 27 31.4	+75 41 45	4.25	−0.3	K4 III	270	0.020	11	11	10	.019	27	104	
11 UMi	136726	15 17 05.8	+71 49 26	5.02	−0.3	K4 III	380	0.009	6	16	−16	.015	25	104	
19 UMi	146926	16 10 49.3	+75 52 39	5.48	0.0	B8 V	410	0.014	330	[8]	−1	[.008]	3.0	79	
RR UMi	132813	14 57 34.9	+65 55 56	4.60$_v$	(−0.4)	M5 III	330	0.088	288	42	7	.010	32	114	
- UMi	118904	13 37 10.9	+71 14 32	5.50	0.2	gK2	370	0.043	259	[28]	15	[.009]	17	65	
- UMi	124730	14 12 04.0	+69 25 57	5.24	−0.5	M2 IIIab	460	0.056	210	28	−23	.016	34	125	
- UMi	136064	15 14 38.2	+67 20 48	5.13	3.6†	F9 IV	67	0.446	152	64	−47	.049	1.4	2.9	

Vela
(Velorum)

a) An attractive double; note that the primary is γ^2. B:$M-1.7$ (assuming the same distance as γ^2), $\mathcal{L}$400. On the other hand, OH gives γ^2 a distance of 1500 l.y., which accords with our distance for γ^1.

South 2° is NGC 2547, a bright open cluster.

b) *Suhail al Muhlif.* The brightest known Wolf–Rayet star, and apparently the closest one to the Solar System. These are highly luminous stars, sometimes approaching 100,000 Suns, and are the hottest stars known, over 50,000 K (and perhaps double that). M and D_s from Burnham.

c) B:$M+0.2$, $\mathcal{L}$70. OH:m1.96.

d) *Markab.*

e) *Al Suhail.* B:$M-4.6$, $\mathcal{L}$5800, Spect. K5 Ib. OH:$M-3.3$, 330 l.y., K4 Ib-IIa.

f) OH:$M+0.8$, 75 l.y.

g) SSE 1° is the open cluster NGC 2660.

h) If the absolute magnitude is estimated to be -4.5, then: 2700 l.y., π.001, V27, D_s4.9, $\mathcal{L}$5000.

i) The parallax suggests a far greater distance, over 1000 l.y.

j) If the absolute magnitude is estimated to be -1, then: 535 l.y., π.006, V28, D_s2.1, $\mathcal{L}$198.

k) The $B-V$ index (-0.18) indicates a size of D_s1–3. From Fig. 2 we might estimate the absolute magnitude at -2; however, this yields a size of only 0.8. Thus we estimate the absolute magnitude of -1, which gives: 520 l.y., π.006, V39, D_s1.8, and $\mathcal{L}$198.

VELA	HD	R.A. 2000.0	Declin.	m	M	Spectra	l.y.	μ	Dir.	V	RV	π	D_s	$\mathscr{L}$	Rmk
γ¹ Vel ∞	68243	08ʰ 09ᵐ 29.2ˢ	−47° 20′ 44″	4.27	−3.9	B1 IV	1400	0.011″	236°	[30]	20	[.002]″	2.7	2858	(a)
γ² Vel	68273	08 09 31.9	−47 20 12	1.78ᵥ	(−5.6)	WC8	800	0.007	304	35	35	.017	17	15000	(b)
δ Vel ∞	74956	08 44 42.2	−54 42 30	2.02	0.5†	A0 V	65	0.082	164	8	2	.050	2.6	50	(c)
κ Vel	81188	09 22 06.8	−55 00 38	2.50	−3.0	B2 IV/V	410	0.011	315	22	22	.013	4.6	1247	(d)
λ Vel	78647	09 07 59.7	−43 25 57	2.21ᵥ	−4.4	K4 III	680	0.025	299	57	18	.002	217	4500	(e)
μ Vel ∞	93497	10 46 46.1	−49 25 12	2.69	0.3	G5 III	98	0.087	125	20	6	.022	11	60	(f)
o Vel	74195	08 40 17.6	−52 55 19	3.62ᵥ	−1.7	B3 IV	380	0.028	314	[22]	16	[.009]	2.6	377	
φ Vel	86440	09 56 51.7	−54 34 04	3.54	−6.0	B5 Ib	2600	0.013	293	[52]	14	[.001]	23	20000	
ψ Vel ∞	82434	09 30 41.9	−40 28 00	3.60	3.18†	F2 IV	50	0.201	290	17	9	.065	1.2	4.2	⊘
a Vel	75063	08 46 01.7	−46 02 30	3.91	−0.6	A1 III	260	0.007	254	27	24	.003	3.9	137	
b Vel	74180	08 40 37.6	−46 38 55	3.84	−8.4	F3 Ia	110	0.004	297	25	25	.031	400	180000	(g)
c Vel	78004	09 04 09.2	−47 05 52	3.75	−0.1	K2 III	190	0.053	253	27	24	.020	19	86	
d Vel	74772	08 44 23.9	−42 38 57	4.07	2.5†	G5 III	67	0.025	310	3	−2	.049	3.8	7.9	
e Vel	73634	08 37 38.6	−42 59 21	4.14	−5.8	A6 II	3200	0.013	293	19	19	.018	56	16500	
f Vel	75821	08 50 33.4	−46 31 45	5.10ᵥ	*	B0 III	*	0.007	243	*	7	*	*	*	(h)
g Vel	75710	08 49 47.7	−45 18 28	4.93	0.05	A2 III	310	0.014	12	8	5	.012	3.3	75	
h Vel	75630	08 49 39.1	−40 19 14	5.48	(3.3)	A2/3 IV	91	0.023	221	17	17	.036	0.8	3.9	
i Vel	95370	11 00 09.2	−42 13 33	4.39	0.6	A3 IV	190	0.021	95	34	−5	.003	2.9	45	(i)
k² Vel	79940	09 15 45.1	−37 24 48	4.62	3.6†	F5 III	51	0.024	123	6	6	.064	1.2	2.9	
l Vel	79917	09 15 36.7	−38 34 12	4.94	−0.1	K0 III	330	0.072	261	13	2	.027	17	86	
m Vel	85622	09 51 40.7	−46 32 52	4.58	0.3	G5 Ib	230	0.013	257	14	11	.007	16	60	
n Vel	74272	08 41 13.0	−47 19 01	4.77	−2.3	A5 II	850	0.018	289	[27]	17	[.004]	10	650	
p Vel	92139	10 37 18.0	−48 13 33	3.84	2.0	F4 IV	81	0.160	263	27	19	.040	1.8	12	
t Vel	91504	10 32 56.9	−47 00 12	5.02	−0.3	K4 III	380	0.014	270	4	4	.010	17	104	
u Vel	85355	09 49 57.1	−45 43 58	5.08	*	B7 III	*	0.032	274	*	12	*	*	*	(j)
w Vel	77258	09 00 05.4	−41 15 14	4.45	2.4	G8 III+	110	0.057	311	11	−7	.030	2.9	8.6	
x Vel ∞	92449	10 39 18.3	−55 36 12	4.28	−2.1	G2/3 Ib	620	0.023	268	21	20	.023	40	545	
B Vel	70930	08 22 31.5	−48 29 25	4.82	−3.6	B1 V	1600	0.019	291	[52]	27	[.002]	16	2168	
C Vel	73155	08 34 43.7	−49 56 39	5.01	(−0.2)	K1/2 II	360	0.017	13	10	4	.009	23	96	
D Vel	74753	08 43 40.5	−49 49 22	5.16	−4.1	B0 IIIn	2300	0.024	90	[117]	28	[.001]	5	3500	
H Vel	76805	08 56 19.4	−52 43 25	4.69	−1.1	B5 V	470	0.007	333	22	22	.020	1.9	217	
I Vel	89890	10 20 55.4	−56 02 36	4.50	−2.3	B3 IIIe	750	0.036	284	24	10	.008	3.2	655	
J Vel	81848	09 26 18.0	−53 22 45	5.11	−1.1	B6 V	570	0.010	264	[25]	24	[.006]	2.0	217	
L Vel	83058	09 34 08.7	−51 15 21	5.01	*	B1.5 V	*	0.023	221	*	35	*	*	*	(k)
M Vel	83446	09 36 49.7	−49 21 18	4.35	2.1	A5 IV/V	92	0.114	283	35	21	.019	1.7	11	
N Vel	82668	09 31 13.3	−57 02 04	3.13ᵥ	−0.3	K4/5 III	160	0.034	268	16	−14	.022	30	104	
Y Vel	91324	10 31 21.8	−53 42 56	4.89ᵥ	3.7	F6 V	60	0.466	296	46	20	.054	1.2	2.6	
FZ Vel	77140	08 58 52.2	−47 14 05	5.18ᵥ	(0.7)	A m	250	0.106	299	43	18	.013	2.9	39	
GU Vel	71935	08 27 36.5	−53 05 19	5.09ᵥ	2.6	A9 III/IV	100	0.072	280	30	25	.021	1.2	7.2	
GX Vel	79186	09 11 04.3	−44 52 04	5.00ᵥ	−6.8	B5 Ia	7500	0.007	270	[83]	34	[.0004]	88	40000	

(Continued)

l) If the absolute magnitude is estimated to be -2, then: 900 l.y., π.004, V25, D_s2.3, $\mathcal{L}$500.

m) This is only one of a half-dozen bright stars in the large open cluster I. 2391, of which **o** Vel is the brightest.

n) If the absolute magnitude is estimated to be 0.0, then: 360 l.y., π.009, V32, D_s1.5, $\mathcal{L}$79.

VELA (CONT.)	HD	2000.0 R.A.	Declin.	m	M	Spectra	l.y.	μ	Dir.	V	RV	π	D_s	$\mathscr{L}$	Rmk
GZ Vel	89682	$10^h\,19^m\,36.8^s$	$-55°\,01'\,46''$	4.57_v	-5.9	K3 II	4000	$0.011''$	$218°$	15	13	$.008''$	418	18000	
HY Vel	74560	08 42 25.4	$-53\,06\,50$	4.86_v	-1.6	B3 IV	650	0.028	319	[34]	22	[.005]	1.8	340	
IS Vel	68324	08 09 43.2	$-47\,56\,14$	5.23_v	-1.7	B1 IVe	790	0.002	270	[6]	5	[.004]	1.3	377	
LN Vel	74371	08 41 56.8	$-45\,24\,39$	5.23_v	-6.3	B6 Iae	6600	0.011	248	[106]	24	[.0005]	67	25000	
- Vel	67582	08 06 40.3	$-45\,15\,59$	5.05	0.3	K3 III	300	0.006	261	25	25	.011	22	62	
- Vel	68217	08 09 35.9	$-44\,07\,23$	5.21	*	B2 IV/V	*	0.018	223	*	8	*	*	*	(l)
- Vel	69144	08 13 36.2	$-46\,59\,31$	5.13	-2.6	B2.5 IV	1100	0.005	202	[27]	25	[.003]	3.3	863	
- Vel	71510	08 25 30.7	$-51\,43\,42$	5.17	-1.6	B2 Ve	740	0.047	254	[53]	18	[.004]	4.3	344	
- Vel	72127	08 29 27.5	$-44\,43\,30$	4.99	-1.0	B2 IV	510	0.005	202	[22]	22	[.006]	3.3	198	
- Vel	74067	08 40 19.2	$-40\,15\,51$	5.20	0.2	B9 V	330	0.050	262	[32]	21	[.010]	2.2	65	
- Vel	74146	08 39 58.6	$-53\,03\,03$	5.19	-1.1	B4 IV	590	0.021	284	[21]	14	[.006]	1.7	215	(m)
- Vel	77653	09 01 44.6	$-52\,11\,18$	5.23	(-0.3)	B9 Si	410	0.020	330	34	32	.008	1.3	99	
- Vel	80108	09 16 23.0	$-44\,15\,57$	5.12	-5.9	K3 Ib	5200	0.005	233	3	-3	.017	437	18000	
- Vel	82694	09 32 19.2	$-40\,38\,58$	5.35	(2.3)	G8 III	140	0.016	153	3	-1	.024	4.5	10	
- Vel	82984	09 33 44.4	$-49\,00\,18$	5.12	-1.4	B4 IV	660	0.022	291	18	17	.015	2.1	286	
- Vel	87783	10 06 11.3	$-47\,22\,12$	5.08	3.2	K1 IV	77	0.059	174	27	21	.017	2.8	4.1	
- Vel	88206	10 08 56.2	$-51\,48\,40$	4.86	-1.6	B3 IV	640	0.012	265	[18]	14	[.005]	2.3	344	
- Vel	88955	10 14 44.1	$-42\,07\,19$	3.85	1.4	A2 V	96	0.155	284	23	7	.034	1.8	22	
- Vel	89998	10 22 19.5	$-41\,39\,00$	4.83	0.0	K1 III	300	0.059	330	24	21	.024	17	79	
- Vel	93563	10 46 57.5	$-56\,45\,26$	5.23	*	B8/9 IIIe	*	0.017	253	*	31	*	*	*	(n)

Virgo
(Virginis)

a) *Spica* (Ear of Wheat). A pulsating variable and also a very large spectroscopic binary; Burnham gives a diameter of eight Suns for the primary and "possibly half" that for the companion.

b) *Porrima*. A well-known visual binary, with the companion currently (1990–95) nearly due west of the primary, and closing to a distance of about 0.3″ by 2007, thereafter rapidly widening (see Orbital Elements Section). B:M+3.6. SC:M+2.6. Y:m3.68.

c) *Auva*. B:$\mathcal{L}$85. OH:M−1.2, 270 l.y.

d) *Vindemiatrix* (Grape Gatherer). B:M+0.6, 90 l.y., $\mathcal{L}$50.

e) *Heze*. B:M+1.1, 90 l.y., $\mathcal{L}$30. OH:M+1.4, 79 l.y.

f) SC:M+0.4 (which yields a luminosity of 54 and size of 8 Suns).

g) Due south just under 4° is the splendid Sombrero Galaxy (M104), a fine spiral, with equatorial dust line visible only in the largest telescopes.

h) A Mira-type variable, with quite rapid period. If the absolute magnitude is estimated to be −1, then: 1350 l.y., π.004, V28, D_s37, $\mathcal{L}$198. Burnham estimates the distance to be 1000 l.y.

i) Mira-type variable; due to its period it will be around 2015 before its maximum should be visible.

   If the absolute magnitude is estimated to be −1, then: 820 l.y., π.004, V57, D_s43, $\mathcal{L}$198.

VIRGO	HD	R.A. 2000.0	Declin.	m	M	Spectra	l.y.	μ	Dir.	V	RV	π	D_s	$\mathscr{L}$	Rmk
α Vir	116658	13ʰ 25ᵐ 11.5ˢ	−11° 09′ 41″	0.98ᵥ	−3.5	B1 III	260	0.054″	232°	11	1	.023″	2.2	1977	(a)
β Vir	102870	11 50 41.6	+01 45 53	3.61	3.60†	F8 V	33	0.790	110	36	5	.100	1.4	2.9	
γ Vir ∞	110379	12 41 39.5	−01 26 58	3.48	3.46†	F0 V	33	0.568	271	34	−20	.099	1.6	3.3	(b)𝒪
δ Vir	112300	12 55 36.1	+03 23 51	3.38	−0.5	M3 III	200	0.474	263	104	−18	.022	34	125	(c)
ε Vir	113226	13 02 10.5	+10 57 33	2.83	0.2	G8 III	76	0.276	274	33	−14	.043	12	65	(d)
ζ Vir	118098	13 34 41.5	−00 35 46	3.37	1.7	A3 V	74	0.288	277	34	−13	.044	1.8	16	(e)
η Vir	107259	12 19 54.3	−00 40 00	3.89	1.4	A2 IV	100	0.068	251	20	2	.016	1.6	22	
θ Vir	114330	13 09 56.9	−05 32 20	4.38	1.2	A1 IV	140	0.050	223	10	−3	.026	1.5	26	
ι Vir	124850	14 16 00.8	−06 00 02	4.08	0.7	F6 III	76	0.432	181	49	12	.043	5.1	41	
κ Vir	124294	14 12 53.7	−10 16 25	4.19	−0.2	K3 III	250	0.136	3	30	−4	.022	23	95	
λ Vir	125337	14 19 06.5	−13 22 16	4.52	(0.7)	A2 m	190	0.031	322	14	−11	.017	3.0	42	
ν Vir	102212	11 45 51.5	+06 31 46	4.03	−0.5	M1 IIIab	260	0.188	186	82	51	.014	31	125	
ξ Vir	102124	11 45 17.0	+08 15 30	4.85	(2.8)	A4 V	84	0.063	110	8	−1	.039	1.3	5.9	
o Vir	104979	12 05 12.5	+08 43 59	4.12	0.3	G8 IIIa+	84	0.225	281	41	−30	.039	12	60	
π Vir	104321	12 00 52.3	+06 36 51	4.66	1.7	A5 V	130	0.034	182	13	−10	.021	1.9	16	
ρ Vir	110411	12 41 53.0	+10 14 08	4.88	0.6	A0 V	230	0.127	139	[43]	2	[.014]	2.8	45	
σ Vir	115521	13 17 36.2	+05 28 12	4.80	−0.5	M2 IIIa	370	0.013	328	28	−27	.011	36	125	
τ Vir	122408	14 01 38.7	+01 32 40	4.26	1.7	A3 V	110	0.030	147	6	−2	.024	1.7	16	
υ Vir	125454	14 19 32.4	−02 15 56	5.14	0.3	G9 III	300	0.140	239	46	−27	.018	13	60	
φ Vir ∞	126868	14 28 12.1	−02 13 40	4.81	3.1†	G2 IV	69	0.141	268	17	−10	.045	2.5	4.5	(f)
χ Vir	110014	12 39 14.7	−07 59 44	4.66	−0.1	K2 III(b)	290	0.085	249	28	−20	.020	20	86	(g)
ψ Vir	112142	12 54 21.1	−09 32 20	4.79ᵥ	−0.5	M3 III+	370	0.034	234	20	18	.021	34	125	
ω Vir	101153	11 38 27.5	+08 08 03	5.36ᵥ	−1.1	M4 III	640	0.010	281	10	4	.005	44	217	
16 Vir	107328	12 20 20.9	+03 18 45	4.96	0.2	K0 IIIb+	290	0.301	257	715	36	.002	16	65	
32 Vir	110951	12 45 37.0	+07 40 24	5.22ᵥ	(1.0)	F0 III	230	0.110	270	38	−9	.014	3.1	33	
49 Vir	114038	13 07 53.7	−10 44 25	5.19	0.0	K2 III	360	0.018	133	10	−9	.025	17	79	
53 Vir	114642	13 12 03.4	−16 11 55	5.04	1.4	F5 III/IV	81	0.307	162	39	−14	.040	3.3	22	
57 Vir	115202	13 15 58.7	−19 56 35	5.22	3.3†	K1 III/IV	80	0.327	112	51	34	.041	3.3	3.8	
59 Vir	115383	13 16 46.4	+09 25 27	5.22	4.65†	G0 V	42	0.385	299	35	−26	.077	0.9	1.1	
61 Vir	115617	13 18 24.2	−18 18 41	4.74	5.12†	G6 V	27	1.518	225	61	−9	.119	0.9	0.7	
69 Vir	116976	13 27 27.1	−15 58 25	4.76	3.5†	K1 III	57	0.124	279	17	−14	.057	3	3	
70 Vir	117176	13 28 25.7	+13 46 43	4.98	3.6†	G2.5 Va	62	0.628	202	56	5	.053	1.8	2.9	
74 Vir	117675	13 31 57.8	−06 15 21	4.69	−0.5	M2 III	360	0.113	245	32	18	.020	35	125	
76 Vir	117818	13 32 58.0	−10 09 54	5.21	0.2	K0 III	330	0.053	220	12	−1	.021	12	65	
78 Vir	118022	13 34 07.8	+03 39 32	4.94ᵥ	(1.6)	A1 p+	160	0.051	125	17	−12	.021	1.6	19	
82 Vir	119149	13 41 36.7	−08 42 11	5.01	−0.5	M2 III	410	0.105	289	53	−37	.013	35	125	
84 Vir ∞	119425	13 43 03.6	+03 32 17	5.36	−0.1	K2 III	400	0.302	256	242	−42	.006	17	86	
89 Vir	120452	13 49 52.2	−18 08 03	4.97	0.0	K0.5 III/b	71	0.109	248	42	−40	.046	15	79	
90 Vir	121299	13 54 42.1	−01 30 12	5.15	−0.1	K2 III	370	0.087	251	17	−7	.027	17	86	
107 Vir	129502	14 43 03.5	−05 39 30	3.88	1.9	F2 III	72	0.338	162	36	5	.045	2.2	14	
109 Vir	130109	14 46 14.9	+01 53 34	3.72	0.6	A0 V	88	0.118	255	16	−6	.037	2.0	45	
110 Vir	133165	15 02 54.0	+02 05 28	4.40	0.2	K0.5 IIIb+	230	0.056	278	19	−16	.025	14	65	
Σ1719 ∞	113984	13 07 19.5	+00 35 13	7.05	3.4	F5 V	180	0.158	228	[100]	−92	[.019]	1.4	3.4	
Σ1833 ∞	125906	14 22 38.5	−07 46 05	6.8	4.4	G0 V	98	0.133	180	40	−35	.033	1.1	1.4	
R Vir	109914	12 38 29.9	+06 59 18	7.08ᵥ	*	M5 IIIe	*	0.029	254	*	−26	*	*	*	(h)
S Vir	117833	13 33 00.6	−07 11 42	6.0ᵥ	*	M7 IIIe	*	0.047	102	*	10	*	*	*	(i)
CU Vir	124224	14 12 15.7	+02 24 34	5.01ᵥ	(−0.2)	A0 VpSi	360	0.060	239	31	−2	.009	1.2	96	
ET Vir	123934	14 10 50.4	−16 18 07	4.91ᵥ	−0.5	M2 IIIa	390	0.011	165	19	18	.012	38	125	

Volans
(Volantis)

a)   If the absolute magnitude is estimated to be 0.0, then: 390 l.y., π.008, V39, D_s1.7, $\mathcal{L}$79.

b)   The $B-V$ index (-0.10) indicates, from Fig. 3, a size of about three Suns. The surface temperature of an A0 star is about 12,000 K. If the star had an absolute magnitude of +1 (as Fig. 2 suggests), then the size would only be about 1.3 Suns, far too small. An absolute magnitude of -1 yields a better fit: 700 l.y., π.005, V41, D_s2.0, and $\mathcal{L}$200.

VOLANS	HD	\multicolumn{3}{c}{2000.0 R.A.}	Declin.	m	M	Spectra	l.y.	μ	Dir.	V	RV	π	D_s	$\mathscr{L}$	Rmk
α Vol	78045	09^h 02^m	26.9^s	−66° 23′ 46″	4.00	2.5†	A2 IV/V	65	0.102″	178°	11	5	.050″	1.3	7.9	
β Vol	71878	08 25	44.3	−66 08 13	3.77	−0.1	K1 III	78	0.164	191	33	27	.042	18	86	
γ^1 Vol ∞	55864	07 08	42.2	−70 29 50	5.67	(1.7)	F0	200	0.097	5	29	−3	.016	1.6	17	
γ^2 Vol	55865	07 08	45.0	−70 29 57	3.78	(−0.2)	K0 III	200	0.105	14	31	3	.016	14	95	
δ Vol	57623	07 16	49.8	−67 57 27	3.98	−5.4	F8 Ib	2500	0.007	236	25	23	.004	130	11500	
ε Vol ∞	68520	08 07	55.9	−68 37 02	4.35	−1.1	B5 III	400	0.031	312	[21]	10	[.008]	2.0	217	
ζ Vol	63295	07 41	49.3	−72 36 22	3.95	0.2	K0 III	180	0.035	63	49	48	.017	14	65	
η Vol	71576	08 22	04.7	−73 24 01	5.29	0.3	A0 IV/V	330	0.027	294	24	20	.010	2.7	60	
θ Vol	74405	08 39	05.3	−70 23 13	5.20	−0.9	A0 V	540	0.052	157	43	13	.006	4.6	180	
ι Vol	51557	06 51	27.0	−70 57 49	5.40	−1.3	B7 IV	710	0.018	3	[27]	19	[.005]	2.2	261	
κ^1 Vol	71046	08 19	49.2	−71 30 54	5.37	∗	B9 III/IV	∗	0.028	339	∗	36	∗	∗	∗	(a)
κ^2 Vol	71066	08 20	00.8	−71 30 19	5.65	∗	A0 IV+	∗	0.040	353	∗	−6	∗	∗	∗	(b)
- Vol	53501	06 59	50.5	−67 54 59	5.17	−0.2	K3 III	88	0.239	352	50	39	.037	25	95	
- Vol	70514	08 18	19.0	−65 36 47	5.07	(0.6)	K1 III	250	0.034	60	12	0	.013	13	44	

Vulpecula
(Vulpeculae)

a) A member of the open cluster C. 399, quite large and bright. The parallax gives a distance of 125 l.y.

b) SE 2° is the Dumbbell Nebula, M27 (NGC 6853), very large and bright, with an m13.5 central star.

VUL-PECULA	HD	R.A.		Declin.			m	M	Spectra	l.y.	μ	Dir.	V	RV	π	D_s	$\mathscr{L}$	Rmk
					2000.0													
α Vul ∞	183439	19^h 28^m	42.2^s	+24° 39′	54″		4.44	(0.2)	M0 III	230	0.164″	231°	102	−86	.014″	23	67	
1 Vul	180554	19 16	12.9	+21 23	26		4.77	−2.3	B4 IV	850	0.006	261	17	−17	.017	5.4	655	
3 Vul	182255	19 22	50.8	+26 15	45		5.18	−1.9	B6 III	850	0.009	201	[16]	−12	[.004]	2.7	453	
4 Vul	182762	19 25	28.5	+19 47	55		5.16	0.2	K0 III	320	0.112	124	21	−1	.026	13	65	(a)
9 Vul	184606	19 34	34.8	+19 46	24		5.00	−0.6	B8 IIIn	430	0.008	67	[7]	5	[.008]	1.8	137	
12 Vul	187811	19 51	04.0	+22 36	36		4.95	−1.7	B2.5 Ve	700	0.027	129	[41]	−31	[.005]	2.2	377	
13 Vul	188260	19 53	27.6	+24 04	47		4.58	−0.6	B9.5 III	350	0.048	33	38	−28	.009	2.3	137	(b)
15 Vul	189849	20 01	06.0	+27 45	13		4.64$_v$	(2.0)	A4 III	110	0.059	80	23	−21	.030	1.8	12	
16 Vul ∞	190004	20 02	01.3	+24 56	17		5.22	−2.0	F2 III	910	0.113	50	139	−37	.004	13	497	
17 Vul	190993	20 06	53.3	+23 36	52		5.07	−1.7	B3 V	740	0.015	70	[17]	−5	[.004]	2.6	377	
21 Vul	192518	20 14	14.4	+28 41	41		5.18$_v$	(0.2)	A7 IVn	330	0.022	148	13	7	.010	4.3	67	
22 Vul	192713	20 15	30.1	+23 30	31		5.15	−4.5	G3 Ib/II	2800	0.012	185	27	−23	.004	120	5000	
23 Vul	192806	20 15	46.0	+27 48	51		4.52	−0.2	K3 III+	290	0.039	287	23	3	.008	21	95	
28 Vul	196740	20 38	31.8	+24 06	58		5.04	−1.1	B5 IV	550	0.010	84	[23]	−22	[.006]	1.6	217	
29 Vul	196724	20 38	31.2	+21 12	04		4.82	0.6	A0 V	230	0.070	83	168	−18	.002	1.9	45	
30 Vul	197752	20 44	52.4	+25 16	15		4.91	−0.1	K2 III	330	0.178	190	144	31	.006	19	86	
31 Vul	198809	20 52	07.6	+27 05	49		4.59	0.3	G7 III+	91	0.091	228	12	1	.036	10	60	
32 Vul	199169	20 54	33.5	+28 03	28		5.01	−0.3	K4 III	380	0.004	304	10	8	.003	28	104	
β 983	192685	20 15	15.8	+25 35	31		4.78	−1.7	B3 V	640	0.008	113	[10]	−7	[.005]	2.6	377	
Σ2525 ∞	183032	19 26	33.6	+27 19	20		7.4	4.2	F9	140	0.134	54	[30]	−11	[.023]	1.1	1.6	∅

Binary Star Section

Double Stars

Note: With some exceptions, only the brightest pair in multiple systems is given.

Const.	>60″	>20″	>10″	6.0″–9.9″	4″–5.9″	2.1″–3.9″	up to 2.0″
And		π, Grb34*		γ^{AB}, h1947	$O\Sigma514$		γ^{BC*}, $\Sigma73$, $\beta1147$
Aqr			·			ζ^{1*}	
Aql			β^{AB}				χ
Ari		γ^{AC}, λ^{AB}, 30, 33		γ^{AB}			ε^{AB}
Aur		R	14^{AC}, $\Sigma872$		4	θ^{AB}	
Boo	μ^{AxBC}	ι^{AB}	κ	ξ^{AB*}, $\Sigma1835$	π^{AB}, τ	ε^{AB}, μ^{BC*}, $\Sigma1785*$, $\Sigma1909*$	ζ^{AB*}
Cam	β^{AB}	$\Sigma1694$	$\Sigma390$			$\Sigma385$	$\Sigma1051^{AB}$, $O\Sigma67$
Cnc		ι		ζ^{AC*}			ζ^{AB*}
CVn			α				25^{AB*}
CMa		h3945			α^*	μ^{AB}	
Cap	α^{2AD}, $\alpha^1 - \alpha^2$	α^{1AC}					
Cas		β	η^{AB}, $\Sigma3053^{AB}$			ι^{AB*}, σ	$\Sigma3062*$
Cen			α^*				γ^*
Cep		δ^{AB}, δ^{AC}	$\Sigma2840^{AB}$	ξ^{AB*}		$O\Sigma482$, Kr 60^{AB*}	
Cet		37				γ	$\beta395*$, $\Sigma186*$
Com		24		$\Sigma1633$			$\Sigma1639*$
CrA		$\kappa^1 - \kappa^2$					h5014*
CrB				ζ, σ^{AB*}			η^{AB*}
Crv		δ					
Crt					γ		
Cyg		β^1, 61^{AB*}				δ^{AB*}, ψ^{AB}	μ^{1AB*}, τ^{AB*}
Del				γ^1			β^{AB*}
Dra	$\nu^1 - \nu^2$, $16 - 17^{AC}$, 39^{AC}, $40 - 41$	o^{AB}, ψ^{1AB}				ε, 39^{AB}, $16 - 17^{AB}$	μ^*, 20*, 26^{AB}
Equ						λ	δ^{AB*}
Eri		o^{2AB}	p^*	$\theta^1 - \theta^2$, 32^{AB}, **f**			
For			ω		α^*		
Gem				λ, 38^{AB*}	δ^*	α^{AB*}, ρ^{AB}	η

*Orbital elements and ephemerides exist for these stars; see the Orbital Elements section.

Const.	>60″	>20″	>10″	6.0″–9.9″	4″–5.9″	2.1″–3.9″	up to 2.0″
Gru							θ
Her		κ	100^{AB}	δ, 95	α^{AB*}, ρ, $\Sigma2319^{AB}$		$\zeta*$, 99^{AB*}
Hor		h3497					
Hya		$\Sigma1474$				ε^{AC*}	β, ε^{AB}, χ^{1*}, $\beta411*$
Lac	$h1823^{AC}$	8^{AB}	$h1823^{AE}$	$\Sigma2902$			
Leo	γ^{AC}			54	γ^{AB*}		$\iota*$
Lep	γ^{AB}, $h3780^{AC}$				h3750	κ	$h3780^{AB}$
Lib		$\alpha^1 - \alpha^2$, ι^{AB}	$\Sigma1962$, 18				μ^{AB}
Lup	$\kappa^1 - \kappa^2$	η, μ^{AC}	$\xi^1 - \xi^2$				γ, ε^{AB}, μ^{AB}
Lyn			19^{AB}	12^{AC}		38^{AB}	12^{AB*}, $\Sigma1338^{AB*}$, Kui 37*
Lyr	$\varepsilon^1 - \varepsilon^2$	β^{AB}, ζ^{AD}	$\Sigma2470$, $\Sigma2474$	$\Sigma2333^{AB}$		ε^{1*}, ε^{2*}	$\beta648*$
Mic		α					θ^{2AB}
Mon		ε^{AB}		β^{AB}		15^{AB}	
Mus							β
Nor		ε					ι^{1AB}
Oct						λ	
Oph	λ^{AD}, ρ^{AD}			$\Sigma2276^{AB}$	36^{AB*}	ξ, ρ^{AB}, 70*	$\eta*$, λ^{AB*}, $\tau*$
Ori		δ^{AC}, $\Sigma747$	θ^{1AC}, ι^{AB}	β^{AB}, θ^{1AB}, ρ^{AB}	λ^{AB}	ζ^{AB*}	η^{AB}, σ^{AB}
Peg		85^{AC}					κ, 37*, 85^{AB*}
Per	ζ^{AD}, η^{AC}	η^{AB}, $\Sigma431$	ζ^{AB}, $\Sigma331$	ε, $\Sigma552$			
Psc		ζ^{AB}			65		$\alpha*$
PsA							η
Pup				$\kappa^1 - \kappa^2$			9*
Sge	ε		θ^{AB}				
Sgr			54^{ABC}			ν^{1AB}	
Sco		ν^{AC}, σ	β^{AC}, $\Sigma1999^{AB}$	ξ^{AC}		$\alpha*$, 2	β^{AB}, ν^{AB}, ξ^{AB*}
Scl					ε^{AB*}	$\tau*$	κ^{AB}
Ser	5^{AC}	β^{AB}, $\theta^1 - \theta^2$, ν	5^{AB}		δ^{AB*}	$\Sigma2375^{(ABxCD)}$	$\Sigma2375^{AB}$
Tau		$\theta^2 - \theta^1$, σ		$\Sigma442*$	$\kappa^1 - \kappa^2$, $\Sigma572$		80*
Tri						6	
Tuc		β, λ^1		δ	κ		
UMa	ζ^{AC}, σ^{2AC}		ζ^{AB}, $\Sigma1415^{AB}$			σ^{2AB}	$\xi*$, 78*
Umi			α				

Const.	>60″	>20″	>10″	6.0″–9.9″	4″–5.9″	2.1″–3.9″	up to 2.0″
Vel	$\gamma^1 - \gamma^{2(AC)}$	$\gamma^1 - \gamma^{2(AB)}$, DUN95				δ	μ, ψ*
Vir				Σ1719	φ^{AB}, Σ1833^{AB}	84	γ^{AB*}
Vol			γ^1	ε			
Vul		α				Σ2525*	16

A Historical Note

It was that indefatigable amateur William Herschel who coined the term *binary star*. In 1802 he defined it as "the union of two stars, that are formed together in one system, by the laws of attraction."

After having discovered Uranus in 1781, Herschel busied himself with the attempt to find the relative distances of stars from each other and from our own Sun. Having noted, in years of observation, that many stars had close neighbors and that these neighboring stars were usually much dimmer, he reasoned that the brighter star would be closer to us and the dimmer one further away. Thus, with this working hypothesis, Herschel set out to detect the *parallactic* displacement of the brighter star to the dimmer. To this end he began making a catalogue of all the double stars he could find.

Soon Herschel realized (as expressed in a 1782 memoir) that the double stars he saw might be dependent: that one might be circling the other following Newton's laws of gravitation. In 1793 he began taking new readings of the position of the fainter stars relative to their brighter neighbors. These observations verified his suspicion; some of the stars were indeed revolving around their neighbor. In 1802 he published his *Catalogue of 500 new Nebulæ . . . and Clusters of Stars; with Remarks on the Construction of the Heavens*. It was here that his discovery of the binary nature of some stars was announced.

Herschel pointed out that caution must be used in deciding whether two close-appearing stars form a true binary system. The dimmer star could be at a considerable distance from the primary one and be independent—not tied to the primary by gravitation. This type of double star is now termed an *optical* double, and is of little interest to observers of true binary systems.

Another kind of binary also exists: the *spectroscopic binary,* in which the neighboring star is so close that its presence can only be detected by examining fluctuations in the spectrum of the combined light emitted by the two stars. This close neighbor, by eclipsing the primary in a regular fashion, can also create a variable magnitude for the primary, but the change in brightness is often too slight to be noticeable. Where the brightness variation is noticeable, the star is an *eclipsing variable,* described in Part Three.

The first true binary discovered predates Herschel. This was Mizar (ζ UMa), whose companion, at 14″ away, was found in 1650 by Jean Baptiste Riccioli. This star is also the first spectroscopic binary to be discovered, in 1889. Thus, Mizar is a complex system, with a visually perceived companion and an "invisible" companion. A number of binaries have complex natures such as this, with companions revolving about other companions.

In 1782 William Herschel presented his first catalogue to the Royal Society. It contained 269 double stars, most of which had been discovered by Herschel. Two years later he had collected another 434 double stars. As time went on, catalogues increased the number of known binary stars greatly. Herschel's son John published in

1874 his *Catalogue of 10,300 Multiple and Double Stars,* which was surpassed in 1906 with S.W. Burnham's classic study, *A General Catalogue of Double Stars within 121° of the North Pole* which contained not only 13,665 double stars, but notes and references to each one of them.

There are currently over 60,000 binary stars known and catalogued. While most of these are out of the reach of amateur telescopes, hundreds of binaries are well within reach. In this section 253 binary stars are listed, most of which can be enjoyed with medium-sized telescopes. Feel free, too, to roam the heavens. With a good atlas or guide book there is every possibility that you will find many more just as intriguing as those listed here.

Color Contrast: The Most Beautiful Binaries

As an introduction to the viewing of binary stars, a list of the most attractive contrasting stars is given below, in order of separation. The first half dozen will all be visible in even the smallest telescopes (or even binoculars) and are therefore not so much a challenge as an invitation.

The last several may be resolved only by medium to large telescopes. See at what point you begin having difficulty resolving the companion. And notice the colors; you may not agree with all the reported colors.

Star	Best Month	Magnitudes	(2000.0) Sep.	(2000.0) P.A.	Colors	Remarks
β Cygni	Sept	3/3.5	34.3″	54°	gold/sapphire	Although only optical, a most spectacular sight; use low power (or binoculars)
o Draconis	Sept	4.5/7.5	34.2″	326°	orange/blue	Possibly optical; a real beauty
h3945 (CMa)	Feb	4.8/6.8	26.6″	55°	gold/blue	One of winter's best!
α CanumVen	May	2.7/5.4	19.4″	229°	yellow/blue	The famous "Cor Caroli"
Σ872 (Aur)	Jan	6/7	11.3″	217°	gold/blue	Best seen in 15-cm (6-inch) scopes or larger
γ^{AxBC} And	Nov	2.3/5.0	9.8″	64°	gold/blue	Finest Autumn binary
ξ Bootis	June	4.8/6.7	6.6″	318°	yellow/red	At 22 l.y. away, one of the closest binaries
99 Herculis	July	5/5	6.3″	258°	green/red	Wide disagreement on colors
α Herculis	July	3/5.5	4.6″	104°	red/green	Primary is a variable, possibly affecting your view of companion
6 Trianguli	Nov	5/6.6	3.9″	71°	yellow/blue	Stunning; best seen in medium to large telescopes
70 Ophiuchi	July	4.3/6.3	3.8″	147°	yellow/red	Both are dwarfs; rapid period of nearly 88 years

Spectral Types and Colors

You will have noticed by now not only that different spectral types create different colors, but that past observers often cannot agree about what those colors are. While the quality of the atmosphere and of the telescope may influence the colors you see, there is also a personal component, which cannot be ignored. Try not to be influenced by foreknowledge. Even if a star is classified F, it doesn't have to be blue! Table I.1, in the Introduction to *StarList 2000,* gives the expected color as a function of the spectral type. Also consult the *Webb Society Deep-Sky Observer's Handbook, vol. 1,* the most thorough guide to the introduction of the study of binaries.

Observing Binaries

Five factors are involved in being able to resolve binary stars:

1. The distance between the two components
2. The size of the objective of one's telescope
3. The apparent magnitudes of the stars in question
4. The condition of the atmosphere
5. The skills of the observer

The distance between the two components.   This is measured in arc-seconds and often represented by the Greek letter rho [ρ]. Sixty arc-seconds make one arc-minute, and sixty arc-minutes equal one degree on the celestial sphere. The full moon extends an angle of 0.5° or 30′ (30 arc-minutes). The maximum size of Venus, when it is at inferior conjunction, is one arc-minute: 60″.

Obviously, the closer the companion is to the primary the more difficult it is to resolve, and extremely close companions can only be observed spectroscopically, that is, by measuring the variation in the stars' radial velocity, shown by the changes in the positions of the lines in their spectra, as the two stars travel around their orbit. Typically, these extremely close binaries have quite rapid periods, usually days rather than the years it takes visual binaries to make one complete circuit.

The size of the telescope's objective.   Telescope size (and quality) will determine how well fairly close binaries can be resolved. A 200-mm reflector will be more effective than a 100-mm reflector; a 100-mm refractor will be superior to a 60 mm-refractor. (There are problems when one begins comparing a refractor to a reflector. Generally, experienced amateurs prefer to use refractors to study binaries, because they will resolve stars more easily than the same-sized reflectors. Yet refractors will distort the colors of the stars more than reflectors do. Many amateurs use medium and large reflectors and are quite happy with the results.)

Note that magnification cannot separate two points of light that are not initially resolved on the focal plane of the telescope. Once the telescope has succeeded in resolving the components, magnification will increase their apparent separation; but high magnification alone will not separate close components.

The apparent magnitudes of the stars.   The brightness of each of the two components is an important determinant. Two stars fairly equal in brightness are more easily seen than is a bright primary with a fainter companion. A number of studies have addressed this issue, and a very rough estimation can be made on the size of telescope in relation to the resolution provided, given the difference in magnitudes between primary and companion:

Size of objective	Magnitudes	Minimum resolvable separation
100 mm	up to 6/7	about 1.0"
	8/9	1.5"
	9/9	2.0"
200 mm	up to 6/7	about 0.6"
	8/9	0.8"
	9/9	1.0"
400 mm	up to 6/7	about 0.3"
	8/9	0.4"
	9/9	0.5"

Note: These tables are based on Rayleigh's formula (in Webb Society, vol. 1, p. 17):

$r' = 13.1/D$ (in cm)   Imperial measures: $r' = 5.15/D$ (in inches)

where r' equals the separation in arc-seconds.

Given a separation of a binary system of $1''$, will a telescope of 200 mm resolve the two components? Here $r' = 1''$. Since r' (the separation in arc-seconds) equals $13.1/D$, then $D = 13.1/r'$ or $13.1/1$. Thus, a telescope of 13.1 cm should be able to resolve the two (given ideal conditions). Hence a telescope of 20 cm should be sufficient.

The quality of the atmosphere and skill of the observer. These last two factors should not be overlooked. Avoid, if possible, sightings over houses, especially in winter, because heat waves will considerably distort the image. Other seemingly innocuous circumstances may also reduce the quality of the atmosphere. For example, if near a lake, the incoming air mass, as the night cools off, may be a hindrance to good sighting. Trial and error will teach the observer when and where the best viewing can be done.

Initial efforts at observing double stars can be frustrating. Being used to marveling at the impressive photographs in books and magazines, including some very close binaries, one then expects to duplicate these sights in one's own scope. Often, instead, nothing seems to be there. The skill to coax up faint images is not quickly achieved. It takes much practice and determination to become adept in the art of observing, whether one is interested in binaries, galaxies, or other elusive inhabitants of our Universe.

The Visual Binaries

Please note the following regarding the Visual Binaries listings:

- The apparent visual magnitudes of the two stars (m_1 and m_2) may differ slightly from those in the StarList, since the present listing is an amalgamation of several sources. The *Lick Observatory Index Catalogue of Visual Binary Stars, 1961.0,* is the standard reference; it has been occasionally updated from the *Sky Catalogue, vol. 2.*

- The PA and Sep. columns indicate in **bold** type the expected position angle and separation at 1 January 2000 of the companion of a rapid-motion binary system, using the orbital elements that follow these listings.

- The "Orbit Info." column indicates whether the PA and separation are increasing or decreasing, or if they appear to be fixed. The bracketed values are the periods, in years, of rapid-motion binaries.

- The "Remarks" column gives the range of observations. $\mathcal{O}$ means that orbital elements exist: this is true for all rapid-motion binaries listed. These orbital elements will be found following this section.

Const.	Star	ADS	vis. magnitudes m_1	m_2	Comb.	2000 PA	Sep.''	(Period) Orbit Info.	Remarks Obs History
And	0Σ514	30	6.1	8.7	6.0	168°	5.2''	fixed	1847–1958
	h 1947	215	6.1	8.8	6.0	76	9.2	fixed	1879–1958
	Grb 34	246	8.1	11.0	8.0	**64**	**35.5**	(2600)	1860$\mathcal{O}$
	π|AB	513	4.4	8.9	4.4	173	35.9	fixed	1821–1937
	|AC		4.4	11.4	—	357	55.2	fixed	1879–1924
	Σ73 (36 And)	755	6.0	6.4	5.4	**313**	**0.9**	(164.7)	1836$\mathcal{O}$
	γ¹|AxBC	1630	2.2	5.5	2.2	64	9.8	fixed	1830–1955
	γ²|BxC		5.5	6.3	5.1	103	0.4	(61.1)	1842:Sep<0.5''
	β1147(2 And)	16467	5.1	8.8	5.1	325	0.5	PA''+	1889–1958
Aqr	ζ¹	15971	4.4	4.6	3.7	**192**	**2.1**	(856)	1781$\mathcal{O}$
Aql	χ AB	12808	5.6	6.8	5.6	77	0.5	PA''−	1844–1958
	β AB	13110	3.7	11.6	3.7	5	12.9	PA−, ''+	1852–1958
Ari	γ|AB	1507	4.8	4.8	4.0	360	7.8	PA fixed, ''−	1830–1969
	|AC		—	9.6		84	21.3		1823–1924
	λ˙AB	1563	4.9	7.7	4.8	46	37.4	fixed	1781–1933
	30	1982	6.6	7.4	6.2	274	38.6	fixed	1835–1937
	33	2033	5.5	8.4	5.5	360	28.6	fixed	1831–1921
	ε|AB	2257	5.2	5.5	4.6	203	1.4	PA+, ''?	1830–1959
	|ABxC		—	12.7		191	146.	PA fixed, ''+	1912–1922

Const.	Star	ADS	vis. magnitudes			2000		(Period)	Remarks
			m_1	m_2	Comb.	PA	Sep."	Orbit Info.	Obs History
Aur	ω (Σ616)	3572	5.0	8.0	4.9	359	5.4	PA+, "−	1858–1950
	14 | AB	3824	5.1	11.1	5.1	352	11.1	PA+, "−	1830–1909
	| AC		—	7.4		226	14.6	fixed	1830–1933
	| AD		—	10.4		356	7.7	PA+, "−	1880–1908
	R	3845	6.4	8.6	6.3	339	47.5	fixed?	1909–1918
	θ AB	4566	2.6	7.1	2.6	313	3.6	PA−, "+	1871–1976
	Σ872 AB	4849	6.9	7.9	6.5	217	11.3	fixed	1828–1949
Boo	τ	9025	4.5	11.1	4.5	11	4.8	PA+, "−	1849–1970
	Σ1785	9031	7.6	8.0	7.0	**174**	**3.3**	(155)	1830⊘
	κ	9173	4.6	6.6	4.4	235	13.4	PA−, "+	1832–1968
	ι | AB	9198	4.9	7.5	4.8	33	38.5	fixed	1836–1942
	| AC		—	12.6		197	85.9	fixed?(2 ob)	1911–1925
	Σ1835	9247A	5.1	7.6		192	6.2	PA" +	1832–1958
	π | AB	9338	4.9	5.8	4.5	108	5.6	PA+, "−	1830–1957
	| AC		—	10.0		163	127.7	PA fixed?	1905–1960
	Σ1865 (ζ Boo) | AB	9343	4.5	4.6	3.8	**300**	**0.8**	(123.4)	1830⊘
	| AC		—	10.9		259	99.3	fixed?(5 ob)	1901–1911
	ε | AB	9372	2.5	4.9	1.9	339	2.8	PA" +	1829–1971
	| AC		—	11.8		255	177.0	PA fixed?, "+	1912–1960
	ξ AB	9413	4.7	7.0	4.6	**318**	**6.6**	(151.505)	1836⊘
	Σ1909	9494	5.3	6.2	4.9	**53**	**2.2**	(225)	1832⊘
	μ^{1,2} | AxBC	9626	4.3	7.0	4.2	171	108.3	fixed	1834–1956
	| BC		7.0	7.6		**9**	**2.3**	(260.1)	1826⊘
Cam	Σ385	2544	4.2	8.5	4.2	162	2.4	fixed	1829–1937
	Σ390	2565	5.1	9.5	5.1	159	14.8	fixed	1832–1920
	OΣ 67	2867	5.3	8.5	5.0	44	1.9	fixed	1847–1959
	β AB	3615	4.0	8.6	4.0	208	80.8	fixed	1825–1923
	Σ1051 | AB	6028	7.1	9.2	7.0	284	1.1	PA+, "−	1831–1953
	| AC		—	7.8		82	31.5	fixed	1831–1935
	Σ1694	8682	5.3	5.8	4.8	326	21.6	PA−, "fixed	1832–1958
Cnc	ζ | AB	6650	5.6	6.0	5.0	**86**	**0.8**	(59.7)	1826⊘
	| ABxC		5.05	6.2	4.7	**72**	**6.0**	(1150)	1841⊘
	| ABxD		—	9.7		108	287.9	PA fixed?, "−	1913–1921
	ι	6988	4.2	6.6	4.1	307	30.5	fixed	1828–1968
CVn	α	8706	2.9	5.5	2.8	229	19.4	fixed?	1830–1970
	25 (Σ1768) | AB	8974	5.0	6.9	4.8	**99**	**1.8**	(240.0)	1831⊘
	| AC		—	8.6		141	217.7	PA+, "−	1918–1959
CMa	α	5423	1.5	8.5	1.5	**150**	**4.6**	(50.09)	1862⊘
	μ | AB	5605	5.3	8.6	5.2	340	3.0	fixed	1831–1944
	| AC		—	10.5		288	88.4	fixed	1865–1912
	| AD		—	10.7		61	101.3	fixed	1865–1912
	h 3945	5951	4.8	6.8	4.6	55	26.6	PA"−	1837–1959

Const.	Star	ADS	vis. magnitudes m_1	m_2	Comb.	2000 PA	Sep.''	(Period) Orbit Info.	Remarks Obs History
Cap	α^1 |AB	13632	4.2	13.7	4.2	182	44.3	PA fixed, ''+	1891–1960
	|AC		—	9.2		221	45.4	PA fixed?, ''+	1830–1932
	α^2 |AB	13645	3.6	11.0	3.6	172	6.6	PA''+	1846–1959
	|AD		—	9.3		156	154.6	fixed	1879–1909
	α^1–α^2		3.6	4.2	3.1	291	377.7	PA fixed, ''+	1835–1924
Cas	Σ3053 AB	1	6.0	7.5	5.8	70	15.2	fixed	1832–1958
	Σ3062	61	6.4	7.5	6.1	**328**	**1.5**	(106.83)	1831⊘
	β	107	2.3	13.6	2.3	243	31.3	PA''+	1889–1935
	η AB	671	3.4	7.5	3.4	**317**	**12.8**	(480)	1832⊘
	ι AB	1806	4.6	6.9	4.5	**230**	**2.5**	(840.0)	1829⊘
	σ AB	17140	5.0	7.1	4.9	326	3.0	fixed	1833–1958
Cen	α AB	—	-0.04	1.17	0.35	**222**	**14.2**	(79.92)	1752⊘
	γ	—	2.9	2.9	2.1	**347**	**1.0**	(84.50)	1835⊘
Cep	Σ2840 AB	15405	5.5	7.3	5.3	196	18.3	PA fixed?, ''–	1832–1958
	ξ AB	15600	4.4	6.5	4.3	**275**	**8.2**	(3800)	1831⊘
	Kr 60|AB	15972	9.8	11.4	9.6	**95**	**3.0**	(44.6)	1890⊘
	|AC		—	10.1		62	73.2	PA''+	1890–1925
	|AI		—	8.5		140	201.5	PA–, ''+	1873–1918
	δ|AB	15987	3.8	13.0	3.8	284	20.4	PA fixed?, ''+	1878–1934
	|AC		—	7.5		191	41.0	fixed	1835–1953
	OΣ482	16294	4.7	9.4	4.7	33	3.5	fixed	1850–1940
Cet	β 395	520	6.3	6.4	5.6	**289**	**0.5**	(25.0)	1886⊘
	37	1003	5.2	8.7	5.2	331	49.7	fixed	1836–1931
	Σ186	1538	7.0	7.0	6.2	**60**	**1.1**	(170.3)	1831⊘
	γ	2080	3.5	7.3	3.5	294	2.8	PA+, ''fixed?	1836–1955
Com	Σ1633	8519	7.0	7.1	6.3	245	9.0	fixed	1831–1958
	Σ1639	8539	6.8	7.8	6.4	**323**	**1.7**	(678)	1836⊘
	24	8600	5.2	6.7	5.0	271	20.3	fixed	1830–1958
CrA	κ^1–κ^2	—	5.9	6.6	5.4	359	21.4	fixed	1836–1936
	h 5014	—	5.7	5.7	4.9	**346**	**0.9**	(191.2)	1836⊘
CrB	η AB	9617	5.6	5.9	5.0	**65**	**0.7**	(41.56)	1826⊘
	ζ	9737	5.1	6.0	4.7	305	6.3	PA''+	1829–1973
	σ AB	9979	5.6	6.6	5.2	**237**	**7.1**	(1000)	1827⊘
Crv	δ	8572	3.0	9.2	3.0	214	24.2	fixed	1823–1958
Crt	γ	8153	4.1	9.6	4.1	96	5.2	fixed	1877–1955
Cyg	β	12540	3.1	5.1	2.9	54	34.3	PA fixed, ''?	1832–1967
	δ AB	12880	2.9	6.3	2.9	**222**	**2.5**	(827.6)	1830⊘
	ψ AB	13148	4.9	7.4	4.8	178	3.2	PA–, ''fixed?	1831–1958

Const.	Star	ADS	vis. magnitudes m_1	m_2	Comb.	2000 PA	Sep.″	(Period) Orbit Info.	Remarks Obs History
Cyg (cont.)	61 AB	14636	5.2	6.0	4.8	**150**	**30.3**	(653.3)	1830○
	AD		—	8.6		282	304.9	(1 obs)	1918
	AE		—	8.1		12	306.0	(1 obs)	1918
	τ AB	14787	3.8	6.4	3.7	**306**	**0.8**	(49.9)	1874○
	AD		—	10.0		210	170.0	PA−, ″+	1851–1924
	μ AB	15270	4.8	6.1	4.5	**320**	**1.2**	(507.5)	1780○
Del	β AB	14073	4.0	4.9	3.6	**343**	**0.5**	(26.65)	1873○
	γ	14279	4.5	5.5	4.1	268	9.6	PA″−	1830–1976
Dra	16–17 AB	10129	5.5	6.4	5.0	108	3.4	PA″−	1831–1958
	AC		—	5.5		194	90.3	fixed	1833–1956
	20	10279	7.1	7.3	6.4	**68**	**1.4**	(729.3)	1832○
	μ AB	10345	5.7	5.7	4.9	**8**	**1.9**	(482.0)	1828○
	ν^1–ν^2	10628	4.9	4.9	4.2	312	61.6	fixed	1833–1955
	26 AB	10660	5.3	8.0	5.2	**331**	**1.7**	(76.0)	1879○
	ψ AB	10759	4.9	6.1	4.6	15	30.3	fixed	1832–1958
	40–41	11061	5.8	6.2	5.2	232	91.3	PA″−	1832–1955
	39 AB	11336	5.0	8.0	5.0	351	3.8	PA−, ″+	1833–1975
	AC		—	7.4		21	88.9	fixed	1834–1956
	o AB	11779	4.8	7.8	4.7	326	34.2	PA−, ″+	1833–1949
	ε	13007	3.8	7.4	3.8	15	3.1	PA″+	1832–1957
Equ	δ AB	14773	5.2	5.3	4.5	**33**	**0.2**	(5.7)	1852:Sep<0.5″
	AC		—	9.4		14	47.7	PA−, ″+	1833–1925
	λ (Σ2742)	14556	7.4	7.4	6.6	218	2.8	PA−, ″+	1831–1955
Eri	32 AB	2850	4.8	6.1	4.5	347	6.8	fixed	1833–1955
	o^2 AB	3093	4.5	9.9	4.5	105	82.8	PA″−	1836–1940
	θ^1–θ^2	—	3.4	4.5	3.1	88	8.2	PA+, ″fixed	1835–1952
	f	—	4.8	5.3	4.3	212	7.9	PA″+	1836–1957
	p	—	5.8	5.8	5.0	**191**	**10.6**	(483.7)	1855○
For	ω	1954	5.0	7.7	4.9	244	10.8	PA+, ″fixed	1836–1952
	α	2402	4.0	7.0	3.9	**299**	**5.1**	(314)	1836○
Gem	η	4841	3.3	8.8	3.3	266	1.4	PA−, ″+	1882–1958
	38 AB	5559	4.7	7.7	4.6	**144**	**7.1**	(3190)	1829○
	AC			10.3		328	111.5	PA fixed, ″+	1912–1932
	λ	5961	3.6	10.7	3.6	33	9.6	fixed	1829–1953
	δ	5983	3.5	8.2	3.5	**225**	**5.8**	(1200)	1829○
	ρ AB	6109	4.2	12.5	4.3	8	3.4	PA−, ″+	1910–1935
	AC			10.6		291	213.7	PA−, ″+	1886–1919
	α AB	6175	1.9	2.9	1.5	**61**	**3.8**	(420.1)	1826○(2)
	AC			8.8		164	72.5	fixed	1835–1955
Gru	θ	--	4.5	7.0	4.4	75	1.1	PA+, ″−	1846–1959

Const.	Star	ADS	vis. magnitudes m_1	m_2	Comb.	2000 PA	Sep."	(Period) Orbit Info.	Remarks Obs History
Her	κ AB	9933	5.3	6.5	5.0	12	28.4	PA+, "–	1832–1958
	ζ	10157	2.9	5.5	2.8	**10**	**0.7**	(34.385)	1949⊘
	α AB	10418	3.5	5.4	3.3	**104**	**4.6**	(3600)	1978⊘
	δ	10424	3.1	8.2	3.1	236	8.9	PA+, "–(optical)	1830–1958
	ρ	10526	4.6	5.6	4.2	316	4.1	PA"+	1830–1958
	95	10993	5.0	5.1	4.3	258	6.3	PA–, "+	1829–1974
	99 AB	11077	5.1	8.4	5.0	**250**	**0.5**	(55.8)	1972⊘
	100 AB	11089	5.9	6.0	5.2	183	14.2	fixed	1831–1955
	Σ2319 AB	11372	8.2	8.6	7.6	191	5.4	fixed	1830–1956
Hya	ε⎮AB	6993	3.8	5.3	3.6	**203**	**0.25**	(15.05)	1888:Sep<0.5"
	⎮ABxC		3.6	7.8		**302**	**2.7**	(890)	1830⊘
	β411	7846	6.7	7.5	6.3	**315**	**1.4**	(211)	1877⊘
	Σ1474⎮AB	7930	6.8	7.9	6.5	24	69.6	fixed	1831–1933
	⎮AC		6.5	6.9		23	75.8	fixed	1889–1924
	β	—	4.8	5.6	4.4	8	0.9	PA+, "–	1834–1954
	χ¹	—	5.8	5.8	5.0	**49**	**0.12**	(7.40)	1927⊘
Lac	Σ2902	15900	7.6	8.5	7.2	89	6.4	fixed	1833–1942
	8⎮AB	16095	5.7	6.5	5.3	186	22.4	fixed	1831–1969
	⎮AD			9.3		144	81.8	fixed	1902–1968
	⎮AE			7.8		239	336.6	1 ob.	1928
	h1823⎮AB	16321	6.8	12.5	6.8	259	19.2	fixed?(3 obs)	1874–1921
	⎮AC			8.5		338	82.1	fixed?(6 obs)	1874–1923
	⎮AE			8.9		263	18.3	fixed?(2 obs)	1885–1921
Leo	γ⎮AB	7724	2.2	3.5	1.9	**125**	**4.4**	(618.6)	1831⊘
	⎮AC			9.2		291	259.9	PA fixed, "+	1904–1915
	⎮AD			9.6		302	333	1 ob	1904
	54	7979	4.5	6.3	4.3	110	6.5	PA"+	1830–1958
	ι	8148	4.0	6.7	3.9	**116**	**1.7**	(192.0)	1832⊘
Lep	κ	3800	4.5	7.4	4.4	358	2.6	fixed	1832–1959
	h3750	3930	4.7	8.5	4.7	282	4.2	fixed	1876–1959
	h3780⎮AB	4254	6.4	7.9	6.2	146	0.8	fixed	1877–1947
	⎮AC		6.2	8.5		136	89.2	fixed?	1876–1916
	⎮AE			8.4		7	76.1	fixed?(5 obs)	1876–1915
	⎮AF			8.1		299	28.8	fixed?(4 obs)	1876–1915
	⎮AG			9.5		49	59.8	fixed?(2 obs)	1878–1916
	γ AB	4334	3.7	6.3	3.6	350	96.3	PA fixed, "+	1825–1957
Lib	α¹–α²	—	2.9	5.3	2.8	314	31.0	fixed	1823–1913
	μ AB	9396	5.8	6.7	5.4	355	1.8	PA"+	1875–1958
	18⎮AB	9456	5.8	10.0	5.8	39	19.7	fixed	1831–1955
	⎮AC			11.3		41	162.3	fixed	1894–1923
	ι AB	9532	5.1	9.4	5.1	111	57.8	fixed	1782–1919
	Σ1962	9728	6.5	6.6	5.8	188	11.9	fixed	1830–1958

Const.	Star	ADS	vis. magnitudes			2000		(Period)	Remarks
			m_1	m_2	Comb.	PA	Sep."	Orbit Info.	Obs History
Lup	γ	—	3.7	3.7	2.9	**274**	**0.7**	(147.0)	1835◌
	ε AB	—	4.0	5.5	3.8	247	0.6	PA"–	1896–1960
	AC			9.1		171	26.5	PA–, "fixed	1826–1955
	η	—	3.6	7.8	3.6	20	15.0	fixed	1834–1934
	κ¹–κ²	—	4.1	6.0	3.9	144	26.8	fixed	1826–1951
	ξ¹–ξ²	—	5.3	5.8	4.8	49	10.4	fixed	1826–1951
	μ AB	—	5.1	5.2	4.4	142	1.2	PA"–	1836–1955
	AC	—		7.2		130	23.7	PA"–	1836–1955
Lyn	12 AB	5400	5.4	6.0	4.8	**69**	**1.7**	(699.0)	1831◌
	AC			7.3		308	8.7	fixed	1831–1959
	19 AB	6012	5.6	6.5	5.2	315	14.8	fixed	1829–1956
	AD			8.9		3	14.9	(2 Obs)	1905–1956
	38 AB	7292	3.9	6.6	3.8	229	2.7	PA–, "fixed	1829–1968
	Σ1338 AB	7307	6.5	6.7	5.8	**16**	**0.4**	(219.7)	1829◌
	Kui 37	—	4.1	6.2	4.0	**46**	**0.6**	(21.85)	1936◌
Lyr	Σ2333 AB	11424	7.8	8.4	7.3	334	6.4	fixed	1831–1952
	ε¹	11635	5.0	6.1	4.7	**350**	**2.6**	(1165)	1831◌
	ε¹–ε²(ABxCD)	11635	5.0	5.2		173	207.7	fixed	1831–1955
	ε²	11635	5.2	5.5	4.6	**82**	**2.3**	(585)	1831◌
	ζ AB	11639	4.3	15	4.3	50	25.5	PA fixed, "–	1889–1934
	AC			13.3		272	46.1	PA–, "+	1880–1923
	AD			5.9		150	43.7	fixed	1835–1955
	β AB	11745	3.5	8.6	3.5	149	45.7	fixed	1835–1955
	AE			9.9		318	66.9	fixed?	1879–1929
	AF			9.9		19	85.8	fixed?	1879–1929
	β648 AB	11871	5.4	7.5	5.3	**317**	**0.7**	(57.0)	1878◌
	Σ2470	12093	6.6	8.6	6.4	271	13.4	fixed	1829–1933
	Σ2474	12101	6.5	8.6	6.4	261	16.4	PA+, "–	1880–1949
Mic	α	—	5.0	10.6	5.0	166	20.5	fixed	1835–1933
	θ² AB	—	6.4	7.0	5.9	267	0.5	PA"–	1879–1959
Mon	ε AB	5012	4.5	6.5	4.3	27	13.4	fixed	1831–1934
	β AB	5107	4.7	5.2	4.2	132	7.3	fixed	1831–1955
	AC			6.1		124	10.0	fixed	1831–1955
	15 AB	5322	4.8	7.6	4.7	213	2.8	PA+, "fixed	1831–1957
	AC			9.9		13	16.6	fixed	1831–1957
	AD			9.7		308	41.3	fixed?(4 obs)	1841–1938
	AE			10.0		139	73.9	fixed	1874–1957
	AF			7.8		222	56.0	fixed?(3 obs)	1874–1924
Mus	β	—	3.7	4.0	3.1	**43**	**1.3**	(383.12)	1880◌
Nor	ε	—	4.8	7.5	4.7	335	22.8	fixed	1826–1951
	ι¹ AB	—	5.6	5.8	4.9	**285**	**0.5**	(26.93)	1897:Sep = <.5"
	ABxC		4.9	8.1		246	10.8	PA–, "+	1836–1946
Oct	λ	—	5.5	7.8	5.4	70	3.1	PA–, "fixed	1835–1946

Const.	Star	ADS	vis. magnitudes m_1	m_2	Comb.	2000 PA	Sep."	(Period) Orbit Info.	Remarks Obs History
Oph	ρ AB	10049	5.3	6.0	4.8	344	3.1	PA"–	1822–1959
	AC			7.9		-	151	?	1846–1925
	AD			7.0		253	156	?	1846–1925
	λ AB	10087	4.2	5.2	3.8	**30**	**1.5**	(129.87)	1825⊘
	ABxC			11.1		170	119.2	PA fixed, "+	1912–1960
	AD			9.9		246	313.8	fixed?	1918–1921
	η	10374	2.9	3.4	2.4	**244**	**0.6**	(88)	1889⊘
	36 AB	10417	5.1	5.1	4.3	**147**	**4.9**	(548.7)	1822⊘
	AC			6.6		-	732	PA?, "fixed	1822–1976
	AD			8.1		315	208	PA"+	1823–1905
	τ AB	11005	5.2	5.9	4.7	**284**	**1.7**	(280.0)	1836⊘
	AC			9.3		127	100.3	fixed	1879–1959
	70 AB	11046	4.2	6.0	4.0	**147**	**3.8**	(87.71)	1825⊘
	ξ	—	4.5	9.0	4.5	50	3.7	PA–, "+	1931–1959
	Σ2276 AB	11056	7.0	7.4	6.4	257	6.9	fixed	1830–1958
Ori	ρ AB	3797	4.5	8.3	4.5	64	7.0	fixed	1832–1972
	β AB	3823	3.4	10.4	3.4	202	9.5	fixed	1831–1954
	η AB	4002	3.8	4.8	3.4	80	1.5	PA–, "+	1849–1959
	δ AB	4134	2.2	13.7	2.2	227	32.8	fixed	1878–1922
	AC			6.3		359	52.6	fixed	1781–1932
	λ AB	4179	3.6	5.5	3.4	43	4.4	fixed	1830–1957
	Σ747	4182	4.7	5.6	4.3	223	35.7	fixed	1833–1924
	θ¹ AB	4186	6.7	7.9	6.4	31	8.8	fixed?	1836–1975
	AC			5.1		132	12.8	PA fixed, "–?	1836–1975
	AD			6.7		96	21.5	fixed	1836–1975
	ι AB	4193	2.8	6.9	2.8	141	11.3	fixed	1831–1932
	σ AB	4241	4.0	6.0	3.8	**115**	**0.2**	(170)	1888:Sep<0.5"
	ABxC			10.3		238	11.4	PA fixed? "+	1831–1969
	ABxD			7.5		84	12.9	fixed	1831–1969
	ABxE			6.5		61	42.6	PA fixed, "+	1869–1970
	ζ AB	4263	1.9	4.0	1.8	**165**	**2.3**	(1509)	1836⊘
	AC			9.9		10	57.6	fixed	1880–1930
Peg	κ AB	15281	4.8	5.3	4.3	**99**	**0.2**	(11.52)	1880:Sep<0.5"
	37	15988	5.8	7.1	5.5	**118**	**0.7**	(140.0)	1831⊘
	85 AB	17175	5.8	8.9	5.7	**184**	**0.7**	(26.27)	1878⊘
	AC			8.6		330	75.5	PA"+	1852–1932
Per	η AB	2157	3.8	8.5	3.8	300	28.3	fixed	1836–1932
	AC			9.8		268	66.6	fixed	1878–1925
	Σ331	2270	5.4	6.8	5.1	85	12.1	fixed	1828–1954
	Σ431	2699	5.0	9.5	5.0	238	20.0	fixed	1830–1925
	ζ AB	2843	2.9	9.5	2.9	208	12.9	PA fixed, "+	1830–1968
	AC			11.3		286	32.8	fixed	1880–1923
	AD			9.5		195	94.2	PA–, "+	1880–1957

Const.	Star	ADS	vis. magnitudes			2000		(Period)	Remarks
			m_1	m_2	Comb.	PA	Sep."	Orbit Info.	Obs History
Per (cont.)	ε	2888	2.9	8.1	2.9	10	8.8	fixed	1832–1938
	Σ552	3273	7.0	7.2	6.3	114	9.0	fixed	1831–1949
Psc	65	683	6.3	6.3	5.5	297	4.4	fixed	1832–1959
	ζ AB	996	5.6	6.5	5.2	63	23.0	PA"–	1832–1974
	α	1615	4.2	5.3	3.8	**272**	**1.8**	(933.05)	1831⊘
PsA	η	15536	5.8	6.8	5.4	115	1.7	fixed	1876–1955
Pup	$κ^1$–$κ^2$	6255	4.5	4.7	3.8	318	9.9	fixed	1826–1951
	β101(9 Pup)	6420	5.6	6.2	5.2	**335**	**0.3**	(23.18)	1875⊘
Sge	ε	12693	5.7	8.0	5.6	81	89.2	PA"–	1782–1949
	θ|AB	13442	6.5	9.0	6.4	325	11.9	PA–, "+	1832–1951
	|AC			7.4		223	83.9	PA–, "+(Optical)	1832–1949
Sgr	$ν^1$ AB	11794	5.0	10.8	5.0	97	2.5	fixed	1888–1930
	54|AB	12767	5.4	11.9	5.4	274	38	PA"+	1832–1951
	|AC			8.9		42	45.6	fixed	1878–1932
Sco	2	9823	4.7	7.4	4.6	274	2.5	PA–, "fixed	1855–1946
	ξ|AB	9909	7.8	7.9	7.1	**308**	**0.4**	(45.69)	1825⊘
	|AC			7.3		51	7.6	PA–, "+	1825–1975
	Σ1999 AB	9910	7.4	8.1	6.9	99	11.6	PA–, "+	1831–1975
	β|AB	9913	2.6	10.3	2.6	132	0.5	PA+, "–	1880–1959
	|AC			4.9		21	13.6	PA–, "fixed	1823–1976
	ν|AB	9951	4.3	6.8	4.2	3	0.9	fixed	1876–1955
	|AC			6.4		337	41.1	fixed	1821–1955
	σ	10009	2.9	8.5	2.9	273	20.0	PA+, "–	1783–1959
	α	10074	1.2	5.4	1.2	**274**	**2.6**	(878)	1847⊘
Scl	κ AB	111	6.1	6.2	5.4	265	1.4	PA–, "+	1876–1954
	ε AB	1394	5.4	8.6	5.3	**23**	**4.7**	(1192)	1836⊘
	τ	—	6.0	7.1	5.7	**340**	**2.1**	(1875.6)	1837⊘
Ser	5|AB	9584	5.1	10.1	5.1	36	11.2	PA–, "+	1831–1958
	|AC			9.1		40	127.2	PA–, "+	1887–1924
	δ AB	9701	4.2	5.2	3.8	**176**	**4.4**	(3168)	1833⊘
	β|AB	9778	3.7	9.9	3.7	265	30.6	fixed	1832–1940
	|AC			10.7		210	201.1	PA"+	1912–1960
	ν	10481	4.3	8.3	4.3	28	46.3	PA"–	1863–1959
	Σ2375|AB	11640	6.5	6.5	5.7	136	0.1	PA fixed?, "–	1953–1960
	|ABxCD			6.6		116	2.4	PA"+	1829–1957
	|CD			7.5		135	0.1		1953–1960
	$θ^1$–$θ^2$AB	11853	4.5	5.4	4.1	104	22.3	PA fixed, "+	1830–1973
Tau	Σ422	2644	5.9	8.8	5.8	**269**	**6.7**	(2101)	1832⊘
	$κ^1$–$κ^2$	3201	9.5	9.9	8.9	328	5.3	fixed	1874–1956

Const.	Star	ADS	vis. magnitudes			2000		(Period)	Remarks
			m_1	m_2	Comb.	PA	Sep."	Orbit Info.	Obs History
Tau (cont.)	80	3264	5.7	8.0	5.6	**17**	**1.8**	(189.5)	1831⊘
	Σ572	3353	7.3	7.3	6.5	94	4.0	PA−, "+	1830–1959
	θ^2–θ^1	—	3.6	4.0	3.0	346	37.4	fixed	1836–1921
	σ	—	4.8	5.2	4.2	193	31.2	fixed	1836–1922
Tri	6	1697	5.3	6.9	5.1	71	3.9	PA−, "fixed?	1836–1973
Tuc	β	—	4.5	4.8	3.9	169	27.1	PA−, "fixed	1835–1952
	δ	—	4.8	9.3	4.8	282	6.9	fixed	1836–1928
	κ	—	5.1	7.3	5.0	336	5.4	PA−, "+	1836–1954
	λ^1	—	6.6	8.0	6.3	81	20.7	PA+, "−	1836–1952
UMa	σ^2 AB	7203	4.8	8.2	4.8	**354**	**3.9**	(1067)	1879⊘
	AC			9.3		148	204.6	PA fixed, "−	1879–1919
	Σ1415 AB	7705	6.7	7.3	6.2	167	16.7	fixed	1832–1968
	AC			10.6		14	150.1	PA"+	1879–1956
	ξ	8119	4.3	4.8	3.8	**273**	**1.8**	(59.84)	1826⊘
	β1082 (78)	8739	5.1	7.4	4.9	**69**	**1.5**	(115.7)	1889⊘
	ζ AB	8891	2.3	4.0	2.1	152	14.4	PA+, "fixed	1830–1977
	AC			4.0		71	708.7	fixed?	1893–1966
UMi	α	1477	2.1	9.1	2.1	218	18.4	PA"+	1834–1955
Vel	γ^1–γ^2 AB	—	2.2	4.4	2.1	220	41.2	fixed	1826–1951
	AC			8.5		151	62.3	fixed	1835–1907
	AD			9.4		141	93.5	fixed?(4obs)	1846–1902
	δ	—	2.1	5.1	2.0	153	2.6	PA−, "fixed	1894–1952
	μ	—	2.9	6.6	2.9	90	0.7	PA+, "fixed?	1880–1942
	ψ	—	4.0	4.9	3.6	**264**	**0.5**	(33.99)	1897⊘
	DUN 95 (x Vel)	—	4.4	6.6	4.3	105	51.9	fixed?(4 obs)	1826–1938
Vir	γ AB	8630	3.5	3.5	2.7	**267**	**1.8**	(171.37)	1825⊘
	Σ1719	8786	7.7	8.2	7.2	1	7.2	fixed	1830–1950
	84	9000	5.5	7.9	5.4	229	2.9	PA"−	1828–1958
	Σ1833 AB	9237	7.6	7.6	6.8	172	5.7	PA"+	1832–1954
	φ AB	9273	4.8	9.3	4.8	110	4.8	fixed	1829–1958
Vol	γ^1	—	3.9	5.8	3.7	300	13.6	fixed	1826–1941
	ε	—	4.5	8.1	4.5	24	6.1	fixed	1835–1922
Vul	Σ2525	12447	8.5	8.7	7.8	**291**	**2.1**	(990.0)	1830⊘
	16	13277	5.9	6.3	5.3	115	0.8	PA"+	1844–1959
	α	—	4.6	6.0	4.3	28	13.7	PA fixed, "−	1835–1924

Orbital Elements of Selected Binaries

(★See next section, "Drawn Orbits," for these short-period binaries.)

Const.	ADS	Mass/Sun*	Year
And			
Grb 34	246	—	1972
36 And	755	—	1836
γ^BxC	1630*	—	1955
Aqr ζ^1	15971	"	1967
Boo			
Σ1785	9031*	—	1953
Σ1865(ζ)	9343*	7.4	1953
Σ1888(ξ)	9413*	1.59	1953
Σ1909	9494*	2.1	1978
μ^2	9626*	2.1	1951
Cnc			
ζ^1AB	6650*	1.9	1951
ζ^1ABxC	6650*	—	1953
CVn			
Σ1768	8974*	—	1955
CMa α	5423*	3.14	1960
Cas			
Σ3062	61*	1.3	1957
η	671	1.42	1969
ι	1860	—	1960
Cen			
α	—*	2.07	1958
γ	—*	7.6	1936
Cep			
ξ	15600	—	1951
Kr 60	15972*	—	1962/52
Cet			
β395	520*	1.8	1937
Σ186	1538*	—	1976
Com			
Σ1639	8539	—	1947
CrA			
h5014	—	—	1836
CrB			
η	9617*	1.58	1938
σ	9979	—	1954

Const.	ADS	Mass/Sun*	Year
Cyg			
δ	12880	5.6	1973
61	14636	1.2	1937
τ	14787*	1.74	1970
μ	15270	2.6	1965
Del β	14073*	4.8	1959
Dra			
20	10279	—	1955
μ	10345	2.6	1965
26	10660*	1.60	1964
Eri			
o^2BC	3093*	—	1962
ρ	—	—	1956
For α	2402	2.03	1978
Gem			
38	5559	—	1949
δ	5983	—	1959
α	6175	4.2	1957
Her			
ζ	10157*	1.86	1976
α	10418	—	1978
99	11077*	1.41	1972
Hya			
ε	6953	3.1	1961
β411	7846*	—	1965
Leo			
γ^1	7724	—	1956
ι	8148*	3.1	1980
Lup γ	—	18	1956
Lyn			
12	5400	—	1955
Σ1338	7307*	—	1966
Kui 37	—	1.2	1936
Lyr			
ε^1AB	11635	—	1955
ε^2CD	11635	—	1955
β648	11871*	3.23	1934

Const.	ADS	Mass/Sun*	Year
Mus β	—	—	1963
Oph			
λ	10087*	—	1955
η	10374	1.25	1958
	"		1958
36	10417	—	1960
τ	11005*	3.6	1959
70	11046*	1.64	1973
Ori ζ	4263	24	1962
Peg			
37	15988	—	1958
85	17175*	1.26	1962
Psc α	1615	—	1983
Pup 9	6420	1.81	1875
Sco			
ξ	9909*	2.7	1941
α	10074	22.5	1978
Scl			
ε	1394	—	1968
τ	—	—	1961
Ser δ	9701	—	1973
Tau			
Σ422	2644	—	1964
80	3264*	2.82	1977
UMa			
σ2	7203	—	1947
ξ	8119*	2.0	1966
β1082	8739	—	1889
Vel ψ	—	2.44	1967
Vir γ	8630*	1.84	1935
Vul			
Σ2525	12447	—	1967

* From Paul Couteau, *Observing Visual Double Stars* (Cambridge, MA, 1981), supplemented by Wulff D. Heintz, *Double Stars* (Dordrecht, Holland, 1978) and the *Bright Star Catalogue*. Those who wish more information on the orbital elements should consult Valerie Illingworth, *Dictionary of Astronomy*, and the *Sky Catalogue*, Volume 2.

Orbital Elements

Const.	Star	ADS	P	T	a	e	i	ω	Ω	Ephemeris		
										yr	PA°	Sep"
And	Grb 34	246	2600	1745	41.15	0.0	61.4	0.0	45.3	1980	62°	36.3"
										2000	64	35.5
										2020	66	34.6
	(36) Σ73	755	164.7	1957.15	1.014	.31	46.4	4.65	171.5	2000	313	0.9
										2010	327	1.1
										2020	338	1.2
	γ^{BC}	1630	61.1	1952.1	.296	.93	111.1	171.15	104.15	1990	106	0.5
										2000	103	0.4
										2020	116	0.3
Aqr	ζ^1	15971	856	1957.6	5.055	.49	131.2	55.12	310.2	1980	227	1.8
										2000	192	2.1
										2020	170	2.7
Boo	Σ1785	9031	155	1916.9	2.423	.44	46.8	200.9	155.1	1990	167	3.4
										2000	174	3.3
										2020	192	2.7
	(ζ) Σ1865	9343	123.44	1897.59	.595	.9572	142.0	1.47	129.99	1990	303	1.0
										2000	300	0.8
										2020	261	0.1
	ξ	9413	151.505	1909.361	4.904	.512	140.04	203.92	348.1	1990	326	7.0
										2000	318	6.6
										2010	308	6.0
										2020	296	5.2
	Σ1909	9494	225	2021	3.77	.43	83.9	38.8	57.8	1980	33	0.9
										2000	53	2.2
										2020	62	1.8
	μ^{2BC}	9626	260.1	1865	1.463	.59	135.4	338.5	174.9	1980	16	2.2
										2000	9	2.3
										2020	2	2.2
Cnc	ζ^{AB}	6650	59.7	1930	.884	.32	172	233	58	1995	125	0.7
										2000	86	0.8
										2005	59	1.0
										2010	38	1.1
										2020	4	1.2
	ζ^{ABxC}	6650	1150	1960	7.96	.26	144.6	163.9	256.7	1990	76	5.9
										2000	72	6.0
										2020	63	6.0
CVn	(25) Σ1768	8974	240	1863.95	1.091	.83	144	137.9	67	2000	99	1.8
										2020	94	1.8
CMa	α	5423	50.09	1894.13	7.5	.592	136.53	147.27	44.57	1990	5	4.5
										1995	231	3.1
										2000	150	4.6
										2005	111	6.7
										2010	91	8.8
										2020	68	11.1
Cas	Σ3062	61	106.83	1943.05	1.432	.45	44.4	278.8	219.1	1990	308	1.5
										2000	328	1.5
										2010	347	1.6
										2020	5	1.6

Const.	Star	ADS	P	T	a	e	i	ω	Ω	Ephemeris		
										yr	PA°	Sep''
Cas	(η) Σ60	671	480	1889.6	11.9939	.497	34.76	268.59	278.42	2000	317	12.8
										2020	326	13.5
	ι^{AB}	1860	840	1550	2.27	.4	132	299	6.3	1980	234	2.4
										2000	230	2.5
										2020	226	2.6
Cen	α^{AB}	—	79.92	1955.56	17.583	.516	79.24	231.56	204.87	1995	218	17.3
										2000	222	14.2
										2005	230	10.6
										2010	245	6.8
										2015	289	4.1
										2020	346	5.5
	γ	—	84.50	1931.22	.93	.79	112.9	187.8	2.4	1995	351	1.2
										2000	347	1.0
										2005	341	0.7
										2010	324	0.4
										2015	196	0.2
										2020	35	0.3
Cep	ξ	15600	3800	1750	11.5	.24	109	114	85	1980	276	8.0
										2000	275	8.2
										2020	273	8.5
orbit 1	Kr 60	15972	44.6	1925.64	2.412	.41	164.5	217.8	161.1	1995	115	3.3
										2000	95	3.0
										2005	68	2.5
orbit 2	Kr 60	15972	44.356	1925.495	2.3717	.411	170.74	223.9	167.51	1995	113	3.3
										2000	92	3.0
										2005	65	2.5
Cet	β395	520	25	1924	.67	.22	78	142	112	1995	132	0.3
										2000	289	0.5
										2005	327	0.2
										2010	97	0.5
										2015	111	0.8
										2020	132	0.3
	Σ186	1538	170.3	1893.35	1.05	.71	73.6	220.7	40.4	1990	57	1.3
										2000	60	1.1
										2010	65	0.9
										2020	71	0.7
Com	Σ1639	8539	678	1891	1.3	.95	161	334	105.7	2000	323	1.7
										2020	321	1.8
CrA	h5014	—	191.2	1841.68	1.062	.52	145.2	190.4	49.2	1993	357	1.1
										1995	354	1.0
										2000	346	0.9
										2010	323	0.7
										2020	287	0.6
CrB	η	9617	41.56	1892.39	0.839	.28	58.9	219.6	24.2	1995	43	0.9
										2000	65	0.7
										2005	110	0.5
										2010	169	0.6
										2015	208	0.6
										2020	284	0.3
	σ	9979	1000	1828	6.599	.78	33.3	84.35	7.7	2000	237	7.1
										2020	240	7.5

Const.	Star	ADS	P	T	a	e	i	ω	Ω	Ephemeris yr	Ephemeris PA°	Ephemeris Sep''
Cyg	δ	12880	827.6	1885.8	3.2	.49	147	134	98.7	2000	222	2.5
										2020	212	2.7
	61	14636	653.34	1676.94	24.307	.4002	55.01	147.03	171.4	2000	150	30.3
										2020	154	31.2
	τ	14787	49.9	1939.6	0.88	.25	134.2	119	159.7	1997	325	0.8
										2000	306	0.8
										2005	272	0.7
										2010	237	0.8
										2015	208	0.9
										2020	186	1.0
	μ	15270	507.5	1962.5	4.278	.58	76.5	340	289.6	2000	320	1.2
										2020	19	0.8
Del	β	14073	26.65	1962.72	.475	.35	63.6	346.4	178.6	1997	324	0.4
										2000	343	0.5
										2005	0	0.6
										2010	23	0.4
										2015	156	0.3
										2020	247	0.2
Dra	20	10279	729.35	1853.5	1.38	.466	97	220.3	66.2	2000	68	1.4
										2020	67	1.6
	μ	10345	482	1964	3.33	.37	143.4	204.3	267.4	2000	8	1.9
										2010	352	2.1
										2020	338	2.2
	26	10660	76	1950.4	1.52	.16	105.7	322	152	2000	331	1.7
										2005	325	1.5
										2010	316	1.1
										2020	207	0.4
Eri	o^{2BC}	3093	251.988	1848.872	7.0453	.4147	108.54	326.497	150.96	2000	336	9.3
										2010	334	9.3
										2020	332	9.0
	p	—	483.66	1813.494	7.8169	.53444	142.82	18.374	13.116	2000	191	11.5
										2020	186	11.8
For	α	2402	314	1947	4.37	.76	81.5	42	117.7	2000	299	5.1
										2020	301	5.8
Gem	38	5559	3190	1636	9.55	.48	148.4	310.5	185.6	2000	144	7.1
										2020	141	7.3
	δ	5983	1200	1437	6.975	.11	63.28	57.19	18.4	2000	225	5.8
										2020	229	5.4
orbit 1	α	6175	420.1	1965.3	6.295	.33	115.9	261.4	40.5	2000	61	3.8
										2020	48	5.2
orbit 2	α	6175	511.3	1950.65	7.37	.36	112.9	239.8	41.7	2000	67	4.0
										2020	55	5.6
Her	ζ	10157	34.385	1933.35	1.369	.47	131.4	291	228.2	1995	59	1.5
										2000	10	0.7
										2005	223	1.0
										2010	175	1.2
										2015	135	1.3
										2020	104	1.5

Const.	Star	ADS	P	T	a	e	i	ω	Ω	Ephemeris		
										yr	PA°	Sep''
Her (cont)	α	10418	3600	3635	4.68	0	155.8	180	119.6	2000	104	4.6
										2020	103	4.6
	99	11077	55.8	1941.8	1.00	.74	32.0	300.6	218.7	1995	57	0.5
										2000	250	0.5
										2005	295	0.9
										2010	314	1.1
										2015	326	1.3
										2020	335	1.5
Hya	ε^{ABxC}	6953	890	1933	4.536	.29	42	203.1	55.5	2000	302	2.7
										2020	318	2.7
	β411	7846	210.1	1948.23	0.9824	.80	126.1	35.8	144.8	2000	315	1.4
										2020	310	1.5
Leo	γ^1	7724	618.6	1743.32	2.505	.84	36.4	162.5	143.2	2000	125	4.4
										2020	126	4.5
	ι	8148	192	1948.47	1.92	.55	130.5	140	52.2	2000	116	1.7
										2020	₍97	2.2
Lup	γ	—	147	1887	0.59	.49	95.6	301	92.8	2000	274	0.7
										2010	272	0.6
										2020	269	0.4
Lyn	12	5400	699	1740	1.66	.03	180	154.8	0	2000	69	1.7
										2020	59	1.7
	Σ1338	7307	219.7	1996.77	1.459	.61	47.8	252.9	91.5	2000	16	0.4
										2010	75	0.8
										2020	94	1.2
	Kui 37	—	21.85	1950.1	0.619	.15	134.8	210	22.8	1993	194	0.5
										2000	46	0.6
										2005	358	0.7
										2010	279	0.5
										2015	192	0.5
										2020	75	0.5
Lyr	ε^{1AB}	11635	1165	1152.4	2.78	.19	138	165.7	29	2000	350	2.6
										2020	345	2.5
	ε^{2CD}	11635	585	1644.5	2.95	.49	120.5	88	17.4	2000	82	2.3
										2020	73	2.4
	β648	11871	61.203	1910.674	1.24	.2489	115.16	279.35	48.13	1995	357	0.8
										2000	317	0.7
										2005	280	0.8
										2010	257	1.0
										2015	243	1.2
										2020	231	1.2
Mus	ρ	—	383.12	1872.29	1.735	.526	61.3	98.32	161.81	2000	43	1.3
										2020	57	1.3
Oph	λ	10087	129.87	1939.54	0.97	.618	26.8	158.9	52.5	1990	22	1.5
										2000	30	1.5
										2010	38	1.5
										2020	46	1.5

Const.	Star		ADS	P	T	a	e	i	ω	Ω	Ephemeris		
											yr	PA°	Sep''
Oph (cont.)	orbit 1	η	10374	88	1936.8	0.86	.84	100.4	279.8	41.4	1995	248	0.6
											2000	244	0.6
											2005	240	0.6
											2010	236	0.6
											2020	227	0.5
	orbit 2	η	10374	84.3	1936.8	1.057	.89	97.3	277.1	38.8	1995	242	0.6
											2000	238	0.6
											2010	231	0.6
											2020	219	0.25
	36		10417	548.7	1643.48	13.91	.9	99.2	90	93.6	2000	147	4.9
											2020	140	5.2
	τ		11005	280	1829	1.494	.72	59.3	49.78	63	2000	284	1.7
											2020	292	1.4
	70		11046	87.892	1895.894	4.5482	.5002	121.083	12.688	301.39	1990	220	1.5
											2000	147	3.8
											2010	131	5.8
											2020	121	6.7
Ori	ζ		4263	1509	2070.6	2.728	.07	72	47.3	155.5	2000	165	2.3
											2020	167	2.2
Peg	37		15988	140	1908	0.75	.51	89	202.3	117.2	2000	118	0.7
											2010	119	0.5
											2020	120	0.2
	orbit 1	85	17175	26.27	1910.11	0.83	.38	50	94.4	288.6	1993	118	0.7
											1995	136	0.8
											2000	184	0.7
											2005	234	0.8
											2010	275	0.8
											2015	16	0.3
											2020	125	0.8
	orbit 2	85	17175	26.386	1910.285	0.8032	.3781	49	93.782	290.954	1993	114	0.7
											1995	134	0.8
											2000	180	0.7
											2005	230	0.8
											2010	272	0.8
											2015	348	0.4
											2020	121	0.7
Psc	α		1615	933.05	2098.64	4	.696	120.9	225.4	23.3	2000	272	1.8
											2020	257	1.7
Pup	(9) β101		6420	23.18	1915.71	0.58	.69	77.8	67.7	103.3	1993	299	0.6
											1995	304	0.5
											2000	335	0.25
											2005	76	0.25
											2010	282	0.4
											2015	296	0.6
											2020	310	0.4
Sco	ξ		9909	45.69	1951.14	0.72	.74	36.9	348.2	201.7	1995	94	0.3
											2000	308	0.4
											2005	343	0.8
											2010	357	1.0
											2015	5	1.2
											2020	13	1.2

Const.	Star	ADS	P	T	a	e	i	ω	Ω	Ephemeris		
										yr	PA°	Sep″
Sco (cont.)	α	10074	878	1461	2.9	.1	90	0	93.7	2000	274	2.6
										2020	274	2.3
Scl	ε	1394	1192	2076.2	4.652	0	180	0	0	2000	23	4.7
										2020	17	4.7
	τ	—	1875.6	1968.6	12.395	.9832	77.82	85.39	138	2000	340	2.1
										2020	344	2.6
Ser	δ	9701	3168	1700	6.02	.31	112.6	274.6	166.8	2000	176	4.4
										2020	175	4.6
Tau	Σ422	2644	2101	1900	8.023	.18	32.1	152	92	2000	269	6.7
										2020	273	6.7
	80	3264	189.5	1888	1.01	.83	108	162	12.8	2000	17	1.8
										2010	16	1.7
										2020	14	1.6
UMa	σ²	7203	1067	1917.7	6.2	.81	146.2	331.5	99.7	2000	354	3.9
										2020	347	4.6
	ξ	8119	59.84	1935.17	2.53	.414	122.65	127.53	101.59	1995	317	1.1
										2000	273	1.8
										2005	243	1.7
										2010	208	1.6
										2015	176	1.8
										2020	152	2.2
	(78) β1082	8739	115.7	1921.74	1.256	.44	51.5	301	269.2	2000	69	1.5
										2010	82	1.4
										2020	99	1.1
Vel	ψ	—	33.99	1935.75	0.795	.44	58.5	48.4	287.2	1993	177	0.6
										1997	227	0.5
										2000	264	0.5
										2005	8	0.25
										2010	100	0.8
										2015	118	1.0
										2020	135	0.9
Vir	γ	8630	171.37	1836.433	3.746	.881	146.05	252.88	31.78	2000	267	1.8
										2010	44	0.9
										2020	1	2.7
Vul	Σ2525	12447	990	1887.9	1.97	.93	133.7	8.5	103.1	2000	291	2.1
										2020	290	2.3

The Drawn Orbits

This chapter contains the most easily resolved binaries with a period of 300 years or less, from the preceding list:

1.	γBC	And		19.	26	Dra
2.	Σ1785	Boo		20.	o²BC	Eri
3.	ζ	Boo		21.	ζ	Her
4.	ξ	Boo		22.	99	Her
5.	Σ1909	Boo		23.	β411	Hya
6.	μ²BC	Boo		24.	ι	Leo
7.	ζ	Cnc		25.	γ	Lup
8.	25	CVn		26.	Σ1338	Lyn
9.	α	CMa		27.	β648	Lyr
10.	Σ3062	Cas		28.	λ	Oph
11.	α	Cen		29.	τ	Oph
12.	γ	Cen		30.	70	Oph
13.	Kr 60	Cep		31.	85	Peg
14.	β395	Cet		32.	ξ	Sco
15.	Σ186	Cet		33.	80	Tau
16.	η	CrB		34.	ξ	UMa
17.	τ	Cyg		35.	γ	Vir
18.	β	Del				

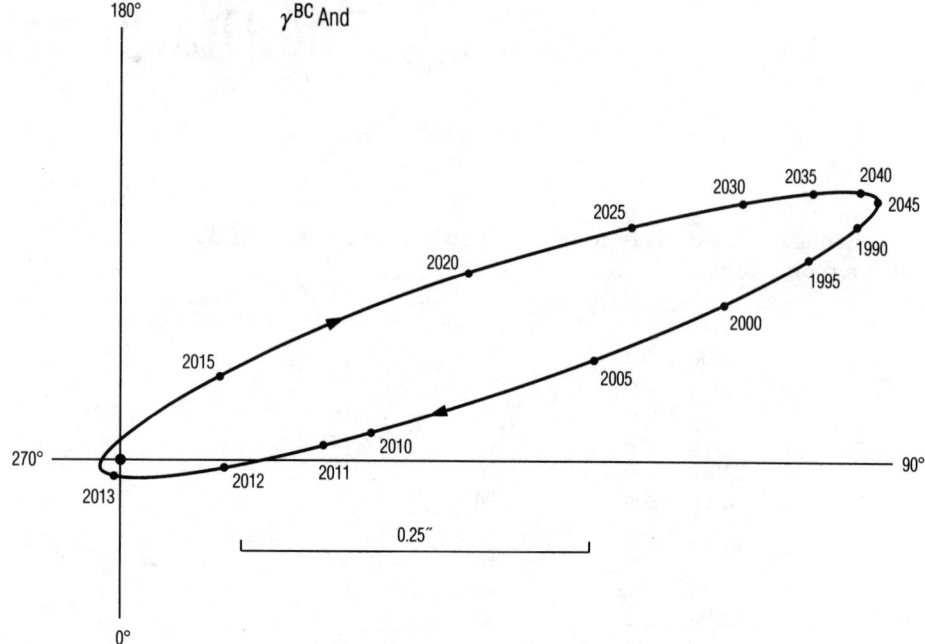

Σ 1785 (Boo)

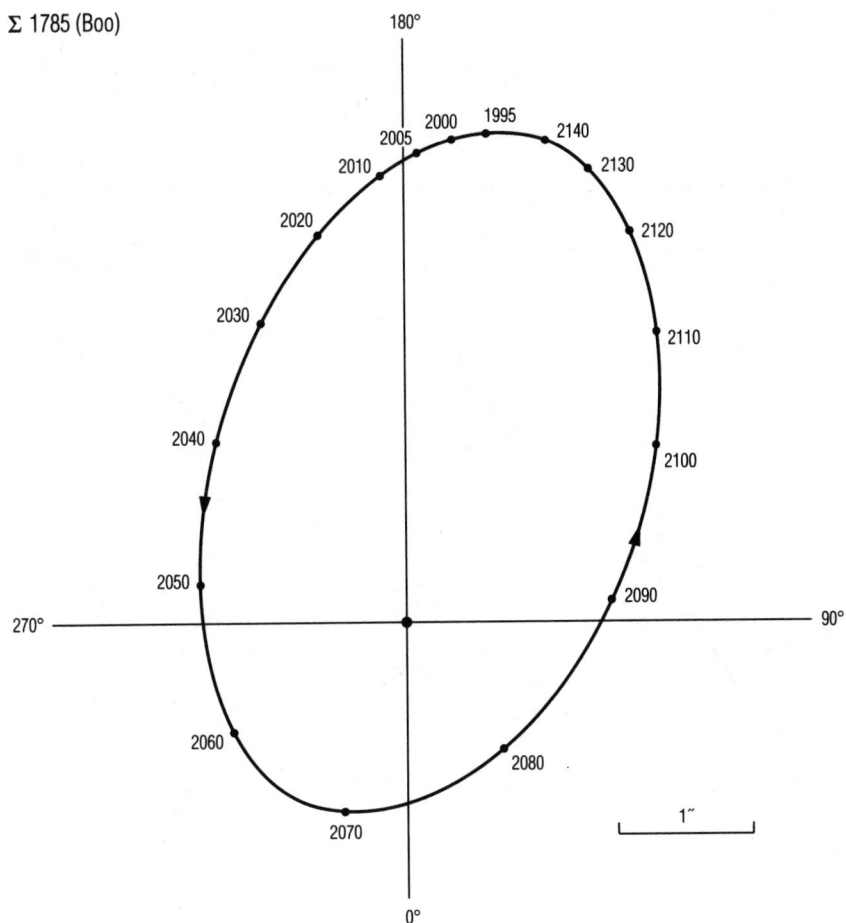

ζ Boo

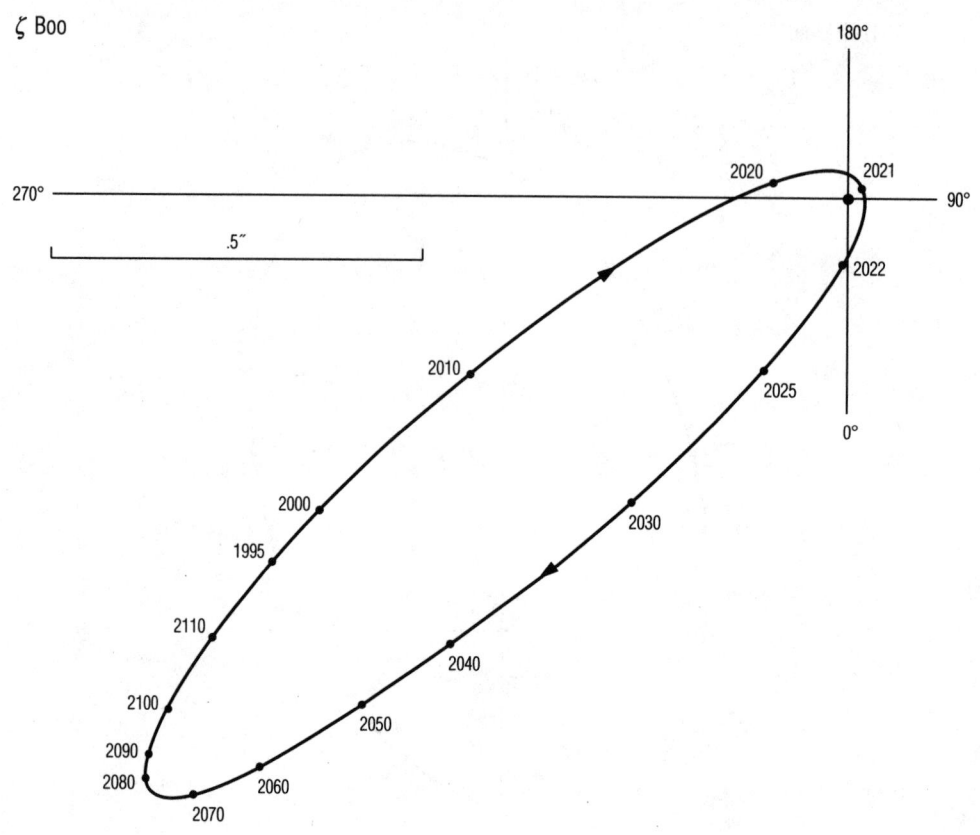

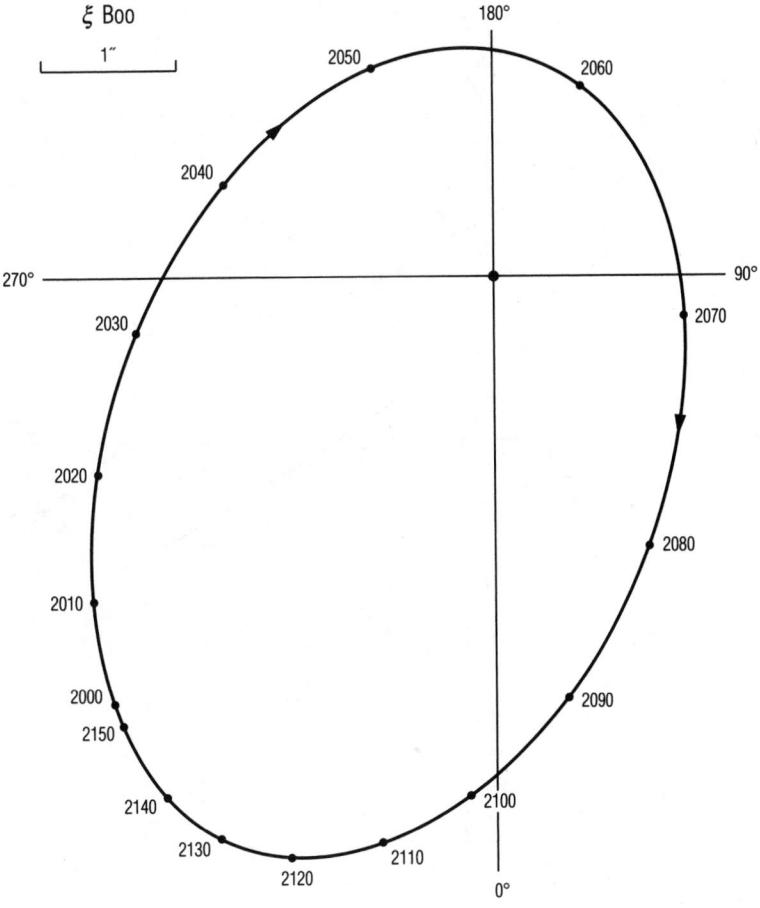

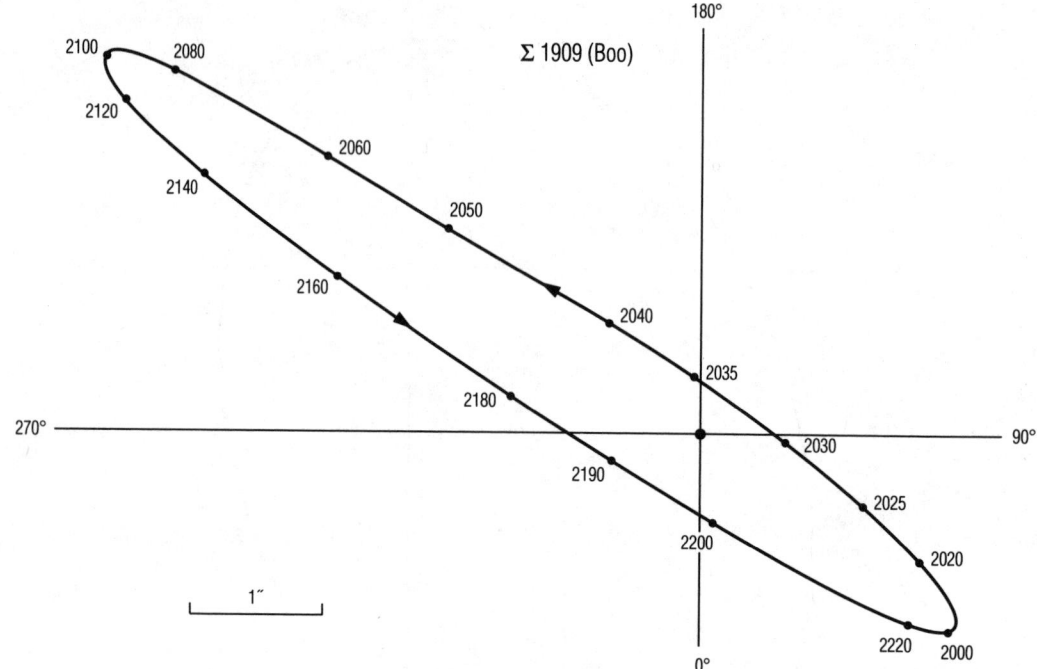

Σ 1909 (Boo)

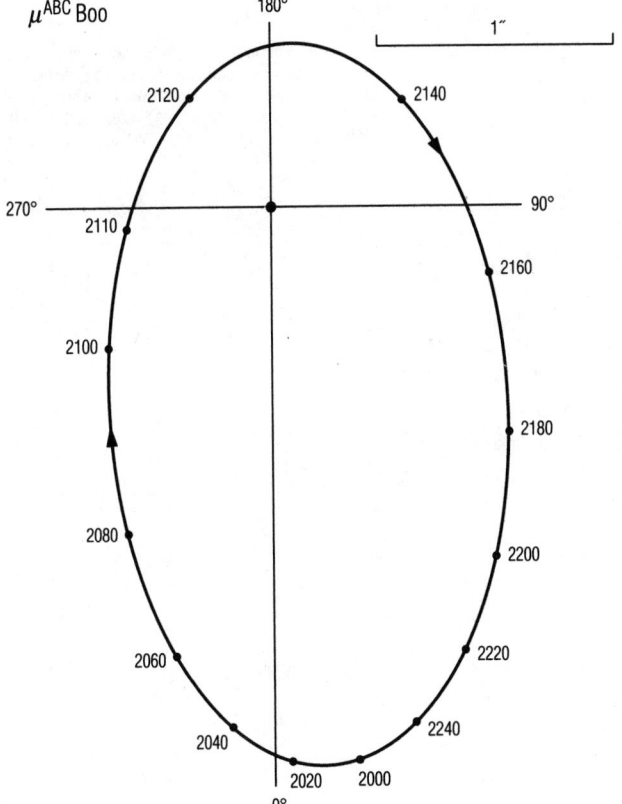

ζ Cnc

The two companion stars to the primary (ζ^B and ζ^C) are shown here with their orbits to scale. The closer companion revolves every 59.7 years; the more distant companion every 1150 years. If the orbital elements are accurate, the two will be in alignment in the summer of 2002. However, this will not be visible to us. In the spring of 2002, just before the system is blotted out in the sunset, ζ^{AB} will be on one side of ζ^C, and when the stars come back into view later that year, ζ^B will have passed its slower companion.

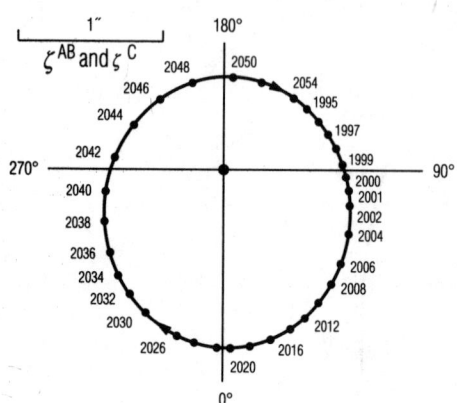

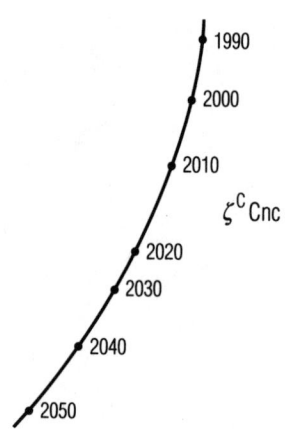

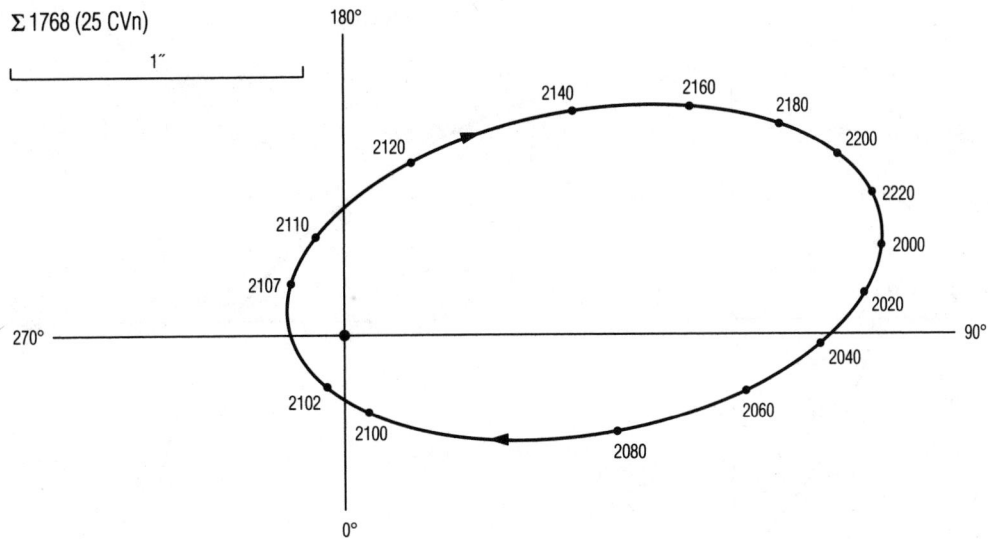

α CMa

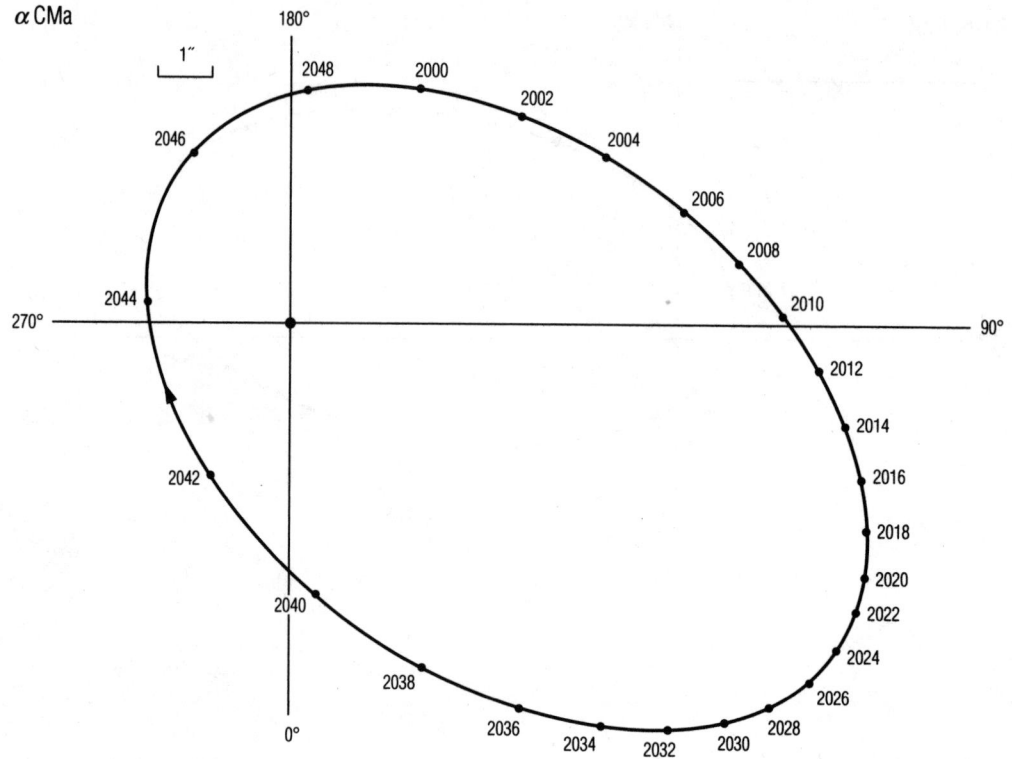

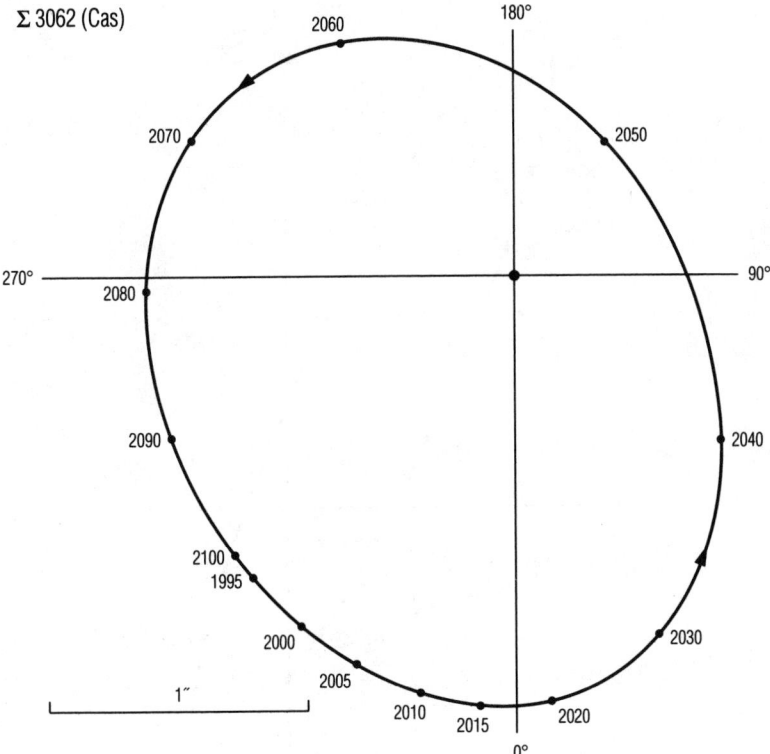

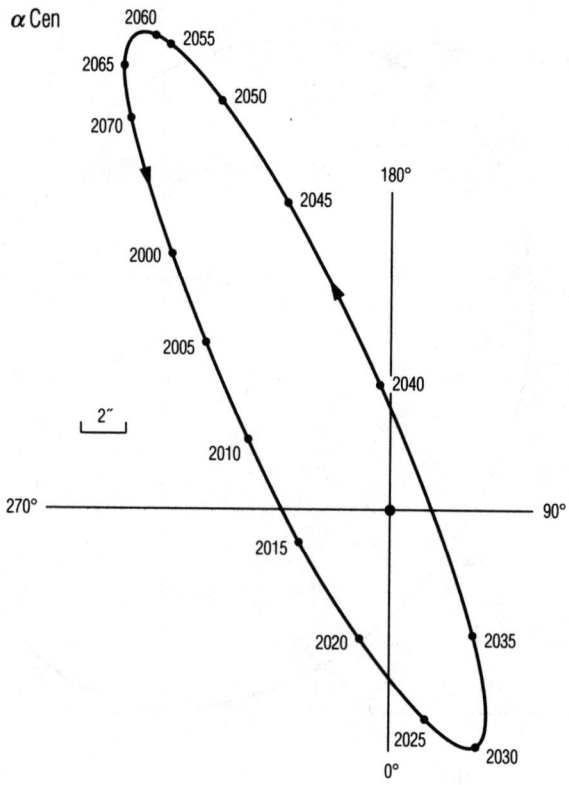

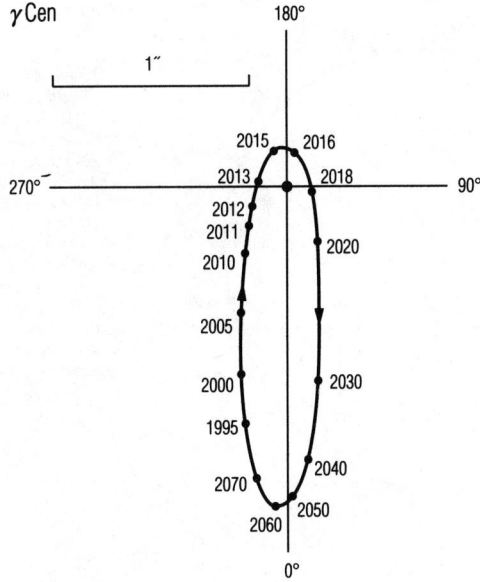

Orbit 1

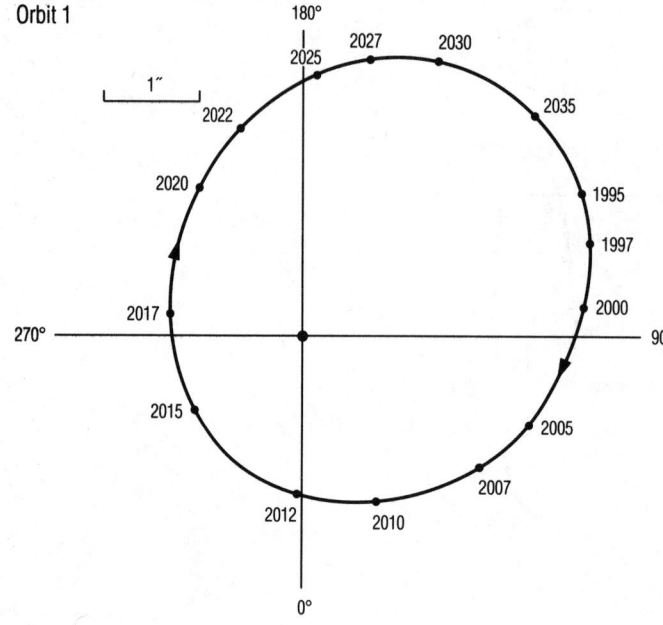

Kr 60 (Cep)

Orbit 1 is from S. L. Lippincott, calculated in 1952. This orbit is considered "Grade 1", that is, of the highest reliability.

Another Grade 1 orbit, by R. Wielen gives a very slight difference of separation, but the PA is quite different. Lippincott's orbit is 2° in advance of Wielen's until 2000, when it reaches 3°. By 2010 Lippincott's orbit is 7 degrees in advance; i.e. Wielen's has a PA of 18° in 2010. This increases to a 10° difference by 2012, and a maximum of 14° in 2015. That is, Wielen's orbit gives a PA of 287° in 2015.

After this date the PA difference decreases quickly, to a minimum of 2° difference by 2030.

Amateur astronomers may therefore be alerted to make their own observations from 2010 to at least 2015, to help decide which of the two orbits is the more accurate. And to make matters even more interesting, a third orbit, calculated in 1950, is also considered a Grade 1 orbit. See Finsen and Worley, p. 245, for all three orbital elements.

Orbit 2: Kr 60 (cep)

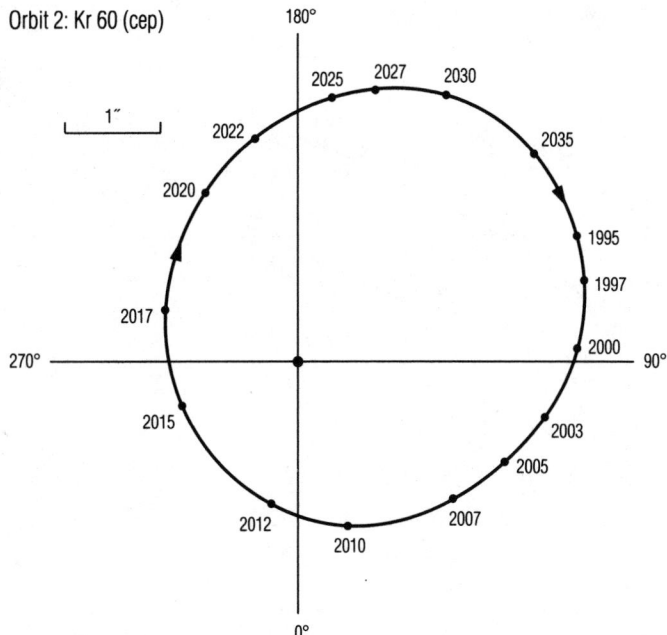

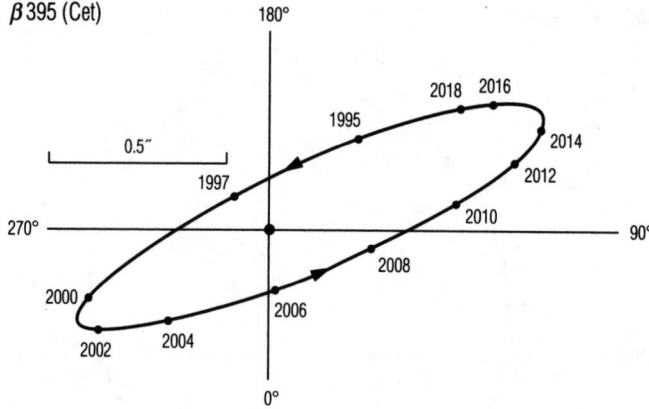

Σ 186 (Cet)

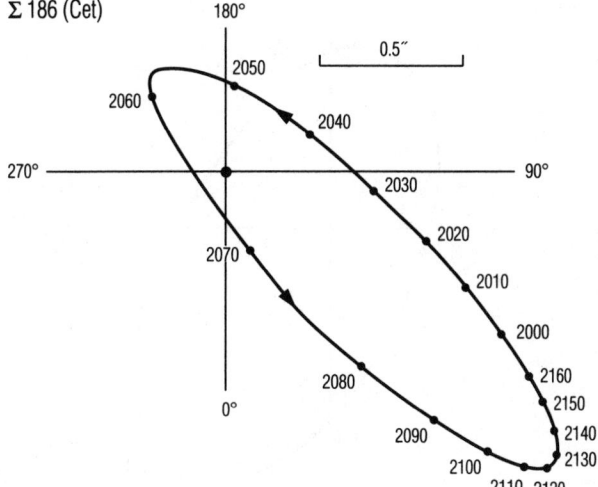

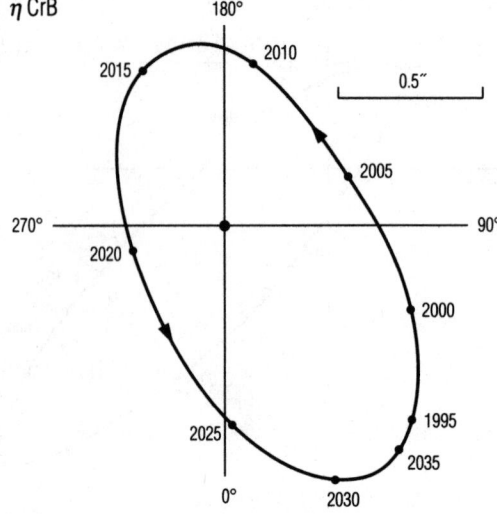

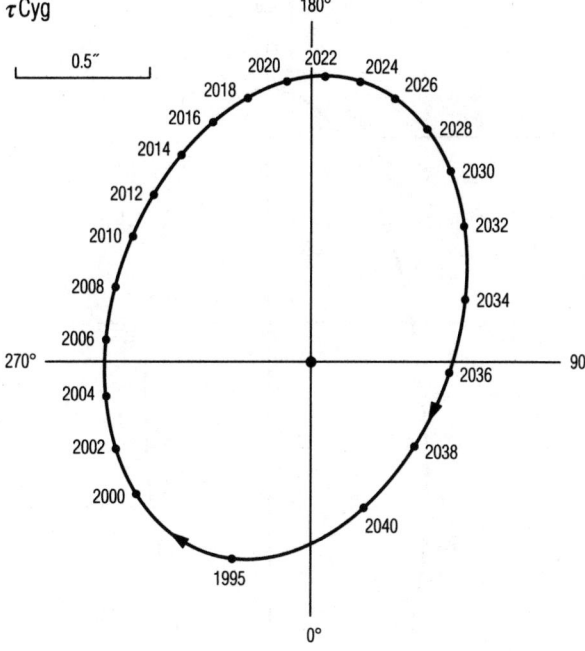

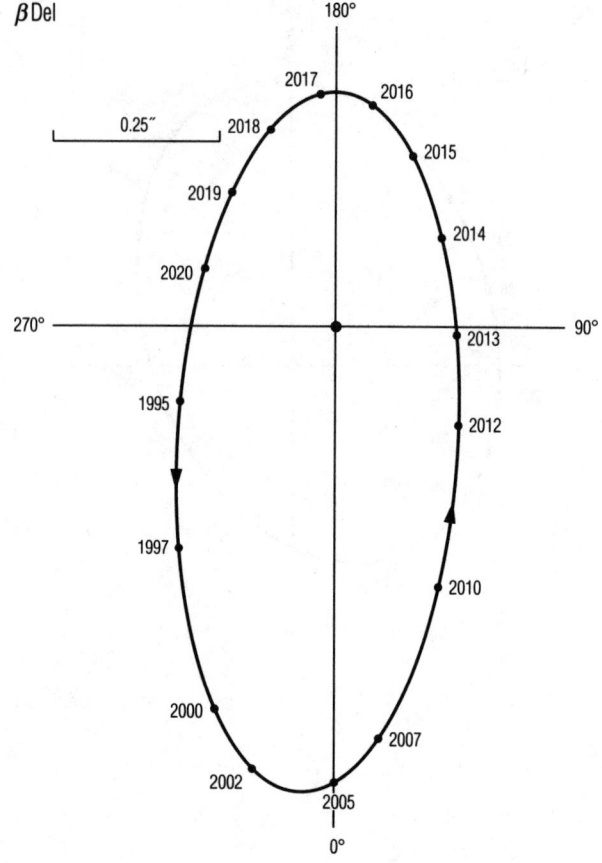

β Del

180°

2017
2016
2018
2015
0.25″
2019
2014
2020
270°   90°
2013
1995
2012
1997
2010
2000
2007
2002
2005
0°

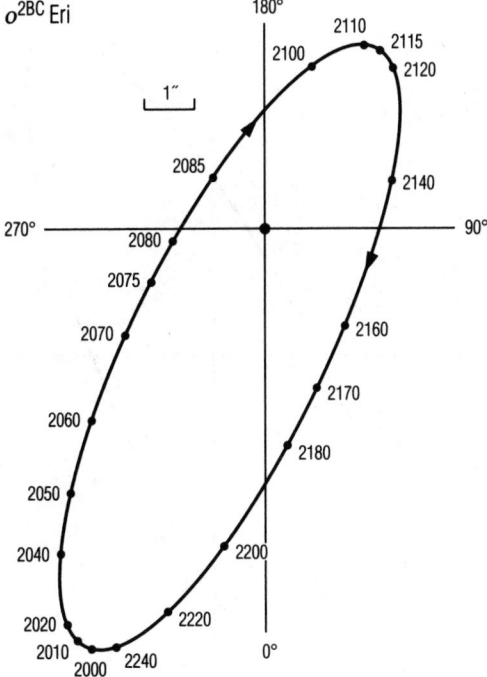

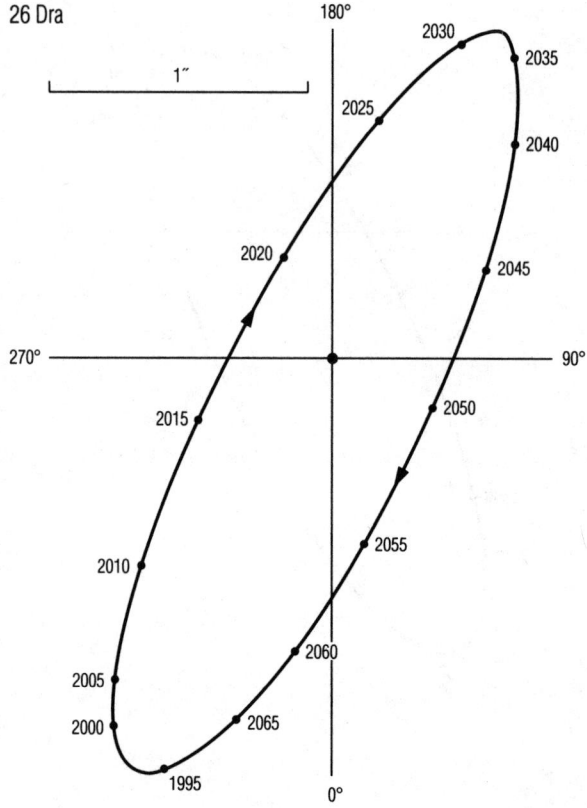

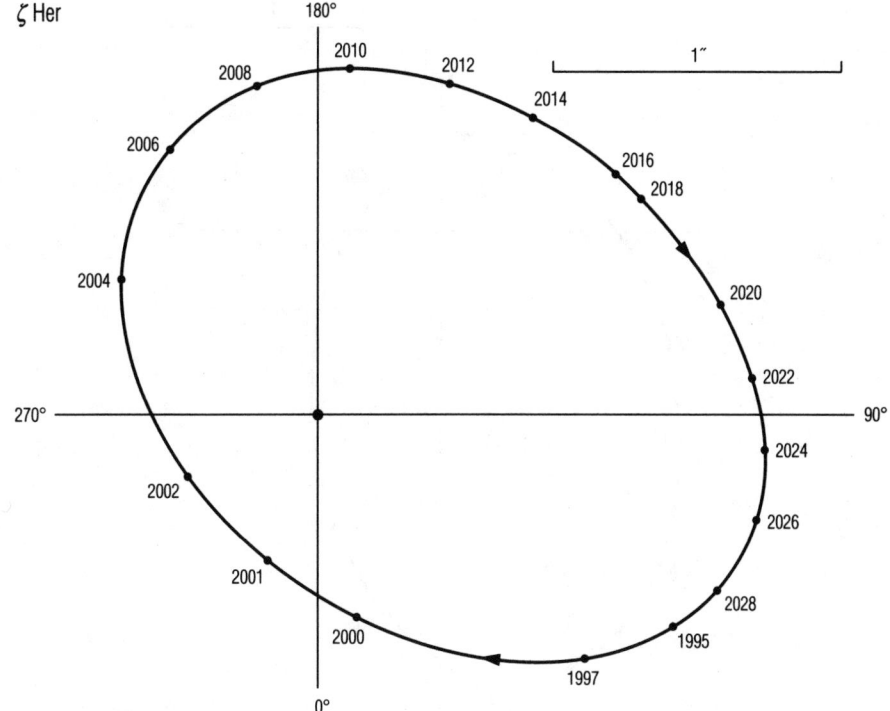

ζ Her

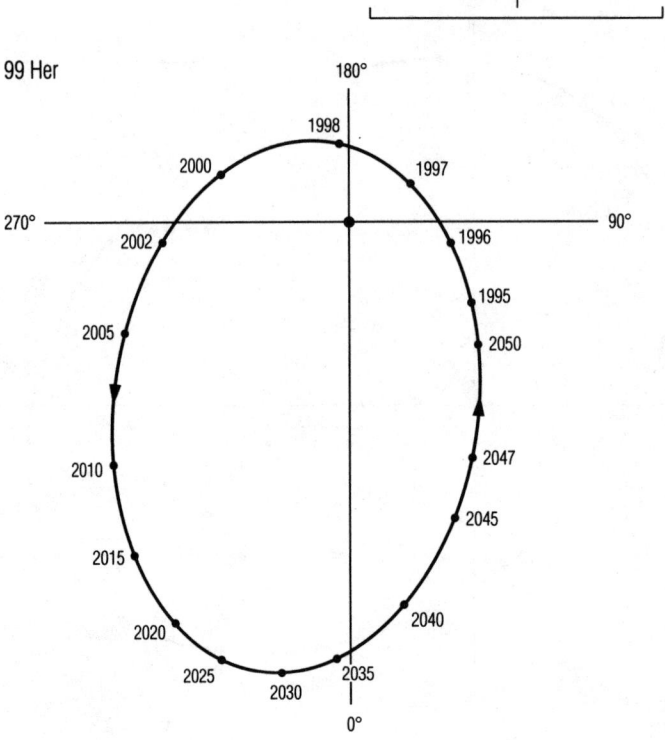

β411 (Hya)

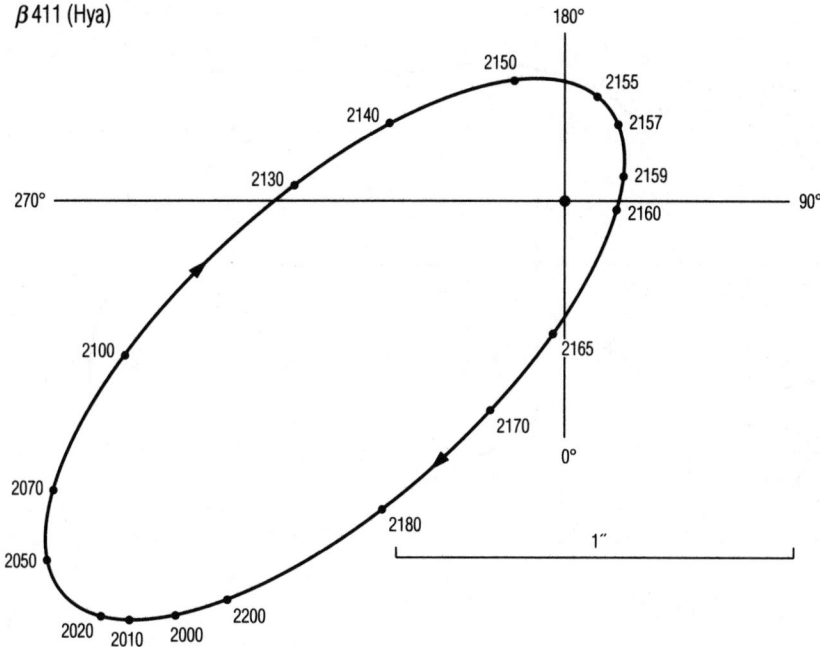

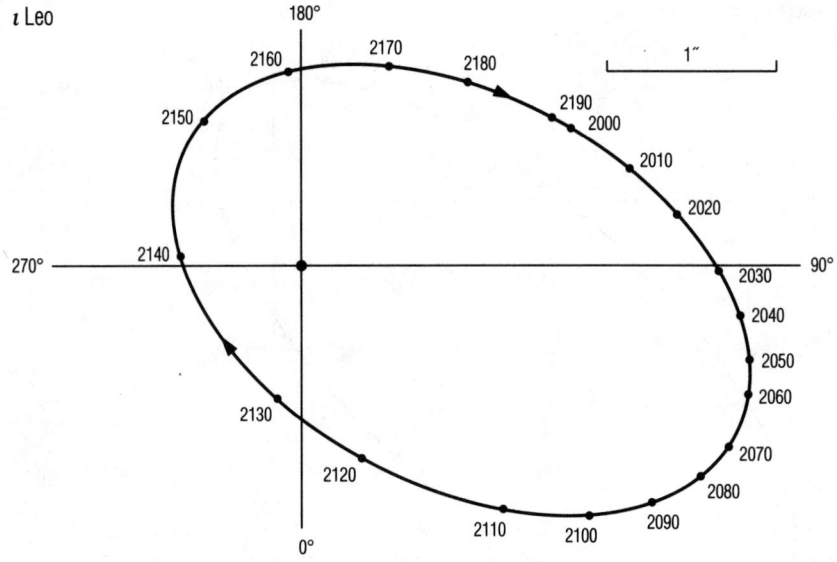

ι Leo

γ Lup

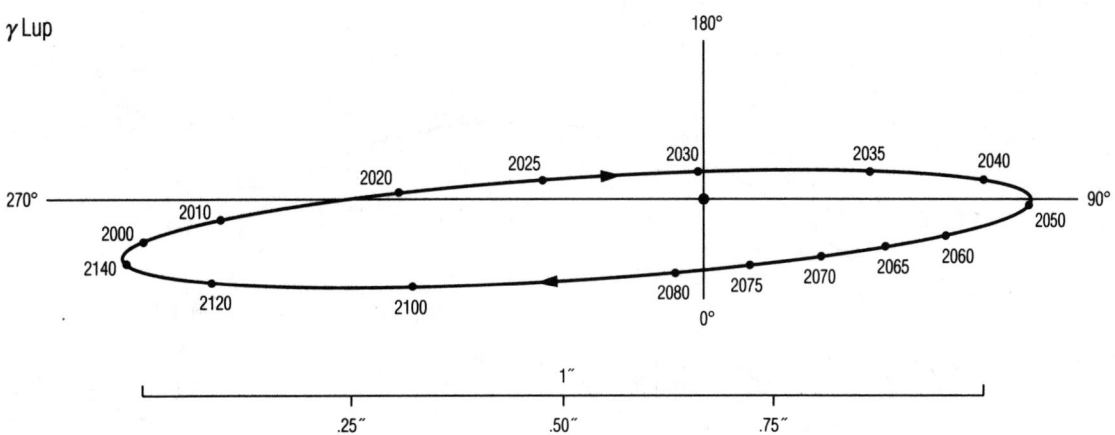

Σ 1338 (Lyn)

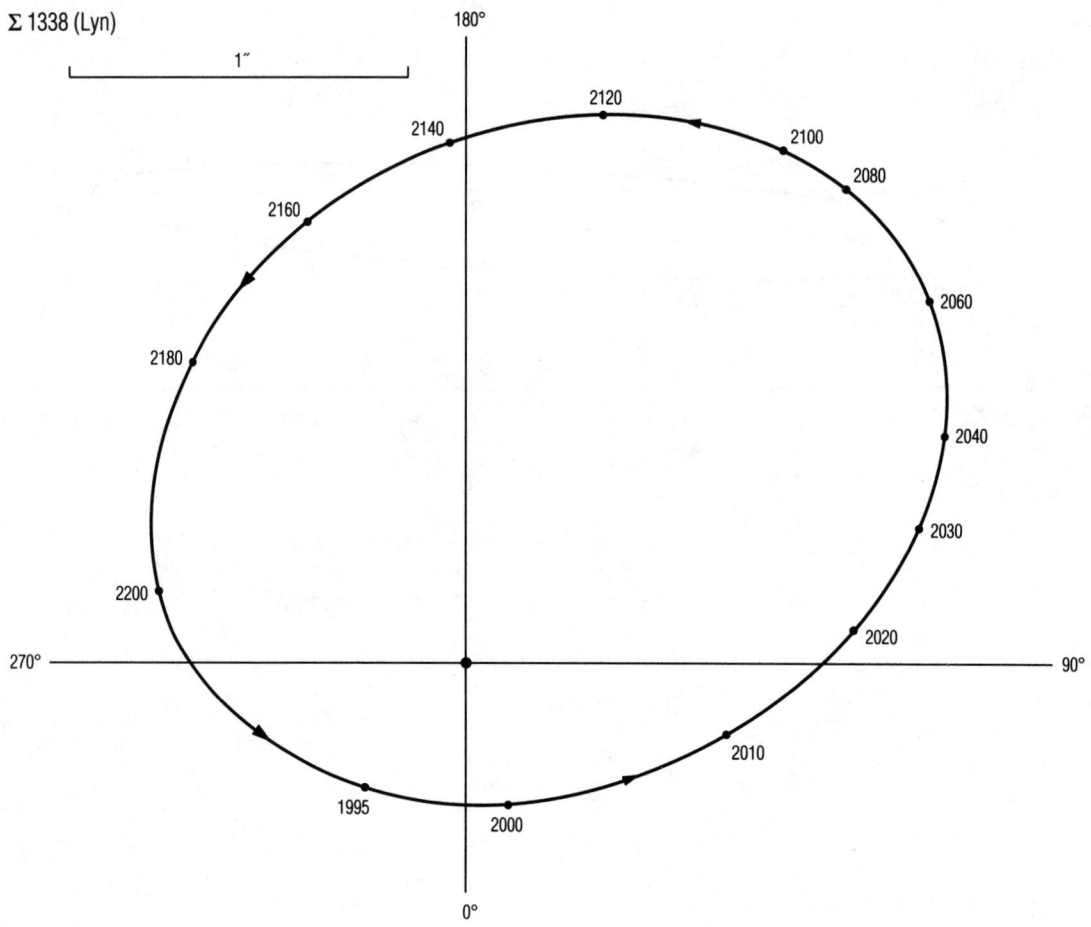

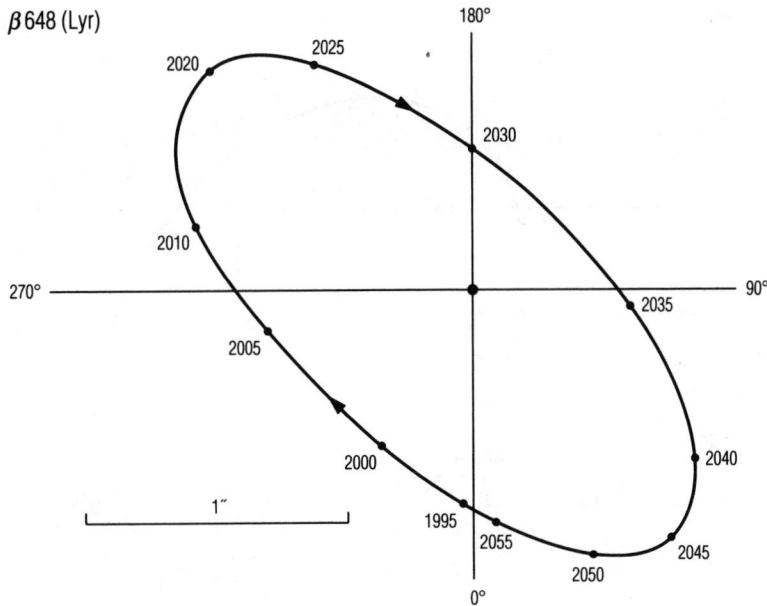

β 648 (Lyr)

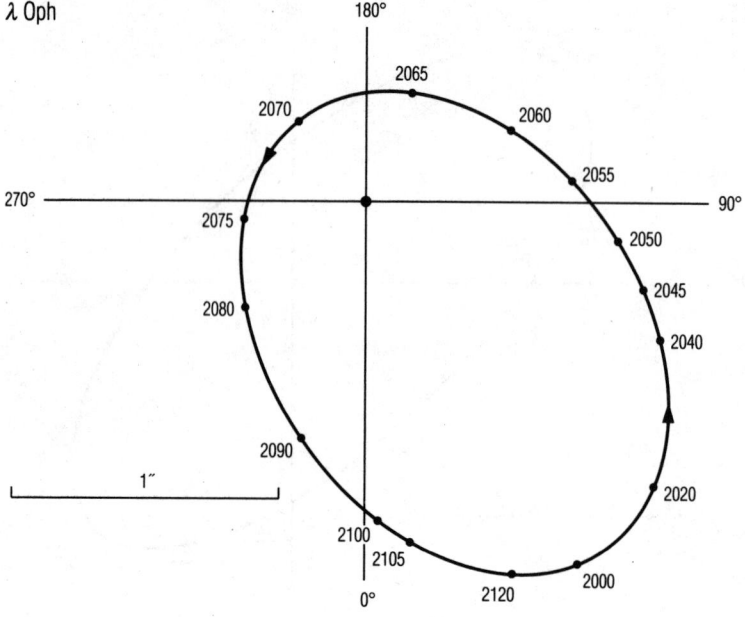

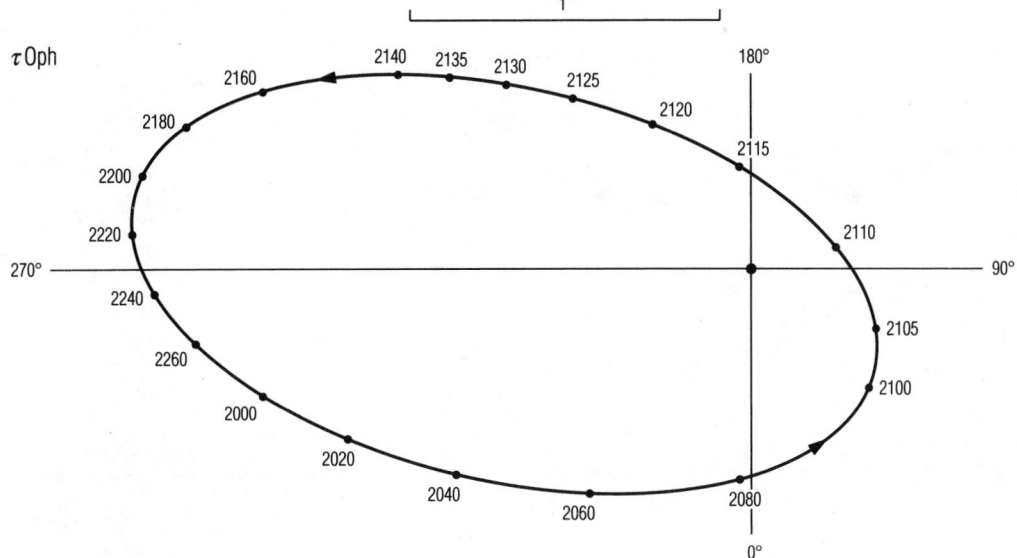

τ Oph

70 Oph

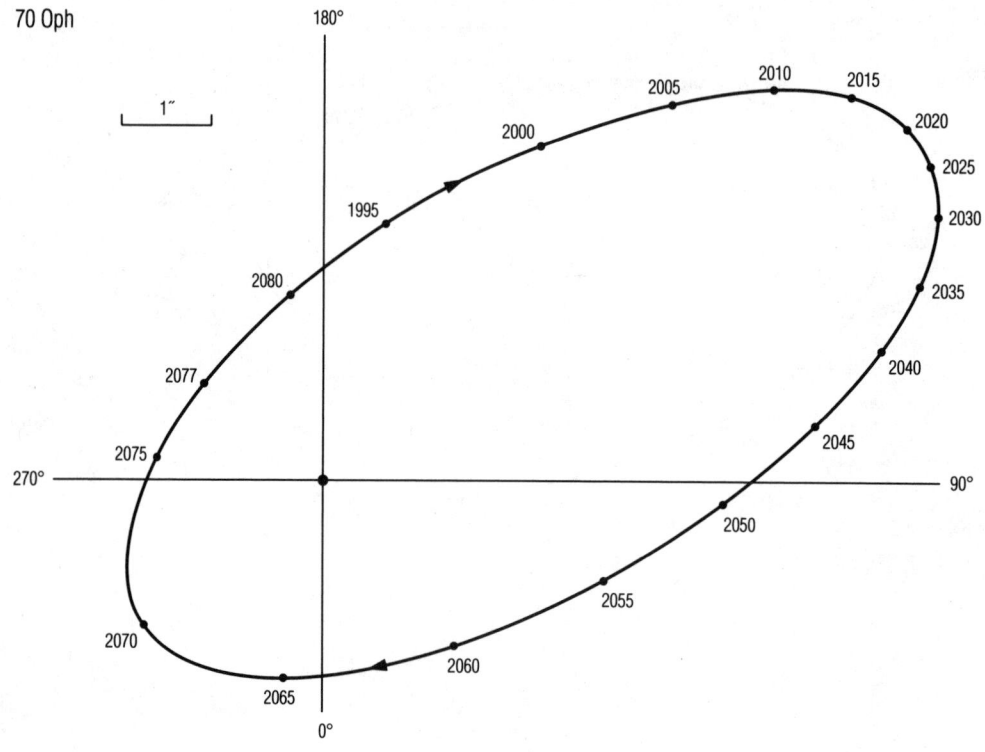

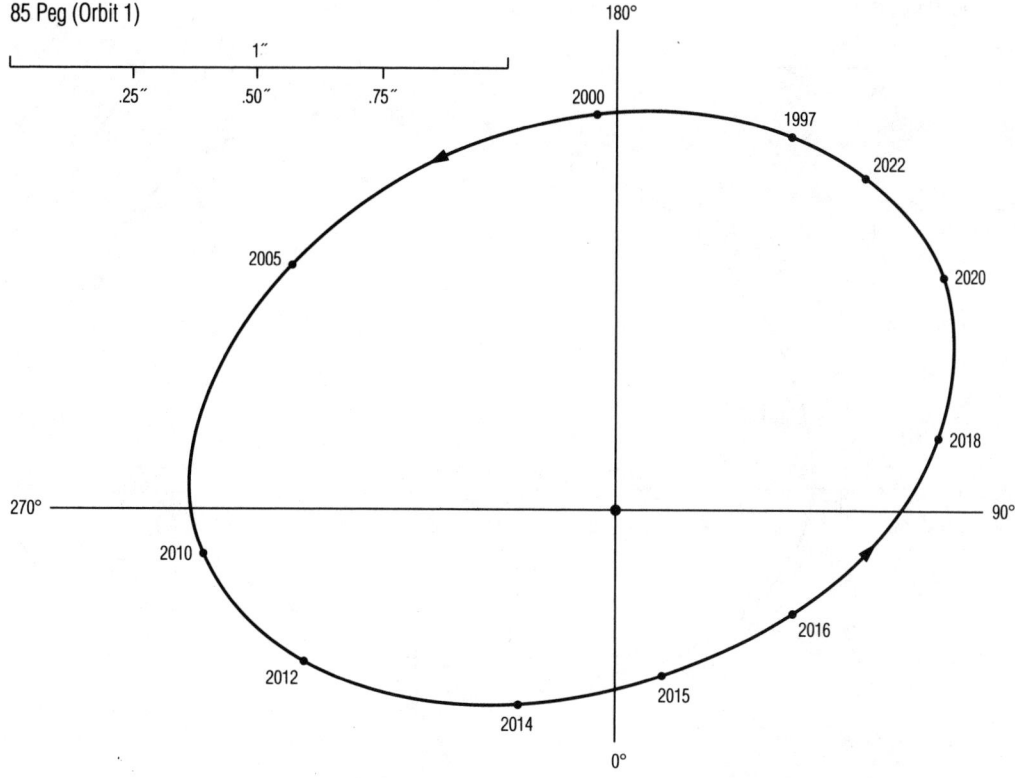

85 Peg (Orbit 1)

85 Peg (Orbit 2)

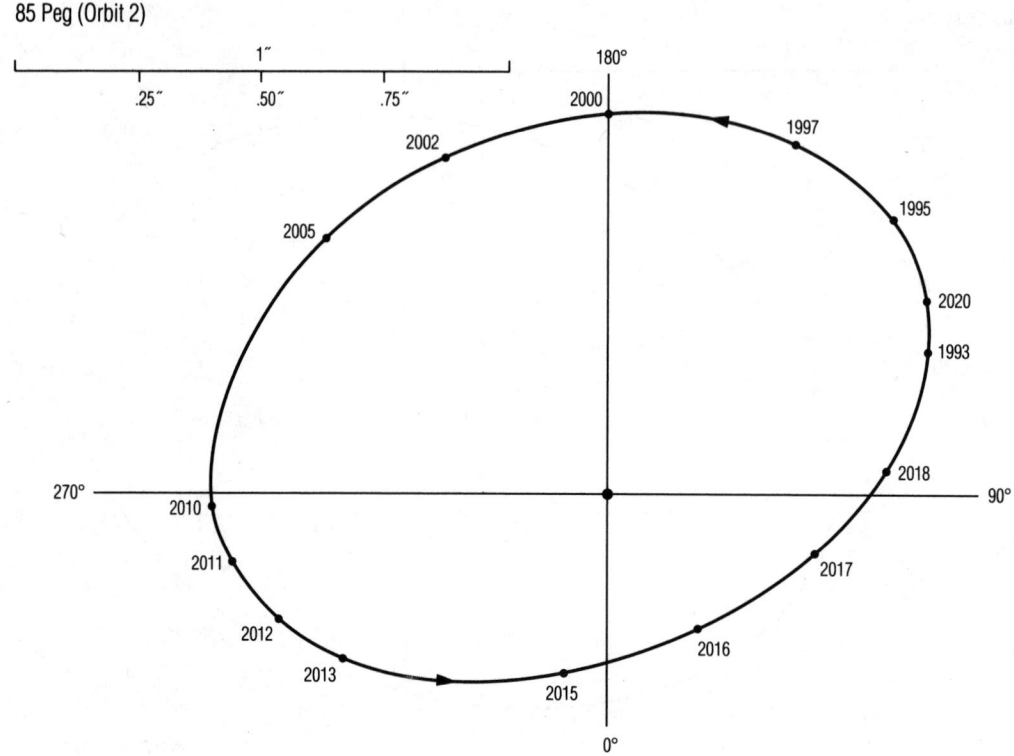

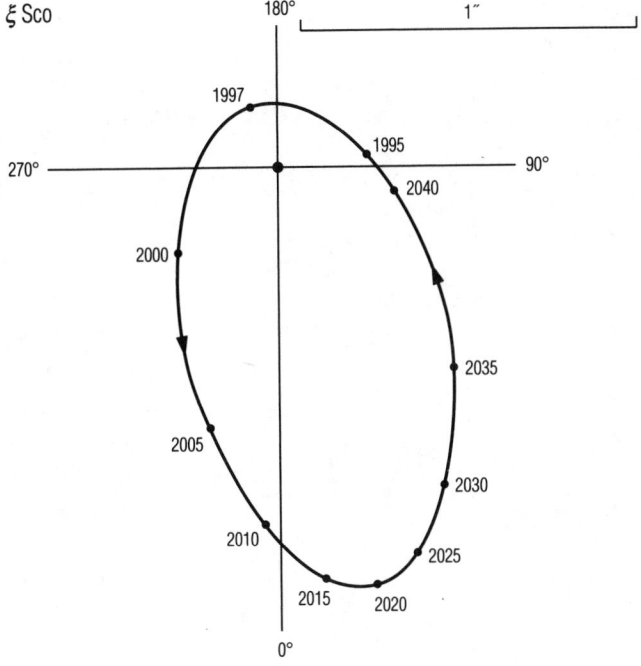

ξ Sco

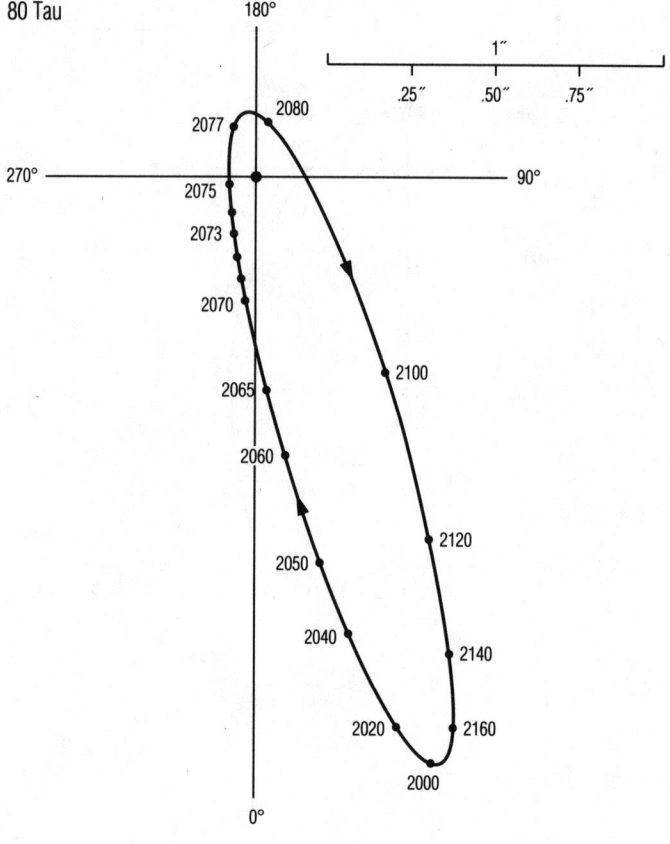

80 Tau

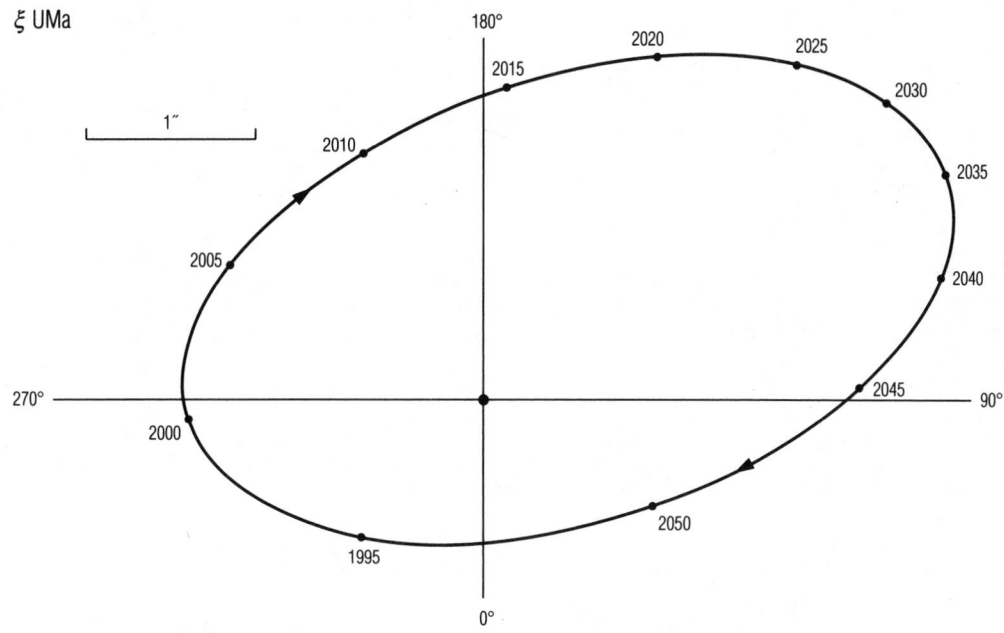

ξ UMa

γ Vir

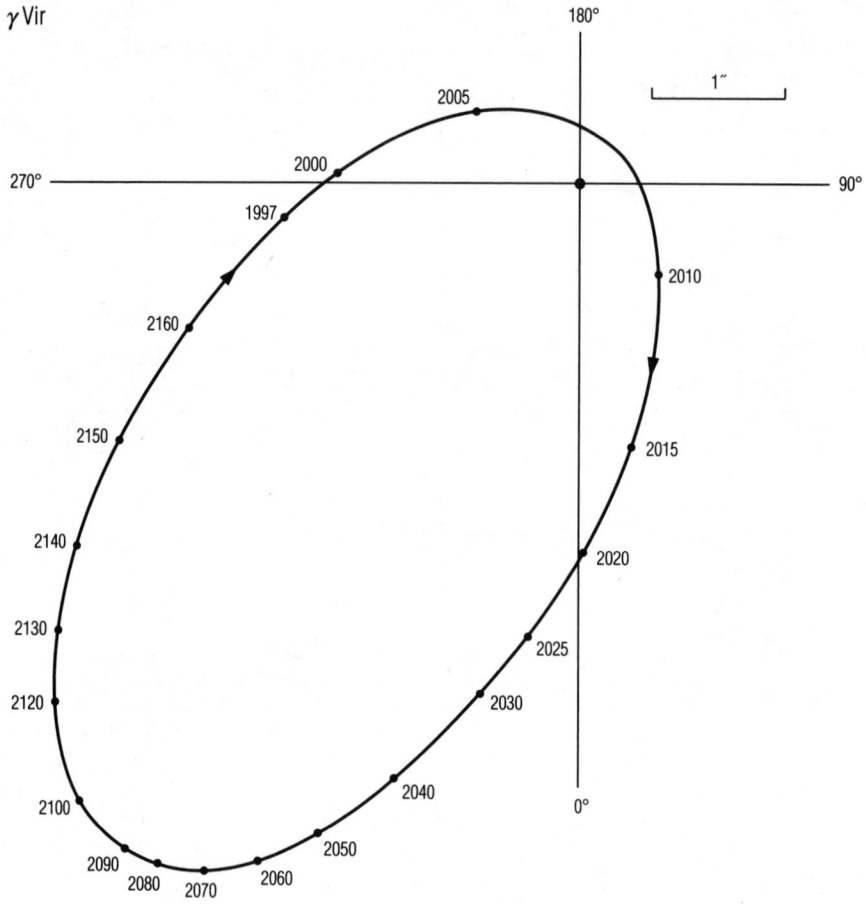

III

Variable Star Section

Variable Stars

It is likely that the ancients were aware of the variable nature of several stars. In particular Algol (β Persei) seems to have been admired for its fluctuating quality; its name—meaning "Demon Star"—was used by the Arabs at a very early date.

Another most probably known in the early days of astronomy was Mira, o Ceti, the most striking of the long-range variables. The year usually given for its discovery is 1596, by the German theologian David Fabricius. However, Fabricius did not realize he had discovered the first variable, and it was left to the Dutch astronomer Phocylides Holworda to study the variable nature of Mira in 1638. The star got its name in 1662, in a treatise written by the German astronomer Johannes Hevelius (who was much better known for his lunar mapping).

At the beginning of the eighteenth century, only Algol, Mira, and χ Cygni were recognized as variable stars. By the end of that century the number had grown to thirteen. The different causes of variability were not understood for a considerable time, and the division of variable stars into precise categories remains an ongoing process, with new classifications being proposed as more is learned about the properties of the variable stars.

Variables fall into three broad groups: pulsating, eruptive, and eclipsing. *StarList 2000* offers many examples from the first and third groups.

Pulsating variables form the largest group, containing eight subgroups. (Authorities do not always agree with either the number of subgroups, or whether a given star belongs to one or another subgroup. Our list of variables by type which precedes the main listing of variable stars, is an amalgam of Kholopov and Petit.) These stars may be of very short period (several minutes or hours), or they may have a period of several days or several hundred days. Generally, the longer the period, the greater the amplitude, or difference in magnitude from dimmest to brightest.

The dynamics at work in the most common kind of variable, the pulsating long-period variables, are poorly understood. It has been suggested that the pulsation may be due to a growing lack of hydrogen—that this gas has been nearly consumed, and as a result, helium now is being burned. Hydrogen is burned apparently only during the maximum brightness period, as shown by spectral lines.

The period of a pulsating variable fluctuates somewhat, yet an average period shows some consistency in that the period will not vary greatly from the observed average. Also, it is common to assign an *epoch* to the star. This is the date—in Julian Days—of one of its maxima, carefully measured to the nearest minute, or even fractions of a second if possible. Depending on the accuracy of the period and on its continued conformity to its average, it is possible to predict any future maximum. However, since stars are seasonal, one cannot count on seeing any given variable at its brightest on any given night. The Variable Section has a column suggesting the best viewing dates, depending on the "season" of the star and its period. Those stars marked (m) are approximately at their transit at midnight on the date indicated.

Since one cannot guarantee these suggested "best viewing dates," the student of variable stars should begin tracking his or her prey when its season first comes around and continue to do so for a month or two to either side of the best viewing date. It would be of some interest to the author to hear from you, with your account of how accurate (or inaccurate!) the proposed dates prove to be.

Eruptive variables, also called cataclysmic variables, are mostly associated with novae—stars suddenly bursting with bright light, then gradually reducing in brightness until they fall below naked-eye visibility. Sometimes the nova recurs, to repeat roughly the same pattern; sometimes once is all there is before it is gone forever. Because of their unpredictability, there are no novae or supernovae included in the StarList. Should one suddenly burst on the scene, it is always fully covered in the periodical literature.

Eclipsing binaries are of three types, based respectively on Algol, β Lyræ, and W UMa. With the last of these, called EW stars, both the primary and companion are dwarfs, and the companion touches the primary, leading to a great deal of mass transfer. This in turn deforms their shapes and contributes to a fluctuating brightness.

In EB (β Lyr) stars, although they may not be in physical contact, there is still a great deal of mass transfer, from the larger—which is becoming a red giant—to the smaller. The final result here is eventually an EA-type variable, based on the model of Algol.

The EA variables, which are the most easily remarked of the eclipsing binaries because of their greater amplitude, find themselves at the end of an evolutionary process. The companion has grown to become a subgiant, roughly equal in size to its primary. Yet the luminosity of the two stars is different, and as the dim companion revolves about the brighter primary, variations in brightness occur. The maximum brightness occurs when the two stars are not eclipsed, each adding its luminosity to the total brightness. Two minima occur: the principal minimum, when the companion eclipses the primary, and a secondary minimum, when the companion is eclipsed by the primary.

The complexities of the dynamics of the many kinds of variable stars are outside the scope of the present work. Those interested in pursuing the subject further should refer to the bibliography. The study of variable stars can be a rewarding pastime, either on one's own or through one of the numerous organizations throughout the world. The principal organization is the American Association of Variable Star Observers (AAVSO), 187 Concord Avenue, Cambridge, Mass. 02138.

Type	Period (days)	Prototypical Star	Amplitude	Spectra
		(Pulsating Variables)		
RR	.05–1.0	RR Lyræ	0.5–1.5m	A, F
βC	0.1–0.5	β CMa	0.2	B0–B4
δ Sct	.05–0.2	δ Scuti	0.2	A, F
ZZ	1 min.–15 min.	ZZ Ceti	0.05	white dwarfs
Cδ	1–50 days	δ Cephei	0.2–2.0	F, G
SR	20–500 days	Semiregular	0.2–2.5	M, C, S
RV	30–150 days	RV Tauri	1.0–3.0	G, K
M	100–600 days	Mira	2.5–10	M, C, S
		(Eclipsing Binaries)		
EA	0.1–10,000 days	Algol (β Persei)	0.1–3	A, B, F
EB	0.5–200 days	β Lyræ	0.1–1.5	O, B, A
EW	0.2–1 day	W Uma	0.2–1	F, G, K

Variable Stars: by Type

I. Pulsating Variables

α Cygni	α Cygni (cont.)	β Cep (β CMa)
Car V371	Leo ρ	CMa β
Cas κ	Nor μ	CMa ι
Cen o^2	Ori ε	CMa ξ^1
Cep V337 (9)	Sco V973	CMa EY (15)
Cyg α	Vel GX	CMa FN
Cyg V1661 (55)	Vel LN	Car χ

I. Pulsating Variables (cont.)

β Cep (β CMa) (cont.)	RV Tau	SR (Semi-Regular)
Car V343 (d)	Sct R: RVa	And λ
Car V376 (b¹)	Mon U: RVb	Cam VZ
Cen β		CVn AW
Cen ε		Cep OV
Cen χ	**δ Sct**	Phe ψ
Cep β		Psc TV (47)
Cet δ	And GN (28)	Ret γ
Cru β	Ari UV (38)	
Cru δ	Aur KW (14)	
Cru θ²	Boo γ	**SRa**
Cru λ	Boo ι	
Eri λ	Boo κ²	Gem η
Eri ν	CVn AO (20)	Peg GZ (57)
Her ι	Cas β	
Hya η	Cep ε	**SRb**
Lac DD (12)	CrB γ	
Lup α	Cyg τ	Aps θ
Lup δ	Cyg V1644 (29)	Boo W (34)
Lup τ¹	Del δ	Cnc BP (27)
Mon V637 (19)	Dra CL	CVn Y
Mus α	Eri o¹	Cen V806 (2)
Oph θ	Leo β	Dor R
Peg γ	Lyr α	Dor WZ
Per ε	Oct σ	Eri DM (54)
Per V469 (53)	Pav ρ	Gem BQ (51)
Sco κ	Peg τ	Her g (30)
Sco λ	Phe ρ	Hya U
Sco σ	Phe SX	Hya II
Tau V971 (23)	Pup ρ	Lib σ
Vel o	Sgr ρ¹	Lyr R
Vel IS	Sct δ	Mus ε
	Ser δ	Oct ε
	Ser o	Oph V2105
Cepheid (Cδ)	Tau θ²	Ori o¹
	Tau ρ	Per ρ
Aql η	Tau τ	Pup L₂
Aql FF	Tau υ	Scl R
Car ZZ	Tau V777 (71)	Ser τ⁴
Car V382	UMa υ	UMi RR
Cep δ	UMa DD (18)	Vir ET
Cru R	UMa DP (67)	
Dor β	UMi γ	**SRc**
Gem ζ	Vel FZ	
Gem ω	Vel GU	Cep μ
Pav κ	Vir FM (32)	Cet T
Sgr γ¹ (W)	Vul NU (21)	Her α
Sgr U		Lyr δ²
Sgr X		Ori α
Sgr Y	**RR Sct**	Per S
UMi α		Sco α
	Eri S (64)	
	Lyr RR	

I. Pulsating Variables (cont.)

SRd	Lc	M (cont.)
Cas ρ	Aur π	Lep R
Cas V509	Aur ψ[1]	Lib S
Cen o[1]	CMa o[1]	Lyn R
Cen V810	CMa σ	Lyn W
Her ν	Cam BE	Nor R
	Car V337	Oph X
L?: Vel N	Gru β	Ori U
	Peg ε	Per R
	Pup KQ	Pup W
Lb	Pup NS	Sgr R
	Vel λ	Sgr RU
Ant U	Vel GZ	Sco RR
Aps δ[1]		Scl S
Aqr χ		Ser R
Aqr EN (3)	**IA**	Tau R
Cam BD		Tri R
Cnc μ[1] (BL)	Mon S (15)	UMa R
Cet α		UMa T
Cet AD		Vel Y
Cet AE (7)	**M (long-period)**	Vir R
Cyg T		Vir S
Cyg V1509 (19)	And R	
Dra CQ (4)	Aqr R	
Dra CU (10)	Aql R	
Eri γ	Aur R	
Eri π	Boo R	
Eri τ[4]	Cam R	
Eri DV (47)	Cnc R	
Gem μ	Car R	
Gru δ[2]	Cas R	
Her V656	Cen R	
Lyn UW (1)	Cep S	
Mus μ	Cep T	
Oph κ	Cet o	
Peg β	Col T	
Phe γ	Com R	
Psc TX (19)	Crv R	
Psc YY (30)	Cyg χ	
Sge δ	Cyg R	
Sgr η	Cyg U	
Sgr V3872 (62)	Cyg RT	
Scl η	Del R	
Tau α	Del S	
Tuc ν	Dra R	
UMa CS	Gem R	
Vir ψ	Her S	
Vir ω	Hor R	
	Hya R	
	Hya T	
	Leo R	
	LMi R	

II. Eruptive Variables

γ Cas

And **o**
Aps κ[1]
Aqr **o**
Aqr π
Cam BK
CMa κ
CMa ω
CMa EW (27)
CMa FT (10)
CMi β
Cap ε
Car PP
Car V344
Car V345
Cas γ
Cas **o**
Cen δ
Cen η
Cen μ
Cen V795

γ Cas (cont.)

Cir θ
Cru μ[2]
Cyg υ
Cyg V832 (59)
Cyg V1746
Dra κ
Her **o**
Lib FX (48)
Oph ζ
Oph χ
Oph V2048 (66)
Ori ω
Pav λ
Per δ
Per φ
Per ψ
Per X
Per MX (48)
Pup MX
Pup NV

γ Cas (cont.)

Pup NW
Pup OS
Tau ζ
Tau BU (28)

S Dor

Car η (?)
Cyg P
Sco ζ[1]

Z And

Lep SS (17)

UV Cet

Cen α[c]

Peculiar

Car η

III. Rotating Variables

α CV (& ACVO)

And α
Aqr ET
Aql V1288 (21)
Ari γ[2]
Aur θ
Cnc κ
CVn α[2]
Cas ι
Cas V566 (6)
Cen I ("el")
Cen V815
Cir α
Com GN (13)
CrB β
Cyg V1741 (4)
Dor α
Dra φ
Dra AF (73)
Equ γ
Eri τ[9]
Eri EG (20)
Eri EN (66)
For ν
Her ω

α CV (cont.)

Her V637 (52)
Hya β
Lep μ
Mic θ[1]
Oph ω
Ori V1032 (11)
Per LT (21)
Phe ι
Psc κ
Pup OU
Ser χ
Sex β
Sex SS
Tau δ[3]
Tau GS (41)
TrA LP
UMa ε
Vir CU
Vir CW (78)
Vul NT (15)

BY Dra

Boo ξ
Hya ε

Elliptical

Cen ν
Col λ
Ori π[5]
Per **o**
Per b[1]
Tri TZ (6)
Vel HY
Vir α

FX Com: Mon 645V

SX Ari

Ari SX (56)
Cen V761
Cyg V1624 (28)
Eri τ[8]

IV. Peculiar: RCB Stars

CrB R
Sgr RY

V. Eclipsing Binaries

E

Aql Y (18)
Car V357
Lyn UZ (2)
Mus η
Mus θ
Mus GT
Per V467 (42)
Vel KX (f)

EA

Aur β
Aur ε
Aur ζ
CMa R
Cap δ
Car V415 ("A")
Cas δ
Cas AR
Cep VV
CrB α
Cyg V695 (31)
Cyg V1488 (32)
Her u (68)
Lib δ
Lyn RR
Oph U

EA (cont.)

Ori δ^A
Ori η
Ori θ^{1A}
Per β
Per τ
Phe ζ
Sge U
Sgr μ
Tau λ
Tau CE (119)
UMi ε

EB

And ζ
Aql σ
Cam TU (31)
CMa UW (29)
Car GM
Lyr β
Pic δ
Pup V
Pup PU
Sgr υ
Sco μ^1

EW

CrA ε
Dor γ

WR (Wolf-Rayet)

Vel γ^2

RS CVn

CVn BH
CrB δ
CrB σ (TZ)
Dra **o**
Eri δ
Gem σ
LMi SU (10)
Psc BC (33)
UMa ξ
UMa DK (24)

VI. Type Uncertain

Car ν: S Dor?
Cen I ("el"): αCV?
Cyg T: Lb?
Her V669: ?
Per ξ: ?
Vel N: L?

NOTE: The following
stars have previously been
designated in various catalogues
as variables, but are now considered not to be variable.

Aps R
Cas α
Eri R
Ori CI (31)
PsA π
UMa SY (31)

Mira-Type Variable Stars

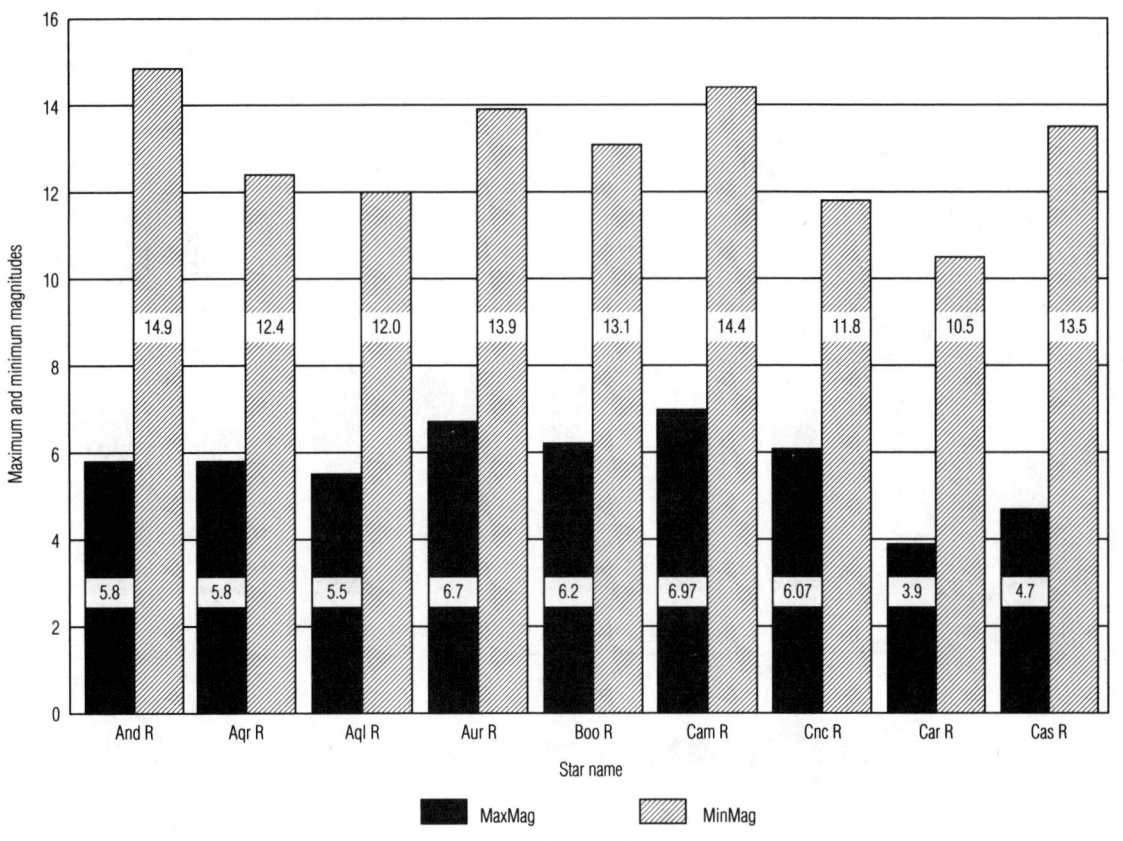

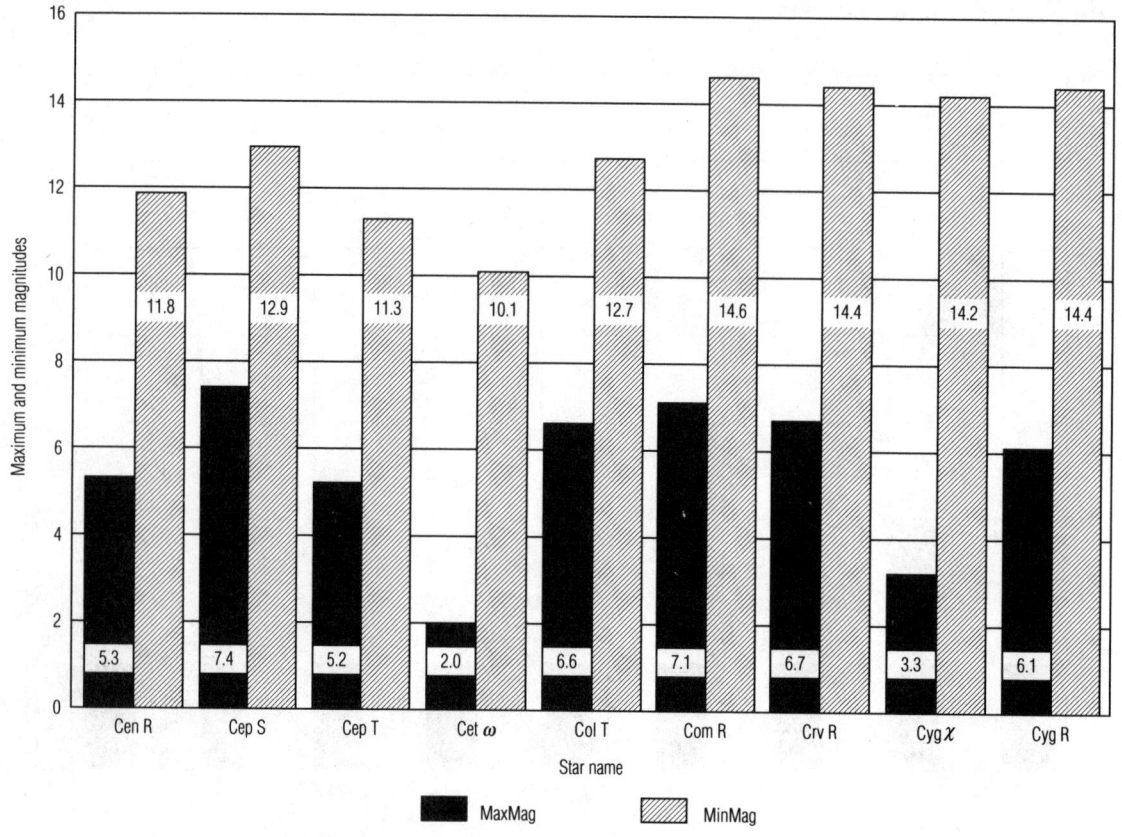

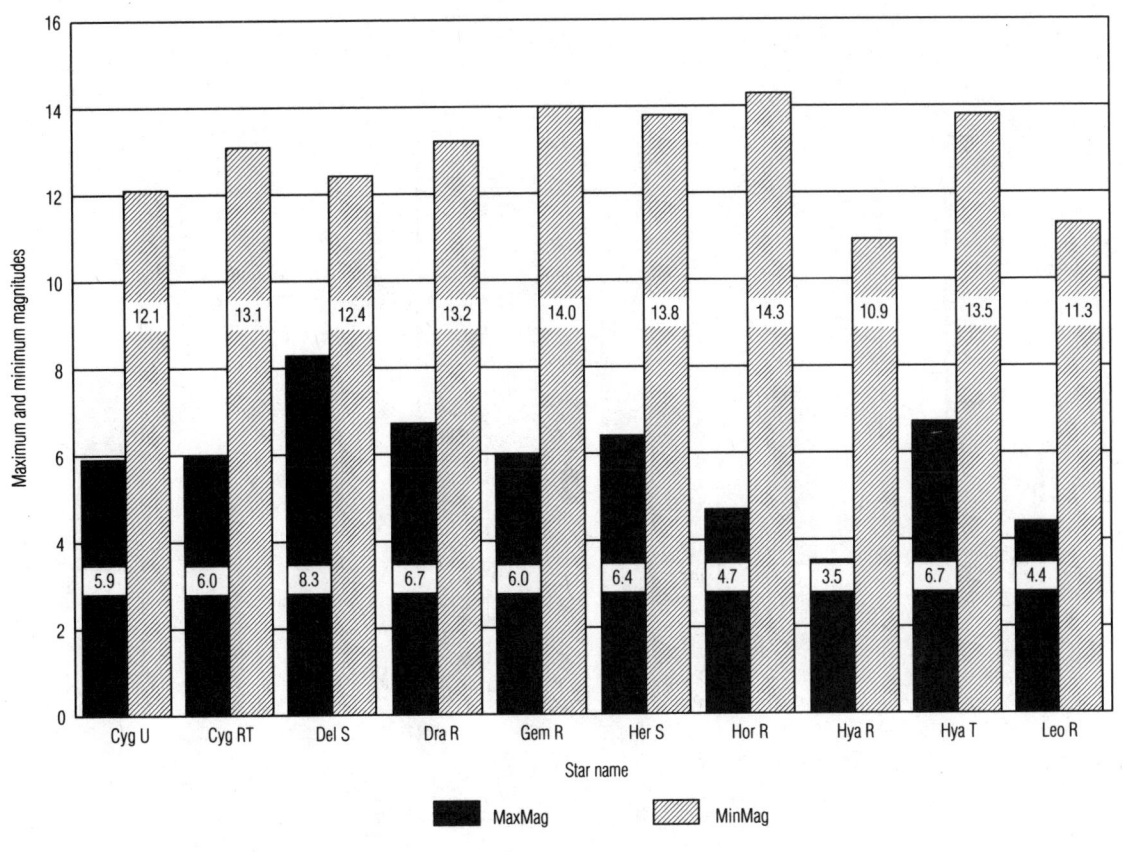

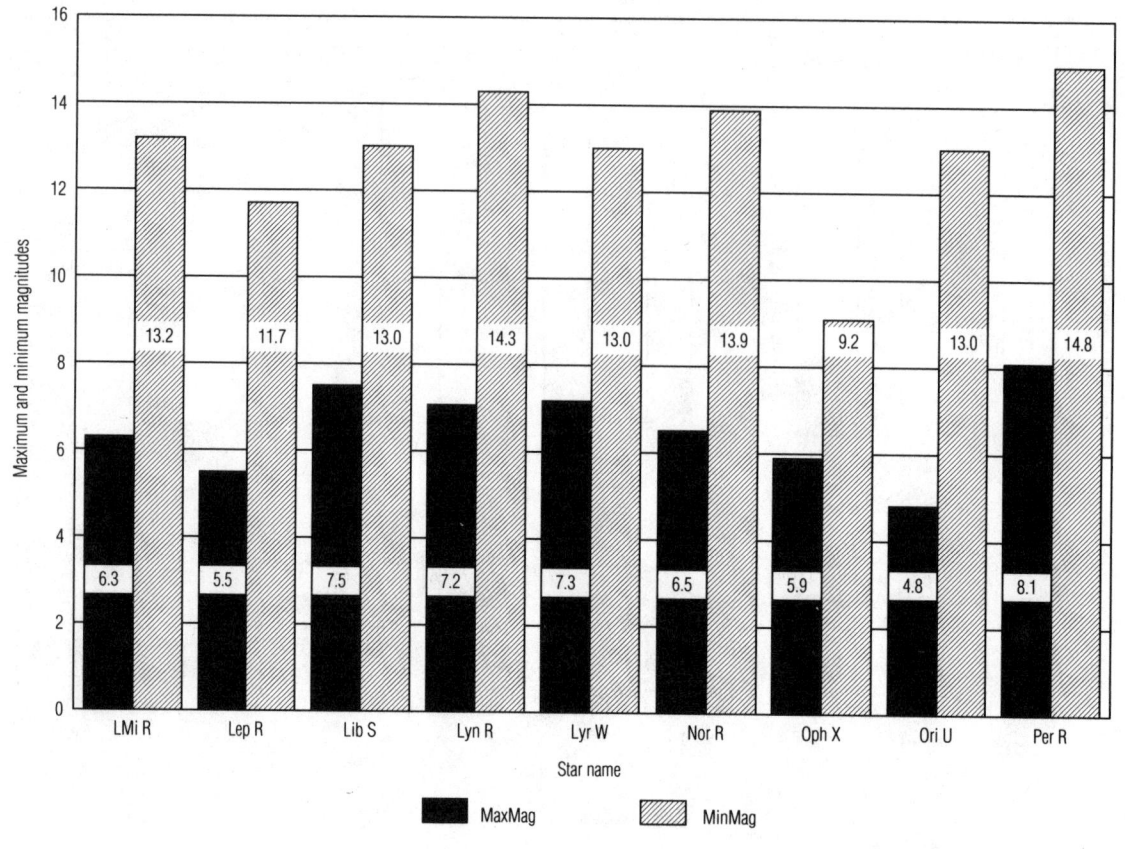

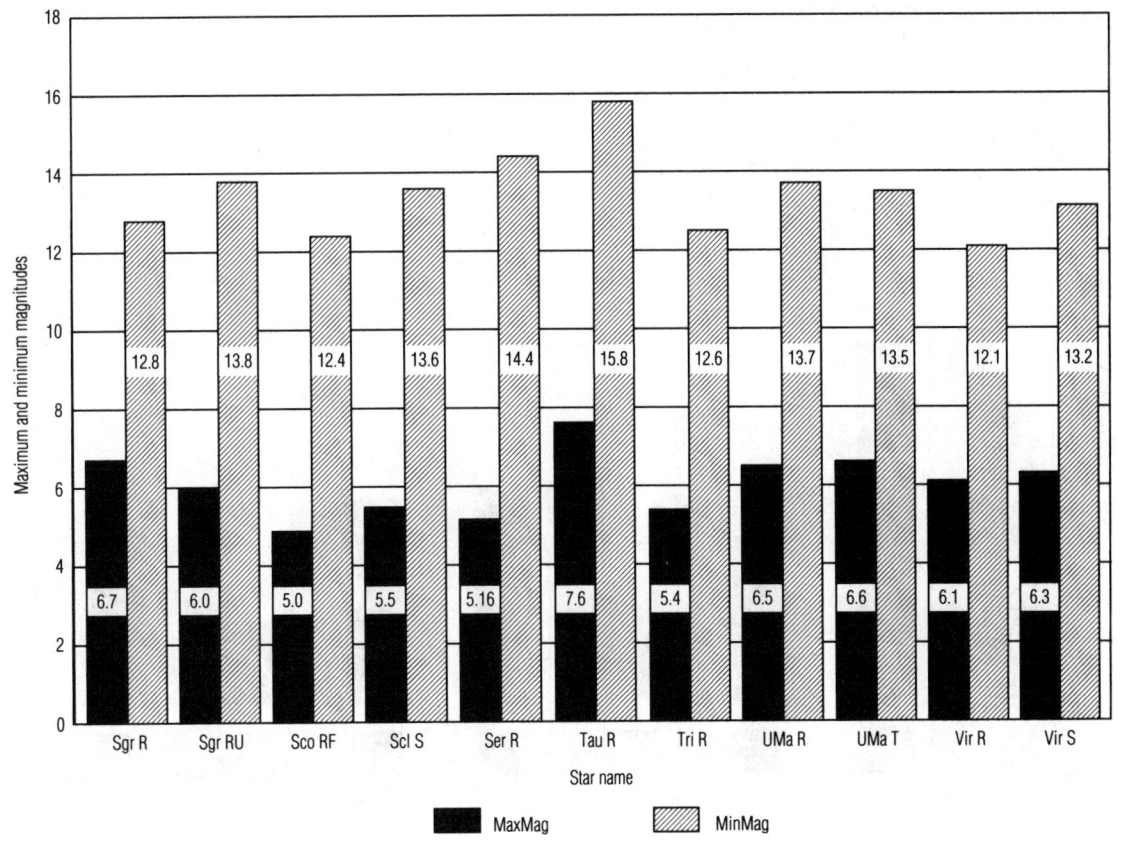

Selected Semiregular Variables

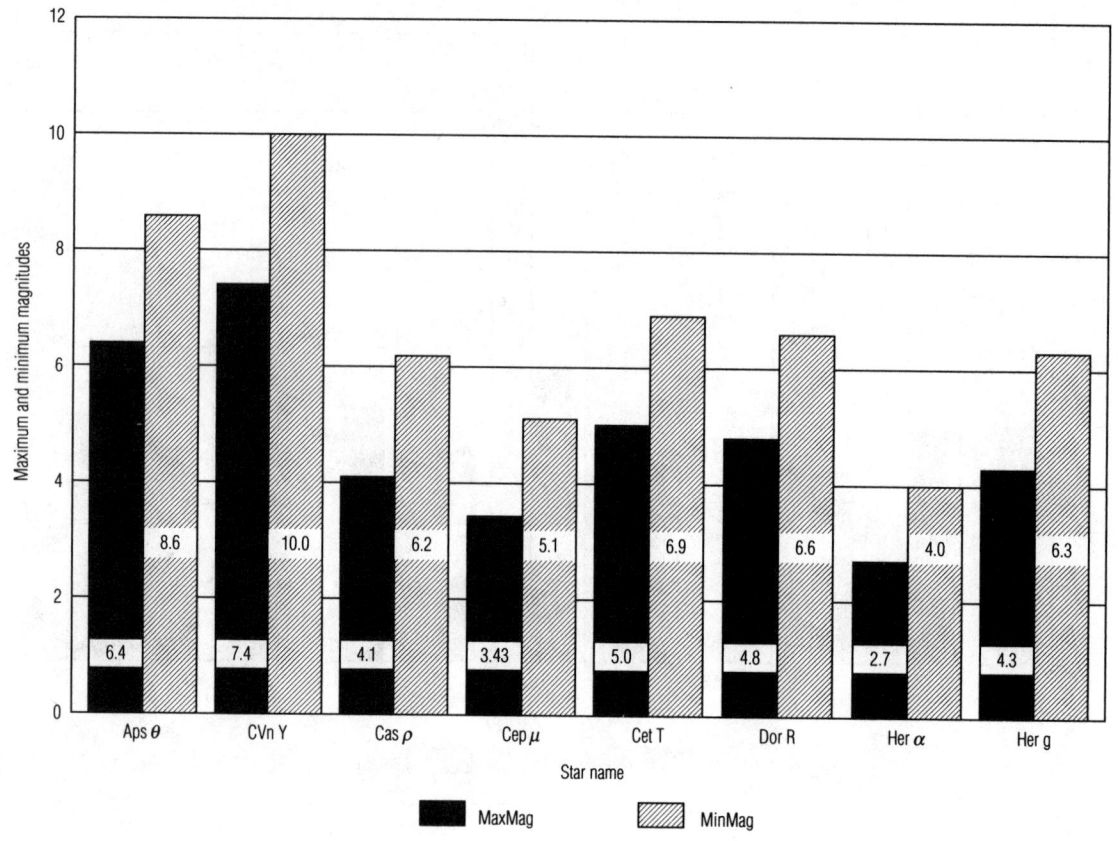

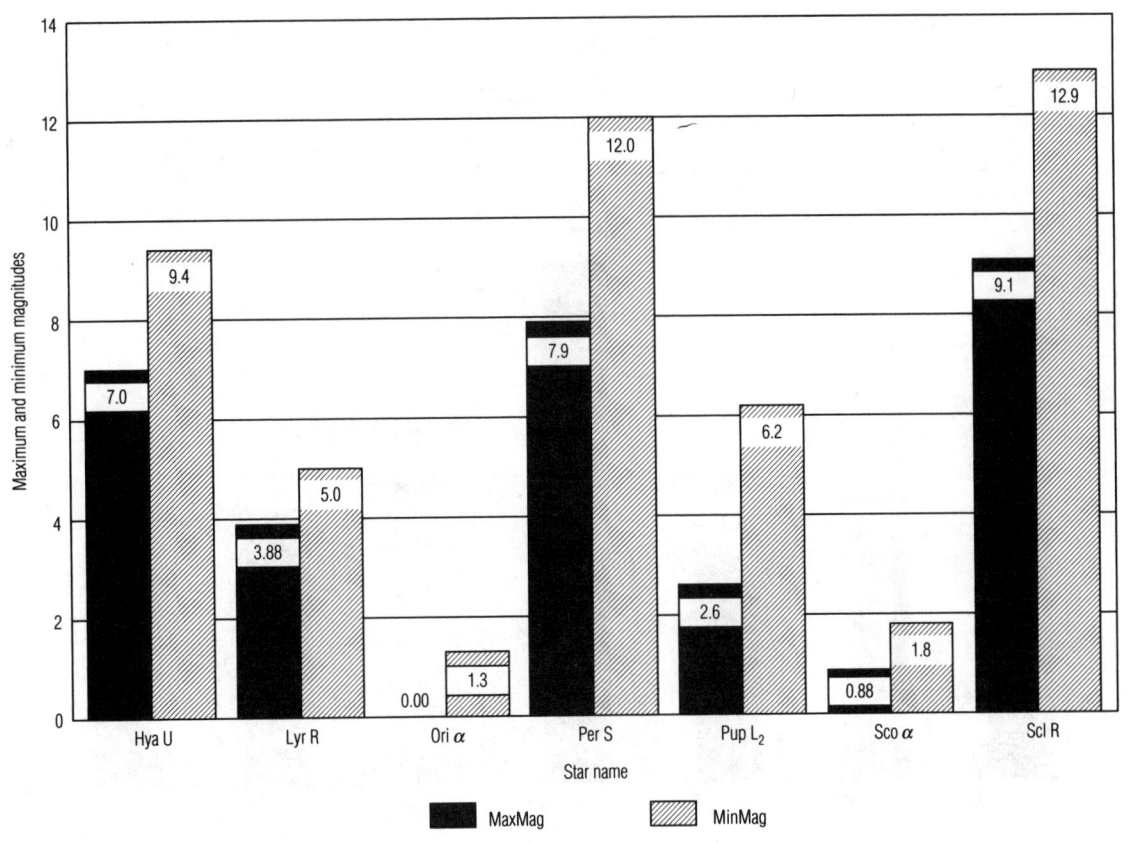

Cepheid Variables

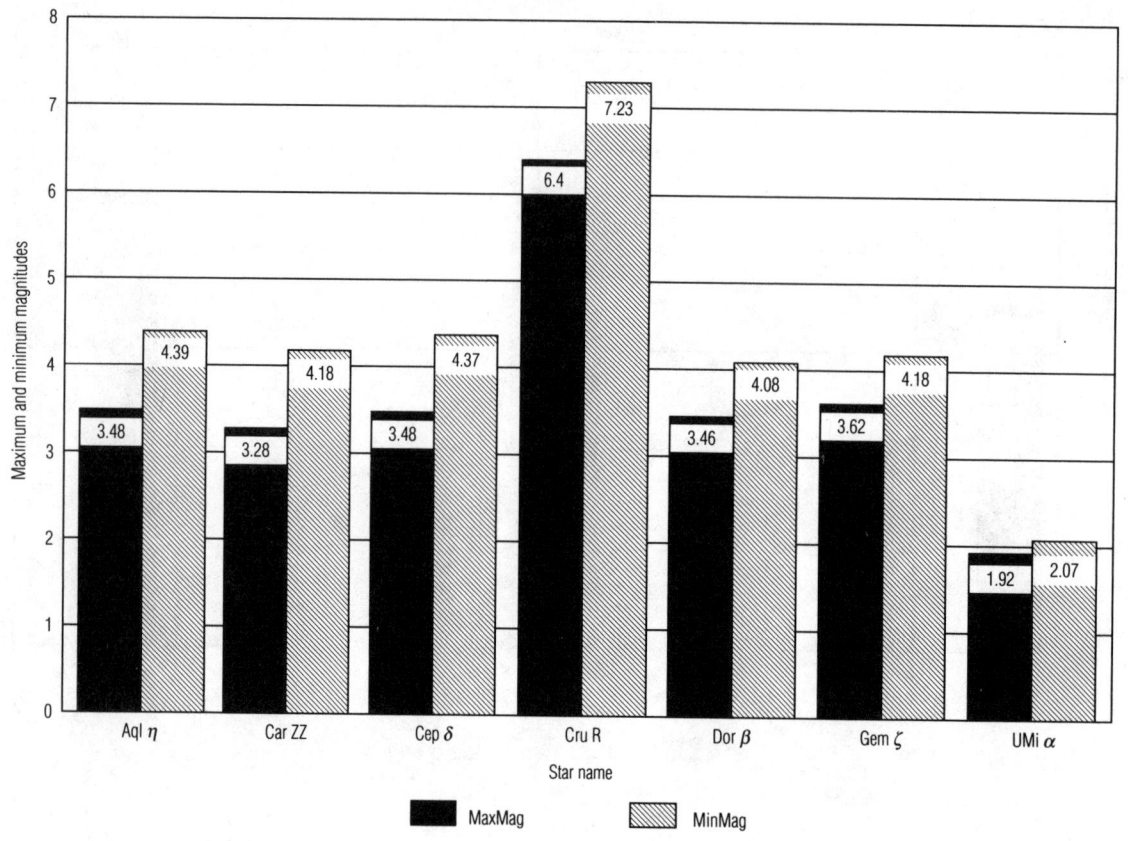

Variable Stars

Const.	Star	Type	Mag. Range Max.	Min.	Epoch (* = SC)	Period (days)	Best viewing date
And	α	αCV	2.02	2.06	2441862.126	.966222	[$23^h11^m21.6^s$]
	ζ	EB	3.92	4.14	2442321.05*	17.7693	[$17^d18^h27^m47.5^s$]
	λ	SR	3.69	3.97	2443886.0	54.20	2000: { 11 Sept. (m) / 05 Nov. / 29 Dec.
	o	γC	3.58	3.78	—	—	
	R	M	5.8	14.9	2443135	409.33	{ 1994: 27 Nov. / 2003: 15 Nov.
	GN (28)	δSct	5.18	5.22	2444236.2559	.0689797	[$1^h39^m19.9^s$]
Ant	U	Lb	8.1	9.7	—	—	—
Aps	δ¹	Lb	4.66	4.87	—	—	—
	θ	SRb	6.4	8.6	—	119	—
	κ¹	γC	5.43	5.61	—	—	—
Aqr	o	γCas	4.68	4.89	—	—	—
	π	γCas	4.42	4.70	—	—	—
	χ	Lb	4.9	5.06	—	—	—
	R	M	5.8	12.4	2442398	386.96	{ 2005: 6 Sept / 2006: 28 Sept
	EN (3)	Lb	4.41	4.45	—	—	—
	ET (108)	αCV	5.16	5.21	2440900.80	3.730	[$3^d17^h31^m12.0^s$]
Aql	η	Cδ	3.48	4.39	2436084.656	7.176641	[$7^d4^h14^m21.8^s$]
	σ	EB	5.14	5.34	2422486.797	1.95026	[$1^d22^h48^m22.5^s$]
	R	M	5.5	12.0	2443458	284.2	{ 1999: 25 Aug. / 2000: 4 Jun
	Y(18)	E	5.02	5.06	2438607.445	1.30227	[$1^d7^h15^m16.1^s$]
	FF	Cδ	5.18	5.68	2441576.428	4.470916	[$4^d11^h18^m7.1^s$]
	V1288 (21)	αCV	5.06	5.16	2444099.23	1.73	[$1^d17^h31^m12.0^s$]
Ari	γ²	αCV	4.62	4.66	2440998.99	2.6095	[$2^d14^h37^m40.8^s$]
	SX (56)	SX Ari	5.67	5.81	2437667.728	0.7278925	[$17^h28^m9.9^s$]
	UV (38)	δSctc	5.18	5.22	—	0.0355	—
Aur	β	EA	1.89	1.98	2431076.719	3.9600421	[$3^d23^h2^m27.6^s$]
	ε	EA	2.92	3.83	2435629	9892	2010: August
	ζ	EA	3.70	3.97	2427692.825	972.160	2003: 25 Nov.(m)
	θ	αCV	2.62	2.70	—	1.3735	[$1^d8^h57^m50.4^s$]
	π	Lc	4.24	4.34	—	—	—
	ψ¹	Lc	4.75	5.70	—	—	—
	R	M	6.7	13.9	2444004	457.51	2001: 25 Nov.(m)
	KW (14)	δSctc	4.95	5.08	—	0.088088	[$2^h6^m50.8^s$]
Boo	γ	δSct	3.02	3.07	—	0.2903137	[$6^h58^m3.1^s$]
	ι	δSct	4.73	4.78	—	—	—
	κ²	δSct	4.50	4.58	—	0.076242	[$1^h49^m47.3^s$]
	ξ	BY	4.52	4.67	—	10.137	[$10^d3^h17^m16.8^s$]
	R	M	6.2	13.1	2444518	223.40	{ 2000: 2 Apr (m) / 2001: 5 Apr
	W (34)	SRb	4.73	5.4	—	450	

Const.	Star	Type	Mag. Range Max.	Min.	Epoch (* = SC)	Period (days)	Best viewing date
Cam	R	M	6.97	14.4	2443978	270.22	1993: 5 Apr 2002: 21 Apr 2007: 25 Apr (m)
	TU (31)	EB	5.12	5.29	2438051.375	2.933241	[$2^d22^h23^m52^s$]
	VZ	SR	4.80	4.96	—	23.7	[$23^d16^h48^m$]
	BD	Lb	5.04	5.17	—	—	—
	BE	Lc	4.35	4.48	—	—	—
	BK	γCas	4.78	4.89	—	—	—
Cnc	κ	αCV	5.22	5.27	2439633.5	5.0035	[$5^d0^h5^m2.4^s$]
	μ¹(BL)	Lb	5.97	6.07	—	—	
	R	M	6.07	11.8	2444231	361.6	1995: 26 Oct. 2000: 7 Oct.
	BP (27)	SRb	5.41	5.75	—	40	
CVn	α²	αCV	2.84	2.98	2439012.61	5.46939	[$5^d11^h15^m55.3^s$]
	Y	SRb	7.4	10.0	—	157	
	AO (20)	δSct	4.70	4.75	2444381.6675	0.12168	[$2^h55^m13.2^s$]
	AW	SR	4.72	4.81	—	—	
	BH	RS	4.94	5.01	2443639.52	2.6131738	[$2^d14^h42^m58.2^s$]
CMa	β	βC	1.93	2.00	2441296.175	0.25003	[$6^h0^m2.6^s$]
	ι	βC	4.36	4.40	—	0.08	[$1^h55^m12.0^s$]
	κ	γCas	3.78	3.97	—	—	
	ξ¹	βC	4.33	4.36	2441296.0514	0.2095755	[$5^h1^m47.3^s$]
	o¹	Lc	3.78	3.99	—	—	
	σ	Lc	3.43	3.51	—	—	—
	ω	γCas	3.60	4.18	—	—	—
	R	EA	5.70	6.34	2444289.361	1.1359405	[$1^d3^h15^m45.3^s$]
	UW (29)	EB	4.84	5.33	2436185.358	4.393407	[$4^d9^h26^m30.4^s$]
	EW (27)	γCas	4.42	4.82	—	—	
	EY (15)	βC	4.79	4.84	2441296.1640	0.184557	[$4^h25^m45.7^s$]
	FN	βC	5.38	5.42	—	0.12377	[$2^h58^m13.7^s$]
	FT (10)	γCas	5.13	5.44	—	—	
CMi	β	γCas	2.84	2.92	—	—	—
Cap	δ	EA	2.81	3.05	2435656.913	1.0227688	[$24^h32^m47.2^s$]
	ε	γCas	4.48	4.72	—	—	
Car	η	S Dor?	5.9*	7.9	—	—	—
	χ	βC	3.46	(0.015)	—	0.101	[$2^h25^m26.4^s$]
	R	M	3.9	10.5	2442000	308.71	2000: 27 Jan. 2000: 30 Nov. 2005: 21 Feb. (m)
	PP	γCas	3.27	3.37	—	—	
	ZZ	Cδ	3.28	4.18	2440736.9	35.53584	[$35^d12^h51^m36.6^s$]
	GM	EB	9.11	9.39	2429344.340	1.535433	[$1^d12^h51^m1.4^s$]
	V337	Lc	3.36	3.44	—	—	—
	V343 (d)	βC	4.20	4.24	—	—	—
	V344	γCas	4.4	4.51	—	—	—
	V345 (E)	γCas	4.67	4.78	—	—	—
	V357	E	3.41	3.44	—	—	—

(* A maximum brightness of −0.8 occurred in 1843. Kholopov points out that since 1880 the star's visual magnitude has varied by the values cited here.)

Const.	Star	Type	Mag. Range Max.	Mag. Range Min.	Epoch (* = SC)	Period (days)	Best viewing date
Car (cont.)	V371	αCyg	5.12	5.19	—	—	—
	V376 (b¹)	βC	4.91	4.96	—	0.0208	[29^{m}57.1^s]
	V382	δC	3.84	4.02	—	—	—
	V415 (A)	EA	4.39	(0.06)	—	—	—
Cas	β	δSct	2.25	2.31	2438991.876	0.10430	[2^{h}30^{m}11.5^s]
	γ	γCas	1.6	3.0	—	—	—
	δ	EA	2.68	2.76	2420161	759	—
	ι	αCV	4.45	4.53	2437248.313	1.74050	[1^{d}17^{h}46^{m}19.2^s]
	κ	αCyg	4.22	4.30	—	—	—
	o	γCas	4.50	4.62	—	—	—
	ρ	SRd	4.1	6.2	—	320	—
	R	M	4.7	13.5	2444463	430.46	{ 2000: 24 Aug. 2001: 29 Oct.
	AR	EA	4.82	4.96	2435792.8948	6.0663309	[6^{d}1^{h}35^{m}31.0^s]
	V509	SRd	4.75	5.5	—	—	—
	V566 (6)	αCV	5.34	5.45	—	—	—
Cen	β	βC	0.61	0.66	—	0.157	[3^{h}46^{m}4.8^s]
	δ	γCas	2.51	2.65	—	—	—
	ε	βC	2.29	2.31	2441040.965	0.169608	[4^{h}4^{m}14.1^s]
	η	γCas	2.30	2.41	—	—	—
	μ	γCas	2.92	3.47	—	—	—
	ν	Ell	3.38	3.41	—	—	—
	o¹	SRd	5.8	6.6	—	200:	—
	o²	αCyg	5.12	5.22	—	46.3	—
	χ	βC	4.15	4.17	—	0.035	[50^{m}24.0^s]
	l ("el")	αCV	4.61	4.66	—	—	—
	R	M	5.3	11.8	2441942	546.2	{ 1999: 18 Feb. 2002: 14 Feb.
	V761	SX Ari	4.38	4.43	2442807.75	8.8171	[8^{d}19^{h}36^{m}37.4^s]
	V795	γCas	4.97	5.10	—	—	—
	V806 (2)	SRb	4.16	4.26	—	12	—
	V810	SRd	4.95	5.12	—	130	—
	V815	αCV	5.14	5.17	—	2.433	[2^{d}10^{h}23^{m}31.2^s]
Cep	β	βC	3.16	3.27	2440444.625	0.1904881	[4^{h}34^{m}18.2^s]
	δ	Cδ	3.48	4.37	2436075.445	5.366341	[5^{d}8^{h}47^{m}31.9^s]
	ε	δSct	4.15	4.21	—	0.041242	[59^{m}53.3^s]
	μ	SRc	3.43	5.1	—	730	—
	S	M	7.4	12.9	2443787	486.84	1993: 23 Aug.(m)
	T	M	5.2	11.3	2444177	388.14	{ 1995: 8 Oct. 2000: 8 Jan.
	VV	EA	4.80	5.36	2443360	7430	[= 619 years]
	OV	SR	5.00	5.07	—	—	—
	V337 (9)	αCyg	4.69	4.78	—	—	—
Cet	α	Lb	2.45	2.54	—	—	—
	δ	βC	4.05	4.10	2438338.4763	0.16113668	[3^{h}52^{m}2.2^s]
	o	M	2.0	10.0	2444839	331.96	{ 1998: 29 Nov. 1999: 26 Oct. (m) 2009: 25 Oct. (m)

Const.	Star	Type	Mag. Range Max.	Min.	Epoch (* = SC)	Period (days)	Best viewing date
Cet (cont.)	T	SRc	5.0	6.9	2440562	158.9	{ 2000: 26 Oct. 2001: 9 Sep.
	AD	Lb	4.9	5.16	—	—	—
	AE (7)	Lb	4.26	4.46	—	—	—
Cir	α	αCV	3.18	3.21	—	—	—
	θ	γCas	5.02	5.44	—	—	—
Col	λ	Ell	4.85	4.92	—	0.640	[15ʰ21ᵐ36.0ˢ]
	T	M	6.6	12.7	2441973	225.84	{ 1993: 7 Oct. 2000: 31 Dec. (m)
Com	R	M	7.1	14.6	2443539	362.82	2000: 5 Dec.
	GN (13)	αCV	5.15	5.18	—	—	—
CrA	ε	EW	4.74	5.00	2439707.6619	0.5914264	[14ʰ11ᵐ39.2ˢ]
CrB	α	EA	2.21	2.32	2423163.770	17.359907	[17ᵈ8ʰ38ᵐ16.0ˢ]
	β	αCV	3.65	3.72	2440335.0	18.487	[18ᵈ11ʰ41ᵐ17.0ˢ]
	γ	δSct	3.80	3.86	—	0.030	[43ᵐ12.0ˢ]
	δ	RS	4.57	4.69	—	—	—
	σ (TZ)	RS+ δSct	5.69	5.74	2423869.561	1.139789	[1ᵈ3ʰ21ᵐ17.8ˢ]
	R	RCB	5.71	14.8	—	—	—
Crv	R	M	6.7	14.4	2442781	317.03	{ 2000: 23 Apr. 2001: 6 Mar. (m)
Cru	β	βC	1.23	1.31	—	0.2365072	[5ʰ40ᵐ34.2ˢ]
	δ	βC	2.78	2.84	—	0.151038	[3ʰ37ᵐ29.7ˢ]
	θ²	βC	4.7	4.74	—	0.0889	[2ʰ8ᵐ1.0ˢ]
	λ	βC	4.62	4.64	2441779.081	0.3951	[9ʰ28ᵐ56.6ˢ]
	μ²	γCas	4.99	5.18	—	—	—
	R	Cδ	6.4	7.23	2434514.629	5.82575	[5ᵈ19ʰ49ᵐ4.8ˢ]
Cyg	α	αCyg	1.21	1.29	—	—	—
	τ	δSct	3.65	3.75	—	—	—
	υ	γCas	4.28	4.50	—	—	—
	χ	M	3.3	14.2	2442140	408.05	{ 1998: 31 Oct. 2003: 20 Apr. 2005: 14 July (m)
	P	S Dor	3.0	6.0	—	—	—
	R	M	6.1	14.4	2444595	426.45	{ 2000: 27 Oct. 2005: 29 June (m)
	T	Lb?	4.91	4.96	—	—	—
	U	M	5.9	12.1	2444558	463.24	{ 1999: 24 Nov. 2002: 8 June
	RT	M	6.0	13.1	2444588	190.28	{ 2000: 1 Oct. 2005: 10 June 2007: 11 July (m)
	V 695 (31)	EA	3.77	3.88	2441470.0	3784.3	[= 10.4 yrs.]
	V 832 (59)	γCas	4.49	4.88	—	—	—
	V1488 (32)	EA	4.11	4.14	2441256.96	1147.4	[= 3.14 yrs.]
	V1509 (19)	Lb	5.08	5.4	—	—	—
	V1624 (28)	SX Ari	4.91	4.97	2443699.12	0.70	[16ʰ48ᵐ]

Const.	Star	Type	Mag. Range Max.	Min.	Epoch (* = SC)	Period (days)	Best viewing date
Cyg (cont.)	V1644 (29)	δSct	4.94	4.97	—	0.031	$[44^m 38.4^s]$
	V1661 (55)	αCyg	4.81	4.87	—	—	—
	V1741 (4)	αCV	4.60	4.62	2441451.03	0.68674	$[16^h 28^m 54.3^s]$
	V1746	γCas+ βC	5.19	5.26	—	—	—
Del	δ	δSct	4.38	4.49	—	0.158	$[3^h 47^m 31.2^s]$
	R	M	7.6	13.8	2444091	285.07	2000: 31 Aug
	S	M	8.3	12.4	2444887	277.75	{ 2000: 13 Oct. 2001: 18 July (m)
Dor	α	αCV	3.26	3.30	2443481.50	2.95	$[2^d 22^h 48^m]$
	β	Cδ	3.46	4.08	2440905.30	9.84260	$[9^d 20^h 12^m 28.8^s]$
	γ	EW	4.23	4.27	—	—	—
	R	SRb	4.8	6.6	—	338	—
	WZ	SRb	5.2	5.32	—	40	—
Dra	κ	γCas	3.82	4.01	—	—	—
	o	RS	4.63	4.73	—	—	—
	φ	αCV	4.22	4.26	2442229.40	1.71646	$[1^d 17^h 11^m 42.1^s]$
	ψ^{1b} (BG)						
	R	M	6.7	13.2	2444779	245.60	{ 2000: 21 Apr. 2002: 28 Apr.
	AF (73)	αCV	5.15	5.22	—	20.2747	$[20^d 6^h 35^m 34.1^s]$
	CL	δSct	4.95	4.97	—	0.063	$[1^h 30^m 43.2^s]$
	CQ (4)	Lb	4.95	5.04	—	—	—
	CU (10)	Lb	4.52	4.67	—	—	—
Equ	γ	αCV	4.58	4.77	—	—	—
Eri	γ	Lb	2.88	2.96	—	—	—
	δ	RS	3.51	3.56	—	—	—
	λ	βC	4.22	4.34	—	0.701538	$[16^h 50^m 12.9^s]$
	ν	βC	3.4	3.6	2433629.277	0.17790414	$[4^h 16^m 10.9^s]$
	o^1	δSct	4.0	4.05	—	0.0815	$[1^h 57^m 21.6^s]$
	π	Lb	4.38	4.44	—	—	—
	τ^4	Lb	3.57	3.72	—	—	—
	τ^8	SX Ari	4.63	4.66	—	—	—
	τ^9	αCV	4.62	4.67	—	1.2094	$[1^d 5^h 1^m 32.2^s]$
	S (64)	RRc	4.77	4.80	—	0.273	$[6^h 33^m 7.2^s]$
	DM (54)	SRb	4.28	4.36	—	30	—
	DV (47)	Lb	5.10	5.13	—	—	—
	EG (20)	αCV	5.23	5.32	2443485.50	1.93	$[1^d 22^h 19^m 12.0^s]$
	EN (66)	αCV	4.89	4.90	—	—	—
For	ν	αCV	4.68	4.73	2443475.0	1.89	$[1^d 21^h 21^m 36.0^s]$
Gem	ζ	Cδ	3.62	4.18	2443805.927	10.15073	$[10^d 3^h 37^m 3.1^s]$
	η	SRa	3.2	3.9	2437725	232.9	—
	μ	Lb	2.75	3.02	—	—	—
	σ	RS	4.13	4.29	2444677.1	19.423	$[19^d 10^h 9^m 7.2^s]$
	ω	Cep	5.14	(.086)	—	0.7282	$[17^h 28^m 36.5^s]$
	R	M	6.0	14.0	2443325	369.91	{ 2000: 15 Oct. 2020: 13 Jan. (m)
	BQ (51)	SRb	6.63	7.02	—	50	—

Const.	Star	Type	Mag. Range Max.	Mag. Range Min.	Epoch (* = SC)	Period (days)	Best viewing date
Gru	β	Lc	2.0	2.3	—	—	—
	δ²	Lb	3.99	4.2	—	—	—
Her	α	SRc	2.74	4.00	—	*:see notes	—
	ι	βC	2.93	2.95	—	—	—
	ν	SRd	4.38	4.48	—	29	—
	o	γCas	3.80	3.87	—	—	—
	ω	αCV	4.57	4.65	2441254.70	2.951	[2^{d}22^{h}49^{m}26.4^s]
	S	M	6.4	13.8	2445058	318.14	{ 2000: 13 July / 2001: 28 May (m)
	g (30)	SRb	4.3	6.3	—	89.2	—
	u (68)	EA	4.69	5.37	2405830.0326	2.0510270	[2^{d}1^{h}13^{m}28.7^s]
	V637 (52)	αCV	4.78	4.85	—	3.8567	[3^{d}20^{h}33^{m}38.9^s]
	V656	Lb	4.9	5.1	—	—	—
	V669 (104)	?	6.62	(0.14)	—	—	—
Hor	R	M	4.7	14.3	2441494	407.6	2003: 24 Sep.
Hya	β	αCV	4.27	4.31	2442451.78	2.344	[2^{d}8^{h}15^{m}21.6^s]
	ε	BY	3.35	3.39	—	—	—
	η	βC	4.27	4.33	—	0.17	[4^{h}4^{m}48.0^s]
	R	M	3.5	10.9	2443596	388.87	{ 1995: 10 Apr. (m) / 2000: 6 Aug.
	T	M	6.7	13.48	2441975	298.7	{ 1994: 31 Mar. / 1999: 21 Dec. / 2000: 15 Oct.
	U	SRb	7.0	9.4	—	450	—
	II	SRb	4.85	5.12	—	61	—
Lac	DD (12)	βC	5.16	5.28	2443063.774	0.1930924	[4^{h}38^{m}3.2^s]
Leo	β	δSct	2.14	(.025)	—	—	—
	ρ	αCyg	3.83	3.90	—	—	—
	R	M	4.4	11.3	2444164	309.95	{ 1990: 29 Oct. / 2000: 28 Feb. (m) / 2001: 3 Jan.
LMi	R	M	6.3	13.2	2445094	372.19	{ 2000: 6 Sep. / 2024: 13 Feb. (m)
	SU (10)	RS	4.54	4.56	—	—	—
Lep	μ	αCV	2.97	3.41	—	2	—
	R	M	5.5	11.7	2442506	427.07	{ 1993: 18 Dec. (m) / 2000: 23 Dec. / 2002: 23 Feb.
	SS (17)	Z And	4.82	5.06	—	—	—
Lib	δ	EA	4.91	5.9	2442960.6994	2.3273543	[2^{d}7^{h}51^{m}25.1^s]
	σ	SRb	3.2	3.46	—	20	—
	S	M	7.5	13.0	2441883	192.9	{ 1997: 25 Apr. / 1999: 6 June / 2000: 25 June
	FX (48)	γCas	4.74	4.96	—	—	—

Const.	Star	Type	Mag. Range Max.	Mag. Range Min.	Epoch (* = SC)	Period (days)	Best viewing date
Lup	α	βC	2.29	2.34	2437418.395	0.2598466	[$6^h14^m12.3^s$]
	δ	βC	3.20	3.24	2441045.172	0.16547	[$3^h58^m16.6^s$]
	τ^1	βC	4.54	4.58	2443602.1269	0.17738884	[$4^h15^m24.4^s$]
Lyn	R	M	7.2	14.3	2445175	378.75	2000: 10 Mar.
	RR	EA	5.52	6.03	2433153.8623	9.945079	[$9^d22^h40^m54.8^s$]
	UW (1)	Lb	4.95	5.06	—	—	—
	UZ (2)	E+ δSct	4.43	4.73	—	—	—
Lyr	α	δSct	-0.02	0.07	—	0.19	[$4^h33^m36.0^s$]
	β	EB	3.25	4.36	2445342.39*	12.93578	[$12^d22^h27^m31.4^s$]
	δ^2	SRc	4.22	4.33	—	—	—
	R	SRb	3.88	5.0	2435920*	46.0	—
	W	M	7.3	13.0	2445084	197.88	{ 2000: 24 Sep. 2001: 10 Apr.
	RR	RRab	7.06	8.12	2442923.4193	0.56686776	[$13^h36^m17.3^s$]
Mic	θ^1	αCV	4.77	4.87	2440345.32	2.1215	[$2^d2^h54^m57.6^s$]
Mon	S (15)	IA	4.62	4.68	—	—	—
	U	RV τ	6.1	8.1	2438496	91.32	2000: 11 Jan.(m)
	V637 (19)	βC	4.96	5.01	2443496.1169	0.19120	[$4^h35^m19.7^s$]
	V645 (28)	FK Com	4.68	4.70	2443100.000	0.207878	[$4^h59^m20.7^s$]
Mus	α	βC	2.68	2.73	—	0.0903	[$2^h10^m1.9^s$]
	ϵ	SRb	3.99	4.31	—	40	—
	η	E	4.76	4.81	—	—	—
	θ	E	5.50	5.52	2440661.4	18.341	[$18^d8^h11^m2.4^s$]
	μ	Lb	4.6	4.8	—	—	—
	GT	E/RS	5.08	5.21	—	—	—
Nor	μ	αCyg	4.87	4.98	—	—	—
	R	M	6.5	13.9	2441874	507.50	2001: 25 Apr.
Oct	ϵ	SRb	4.58	5.30	—	55	—
	σ	δSct	5.45	5.50	—	0.097	[$2^h19^m40.8^s$]
Oph	ζ	γCas	2.56	2.58	—	—	—
	θ	βC	3.25	3.31	2440324.23	0.140531	[$3^h22^m21.9^s$]
	κ	Lb	4.1	5.0	—	—	—
	χ	γCas	4.18	5.0	—	—	—
	ω	αCV	4.44	4.51	—	2.99	—
	U	EA	5.84	6.56	2444416.3864	1.67734617	[$1^d16^h15^m22.7^s$]
	X	M	5.9	9.2	2444729	328.85	{ 1997: 19 July (m) 2000: 31 Mar.
	V2048 (66)	γCas	4.55	4.85	—	—	—
	V2105	SRb	5.0	5.38	—	—	—
Ori	α	SRc	0.0	1.3	—	2335	—
	δ^A	EA	2.14	2.26	2443872.589	5.732476	[$5^d17^h34^m45.9^s$]
	ϵ	αCyg	1.64	1.74	—	—	—
	η	EA	3.31	3.60	2415761.826	7.989268	[$7^d23^h44^m32.8^s$]
	θ^{1A}	EA	6.72	7.65	2443144.6	65.43233	[$65^d10^h22^m33.3^s$]
	o^1	SRb	4.65	4.88	—	30	—
	π^5	Ell	3.66	3.73	2417922.565	3.700363	[$3^d16^h48^m31.4^s$]
	ω	γCas	4.40	4.59	—	—	—

Const.	Star	Type	Mag. Range Max.	Min.	Epoch (* = SC)	Period (days)	Best viewing date
Ori (cont.)	U	M	4.8	13.0	2445254	368.3	$\begin{cases} \text{2000: 5 Dec.} \\ \text{2005: 20 Dec. (m)} \end{cases}$
	V1032 (11)	αCV	4.65	4.69	2443864.78	4.6398	$[4^d15^h21^m18.7^s]$
Pav	κ	Cδ	3.91	4.78	2440858.53*	9.088	$[9^d2^h6^m43.2^s]$
	λ	γCas	4.0	4.26	—	—	—
	ρ	δSct	4.85	(.055)	—	0.1141	$[2^h44^m18.2^s]$
Peg	β	Lb	2.31	2.74	—	—	—
	γ	βC	2.78	2.89	2441224.64	0.151750125	$[3^h38^m31.2^s]$
	ϵ	Lc	0.7	3.5	—	—	—
	τ	δSct	4.60	4.62	—	0.05433	$[1^h18^m14.1^s]$
	GZ (57)	SRa	4.95	5.23	2443085.7	92.66	$[92^d15^h50^m24.0^s]$
Per	β	EA	2.12	3.39	2445641.5135	2.8673043	$[2^d20^h48^m55.1^s]$
	δ	γCas	2.99	3.04	—	—	—
	ϵ	βC	2.88	3.00	—	—	—
	ξ	—	4.00	4.06	—	—	—
	o	Ell	3.79	3.88	2436459.0	4.4191666	$[4^d10^h3^m36.0^s]$
	ρ	SRb	3.30	4.0	—	50	—
	τ	EA	3.94	4.07	—	—	—
	φ	γCas	3.96	4.11	—	19.5	—
	ψ	γCas	4.17	4.28	—	—	—
	b^1	Ell	4.52	4.68	2443141.728	1.5273643	$[1^d12^h39^m24.3^s]$
	R	M	8.1	14.8	2445339	209.89	2000: 28 Oct.
	S	SRc	7.9	12.0	2432200*	822 = 2.25yr	$\begin{cases} \text{1998: 20 Oct. (m)} \\ \text{2007: 20 Oct. (m)} \end{cases}$
	X	γCas	6.03	7.0	—	—	—
	LT (21)	αCV	5.03	5.14	2439837.7	2.88422	$[2^d21^h13^m16.6^s]$
	MX (48)	γCas	4.00	4.09	—	72	—
	V467 (42)	E	5.05	5.18	2443101.24	22.58	$[22^d13^h55^m12.0^s]$
	V469 (53)	βC	4.81	4.86	—	0.304	$[7^h17^m45.6^s]$
Phe	γ	Lb	3.39	3.49	—	—	—
	ζ	EA	3.91	4.42	2441643.6890	1.6697671	$[1^d16^h4^m27.9^s]$
	ι	αCV	4.70	4.75	—	12.5	—
	ρ	δSct	5.17	5.27	—	0.110	$[2^h38^m24.0^s]$
	ψ	SR	4.3	4.5	—	30	—
	SX	δSct	6.76	7.53	2438636.6170	0.054964438	$[1^h19^m8.9^s]$
Pic	δ	EB	4.65	4.90	2441695.336	1.672541	$[1^d16^h8^m27.5^s]$
Psc	κ	αCV	4.87	4.95	—	0.58525	$[14^h2^m45.6^s]$
	TV (47)	SR	4.65	5.42	2431387	49.1	—
	TX (19)	Lb	4.79	5.20	—	—	—
	YY (30)	Lb	4.31	4.41	—	—	—
	BC (33)	RS	4.61	4.69	—	—	—
Pup	ρ	δSct	2.68	2.87	2444995.905	0.1408809	$[3^h22^m52.1^s]$
	L_2	SRb	2.6	6.2	2440813	140.6	2001: 11 Jan.(m)
	V	EB	4.35	4.92	2445367.60633	1.4544859	$[1^d10^h54^m27.6^s]$
	W	M	7.15	13.6	2444956	119.7	2000: 20 Dec.
	KQ	Lc	4.82	5.17	—	—	—
	MX	γCas	4.60	4.92	—	—	—
	NS	Lc	4.4	4.5	—	—	—
	NV	γCas	4.58	4.78	—	—	—

Const.	Star	Type	Mag. Range Max.	Min.	Epoch (* = SC)	Period (days)	Best viewing date
Pup (cont.)	NW	γCas+Ell	5.11	5.18	—	0.125	$[3^h0^m0.0^s]$
	OS	γCas	5.07	5.2	—	—	—
	OU	αCV	4.86	4.93	—	0.9183	$[22^h2^m21.1^s]$
	PU	EB	4.69	4.75	2443100.000	2.57895	$[2^d13^h53^m41.3^s]$
Ret	γ	SR	4.42	4.64	—	25	—
Sge	δ	Lb	3.75	3.83	—	—	—
	U	EA	6.45	9.28	2440774.4638*	3.3806260	$[3^d9^h8^m6.1^s]$
Sgr	γ^1 (W)	Cδ	4.29	5.14	2443374.77	7.59503	$[7^d14^h16^m50.6^s]$
	η	Lb	3.05	3.15	—	—	—
	μ	EA	3.80	3.88	2444035	180.55	—
	ρ^1	δSct	3.90	3.94	—	0.050	$[1^h12^m]$
	υ	EB	4.53	4.61	2433134*	137.939	—
	R	M	6.7	12.83	2443371	269.84	2000: 11 July(m)
	U	Cδ	6.28	7.15	2438084.23*	6.744925	$[6^d17^h52^m41.5^s]$
	X	Cδ	4.20	4.90	2440741.70	7.01283	$[7^d0^h18^m28.5^s]$
	Y	Cδ	5.25	6.24	2440762.38	5.77335	$[5^d18^h33^m37.4^s]$
	RU	M	6.0	13.8	2441900	240.49	2000: 4 Aug.
	RY	RCb	5.8	14.0	—	—	—
	V3872 (62)	Lb	4.45	4.64	—	—	—
Sco	α	SRc	0.88	1.8	2408600*	1733 = 4.75yr	—
	ζ^1	S Dor	4.66	4.86	—	—	—
	κ	βC	2.41	2.42	2440690.062	0.19987	$[4^d47^m48.8^s]$
	λ	βC	1.59	1.65	2440380.1225	0.2137015	$[5^h7^m43.8^s]$
	μ^1	EB	2.94	3.22	2432001.0451*	1.44626907	$[1^d10^h42^m37.7^s]$
	σ	βC	2.86	2.94	2444450.548	0.2468390	$[5^d55^m26.9^s]$
	RR	M	5.0	12.4	2445418	281.45	1998: 22 Aug. 1999: 30 May 2001: 20 Sep.
	V973	αCyg	5.22	5.28	—	—	—
Scl	η	Lb	4.80	4.90	—	—	—
	R	SRb	9.1	12.9	2440587*	370	2025: 18 Sep. 2030: 13 Oct.
	S	M	5.5	13.6	2442345	362.57	2000: 24 Oct. [A permanent fixture this century.]
Sct	δ	δSct	4.60	4.79	2443379.05	0.1937697	$[4^h39^m1.7^s]$
	R	RVa	4.2	8.6	2444872	146.5	2000: 1 Aug. 2001: 21 May 2002: 4 Aug.
Ser	δ	δSct	4.23	4.27	—	0.134	$[3^h12^m57.6^s]$
	o	δSct	4.26	4.27	—	0.053	$[1^h16^m19.2^s]$
	τ^4	SRb	5.89	7.07	—	—	—
	χ	αCV	5.33	5.36	2434134.06	1.59584	$[1^d14^h18^m0.6^s]$
	R	M	5.16	14.4	2445521	356.41	2000: 5 Feb.
Sex	β	αCV	5.00	5.10	—	—	—
	SS	αCV	5.94	5.98	2444318.00	4.37	$[4^d8^h52^m48.0^s]$

Const.	Star	Type	Mag. Range Max.	Mag. Range Min.	Epoch (* = SC)	Period (days)	Best viewing date
Tau	α	Lb	0.75	0.95	—	—	—
	δ³	αCV	4.29	4.32	2440501.35	57.25	—
	ζ	γCas	2.88	3.17	2444936.781	132.9735	—
	θ²	δSct	3.35	3.42	—	0.07564	[$1^h48^m55.3^s$]
	λ	EA	3.3	3.8	2435089.204*	3.952955	[$3^d22^h52^m15.3^s$]
	ρ	δSct	4.90	4.91	—	0.067	[$1^h36^m28.8^s$]
	τ	δSct	5.09	5.13	—	0.042	[$1^h0^m28.8^s$]
	υ	δSct	4.28	4.31	—	0.1484	[$3^h33^m41.8^s$]
	R	M	7.6	15.8	2445250	320.9	{ 1995: 12 Dec. (m) 2000: 4 May
	RW	EA	7.98	11.47	2442776.9313	2.7688396	[$2^d18^h27^m7.7^s$]
	BU (28)	γCas	4.77	5.50	—	—	—
	CE (119)	EA	4.23	4.54	—	165	—
	GS (41)	αCV	5.15	5.22	2421944.74	7.227424	[$7^d5^h27^m29.4^s$]
	V480 (97) = τ V776 (68) = δ³						
	V777 (71)	δSct	4.73	4.75	—	0.16	[$3^h50^m24.0^s$]
	V971 (23)	βC	4.18	4.19	—	—	—
Tri	R	M	5.4	12.6	2445215	266.9	2000: 9 Dec.
	TZ (6)	Ell/RS	5.19	5.28	2443729.8	14.732	[$14^d17^h34^m4.8^s$]
TrA	LP	αCV	5.12	(.033)	—	3.76	[$3^d18^h14^m24.0^s$]
Tuc	ν	Lb	4.75	4.93	—	—	—
UMa	ε	αCV	1.76	1.78	2426437.01	5.0887	[$5^d2^h7^m43.7^s$]
	ξ	RS	4.38	4.39	—	—	—
	υ	δSct	3.68	3.86	2441353.54	0.1327	[$3^h11^m5.3^s$]
	R	M	6.5	13.7	2445593	301.62	2000: 22 Mar.
	T	M	6.6	13.5	2445623	256.6	2001: 9 May
	CS	Lb	6.78	6.94	—	—	—
	DD (18)	δSct	5.02	5.05	—	0.121	[$2^h54^m14.4^s$]
	DK (24)	RS	4.56	(.058)	—	0.9202	[$22^h5^m5.3^s$]
	DP (67)	δSct	5.21	5.24	—	—	—
UMi	α	Cδ	1.92	2.07	2439253.01*	3.969778	[$3^d23^h16^m28.8^s$]
	γ	δSct	3.04	3.09	2439950.367	0.143009	[$3^h25^m56.0^s$]
	ε	EA	4.19	4.23	2433077.75	39.4809	[$39^d11^h32^m29.8^s$]
	RR	SRb	4.53	4.73		43.3	[$43^d7^h12^m$]
Vel	γ²	WR	1.81	1.87	—	154 sec.	—
	λ	Lc	2.14	2.30	—	—	—
	o	βC	3.55	3.67	2444651.6922	2.779	[$2^d18^h41^m45.6^s$]
	N	L?	3.12	3.15	—	—	—
	Y	M	8.0	14.2	2440875*	444.61	2000: 2 Jan.
	FZ	δSct	5.14	5.17	—	0.065	[$1^h33^m36.0^s$]
	GU	δSct	5.08	5.11	—	0.07	[$1^h40^m48.0^s$]
	GX	αCyg	4.97	5.04	—	—	—
	GZ	Lc	3.43	3.81	—	—	—
	HY	Ell	4.83	4.90	2444627.727	3.106	[$3^d2^h32^m38.4^s$]
	IS	βC	5.23	—	—	0.108	[$2^h35^m31.2^s$]
	KX (f)	E	4.87	(0.08″)	—	—	—
	LN	αCyg	5.19	5.25	—	—	—

Const.	Star	Type	Mag. Range		Epoch (* = SC)	Period (days)	Best viewing date
			Max.	Min.			
Vir	α	Ell	0.95	1.05	2419530.49	4.014604	$[4^d0^h21^m1.8^s]$
	ψ	Lb	4.73	4.96	—	—	—
	ω	Lb	5.23	5.50	—	—	—
	R	M	6.1	12.1	2445872	145.63	⎧ 1995: 28 Mar. (m) ⎨ 1997: 25 Mar. (m) ⎩ 2000: 2 June
	S	M	6.3	13.2	2445046	375.10	⎧ 1991: 14 June ⎨ 1993: 4 July ⎩ 1995: 24 July
	FM (32)	δSct	5.20	5.28	—	0.07188	$[1^h43^m30.4^s]$
	CU	αCV	4.92	5.07	2441455.685	0.5206794	$[12^h29^m46.7^s]$
	CW (78)	αCV	4.91	4.99	2434816.9	3.7220	$[3^d18^h31^m40.8^s]$
	ET	SRb	4.8	5.0	2440697	80	—
Vul	NT (15)	αCV	4.62	4.67	2441885.2	14.0	—
	NU (21)	δSct	5.36	5.41	—	16.478*	—

Computer Programs

This Appendix presents a number of programs written in BASIC for the use of amateur astronomers. Since space limitations prevent more rigorous programs from being included here, the user should realize that these programs—while accurate for almost all amateur needs—are not precise enough for scientific work.

The present programs are written in BASIC and require GWBASIC, as found in DOS 3.2–4.01. Place GWBASIC.EXE in a separate directory and include all these programs in the same directory. (The programs have been specifically written for GWBASIC. If you have DOS 5.0, you have QuickBASIC. These programs will not run under QuickBASIC.)

To copy the programs presented here, first enter GWBASIC. You are presented with a quasi-blank screen. Begin typing, with the first line of code (line 100). Please note: Do not type in the program name, which appears at the top of each program (i.e., DAY). This is for identification only; if you include it, the program will not run! Type exactly what you see, including the same case— upper or lower. After the last line ("END"), press <Enter> again and then press F4 ("Save"). Now type in the name of the program, exactly as it is named. You cannot rename any of these programs because a number of them are interactive— they require each other in order to run properly. To save the program you have just typed, after having pressed F4 and having typed in the name of the program, finish by typing a comma, followed by the letter A and another <Enter>. Here is an example: SAVE"TRA,A <Enter>. Now you have an executable program, called TRA.BAS.

You should place all these programs, along with GWBASIC.EXE, in the same directory. Make a backup file of the whole thing on a floppy. You won't want to type these programs all over again if you happen to lose the files.

Run any of the programs by first entering into the directory, then typing GWBASIC followed by the name of the program. For example, if you want to run JD, enter the directory in which GWBASIC and all the astronomy files are found, then type GWBASIC JD.

Pressing Ctrl-C will abort the program at practically any stage. To exit GWBA-SIC, type SYSTEM.

The following is a list of the programs in this appendix:

- DAY   to find the day of the week, given the Julian Date
- JD   to find the Julian Date, given the calendar date and time (UT)
- JDR   to find the calendar date, and the day of the week, given the Julian Date
- POS   to find the position (azimuth and altitude) of a star, given its right ascension and declination, the latitude and longitude of the observer, and the date
- RA   to calculate the right ascension on the meridian (sidereal time) at midnight, given the calendar date
- TRA   to calculate the date of midnight transit of a star, given its right ascension
- VAR   to calculate the approximate date of maximum brightness of a long-period variable star

Limitations

No error checking is performed on any of the inputs on these programs. One of the requirements imposed on the development of these BASIC programs for inclusion in *StarList 2000* was that the number of lines of code produced would not be excessively large. The introduction of sophisticated error–checking logic would have added greatly to the volume of code that the user of these programs would have to type into his/her computer.

Therefore, care needs to be exercised by the user to ensure that all the inputs are valid. For example, even though the programs would accept a month of 13, the results produced by the programs would be questionable. As another example, a date of February 31 would also be accepted by the program.

Calendar dates prior to 1 January −4712 should not be entered, as this date is (by definition) Julian Date zero.

Notes concerning each program:

- If you get the message "File not found in ____ ," look up that line number of the program. Chances are it will indicate another program that you have failed to put in the same directory. The best course is just to do all the programs and keep them in the same directory as your BASIC program.

- Before running JD or JDR, the program DAY must have been previously entered into GWBASIC and saved via the SAVE command (F4).

- Before running VAR, TRA, RA, or POS, the program JD must have ben previously entered into GWBASIC and saved via the SAVE command (F4).

For your convenience, you may download all these programs from CompuServe: STRPRG.ZIP in the Astronomy forum.

DAY

```
100 COMMON WHO$,  OLDWHO$, JD#, YEAR#, MON!, DATE!, HOUR#, MIN#, SEC#
110 COMMON EPOCH#,  PERIOD#, UT#, RA#, DECL#, LAT#, LON#
120 '
130 '  Figure out if we were called by someone or have just been invoked.
140 '
150 IF  WHO$ = "" THEN WHO$ = "day"
160 IF  WHO$ <> "day" THEN GOTO 230
170 '
180 CLS
190 PRINT  "Calculates the day of the week"
200 PRINT
210 INPUT  "Julian Date"; JD#
220 '
230 J# = INT( JD# + .5# )  / 7
240 I# = INT( 7 * ( J# -  INT( J# )) + .1) + 1
250 '
260 IF JD# < 0 THEN I# =  I# + 7
270 '
280 IF WHO$ = "day" THEN PRINT
290 '
300 IF I# = 1 THEN PRINT "MONDAY"
310 IF I# = 2 THEN PRINT "TUESDAY"
320 IF I# = 3 THEN PRINT "WEDNESDAY"
330 IF I# = 4 THEN PRINT "THURSDAY"
340 IF I# = 5 THEN PRINT "FRIDAY"
350 IF I# = 6 THEN PRINT "SATURDAY"
360 IF I# = 7 THEN PRINT "SUNDAY"
370 '
380 IF WHO$ = "day" THEN GOTO 430      ' Don't return if we weren't called.
390 OLDWHO$ = WHO$
400 WHO$ = "day"
410 CHAIN OLDWHO$
420 '
430 PRINT
440 INPUT "Compute another (y/n)"; A$
450 IF LEFT$( A$, 1 ) = "Y" THEN GOTO 200
460 IF LEFT$( A$, 1 ) = "y" THEN GOTO 200
470 END
```

Purpose: Calculates the day of the week, given the Julian Date.

Input: The given Julian Date.

Output: The day of the week, corresponding to the given Julian Date.

Examples

Following are two examples on the use of this program. If the program you have entered into your machine produces the correct result with both of these examples, the chances are that you have entered it correctly. Congratulations!

Example 1: What day of the week was Julian date 2435466?

Enter the following value when prompted:

```
Julian Date? 2435466
```

The answer is displayed:

```
Saturday

Compute another (y/n)? y(Enter)
```

Example 2: What day of the week was Julian date zero?

Enter the following value when prompted:

```
Julian Date? 0
```

The answer is displayed:

```
Monday

Compute another (y/n)? n(Enter)
```

JD

```
100 COMMON WHO$, OLDWHO$, JD#, YEAR#, MON!, DATE!, HOUR#, MIN#, SEC#
110 COMMON EPOCH#, PERIOD#, UT#, RA#, DECL#, LAT#, LON#
120 '
130 ' Figure out if we are being called by someone else or are returning
140 ' after a call.
150 '
160 IF WHO$ = "" THEN WHO$ = "jd"
170 IF WHO$ = "ra" THEN GOTO 440
180 IF WHO$ = "var" THEN GOTO 440
190 IF WHO$ = "pos" THEN GOTO 440
200 IF WHO$ = "day" THEN GOTO 820    ' get back to where we were
210 '
220 CLS
230 PRINT "Program to compute the Julian date"
240 PRINT
250 INPUT "Date (yyyy.mmdd)"; YEAR#
260 '
270 MON! = INT( 100 * (YEAR# - INT( YEAR# )) + .1 )
280 DATE! = INT( 100 * ( 100 * ( YEAR# - INT(Year#)) - MON! ) + .1 )
290 YEAR# = INT( YEAR# )
300 '
310 INPUT "Universal Time (hh.mmss) [default 12h]"; HOUR$
320 IF LEN( HOUR$) ) 0  THEN GOTO 350
330 HOUR# = 12
340 GOTO 440
350 X# = VAL( HOUR$)
360 '
370 ' convert HOUR# from hours, minutes, seconds to decimal hours
380 '
390 M# = INT( 100 * ( X# - INT( X# )) + .1)
400 S# = 100 * ( 100 * (X# -  INT( X# )) -M# )
410 H# = INT( X# )
415 print h#, m#, s#
420 HOUR# = H# + ( M# / 60 ) + ( S# / 3600 )
430 '
440 IF MON! ) 2 THEN GOTO 500
450    YEAR# = YEAR# - 1
460    MON! = MON! + 12
470 '
480 ' Check to see if we have a valid date in the Gregorian calendar.
490 '
500 IF YEAR# ) 1582 THEN GOTO 580
510 IF YEAR# ( 1582 THEN GOTO 610
520 '
530 IF MON! ) 10 THEN GOTO 580
540 IF MON! ( 10 THEN GOTO 610
550 '
560 IF DATE! (= 15 THEN GOTO 610
570 '
580 B# = 2 - INT( YEAR# / 100 ) + INT( INT( YEAR# / 100 ) / 4 )
590 GOTO 630
600 '
610 B# = 0
620 '
630 IF YEAR# )= 0 THEN GOTO 670
640    C# = INT(( 365.25 * YEAR# ) - .75 )
650    GOTO 690
660 '
670 C# = INT( 365.25 * YEAR# )
680 '
690 D# = INT( 30.6001 * (MON! + 1 ))
700 '
710 JD# = B# + C# + D# + DATE! + 1720994.5# + ( HOUR# / 24 )
720 '
730 IF WHO$ = "jd" THEN GOTO 780    ' don't return if we weren't called.
740 OLDWHO$ = WHO$
750 WHO$ = "jd"
760 CHAIN OLDWHO$
770 '
780 PRINT
790 PRINT "Julian Date is"; JD#
800 CHAIN "day"
810 '
820 WHO$ = "jd"
```

```
830 PRINT
840 INPUT "Compute another (y/n)"; A$
850 IF LEFT$( A$, 1 ) = "Y" THEN GOTO 240
860 IF LEFT$( A$, 1 ) = "y" THEN GOTO 240
870 END
```

Purpose: To calculate the Julian date, given the calendar date and the time (UT).

Input:

> **Date (yyyy.mmdd)**   The calendar date, with the year to the left of the decimal point and the month and day to the right. For example, a date of 5 January 1900 would be entered as 1900.0105.

> **Universal Time (hh.mmss) [default is 12h]**   The universal time (equivalent to GMT) of the observation, with the number of hours to the left of the decimal point and the minutes and seconds to the right. For example, a UT of 18:23:54 would be entered at 18.2354. If no value is entered, 12h0m0s UT (or Noon, GMT) is assumed.

Output: The Julian Date that corresponds to the calendar date entered, and the day of the week.

Examples

Following are three examples on the use of this program. If the program you have entered into your machine produces the correct result with all of these examples, the chances are that you have entered it correctly. Congratulations!

Example 1: Find the Julian date for 20 March 1995.

Enter the following values when prompted:

```
Date (yyyy.mmdd)? 1995.0320
Universal Time (hh.mmss) [default is 12h]? (Enter)
```

The answer is then displayed:

```
Julian Date is 2449797
Monday

Compute another (y/n)? y(Enter)
```

Example 2: Find the Julian date corresponding to 18:15 UT on 14 July 1987.

Enter the following values when prompted:

```
Date (yyyy.mmdd)? 1987.0714
Universal Time (hh.mmss) [default is 12h]? 18.15
```

The answer is then displayed:

```
Julian Date is 2446991.260416667
Tuesday

Compute another (y/n)? y(Enter)
```

Example 3: What is the Julian date for 11:50 on 19 January 1958?

Enter the following values when prompted:

```
Date (yyyy.mmdd)? 1958.0119
Universal Time (hh.mmss) [default is 12h]? 11.50
```

The answer is then displayed:

```
Julian Date is 2436222.993055556
Sunday

Compute another (y/n)? n(Enter)
```

JDR

```
100 COMMON WHO$, OLDWHO$, JD#, YEAR#, MON!, DATE!, HOUR#, MIN#, SEC#
110 COMMON EPOCH#, PERIOD#, UT#, RA#, DECL#, LAT#, LON#
120 '
130 ' Figure out if we were called by someone else or are being returned to
140 ' by someone we called.
150 '
160 IF WHO$ = "" THEN WHO$ = "jdr"
170 IF WHO$ = "var" THEN GOTO 270
180 IF WHO$ = "tra" THEN GOTO 270      ' input already in JD# — don't prompt
190 IF WHO$ = "ra" THEN GOTO 270
200 IF WHO$ = "day" THEN GOTO 670      ' get back to where we were
210 '
220 CLS
230 PRINT "Program to calculate the calendar date"
240 PRINT
250 INPUT "Julian Date"; JD#
260 '
270 I# = INT( JD# + .5 )
280 F# = ( JD# + .5 ) − INT( JD# + .5 )
290 '
300 IF I# <= 2299160! THEN GOTO 350
310    A# = INT(( I# − 1867216.25# ) / 36524.25 )
320    B# = I# + 1 + A# − INT( A# / 4 )
330    GOTO 370
340 '
350 B# = I#
360 '
370 C# = B# + 1524
380 D# = INT(( C# − 122.1 ) / 365.25 )
390 E# = INT( 365.25 * D# )
400 G! = INT(( C# − E# ) / 30.6001 )
410 '
420 H# = C# − E# + F# − INT( 30.6001 * G! )
430 DATE! = INT( H# )
440 '
450 HOUR# = 24 * ( H# − INT( H# ))
460 MIN# = 60 * ( HOUR# − INT(HOUR# ))
470 SEC# = 60 * ( MIN# − INT( MIN# ))
480 HOUR# = INT( HOUR# )
490 MIN# = INT( MIN# )
500 SEC# = INT(10 * SEC# ) / 10
510 '
520 IF G! <= 13 THEN MON! = G! − 1 ELSE MON! = G! − 13
530 '
540 IF MON! > 2 THEN YEAR# = D# − 4716 ELSE YEAR# = D# − 4715
550 '
560 IF WHO$ <> "jdr" THEN GOTO 710
570 '
580 PRINT
590 PRINT "The Calendar Date for "; JD#; "is"
600 PRINT HOUR#; "h"; MIN#; "m"; SEC#; "s UT on"; DATE!; "/"; MON!; "/"; YEAR#
610 '
620 ' chain to "day" to print day-of-week
630 '
640 OLDWHO$ = WHO$
650 WHO$ = "jdr"
660 CHAIN "day"
670 WHO$ = OLDWHO$
680 '
690 IF WHO$ = "jdr" THEN GOTO 750   ' Don't return if we weren't called
700 '
710 OLDWHO$ = WHO$
720 WHO$ = "jdr"
730 CHAIN OLDWHO$
740 '
750 PRINT
760 INPUT "Compute another (y/n)"; A$
770 IF LEFT$( A$, 1 ) = "Y" THEN GOTO 240
780 IF LEFT$( A$, 1 ) = "y" THEN GOTO 240
790 END
```

Purpose: To calculate the calendar date, given the Julian date.

Input: The given Julian Date.

Output:

Time—The Universal Time on the calendar date corresponding to the input Julian date.

Calendar Date—The calendar date, expressed in the form Date/Month/Year.

Day of Week—The day of the week represented by the Julian date entered.

Examples

Following are two examples of the use of this program. If the program you have entered into your machine produces the correct result with both of these examples, the chances are that you have entered it correctly. Congratulations!

Example 1: You note that the epoch of the variable Antares (α Scorpii) is 2408600. What calendar date does this represent?

Enter the following value when prompted:

```
Julian Date? 2408600
```

The answer is then displayed:

```
The Calendar Date for 2408600 is 12 h 0 m 0 s UT on 3/6/1882
Saturday

Compute another (y/n)? y(Enter)
```

Example 2: The *Sky Catalogue* gives an epoch of 2442776.9313 for the variable RW Tauri. What is the corresponding date?

Enter the following value when prompted:

```
Julian Date? 2442776.9313
```

The answer will then be displayed:

```
The Calendar Date for 2442776.9313 is 10 h 21 m 4.3 s UT on 30/12/1975
Tuesday

Compute another (y/n)? n(Enter)
```

POS

```
100 '
110 COMMON WHO$, OLDWHO$, JD#, YEAR#, MON!, DATE!, HOUR#, MIN#, SEC#
120 COMMON EPOCH#, PERIOD#, UT#, RA#, DECL#, LAT#, LON#
130 '
140 GOTO 390    'jump around the subroutine definitions
150 '
160 ' subroutine to convert from decimal degrees to degrees, minutes, seconds
170 '
180 ' Input must be in DEG#; output returned in D#, M#, S#
190 '
200 D# = INT( DEG# )
210 M# = 60 * ( DEG# - D# )
220 S# = 60 * ( M# - INT( M#))
230 M# = INT( M# )
240 S# = INT( S# * 10 ) / 10
250 RETURN
260 '
270 ' subroutine to convert degrees, minutes, seconds to decimal degrees
280 '
290 ' Input must be in DEG#; output returned in DEG#
300 '
310 M# = INT( 100* ( DEG# - INT( DEG# )) + .1)
320 S# = 100 * ( 100 * ( DEG# - INT( DEG# )) -M# )
330 H# = INT( DEG# )
340 DEG# = H# + ( M# / 60 ) + ( S# / 3600 )
350 RETURN
360 '
370 ' function to convert degrees to radians
380 '
390 DEF FNRAD( DEG# ) = DEG# / 57.2957795132#
400 '
410 ' function to convert radians to degrees
420 '
430 DEF FNDEG( RAD# ) = RAD# * 57.2957795132#
440 '
450 ' function to compute the arcsin
460 '
470 DEF FNARCSIN( X# ) = ATN( X# / SQR( 1 - X#^2 ))
480 '
490 ' function to compute the arccos
500 '
510 DEF FNARCCOS ( X# ) = ATN( SQR( 1 - X#^ 2 ) / X# )
520 '
530 ' Figure out if we are returning after calling a subroutine or have
540 ' just been invoked.
550 '
560 IF WHO$ = "" THEN WHO$ = "pos"
570 IF WHO$ = "jd" THEN GOTO 1440
580 '
590 CLS
600 PRINT "Program to convert equatorial coordinates to azimuth and elevation"
610 PRINT
620 INPUT "Do you know the hour angle of the star (y/n)"; A$
630 PRINT
640 IF LEFT$( A$, 1 ) = "N" THEN GOTO 900
650 IF LEFT$( A$, 1 ) = "n" THEN GOTO 900
660 '
670 INPUT "Declination of star (dd.mmss)"; DECL#
680 INPUT "Hour Angle of star (hh.mmss)"; HA#
690 INPUT "Latitude of observer (dd.mmss)"; LAT#
700 '
710 ' convert inputs to decimal degrees
720 '
730 DEG# = DECL#
740 GOSUB 310
750 DECL# = DEG#
760 '
770 DEG# = LAT#
780 GOSUB 310
790 LAT# = DEG#
800 '
810 DEG# = HA#
```

```
820 GOSUB 310
830 HA# = DEG#
840 '
850 GOTO 1710
860 '
870 ' Since we don't know the star's hour angle, we're going to have to
880 ' do this the hard way...
890 '
900 INPUT "Date (yyyy.mmdd)"; YEAR#
910 '
920 MON! = INT( 100 * ( YEAR# - INT( YEAR# )) + .1 )
930 DATE! = INT( 100 * ( 100 * ( YEAR# - INT( YEAR# )) -MON! ) + .1 )
940 YEAR# = INT( YEAR# )
950 '
960 PRINT
970 INPUT "Local Time (hh.mmss)"; T#
980 INPUT "Time Zone (hours from GMT)"; ZONE#
990 PRINT
1000 INPUT "Right Ascension of star (hh.mmss)"; RA#
1010 INPUT "Declination of star (dd.mmss)"; DECL#
1020 PRINT
1030 INPUT "Latitude of observer (dd.mmss)"; LAT#
1040 INPUT "Longitude of observer (dd.mmss)"; LON#
1050 '
1060 ' convert local time to UT and adjust date if necessary
1070 '
1080 UT# = T# - ZONE#
1090 IF UT# < 24 THEN GOTO 1130
1100 DATE! = DATE! + 1
1110 UT# = UT# - 24
1120 '
1130 If UT# >= 0 THEN GOTO 1190
1140 THEN DATE! = DATE! - 1
1150 UT# = UT# + 24
1160 '
1170 ' convert inputs to decimal degrees
1180 '
1190 DEG# = UT#
1200 GOSUB 310
1210 UT# = DEG#
1220 '
1230 DEG# = RA#
1240 GOSUB 310
1250 RA# = DEG#
1260 '
1270 DEG# = DECL#
1280 GOSUB 310
1290 DECL# = DEG#
1300 '
1310 DEG# = LAT#
1320 GOSUB 310
1330 LAT# = DEG#
1340 '
1350 DEG# = LON#
1360 GOSUB 310
1370 LON# = DEG#
1380 '
1390 ' We begin the arduous task of converting UT to local sidereal time
1400 '
1410 HOUR# = 0
1420 CHAIN "jd"
1430 '
1440 T# = ( JD# - 2451545! ) / 36525!
1450 TO# = 6.697374558# + ( 2400.051336# * T# ) + ( 2.5862E-05 * T#^2 )
1460 '
1470 IF TO# > 0 THEN GOTO 1510
1480    TO# = TO# + 24
1490    IF TO# < 0 THEN GOTO 1480
1500 '
1510 IF TO# < 24 THEN GOTO 1550
1520    TO# = TO# - 24
1530    IF TO# >= 24 THEN GOTO 1520
1540 '
1550 UT# = UT# * 1.002737909#
1560 '
```

```
1570 GST# = UT# + TO#
1580 '
1590 IF GST# < 0 THEN GST# = GST# + 24
1600 IF GST# >= 24 THEN GST# = GST# - 24
1610 '
1620 LST# = GST# - ( LON# / 15 )
1630 '
1640 IF LST# < 0 THEN LST# = LST# + 24
1650 IF LST# >= 24 THEN LST# = LST# - 24
1660 '
1670 HA# = LST# - RA#    ' At last!  We have the hour angle of the star.
1680 '
1690 ' convert inputs to radian so the trig functions will work
1700 '
1710 DECL# = FNRAD( DECL# )
1720 LAT# = FNRAD( LAT# )
1730 HA# = FNRAD( 15 * HA# )
1740 '
1750 EL# = SIN( DECL# ) * SIN( LAT# )
1760 EL# = EL# + ( COS( DECL# ) * COS( LAT# ) * COS( HA# ))
1770 EL# = FNARCSIN( EL# )
1780 '
1790 AZ# = SIN( DECL# ) - ( SIN( LAT# ) * SIN( EL# ))
1800 AZ# = AZ# / ( COS( LAT# ) * COS( EL# ))
1810 '
1820 IF AZ# > 1 THEN AZ# = 1
1830 IF AZ# < -1 THEN AZ# = -1
1840 AZ# = FNARCCOS( AZ# )
1850 IF AZ# < 0 THEN AZ# = AZ# + 3.14159265359#
1860 '
1870 AZ# = FNDEG( AZ# )
1880 EL# = FNDEG( EL# )
1890 '
1900 IF SIN( HA# ) > 0 THEN AZ# = 360 - AZ#
1910 '
1920 PRINT
1930 '
1940 ' convert az to degrees, minutes, seconds
1950 '
1960 DEG# = AZ#
1970 GOSUB 200
1980 '
1990 PRINT "Azimuth = "; D#; CHR$( 248 ); M#; "'"; S#; CHR$( 34 )
2000 '
2010 ' convert el to degrees, minutes, seconds
2020 '
2030 DEG# = EL#
2040 GOSUB 200
2050 '
2060 PRINT "Altitude = "; D#; CHR$( 248 ); M#; "'"; S#; CHRS#( 34 )
2070 '
2080 WHO$ = "pos"
2090 PRINT
2100 INPUT "Compute another (y/n)"; A$
2110 IF LEFT$( A$, 1 ) = "Y" THEN GOTO 610
2120 IF LEFT$( A$, 1 ) = "y" THEN GOTO 610
2130 END
```

Purpose: To compute the position (azimuth and altitude) of a star, given its Right Ascension and Declination, the observer's latitude and longitude, the date and time. Alternatively, if the star's hour angle is known, the program requires merely the declination of the object and the observer's latitude.

Input: Do you know the hour angle of the star? (y/n)? <Enter>

If the hour angle of the object is known:

Declination of star (dd.mmss)?—The Declination of the star, with the number of degrees to the left of the decimal point and the minutes and seconds to the right. For example, a Declination of 47°23′57.2″ would be entered as 47.23572.

Hour Angle of star (hh.mmss)?—The hour angle of the star. This is simply the number of hours of Right Ascension that the star is west of the local meridian; thus a star at transit would have an hour angle of zero. The hour angle is entered with the number of hours to the left of the decimal point and the minutes and seconds to the right. For example, an hour angle of 3h31m44.9s would be entered as 3.31449.

Latitude of observer (dd.mmss)?—The latitude of the observer, with the number of degrees to the left of the decimal point and the minutes and seconds to the right. For example, a latitude of 38°45′10″ would be entered as 38.4510.

If the hour angle is not known:

Date (yyyy.mmdd)?—The date of the observation, with the year to the left of the decimal point and the month and days to the right. Thus, 9 March 1950 would be entered as 1950.0309.

Local Time (hh.mmss)?—The local time of the observation, with the number of hours to the left of the decimal point and the minutes and seconds to the right. For example, a time of 18:23:54 would be entered as 18.2354.

Time Zone (hours from GMT)?—The observer's time zone, expressed as the number of hours ahead or behind GMT. For example, North American Eastern Standard Time would be entered as −5; Pacific Standard Time would be entered as −8; Central European Time would be entered as +1.

Right Ascension of star (hh.mmss)?—The Right Ascension of the star, with the number of hours to the left of the decimal point and the minutes and seconds to the right. For example, a Right Ascension of 10h18m01.2s would be entered as 10.18012.

Declination of star (dd.mmss)?—The Declination of the star, with the number of degrees to the left of the decimal point and the minutes and seconds to the right. A Declination of −30°24′44″ would be entered as −30.2444.

Latitude of observer (dd.mmss)?—The latitude of the observer, with the number of degrees to the left of the decimal point and the minutes and seconds to the right. For example, a latitude of 46°15m21s would be entered as 46.1521.

Longitude of observer (dd.mmss)?—The longitude of the observer. Longitudes west of the Greenwich meridian are expressed as positive numbers, while longitudes east of Greenwich are expressed as the negative numbers. The longitude must be entered with degrees to the left of the decimal point and minutes and seconds to the right. Thus, a longitude of 140° east would be entered as −140.

Output:

Azimuth—The star's azimuth, expressed in degrees, minutes, and seconds.

Altitude—The star's elevation above the horizon, expressed in degrees, minutes, and seconds.

Examples

Following are two examples on the use of this program. If the program you have entered into your machine produces the correct result with both of these examples, the chances are that you have entered it correctly. Congratulations!

Example 1: We would like to locate Betelgeuse (α Ori). We know that its R.A. is 5h53m32.8s, and its declination is 7°24'10". The date is 28 February 1995, and the local time is 9 pm, PST. We are located at 45°N latitude and 120°W longitude.

We don't know the hour angle of Betelgeuse. Answer **N** to the first question concerning the hour angle. Then enter these values when prompted:

```
Date? 1995.0228

Local Time (hh.mmss)? 21
Time  Zone (hours from GMT)? −8

Right Ascension of star (hh.mmss)? 5.53328
Declination of star (dd.mmss)? 7.2410

Latitude of observer (dd.mmss)? 45
Longitude of observer (dd.mmss)? 120
```

After a brief pause, the answer will be displayed:

```
Azimuth = 217° 46' 52.6"
Altitude = 46° 32' 24.3"

Compute another (y/n)? y(Enter)
```

Example 2: Find the azimuth and altitude of a star whose declination is 23°13'10" and whose hour angle at the time of the observation is 5h51m44s. The observer's latitude is 52°N.

Answer **Y** to the question about the hour angle. Enter the following values when prompted:

```
Declination of star (dd.mmss)? 23.1310
Hour Angle of star (hh.mmss)? 5.5144
Latitude of observer (dd.mmss)? 52
```

The answer will be displayed:

```
Azimuth = 283° 16' 15.6"
Altitude = 19° 20' 3.6"

Compute another (y/n)? n(Enter)
```

RA

```
100 COMMON WHO$, OLDWHO$, JD#, YEAR#, MON!, DATE!, HOUR#, MIN#, SEC#
110 COMMON EPOCH#, PERIOD#, UT#, RA#, DECL#, LAT#, LON#
120 '
130 ' Figure out if we're returning from a subroutine call or have just
140 ' been invoked.
150 '
160 IF WHO$ = "" THEN WHO$ = "ra"
170 IF WHO$ = "jd" THEN GOTO 310
180 '
190 CLS
200 PRINT "Program to compute the right ascension at midnight"
210 PRINT
220 INPUT "Date (mm.dd)"; X#
230 '
240 MON! = INT( X# )
250 DATE! = 100 * ( X# - MON! )
260 YEAR# = 2000
270 HOUR# = 0
280 '
290 CHAIN "jd"    ' we need the Julian date of the requested date
300 '
310 RA# = ( JD# - 2451442.5# ) / 15.208333333333#
320 IF RA# )= 24 THEN RA# = RA# - 24
330 '
340 ' convert from decimal hours to hours and minutes
350 '
360 H# = INT( RA# )
370 M# = INT( 60 * ( RA# - INT( RA# )))
380 '
390 PRINT
400 PRINT "Right Ascension is"; H#; "h"; M#; "m"
410 '
420 WHO$ = "ra"
430 PRINT
440 INPUT "Compute another (y/n)"; A$
450 IF LEFT$( A$, 1 ) = "Y" THEN GOTO 210
460 IF LEFT$( A$, 1 ) = "y" THEN GOTO 210
470 END
```

Purpose: To calculate the Right Ascension on the meridian (sidereal time) at midnight, given the month and day.

Input:

> **Date (mm.dd)?** The date, entered with the month to the left of the decimal point, and the date to the right. A date of 4 July would be entered as 07.04.

Output: The Right Ascension (at midnight for the given date.)

Examples

Following are two examples on the use of this program. If the program you have entered into your machine produces the correct result with both of these examples, the chances are that you have entered it correctly. Congratulations!

Example 1: What is the Right Ascension at midnight on July 4?

Enter the following values when prompted:

```
Date(mm.dd)? 07.04
```

The answer is then displayed:

```
Right Ascension is 18 h 52 m

Compute another (y/n)? y(Enter)
```

Example 2: What is the Right Ascension at midnight on April 7?

Enter the following values when prompted:

```
Date (mm.dd)? 04.07
```

The answer is then displayed:

```
Right Ascension is 13 h 5 m

Compute another? (y/n)? n(Enter)
```

TRA

```
100 COMMON WHO$, OLDWHO$, JD#, YEAR#, MON!, DATE!, HOUR#, MIN#, SEC#
110 COMMON EPOCH#, PERIOD#, UT#, RA#, DECL#, LAT#, LON#
120 '
130 ' Figure out if we're returning from a subroutine or have just been
140 ' invoked.
150 '
160 IF WHO$ = "" THEN WHO$ = "tra"
170 IF WHO$ = "jdr" THEN GOTO 340    ' go back to where we were
180 '
190 CLS
200 PRINT "Program to compute the midnight transit date of a star"
210 PRINT
220 INPUT "Right Ascension (hh.mmss)"; X#
230 '
240 ' convert RA from hours, minutes, seconds to decimal hours
250 '
260 M# = INT( 100 * ( X# - INT( X# )) + .1 )
270 S# = 100 * ( 100 * ( X# - INT( X# )) - M# )
280 H# = INT( X# )
290 RA# = H# + ( M# / 60 ) + ( S# / 3600 )
300 '
310 JD# = ( 15.20833333333# * RA# ) + 2451808.5#
320 '
330 CHAIN "jdr"    ' Convert JD to calendar date.
340 PRINT
350 PRINT "Midnight transit date is"; MON!; "/"; DATE!
360 '
370 WHO$ = "tra"
380 PRINT
390 INPUT "Compute another (y/n)"; A$
400 IF LEFT$ ( A$, 1 ) = "Y" THEN GOTO 210
410 IF LEFT$ ( A$, 1 ) = "y" THEN GOTO 210
420 END
```

Purpose: To calculate the date of midnight transit of a given star, given its Right Ascension.

Input:

> **Right Ascension (hh.mmss)?**   The star's Right Ascension, with the number of hours to the left of the decimal point and the minutes and seconds to the right. For example, a Right Ascension of 20h39m14s would be entered as 20.3914.

Output:

> **Transit Date (m/d)**   The date on which the star will transit at (or near) midnight. The accuracy is should be within about two minutes of midnight (plus or minus), local time.

Examples

Following are two examples on the use of this program. If the program you have entered into your machine produces the correct result with both of these examples, the chances are that you have entered it correctly. Congratulations!

Example 1: The Right Ascension of Sirus (α CMa) is 6h43m49.6s. When will it cross the local meridian at midnight?

Enter the following value when prompted:

```
Right Ascension (hh.mmss)? 6.43496
```

The answer is then displayed:

```
Midnight transit date is 1 / 1 (that is, on January first)

Compute another (y/n) y(Enter)
```

Example 2: Antares has a Right Ascension of 16h27m33.9s. On what date will it transit nearest to midnight?

Enter the following values when prompted:

```
Right Ascension (hh.mmss)? 16.27339
```

The answer is then displayed:

```
Midnight transit date is 5/29 (i.e., 29 May)

Compute another (y/n)? n(Enter)
```

VAR

```
100 COMMON WHO$, OLDWHO$, JD#, YEAR#, MON!, DATE!, HOUR#, MIN#, SEC#
110 COMMON EPOCH#, PERIOD#, UT#, RA#, DECL#, LAT#, LON#
120 '
130 ' Figure out if we are returning after calling a subroutine or have
140 ' just been invoked.
150 '
160 IF WHO$ = "" THEN WHO$ = "var"
170 IF WHO$ = "jd" THEN GOTO 330
180 IF WHO$ = "jdr" THEN GOTO 410
190 '
200 CLS
210 PRINT "Program to figure the approximate time of maximum brightness"
220 PRINT "  prior to the requested date"
230 PRINT
250 INPUT "Date (yyyy.mmdd)"; Year#
260 '
270 MON! = INT( 100 * (YEAR# - INT(YEAR# )) + .1)
280 DATE! = INT( 100 * ( 100 * (YEAR# - INT( YEAR# )) - MON! ) + .1 )
290 YEAR# = INT(YEAR# )
291 PRINT
292 INPUT "Epoch of Maximum"; EPOCH#
293 INPUT "Period of varability (days)"; PERIOD#
300 '
310 HOUR# = 0
320 CHAIN "jd"    ' we need the Julian date of the requested date
330 WHO$ = "var"
340 '
350 NPERIODS = INT(( JD# - EPOCH# ) / PERIOD# )
360 IF NPERIODS (= 0 THEN NPERIODS = NPERIODS - 1
370 '
380 JD# = EPOCH#  + ( PERIOD# * NPERIODS )
390 CHAIN "jdr"       ' convert the answer back to a calendar date
400 '
410 PRINT
420 PRINT "Maximum brightness should occur on"; DATE!; "/"; MON!; "/"; YEAR#
430 '
440 WHO$ = "var"
450 PRINT
460 INPUT "Compute another (y/n)"; A$
470 IF LEFT$( A$, 1 ) = "Y" THEN GOTO 230
480 IF LEFT$( A$, 1 ) = "y" THEN GOTO 230
490 END
```

Purpose: To find the approximate date of maximum brightness of a long-period variable star.

Input:

> **Date (yyyy.mmdd)?**   The approximate date desired. This is the last possible date in the year indicated. In other words, if you wish to find the best viewing date for a given Mira-type variable in 1995, the date to enter is 1995.1231. This will give you the best date prior to that time. But see the two frames below for the best way to use this program.
>
> **Epoch of Maximum?**   The Julian date of a verified maximum of the star. This is usually given as the star's Epoch.
>
> **Period of variability(days)?**   The period of the star, given in days.

Output: Maximum brightness should occur on (m/d/yr)—An approximate date for the maximum to occur.

Example 1: Find the date of the maximum brightness of Mira in the year 2000. The epoch of maximum for Mira is 2444839 and its period is 331.96 days.

Enter the following values when prompted:

```
Date? 2000.1231

Epoch of Maximum? 2444839
Period of variability (days)? 331.96
```

The answer is then displayed:

```
Maximum brightness should occur on 22/9/2000

Compute another (y/n)? y(Enter)
```

Example 2: Determine the date of maximum brightness for R Draconis in the year 2000. The epoch of maximum for R Draconis is 2444779 and its period is 245.6 days.

Enter the following values when prompted for them:

```
Date? 2000.0630

Epoch of Maximum? 2444779
Period of variability (days)? 245.6
```

The answer is then displayed:

```
Maximum brightness should occur on 21/4/2000

Compute another (y/n)? n(Enter)
```

NOTE: A little thought is required to get the most out of this program. Except for circumpolar stars, each star has its own season. You must verify that a star's season corresponds to its most favorable date that this program calculates.

In Example 2, if we used the usual input of 2000.1231 to find the best viewing date of this star for the year 2000, we would get the answer 22 December. However, this date is not favorable for viewing R Draconis. Spring is much better.

Therefore we should put 30 June as the latest "best date." When we do so, the answer is 21 April, an excellent time.

Always use a planisphere or other star guide to determine the best time to view a star, then input accordingly.

Bibliography

Some of these titles also appear on the Primary Sources list, which precedes the StarList.

Titles marked with an (★) are recommended for the general reader.

Aitken, R. G. *The Binary Stars* (New York, 1935; 2nd ed.).

Barbier, M. and Petit, M. *Catalogue bibliographique de vitesses radiales stellaires* (Strasbourg, 1976).

★Bishop, Roy L. (ed.). *Observer's Handbook* (Toronto, 1989 ed.) (published annually).

Boss, Benjamin. *General Catalogue of 33342 Stars for the Epoch 1950.0* (Washington, DC, 1963).

★Burnham, Robert. *Celestial Handbook* (New York, 1978 ed.). 3 vols.

Couteau, P. *Observing Visual Double Stars* (Cambridge, MA, 1981).

Dickinson, Terence. *Nightwatch* (Toronto, 1989).

Dickinson, Terence, and Dyer, Alan. *The Backyard Astronomer's Guide* (Columbia, SC, 1991).

Duffett-Smith, Peter. *Practical Astronomy with Your Calculator* (Cambridge, UK, 1988; 3rd ed.).

★Eicher, David J. (ed.). *Deep-Sky Observing with Small Telescopes* (Hillside, NJ, 1989).

Evans, David S. *Catalogue of Stellar Radial Velocities* (Strasbourg, 1967).

Finsen, W. S. and Worley, C. E. *Third Catalogue of Orbits of Visual Binary Stars* (Johannesburg, *Republic Observatory Circular* vol. 129, 1970: pp. 203–54).

Gliese, W. *Catalogue of Nearby Stars* (Karlsruhe, 1969).

Hirshfeld, Alan and Sinnott, R. W. (eds.). *Sky Catalogue 2000.0* (Cambridge, MA, 1982). 2 vols.

Hoffleit, Dorrit and Jaschek, Carlos. *The Bright Star Catalogue* (New Haven, CT, 1982).

Hoffleit, Dorrit; Saladyga, Michael; and Wlasuk, Peter. *A Supplement to the Bright Star Catalogue* (New Haven, CT, 1983).

Hoffleit, Dorrit. "Additions and Corrections to the Bright Star Catalogue." (*Bulletin d'Information du Centre de Données Stellaires,* Strasbourg, 1984; pp. 161–195).

Hoffmeister, Cuno; Richter, G.; and Wenzel, W. *Variable Stars* (Berlin, 1985; 2nd ed.).

IBVS: *Information Bulletin of Variable Stars* (Budapest; periodical).

★Illingworth, Valerie (ed.). *The Dictionary of Astronomy* (New York, 1985; 2nd ed.).

Jeffers, H. M. and van den Bos, W. H. *Lick Observatory Index Catalogue of Visual Binary Stars, 1961.0* (Mount Hamilton, California, 1963). 2 vols.

Jenkins, Louise F. *General Catalogue of Trigonometic Stellar Parallaxes* (New Haven, CT, 1963).

★Jones, Kenneth Glyn (ed.) *Webb Society Deep-Sky Observer's Handbook, vol. 1: Double Stars* (Hillside, NJ, 1986; 2nd ed.) & *vol. 8: Variable Stars* (Hillside, NJ, 1990).

Kaler, James B. *Stars and Their Spectra* (Cambridge, UK, 1989).

Kholopov, R. N. (ed.) *General Catalogue of Variable Stars* (Moscow, 1985–87; 4th ed.). 4 vols.

★Levy, David H. *Observing Variable Stars* (Cambridge, UK, 1989).

Meeus, Jean. *Astronomical Formulae for Calculators* (Richmond, VA, 1982).

Michigan Catalogue of Two-Dimensional Spectral Type for the HD Stars (Ann Arbor, 1988). 4 vols.

Mills, H. R. *Positional Astronomy and Astro-Navigation Made Easy* (Cheltenham, UK, 1978).

★Motz, Lloyd, and Nathanson, Carol. *The Constellations* (New York, 1988).

*Muirden, James. *The Amateur Astronomer's Handbook* (New York, 1982; 3rd ed.).

—. *How to Use an Astronomical Telescope* (New York, 1985).

*Newton, Jack, and Teece, Philip. *The Guide to Amateur Astronomy* (Cambridge, UK, 1988).

*Nicolson, Iain, and Moore, Patrick. *The Universe* (London, 1985).

Petit, Michel. *Variable Stars* (New York, 1987).

*Ridpath, Ian and Tirion, Wil. *Universe Guide to Stars and Planets* (New York, 1984).

Smithsonian Astrophysical Observatory Catalogue (Washington, DC, 1966). 4 vols.

*Tirion, Wil. *Sky Atlas 2000.0* (Cambridge, MA, 1981).

Wyatt, Stanley P. *Principles of Astronomy* (Boston, 1977; 3rd ed.).

INDEXES

The star names in the "Also Known As" column refer to the following individuals:

B	W. H. van den Bos
β	S. W. Burnham
Dawes	William R. Dawes
DUN	David Dunlap Observatory, Ontario
h	Sir John Herschel
Ho	G. W. Hough
Hu	W. J. Hussey
I	R. T. Innes
Kui	G. P. Kuiper
S	J. South
See	T. J. J. See
OΣ	Otto Struve
Σ	F. G. W. Struve

I have added a few last-minute variable names in the "also known as" column for a number of stars, although these late additions are not so indicated on the Starlist tables or in the Variable Star section.

Stars Arranged by Right Ascension

R.A.	Declin.	HD	Star	Const.	ADS	Also Known As	R(30)	S(30)	R(40)	S(40)	R(50)	S(50)
00 01 35.8	−77 03 57	224889	θ	Oct			nv	nv	(cp)	(cp)	(cp)	(cp)
00 01 49.3	−03 01 39	224926	29	Psc			93	267	94	266	95	265
00 01 57.5	−06 00 51	224935	30	Psc		YY	97	263	98	262	99	261
00 02 10.1	+27 04 56	224930	85	Peg	17175	β733	58	302	54	306	45	315
00 02 19.9	−29 43 15	224990	ζ	Scl			124	236	129	231	139	221
00 02 36.0	+66 05 57	225009	Σ3053	(Cas)	1		cp	cp	cp	cp	cp	cp
00 03 44.3	−17 20 10	225132	2	Cet			110	250	112	248	117	243
00 04 30.0	−10 30 35	225212	3	Cet			102	258	103	257	106	254
00 04 36.6	+42 05 32	225218	OΣ514	(And)	30		39	321	29	331	cp	cp
00 05 20.1	+05 42 27	28	33	Psc		BC	84	276	83	277	82	278
00 06 15.9	+58 26 12	123	Σ3062	(Cas)	61		12	348	cp	cp	cp	cp
00 08 23.2	+29 05 26	358	α	And	94	21, δPeg	56	304	51	309	41	319
00 09 10.6	+59 08 59	432	β	Cas	107	11	8	352	cp	cp	cp	cp
00 09 20.9	−27 59 16	493	κ¹	Scl	111	β391	122	238	126	234	135	225
00 09 24.6	−45 44 51	496	ε	Phe			145	215	157	203	nv	nv
00 10 02.3	−82 13 27	636	γ³	Oct			nv	nv	(cp)	(cp)	(cp)	(cp)
00 10 19.2	+46 04 20	571	22	And			34	326	20	340	cp	cp
00 11 15.8	−15 28 05	693	6	Cet			107	253	110	250	114	246
00 11 34.4	−27 47 59	720	κ²	Scl			122	238	126	234	135	225
00 11 43.9	−35 07 59	739	θ	Scl			131	229	138	222	153	207
00 13 14.1	+15 11 01	886	γ	Peg		88	73	287	70	290	66	294
00 14 27.5	−07 46 50	1014	AD	Cet			98	262	99	261	101	259
00 14 36.1	+20 12 24	1013	χ	Peg		89	67	293	63	297	58	302
00 14 38.3	−18 55 58	1038	7	Cet		AE	111	249	114	246	119	241
00 15 22.6	−32 02 41	1115	S	Scl			128	232	134	226	146	214
00 16 21.5	+43 35 42	1185	h1947	(And)	215		38	322	27	333	cp	cp
00 17 05.4	+38 40 54	1280	θ	And		24	45	315	37	323	17	343
00 18 12.9	+44 01 22	1326	Grb34	And	246		37	323	25	335	cp	cp
00 18 19.6	+36 47 07	1404	σ	And		25	47	313	40	320	24	336
00 19 25.6	−08 49 26	1522	ι	Cet		8, h1953	99	261	100	260	103	257
00 20 04.2	−64 52 30	1581	ζ	Tuc			nv	nv	(cp)	(cp)	(cp)	(cp)
00 21 07.2	+37 58 07	1671	ρ	And		27	46	314	38	322	21	339
00 21 31.2	−28 58 54	1737	ι	Scl			123	237	128	232	137	223
00 21 46.3	−20 03 28	1760	T	Cet			113	247	117	243	122	238
00 24 01.9	+38 34 38	1967	R	And			45	315	37	323	17	343
00 25 45.3	−77 15 16	2151	β	Hyi			nv	nv	(cp)	(cp)	(cp)	(cp)
00 26 12.1	−43 40 48	2262	κ	Phe			142	218	153	207	nv	nv
00 26 17.0	−42 18 22	2261	α	Phe			141	219	151	209	nv	nv
00 27 55.7	−33 00 26	2429	η	Scl			129	231	135	225	148	212
00 28 02.9	+17 53 36	2411	47	Psc		TV	70	290	68	292	63	297
00 28 13.7	+44 23 40	2421	—	And			37	323	25	335	cp	cp
00 30 07.3	+29 45 06	2628	28	And		GN	56	304	51	309	41	319
00 30 22.6	−23 47 16	2696	—	Cet			117	243	121	239	127	233
00 31 24.9	−48 48 13	2834	λ¹	Phe			149	211	166	194	nv	nv
00 31 32.7	−62 57 30	2884	β¹	Tuc			nv	nv	(cp)	(cp)	(cp)	(cp)

2000.0 R.A.			2000.0 Declin.			HD	Star	Const.	ADS	Also Known As	Rising and Setting Azimuths					
											R(30)	S(30)	R(40)	S(40)	R(50)	S(50)
00	31	33.6	−62	57	57	2885	β²	Tuc			nv	nv	(cp)	(cp)	(cp)	(cp)
00	31	46.3	+54	31	20	2772	λ	Cas	434	14, OΣ12	21	339	cp	cp	cp	cp
00	32	43.8	−63	01	53	3003	β³	Tuc			nv	nv	(cp)	(cp)	(cp)	(cp)
00	32	59.9	+62	55	55	2905	κ	Cas		15	cp	cp	cp	cp	cp	cp
00	35	14.8	−03	35	34	3196	13	Cet	490	Ho 212	93	267	94	266	95	265
00	36	08.2	+54	10	07	3240	—	Cas			21	339	cp	cp	cp	cp
00	36	46.5	+44	29	19	3346	—	And			37	323	25	335	cp	cp
00	36	52.8	+33	43	10	3369	π	And	513	29	51	309	45	315	32	328
00	36	58.2	+53	53	49	3360	ζ	Cas		17	23	337	cp	cp	cp	cp
00	37	20.6	−24	46	02	3443	β395	(Cet)	520		118	242	122	238	129	231
00	38	33.3	+29	18	43	3546	ε	And		30	56	304	51	309	41	319
00	39	09.8	+49	21	16	3574	OΣ16	(Cas)	546		29	331	10	350	cp	cp
00	39	19.6	+30	51	40	3627	δ	And	548	31, β491	55	305	49	311	39	321
00	40	30.4	+56	32	15	3712	α	Cas	561	18	17	343	cp	cp	cp	cp
00	41	19.5	−46	05	06	3919	μ	Phe			146	214	160	200	nv	nv
00	42	03.8	+50	30	45	3901	ξ	Cas		19	28	332	cp	cp	cp	cp
00	42	28.4	−65	28	05	4089	ρ	Tuc			nv	nv	(cp)	(cp)	(cp)	(cp)
00	42	42.8	−38	27	48	4065	λ¹	Scl			135	225	143	217	163	197
00	43	21.2	−57	27	47	4150	η	Phe		h3391	166	194	nv	nv	nv	nv
00	43	28.0	+47	01	29	4058	π	Cas		20	32	328	17	343	cp	cp
00	43	35.3	−17	59	12	4128	β	Cet		16	110	250	112	248	117	243
00	44	11.3	−10	36	34	4188	φ¹	Cet		17	102	258	103	257	106	254
00	44	43.5	+48	17	04	4180	o	Cas	622	22, β231	31	329	14	346	cp	cp
00	44	44.3	−22	00	22	4247	—	Cet			116	244	119	241	126	234
00	47	20.3	+24	16	02	4502	ζ	And		34	62	298	58	302	51	309
00	48	35.4	−74	55	25	4815	λ	Hyi			nv	nv	(cp)	(cp)	(cp)	(cp)
00	48	40.9	+07	35	06	4656	δ	Psc		63	82	278	81	279	79	281
00	48	50.0	+50	58	06	4636	ν	Cas		25	28	332	cp	cp	cp	cp
00	48	58.6	+16	56	26	4676	64	Psc			71	289	69	291	65	295
00	49	06.0	+57	48	58	4614	η	Cas	671	24, Σ60	14	346	cp	cp	cp	cp
00	49	48.8	+41	04	44	4727	ν	And		35	41	319	31	329	cp	cp
00	49	53.1	+27	42	37	4757	65ᴮ	Psc	683		58	302	54	306	45	315
00	49	53.5	+27	42	35	4758	65ᴬ	Psc	683	Σ61	58	302	54	306	45	315
00	50	07.5	−10	38	40	4813	φ²	Cet		19	102	258	103	257	106	254
00	50	41.0	−50	59	13	4919	ρ	Phe			152	208	180	180	nv	nv
00	52	24.4	−69	30	16	5190	λ¹	Tuc			nv	nv	(cp)	(cp)	(cp)	(cp)
00	53	00.4	−01	08	40	5112	20	Cet			91	269	91	269	92	268
00	53	04.1	+61	07	27	5015	β497	(Cas)	721		cp	cp	cp	cp	cp	cp
00	54	58.0	+23	37	42	5286	36	And	755	Σ73	63	297	59	301	53	307
00	55	00.0	+58	58	22	5234	υ¹	Cas	748	26, β1098	12	348	cp	cp	cp	cp
00	55	00.3	−69	31	38	5457	λ²	Tuc			nv	nv	(cp)	(cp)	(cp)	(cp)
00	56	01.4	−11	16	00	5437	φ³	Cet		22	103	257	104	256	107	253
00	56	39.7	+59	10	52	5395	υ²	Cas		28	8	352	cp	cp	cp	cp
00	56	42.4	+60	43	00	5394	γ	Cas	782	27, β1028	cp	cp	cp	cp	cp	cp
00	56	45.1	+38	29	58	5448	μ	And	788	37, h1057	45	315	37	323	17	343
00	57	12.4	+23	25	04	5516	η	And		38	63	297	59	301	53	307
00	58	36.3	−29	21	28	5737	α	Scl			124	236	129	231	139	221
01	02	26.3	−31	33	07	6178	σ	Scl			126	234	132	228	143	217
01	02	49.0	+31	48	16	6118	σ	Psc		69	54	306	48	312	37	323
01	02	56.5	+07	53	24	6186	ε	Psc		71	82	278	81	279	79	281

2000.0 R.A.	Declin.	HD	Star	Const.	ADS	Also Known As	Rising and Setting Azimuths R(30)	S(30)	R(40)	S(40)	R(50)	S(50)
01 05 40.9	+21 28 24	6456	ψ¹	Psc		74, Σ88	66	294	62	298	56	304
01 06 05.0	−46 43 08	6595	β	Phe			146	214	160	200	nv	nv
01 07 18.7	−61 46 31	6793	ι	Tuc			nv	nv	(cp)	(cp)	(cp)	(cp)
01 07 47.8	−41 29 14	6767	υ	Phe			139	221	149	211	nv	nv
01 08 00.8	+43 56 32	6658	41	And			38	322	27	333	cp	cp
01 08 16.3	+54 55 14	6582	μ	Cas		30	21	339	cp	cp	cp	cp
01 08 23.0	−55 14 45	6882	ζ	Phe			161	199	nv	nv	nv	nv
01 08 35.3	−10 10 56	6805	η	Cet		31	102	258	103	257	106	254
01 08 44.9	+86 15 26	5848	—	Cep		2 UMi	cp	cp	cp	cp	cp	cp
01 09 30.1	+47 14 31	6811	φ	And	940	42, OΣ515	32	328	17	343	cp	cp
01 09 43.9	+35 37 14	6860	β	And	949	43	49	311	42	318	27	333
01 11 06.1	+55 09 00	6961	θ	Cas		33	19	341	cp	cp	cp	cp
01 11 06.7	+31 25 29	7034	82	Psc			54	306	48	312	37	323
01 11 27.1	+21 02 05	7087	χ	Psc		84	66	294	62	298	56	304
01 11 39.6	+30 05 23	7106	τ	Psc		83	55	305	49	311	39	321
01 13 43.8	+07 34 31	7344	ζᴬ	Psc	996	86, Σ100/β1029	82	278	81	279	79	281
01 13 44.8	+24 35 01	7318	φ	Psc		85, Σ99	62	298	58	302	51	309
01 13 45.2	+07 34 42	7345	ζᴮ	Psc		86	82	278	81	279	79	281
01 14 24.0	−07 55 23	7439	37	Cet	1003	Σ3	98	262	99	261	101	259
01 15 11.1	−45 31 54	7570	ν	Phe			145	215	157	203	nv	nv
01 15 46.2	−68 52 34	7788	κ	Tuc		h3423	nv	nv	(cp)	(cp)	(cp)	(cp)
01 17 47.9	+03 36 52	7804	89	Psc			87	273	86	274	85	275
01 19 27.9	+27 15 51	7964	υ	Psc		90	58	302	54	306	45	315
01 20 04.8	+58 13 54	7927	φ	Cas	1073	34	12	348	cp	cp	cp	cp
01 21 07.3	+28 44 18	8126	91	Psc			57	303	52	308	43	317
01 22 20.3	+45 31 44	8207	ξ	And		46	35	325	23	337	cp	cp
01 24 01.3	−08 11 01	8512	θ	Cet	1118	45, β505	99	261	100	260	103	257
01 25 37.1	−14 35 56	8705	46	Cet			106	254	108	252	112	248
01 25 48.9	+60 14 07	8538	δ	Cas		37	cp	cp	cp	cp	cp	cp
01 25 56.0	+68 07 48	8491	ψ	Cas	1129	36	cp	cp	cp	cp	cp	cp
01 26 15.2	+19 10 20	8723	ρ	Psc		93	68	292	65	295	60	300
01 26 58.0	−32 32 36	8879	R	Scl			128	232	134	226	146	214
01 27 39.2	+45 24 25	8799	ω	And	1152	48, β999	35	325	23	337	cp	cp
01 28 21.9	−43 19 06	9053	γ	Phe			142	218	153	207	nv	nv
01 29 36.1	−21 37 46	9132	48	Cet	1184	See 14	114	246	118	242	124	236
01 30 11.1	+06 08 38	9138	μ	Psc		98	83	277	82	278	81	279
01 31 15.0	−49 04 22	9362	δ	Phe			151	209	170	190	nv	nv
01 31 28.9	+15 20 45	9270	η	Psc	1199	99, β506	73	287	70	290	66	294
01 33 55.9	+59 13 56	9408	χ	Cas		39	8	352	cp	cp	cp	cp
01 36 08.3	−29 54 27	9906	τ	Scl		h3447	124	236	129	231	139	221
01 36 47.8	+41 24 20	9826	υ	And		50	41	319	31	329	cp	cp
01 37 42.9	−57 14 12	10144	α	Eri			166	194	nv	nv	nv	nv
01 39 20.9	+44 23 10	10072	χ	And		52	37	323	25	335	cp	cp
01 39 47.4	−56 11 53	10360	pᴮ	Eri			163	197	nv	nv	nv	nv
01 39 47.7	−56 11 41	10361	pᴬ	Eri		DUN 5	163	197	nv	nv	nv	nv
01 40 34.7	+40 34 37	10205	τ	And		53	42	318	33	327	1	359
01 41 25.8	+05 29 15	10380	ν	Psc		106	84	276	83	277	82	278
01 41 47.1	+42 36 49	10307	—	And			39	321	29	331	cp	cp
01 42 08.5	−32 19 37	10537	π	Scl			128	232	134	226	146	214
01 42 29.7	+20 16 07	10476	107	Psc			67	293	63	297	58	302

| 2000.0 | | | HD | Star | Const. | ADS | Also Known As | Rising and Setting Azimuths | | | | | |
R.A.		Declin.						R(30)	S(30)	R(40)	S(40)	R(50)	S(50)
01 42 43.4	−03 41 25		10550	—	Cet			93	267	94	266	95	265
01 42 55.8	+70 37 22		10250	42	Cas			cp	cp	cp	cp	cp	cp
01 43 39.6	+50 41 20		10516	φ	Per			28	332	cp	cp	cp	cp
01 44 04.0	−15 56 15		10700	τ	Cet		52	107	253	110	250	114	246
01 45 23.6	+09 09 28		10761	o	Psc		110	80	280	78	282	76	284
01 45 38.7	−25 03 10		10830	ε	Scl	1394	h3461	119	241	123	237	131	229
01 46 06.3	−53 31 19		10939	q²	Eri			157	203	nv	nv	nv	nv
01 49 35.0	−10 41 11		11171	χ	Cet		53	102	258	103	257	106	254
01 51 27.5	−10 20 06		11353	ζ	Cet		55	102	258	103	257	106	254
01 52 34.8	−67 56 40		11733	η¹	Hyi			nv	nv	(cp)	(cp)	(cp)	(cp)
01 53 04.8	+29 34 44		11443	α	Tri		2	56	304	51	309	41	319
01 53 31.7	+19 17 45		11503	γ¹	Ari		5	68	292	65	295	60	300
01 53 31.8	+19 17 37		11502	γ²	Ari	1507	5, Σ180	68	292	65	295	60	300
01 53 33.3	+03 11 15		11559	ξ	Psc		111	87	273	86	274	85	275
01 53 38.7	−46 18 10		11695	ψ	Phe			146	214	160	200	nv	nv
01 54 21.9	−42 29 50		11753	φ	Phe			141	219	151	209	nv	nv
01 54 23.6	+63 40 13		11415	ε	Cas		45	cp	cp	cp	cp	cp	cp
01 54 38.3	+20 48 29		11636	β	Ari		6	67	293	63	297	58	302
01 54 56.1	−67 38 51		11977	η²	Hyi			nv	nv	(cp)	(cp)	(cp)	(cp)
01 55 53.7	+01 50 59		11803	Σ186	(Cet)	1538		89	271	89	271	88	272
01 55 57.5	−51 36 32		11937	χ	Eri		h3473	154	206	nv	nv	nv	nv
01 55 59.9	+68 41 07		11529	ω	Cas		46	cp	cp	cp	cp	cp	cp
01 56 40.1	−22 31 36		11930	56	Cet			116	244	119	241	126	234
01 57 10.0	−47 23 06		12055	—	Phe			148	212	163	197	nv	nv
01 57 21.0	+17 49 03		11909	ι	Ari		8	70	290	68	292	63	297
01 57 55.7	+23 35 46		11973	λ	Ari	1563	9	63	297	59	301	53	307
01 58 46.2	−61 34 12		12311	α	Hyi			nv	nv	(cp)	(cp)	(cp)	(cp)
01 59 37.9	+64 37 18		11946	h1100	(Cas)	1571		cp	cp	cp	cp	cp	cp
02 00 00.2	−21 04 40		12274	υ	Cet		59	114	246	118	242	124	236
02 01 14.7	−30 00 07		12438	π	For			125	235	131	229	141	219
02 01 42.3	−44 42 48		12524	χ	Phe			143	217	155	205	nv	nv
02 01 57.3	+70 54 26		12111	48	Cas			cp	cp	cp	cp	cp	cp
02 02 02.7	+02 45 49		12446	αᴮ	Psc		13	88	272	87	273	87	273
02 02 02.7	+02 45 49		12447	αᴬ	Psc	1615	113, Σ202	88	272	87	273	87	273
02 02 18.0	+54 29 16		12303	4	Per			21	339	cp	cp	cp	cp
02 02 57.9	+33 17 03		12471	ε	Tri	1621	3, Σ201	51	309	45	315	32	328
02 03 26.0	+72 25 17		12216	50	Cas			cp	cp	cp	cp	cp	cp
02 03 53.9	+42 19 47		12533	γ¹	And	1630	57, Σ205	39	321	29	331	cp	cp
02 03 54.7	+42 19 51		12534	γ²	And	1630	57, OΣ38	39	321	29	331	cp	cp
02 04 29.4	−29 17 49		12767	ν	For			124	236	129	231	139	221
02 05 31.2	+76 06 55		12339	49	Cas			cp	cp	cp	cp	cp	cp
02 06 33.8	+22 38 54		12869	κ	Ari		12	64	296	61	299	54	306
02 07 10.3	+23 27 45		12929	α	Ari		13	63	297	59	301	53	307
02 08 29.2	+37 51 33		13041	58	And			46	314	38	322	21	339
02 09 25.3	+25 56 24		13174	14	Ari			61	299	57	303	49	311
02 09 32.5	+34 59 14		13161	β	Tri		4	50	310	43	317	30	330
02 12 22.2	+30 18 11		13480	ι	Tri	1697	6, Σ227	55	305	49	311	39	321
02 12 48.0	+21 12 39		13555	η	Ari		17	66	294	62	298	56	304
02 12 54.4	−30 43 26		13709	μ	For			125	235	131	229	141	219
02 12 59.9	+08 50 48		13611	ξ¹	Cet		65	81	279	80	280	77	283

R.A. 2000.0	Declin.	HD	Star	Const.	ADS	Also Known As	R(30)	S(30)	R(40)	S(40)	R(50)	S(50)
02 13 13.2	+44 13 55	13520	60	And			37	323	25	335	cp	cp
02 14 14.8	−67 50 31	14141	π¹	Hyi			nv	nv	(cp)	(cp)	(cp)	(cp)
02 15 28.6	−67 44 48	14287	π²	Hyi			nv	nv	(cp)	(cp)	(cp)	(cp)
02 16 30.6	−51 30 44	14228	φ	Eri		DUN 6	154	206	nv	nv	nv	nv
02 17 03.2	+34 13 28	13974	δ	Tri	1739	8	50	310	43	317	30	330
02 17 18.8	+33 50 50	14055	γ	Tri		9	51	309	45	315	32	328
02 18 57.0	+28 38 33	14252	10	Tri			57	303	52	308	43	317
02 19 20.7	−02 58 39	14386	o	Cet	1778	68	92	268	93	267	93	267
02 21 45.1	−68 39 34	15008	δ	Hyi			nv	nv	(cp)	(cp)	(cp)	(cp)
02 22 21.3	+55 50 45	14489	9	Per		V474	19	341	cp	cp	cp	cp
02 22 32.5	−23 48 59	14802	κ	For			117	243	121	239	127	233
02 22 51.7	+58 35 13	14528	S	Per			12	348	cp	cp	cp	cp
02 22 52.3	−73 38 45	15248	κ	Hyi			nv	nv	(cp)	(cp)	(cp)	(cp)
02 24 24.8	+50 00 24	14770	64	And			28	332	cp	cp	cp	cp
02 24 49.0	+10 36 38	14951	ξ	Ari		24	78	282	77	283	74	286
02 24 53.9	−60 18 43	15233	λ	Hor			180	180	nv	nv	nv	nv
02 25 37.3	+50 16 43	14872	65	And			28	332	cp	cp	cp	cp
02 25 56.9	−12 17 26	15130	ρ	Cet		72	104	256	106	254	109	251
02 26 59.1	−47 42 14	15371	κ	Eri			148	212	163	197	nv	nv
02 28 01.6	−33 48 40	15427	φ	For			129	231	135	225	148	212
02 28 09.5	+08 27 36	15318	ξ²	Cet		73	81	279	80	280	77	283
02 29 03.9	+67 24 09	15089	ι	Cas	1860	Σ262	cp	cp	cp	cp	cp	cp
02 31 40.7	−79 06 34	16522	μ	Hyi			nv	nv	(cp)	(cp)	(cp)	(cp)
02 31 50.5	+89 15 51	8890	α	UMi	1477	1, Σ93	cp	cp	cp	cp	cp	cp
02 32 05.1	−15 14 41	15798	σ	Cet		76	107	253	110	250	114	246
02 32 06.1	+36 08 50	15656	14	Tri			47	313	40	320	24	336
02 33 50.6	−28 13 57	16046	ω	For	1954	h3506	123	237	128	232	137	223
02 35 52.4	+05 35 36	16161	ν	Cet	1971	78, Σ281	84	276	83	277	82	278
02 36 57.7	+24 38 54	16232	30B	Ari	1982		62	298	58	302	51	309
02 36 58.5	−34 34 42	16417	λ²	For			130	230	137	223	150	210
02 37 00.4	+24 38 51	16246	30A	Ari	1982		62	298	58	302	51	309
02 37 02.4	+34 15 50	16210	R	Tri			50	310	43	317	30	330
02 37 24.2	−52 32 36	16555	η	Hor			155	205	nv	nv	(cp)	(cp)
02 38 01.9	+72 49 06	15920	—	Cas			cp	cp	cp	cp	cp	cp
02 38 48.9	+21 57 41	16432	ν	Ari		32	66	294	62	298	56	304
02 39 28.9	+00 19 43	16582	δ	Cet		82	90	270	90	270	90	270
02 39 33.7	−11 52 20	16620	ε	Cet		83	103	257	104	256	107	253
02 39 35.5	−68 16 01	16978	ε	Hyi			nv	nv	(cp)	(cp)	(cp)	(cp)
02 39 47.9	−42 53 30	16754	—	Eri			141	219	151	209	nv	nv
02 40 39.6	−54 33 00	16920	ζ	Hor			159	201	nv	nv	nv	nv
02 40 40.0	−39 51 19	16815	ι	Eri			137	223	145	215	168	192
02 40 41.0	+27 03 39	16628	33	Ari	2033	Σ289	58	302	54	306	54	315
02 42 14.9	+40 11 38	16739	12	Per			42	318	33	327	cp	cp
02 42 33.4	−50 48 01	17051	ι	Hor			152	208	180	180	nv	nv
02 43 18.0	+03 14 09	16970	γ	Cet	2080	86, Σ299	87	273	86	274	85	275
02 43 27.0	+27 42 26	16908	35	Ari			58	302	54	306	45	315
02 44 07.3	−13 51 32	17081	π	Cet		89	105	255	107	253	110	250
02 44 11.9	+49 13 43	16895	θ	Per	2081	13, Σ296	29	331	10	350	cp	cp
02 44 56.5	+10 06 51	17094	μ	Cet		87	78	282	77	283	74	286
02 44 57.5	+12 26 45	17093	38	Ari		UV	76	284	74	286	71	289

R.A.	Declin.	HD	Star	Const.	ADS	Also Known As	R(30)	S(30)	R(40)	S(40)	R(50)	S(50)
02 45 06.1	−18 34 21	17206	τ^1	Eri		1	111	249	114	246	119	241
02 45 32.6	−67 37 00	17566	ζ	Hyi			nv	nv	(cp)	(cp)	(cp)	(cp)
02 47 54.5	+29 14 50	17361	39	Ari			56	304	51	309	41	319
02 49 01.5	−62 48 24	17848	ν	Hor			nv	nv	(cp)	(cp)	(cp)	(cp)
02 49 05.4	−32 24 22	17652	β	For			128	232	134	226	146	214
02 49 17.5	+17 27 51	17543	π	Ari	2151	42, Σ311	70	290	68	292	63	297
02 49 50.9	−24 33 37	17713	γ^1	For	2167	β877	118	242	122	238	129	231
02 49 54.1	−27 56 31	17729	γ^2	For			122	238	126	234	135	225
02 49 59.0	+27 15 38	17573	41	Ari	2159	OΣ47rej	58	302	54	306	45	315
02 50 14.7	−35 50 37	17793	η^2	For		h3536	131	229	138	222	153	207
02 50 28.7	−75 04 01	18293	ν	Hyi			nv	nv	(cp)	(cp)	(cp)	(cp)
02 50 34.9	+38 19 07	17584	16	Per			45	315	37	323	17	343
02 50 40.3	−35 40 34	17829	η^3	For			131	229	138	222	153	207
02 50 41.8	+55 53 44	17506	η	Per	2157	15, Σ307	19	341	cp	cp	cp	cp
02 51 02.2	−21 00 15	17824	τ^2	Eri	2179	2	114	246	118	242	124	236
02 51 29.5	+15 04 55	17769	σ	Ari		43	73	287	70	290	66	294
02 51 30.8	+35 03 35	17709	17	Per			49	311	42	318	27	333
02 53 52.8	−49 53 25	18242	R	Hor			151	209	170	190	nv	nv
02 54 15.4	+52 45 45	17878	τ	Per	2202	18	25	335	cp	cp	cp	cp
02 56 25.6	−08 53 53	18322	η	Eri		3	99	261	100	260	103	257
02 56 37.4	−03 42 44	18331	—	Eri			93	267	94	266	95	265
02 57 17.2	+31 56 03	18296	21	Per		LT	54	306	48	312	37	323
02 58 15.6	−40 18 17	18622	θ^1	Eri			138	222	147	213	179	181
02 58 16.2	−40 18 16	18623	θ^2	Eri			138	222	147	213	179	181
02 58 42.0	−02 46 57	18543	—	Eri			92	268	93	267	93	267
02 58 45.6	+39 39 46	18411	π	Per		22	43	317	35	325	12	348
02 58 47.8	−64 04 16	18866	β	Hor			nv	nv	(cp)	(cp)	(cp)	(cp)
02 59 03.6	+35 10 59	18449	24	Per			49	311	42	318	27	333
02 59 12.6	+21 20 25	18520	ε	Ari	2257	48, Σ333	66	294	62	298	56	304
02 59 42.8	+08 54 27	18604	λ	Cet		91	81	279	80	280	77	283
03 00 52.1	+52 21 06	18537	Σ331A	(Per)	2270		25	335	cp	cp	cp	cp
03 00 53.3	+52 21 08	18538	Σ331B	(Per)			25	335	cp	cp	cp	cp
03 02 16.7	+04 05 23	18884	α	Cet		92	85	275	85	275	84	276
03 02 23.5	−23 37 28	18978	τ^3	Eri		11	117	243	121	239	127	233
03 02 42.2	−07 41 07	18953	ρ^2	Eri	2312	9, β11	98	262	99	261	101	259
03 03 36.8	−59 44 16	19319	μ	Hor			172	188	nv	nv	nv	nv
03 04 16.3	−07 36 03	19107	ρ^3	Eri		10	98	262	99	261	101	259
03 04 47.7	+53 30 23	18925	γ	Per	2324	23, h2170	23	337	cp	cp	cp	cp
03 05 10.5	+38 50 25	19058	ρ	Per		25	45	315	37	323	17	343
03 05 32.4	+56 42 21	18970	k	Per			17	343	cp	cp	cp	cp
03 08 10.1	+40 57 21	19356	β	Per	2362	26, β526	42	318	33	327	cp	cp
03 09 04.0	+49 36 48	19373	ι	Per			29	331	10	350	cp	cp
03 09 29.7	+44 51 27	19476	κ	Per	2368	27	37	323	25	335	cp	cp
03 11 17.3	+39 36 42	19656	ω	Per		28	43	317	35	325	12	348
03 11 37.7	+19 43 36	19787	δ	Ari		57	68	292	65	295	60	300
03 11 56.3	+74 23 37	19275	—	Cas			cp	cp	cp	cp	cp	cp
03 12 04.2	−28 59 14	20010	α	For	2402	h3555	123	237	128	232	137	223
03 12 14.2	+27 15 26	19832	SX	Ari		56	58	302	54	306	45	315
03 12 46.4	−01 11 46	19994	94	Cet	2406	h663	91	269	91	269	92	268
03 14 54.0	+21 02 40	20150	ζ	Ari		58	66	294	62	298	56	304

The header rows:

	2000.0						Also	Rising and Setting Azimuths					

2000.0 R.A.			Declin.			HD	Star	Const.	ADS	Also Known As	Rising and Setting Azimuths					
											R(30)	S(30)	R(40)	S(40)	R(50)	S(50)
03	15	49.9	−08	49	11	20320	ζ	Eri		13	99	261	100	260	103	257
03	16	12.1	+50	56	16	20123	—	Per			28	332	cp	cp	cp	cp
03	17	46.1	−62	34	32	20766	ζ¹	Ret			nv	nv	(cp)	(cp)	(cp)	(cp)
03	18	12.8	−62	30	23	20807	ζ²	Ret			nv	nv	(cp)	(cp)	(cp)	(cp)
03	18	22.1	−22	30	41	20610	15	Eri	2463	See 23	116	244	119	241	126	234
03	18	37.7	+50	13	20	20365	29	Per			28	332	cp	cp	cp	cp
03	18	43.7	+34	13	21	20468	—	Per			50	310	43	317	30	330
03	19	07.6	+50	05	42	20418	31	Per			28	332	cp	cp	cp	cp
03	19	21.6	+03	22	13	20630	κ¹	Cet		96	87	273	86	274	85	275
03	19	30.9	−21	45	28	20720	τ⁴	Eri	2472	16	114	246	118	242	124	236
03	19	55.6	−43	04	11	20794	82	Eri			142	218	153	207	nv	nv
03	19	59.3	+65	39	09	20336	BK	Cam			cp	cp	cp	cp	cp	cp
03	20	20.3	+29	02	55	20644	—	Ari			56	304	51	309	441	319
03	21	13.6	+21	08	49	20756	τ¹	Ari		61	66	294	62	298	56	304
03	21	26.5	+43	19	47	20677	32	Per			38	322	27	333	cp	cp
03	22	45.2	+20	44	31	20893	τ²	Ari		61	67	293	63	297	58	302
03	24	19.3	+49	51	41	20902	α	Per		33	29	331	10	350	cp	cp
03	24	48.7	+09	01	44	21120	o	Tau		1	80	280	78	282	76	284
03	27	10.1	+09	43	58	21364	ξ	Tau		2	80	280	78	282	76	284
03	28	03.0	+49	03	46	21278	—	Per			29	331	10	350	cp	cp
03	29	04.1	+59	56	25	21291	Σ385	(Cam)	2544		8	352	cp	cp	cp	cp
03	29	22.0	+49	30	32	21428	34	Per	2558	β1179	29	331	10	350	cp	cp
03	29	22.6	−62	56	16	22001	κ	Ret			nv	nv	(cp)	(cp)	(cp)	(cp)
03	29	54.8	+58	52	44	21389	—	Cam			12	348	cp	cp	cp	cp
03	30	00.2	+55	27	07	21447	Σ390	(Cam)	2565		19	341	cp	cp	cp	cp
03	30	03.2	+35	40	17	21567	R	Per			49	311	42	318	27	333
03	30	24.4	+11	20	11	21686	4	Tau			77	283	76	284	73	287
03	30	34.4	+47	59	43	21552	σ	Per		35	32	328	17	343	cp	cp
03	30	37.0	−05	04	31	21790	17	Eri			96	264	97	263	98	262
03	30	52.3	+12	56	12	21754	5	Tau			76	284	74	286	71	289
03	32	55.8	−09	27	30	22049	ε	Eri		18	100	260	102	258	104	256
03	33	47.2	−21	37	59	22203	τ⁵	Eri		19	114	246	118	242	124	236
03	36	17.3	−17	28	02	22470	20	Eri		EG	110	250	112	248	117	243
03	36	29.3	+48	11	34	22192	ψ	Per		37	31	329	14	346	cp	cp
03	36	47.2	+00	35	16	22468	Σ422	(Tau)	2644	V711	90	270	90	270	90	270
03	36	52.3	+00	24	06	22484	10	Tau			90	270	90	270	90	270
03	37	05.6	−40	16	29	22663	y	Eri			138	222	147	213	179	181
03	42	09.3	+63	13	01	22649	BD	Cam			cp	cp	cp	cp	cp	cp
03	42	14.9	−31	56	18	23227	δ	For			126	234	132	228	143	217
03	42	22.5	+33	57	54	22951	Σ431	(Per)	2699		51	309	45	315	32	328
03	42	50.0	−37	18	49	23319	—	Eri			134	226	142	218	159	201
03	42	55.4	+47	47	15	22928	δ	Per		39	32	328	17	343	cp	cp
03	43	14.8	−09	45	48	23249	δ	Eri		23	100	260	102	258	104	256
03	44	12.0	−64	48	26	23817	β	Ret			nv	nv	(cp)	(cp)	(cp)	(cp)
03	44	19.1	+32	17	18	23180	o	Per	2726	38, β535	52	308	46	314	34	326
03	44	48.1	+24	17	22	23288	16	Tau			62	298	58	302	51	309
03	44	52.5	+24	06	48	23302	17	Tau			62	298	58	302	51	309
03	45	11.6	+42	34	43	23230	ν	Per	2738	41	39	321	29	331	cp	cp
03	45	12.4	+24	28	02	23338	19	Tau		h3251	62	298	58	302	51	309
03	45	49.5	+24	22	04	23408	20	Tau			62	298	58	302	51	309

2000.0 R.A.			Declin.			HD	Star	Const.	ADS	Also Known As	Rising and Setting Azimuths R(30)	S(30)	R(40)	S(40)	R(50)	S(50)
03	45	54.3	+24	33	17	23432	21	Tau			62	298	58	302	51	309
03	46	02.3	+63	20	42	23089	—	Cam			cp	cp	cp	cp	cp	cp
03	46	08.4	−12	06	06	23614	π	Eri		26	104	256	106	254	109	251
03	46	19.5	+23	56	54	23480	23	Tau		V971	63	297	59	301	53	307
03	46	50.8	−23	14	59	23754	τ⁶	Eri		27	117	243	121	239	127	233
03	47	14.5	−74	14	21	24512	γ	Hyi			nv	nv	(cp)	(cp)	(cp)	(cp)
03	47	29.0	+24	06	18	23630	η	Tau		25	62	298	58	302	51	309
03	47	39.6	−23	52	29	23878	τ⁷	Eri		28	117	243	121	329	127	233
03	48	16.2	+11	08	36	23793	30	Tau	2778	Σ452	77	283	76	284	73	287
03	48	35.3	−37	37	20	24071	fᴮ	Eri			134	226	142	218	159	201
03	48	35.8	−37	37	14	24072	fᴬ	Eri		DUN 16	134	226	142	218	159	201
03	49	09.7	+24	03	12	23850	27	Tau	2786	Σ453	62	298	58	302	51	309
03	49	11.1	+24	08	12	23862	28	Tau		BU	62	298	58	302	51	309
03	49	27.2	−36	12	01	24160	g	Eri			133	227	140	220	156	204
03	49	31.2	+65	31	34	23475	BE	Cam			cp	cp	cp	cp	cp	cp
03	49	32.6	+33	05	29	23848	42	Per		V467	51	309	45	315	32	328
03	50	21.5	+71	19	57	23401	γ	Cam		h2200	cp	cp	cp	cp	cp	cp
03	53	38.9	−34	43	57	24626	i	Eri			130	230	137	223	150	210
03	53	42.6	−24	36	45	24587	τ⁸	Eri		33	118	242	122	238	129	231
03	54	07.9	+31	53	01	24398	ζ	Per	2843	44, Σ464	54	306	48	312	37	323
03	54	17.3	−02	57	10	24554	32B	Eri			92	268	93	267	93	267
03	54	17.4	−02	57	17	24555	32A	Eri	2850	w, Σ470	92	268	93	267	93	267
03	55	22.9	+31	02	45	24534	X	Per	2859		54	306	48	312	37	323
03	57	08.2	+61	06	32	24480	OΣ67	(Cam)	2867		cp	cp	cp	cp	cp	cp
03	57	25.3	+63	04	20	24479	—	Cam			cp	cp	cp	cp	cp	cp
03	57	51.2	+40	00	37	24760	ε	Per	2888	45, Σ471	42	318	33	327	cp	cp
03	58	01.7	−13	30	31	25025	γ	Eri	2904	34, h3608	105	255	107	253	110	250
03	58	44.7	−61	24	01	25422	δ	Ret			nv	nv	(cp)	(cp)	(cp)	(cp)
03	58	57.8	+35	47	28	24912	ξ	Per		46	49	311	42	318	27	333
03	59	55.4	−24	00	59	25267	τ⁹	Eri		36	118	242	122	238	129	231
04	00	40.8	+12	29	25	25204	λ	Tau		35	76	284	74	286	71	289
04	00	53.8	−62	09	34	25705	γ	Ret			nv	nv	(cp)	(cp)	(cp)	(cp)
04	01	18.2	−61	04	44	25728	ι	Ret			nv	nv	(cp)	(cp)	(cp)	(cp)
04	03	09.3	+05	59	22	25490	ν	Tau		38	84	276	83	277	82	278
04	03	54.4	+28	07	33	25487	RW	Tau			57	303	52	308	43	317
04	04	27.1	+59	09	20	25291	—	Cam			8	352	cp	cp	cp	cp
04	04	41.7	+22	04	55	25604	37	Tau			64	296	61	299	54	306
04	06	35.0	+50	21	05	25642	λ	Per		47	28	332	cp	cp	cp	cp
04	06	36.3	+27	36	00	25823	41	Tau		GS	58	302	54	306	45	315
04	07	00.4	+29	00	05	25867	ψ	Tau		42	56	304	51	309	41	319
04	08	39.6	+47	42	45	25940	48	Per		MX	32	328	17	343	cp	cp
04	09	09.9	+19	36	33	26162	ω¹	Tau		50	68	292	65	295	60	300
04	10	02.8	+80	41	55	25007	Σ460	(Cep)	2963		cp	cp	cp	cp	cp	cp
04	10	50.5	−41	59	37	26612	δ	Hor			139	221	149	211	nv	nv
04	11	51.9	−06	50	16	26574	o¹	Eri		38	97	263	98	262	99	261
04	13	56.3	+09	15	49	26722	47	Tau	3072	β547	80	280	78	282	76	284
04	14	00.1	−42	17	40	26967	α	Hor			141	219	151	209	nv	nv
04	14	23.6	−10	15	23	26846	39	Eri	3079	Σ516	102	258	103	257	106	254
04	14	25.5	−62	28	26	27256	α	Ret		h3638	nv	nv	(cp)	(cp)	(cp)	(cp)
04	14	36.2	+10	00	40	26793	—	Tau			78	282	77	283	74	286

R.A.	Declin.	HD	Star	Const.	ADS	Also Known As	R(30)	S(30)	R(40)	S(40)	R(50)	S(50)
	2000.0					Also	Rising and Setting Azimuths					
04 14 53.3	+40 29 02	26673	52	Per			42	318	33	327	cp	cp
04 14 53.8	+48 24 34	26630	μ	Per	3071	51, OΣ73	31	329	14	346	cp	cp
04 15 16.3	−07 39 10	26965	o²	Eri	3093	40, Σ518	98	262	99	261	101	259
04 15 32.0	+08 53 32	26912	μ	Tau		49	81	279	80	280	77	283
04 16 01.6	−51 29 12	27290	γ	Dor			154	206	nv	nv	nv	nv
04 16 28.9	−59 18 07	27442	ε	Ret			nv	nv	(cp)	(cp)	(cp)	(cp)
04 16 43.1	+53 36 43	26764	—	Cam			23	337	cp	cp	cp	cp
04 17 15.6	+20 34 43	27045	ω²	Tau		50	67	293	63	297	58	302
04 17 53.6	−33 47 54	27376	41	Eri		υ⁴	129	231	135	225	148	212
04 17 59.2	−80 12 51	28525	δ	Men			nv	nv	(cp)	(cp)	(cp)	(cp)
04 18 14.6	+50 17 44	26961	b¹	Per			28	332	cp	cp	cp	cp
04 19 47.5	+15 37 39	27371	γ	Tau		54	73	287	70	290	66	294
04 20 21.2	+27 21 03	27382	φ	Tau		52	58	302	54	306	45	315
04 20 24.6	+34 34 00	27348	54	Per			50	310	43	317	30	330
04 21 33.1	+46 29 56	27396	53	Per		V469	34	326	20	340	cp	cp
04 21 53.4	−63 23 11	28093	η	Ret			nv	nv	(cp)	(cp)	(cp)	(cp)
04 22 34.9	+25 37 45	27638	χ	Tau	3161	59, Σ528	61	299	57	303	49	311
04 22 56.0	+17 32 33	27697	δ¹	Tau		61	70	290	68	292	63	297
04 23 40.8	−03 44 44	27861	ξ	Eri		42	93	267	94	266	95	265
04 23 51.8	+09 27 39	27820	66	Tau	3182	Hu 304	80	280	78	282	76	284
04 24 02.1	−34 01 01	28028	43	Eri		υ³	130	230	137	223	150	210
04 24 05.7	+17 26 38	27819	δ²	Tau		64	70	290	68	292	63	297
04 25 22.1	+22 17 38	27934	κ¹	Tau	3201	65, Σ541	64	296	61	299	54	306
04 25 24.9	+22 11 59	27946	κ²	Tau		67	64	296	61	299	54	306
04 25 29.3	+17 55 41	27962	δ³	Tau	3206	68, Kui17, V776	70	290	68	292	63	297
04 26 18.4	+22 48 49	28024	υ	Tau		69	64	296	61	299	54	306
04 26 20.7	+15 37 06	28052	71	Tau		V777	73	287	70	290	66	294
04 26 36.4	+14 42 49	28100	π	Tau		73	74	286	72	288	68	292
04 28 18.1	+10 09 45	28309	R	Tau			78	282	77	283	74	286
04 28 26.3	+16 21 35	28292	75	Tau			71	289	69	291	65	295
04 28 34.4	+15 57 44	28307	θ¹	Tau		77	73	287	70	290	66	294
04 28 36.9	+19 10 49	28305	ε	Tau		74	68	292	65	295	60	300
04 28 39.7	+15 52 15	28319	θ²	Tau		78	73	287	70	290	66	294
04 28 50.2	+13 02 52	28355	79	Tau			75	285	73	287	70	290
04 30 08.3	+15 38 17	28485	80	Tau	3264	Σ554	73	287	70	290	66	294
04 30 33.6	+16 11 38	28527	—	Tau			71	289	69	291	65	295
04 30 50.1	−44 57 14	28873	δ	Cae			143	217	155	205	nv	nv
04 31 24.0	+40 00 37	28503	Σ552	(Per)	3273		42	318	33	327	cp	cp
04 31 52.6	−00 02 39	28749	45	Eri			90	270	90	270	90	270
04 33 30.6	−29 46 00	29085	υ¹	Eri		50	124	236	129	231	139	221
04 33 50.8	+14 50 40	28910	ρ	Tau		86	74	286	72	288	68	292
04 33 59.8	−55 02 42	29305	α	Dor			161	199	nv	nv	nv	nv
04 34 11.5	−08 13 53	29064	47	Eri		DV	99	261	100	260	103	257
04 35 33.0	−30 33 45	29291	52	Eri		υ²	125	235	131	229	141	219
04 35 39.2	+10 09 39	29140	88	Tau	3317		78	282	77	283	74	286
04 35 55.2	+16 30 33	29139	α	Tau	3321	87, β550	71	289	69	291	65	295
04 36 19.1	−03 21 09	29248	ν	Eri		48	93	267	94	266	95	265
04 36 41.3	+41 15 53	29094	58	Per			41	319	31	329	cp	cp
04 36 45.6	−62 04 39	29712	R	Dor			nv	nv	nv	nv	nv	nv
04 37 36.0	−02 28 25	29391	51	Eri		c	92	268	93	267	93	267

R.A.	2000.0 Declin.	HD	Star	Const.	ADS	Also Known As	R(30)	S(30)	R(40)	S(40)	R(50)	S(50)
04 38 09.4	+12 30 39	29388	90	Tau			76	284	74	286	71	289
04 38 10.7	−14 18 15	29503	53	Eri			106	254	108	252	112	248
04 38 29.5	+26 56 24	29364	Σ572	(Tau)	3353		60	300	55	305	47	313
04 38 53.5	−12 07 23	29573	—	Eri			104	256	106	254	109	251
04 39 09.2	+15 47 59	29479	σ¹	Tau		91	73	287	70	290	66	294
04 39 16.4	+15 55 05	29488	σ²	Tau		92	73	287	70	290	66	294
04 39 54.7	+53 04 47	29317	3	Cam	3359	β1043	23	337	cp	cp	cp	cp
04 40 26.4	−19 40 18	29755	54	Eri	3380	DM	112	248	115	245	120	240
04 40 33.6	−41 51 50	29875	α	Cae			139	221	149	211	nv	nv
04 42 03.4	−37 08 40	29992	β	Cae			134	226	142	218	159	201
04 42 14.6	+22 57 25	29763	τ	Tau		94, OΣ54	64	296	61	299	54	306
04 42 46.3	−50 28 52	30185	λ	Pic			152	208	180	180	nv	nv
04 44 21.2	−59 43 58	30478	κ	Dor			172	188	nv	nv	nv	nv
04 45 30.1	−03 15 17	30211	μ	Eri		57	93	267	94	266	95	265
04 49 50.3	+06 57 41	30652	π³	Ori		1	83	277	82	278	81	279
04 49 54.6	+37 29 18	30504	1	Aur			46	314	38	322	21	339
04 50 11.5	−16 13 02	30814	60	Eri			109	251	111	249	115	245
04 50 36.7	+08 54 01	30739	π²	Ori		2	81	279	80	280	77	283
04 51 12.3	+05 36 18	30836	π⁴	Ori		3	84	276	83	277	82	278
04 51 22.4	+18 50 23	30780	97	Tau		V480	69	291	66	294	61	299
04 52 31.9	+14 15 02	30959	o¹	Ori		4	74	286	72	288	68	292
04 52 37.9	+36 42 11	30834	2	Aur			47	313	40	320	24	336
04 52 53.6	−05 27 10	31109	ω	Eri		61	96	264	97	263	98	262
04 54 03.0	+66 20 34	30614	α	Cam		9	cp	cp	cp	cp	cp	cp
04 54 15.0	+02 26 26	31237	π⁵	Ori		8	88	272	87	273	87	273
04 54 46.8	+11 25 34	31283	6	Ori			77	283	76	284	73	287
04 54 53.7	+10 09 03	31295	π¹	Ori		7	78	282	77	283	74	286
04 55 11.3	−74 56 13	32440	η	Men			nv	nv	(cp)	(cp)	(cp)	(cp)
04 55 18.5	−16 25 04	31444	R	Eri			109	251	111	249	115	245
04 56 22.2	+13 30 52	31421	o²	Ori	3540	9, β553	75	285	73	287	70	290
04.56 59.6	+33 09 58	31398	ι	Aur		3	51	309	45	315	32	328
04 57 17.1	+53 45 08	31278	7	Cam	3536		23	337	cp	cp	cp	cp
04 58 32.8	+01 42 51	31767	π⁶	Ori		10	89	271	89	271	88	272
04 59 15.3	+37 53 24	31647	ω	Aur	3572	4, Σ616	46	314	38	322	21	339
04 59 36.4	−14 48 21	31996	R	Lep			106	254	108	252	112	248
04 59 55.7	−12 32 15	32045	64	Eri		S	104	256	106	254	109	251
05 00 20.6	+81 11 39	30338	—	Cep			cp	cp	cp	cp	cp	cp
05 01 25.5	−20 03 07	32309	—	Lep			113	247	117	243	122	238
05 01 26.3	−07 10 26	32249	ψ	Eri		65	98	262	99	261	101	259
05 01 58.1	+43 49 24	31964	ε	Aur	3605	7, β554	38	322	27			
05 02 09.8	−26 16 31	32436	—	Lep			120	240	125	235	133	227
05 02 28.6	+41 04 33	32068	ζ	Aur		8	41	319	31	329	cp	cp
05 02 43.2	−71 18 50	33285	β	Men			nv	nv	(cp)	(cp)	(cp)	(cp)
05 02 48.6	−49 09 05	32743	η¹	Pic			151	209	170	190	nv	nv
05 03 05.7	+21 35 24	32301	ι	Tau		102	66	294	62	298	56	304
05 03 25.1	+60 26 32	31910	β	Cam	3615	10, OΣ57	cp	cp	cp	cp	cp	cp
05 04 24.3	−35 29 00	32831	γ¹	Cae			131	229	138	222	153	207
05 04 26.0	−35 42 19	32846	γ²	Cae			131	229	138	222	153	207
05 04 34.1	+15 24 14	32549	11	Ori		V1032	73	287	70	290	66	294
05 04 57.9	−49 34 41	33042	η²	Pic			151	209	170	190	nv	nv

R.A.		Declin.			HD	Star	Const.	ADS	Also Known As	R(30)	S(30)	R(40)	S(40)	R(50)	S(50)
		2000.0										Rising and Setting Azimuths			
05 05 27.6	−22	22	16	32887	ε	Lep		2		116	244	119	241	126	234
05 05 30.6	−57	28	22	33262	ζ	Dor				166	194	nv	nv	nv	nv
05 06 08.4	+58	58	21	32343	11	Cam		BV		12	348	cp	cp	cp	cp
05 06 30.8	+41	14	04	32630	η	Aur		10		41	319	31	329	cp	cp
05 06 40.6	+51	35	52	32537	9	Aur	3675	β1046		26	334	cp	cp	cp	cp
05 06 45.6	−04	39	18	32964	66	Eri	3698	Σ642, EN		95	265	95	265	96	264
05 07 27.0	+18	38	42	32923	104	Tau	3701			69	291	66	294	61	299
05 07 34.1	−63	23	59	33684	WZ	Dor				nv	nv	nv	nv	(cp)	(cp)
05 07 50.9	−05	05	11	33111	β	Eri		67		96	264	97	263	98	262
05 08 43.6	−04	27	22	33256	68	Eri				95	265	95	265	96	264
05 09 08.7	−08	45	15	33328	λ	Eri		69		99	261	100	260	103	257
05 09 41.9	+15	35	50	33276	15	Ori				73	287	70	290	66	294
05 11 17.8	−44	59	04	33793	Kapteyn's	(Pic)				143	217	155	205	nv	nv
05 11 41.5	+16	02	44	33554	—	Ori				71	289	69	291	65	295
05 12 17.8	−11	52	09	33802	ι	Lep	3778	3, Σ655		103	257	104	256	107	253
05 12 55.8	−16	12	20	33904	μ	Lep		5		109	251	111	249	115	245
05 13 13.8	−12	56	30	33949	κ	Lep	3800	4, Σ661		104	256	106	254	109	251
05 13 17.4	+02	51	40	33856	ρ	Ori	3797	17, Σ654		88	272	87	273	87	273
05 13 25.6	+38	29	04	33641	μ	Aur		11		45	315	37	323	17	343
05 13 45.4	−67	11	08	34649	θ	Dor				nv	nv	(cp)	(cp)	(cp)	(cp)
05 14 32.2	−08	12	06	34085	β	Ori	3823	19, Σ668		99	261	100	260	103	257
05 15 24.3	+32	41	16	33959	14	Aur	3824	Σ653, KW		52	308	46	314	34	326
05 15 24.3	−26	56	36	34310	—	Lep				120	240	125	235	133	227
05 16 41.3	+45	59	53	34029	α	Aur	3841	13		35	325	23	337	cp	cp
05 17 17.8	+53	35	10	34019	R	Aur	3845			23	337	cp	cp	cp	cp
05 17 29.0	−34	53	43	34642	o	Col				130	230	137	223	150	210
05 17 36.3	−06	50	40	34503	τ	Ori	3877	20, β188		97	263	98	262	99	261
05 18 10.6	+33	22	18	34334	16	Aur	3872	OΣ103		51	309	45	315	32	328
05 19 08.4	+40	05	57	34411	λ	Aur	3886	15, ΣII3		42	318	33	327	cp	cp
05 19 16.5	+22	05	47	34559	109	Tau				64	296	61	299	54	306
05 19 17.5	−33	42	27	34897	T	Col				129	231	135	225	148	212
05 19 22.0	−50	36	22	35072	ζ	Pic				152	208	180	180	nv	nv
05 19 34.4	−13	10	37	34816	λ	Lep		6		105	255	107	253	110	250
05 19 59.0	−12	18	56	34863	ν	Lep		7		104	256	106	254	109	251
05 20 00.8	+33	57	28	34578	19	Aur				51	309	45	315	32	328
05 20 26.8	−21	14	23	34968	h3750	(Lep)	3930			114	246	118	242	124	236
05 21 45.7	−00	22	57	35039	22	Ori				90	270	90	270	90	270
05 21 46.2	−24	46	23	35162	h3752	(Lep)	3954			118	242	122	238	129	231
05 21 48.4	+41	48	17	34759	ρ	Aur		20		41	319	31	329	cp	cp
05 22 33.5	+79	13	52	33564	—	Cam	3864	Σ634		cp	cp	cp	cp	cp	cp
05 22 49.9	+03	32	40	35149	23	Ori	3962	Σ696		87	273	86	274	85	275
05 23 27.6	+57	32	40	34787	16	Cam				14	346	cp	cp	cp	cp
05 23 56.8	−07	48	29	35369	29	Ori				98	262	99	261	101	259
05 24 25.4	+17	23	00	35296	111	Tau				70	290	68	292	63	297
05 24 28.6	−02	23	49	35411	η	Ori	4002	28		92	268	93	267	93	267
05 24 28.9	−00	53	29	35410	27	Ori				90	270	90	270	90	270
05 24 39.1	+37	23	08	35186	σ	Aur	3984	21, β888		46	314	38	322	21	339
05 24 44.8	+01	50	47	35439	ψ¹	Ori		25, V1086		89	271	89	271	88	272
05 25 07.8	+06	20	59	35468	γ	Ori		24		83	277	82	278	81	279
05 26 17.5	+28	36	27	35497	β	Tau		112, γAur		57	303	52	308	43	317

2000.0 R.A.	Declin.	HD	Star	Const.	ADS	Also Known As	R(30)	S(30)	R(40)	S(40)	R(50)	S(50)
05 26 19.2	−58 54 46	36189	λ	Dor			168	192	nv	nv	nv	nv
05 26 50.2	+03 05 44	35715	ψ²	Ori	4039	30	87	273	86	274	85	275
05 27 38.0	+21 56 13	35708	114	Tau	4048	h365	66	294	62	298	56	304
05 27 38.8	+34 28 33	35620	φ	Aur		24	50	310	43	317	30	330
05 28 14.7	−20 45 34	36079	β	Lep	4066	9, β320	113	247	117	243	122	238
05 29 43.9	−01 05 32	36167	31	Ori	4097	Σ725, Cl	91	269	91	269	92	268
05 30 47.0	+05 56 53	36267	32	Ori	4115	Σ728	84	276	83	277	82	278
05 31 12.7	−35 28 14	36597	ε	Col			131	229	138	222	153	207
05 31 53.0	−76 20 28	37763	γ	Men		h3795	nv	nv	(cp)	(cp)	(cp)	(cp)
05 31 55.8	−07 18 06	36512	υ	Ori		36	98	262	99	261	101	259
05 32 00.3	−00 17 57	36486	δ^A	Ori	4134	34, β558	90	270	90	270	90	270
05 32 00.4	−00 17 04	36485	δ^C	Ori			90	270	90	270	90	270
05 32 12.7	+18 35 39	36389	119	Tau		CE	69	291	66	294	61	299
05 32 43.6	+32 11 31	36371	χ	Aur		25	52	308	46	314	34	326
05 32 43.7	−17 49 20	36673	α	Lep	4146	11, h3766	110	250	112	248	117	243
05 33 37.5	−62 29 24	37350	β	Dor			nv	nv	nv	nv	(cp)	(cp)
05 34 15.8	−05 23 14	37020	θ^1A	Ori	4186	41, Σ748, V1016	96	264	97	263	98	262
05 34 49.2	+09 29 22	36822	φ¹	Ori		37	80	280	78	282	76	284
05 35 00.8	−06 00 34	36959	Σ747B	(Ori)			97	263	98	262	99	261
05 35 02.6	−06 00 07	36960	Σ747A	(Ori)	4182		97	263	98	262	99	261
05 35 08.2	+09 56 03	36861	λ^A	Ori	4179	39, Σ738	80	280	78	282	76	284
05 35 08.4	+09 56 06	36862	λ^B	Ori	4179	39	80	280	78	282	76	284
05 35 16.0	−05 23 07	37021	θ^1B	Ori	4186	BM	96	264	97	263	98	262
05 35 16.4	−05 23 23	37022	θ^1C	Ori	4186		96	264	97	263	98	262
05 35 17.2	−05 23 16	37023	θ^1D	Ori	4186		96	264	97	263	98	262
05 35 22.8	−05 24 58	37041	θ^2A	Ori	4188	43	96	264	97	263	98	262
05 35 25.9	−05 54 36	37043	ι	Ori	4193	44, Σ752	96	264	97	263	98	262
05 36 12.7	−01 12 07	37128	ε	Ori		46	91	269	91	269	92	268
05 36 54.3	+09 17 26	37160	φ²	Ori		40	80	280	78	282	76	284
05 37 38.6	+21 08 33	37202	ζ	Tau		123	66	294	62	298	56	304
05 37 44.6	−28 41 22	37495	ν²	Col			123	237	128	232	137	223
05 38 44.7	−02 36 00	37468	σ^A	Ori	4241	48, β1032/Σ762	92	268	93	267	93	267
05 38 47.0	−02 35 39	37479	σ^E	Ori			92	268	93	267	93	267
05 38 53.0	−07 12 47	37507	49	Ori			98	262	99	261	101	259
05 39 11.1	+04 07 17	37490	ω	Ori		47	85	275	85	275	84	276
05 39 16.2	−17 50 58	37643	h3780	(Lep)	4254		110	250	112	248	117	243
05 39 38.9	−34 04 27	37795	α	Col			130	230	137	223	150	210
05 39 44.2	+25 53 50	37438	125	Tau			61	299	57	303	49	311
05 40 45.5	−01 56 34	37742	ζ^A	Ori	4263	50, Σ774	91	269	91	269	92	268
05 40 45.5	−01 56 34	37743	ζ^B	Ori	4263	50	91	269	91	269	92	268
05 40 50.6	−01 07 44	37756	—	Ori			91	269	91	269	92	268
05 41 17.7	+16 32 02	37711	126	Tau	4265	β1007	71	289	69	291	65	295
05 42 28.6	+01 28 29	37984	51	Ori			89	271	89	271	88	272
05 44 26.4	−22 25 19	38392	γ^B	Lep	4334	13	116	244	119	241	126	234
05 44 27.8	−22 26 54	38393	γ^A	Lep	4334	13	116	244	119	241	126	234
05 44 46.5	−65 44 08	39014	δ	Dor			nv	nv	nv	nv	(cp)	(cp)
05 45 59.9	−32 18 23	38666	μ	Col			128	232	134	226	146	214
05 46 57.3	−14 49 19	38678	ζ	Lep		14	106	254	108	252	112	248
05 47 17.1	−51 03 59	39060	β	Pic			154	206	nv	nv	nv	nv
05 47 45.3	−09 40 11	38771	κ	Ori		53	100	260	102	258	104	256

R.A. 2000.0		Declin.		HD	Star	Const.	ADS	Also Known As	Rising and Setting Azimuths					
									R(30)	S(30)	R(40)	S(40)	R(50)	S(50)
05 49 00.9	+24 34 03			38751	132	Tau			62	298	58	302	51	309
05 49 10.4	+39 10 52			38656	τ	Aur	4398	29, β192	43	317	35	325	12	348
05 49 32.9	+12 39 04			38899	134	Tau			76	284	74	286	71	289
05 49 49.6	−56 10 00			39523	γ	Pic			163	197	nv	nv	nv	nv
05 49 53.7	−66 54 05			39844	ε	Dor			nv	nv	nv	nv	nv	nv
05 50 16.5	−79 21 41			40953	κ	Men			nv	nv	(cp)	(cp)	(cp)	(cp)
05 50 53.3	−52 06 32			39640	—	Pic			155	205	nv	nv	nv	nv
05 50 57.5	−35 46 06			39425	β	Col			131	229	138	222	153	207
05 51 02.4	+37 18 20			38944	υ	Aur		31	46	314	38	322	21	339
05 51 19.2	−20 52 45			39364	δ	Lep		15	113	247	117	243	122	238
05 51 29.3	+39 08 55			39003	ν	Aur	4440	32	43	317	35	325	12	348
05 52 26.4	+01 51 19			39400	56	Ori	4467		89	271	89	271	88	272
05 53 06.8	−33 48 05			39764	λ	Col			129	231	135	225	148	212
05 53 19.6	+27 36 44			39357	136	Tau	4474	β1054	58	302	54	306	45	315
05 54 06.1	−63 05 23			40409	—	Dor			nv	nv	nv	nv	(cp)	(cp)
05 54 22.9	+20 16 34			39587	χ¹	Ori		54	67	293	63	297	58	302
05 54 50.7	+55 42 25			39283	ξ	Aur		30	19	341	cp	cp	cp	cp
05 54 57.7	+59 53 18			39220	31	Cam		TU	8	352	cp	cp	cp	cp
05 55 10.3	+07 24 25			39801	α	Ori	4506	58	82	278	81	279	79	281
05 55 29.8	−37 07 15			40176	ξ	Col			134	226	142	218	159	201
05 55 49.2	+20 10 30			39816	U	Ori			67	293	63	297	58	302
05 56 20.9	−31 22 57			40248	σ	Col			126	234	132	228	143	217
05 56 24.2	−14 10 04			40136	η	Lep		16	106	254	108	252	112	248
05 57 32.2	−35 17 00			40494	γ	Col		h3819	131	229	138	222	153	207
05 57 59.6	+25 57 14			40111	139	Tau			61	299	57	303	49	311
05 58 49.5	+00 33 11			40446	60	Ori			90	270	90	270	90	270
05 59 04.3	−09 33 30			40536	2	Mon			100	260	102	258	104	256
05 59 08.7	−42 48 55			40808	η	Col			141	219	151	209	nv	nv
05 59 31.6	+54 17 05			40035	δ	Aur		33	21	339	cp	cp	cp	cp
05 59 31.7	+44 56 51			40183	β	Aur	4556	34	37	323	25	335	cp	cp
05 59 43.2	+37 12 45			40312	θ	Aur	4566	37, OΣ545	46	314	38	322	21	339
05 59 56.1	+45 56 13			40239	π	Aur		35	35	325	23	337	cp	cp
06 00 03.3	−03 04 27			40657	—	Ori			93	267	94	266	95	265
06 01 50.3	−10 35 53			40967	3	Mon	4615	β16	102	258	103	257	106	254
06 02 23.0	+09 38 51			40932	μ	Ori	4617	61, Kui23	80	280	78	282	76	284
06 03 15.5	−26 17 04			41312	—	Lep	4645		120	240	125	235	133	227
06 03 27.3	+19 41 26			41040	64	Ori			68	292	65	295	60	300
06 03 55.2	+20 08 18			41117	χ²	Ori		62	67	293	63	297	58	302
06 04 07.2	+23 15 48			41116	1	Gem			63	297	59	301	53	307
06 04 13.4	−06 42 33			41335	—	Mon			97	263	98	262	99	261
06 04 59.0	−16 29 04			41511	17	Lep		SS	109	251	111	249	115	245
06 06 09.3	−14 56 07			41695	θ	Lep		18	106	254	108	252	112	248
06 06 09.5	−66 02 23			42525	η¹	Dor			nv	nv	nv	nv	(cp)	(cp)
06 07 03.4	−62 09 17			42540	—	Pic			nv	nv	nv	nv	(cp)	(cp)
06 07 31.6	−37 15 10			42167	θ	Col			134	226	142	218	159	201
06 07 34.3	+14 46 06			41753	ν	Ori		67	74	286	72	288	68	292
06 07 52.9	−42 09 14			42303	π²	Col			141	219	151	209	nv	nv
06 08 44.3	−68 50 36			43107	ν	Dor			nv	nv	nv	nv	nv	nv
06 10 14.6	−74 45 11			43834	α	Men			nv	nv	(cp)	(cp)	(cp)	(cp)
06 10 17.9	−54 58 07			42933	δ	Pic			159	201	nv	nv	nv	nv

R.A.			Declin.			HD	Star	Const.	ADS	Also Known As	R(30)	S(30)	R(40)	S(40)	R(50)	S(50)
		2000.0										Rising and Setting Azimuths				
06	11	15.0	−65	35	22	43455	η²	Dor			nv	nv	nv	nv	nv	nv
06	11	51.7	−06	33	02	42690	—	Mon			97	263	98	262	99	261
06	11	56.4	+14	12	31	42560	ξ	Ori		70	74	286	72	288	68	292
06	12	03.3	+16	07	50	42545	69	Ori			71	289	69	291	65	295
06	14	50.8	+19	09	23	43042	71	Ori	4842	h2302	68	292	65	295	60	300
06	14	51.3	−06	16	29	43232	γ	Mon	4853	5, h384	97	263	98	262	99	261
06	14	52.6	+22	30	24	42995	η	Gem	4841	7, β1008	64	296	61	299	54	306
06	15	22.6	+29	29	53	43039	κ	Aur		44	56	304	51	309	41	319
06	15	39.0	+36	08	55	43017	Σ872	(Aur)	4849		47	313	40	320	24	336
06	15	44.8	−13	43	06	43445	—	CMa			105	255	107	253	110	250
06	16	26.6	+12	16	20	43386	74	Ori			76	284	74	286	71	289
06	16	33.0	−35	08	26	43785	κ	Col			131	229	138	222	153	207
06	17	41.7	−16	48	57	43827	—	CMa			109	251	111	249	115	245
06	17	54.9	+61	30	55	42973	1	Lyn		UW	cp	cp	cp	cp	cp	cp
06	18	50.8	+69	19	12	42818	L	Cam			cp	cp	cp	cp	cp	cp
06	19	37.3	+59	00	39	43378	2	Lyn		UZ	8	352	cp	cp	cp	cp
06	19	59.5	−02	56	40	44131	—	Ori			92	268	93	267	93	267
06	20	18.7	−30	03	48	44402	ζ	CMa		1	125	235	131	229	141	219
06	22	06.7	−33	26	11	44762	δ	Col		3 CMa	129	231	135	225	148	212
06	22	41.9	−17	57	22	44743	β	CMa		2	110	250	112	248	117	243
06	22	57.6	+22	30	49	44478	μ	Gem	4990	13, β1059	64	296	61	299	54	306
06	23	46.0	+04	35	34	44769	εᴬ	Mon	5012	8A, Σ900	85	275	85	275	84	276
06	23	46.9	+04	35	44	44770	εᴮ	Mon	5012	8B	85	275	85	275	84	276
06	23	57.2	−52	41	44	45348	α	Car			155	205	nv	nv	nv	nv
06	24	10.2	−11	31	49	44951	—	CMa			103	257	104	256	107	253
06	24	53.8	+49	17	17	44537	ψ¹	Aur		46	29	331	10	350	cp	cp
06	25	28.7	−69	41	25	46116	π²	Dor			nv	nv	nv	nv	(cp)	(cp)
06	26	25.8	+56	17	06	44691	RR	Lyn			17	343	cp	cp	cp	cp
06	26	48.8	+58	25	02	44708	5	Lyn	5036		12	348	cp	cp	cp	cp
06	27	13.7	+00	17	57	45416	77	Ori			90	270	90	270	90	270
06	27	57.5	−04	45	44	45546	10	Mon			95	265	95	265	96	264
06	28	10.1	−32	34	49	45813	λ	CMa			128	232	134	226	146	214
06	28	48.9	−07	01	59	45725	βᴬ	Mon	5107	11, Σ919	98	262	99	261	101	259
06	28	49.4	−07	02	04	45726	βᴮ	Mon	5107	11	98	262	99	261	101	259
06	28	57.7	+20	12	43	45542	ν	Gem	5103	18, OΣ77	67	293	63	297	58	302
06	29	28.4	−56	51	11	46355	—	Pic			163	197	nv	nv	nv	nv
06	31	22.9	−12	23	30	46184	—	CMa			104	256	106	254	109	251
06	31	48.2	+11	32	40	46089	—	Mon			77	283	76	284	73	287
06	31	51.3	−23	25	06	46328	ξ¹ₛ	CMa	5176	4, See 68	117	243	121	239	127	233
06	32	21.3	−37	41	48	46568	—	Col			134	226	142	218	159	201
06	32	54.2	+07	19	58	46300	13	Mon			82	278	81	279	79	281
06	33	37.8	−01	13	13	46487	—	Mon			91	269	91	269	92	268
06	34	58.5	−52	58	32	47306	N	Car			155	205	nv	nv	nv	nv
06	35	03.3	−22	57	53	46933	ξ²	CMa		5	116	244	119	241	126	234
06	36	41.0	−19	15	22	47205	ν²	CMa		7	112	248	115	245	120	240
06	37	24.0	+06	08	07	47129	Plaskett's	Mon			83	277	82	278	81	279
06	37	42.7	+16	23	57	47105	γ	Gem		24	71	289	69	291	65	295
06	37	45.6	−43	11	45	47670	ν	Pup			142	218	153	207	nv	nv
06	37	47.5	−32	20	23	47536	—	CMa			128	232	134	226	146	214
06	37	53.3	−18	14	15	47442	ν³	CMa		8	111	249	114	246	119	241

R.A.	2000.0 Declin.		HD	Star	Const.	ADS	Also Known As	Rising and Setting Azimuths					
								R(30)	S(30)	R(40)	S(40)	R(50)	S(50)
06 38 37.6	−48 13 13		47973	y	Pup			149	211	166	194	nv	nv
06 38 49.1	+39 54 09		47100	ψ³	Aur		52	43	317	35	325	12	348
06 39 16.6	−14 08 45		47667	—	CMa			106	254	108	252	112	248
06 39 19.8	+42 29 20		47174	ψ²	Aur		50	39	321	29	331	cp	cp
06 40 58.6	+09 53 44		47839	15	Mon	5322	Σ950, S	80	280	78	282	76	284
06 41 56.4	−09 10 03		48217	—	Mon			100	260	102	258	104	256
06 42 24.3	+17 38 43		48097	26	Gem			70	290	68	292	63	297
06 43 04.9	+44 31 28		47914	ψ⁴	Aur		55	37	323	25	335	cp	cp
06 43 55.9	+25 07 52		48329	ε	Gem	5381	27	61	299	57	303	49	311
06 43 59.2	+13 13 40		48433	30	Gem	5387		75	285	73	287	70	290
06 44 28.3	−31 04 14		48917	10	CMa		FT	126	234	132	228	143	217
06 45 08.9	−16 42 58		48915	α	CMa	5423	9	109	251	111	249	115	245
06 45 17.3	+12 53 44		48737	ξ	Gem		31	76	284	74	286	71	289
06 46 14.1	+59 26 30		48250	12	Lyn	5400	Σ948	8	352	cp	cp	cp	cp
06 46 44.3	+43 34 39		48682	ψ⁵	Aur	5425	56	38	322	27	333	cp	cp
06 46 51.0	−14 25 34		49229	11	CMa			106	254	108	252	112	248
06 47 19.8	+08 02 14		49161	17	Mon			81	279	80	280	77	283
06 47 37.1	−08 59 54		49331	—	Mon			99	261	100	260	103	257
06 47 39.5	+48 47 22		48781	ψ⁶	Aur		57	31	329	14	346	cp	cp
06 47 51.6	+02 24 44		49293	18	Mon			88	272	87	273	87	273
06 48 11.4	−61 56 29		50241	α	Pic			nv	nv	nv	nv	(cp)	(cp)
06 49 50.4	−32 30 31		50013	κ	CMa		13	128	232	134	226	146	214
06 49 51.3	−53 37 20		50337	A	Car		V415	157	203	nv	nv	nv	nv
06 49 54.5	−46 36 52		50223	—	Car			146	214	160	200	nv	nv
06 49 56.1	−50 36 53		50310	τ	Pup			152	208	180	180	nv	nv
06 50 45.9	+41 46 53		49520	ψ⁷	Aur		58	41	319	31	329	cp	cp
06 50 52.3	−34 22 02		50235	—	Pup			130	230	137	223	150	210
06 50 57.1	+67 34 19		48879	42	Cam			cp	cp	cp	cp	cp	cp
06 51 27.0	−70 57 49		51557	ι	Vol			nv	nv	(cp)	(cp)	(cp)	(cp)
06 52 47.3	+33 57 40		50019	θ	Gem	5532	34	51	309	45	315	32	328
06 53 32.8	−20 13 27		50707	15	CMa		EY	113	247	117	243	122	238
06 53 42.2	+68 53 18		49340	43	Cam			cp	cp	cp	cp	cp	cp
06 54 07.8	−24 11 02		50877	o¹	CMa		16	118	242	122	238	129	231
06 54 11.3	−12 02 19		50778	θ	CMa		14	104	256	106	254	109	251
06 54 38.6	+13 10 40		50635	38	Gem	5559	Σ982	75	285	73	287	70	290
06 55 37.3	−20 08 11		51199	π	CMa	5602	19	113	247	117	243	122	238
06 56 06.6	−14 02 37		51250	μ	CMa	5605	18, Σ997	106	254	108	252	112	248
06 56 08.1	−17 03 15		51309	ι	CMa		20	110	250	112	248	117	243
06 56 16.0	−48 43 16		51799	—	Car			149	211	166	194	nv	nv
06 56 34.5	−79 25 13		54239	θ	Men			nv	nv	(cp)	(cp)	(cp)	(cp)
06 57 16.5	+58 25 21		50522	15	Lyn	5586	OΣ159	12	348	cp	cp	cp	cp
06 57 37.0	+45 05 39		50973	16	Lyn			35	325	23	337	cp	cp
06 58 25.0	−34 06 42		52092	t	Pup			130	230	137	223	150	210
06 58 37.5	−28 58 20		52089	ε	CMa	5654	21	123	237	128	232	137	223
06 59 50.5	−67 54 59		53501	—	Vol			(cp)	(cp)	(cp)	(cp)	(cp)	(cp)
07 00 04.0	+76 58 39		49878	—	Cam			cp	cp	cp	cp	cp	cp
07 00 51.5	−51 24 09		53047	—	Car			154	206	nv	nv	nv	nv
07 01 17.9	+55 19 51		51610	R	Lyn			19	341	cp	cp	cp	cp
07 01 43.1	−27 56 06		52877	σ	CMa	5719	22	122	238	126	234	135	225
07 01 56.3	−05 43 20		52666	—	Mon			96	264	97	263	98	262

	2000.0						Also	Rising and Setting Azimuths					
R.A.		Declin.	HD	Star	Const.	ADS	Known As	R(30)	S(30)	R(40)	S(40)	R(50)	S(50)
07 02 24.7	+24 12 56		52497	ω	Gem		42	62	298	58	302	51	309
07 02 54.6	−04 14 21		52918	19	Mon		V637	95	265	95	265	96	264
07 03 01.4	−23 50 00		53138	o²	CMa		24	117	243	121	239	127	233
07 03 38.0	+10 57 06		52960	—	Gem			78	282	77	283	74	286
07 03 45.4	−15 38 00		53244	γ	CMa		23	107	253	110	250	114	246
07 03 53.7	−49 35 02		53811	H	Pup			151	209	170	190	nv	nv
07 03 57.2	−43 36 29		53705	—	Pup(A)		DUN 38	142	218	153	207	nv	nv
07 03 58.8	−43 36 42		53706	—	Pup(B)		DUN 38	142	218	153	207	nv	nv
07 04 02.7	−42 20 15		53704	c	Pup			141	219	151	209	nv	nv
07 04 06.5	+20 34 13		52973	ζ	Gem	5742	43	67	293	63	297	58	302
07 04 18.3	−56 44 59		54118	—	Car			163	197	nv	nv	nv	nv
07 06 40.6	−11 17 39		53974	FN	CMa	5795	β328/Σ1026	103	257	104	256	107	253
07 07 21.3	+22 42 13		53791	R	Gem			64	296	61	299	54	306
07 08 23.4	−26 23 35		54605	δ	CMa		25	120	240	125	235	133	227
07 08 42.2	−70 29 50		55864	γ¹	Vol		DUN 42	nv	nv	(cp)	(cp)	(cp)	(cp)
07 08 45.0	−70 29 57		55865	γ²	Vol			nv	nv	(cp)	(cp)	(cp)	(cp)
07 08 51.0	−39 39 21		54893	A	Pup			137	223	145	215	168	192
07 10 13.6	−04 14 14		54810	20	Mon			95	265	95	265	96	264
07 10 47.4	−48 55 55		55526	—	Pup			149	211	166	194	nv	nv
07 11 08.3	+30 14 43		54719	τ	Gem	5846	46, β1009	55	305	49	311	39	321
07 11 39.3	+39 19 14		54716	63	Aur			43	317	35	325	12	348
07 11 51.8	−00 29 34		55185	δ	Mon	5864	22	90	270	90	270	90	270
07 12 33.6	−46 45 34		55892	I	Pup		QW	146	214	160	200	nv	nv
07 13 13.3	−45 10 59		56022	OU	Pup			145	215	157	203	nv	nv
07 13 22.2	+16 09 32		55383	51	Gem		BQ	71	289	69	291	65	295
07 13 32.3	−44 38 23		56096	L₂	Pup			143	217	155	205	nv	nv
07 14 15.1	−26 21 09		56014	27	CMa		EW	120	240	125	235	133	227
07 14 38.1	−48 16 18		56456	—	Pup			149	211	166	194	nv	nv
07 14 48.6	−26 46 22		56139	ω	CMa		28	120	240	125	235	133	227
07 15 54.8	+59 38 15		55280	18	Lyn			8	352	cp	cp	cp	cp
07 16 34.9	−27 52 52		56618	—	CMa			122	238	126	234	135	225
07 16 36.7	−23 18 56		56577	h3945	(CMa)	5951		117	243	121	239	127	233
07 16 49.4	−36 35 34		56779	v¹	Pup			133	227	140	220	156	204
07 16 49.8	−67 57 27		57623	δ	Vol			nv	nv	(cp)	(cp)	(cp)	(cp)
07 17 08.5	−37 05 51		56855	π	Pup			134	226	142	218	159	201
07 18 05.5	+16 32 25		56537	λ	Gem	5961	54, Σ1061	71	289	69	291	65	295
07 18 18.4	−36 44 03		57150	NV	Pup			133	227	140	220	156	204
07 18 31.9	+49 27 54		56169	—	Lyn			29	331	10	350	cp	cp
07 18 38.2	−36 44 34		57219	NW	Pup			133	227	140	220	156	204
07 18 40.3	−24 33 32		57060	29	CMa		UW	118	242	122	238	129	231
07 18 42.4	−24 57 15		57061	τ	CMa	5977	30, h3948	118	242	122	238	129	231
07 19 28.1	−16 23 43		57167	R	CMa			109	251	111	249	115	245
07 20 07.3	+21 58 56		56986	δ	Gem	5983	55, Σ1066	66	294	62	298	56	304
07 21 56.8	+20 26 37		57423	56	Gem	6016		67	293	63	297	58	303
07 22 02.6	+36 45 38		57264	65	Aur	6009	β901	47	313	40	320	24	336
07 22 13.5	−19 01 00		57821	—	CMa			112	248	115	245	120	240
07 22 50.8	+55 17 04		57102	19B	Lyn	6012		19	341	cp	cp	cp	cp
07 22 52.0	+55 16 53		57103	19A	Lyn	6012	Σ1062	19	341	cp	cp	cp	cp
07 23 28.4	+25 03 02		57727	57	Gem			61	299	57	303	49	311
07 24 05.6	−29 18 11		58350	η	CMa		31	124	236	129	231	139	221

R.A.			Declin.			HD	Star	Const.	ADS	Also Known As	R(30)	S(30)	R(40)	S(40)	R(50)	S(50)
07	24	08.4	+40	40	20	57669	66	Aur			42	318	33	327	cp	cp
07	25	38.8	+09	16	34	58367	ε	CMi		2	80	280	78	282	76	284
07	25	43.5	+27	47	53	58207	ι	Gem		60	58	302	54	306	45	315
07	26	21.8	−51	01	07	59219	—	Pup			154	206	nv	nv	nv	nv
07	26	35.1	+73	04	57	57044	Σ1051	(Cam)	6028		cp	cp	cp	cp	cp	cp
07	26	42.8	+49	12	42	58142	21	Lyn			29	331	10	350	cp	cp
07	27	09.0	+08	17	21	58715	β	CMi		3	81	279	80	280	77	283
07	27	44.3	+21	26	42	58728	63	Gem	6089		66	294	62	298	56	304
07	28	02.0	+06	56	31	58923	η	CMi	6101	5, β21	83	277	82	278	81	279
07	28	09.7	+08	55	32	58972	γ	CMi	6100	4	81	279	80	280	77	283
07	29	06.6	+31	47	04	58946	ρ	Gem	6109	62	54	306	48	312	37	323
07	29	13.8	−43	18	05	59717	σ	Pup		DUN 51	142	218	153	207	37	323
07	29	20.3	+28	07	05	59037	64	Gem			57	303	52	308	43	317
07	29	47.7	+12	00	24	59294	6	CMi			76	284	74	286	71	289
07	29	48.7	+27	54	58	59148	65	Gem	6119		58	302	54	306	45	315
07	29	51.4	−23	01	28	59612	—	Pup			117	243	121	239	127	233
07	30	42.5	−30	57	44	59890	—	Pup			125	235	131	229	141	219
07	30	47.3	−09	46	37	59693	U	Mon			100	260	102	258	104	256
07	31	04.5	+82	24	42	55966	VZ	Cam			cp	cp	cp	cp	cp	cp
07	31	48.3	+17	05	09	59686	—	Gem			70	290	68	292	63	297
07	32	05.8	+01	54	52	59881	δ¹	CMi		7	89	271	89	271	88	272
07	33	47.8	−14	31	26	60414	KQ	Pup			106	254	108	252	112	248
07	34	03.1	−22	17	46	60532	—	CMa			116	244	119	241	126	234
07	34	35.9	+31	53	18	60179	α	Gem	6175	66, Σ1110	54	306	48	312	37	323
07	35	22.8	−28	22	10	60863	p	Pup	6205	h3982	123	237	128	232	137	223
07	35	39.7	−52	32	02	61248	Q	Car			155	205	nv	nv	nv	nv
07	35	55.3	+26	53	44	60522	υ	Gem		69	60	300	55	305	47	313
07	37	16.6	−04	06	40	61064	25	Mon			95	265	95	265	96	264
07	37	22.0	−34	58	06	61330	f	Pup			130	230	137	223	150	210
07	38	17.9	−25	21	54	61429	PU	Pup	6246		119	241	123	237	131	229
07	38	49.3	−26	48	07	61555	k¹	Pup	6255A		120	240	125	235	133	227
07	38	49.7	−26	48	13	61556	k²	Pup	6255B		120	240	125	235	133	227
07	39	09.9	+34	35	04	61110	o	Gem		71	50	310	43	317	30	330
07	39	18.1	+05	13	30	61421	α	CMi	6251	10	84	276	83	277	82	278
07	39	27.3	−38	18	30	61831	—	Pup			135	225	143	217	163	197
07	39	28.6	+17	40	29	61338	74	Gem			70	290	68	292	63	297
07	40	06.9	+05	13	51	61563	Σ1126	(CMi)	6263		84	276	83	277	82	278
07	40	23.1	−15	15	49	61772	—	Pup			107	253	110	250	114	246
07	40	31.1	+87	01	12	51802	OV	Cep			cp	cp	cp	cp	cp	cp
07	41	14.8	−09	33	04	61935	α	Mon		26	100	260	102	258	104	256
07	41	49.3	−72	36	22	63295	ζ	Vol			nv	nv	(cp)	(cp)	(cp)	(cp)
07	42	57.2	−45	10	24	62644	—	Pup			145	215	157	203	nv	nv
07	43	00.4	+58	42	37	61497	24	Lyn	6285	h2405	12	348	cp	cp	cp	cp
07	43	18.7	+28	53	00	62044	σ	Gem		75	57	303	52	308	43	317
07	43	32.3	−28	24	40	62576	1	Pup	6324		123	237	128	232	137	223
07	43	41.9	−40	56	03	62713	—	Pup			138	222	147	213	179	181
07	43	48.4	−28	57	18	62623	3	Pup			123	237	128	232	137	223
07	44	04.1	+50	26	01	61931	—	Lyn			28	332	cp	cp	cp	cp
07	44	26.8	+24	23	53	62345	κ	Gem	6321	77, OΣ179	62	298	58	302	51	309
07	45	15.2	−37	58	07	63032	—	Pup			134	226	142	218	159	201

2000.0 R.A.			Declin.			HD	Star	Const.	ADS	Also Known As	R(30)	S(30)	R(40)	S(40)	R(50)	S(50)
07	45	18.9	+28	01	34	62509	β	Gem	6335	78, β580	57	303	52	308	43	317
07	45	56.8	−14	33	50	62952	4	Pup			106	254	108	252	112	248
07	46	07.4	+18	30	36	62721	81	Gem			69	291	66	294	61	299
07	46	39.2	+37	31	03	62647	—	Lyn			46	314	38	322	21	339
07	47	24.9	−38	30	40	63465	—	Pup			135	225	143	217	163	197
07	47	30.3	+33	24	56	62898	π	Gem	6364	80, Σ1135	51	309	45	315	32	328
07	47	31.5	−46	36	31	63578	p	Pup			146	214	160	200	nv	nv
07	48	05.1	−25	56	14	63462	o	Pup	6384	See 86	119	241	123	237	131	229
07	48	20.2	−47	04	40	63744	Q	Pup			148	212	163	197	nv	nv
07	49	14.3	−46	22	24	63922	P	Pup			146	214	160	200	nv	nv
07	49	17.6	−24	51	35	63700	ξ	Pup	6393	7, β1063	118	242	122	238	129	231
07	49	41.1	−17	13	43	63697	6	Pup			110	250	112	248	117	243
07	51	41.9	+01	46	01	63975	ζ	CMi		13	89	271	89	271	88	272
07	51	46.2	−13	53	53	64096	9	Pup	6420	β101	105	255	107	253	110	250
07	52	13.0	−40	34	33	64440	a	Pup			138	222	147	213	179	181
07	52	15.6	−34	42	19	64379	—	Pup			130	230	137	223	150	210
07	52	38.6	−38	51	47	64503	b	Pup		QZ	135	225	143	217	163	197
07	53	03.7	−49	36	47	64740	—	Pup			151	209	170	190	nv	nv
07	53	18.2	−48	06	11	64760	J	Pup			149	211	166	194	nv	nv
07	53	29.7	+26	45	57	64145	φ	Gem		83	60	300	55	305	47	313
07	56	46.7	−52	58	56	65575	χ	Car			155	205	nv	nv	nv	nv
07	56	51.5	−22	52	49	65228	11	Pup			116	244	119	241	126	234
07	57	18.5	−44	06	35	65551	N	Pup			143	217	155	205	nv	nv
07	57	40.1	−30	20	04	65456	—	Pup			125	235	131	229	141	219
07	57	51.7	−45	34	40	65685	O	Pup			145	215	157	203	nv	nv
07	58	14.3	−49	14	42	65818	V	Pup		h4025	151	209	170	190	nv	nv
07	59	05.6	−23	18	38	65699	12	Pup			117	243	121	239	127	233
07	59	28.3	−39	17	50	65925	—	Pup			137	223	145	215	168	192
07	59	37.6	−60	35	13	66342	—	Car			180	180	nv	nv	nv	nv
07	59	44.1	−03	40	47	65695	27	Mon			93	267	94	266	95	265
07	59	52.0	−18	23	58	65810	—	Pup			111	249	114	246	119	241
08	00	20.0	−63	34	03	66591	D¹	Car			nv	nv	nv	nv	nv	nv
08	01	13.2	−01	23	33	65953	28	Mon		V645	91	269	91	269	92	268
08	02	15.9	+02	20	04	66141	—	CMi			88	272	87	273	87	273
08	03	31.0	+27	47	39	66216	χ	Gem			58	302	54	306	45	315
08	03	35.0	−40	00	11	66811	ζ	Pup			138	222	147	213	179	181
08	05	04.4	+13	07	05	66664	8	Cnc			75	285	73	287	70	290
08	06	18.3	+22	38	08	66875	μ¹	Cnc		10, BL	64	296	61	299	54	306
08	06	40.3	−45	15	59	67582	—	Vel			145	215	157	203	nv	nv
08	07	32.6	−24	18	15	67523	ρ	Pup		15	118	242	122	238	129	231
08	07	45.8	+21	34	54	67228	μ²	Cnc			66	294	62	298	56	304
08	07	55.9	−68	37	02	68520	ε	Vol			nv	nv	(cp)	(cp)	(cp)	(cp)
08	08	27.4	+51	30	24	67006	27	Lyn	6600		26	334	cp	cp	cp	cp
08	08	35.6	−02	59	02	67594	ζ	Mon	6617	29, Σ1190	92	268	93	267	93	267
08	09	00.7	−61	18	07	68456	B	Car			nv	nv	nv	nv	nv	nv
08	09	01.5	−19	14	42	67797	16	Pup			112	248	115	245	120	240
08	09	29.2	−47	20	44	68243	γ¹	Vel		DUN 65	148	212	163	197	nv	nv
08	09	31.9	−47	20	12	68273	γ²	Vel			148	212	163	197	nv	nv
08	09	35.9	−44	07	23	68217	—	Vel			143	217	155	205	nv	nv
08	09	43.2	−47	56	14	68324	IS	Vel			148	212	163	197	nv	nv

2000.0 R.A.			2000.0 Declin.			HD	Star	Const.	ADS	Also Known As	R(30)	S(30)	R(40)	S(40)	R(50)	S(50)
08	11	16.2	−12	55	37	68290	19	Pup	6647	β1064	104	256	106	254	109	251
08	11	21.5	−39	37	07	68553	NS	Pup			137	223	145	215	168	192
08	11	25.9	−42	59	14	68601	−	Pup			141	219	151	209	nv	nv
08	12	12.6	+17	38	52	68257	ζ^{1A}	Cnc	6650A	16, Σ1196	70	290	68	292	63	297
08	12	12.6	+17	38	52	68255	ζ^{1C}	Cnc	6650C	16	70	290	68	292	63	297
08	12	13.2	+17	38	51	68256	ζ^{2B}	Cnc	6650B	16	70	290	68	292	63	297
08	13	19.9	−15	47	18	68752	20	Pup			107	253	110	250	114	246
08	13	29.5	−35	53	59	68980	MX	Pup			131	229	138	222	153	207
08	13	36.2	−46	59	31	69144	−	Vel			146	214	160	200	nv	nv
08	13	58.3	−36	19	21	69081	OS	Pup			133	227	140	220	156	204
08	14	02.8	−40	20	53	69142	h^2	Pup			138	222	147	213	179	181
08	15	15.9	−62	54	57	69863	C	Car			nv	nv	nv	nv	nv	nv
08	16	30.9	+09	11	08	69267	β	Cnc	6704	17, β1065	80	280	78	282	76	284
08	16	33.9	+11	43	35	69243	R	Cnc			77	283	76	284	73	287
08	18	19.0	−65	36	47	70514	−	Vol			nv	nv	(cp)	(cp)	(cp)	(cp)
08	18	31.7	−76	55	11	71243	α	Cha			nv	nv	(cp)	(cp)	(cp)	(cp)
08	18	33.3	−36	39	34	70060	q	Pup			133	227	140	220	156	204
08	19	49.2	−71	30	54	71046	κ^1	Vol			nv	nv	(cp)	(cp)	(cp)	(cp)
08	20	00.8	−71	30	19	71066	κ^2	Vol			nv	nv	(cp)	(cp)	(cp)	(cp)
08	20	03.8	+27	13	03	69897	χ	Cnc		18	58	302	54	306	45	315
08	20	38.7	−77	29	04	71701	θ	Cha			nv	nv	(cp)	(cp)	(cp)	(cp)
08	21	21.0	−36	29	04	70556	−	Pup			133	227	140	220	156	204
08	21	23.0	−33	03	16	70555	W	Pup			129	231	135	225	148	212
08	22	04.7	−73	24	01	71576	η	Vol		h4103	nv	nv	(cp)	(cp)	(cp)	(cp)
08	22	30.8	−59	30	34	71129	ε	Car			172	188	nv	nv	nv	nv
08	22	31.5	−48	29	25	70930	B	Vel			149	211	166	194	nv	nv
08	22	50.1	+43	11	17	70272	31	Lyn			38	322	27	333	cp	cp
08	25	30.7	−51	43	42	71510	−	Vel			154	206	nv	nv	nv	nv
08	25	39.6	−03	54	23	71155	C	Hya		30 Mon	93	267	94	266	95	265
08	25	44.3	−66	08	13	71878	β	Vol			nv	nv	(cp)	(cp)	(cp)	(cp)
08	25	54.7	+07	33	53	71115	h785	(Cnc)	6805		82	278	81	279	79	281
08	26	43.8	+12	39	17	71250	27	Cnc		BP	76	284	74	286	71	289
08	27	36.5	−53	05	19	71935	GU	Vel			157	203	nv	nv	nv	nv
08	29	27.5	−44	43	30	72127	−	Vel			143	217	155	205	nv	nv
08	30	15.8	+60	43	05	71369	o	UMa	6830	1, β1067	cp	cp	cp	cp	cp	cp
08	31	35.7	+18	05	40	72094	θ	Cnc		31	69	291	66	294	61	299
08	32	42.4	+20	26	28	72292	η	Cnc		33	67	293	63	297	58	302
08	34	43.7	−49	56	39	73155	C	Vel			151	209	170	190	nv	nv
08	35	19.6	−58	00	33	73389	e^2	Car			168	192	nv	nv	nv	nv
08	37	38.6	−42	59	21	73634	e	Vel			141	219	151	209		
08	37	39.3	+05	42	13	73262	δ	Hya		4	84	276	83	277	82	278
08	37	52.1	−26	15	18	73495	η	Pyx			120	240	125	235	133	227
08	38	45.4	+03	20	29	73471	σ	Hya		5	87	273	86	274	85	275
08	39	05.3	−70	23	13	74405	θ	Vol		h4134	nv	nv	(cp)	(cp)	(cp)	(cp)
08	39	07.9	−22	39	43	73752	−	Pyx	6914	β208	116	244	119	241	126	234
08	39	42.5	−29	33	40	73898	ζ	Pyx	6923	h4120	124	236	129	231	139	221
08	39	58.6	−53	03	03	74146	−	Vel			157	203	nv	nv	nv	nv
08	40	01.4	−12	28	32	73840	6	Hya			104	256	106	254	109	251
08	40	06.2	−35	18	29	74006	β	Pyx			131	229	138	222	153	207
08	40	12.9	+64	19	41	73108	π^2	UMa		4	cp	cp	cp	cp	cp	cp

R.A. 2000.0		Declin.			HD	Star	Const.	ADS	Also Known As	Rising and Setting Azimuths					
										R(30)	S(30)	R(40)	S(40)	R(50)	S(50)
08 40 17.6		−52 55	19		74195	o	Vel			155	205	nv	nv	nv	nv
08 40 19.2		−40 15	51		74067	—	Vel			138	222	147	213	179	181
08 40 37.0		−59 45	40		74375	d	Car		V343	172	188	nv	nv	nv	nv
08 40 37.6		−46 38	55		74180	b	Vel			146	214	160	200	nv	nv
08 41 13.0		−47 19	01		74272	n	Vel			148	212	163	197	nv	nv
08 41 19.9		−78 57	48		75416	η	Cha			nv	nv	(cp)	(cp)	(cp)	(cp)
08 41 43.2		−15 56	36		74137	9	Hya	6937	h4124	107	253	110	250	114	246
08 41 56.8		−45 24	39		74371	LN	Vel			145	215	157	203	nv	nv
08 42 25.4		−53 06	50		74560	HY	Vel			157	203	nv	nv	nv	nv
08 43 13.4		+03 23	55		74280	η	Hya		7	87	273	86	274	85	275
08 43 17.1		+21 28	06		74198	γ	Cnc		43	66	294	62	298	56	304
08 43 35.5		−33 11	11		74575	α	Pyx			129	231	135	225	148	212
08 43 40.4		−07 14	01		74395	F	Hya			98	262	99	261	101	259
08 43 40.5		−49 49	22		74753	D	Vel			151	209	170	190	nv	nv
08 44 23.9		−42 38	57		74772	d	Vel			141	219	151	209	nv	nv
08 44 41.0		+18 09	15		74442	δ	Cnc	6967	47, h457	69	291	66	294	61	299
08 44 42.2		−54 42	30		74956	δ	Vel		h4136	159	201	nv	nv	nv	nv
08 46 01.7		−46 02	30		75063	a	Vel			146	214	160	200	nv	nv
08 46 22.5		−13 32	52		74918	12	Hya		D	105	255	107	253	110	250
08 46 40.0		+28 45	55		74738	ι^B	Cnc	6988	48	57	303	52	308	43	317
08 46 41.8		+28 45	36		74739	ι^A	Cnc	6988	48, Σ1268	57	303	52	308	43	317
08 46 42.7		−56 46	11		75311	V344	Car			163	197	nv	nv	nv	nv
08 46 46.5		+06 25	08		74874	ε	Hya	6993	11, Σ1273	83	277	82	278	81	279
08 48 25.9		+05 50	16		75137	ρ	Hya	7006	13	84	276	83	277	82	278
08 49 39.1		−40 19	14		75630	h	Vel			138	222	147	213	179	181
08 49 47.7		−45 18	28		75710	g	Vel			145	215	157	203	nv	nv
08 49 51.5		−32 46	50		75605	—	Pyx			128	232	134	226	146	214
08 50 31.9		−27 42	36		75691	γ	Pyx			122	238	126	234	135	225
08 50 33.4		−46 31	45		75821	f	Vel		KX	146	214	160	200	nv	nv
08 51 56.8		+43 43	36		75506	35	Lyn			38	322	27	333	cp	cp
08 55 02.8		−60 38	40		76728	c	Car			180	180	nv	nv	nv	nv
08 55 23.6		+05 56	44		76294	ζ	Hya		16	84	276	83	277	82	278
08 55 31.5		−27 40	55		76483	δ	Pyx	7095	See 107	122	238	126	234	135	225
08 55 39.6		+27 55	39		76219	ρ²	Cnc		58	58	302	54	306	45	315
08 55 39.7		−09 08	29		76400	T	Hya			100	260	102	258	104	256
08 56 19.4		−52 43	25		76805	H	Vel			155	205	nv	nv	nv	nv
08 56 41.9		−85 39	47		79837	ζ	Oct			nv	nv	(cp)	(cp)	(cp)	(cp)
08 56 56.6		+32 54	37		76398	σ²	Cnc		59	52	308	46	314	34	326
08 56 58.3		−59 13	46		77002	b¹	Car		V376	172	188	nv	nv	nv	nv
08 57 14.9		+15 19	21		76543	o¹	Cnc		62	73	287	70	290	66	294
08 58 29.2		+11 51	28		76756	α	Cnc	7115	65, h110	77	283	76	284	73	287
08 58 52.2		−47 14	05		77140	FZ	Vel			148	212	163	197	nv	nv
08 59 12.4		+48 02	30		76644	ι	UMa	7114	9, h2477	31	329	14	346	cp	cp
08 59 24.1		−59 05	01		77370	b²	Car			172	188	nv	nv	nv	nv
08 59 32.6		+32 25	07		76813	σ³	Cnc		64	52	308	46	314	34	326
09 00 05.4		−41 15	14		77258	w	Vel			139	221	149	211	nv	nv
09 00 38.3		+41 46	58		76943	Kui 37	(Lyn)		10 UMa	41	319	31	329	cp	cp
09 01 44.6		−52 11	18		77653	—	Vel			155	205	nv	nv	nv	nv
09 02 26.9		−66 23	46		78045	α	Vol			nv	nv	(cp)	(cp)	(cp)	(cp)
09 02 32.7		+67 37	47		76827	ρ	UMa		8	cp	cp	cp	cp	cp	cp

2000.0 R.A.									Also	Rising and Setting Azimuths					
			Declin.			HD	Star	Const.	ADS	Known As	R(30)	S(30)	R(40)	S(40)	R(50)	S(50)

R.A.			Declin.			HD	Star	Const.	ADS	Known As	R(30)	S(30)	R(40)	S(40)	R(50)	S(50)
09	02	44.2	+24	27	11	77350	ν	Cnc		69	62	298	58	302	51	309
09	03	37.5	+47	09	24	77327	κ	UMa	7158	12	32	328	17	343	cp	cp
09	04	09.2	−47	05	52	78004	c	Vel			148	212	163	197	nv	nv
09	05	09.3	−72	36	10	78791	G	Car			nv	nv	nv	nv	nv	nv
09	05	38.4	−70	32	19	78764	E	Car		V345	nv	nv	nv	nv	nv	nv
09	05	58.3	+05	05	32	77996	ω	Hya		18	84	276	83	277	82	278
09	06	31.7	+38	27	08	77912	—	Lyn			45	315	37	323	17	343
09	07	44.8	+10	40	06	78316	κ	Cnc		76	78	282	77	283	74	286
09	07	59.7	−43	25	57	78647	λ	Vel		See 109	142	218	153	207	nv	nv
09	08	00.0	+29	39	15	78235	τ	Cnc		72	56	304	51	309	41	319
09	08	02.8	−25	51	30	78541	κ	Pyx	7202		119	241	123	237	131	229
09	08	23.5	+66	52	24	77800	σ¹	UMa		11	cp	cp	cp	cp	cp	cp
09	08	52.2	+51	36	16	78209	15	UMa			26	334	cp	cp	cp	cp
09	09	21.5	+22	02	43	78515	ξ	Cnc		77	64	296	61	299	54	306
09	10	23.1	+67	08	04	78154	σ²	UMa	7203	13, Σ1306	cp	cp	cp	cp	cp	cp
09	10	55.0	+63	30	49	78362	τ	UMa	7211	14	cp	cp	cp	cp	cp	cp
09	10	57.9	−58	58	01	79351	V357	Car		a	168	192	nv	nv	nv	nv
09	11	04.3	−44	52	04	79186	GX	Vel			143	217	155	205	nv	nv
09	11	16.7	−62	19	02	79447	i	Car			nv	nv	(cp)	(cp)	(cp)	(cp)
09	13	12.1	−69	43	02	80007	β	Car			nv	nv	(cp)	(cp)	(cp)	(cp)
09	14	20.6	+61	25	24	79028	16	UMa			cp	cp	cp	cp	cp	cp
09	14	21.8	+02	18	51	79469	θ	Hya	7253	22, h2489	88	272	87	273	87	273
09	15	13.8	+14	56	29	79554	π²	Cnc		82	74	286	72	288	68	292
09	15	36.7	−38	34	12	79917	l ("ell")	Vel			135	225	143	217	163	197
09	15	45.1	−37	24	48	79940	k2	Vel			134	226	142	218	159	201
09	16	11.3	+54	01	18	79439	18	UMa		DD	21	339	cp	cp	cp	cp
09	16	12.2	−57	32	28	80230	g	Car			166	194	nv	nv	nv	nv
09	16	23.0	−44	15	57	80108	—	Vel			143	217	155	205	nv	nv
09	16	41.6	−06	21	11	79910	23	Hya			97	263	98	262	99	261
09	18	50.6	+36	48	09	80081	38	Lyn	7292	Σ1334	47	313	40	320	24	336
09	19	46.3	−11	58	30	80499	26	Hya			103	257	104	256	107	253
09	20	28.9	−09	33	21	80586	27	Hya	7311	h105	100	260	102	258	104	256
09	20	57.1	−62	24	17	81101	k	Car			nv	nv	nv	nv	nv	nv
09	20	59.2	+38	11	18	80441	Σ1338	(Lyn)	7307		45	315	37	323	17	343
09	21	03.2	+34	23	33	80493	α	Lyn		40	50	310	43	317	30	330
09	21	29.6	−25	57	56	80874	θ	Pyx			119	241	123	237	131	229
09	22	06.8	−55	00	38	81188	κ	Vel			161	199	nv	nv	nv	nv
09	23	12.1	−28	50	02	81169	λ	Pyx			123	237	128	232	137	223
09	24	09.2	−80	47	13	82554	ι	Cha			nv	nv	(cp)	(cp)	(cp)	(cp)
09	24	39.2	+26	10	56	81146	κ	Leo	7351	1, β105	60	300	55	305	47	313
09	26	18.0	−53	22	45	81848	J	Vel			157	203	nv	nv	nv	nv
09	27	18.3	−22	20	38	81799	G	Hya			116	244	119	241	126	234
09	27	35.2	−08	39	31	81797	α	Hya		30	99	261	100	260	103	257
09	28	27.4	+09	03	24	81858	ω	Leo	7390	2, Σ1356	80	280	78	282	76	284
09	29	08.8	−02	46	08	81997	τ¹	Hya		31	92	268	93	267	93	267
09	29	14.7	−35	57	06	82150	ε	Ant			131	229	138	222	153	207
09	30	41.9	−40	28	00	82434	ψ	Vel			138	222	147	213	179	181
09	30	45.4	−31	53	29	82383	ζ¹ᴮ	Ant			126	234	132	228	143	217
09	30	46.1	−31	53	22	82384	ζ¹ᴬ	Ant		DUN 78	126	234	132	228	143	217
09	31	13.3	−57	02	04	82668	N	Vel			166	194	nv	nv	nv	nv

R.A. 2000.0	Declin.	HD	Star	Const.	ADS	Also Known As	R(30)	S(30)	R(40)	S(40)	R(50)	S(50)
09 31 31.7	+63 03 43	81937	23	UMa	7402	h, Σ1351	cp	cp	cp	cp	cp	cp
09 31 32.2	−31 52 18	82513	ζ²	Ant			126	234	132	228	143	217
09 31 32.3	+35 06 11	82198	8	LMi			49	311	42	318	27	333
09 31 43.1	+22 58 04	82308	λ	Leo		4	64	296	61	299	54	306
09 31 56.7	+11 17 59	82395	ξ	Leo		5	77	283	76	284	73	287
09 31 57.5	+09 42 57	82381	6	Leo	7416	h107	80	280	78	282	76	284
09 31 58.9	−01 11 05	82446	τ²	Hya		32	91	269	91	269	92	268
09 32 14.7	−62 47 19	82901	R	Car			nv	nv	(cp)	(cp)	(cp)	(cp)
09 32 19.2	−40 38 58	82694	—	Vel			138	222	147	213	1779	181
09 32 51.3	+51 40 38	82328	θ	UMa	7420	25, β1071	26	334	cp	cp	cp	cp
09 33 12.4	−21 06 57	82734	—	Hya			114	246	118	242	124	236
09 33 44.4	−49 00 18	82984	—	Vel			151	209	170	190	nv	nv
09 33 53.4	−80 56 29	83979	ζ	Cha			nv	nv	(cp)	(cp)	(cp)	(cp)
09 34 08.7	−51 15 21	83058	L	Vel			154	206	nv	nv	nv	nv
09 34 13.3	+36 23 51	82635	10	LMi		SU	47	313	40	320	24	336
09 34 26.6	−59 13 46	83183	h	Car			172	188	nv	nv	nv	nv
09 34 28.8	+69 49 49	82210	24	UMa		DK	cp	cp	cp	cp	cp	cp
09 34 49.4	+52 03 05	82621	26	UMa			25	335	cp	cp	cp	cp
09 35 03.8	+39 37 17	82741	—	Lyn			43	317	35	325	12	348
09 36 49.7	−49 21 18	83446	M	Vel			151	209	170	190	nv	nv
09 37 05.2	+81 19 35	81817	—	Dra			cp	cp	cp	cp	cp	cp
09 37 12.6	+06 50 09	83240	10	Leo			83	277	82	278	81	279
09 38 27.2	+04 38 57	83425	—	Hya			85	275	85	275	84	276
09 39 21.0	−61 19 41	83944	m	Car			nv	nv	nv	nv	nv	nv
09 39 51.3	−01 08 34	83618	ι	Hya		35	91	269	91	269	92	268
09 40 18.3	−14 19 56	83754	κ	Hya		38	106	254	108	252	112	248
09 41 09.0	+09 53 32	83808	o	Leo	7480	14	80	280	78	282	76	284
09 41 16.9	−23 35 30	83953	I	Hya			117	243	121	239	127	233
09 42 14.4	−23 54 56	84117	—	Hya			117	243	121	239	127	233
09 42 57.1	+72 15 09	83506	27	UMa			cp	cp	cp	cp	cp	cp
09 43 43.8	+14 01 18	84194	ψ	Leo		16	74	286	72	288	68	292
09 44 12.1	−27 46 10	84367	θ	Ant			122	238	126	234	135	225
09 45 14.8	−62 30 28	84810	ZZ	Car		l ["ell"]	nv	nv	(cp)	(cp)	(cp)	(cp)
09 45 34.1	+34 30 44	84346	R	LMi			50	310	43	317	30	330
09 45 51.0	+23 46 27	84441	ε	Leo		17	63	297	59	301	53	307
09 46 21.3	−76 46 33	85396	ν	Cha			(cp)	(cp)	(cp)	(cp)	(cp)	(cp)
09 46 31.6	+57 07 41	84335	CS	UMa			14	346	cp	cp	cp	cp
09 47 05.4	−59 16 31	80404	ι	Car			172	188	nv	nv	nv	nv
09 47 06.1	−65 04 18	85123	υ^A	Car			nv	nv	nv	nv	(cp)	(cp)
09 47 06.7	−65 04 21	85124	υ^B	Car			nv	nv	nv	nv	nv	nv
09 47 33.4	+11 25 43	84748	R	Leo			77	283	76	284	73	287
09 48 35.3	+46 01 15	84737	—	UMa			34	326	20	340	cp	cp
09 49 57.1	−45 43 58	85355	u	Vel			145	215	157	203	nv	nv
09 50 59.3	+59 02 19	84999	υ	UMa	7534	29, OΣ521	8	352	cp	cp	cp	cp
09 51 28.6	−14 50 48	85444	υ¹	Hya		39	106	254	108	252	112	248
09 51 40.7	−46 32 52	85622	m	Vel			146	214	160	200	nv	nv
09 52 06.3	+54 03 51	85235	φ	UMa	7545	30, OΣ208	21	339	cp	cp	cp	cp
09 52 30.4	−08 06 18	85558	γ	Sex	7555	8, h4256	99	261	100	260	103	257
09 52 45.8	+26 00 25	85503	μ	Leo		24	60	300	55	305	47	313
09 54 12.2	−25 55 55	85859	—	Hya			119	241	123	237	131	229

2000.0 R.A.	Declin.	HD	Star	Const.	ADS	Also Known As	R(30)	S(30)	R(40)	S(40)	R(50)	S(50)
09 54 52.1	−19 00 34	85951	—	Hya			112	248	115	245	120	240
09 55 42.9	+49 49 12	85795	31	UMa		SY	29	331	10	350	cp	cp
09 56 51.7	−54 34 04	86440	φ	Vel			159	201	nv	nv	nv	nv
09 57 41.0	+41 03 20	86146	19	LMi			41	319	31	329	cp	cp
09 58 13.3	+12 26 41	86360	ν	Leo		27	76	284	74	286	71	289
09 58 52.2	−35 53 28	86629	η	Ant		h4271	131	229	138	222	153	207
10 00 12.7	+08 02 39	86663	π	Leo		29	81	279	80	280	77	283
10 05 07.4	−13 03 53	87504	ν²	Hya		40	105	255	107	253	110	250
10 06 11.3	−47 22 12	87783	—	Vel			148	212	163	197	nv	nv
10 07 19.9	+16 45 45	87737	η	Leo		30	71	289	69	291	65	295
10 07 25.7	+35 14 41	87696	21	LMi			49	311	42	318	27	333
10 07 54.2	+09 59 51	87837	31	Leo	7649		80	280	78	282	76	284
10 07 56.2	−00 22 18	87887	α	Sex		15	90	270	90	270	90	270
10 08 22.2	+11 58 02	87901	α	Leo	7654	32	77	283	76	284	73	287
10 08 56.2	−51 48 40	88206	—	Vel			154	206	nv	nv	nv	nv
10 10 35.2	−12 21 15	88284	λ	Hya	7671	41, β593	104	256	106	254	109	251
10 13 30.6	−66 22 22	88981	M	Car			nv	nv	nv	nv	nv	nv
10 13 44.3	−70 02 16	89080	ω	Car			nv	nv	nv	nv	nv	nv
10 14 44.1	−42 07 19	88955	—	Vel			141	219	151	209	nv	nv
10 16 41.4	+23 25 02	89025	ζ	Leo		36	63	297	59	301	53	307
10 17 04.9	−61 19 56	89388	V337	Car			nv	nv	nv	nv	nv	nv
10 17 05.7	+42 54 52	89021	λ	UMa		33	39	321	29	331	cp	cp
10 17 37.7	−08 04 08	89254	ε	Sex		22	99	261	100	260	103	257
10 17 51.3	+71 03 22	88849	Σ1415	(UMa)	7705		cp	cp	cp	cp	cp	cp
10 19 36.8	−55 01 46	89682	GZ	Vel			161	199	nv	nv	nv	nv
10 19 44.1	+19 28 15	89449	40	Leo			68	292	65	295	60	300
10 19 58.3	+19 50 30	89484	γ¹	Leo	7724	41, Σ1424	68	292	65	295	60	300
10 19 58.6	+19 50 25	89485	γ²	Leo	7724	41	68	292	65	295	60	300
10 20 55.4	−56 02 36	89890	I	Vel			163	197	nv	nv	nv	nv
10 22 19.5	−41 39 00	89998	—	Vel			139	221	149	211	nv	nv
10 22 19.7	+41 29 58	89758	μ	UMa		34	41	319	31	329	cp	cp
10 22 58.1	−66 54 06	90264	L	Car			nv	nv	nv	nv	(cp)	(cp)
10 23 26.4	−04 04 27	90044	SS	Sex		25	95	265	95	265	96	264
10 24 07.8	+65 33 59	89822	—	UMa			cp	cp	cp	cp	cp	cp
10 24 23.7	−74 01 54	90589	I	Car			nv	nv	(cp)	(cp)	(cp)	(cp)
10 25 54.8	+33 47 46	90277	30	LMi			51	309	45	315	32	328
10 26 05.4	−16 50 11	90432	μ	Hya		42	109	251	111	249	115	245
10 27 09.1	−31 04 04	90610	α	Ant			126	234	132	228	143	217
10 27 24.4	−57 38 20	90772	—	Car			166	194	nv	nv	nv	nv
10 27 52.7	−58 44 22	90853	s	Car			168	192	nv	nv	nv	nv
10 27 52.9	+36 42 26	90537	β	LMi	7780	31, Hu 879	47	313	40	320	24	336
10 29 28.6	−02 44 21	90882	δ	Sex		29	92	268	93	267	93	276
10 30 17.4	−00 38 13	90994	β	Sex		30	90	270	90	270	90	270
10 30 20.0	−71 59 34	91375	K	Car			nv	nv	nv	nv	(cp)	(cp)
10 30 37.5	+55 58 50	90839	36	UMa			19	341	cp	cp	cp	cp
10 31 02.0	−73 13 18	91496	—	Car			nv	nv	nv	nv	nv	nv
10 31 21.8	−53 42 56	91324	Y	Vel			157	203	nv	nv	nv	nv
10 32 01.4	−61 41 07	91465	PP	Car		p Car	nv	nv	nv	nv	(cp)	(cp)
10 32 48.6	+09 18 24	91316	ρ	Leo		47	80	280	78	282	76	284
10 32 56.9	−47 00 12	91504	t	Vel		h4330	148	212	163	197	nv	nv

2000.0 R.A.			Declin.			HD	Star	Const.	ADS	Also Known As	Rising and Setting Azimuths R(30)	S(30)	R(40)	S(40)	R(50)	S(50)
10	33	13.8	+40	25	31	91312	—	UMa	7826		42	318	33	327	cp	cp
10	34	00.8	−23	44	32	91550	44	Hya	7834	β1269	117	243	121	239	127	233
10	34	47.9	+06	57	14	91612	48	Leo			83	277	82	278	81	279
10	35	05.5	+75	42	46	91190	—	Dra			cp	cp	cp	cp	cp	cp
10	35	09.6	+57	04	57	91480	37	UMa			14	346	cp	cp	cp	cp
10	35	12.8	−39	33	45	91793	U	Ant			137	223	145	215	168	192
10	35	28.1	−78	36	27	92305	γ	Cha			nv	nv	(cp)	(cp)	(cp)	(cp)
10	35	35.2	−57	33	27	91942	r	Car			166	194	nv	nv	nv	nv
10	36	04.5	−26	40	30	91881	β411	(Hya)	7846		120	240	125	235	133	227
10	36	20.3	−59	33	53	92063	—	Car			172	188	nv	nv	nv	nv
10	37	13.7	−27	24	46	92036	—	Hya			122	238	126	234	135	225
10	37	18.0	−48	13	33	92139	p	(Vel)		See 119	149	211	166	194	nv	nv
10	37	33.1	−13	23	04	92055	U	Hya			105	255	107	253	110	250
10	38	34.9	−16	52	36	92214	φ³	Hya			109	251	111	249	115	245
10	38	43.2	+31	58	34	92125	37	LMi			54	306	48	312	37	323
10	38	45.1	−59	10	59	92397	GM	Car			172	188	nv	nv	nv	nv
10	39	18.3	−55	36	12	92449	x	Vel		DUN 95, h4341	161	199	nv	nv	nv	nv
10	41	56.5	+65	42	58	92424	38	UMa			cp	cp	cp	cp	cp	cp
10	42	14.0	−64	27	58	92938	—	Car			nv	nv	nv	nv	(cp)	(cp)
10	42	57.4	−64	23	40	93030	θ	Car			nv	nv	nv	nv	(cp)	(cp)
10	43	04.0	+69	04	34	92523	—	UMa			cp	cp	cp	cp	cp	cp
10	43	24.9	+23	11	18	92825	41	LMi			63	297	59	301	53	307
10	43	32.1	−60	33	59	93070	—	Car			180	180	nv	nv	(cp)	(cp)
10	43	32.8	+46	12	14	92787	—	UMa			34	326	20	340	cp	cp
10	44	06.9	−63	57	40	93194	—	Car			nv	nv	nv	nv	(cp)	(cp)
10	44	38.3	+68	46	32	92763	R	UMa			cp	cp	cp	cp	cp	cp
10	45	03.6	−59	41	03	93308	η	Car			172	188	nv	nv	(cp)	(cp)
10	45	15.8	−80	28	10	93779	δ¹	Cha			nv	nv	(cp)	(cp)	(cp)	(cp)
10	45	46.6	−80	32	24	93845	δ²	Cha			nv	nv	(cp)	(cp)	(cp)	(cp)
10	45	51.8	+30	40	56	93152	42	LMi			55	305	49	311	39	321
10	46	29.7	−64	15	47	93549	—	Car			nv	nv	nv	nv	(cp)	(cp)
10	46	46.1	−49	25	12	93497	μ	Vel			151	209	170	190	nv	nv
10	46	51.2	−64	23	00	93607	—	Car			nv	nv	nv	nv	(cp)	(cp)
10	46	57.5	−56	45	26	93563	—	Vel			163	197	nv	nv	(cp)	(cp)
10	47	37.9	−15	15	44	93526	Σ1474	(Hya)	7930		107	253	110	250	114	246
10	49	37.4	−16	11	37	93813	ν	Hya			109	251	111	249	115	245
10	53	18.6	+34	12	53	94264	46	LMi			50	310	43	317	30	330
10	53	29.4	−20	08	20	94388	b³	Hya			113	247	117	243	122	238
10	53	29.6	−58	51	12	94510	u	Car			168	192	nv	nv	nv	nv
10	53	34.3	+54	35	06	94247	44	UMa			21	339	cp	cp	cp	cp
10	53	58.7	+43	11	24	94334	ω	UMa		45	38	322	27	333	cp	cp
10	55	36.7	+24	44	59	94601	54A	Leo	7979	Σ1487	62	298	58	302	51	309
10	55	37.2	+24	44	46	94602	54B	Leo			62	298	58	302	51	309
10	55	44.3	+33	30	25	94600	46	UMa			51	309	45	315	32	328
10	56	43.0	−37	08	16	94890	ι	Ant			134	226	142	218	159	201
10	59	27.9	+40	25	49	95128	47	UMa			42	318	33	327	cp	cp
10	59	46.4	−18	17	56	95272	α	Crt		7	111	249	114	246	119	241
11	00	09.2	−42	13	33	95370	i	Vel			141	219	151	209	nv	nv
11	00	33.6	+03	37	03	95345	58	Leo			87	273	86	274	85	275
11	00	44.7	+06	06	05	95382	59	Leo	8019		83	277	82	278	81	279

2000.0 R.A.	Declin.	HD	Star	Const.	ADS	Also Known As	R(30)	S(30)	R(40)	S(40)	R(50)	S(50)
11 00 50.3	+39 12 43	95310	49	UMa			43	317	35	325	12	348
11 01 49.6	−02 29 04	95578	61	Leo			92	268	93	267	93	267
11 01 50.4	+56 22 56	95418	β	UMa		48	17	343	cp	cp	cp	cp
11 02 19.7	+20 10 47	95608	60	Leo			67	293	63	297	58	302
11 03 20.2	+35 58 13	95735	Lalande 21185	UMa			49	311	42	318	27	333
11 03 43.6	+61 45 03	95689	α	UMa	8035	50, β1077	cp	cp	cp	cp	cp	cp
11 05 01.0	+07 20 10	96097	χ	Leo		63, Kui 54	82	278	81	279	79	281
11 05 19.9	−27 17 36	96202	χ¹	Hya			122	238	126	234	135	225
11 05 57.5	−27 17 16	96314	χ²	Hya			122	238	126	234	135	225
11 06 32.4	−62 25 26	96566	z¹	Car			nv	nv	nv	nv	(cp)	(cp)
11 07 16.5	−42 38 19	96616	V815	Cen		h4409	141	219	151	209	nv	nv
11 08 33.8	−61 56 49	96919	V371	Car			nv	nv	nv	nv	(cp)	(cp)
11 08 35.3	−58 58 30	96918	V382	Car			168	192	nv	nv	(cp)	(cp)
11 09 39.7	+44 29 54	96833	ψ	UMa		52	37	323	25	335	cp	cp
11 11 39.4	−22 49 33	97277	β	Crt		11	116	244	119	241	126	234
11 12 36.0	−60 19 03	97534	y	Car			180	180	nv	nv	(cp)	(cp)
11 12 45.3	−64 10 12	97583	—	Car			nv	nv	nv	nv	(cp)	(cp)
11 14 06.4	+20 31 25	97603	δ	Leo		68, β1282	67	293	63	297	58	302
11 14 14.3	+15 25 46	97633	θ	Leo		70	73	287	70	290	66	294
11 15 12.2	+23 05 44	97778	72	Leo			63	297	59	301	53	307
11 16 39.6	−03 39 06	98058	φ	Leo		74	93	267	94	266	95	265
11 17 17.3	+02 00 38	98118	75	Leo			88	272	87	273	87	273
11 18 10.9	+31 31 45	98231	ξ^A	UMa	8119	53, Σ1523	54	306	48	312	37	323
11 18 10.9	+31 31 45	98230	ξ^B	UMa		53	54	306	48	312	37	323
11 18 28.7	+33 05 39	98262	ν	UMa	8123	54, Σ1524	51	309	45	315	32	328
11 19 07.8	+38 11 08	98353	55	UMa			45	315	37	323	17	343
11 19 20.4	−14 46 43	98430	δ	Crt		12	106	254	108	252	112	248
11 21 00.4	−54 29 27	98718	π	Cen			159	201	nv	nv	nv	nv
11 21 08.1	+06 01 46	98664	σ	Leo		77	83	277	82	278	81	279
11 22 49.5	+45 28 58	98839	56	UMa			35	325	23	337	cp	cp
11 23 12.5	−36 09 54	98993	—	Cen			133	227	140	220	156	204
11 23 21.8	−18 46 48	98991	λ	Crt		13	111	249	114	246	119	241
11 23 21.8	−64 57 18	99104	—	Mus			nv	nv	(cp)	(cp)	(cp)	(cp)
11 23 55.4	+10 31 45	99028	ι	Leo	8148	78, Σ1536	78	282	77	283	74	286
11 24 36.5	−10 51 34	99167	ε	Crt		14	102	258	103	257	106	254
11 24 52.8	−17 41 03	99211	γ	Crt	8153	15, h840	110	250	112	248	117	243
11 25 29.3	−36 03 47	99322	—	Cen			133	227	140	220	156	204
11 25 43.2	−63 58 22	99453	—	Cru			nv	nv	nv	nv	nv	nv
11 27 56.2	+02 51 22	99648	τ	Leo		84	88	272	87	273	87	273
11 28 35.0	−42 40 27	99803	—	Cen			141	219	151	209	nv	nv
11 30 18.8	−03 00 13	99998	87	Leo			93	267	94	266	95	265
11 31 24.2	+69 19 52	100029	λ	Dra		1	cp	cp	cp	cp	cp	cp
11 31 46.1	−59 26 32	100261	o¹	Cen			172	188	nv	nv	nv	nv
11 31 48.6	−59 30 56	100262	o²	Cen			172	188	nv	nv	nv	nv
11 32 54.0	−31 05 14	100393	—	Hya			126	234	132	228	143	217
11 33 00.1	−31 51 27	100407	ξ	Hya			126	234	132	228	143	217
11 34 45.6	−54 15 51	100673	—	Cen			159	201	nv	nv	nv	nv
11 35 46.8	−63 01 11	100841	λ	Cen			nv	nv	nv	nv	(cp)	(cp)
11 36 02.7	+69 19 22	100696	2	Dra			cp	cp	cp	cp	cp	cp
11 36 40.8	−09 48 08	100889	θ	Crt		21	100	260	102	258	104	256

	2000.0						Also	Rising and Setting Azimuths					
R.A.		Declin.		HD	Star	Const.	ADS	Known As	R(30)	S(30)	R(40)	S(40)	R(50)	S(50)
11 36 56.9	−00 49 26			100920	91	Leo			90	270	90	270	90	270
11 37 00.6	−61 17 00			101021	—	Cen			nv	nv	nv	nv	(cp)	(cp)
11 38 07.3	−61 49 35			101189	—	Cen			nv	nv	nv	nv	(cp)	(cp)
11 38 27.5	+08 08 03			101153	ω	Vir		1	81	279	80	280	77	283
11 38 40.0	−13 12 07			101198	ι	Crt		24, Kui 58	105	255	107	253	110	250
11 39 29.5	−65 23 52			101379	—	Mus			nv	nv	(cp)	(cp)	(cp)	(cp)
11 40 12.7	−34 44 41			101431	o	Hya			130	230	137	223	150	210
11 40 53.6	−62 05 23			101570	—	Cen			nv	nv	nv	nv	(cp)	(cp)
11 41 43.9	−32 29 59			101666	—	Hya			128	232	134	226	146	214
11 43 31.2	−62 29 21			101947	V810	Cen			nv	nv	nv	nv	(cp)	(cp)
11 44 45.7	−18 21 03			102070	ζ	Crt		27	111	249	114	246	119	241
11 45 17.0	+08 15 30			102124	ξ	Vir		2	81	279	80	280	77	283
11 45 36.4	−66 43 43			102249	λ	Mus		h4471	nv	nv	(cp)	(cp)	(cp)	(cp)
11 45 51.5	+06 31 46			102212	ν	Vir		3	83	277	82	278	81	279
11 46 03.0	+47 46 46			102224	χ	UMa		63	32	328	17	343	cp	cp
11 46 30.7	−61 10 42			102350	—	Cen			nv	nv	(cp)	(cp)	(cp)	(cp)
11 46 31.0	−40 30 01			102365	—	Cen			138	222	147	213	179	181
11 47 59.1	+20 13 08			102509	93	Leo			67	293	63	297	58	302
11 48 14.4	−66 48 53			102584	μ	Mus			nv	nv	(cp)	(cp)	(cp)	(cp)
11 48 45.0	−26 44 59			102620	II	Hya			120	240	125	235	133	227
11 49 03.5	+14 34 19			102647	β	Leo	8314	94	74	286	72	288	68	292
11 49 41.0	−63 47 18			102776	j	Cen			nv	nv	(cp)	(cp)	(cp)	(cp)
11 49 56.3	−70 13 32			102839	—	Mus			nv	nv	(cp)	(cp)	(cp)	(cp)
11 50 41.6	+01 45 53			102870	β	Vir		5	89	271	89	271	88	272
11 51 08.1	−45 10 26			102964	—	Cen			145	215	157	203	nv	nv
11 51 51.2	−65 12 22			103079	—	Mus			nv	nv	(cp)	(cp)	(cp)	(cp)
11 52 54.5	−33 54 28			103192	β	Hya		h4478	129	231	135	225	148	212
11 52 58.7	+37 43 07			103095	Groombridge 1830	(UMa)			46	314	38	322	21	339
11 53 49.8	+53 41 41			103287	γ	UMa		64	23	337	cp	cp	cp	cp
11 56 00.9	−17 09 03			103632	η	Crt		30	110	250	112	248	117	243
11 59 37.3	−78 13 18			104174	ε	Cha		h4486	nv	nv	(cp)	(cp)	(cp)	(cp)
12 00 52.3	+06 36 51			104321	π	Vir		8	83	277	82	278	81	279
12 02 06.8	+43 02 44			104513	67	UMa		DP	38	322	27	333	cp	cp
12 03 01.5	−63 18 46			104671	θ¹	Cru			nv	nv	nv	nv	nv	nv
12 03 39.5	−42 26 03			104731	—	Cen			141	219	151	209	nv	nv
12 04 00.9	+18 48 53			104785	R	Com			69	291	66	294	61	299
12 04 19.2	−63 09 56			104841	θ²	Cru			nv	nv	nv	nv	nv	nv
12 04 46.5	−76 31 08			104902	κ	Cha			nv	nv	(cp)	(cp)	(cp)	(cp)
12 05 12.5	+08 43 59			104979	o	Vir		9	81	279	80	280	77	283
12 06 52.8	−64 36 49			105211	η	Cru		h4501	nv	nv	nv	nv	nv	nv
12 07 49.9	−75 22 00			105340	—	Mus			nv	nv	(cp)	(cp)	(cp)	(cp)
12 08 05.1	−50 39 40			105382	—	Cen			152	208	180	180	nv	nv
12 08 21.5	−50 43 20			105435	δ	Cen			152	208	180	180	nv	nv
12 08 24.7	−24 43 44			105452	α	Crv		1	118	242	122	238	129	231
12 10 07.4	−22 37 11			105707	ε	Crv		2	116	244	119	241	126	234
12 11 39.1	−52 22 06			105937	ρ	Cen			155	205	nv	nv	nv	nv
12 12 11.8	+77 36 58			106112	—	Cam			cp	cp	cp	cp	cp	cp
12 15 08.6	−58 44 56			106490	δ	Cru			168	192	nv	nv	nv	nv
12 15 25.5	+57 01 57			106591	δ	UMa		69	14	346	cp	cp	cp	cp
12 15 48.3	−17 32 31			106625	γ	Crv		4	110	250	112	248	117	243

2000.0 R.A.	Declin.	HD	Star	Const.	ADS	Also Known As	Rising and Setting Azimuths R(30)	S(30)	R(40)	S(40)	R(50)	S(50)
12 16 00.1	+14 53 57	106661	6	Com			74	286	72	288	68	292
12 16 07.5	+40 39 36	106690	2	CVn	8489	Σ1622	42	318	33	327	cp	cp
12 16 20.5	+23 56 43	106714	7	Com			63	297	59	301	53	307
12 16 30.1	+33 03 41	106760	—	Com			51	309	45	315	32	328
12 17 34.2	−67 57 38	106849	ε	Mus			nv	nv	(cp)	(cp)	(cp)	(cp)
12 18 20.7	−79 18 43	106911	β	Cha			nv	nv	(cp)	(cp)	(cp)	(cp)
12 18 26.1	−64 00 11	106983	ζ	Cru		h4512	nv	nv	nv	nv	nv	nv
12 18 59.7	−55 08 35	107079	F	Cen			161	199	nv	nv	nv	nv
12 19 37.9	−19 15 21	107199	R	Crv			112	248	115	245	120	240
12 19 48.7	+48 59 03	107274	3	CVn			31	329	14	346	cp	cp
12 19 54.3	−00 40 00	107259	η	Vir		15	90	270	90	270	90	270
12 20 20.9	+03 18 45	107328	16	Vir			87	273	86	274	85	275
12 20 33.6	−22 12 57	107348	ζ	Crv	8517	5	116	244	119	241	126	234
12 20 41.3	+27 03 17	107398	Σ1633	(Com)	8519		58	302	54	306	45	315
12 20 42.9	+17 47 34	107383	11	Com	8521	Ho 52	70	290	68	292	63	297
12 20 55.7	−13 33 56	107418	—	Crv			105	255	107	253	110	250
12 21 21.5	−60 24 04	107446	ε	Cru			180	180	nv	nv	nv	nv
12 22 07.4	−67 31 20	107566	ζ²	Mus			nv	nv	(cp)	(cp)	(cp)	(cp)
12 22 11.9	−68 18 27	107567	ζ¹	Mus			nv	nv	(cp)	(cp)	(cp)	(cp)
12 22 30.2	+25 50 46	107700	12	Com	8530		61	299	57	303	49	311
12 23 37.9	−61 37 44	107805	R	Cru			nv	nv	nv	nv	nv	nv
12 24 01.4	+51 33 44	107950	5	CVn			26	334	cp	cp	cp	cp
12 24 18.4	+26 05 55	107966	13	Com		GN	60	300	55	305	47	313
12 24 26.7	+25 34 58	108007	Σ1639	(Com)	8539		61	299	57	303	49	311
12 25 50.9	+39 01 07	108225	6	CVn			43	317	35	325	12	348
12 26 24.0	+27 16 05	108283	14	Com			58	302	54	306	45	315
12 26 30.9	−63 07 21	108250	—	Cru			nv	nv	nv	nv	nv	nv
12 26 31.5	−51 27 02	108257	—	Cen			154	206	nv	nv	nv	nv
12 26 35.9	−63 05 56	108248	α¹	Cru			nv	nv	nv	nv	nv	nv
12 26 36.5	−63 05 58	108249	α²	Cru			nv	nv	nv	nv	nv	nv
12 26 56.2	+28 16 06	108381	γ	Com		15	57	303	52	308	43	317
12 26 59.3	+26 49 32	108382	16	Com			60	300	55	305	47	313
12 28 02.3	−50 13 51	108483	σ	Cen			152	208	180	180	nv	nv
12 29 51.8	−16 30 56	108767	δ	Crv	8572	7	109	251	111	249	115	245
12 30 06.6	+69 12 04	108907	4	Dra		CQ	cp	cp	cp	cp	cp	cp
12 31 09.9	−57 06 47	108903	γ^A	Cru		DUN 124	166	194	nv	nv	nv	nv
12 31 16.7	−57 04 51	108925	γ^B	Cru			166	194	nv	nv	nv	nv
12 32 04.1	−16 11 46	109085	η	Crv		8	109	251	111	249	115	245
12 32 28.0	−72 07 58	109026	γ	Mus			nv	nv	(cp)	(cp)	(cp)	(cp)
12 33 28.9	+69 47 17	109387	κ	Dra		5	cp	cp	cp	cp	cp	cp
12 33 44.5	+41 21 27	109358	β	CVn		8	41	319	31	329	cp	cp
12 34 23.2	−23 23 48	109379	β	Crv		9	117	243	121	239	127	233
12 34 43.9	+70 01 18	109551	6	Dra			cp	cp	cp	cp	cp	cp
12 34 51.0	+22 37 45	109485	23	Com			64	296	61	299	54	306
12 35 07.7	+18 22 37	109511	24	Com	8600	Σ1657	69	291	66	294	61	299
12 35 45.4	−41 01 19	109536	—	Cen			139	221	149	211	nv	nv
12 36 23.2	+59 29 12	109729	T	UMa			8	352	cp	cp	cp	cp
12 37 11.0	−69 08 08	109668	α	Mus			nv	nv	(cp)	(cp)	(cp)	(cp)
12 37 42.1	−48 32 28	109787	τ	Cen			149	211	166	194	nv	nv
12 38 29.9	+06 59 18	109914	R	Vir			83	277	82	278	81	279

R.A.			Declin.			HD	Star	Const.	ADS	Also Known As	R(30)	S(30)	R(40)	S(40)	R(50)	S(50)
			2000.0								Rising and Setting Azimuths					
12	38	29.9	+06	59	18	109914	R	Vir			83	277	82	278	81	279
12	39	14.7	−07	59	44	110014	χ	Vir		26	98	262	99	261	101	259
12	39	52.4	−39	59	15	110073	l ("ell")	Cen			137	223	145	215	168	192
12	41	30.9	−48	57	34	110304	γ	Cen		h4539	149	211	166	194	nv	nv
12	41	39.5	−01	26	58	110379	γ	Vir	8630	29, Σ1670	91	269	91	269	92	268
12	41	53.0	+10	14	08	110411	ρ	Vir		30	78	282	77	283	74	286
12	41	56.6	−59	41	08	110335	—	Cru			172	188	nv	nv	nv	nv
12	42	35.3	−48	48	47	110458	—	Cen			149	211	166	194	nv	nv
12	45	07.8	+45	26	25	110914	Y	CVn			35	325	23	337	cp	cp
12	45	37.0	+07	40	24	110951	32	Vir		FM	82	278	81	279	79	281
12	45	37.8	−60	58	52	110829	ι	Cru			180	180	nv	nv	nv	nv
12	46	16.9	−68	06	29	110879	β	Mus			nv	nv	(cp)	(cp)	(cp)	(cp)
12	46	22.6	−56	29	30	110956	—	Cru			163	197	nv	nv	nv	nv
12	46	38.7	+16	34	39	111067	27	Com			71	289	69	291	65	295
12	47	43.3	−59	41	19	111123	β	Cru			172	188	nv	nv	nv	nv
12	49	06.5	+83	25	04	112014	Σ1694B	(Cam)	8682		cp	cp	cp	cp	cp	cp
12	49	13.5	+83	24	46	112028	Σ1694A	(Cam)	8682		cp	cp	cp	cp	cp	cp
12	50	41.1	−33	59	57	111597	—	Cen			129	231	135	225	148	212
12	51	41.8	+27	32	26	111812	31	Com			58	302	54	306	45	315
12	53	06.8	−48	56	35	111915	—	Cen			149	211	166	194	nv	nv
12	53	19.3	+21	14	25	112033	35	Com	8695	Σ1687	66	294	62	298	56	304
12	53	26.1	−40	10	44	111968	—	Cen			138	222	147	213	179	181
12	53	49.0	−60	22	36	111973	κ	Cru			nv	nv	nv	nv	(cp)	(cp)
12	54	01.7	+55	57	35	112185	ε	UMa		77	19	341	cp	cp	cp	cp
12	54	21.1	−09	32	20	112142	ψ	Vir		40	100	260	102	258	104	256
12	54	35.6	−57	10	40	112092	μ¹	Cru		DUN 126	166	194	nv	nv	nv	nv
12	54	36.8	−57	10	05	112091	μ²	Cru			166	194	nv	nv	nv	nv
12	54	39.1	−59	08	47	112078	λ	Cru			172	188	nv	nv	nv	nv
12	54	58.9	−85	07	24	111482	ι	Oct			(cp)	(cp)	(cp)	(cp)	(cp)	(cp)
12	55	28.4	+65	26	18	112429	8	Dra			cp	cp	cp	cp	cp	cp
12	55	36.1	+03	23	51	112300	δ	Vir		43	87	273	86	274	85	275
12	56	00.3	+38	18	53	112412	α¹	CVn	8706	12, Σ1692	45	315	37	323	17	343
12	56	01.6	+38	19	06	112413	α²	CVn	8706		45	315	37	323	17	343
12	57	04.3	−51	11	55	112409	—	Cen			154	206	nv	nv	nv	nv
12	58	55.4	+17	24	33	112769	36	Com			70	290	68	292	63	297
13	00	16.4	+30	47	06	112989	37	Com	8731	β1081	55	305	49	311	39	321
13	00	43.7	+56	21	59	113139	78	UMa	8739	β1082	17	343	cp	cp	cp	cp
13	02	10.5	+10	57	33	113226	ε	Vir		47	78	282	77	283	74	286
13	02	16.3	−71	32	56	112985	δ	Mus			nv	nv	(cp)	(cp)	(cp)	(cp)
13	03	33.1	−49	31	38	113314	ξ¹	Cen			151	209	170	190	nv	nv
13	05	44.4	+35	47	56	113797	14	CVn			49	311	42	318	27	333
13	06	16.6	−48	27	48	113703	—	Cen			149	211	166	194	nv	nv
13	07	10.6	+27	37	29	113996	41	Com			58	302	54	306	45	315
13	07	19.5	+00	35	13	113984	Σ1719	(Vir)	8786		90	270	90	270	90	270
13	07	53.7	−10	44	25	114038	49	Vir			102	258	103	257	106	254
13	08	07.0	−65	18	22	113904	θ	Mus			nv	nv	(cp)	(cp)	(cp)	(cp)
13	09	03.2	−23	07	05	114149	ψ	Hya		45	117	243	121	329	127	233
13	09	56.9	−05	32	20	114330	θ	Vir	8801	51, Σ1724	96	264	97	263	98	262
13	09	59.2	+17	31	46	114378	α	Com	8804	42, Σ1728	70	290	68	292	63	297
13	11	52.3	+27	52	41	114710	β	Com		43	58	302	54	306	45	315

2000.0 R.A.	Declin.	HD	Star	Const.	ADS	Also Known As	R(30)	S(30)	R(40)	S(40)	R(50)	S(50)
13 12 03.1	−37 48 11	114613	—	Cen			134	226	142	218	159	201
13 12 03.4	−16 11 55	114642	53	Vir			109	251	111	249	115	245
13 12 17.4	−59 55 15	114529	—	Cen			172	188	nv	nv	nv	nv
13 13 42.9	+40 09 10	115004	—	CVn			42	318	33	327	cp	cp
13 14 14.7	−59 06 12	114837	—	Cen			172	188	nv	nv	nv	nv
13 15 14.9	−67 53 41	114911	η	Mus			nv	nv	(cp)	(cp)	(cp)	(cp)
13 15 58.7	−19 56 35	115202	57	Vir			112	248	115	245	120	240
13 16 46.4	+09 25 27	115383	59	Vir			80	280	78	282	76	284
13 16 53.1	−31 30 23	115310	—	Cen			126	234	132	228	143	217
13 17 13.0	−66 47 01	115211	—	Mus			nv	nv	(cp)	(cp)	(cp)	(cp)
13 17 32.5	+40 34 21	115604	20	CVn		AO	42	318	33	327	cp	cp
13 17 36.2	+05 28 12	115521	σ	Vir		60	84	276	83	277	82	278
13 18 14.5	+49 40 55	115735	21	CVn			29	331	10	350	cp	cp
13 18 24.2	−18 18 41	115617	61	Vir			111	249	114	246	119	241
13 18 55.2	−23 10 18	115659	γ	Hya		46	117	243	121	329	127	233
13 20 35.7	−36 42 44	115892	ι	Cen			133	227	140	220	156	204
13 22 37.9	−60 59 18	116087	—	Cen			180	180	nv	nv	nv	nv
13 23 55.5	+54 55 31	116656	ζ^A	UMa	8891	79, Σ1744	21	339	cp	cp	cp	cp
13 23 56.3	+54 55 18	116657	ζ^B	UMa		79	21	339	cp	cp	cp	cp
13 24 00.5	−64 32 09	116243	m	Cen			nv	nv	nv	nv	nv	nv
13 25 07.2	−74 53 16	116244	ι	Mus			nv	nv	(cp)	(cp)	(cp)	(cp)
13 25 11.5	−11 09 41	116658	α	Vir		67	103	257	104	256	107	253
13 25 13.4	+54 59 17	116842	80	UMa		g	21	339	cp	cp	cp	cp
13 26 07.7	−39 45 19	116713	—	Cen			137	223	145	215	168	192
13 27 27.1	−15 58 25	116976	69	Vir			107	253	110	250	114	246
13 28 25.7	+13 46 43	117176	70	Vir			75	285	73	287	70	290
13 29 25.2	−51 09 55	117150	—	Cen			154	206	nv	nv	nv	nv
13 29 42.7	−23 16 52	117287	R	Hya	8920		117	243	121	329	127	233
13 31 02.6	−39 24 26	117440	—	Cen			137	223	145	215	168	192
13 31 57.8	−06 15 21	117675	74	Vir			97	263	98	262	99	261
13 32 58.0	−10 09 54	117818	76	Vir			102	258	103	257	106	254
13 33 00.6	−07 11 42	117833	S	Vir			98	262	99	261	101	259
13 34 07.8	+03 39 32	118022	78	Vir		CW	87	273	86	274	85	275
13 34 27.2	+49 00 57	118232	24	CVn			29	331	10	350	cp	cp
13 34 41.5	−00 35 46	118098	ζ	Vir		79	90	270	90	270	90	270
13 34 47.7	+37 10 57	118216	BH	CVn			46	314	38	322	21	339
13 37 10.9	+71 14 32	118904	—	UMi			cp	cp	cp	cp	cp	cp
13 37 27.5	+36 17 41	118623	25	CVn	8974	Σ1768	47	313	40	320	24	336
13 39 53.2	−53 27 59	118716	ε	Cen			157	203	nv	nv	nv	nv
13 40 44.1	+54 40 54	119228	83	UMa			21	339	cp	cp	cp	cp
13 41 36.7	−08 42 11	119149	82	Vir			99	261	100	260	103	257
13 41 44.6	−54 33 36	118991	—	Cen			159	201	nv	nv	nv	nv
13 43 03.6	+03 32 17	119425	84	Vir	9000	Σ1777	87	273	86	274	85	275
13 45 41.2	−33 02 37	119756	1	Cen			129	231	135	225	148	212
13 46 39.3	−51 25 58	119834	—	Cen			154	206	nv	nv	nv	nv
13 46 56.3	−36 15 08	119921	—	Cen			133	227	140	220	156	204
13 47 15.7	+17 27 24	120136	τ	Boo	9025	4, OΣ270	70	290	68	292	63	297
13 47 32.3	+49 18 48	120315	η	UMa		85	29	331	10	350	cp	cp
13 49 05.0	+26 58 46	120476	Σ1785	(Boo)	9031		60	300	55	305	47	313
13 49 26.6	−34 27 02	120323	2	Cen		V806	130	230	137	223	150	210

R.A.			Declin.			HD	Star	Const.	ADS	Also Known As	R(30)	S(30)	R(40)	S(40)	R(50)	S(50)
			2000.0										Rising and Setting Azimuths			
13	49	28.5	+15	47	52	120477	υ	Boo		5	73	287	70	290	66	294
13	49	30.2	−41	41	16	120307	ν	Cen			139	221	149	211	nv	nv
13	49	36.9	−42	28	26	120324	μ	Cen			141	219	151	209	nv	nv
13	49	42.7	+21	15	51	120539	6	Boo			66	294	62	298	56	304
13	49	52.2	−18	08	03	120452	89	Vir			111	249	114	246	119	241
13	51	25.8	+64	43	23	121130	10	Dra	9039	h3342, CU	cp	cp	cp	cp	cp	cp
13	51	47.4	+34	26	39	120933	AW	CVn			50	310	43	317	30	330
13	51	49.5	−32	59	40	120709	3A	Cen		k, DUN 148	128	232	134	226	146	214
13	51	50.0	−32	59	41	120710	3B	Cen			128	232	134	226	146	214
13	53	12.4	−31	55	39	120955	4	Cen			126	234	132	228	143	217
13	54	41.0	+18	23	52	121370	η	Boo		8	69	291	66	294	61	299
13	54	42.1	−01	30	12	121299	90	Vir			91	269	91	269	92	268
13	55	32.3	−47	17	18	121263	ζ	Cen			148	212	163	197	nv	nv
13	56	34.1	+27	29	31	121710	9	Boo			58	302	54	306	45	315
13	57	38.9	−63	41	12	121474	—	Cen			nv	nv	nv	nv	nv	nv
13	58	16.2	−42	06	03	121743	φ	Cen			141	219	151	209	nv	nv
13	58	31.1	−24	58	20	121847	47	Hya			118	242	122	238	129	231
13	58	40.7	−44	48	13	121790	υ¹	Cen			143	217	155	205	nv	nv
14	01	38.7	+01	32	40	122408	τ	Vir	9085	93	89	271	89	271	88	272
14	01	43.3	−45	36	12	122223	υ²	Cen			145	215	157	203	nv	nv
14	03	49.4	−60	22	22	122451	β	Cen			180	180	nv	nv	nv	nv
14	04	23.2	+64	22	33	123299	α	Dra		11	cp	cp	cp	cp	cp	cp
14	05	19.8	−76	47	48	122250	θ	Aps			nv	nv	(cp)	(cp)	(cp)	(cp)
14	06	02.7	−41	10	46	122980	χ	Cen			139	221	149	211	nv	nv
14	06	22.2	−26	40	56	123123	π	Hya		49	120	240	125	235	133	227
14	06	40.8	−36	22	12	123139	θ	Cen		5, See 196	133	227	140	220	156	204
14	08	50.8	+77	32	51	124547	4	UMi			cp	cp	cp	cp	cp	cp
14	09	54.7	−53	26	20	123569	—	Cen			157	203	nv	nv	nv	nv
14	10	23.9	+25	05	30	123999	12	Boo			61	299	57	303	49	311
14	10	50.4	−16	18	07	123934	ET	Vir			109	251	111	249	115	245
14	12	04.0	+69	25	57	124730	—	UMi			cp	cp	cp	cp	cp	cp
14	12	15.7	+02	24	34	124224	CU	Vir	9152	h3343	88	272	87	273	87	273
14	12	45.9	−27	15	40	124206	50	Hya			122	238	126	234	135	225
14	12	53.7	−10	16	25	124294	κ	Vir		98	102	258	103	257	106	254
14	13	28.9	+51	47	24	124675	κ²	Boo	9173	17, Σ1821	26	334	cp	cp	cp	cp
14	14	56.9	−57	05	09	124367	V795	Cen			166	194	nv	nv	nv	nv
14	15	39.6	+19	10	57	124897	α	Boo		16	68	292	65	295	60	300
14	16	00.8	−06	00	02	124850	ι	Vir		99	97	263	98	262	99	261
14	16	09.8	+51	22	02	125161	ι	Boo	9198	21	26	334	cp	cp	cp	cp
14	16	22.9	+46	05	18	125162	λ	Boo		19	34	326	20	340	cp	cp
14	16	34.2	−59	54	50	124601	R	Cen			172	188	nv	nv	nv	nv
14	17	51.2	+83	49	56	127226	R	Cam			cp	cp	cp	cp	cp	cp
14	17	59.7	+35	30	34	125351	—	Boo			49	311	42	318	27	333
14	18	13.6	−81	00	27	123998	η	Aps			nv	nv	(cp)	(cp)	(cp)	(cp)
14	19	06.5	−13	22	16	125337	λ	Vir		100	105	255	107	253	110	250
14	19	24.1	−46	03	28	125238	ι	Lup			146	214	160	200	nv	nv
14	19	32.4	−02	15	56	125454	υ	Vir		102	92	268	93	267	93	267
14	19	45.1	+16	18	25	125560	20	Boo			71	289	69	291	65	295
14	19	51.4	−61	16	23	125158	—	Cen			nv	nv	nv	nv	(cp)	(cp)
14	20	19.4	−56	23	12	125288	—	Cen			163	197	nv	nv	nv	nv

2000.0 R.A.	Declin.	HD	Star	Const.	ADS	Also Known As	R(30)	S(30)	R(40)	S(40)	R(50)	S(50)
14 20 33.3	−37 53 07	125473	ψ	Cen			134	226	142	218	159	201
14 20 42.4	−45 11 14	125442	—	Lup			145	215	157	203	nv	nv
14 22 22.7	−80 06 32	124771	ε	Aps			nv	nv	(cp)	(cp)	(cp)	(cp)
14 22 36.9	−58 27 34	125628	—	Cen			168	192	nv	nv	nv	nv
14 22 38.5	−07 46 05	125906	Σ1833	(Vir)	9237		98	262	99	261	101	259
14 23 02.1	−39 30 44	125823	V761	Cen			137	223	145	215	168	192
14 23 05.7	−27 45 14	125932	51	Hya			122	238	126	234	135	225
14 23 22.5	+08 26 42	126128	Σ1835	(Boo)	9247BC		81	279	80	280	77	283
14 23 22.6	+08 26 48	126129	β1111	(Boo)	9247		81	279	80	280	77	283
14 25 11.7	+51 51 03	126660	θ	Boo		23	26	334	cp	cp	cp	cp
14 26 08.1	−45 13 17	126341	τ¹	Lup		DUN 160	145	215	157	203	nv	nv
14 26 10.7	−45 22 46	126354	τ²	Lup		I.402	145	215	157	203	nv	nv
14 26 54.8	−83 40 04	124882	δ	Oct			(cp)	(cp)	(cp)	(cp)	(cp)	(cp)
14 27 31.4	+75 41 45	127700	5	UMi	9286		cp	cp	cp	cp	cp	cp
14 28 10.3	−29 29 30	126769	52	Hya	9270	β940(ABxC)	124	236	129	231	139	221
14 28 12.1	−02 13 40	126868	φ	Vir	9273	105, Σ1846	92	268	93	267	93	267
14 29 42.0	−62 41 07	—	α^C	Cen		V645	nv	nv	nv	nv	(cp)	(cp)
14 31 49.7	+30 22 17	127665	ρ	Boo	9296	25, h2728	55	305	49	311	39	321
14 32 04.6	+38 18 29	127762	γ	Boo		27	45	315	37	323	17	343
14 32 36.8	−50 27 25	127381	σ	Lup			152	208	180	180	nv	nv
14 34 40.7	+29 44 42	128167	σ	Boo		28	56	304	51	309	41	319
14 35 30.3	−42 09 28	127972	η	Cen		See 207	141	219	151	209	nv	nv
14 37 11.7	+26 44 11	128609	R	Boo			60	300	55	305	47	313
14 37 53.1	−49 25 32	128345	ρ	Lup			151	209	170	190	nv	nv
14 39 36.2	−60 50 07	128620	α^A	Cen			180	180	nv	nv	nv	nv
14 39 36.2	−60 50 07	128621	α^B	Cen			180	180	nv	nv	nv	nv
14 40 43.5	+16 25 06	129174	π¹	Boo	9338	29, Σ1864	71	289	69	291	65	295
14 40 43.8	+16 25 04	129175	π²	Boo	9338	29	71	289	69	291	65	295
14 41 08.8	+13 43 42	129247	ζ	Boo	9343	30, Σ1865	75	285	73	287	70	290
14 41 38.7	+08 09 42	129312	31	Boo			81	279	80	280	77	283
14 41 55.7	−47 23 17	129056	α	Lup			148	212	163	197	nv	nv
14 41 57.5	−37 47 37	129116	—	Cen			134	226	142	218	159	201
14 42 30.3	−65 58 31	128898	α	Cir		DUN 166	nv	nv	(cp)	(cp)	(cp)	(cp)
14 43 03.5	−05 39 30	129502	107	Vir			96	264	97	263	98	262
14 43 25.3	+26 31 40	129712	34	Boo		W	60	300	55	305	47	313
14 43 39.3	−35 10 26	129456	—	Cen			131	229	138	222	153	207
14 44 59.1	+27 04 27	129989	ε^A	Boo	9372	36, Σ1877	58	302	54	306	45	315
14 44 59.1	+27 04 30	129988	ε^B	Boo	9372	36	58	302	54	306	45	315
14 44 59.1	−35 11 31	129685	—	Cen			131	229	138	222	153	207
14 45 14.4	+16 57 52	129972	o	Boo		35	71	289	69	291	65	295
14 46 00.0	−25 26 35	129926	54	Hya	9375	m	119	241	123	237	131	229
14 46 14.9	+01 53 34	130109	109	Vir			89	271	89	271	88	272
14 47 01.2	−52 23 01	129893	—	Lup			155	205	nv	nv	nv	nv
14 47 44.7	−26 05 15	130259	56	Hya			120	240	125	235	133	227
14 47 51.6	−79 02 41	129078	α	Aps			nv	nv	(cp)	(cp)	(cp)	(cp)
14 49 19.0	−14 08 56	130559	μ	Lib	9396	7, β106	106	254	108	252	112	248
14 50 17.2	−27 57 37	130694	58	Hya			122	238	126	234	135	225
14 50 41.1	−15 59 50	130819	α¹	Lib		8	107	253	110	250	114	246
14 50 42.2	+74 09 20	131873	β	UMi		7	cp	cp	cp	cp	cp	cp
14 50 52.6	−16 02 31	130841	α²	Lib		9	109	251	111	249	115	245

| 2000.0 | | | | | | | Also | Rising and Setting Azimuths | | | | | |
R.A.		Declin.		HD	Star	Const.	ADS	Known As	R(30)	S(30)	R(40)	S(40)	R(50)	S(50)
14 51 00.9	−02 17 57			130952	11	Lib			92	268	93	267	93	267
14 51 23.2	+19 06 04			131156	ξ	Boo	9413	37, Σ1888	68	292	65	295	60	300
14 51 38.3	−43 34 31			130807	o	Lup			142	218	153	207	nv	nv
14 52 50.9	−37 48 11			131120	—	Cen			134	226	142	218	159	201
14 54 20.0	−24 38 32			131430	12	Lib			118	242	122	238	129	231
14 55 34.4	−60 06 50			131342	—	Cir			180	180	nv	nv	nv	nv
14 56 44.0	−62 46 51			131492	θ	Cir			nv	nv	(cp)	(cp)	(cp)	(cp)
14 56 46.0	−11 24 35			131918	ξ²	Lib		15	103	257	104	256	107	253
14 57 10.9	−04 20 47			132052	16	Lib			95	265	95	265	96	264
14 57 34.9	+65 55 56			132813	RR	UMi			cp	cp	cp	cp	cp	cp
14 57 52.8	−76 39 45			131109	R	Aps			nv	nv	(cp)	(cp)	(cp)	(cp)
14 58 31.8	−43 08 02			132058	β	Lup			142	218	153	207	nv	nv
14 58 53.5	−11 08 39			132345	18	Lib	9456	Σ1894	103	257	104	256	107	253
14 59 09.6	−42 06 15			132200	κ	Cen			141	219	151	209	nv	nv
15 00 58.3	−08 31 08			132742	δ	Lib		19	99	261	100	260	103	257
15 01 56.6	+40 23 26			133208	β	Boo		42	42	318	33	327	cp	cp
15 02 06.4	+25 00 29			133124	ω	Boo		41	61	299	57	303	49	311
15 02 54.0	+02 05 28			133165	110	Vir			88	272	87	273	87	273
15 03 47.3	+47 39 16			133640	Σ1909	(Boo)	9494	44, i	32	328	17	343	cp	cp
15 04 04.1	−25 16 55			133216	σ	Lib		20	119	241	123	237	131	229
15 04 26.7	+26 56 51			133582	ψ	Boo		43	60	300	55	305	47	313
15 04 46.6	−83 02 17			131246	π²	Oct			nv	nv	(cp)	(cp)	(cp)	(cp)
15 04 48.1	−64 01 54			132905	η	Cir			nv	nv	(cp)	(cp)	(cp)	(cp)
15 05 07.1	−47 03 04			133242	π¹	Lup		h4728	148	212	163	197	nv	nv
15 05 07.1	−47 03 04			133243	π²	Lup			148	212	163	197	nv	nv
15 05 19.0	−41 04 02			133340	—	Lup			139	221	149	211	nv	nv
15 06 37.5	−16 15 24			133774	ν	Lib		21	109	251	111	249	115	245
15 07 18.0	+24 52 09			134083	45	Boo			62	298	58	302	51	309
15 08 50.5	−45 16 47			133955	λ	Lup		See 219	145	215	157	203	nv	nv
15 11 56.0	−48 44 16			134481	κ¹	Lup		DUN 177	149	211	166	194	nv	nv
15 11 57.5	−48 44 37			134482	κ²	Lup			149	211	166	194	nv	nv
15 12 13.2	−19 47 30			134759	ι¹	Lib	9532	24	112	248	115	245	120	240
15 12 17.0	−52 05 57			134505	ζ	Lup		DUN 176	155	205	nv	nv	nv	nv
15 12 49.4	−44 30 02			134687	—	Lup			143	217	155	205	nv	nv
15 14 29.1	+29 09 51			135502	χ	Boo		48	56	304	51	309	41	319
15 14 37.2	−31 31 09			135153	1	Lup			126	234	132	228	143	217
15 14 38.2	+67 20 48			136064	—	UMi			cp	cp	cp	cp	cp	cp
15 15 11.3	+04 56 22			135482	3	Ser			85	275	85	275	84	276
15 15 30.1	+33 18 53			135722	δ	Boo	9559	49	51	309	45	315	32	328
15 16 03.9	−41 29 28			135345	—	Lup			139	221	149	211	nv	nv
15 16 56.7	−60 57 27			135240	δ	Cir			180	180	nv	nv	nv	nv
15 17 00.3	−09 22 58			135742	β	Lib		27	100	260	102	258	104	256
15 17 05.8	+71 49 26			136726	11	UMi			cp	cp	cp	cp	cp	cp
15 17 30.8	−58 48 04			135379	β	Cir			168	192	nv	nv	nv	nv
15 17 38.8	−63 36 38			135291	ε	Cir			nv	nv	(cp)	(cp)	(cp)	(cp)
15 17 49.7	−30 08 55			135758	2	Lup			125	235	131	229	141	219
15 18 31.9	−47 52 30			135734	μ	Lup		h4753	148	212	163	197	nv	nv
15 18 54.6	−68 40 46			135382	γ	TrA			nv	nv	(cp)	(cp)	(cp)	(cp)
15 19 18.7	+01 45 55			136202	5	Ser		MQ	89	271	89	271	88	272
15 20 43.6	+71 50 02			137422	γ	UMi		13	cp	cp	cp	cp	cp	cp

2000.0 R.A.			Declin.			HD	Star	Const.	ADS	Also Known As	Rising and Setting Azimuths					
											R(30)	S(30)	R(40)	S(40)	R(50)	S(50)
15	21	22.2	−40	38	52	136298	δ	Lup			138	222	147	213	179	181
15	21	23.6	−20	23	16	136458	S	Lib			113	247	117	243	122	238
15	21	48.3	−36	15	41	136422	φ^1	Lup		See 229	133	227	140	220	156	204
15	22	08.2	−47	55	40	136351	ν^1	Lup			148	212	163	197	nv	nv
15	22	40.8	−44	41	22	136504	ε	Lup		DUN 182	143	217	155	205	nv	nv
15	23	09.2	−36	51	30	136664	φ^2	Lup			133	227	140	220	156	204
15	23	12.2	+30	17	16	137107	η	CrB	9617	2, Σ1937	55	305	49	311	39	321
15	23	22.6	−59	19	15	136415	γ	Cir		h4757	172	188	nv	nv	nv	nv
15	24	11.8	−10	19	20	137052	ε	Lib		31	102	258	103	257	106	254
15	24	29.3	+37	22	38	137391	μ^1	Boo	9626	51, Σ1938	46	314	38	322	21	339
15	24	30.8	+37	20	51	137392	μ^2	Boo	9626	51	46	314	38	322	21	339
15	24	44.8	−39	42	37	136933	υ	Lup			137	223	145	215	168	192
15	24	55.6	+58	57	57	137759	ι	Dra		12	12	348	cp	cp	cp	cp
15	25	20.1	−38	44	01	137058	—	Lup			135	225	143	217	163	197
15	25	47.3	+15	25	41	137471	τ^1	Ser		9	73	287	70	290	66	294
15	27	49.7	+29	06	20	137909	β	CrB		3	56	304	51	309	41	319
15	28	38.1	+01	50	31	137898	10	Ser			89	271	89	271	88	272
15	29	24.2	−46	43	58	137709	—	Lup			146	214	160	200	nv	nv
15	30	55.7	+40	49	59	138481	ν^1	Boo		52	42	318	33	327	cp	cp
15	31	24.7	+77	20	57	139669	θ	UMi		15	cp	cp	cp	cp	cp	cp
15	31	30.8	−73	23	22	137387	κ^1	Aps		h4764	nv	nv	(cp)	(cp)	(cp)	(cp)
15	31	46.9	+40	53	58	138629	ν^2	Boo	9688	53	42	318	33	327	cp	cp
15	32	55.1	−16	51	11	138485	ζ^4	Lib		35	109	251	111	249	115	245
15	32	55.7	+31	21	32	138749	θ	CrB		4	54	306	48	312	37	323
15	34	10.6	−10	03	53	138716	37	Lib			102	258	103	257	106	254
15	34	26.5	−09	11	00	138764	—	Lib			100	260	102	258	104	256
15	34	37.2	−28	02	49	138688	36	Lib			123	237	128	232	137	223
15	34	41.2	+26	42	53	139006	α	CrB		5	60	300	55	305	47	313
15	34	48.0	+10	32	15	138917	δ^B	Ser		13	78	282	77	283	74	286
15	34	48.1	+10	32	21	138918	δ^A	Ser	9701	13, Σ1954	78	282	77	283	74	286
15	35	08.3	−41	10	00	138690	γ	Lup		h4786	139	221	149	211	nv	nv
15	35	14.8	+39	00	36	139153	μ	CrB		6	43	317	35	325	12	348
15	35	31.5	−41	47	22	138905	γ	Lib	9704	38	139	221	149	211	nv	nv
15	35	53.1	−44	57	31	138769	—	Lup			143	217	155	205	nv	nv
15	35	57.5	−49	30	29	138743	R	Nor			151	209	170	190	nv	nv
15	36	28.1	+15	06	05	139216	τ^4	Ser		17	73	287	70	290	66	294
15	36	43.1	−66	19	02	138538	ε	TrA		DUN 188	nv	nv	(cp)	(cp)	(cp)	(cp)
15	37	01.4	−28	08	06	139063	υ	Lib	9705	39	123	237	128	232	137	223
15	37	49.5	+40	21	12	139641	φ	Boo		54	42	318	33	327	cp	cp
15	38	03.1	−42	34	02	139127	ω	Lup			141	219	151	209	nv	nv
15	38	39.3	−29	46	40	139365	ρ	Lib		40	124	236	129	231	139	221
15	38	39.9	−08	47	40	139460	Σ1962B	(Lib)	9728		99	261	100	260	103	257
15	38	40.0	−08	47	28	139461	Σ1962A	(Lib)	9728		99	261	100	260	103	257
15	39	22.6	+36	38	09	139892	ζ^2	CrB		7, Σ1965	47	313	40	320	24	336
15	39	45.9	−34	24	42	139521	ψ^1	Lup		3	130	230	137	223	150	210
15	40	16.8	−23	49	05	139663	42	Lib			117	243	121	239	127	233
15	40	21.2	−73	26	48	138800	κ^2	Aps			nv	nv	(cp)	(cp)	(cp)	(cp)
15	41	11.2	−44	39	40	139664	—	Lup			143	217	155	205	nv	nv
15	41	33.0	+19	40	13	140159	ι	Ser	9744	21, Hu 580	68	292	65	295	60	300
15	41	47.3	+12	50	50	140160	χ	Ser		20	76	284	74	286	71	289

2000.0 R.A.				Declin.			HD	Star	Const.	ADS	Also Known As	R(30)	S(30)	R(40)	S(40)	R(50)	S(50)
15	41	56.7	−19	40	44		139997	κ	Lib		43	112	248	115	245	120	240
15	42	38.2	−37	25	30		139980	h	Lup			134	226	142	218	159	201
15	42	40.9	−34	42	38		140008	ψ²	Lup		4	130	230	137	223	150	210
15	42	44.5	+26	17	44		140436	γ	CrB	9757	8, Σ1967	60	300	55	305	47	313
15	44	03.3	+77	47	40		142105	ζ	UMi		16	cp	cp	cp	cp	cp	cp
15	44	04.3	−15	40	22		140417	η	Lib		44	107	253	110	250	114	246
15	44	16.0	+06	25	32		140573	α	Ser	9765	24	83	277	82	278	81	279
15	46	11.2	+15	25	18		141003	β	Ser	9778	28, β1970	73	287	70	290	66	294
15	46	26.5	+07	21	11		141004	λ	Ser		27	82	278	81	279	79	281
15	46	39.8	+62	35	58		141653	—	Dra			cp	cp	cp	cp	cp	cp
15	48	34.3	+28	09	24		141527	R	CrB			57	303	52	308	43	317
15	48	44.3	+18	08	29		141477	κ	Ser		35	69	291	66	294	61	299
15	49	35.6	+26	04	06		141714	δ	CrB		10	60	300	55	305	47	313
15	49	37.1	−03	25	49		141513	μ	Ser		32	93	267	94	266	95	265
15	50	17.5	+02	11	47		141680	ω	Ser		34	88	272	87	273	87	273
15	50	41.6	+15	08	00		141850	R	Ser			73	287	70	290	66	294
15	50	48.9	+04	28	40		141795	ε	Ser		37	85	275	85	275	84	276
15	50	57.4	−33	37	38		141556	χ	Lup		5	129	231	135	225	148	212
15	50	58.6	−25	45	05		141637	1	Sco			119	241	123	237	131	229
15	51	13.8	+35	39	26		142091	κ	CrB		11	49	311	42	318	27	333
15	51	15.5	−03	05	26		141851	36	Ser			93	267	94	266	95	265
15	51	15.8	+20	58	40		141992	ρ	Ser		38	67	293	63	297	58	302
15	52	40.4	+42	27	06		142373	χ	Her		1	39	321	29	331	cp	cp
15	53	20.0	−20	10	02		142096	λ	Lib		45	113	247	117	243	122	238
15	53	36.6	−25	19	38		142114	2	Sco	9823	β36	119	241	123	237	131	229
15	53	49.4	−16	43	46		142198	θ	Lib		46	109	251	111	249	115	245
15	55	08.4	−63	25	40		141891	β	TrA			nv	nv	(cp)	(cp)	(cp)	(cp)
15	55	29.5	−68	36	11		141767	κ	TrA			nv	nv	(cp)	(cp)	(cp)	(cp)
15	55	47.6	+37	56	49		142908	λ	CrB		12	46	314	38	322	21	339
15	56	27.1	+15	39	42		142860	γ	Ser		41	73	287	70	290	66	294
15	56	53.0	−29	12	50		142669	ρ	Sco	9846	5, See 251	124	236	129	231	139	221
15	56	53.4	−33	57	59		142629	ξ¹	Lup		DUN 196	129	231	135	225	148	212
15	56	54.1	−33	57	51		142630	ξ²	Lup			129	231	135	225	148	212
15	57	35.2	+26	52	40		143107	ε	CrB	9859	13	60	300	55	305	47	313
15	57	47.3	+54	44	59		143466	CL	Dra			21	339	cp	cp	cp	cp
15	58	11.3	−14	16	46		142983	48	Lib		FX	106	254	108	252	112	248
15	58	51.0	−26	06	51		143018	π	Sco	9862	6	120	240	125	235	133	227
15	59	30.2	−41	44	39		143009	—	Lup			139	221	149	211	nv	nv
16	00	07.2	−38	23	49		143118	η	Lup		DUN 197	135	225	143	217	163	197
16	00	19.9	−22	37	18		143275	δ	Sco		7	116	244	119	241	126	234
16	01	02.6	+33	18	13		143761	ρ	CrB		15	51	309	45	315	32	328
16	01	14.2	+17	49	06		143666	5	Her			70	290	68	292	63	297
16	01	26.6	+29	51	04		143807	ι	CrB		14	56	304	51	309	41	319
16	01	53.2	+58	33	55		144284	θ	Dra		13	12	348	cp	cp	cp	cp
16	02	17.7	+22	48	16		143894	π	Ser		44	64	296	61	299	54	306
16	02	47.8	+46	02	12		144206	υ	Her		6	34	326	20	340	cp	cp
16	03	12.7	−49	13	47		143546	η	Nor			151	209	170	190	nv	nv
16	03	20.5	−25	51	55		143787	—	(Sco)			119	241	123	237	131	229
16	03	24.0	−38	36	09		143699	—	Lup			135	225	143	217	163	197
16	03	31.9	−57	46	31		143474	ι¹	Nor		See 258/h4825	166	194	nv	nv	nv	nv

2000.0 R.A.	Declin.	HD	Star	Const.	ADS	Also Known As	R(30)	S(30)	R(40)	S(40)	R(50)	S(50)
16 04 22.0	−11 22 23	144069	ξ^B	Sco	9909		103	257	104	256	107	253
16 04 22.0	−11 22 23	144070	ξ^A	Sco	9909	Σ1998	103	257	104	256	107	253
16 04 25.7	−11 26 56	144087	Σ1999	(Sco)	9910		103	257	104	256	107	253
16 05 26.1	−19 48 19	144217	β^1	Sco	9913	8, β947	112	248	115	245	120	240
16 05 26.4	−19 48 07	144218	β^2	Sco	9913	8	112	248	115	245	120	240
16 06 29.3	−45 10 23	144197	δ	Nor			145	215	157	203	nv	nv
16 06 35.4	−36 48 08	144294	θ	Lup			133	227	140	220	156	204
16 06 48.3	−20 40 09	144470	ω^1	Sco		9	113	247	117	243	122	238
16 07 24.2	−20 52 07	144608	ω^2	Sco		10	113	247	117	243	122	238
16 08 04.4	+17 02 49	145001	κ^A	Her	9933	7, Σ2010	70	290	68	292	63	297
16 08 04.8	+17 03 16	145000	κ^B	Her		7	70	290	68	292	63	297
16 08 46.1	+44 56 06	145389	φ	Her		11	37	323	25	335	cp	cp
16 08 58.2	+36 29 27	145328	τ	CrB	9939	16, β1087	47	313	40	320	24	336
16 10 49.3	+75 52 39	146926	19	UMi			cp	cp	cp	cp	cp	cp
16 11 01.9	−29 24 59	145250	—	Sco			124	236	129	231	139	221
16 11 58.5	−19 26 59	145501	ν^C	Sco	9951		112	248	115	245	120	240
16 11 59.6	−19 27 38	145502	ν^{AB}	Sco	9951	14, β120	112	248	115	245	120	240
16 11 59.9	−10 03 51	145570	ψ	Sco		15	102	258	103	257	106	254
16 12 18.1	−27 55 35	145482	13	Sco			122	238	126	234	135	225
16 13 28.6	−54 37 50	145397	κ	Nor			159	201	nv	nv	nv	nv
16 13 50.7	−11 50 16	145897	χ	Sco		17	103	257	104	256	107	253
16 14 20.6	−03 41 39	146051	δ	Oph		1	93	267	94	266	95	265
16 14 40.7	+33 51 30	146361	σ^A	CrB	9979	17, Σ2032, TZ	51	309	45	315	32	328
16 14 40.7	+33 51 30	146362	σ^B	CrB	9979	17	51	309	45	315	32	328
16 15 15.2	−47 22 20	145842	θ	Nor			148	212	163	197	nv	nv
16 15 26.2	−63 41 08	145544	δ	TrA			nv	nv	(cp)	(cp)	(cp)	(cp)
16 17 00.8	−50 04 05	146143	γ^1	Nor			152	208	180	180	nv	nv
16 17 30.2	+75 45 19	148048	η	UMi		21	cp	cp	cp	cp	cp	cp
16 18 17.8	−28 36 51	146624	—	Sco			123	237	128	232	137	223
16 18 19.1	−04 41 33	146791	ε	Oph		2	95	265	95	265	96	264
16 19 17.6	−42 40 26	146667	λ	Nor		See 271	141	219	151	209	nv	nv
16 19 44.3	+46 18 48	147394	τ	Her	10010	22, β1198	34	326	20	340	cp	cp
16 19 50.3	−50 09 20	146686	γ^2	Nor		h4841	152	208	180	180	nv	nv
16 20 20.7	−78 41 45	145366	δ^1	Aps			nv	nv	(cp)	(cp)	(cp)	(cp)
16 20 26.7	−78 40 02	145388	δ^2	Aps			nv	nv	(cp)	(cp)	(cp)	(cp)
16 20 38.1	−24 10 10	147084	o	Sco		19	118	242	122	238	129	231
16 21 11.2	−25 35 34	147165	σ	Sco	10009	20	119	241	123	237	131	229
16 21 55.1	+19 09 11	147547	γ	Her	10022	20	68	292	65	295	60	300
16 22 04.3	+01 01 45	147449	σ	Ser		50	89	271	89	271	88	272
16 22 05.7	+30 53 32	147677	ξ	CrB		19	55	305	49	311	39	321
16 22 21.3	+33 47 56	147749	ν^{1AB}	CrB		20	51	309	45	315	32	328
16 22 29.1	+33 42 13	147767	ν^2	CrB		21	51	309	45	315	32	328
16 23 59.3	+61 30 51	148387	η	Dra	10058	14, OΣ312	cp	cp	cp	cp	cp	cp
16 24 06.1	−20 02 15	147700	ψ	Oph		4	113	247	117	243	122	238
16 25 24.9	+14 02 00	148112	ω	Her		24, β625	74	286	72	288	68	292
16 25 34.9	−23 26 46	147933	ρ	Oph	10049	5	117	243	121	239	127	233
16 27 01.3	−18 27 23	148184	χ	Oph		7	111	249	114	246	119	241
16 27 11.0	−47 33 18	147971	ε	Nor		h4853	148	212	163	197	nv	nv
16 27 43.4	−07 35 53	148349	V2105	Oph			98	262	99	261	101	259
16 27 48.1	−08 22 18	148367	υ	Oph		3	99	261	100	260	103	257

	2000.0								Also	Rising and Setting Azimuths					
R.A.			Declin.			HD	Star	Const.	ADS	Known As	R(30)	S(30)	R(40)	S(40)	R(50)	S(50)
16	27	57.2	−64	03	29	147787	ι	TrA		DUN 201	nv	nv	(cp)	(cp)	(cp)	(cp)
16	27	58.8	+68	46	05	149212	15	Dra			cp	cp	cp	cp	cp	cp
16	28	28.1	−70	05	04	147584	ζ	TrA			nv	nv	(cp)	(cp)	(cp)	(cp)
16	28	38.4	+41	52	54	148783	30	Her		g	41	319	31	329	cp	cp
16	29	24.4	−26	25	55	148478	α	Sco	10074	21	120	240	125	235	133	227
16	30	12.4	−25	06	54	148605	22	Sco			119	241	123	237	131	229
16	30	13.1	+21	29	22	148856	β	Her		27	66	294	62	298	56	304
16	30	49.3	−61	38	00	148291	—	TrA			nv	nv	nv	nv	(cp)	(cp)
16	30	54.7	+01	59	02	148857	λ	Oph	10087	10, Σ2055	89	271	89	271	88	272
16	31	08.2	−16	36	46	148786	φ	Oph	10086	8	109	251	111	249	115	245
16	31	22.8	−34	42	16	148703	N	Sco			130	230	137	223	150	210
16	32	08.0	−21	27	59	148898	ω	Oph		9	114	246	118	242	124	236
16	32	36.2	+11	29	17	149161	29	Her			77	283	76	284	73	287
16	32	40.0	+66	45	13	149880	R	Dra			cp	cp	cp	cp	cp	cp
16	33	27.1	−78	53	49	147675	γ	Aps			nv	nv	(cp)	(cp)	(cp)	(cp)
16	34	04.8	−44	02	43	149038	μ	Nor			143	217	155	205	nv	nv
16	34	06.1	+42	26	13	149630	σ	Her		35	39	321	29	331	cp	cp
16	35	44.7	−65	29	44	148890	θ	TrA			(cp)	(cp)	(cp)	(cp)	(cp)	(cp)
16	35	52.9	−28	12	58	149438	τ	Sco		23	123	237	128	232	137	223
16	36	11.3	+52	54	00	150100	16	Dra			25	335	cp	cp	cp	cp
16	36	13.6	+52	55	28	150117	17A	Dra	10129	Σ2078	25	335	cp	cp	cp	cp
16	36	14.0	+52	55	27	150118	17B	Dra			25	335	cp	cp	cp	cp
16	36	22.4	−35	15	20	149447	H	Sco			131	229	138	222	153	207
16	37	09.4	−10	34	02	149757	ζ	Oph		13	102	258	103	257	106	254
16	38	44.7	+48	55	42	150450	42	Her	10144	Σ2082	31	329	14	346	cp	cp
16	40	55.0	+64	35	20	151101	18	Dra			cp	cp	cp	cp	cp	cp
16	41	17.1	+31	36	10	150680	ζ	Her	10157	40, Σ2084	54	306	48	312	37	323
16	41	34.3	−17	44	32	150416	—	Oph			110	250	112	248	117	243
16	42	53.7	+38	55	20	150997	η	Her		44	45	315	37	323	17	343
16	43	04.4	−77	31	03	149324	β	Aps		h4858	nv	nv	(cp)	(cp)	(cp)	(cp)
16	45	17.7	+56	46	55	151613	—	Dra			17	343	cp	cp	cp	cp
16	45	49.8	+08	34	57	151217	43	Her			81	279	80	280	77	283
16	45	57.8	+82	02	14	153751	ε	UMi	10742	22	cp	cp	cp	cp	cp	cp
16	46	40.0	−67	06	35	150549	LP	TrA			nv	nv	(cp)	(cp)	(cp)	(cp)
16	46	40.0	−67	06	35	150549	—	TrA			nv	nv	(cp)	(cp)	(cp)	(cp)
16	48	39.9	−69	01	40	150798	α	TrA			nv	nv	(cp)	(cp)	(cp)	(cp)
16	49	14.1	+45	59	00	152107	52	Her	10227	β627, V637	35	325	23	337	cp	cp
16	49	47.0	−59	02	29	151249	η	Ara			172	188	nv	nv	nv	nv
16	49	49.9	−10	46	59	151769	20	Oph			102	258	103	257	106	254
16	50	09.7	−34	17	36	151680	ε	Sco		26	130	230	137	223	150	210
16	51	33.6	−41	13	50	151804	V973	Sco			139	221	149	211	nv	nv
16	51	45.2	+24	39	23	152326	51	Her			62	298	58	302	51	309
16	51	52.1	−38	02	51	151890	μ¹	Sco			135	225	143	217	163	197
16	51	53.7	+14	56	29	152276	S	Her			74	286	72	288	68	292
16	52	20.0	−38	01	03	151985	μ²	Sco			135	225	143	217	163	197
16	53	59.6	−42	21	43	152236	ζ¹	Sco			141	219	151	209	nv	nv
16	54	00.4	+10	09	55	152614	ι	Oph		25	78	282	77	283	74	286
16	54	01.7	−41	48	23	152234	B1833	(Sco)	11024		139	221	149	211	nv	nv
16	54	34.9	−42	21	41	152334	ζ²	Sco			141	219	151	209	nv	nv
16	56	01.6	+65	08	05	153597	19	Dra			cp	cp	cp	cp	cp	cp

R.A.			Declin.			HD	Star	Const.	ADS	Also Known As	Rising and Setting Azimuths					
	2000.0										R(30)	S(30)	R(40)	S(40)	R(50)	S(50)
16	56	25.1	+65	02	20	153697	20	Dra	10279	Σ2118	cp	cp	cp	cp	cp	cp
16	56	37.9	−30	34	47	152783	RR	Sco			125	235	131	229	141	219
16	57	40.0	+09	22	30	153210	κ	Oph		27	80	280	78	282	76	284
16	58	37.1	−55	59	24	152786	ζ	Ara			161	199	nv	nv	nv	nv
16	59	35.0	−53	09	38	152980	ε¹	Ara			157	203	nv	nv	nv	nv
17	00	17.3	+30	55	35	153808	ε	Her		58	55	305	49	311	39	321
17	01	03.5	−04	13	21	153687	30	Oph			95	265	95	265	96	264
17	01	52.6	−32	08	37	153613	—	Sco			128	232	134	226	146	214
17	03	07.8	+14	05	31	154143	—	Her			74	286	72	288	68	292
17	03	08.6	−53	14	13	153580	ε²	Ara			157	203	nv	nv	nv	nv
17	04	49.3	−34	07	23	154090	—	Sco			130	230	137	223	150	210
17	05	19.5	+54	28	13	154906	μ	Dra	10345	21, Σ2130	21	339	cp	cp	cp	cp
17	05	22.6	+12	44	27	154494	60	Her	10334		76	284	74	286	71	289
17	08	01.9	+35	56	07	155103	Hu1176	(Her)			49	311	42	318	27	333
17	08	47.1	+65	42	53	155763	ζ	Dra		22	cp	cp	cp	cp	cp	cp
17	09	33.1	+40	46	37	155410	—	Her			42	318	33	327	1	359
17	10	22.6	−15	43	29	155125	η	Oph	10374	35, β1118	107	253	110	250	114	246
17	10	42.2	−44	33	27	154948	—	Sco			143	217	155	205	nv	nv
17	12	09.1	−43	14	21	155203	η	Sco			142	218	153	207	nv	nv
17	14	38.8	+14	23	25	156014	α¹	Her	10418	64, Σ2140	74	286	72	288	68	292
17	14	39.1	+14	23	24	156105	α²	Her	10418	64	74	286	72	288	68	292
17	15	01.8	+24	50	21	156164	δ	Her	10424	65, Σ2127	62	298	58	302	51	309
17	15	02.7	+36	48	33	156283	π	Her		67	47	313	40	320	24	336
17	15	20.7	−23	36	05	155886	36	Oph	10417		117	243	121	239	127	233
17	16	31.6	+01	12	38	156247	U	Oph	10428	h854	89	271	89	271	88	272
17	16	36.6	−00	26	43	156266	41	Oph	10429		90	270	90	270	90	270
17	16	56.0	+89	02	15	183030	λ	UMi			cp	cp	cp	cp	cp	cp
17	17	19.4	+33	06	00	156633	68	Her	10449	u, OΣ328	51	309	45	315	32	328
17	17	40.2	+37	17	29	156729	69	Her			46	314	38	322	21	339
17	18	00.4	−24	17	03	156350	oᴮ	Oph	10442B	39	118	242	122	238	129	231
17	18	00.6	−24	17	13	156349	oᴬ	Oph	10442A	39	118	242	122	238	129	231
17	18	36.9	+10	51	53	156681	—	Oph			78	282	77	283	74	286
17	20	18.8	+18	03	25	157049	V656	Her			69	291	66	294	61	299
17	20	39.5	+32	28	04	157214	72	Her	10488	Dorpat 544	52	308	46	314	34	326
17	20	49.5	−12	50	48	156928	ν	Ser		53	104	256	106	254	109	251
17	20	54.1	+24	29	58	157198	70	Her			62	298	58	302	51	309
17	21	00.1	−21	06	46	156897	ξ	Oph		40	114	246	118	242	124	236
17	21	59.5	−67	46	13	156277	ζ	Aps			nv	nv	(cp)	(cp)	(cp)	(cp)
17	22	00.5	−24	59	58	157056	θ	Oph		42	118	242	122	238	129	231
17	22	05.8	−70	07	24	156190	ι	Aps			nv	nv	(cp)	(cp)	(cp)	(cp)
17	23	16.0	−47	28	05	157042	ι	Ara			148	212	163	197	nv	nv
17	23	40.6	+37	08	48	157778	ρᴮ	Her		75	46	314	38	322	21	339
17	23	40.9	+37	08	45	157779	ρᴬ	Her	10526	75, Σ2161	46	314	38	322	21	339
17	24	12.9	−44	09	45	157243	—	Sco			143	217	155	205	nv	nv
17	25	17.9	−55	31	47	157244	β	Ara			161	199	nv	nv	nv	nv
17	25	23.5	−56	22	39	157246	γ	Ara		h4972	163	197	nv	nv	nv	nv
17	25	59.9	−50	38	01	157457	κ	Ara			152	208	180	180	nv	nv
17	26	22.1	−24	10	31	157792	44	Oph			118	242	122	238	129	231
17	26	30.8	+04	08	25	157999	σ	Oph		49	85	275	85	275	84	276
17	26	37.8	−05	05	12	157950	—	Oph			96	264	97	263	98	262

2000.0							Also	Rising and Setting Azimuths					
R.A.		Declin.		HD	Star	Const.	ADS	Known As	R(30)	S(30)	R(40)	S(40)	R(50)	S(50)
17 27 21.2	−29 52 01			157919	45	Oph			124	236	129	231	139	221
17 30 23.7	−01 03 45			158614	Σ2178	(Oph)	10598		91	269	91	269	92	268
17 30 25.8	+52 18 05			159181	β	Dra	10611	23, β1090	25	335	cp	cp	cp	cp
17 30 44.2	+26 06 38			158899	λ	Her		76	60	300	55	305	47	313
17 30 45.7	−37 17 45			158408	υ	Sco		34	134	226	142	218	159	201
17 31 05.9	−60 41 01			158094	δ	Ara			180	180	nv	nv	nv	nv
17 31 24.8	−23 57 46			158643	51	Oph			117	243	121	239	127	233
17 31 50.4	−49 52 34			158427	α	Ara		h4955	151	209	170	190	nv	nv
17 31 57.7	+68 08 06			159966	27	Dra			cp	cp	cp	cp	cp	cp
17 32 10.4	+55 11 03			159541	ν¹	Dra	10628	24	19	341	cp	cp	cp	cp
17 32 12.5	+86 35 11			166205	δ	UMi		23	cp	cp	cp	cp	cp	cp
17 32 15.9	+55 10 22			159560	ν²	Dra		25	19	341	cp	cp	cp	cp
17 33 36.4	−37 06 13			158926	λ	Sco		35, See 334	134	226	142	218	159	201
17 34 55.9	+12 33 36			159561	α	Oph		55	76	284	74	286	71	289
17 34 59.4	+61 52 30			160269	26	Dra	10660	β962	cp	cp	cp	cp	cp	cp
17 35 39.4	−46 30 20			159217	σ	Ara			146	214	160	200	nv	nv
17 36 32.7	−38 38 07			159433	—	Sco			135	225	143	217	163	197
17 36 56.9	+68 45 29			160922	ω	Dra		28	cp	cp	cp	cp	cp	cp
17 37 19.0	−42 59 52			159532	θ	Sco			141	219	151	209	nv	nv
17 37 35.1	−15 23 55			159876	ξ	Ser		55	107	253	110	250	114	246
17 37 50.6	−08 07 08			159975	μ	Oph		57	99	261	100	260	103	257
17 38 05.5	−54 30 01			159492	π	Ara			159	201	nv	nv	nv	nv
17 39 27.8	+46 00 23			160762	ι	Her		85	34	326	20	340	cp	cp
17 40 23.4	−49 24 56			160032	λ	Ara			151	209	170	190	nv	nv
17 41 24.8	−12 52 31			160613	o	Ser		56	104	256	106	254	109	251
17 41 56.1	+72 08 56			162003	ψ¹ᴬ	Dra	10759	31, Σ2241	cp	cp	cp	cp	cp	cp
17 41 57.8	+72 09 25			162004	ψ¹ᴮ	Dra		31	cp	cp	cp	cp	cp	cp
17 42 29.1	−39 01 48			160578	κ	Sco			137	223	145	215	168	192
17 43 25.7	−21 41 00			160915	58	Oph			114	246	118	242	124	236
17 43 28.3	+04 34 02			161096	β	Oph		60	85	275	85	275	84	276
17 44 08.6	−51 50 03			160691	μ	Ara			154	206	nv	nv	nv	nv
17 45 43.9	−64 43 26			160635	η	Pav			nv	nv	nv	nv	(cp)	(cp)
17 46 27.5	+27 43 15			161797	μ	Her	10786	86, Σ2220	58	302	54	306	45	315
17 47 33.5	−27 49 51			161592	X	Sgr			122	238	126	234	135	225
17 47 35.0	−40 07 37			161471	ι¹	Sco		See 338	138	222	147	213	179	181
17 47 53.5	+02 42 26			161868	γ	Oph		62	88	272	87	273	87	273
17 48 49.0	+25 37 22			162211	87	Her			61	299	57	303	49	311
17 49 04.1	+50 46 52			162579	30	Dra			28	332	cp	cp	cp	cp
17 49 10.4	−31 42 12			161840	—	Sco			126	234	132	228	143	217
17 49 26.8	+76 57 46			163989	35	Dra			cp	cp	cp	cp	cp	cp
17 49 51.4	−37 02 36			161892	G	Sco			134	226	142	218	159	201
17 50 11.0	−40 05 26			161912	ι²	Sco			138	222	147	213	179	181
17 53 17.9	+40 00 29			163217	90	Her	10875		42	318	33	327	cp	cp
17 53 31.6	+56 52 21			163588	ξ	Dra		32	17	343	cp	cp	cp	cp
17 55 10.9	+72 00 19			164613	ψ²	Dra		34	cp	cp	cp	cp	cp	cp
17 56 15.1	+37 15 02			163770	θ	Her		91	46	314	38	322	21	339
17 56 36.2	+51 29 20			164058	γ	Dra	10923	33, β633	26	334	cp	cp	cp	cp
17 56 47.3	−44 20 32			163145	—	Sco			143	217	155	205	nv	nv
17 57 45.8	+29 14 52			163993	ξ	Her		92	56	304	51	309	41	319
17 57 47.6	−41 42 58			163376	—	Sco			139	221	149	211	nv	nv

2000.0 R.A.	Declin.	HD	Star	Const.	ADS	Also Known As	R(30)	S(30)	R(40)	S(40)	R(50)	S(50)
17 57 50.4	+04 38 19	—	Barnard's	Oph			85	275	85	275	84	276
17 58 30.1	+30 11 22	164136	ν	Her		94	55	305	49	311	39	321
17 59 01.5	−09 46 25	163917	ν	Oph		3	100	260	102	258	104	256
17 59 47.5	−23 48 58	163955	4	Sgr			117	243	121	239	127	233
18 00 03.1	+80 00 03	166865	40	Dra	11061B		cp	cp	cp	cp	cp	cp
18 00 03.3	+16 45 03	164349	93	Her			71	289	69	291	65	295
18 00 09.0	+80 00 14	166866	41	Dra	11061A	Σ2308	cp	cp	cp	cp	cp	cp
18 00 15.7	+04 22 07	164284	66	Oph		V2048	85	275	85	275	84	276
18 00 28.8	−03 41 25	164259	ζ	Ser		57	93	267	94	266	95	265
18 00 38.6	+02 55 53	164353	67	Oph	10966	β1124	88	272	87	273	87	273
18 01 29.8	+21 35 43	164668	95B	Her	10993		66	294	62	298	56	304
18 01 30.3	+21 35 44	164669	95A	Her	10993	Σ2264	66	294	62	298	56	304
18 01 45.1	+01 18 19	164577	68	Oph	10990	β1125	89	271	89	271	88	272
18 03 04.8	−08 10 50	164764	τ^B	Oph	11005B	69	99	261	100	260	103	257
18 03 04.8	−08 10 50	164765	τ	Oph	11005	69, Σ2262	99	261	100	260	103	257
18 05 01.2	−29 34 48	164975	γ¹	Sgr	11029	See 346, W	124	236	129	231	139	221
18 05 27.2	+02 29 58	165341	70	Oph	11046	p, Σ2272	88	272	87	273	87	273
18 05 43.2	+12 00 14	165475	Σ2276	(Oph)	11056		76	284	74	286	71	289
18 05 48.4	−30 25 27	165135	γ²	Sgr			125	235	131	229	141	219
18 06 01.8	+22 13 08	165625	98	Her			64	296	61	299	54	306
18 06 37.7	−50 05 30	165024	θ	Ara			152	208	180	180	nv	nv
18 06 49.7	−43 25 29	165189	h5014	(CrA)			142	218	153	207	nv	nv
18 07 01.3	+30 33 43	165908	99	Her	11077	b	55	305	49	311	39	321
18 07 18.3	+08 44 02	165760	71	Oph			81	279	80	280	77	283
18 07 20.9	+09 33 50	165777	72	Oph	11076	OΣ342	80	280	78	282	76	284
18 07 28.7	+43 27 42	166208	—	Her			38	322	27	333	cp	cp
18 07 32.5	+28 45 45	166014	o	Her		103	57	303	52	308	43	317
18 07 49.4	+26 05 51	166045	100A	Her	11089	Σ2280	60	300	55	305	47	313
18 07 49.4	+26 06 05	166046	100B	Her	11089		60	300	55	305	47	313
18 08 04.9	−28 27 25	165634	—	Sgr			123	237	128	232	137	223
18 08 34.7	−63 40 06	165040	π	Pav			nv	nv	nv	nv	(cp)	(cp)
18 08 45.4	+20 48 52	166182	102	Her	11102		67	293	63	297	58	302
18 10 26.1	−62 00 08	165499	ι	Pav			nv	nv	nv	nv	(cp)	(cp)
18 11 13.7	−45 57 15	166063	ε	Tel			145	215	157	203	nv	nv
18 11 43.3	−23 42 04	166464	11	Sgr	11133	h5030	117	243	121	239	127	233
18 11 54.1	+31 24 19	167006	104	Her		V669	54	306	48	312	37	323
18 13 45.7	−21 03 32	166937	μ	Sgr	11169	13, h2822	114	246	118	242	124	236
18 13 53.6	+64 23 50	168151	36	Dra			cp	cp	cp	cp	cp	cp
18 14 55.8	+36 40 13	167740	W	Lyr			47	313	40	320	24	336
18 17 37.5	−36 45 42	167618	η	Sgr		β760	133	227	140	220	156	204
18 18 03.1	−27 02 33	167818	—	Sgr			122	238	126	234	135	225
18 19 51.6	+36 03 52	168775	κ	Lyr		1	47	313	40	320	24	336
18 20 17.8	+21 57 41	168720	106	Her			66	294	62	298	56	304
18 20 45.3	+71 20 16	170000	φ	Dra	11311	43, OΣ353	cp	cp	cp	cp	cp	cp
18 20 52.0	+03 22 38	168656	74	Oph	11271	h5495	87	273	86	274	85	275
18 20 59.6	−29 49 41	168454	δ	Sgr	11264	19, See 350	124	236	129	231	139	221
18 21 00.9	+28 52 12	168914	107	Her			57	303	52	308	43	317
18 21 03.2	+72 43 58	170153	χ	Dra		44	cp	cp	cp	cp	cp	cp
18 21 18.5	−02 53 56	168723	η	Ser		58	92	268	93	267	93	267
18 21 22.9	−18 51 36	168608	Y	Sgr			111	249	114	246	119	241

2000.0 R.A.			2000.0 Declin.			HD	Star	Const.	ADS	Also Known As	Rising and Setting Azimuths R(30)	S(30)	R(40)	S(40)	R(50)	S(50)
18	21	32.5	+49	07	18	169305	—	Dra			29	331	10	350	cp	cp
18	22	18.5	−38	39	25	168592	—	CrA			135	225	143	217	163	197
18	23	13.5	−61	29	38	168339	ξ	Pav			nv	nv	nv	nv	(cp)	(cp)
18	23	36.0	−75	02	39	167468	φ	Oct			nv	nv	(cp)	(cp)	(cp)	(cp)
18	23	39.4	−08	56	04	169156	ζ	Sct			96	264	97	263	98	262
18	23	41.8	+21	46	11	169414	109	Her			66	294	62	298	56	304
18	23	54.4	+58	48	02	170073	39	Dra	11336	b, Σ2323	12	348	cp	cp	cp	cp
18	24	10.3	−34	23	05	169022	ε	Sgr		20, See 351	130	230	137	223	150	210
18	24	13.7	+39	30	26	169702	μ	Lyr		2	43	317	35	325	12	348
18	25	20.9	−20	32	30	169420	21	Sgr	11325		113	247	117	243	122	238
18	25	58.9	+65	33	49	170693	42	Dra			cp	cp	cp	cp	cp	cp
18	26	58.3	−45	58	06	169467	α	Tel			145	215	157	203	nv	nv
18	27	12.3	+00	11	46	169985	59	Ser	11353	d, Σ2316	90	270	90	270	90	270
18	27	43.8	+19	17	45	170267	Σ2319	(Her)	11372		68	292	65	295	60	300
18	27	58.1	−25	25	18	169916	λ	Sgr		22	119	241	123	237	131	229
18	28	49.8	−49	04	15	169767	ζ	Tel			151	209	170	190	nv	nv
18	29	11.7	−14	33	57	170296	γ	Sct			100	260	102	258	104	256
18	31	06.9	+32	14	44	171026	Σ2333	(Lyr)	11424		52	308	46	314	34	326
18	31	22.3	−62	16	42	169978	ν	Pav			nv	nv	nv	nv	(cp)	(cp)
18	31	26.2	−18	24	10	170680	—	Sgr	11411	See 354	111	249	114	246	119	241
18	31	45.3	−45	54	54	170465	δ¹	Tel			145	215	157	203	nv	nv
18	31	53.0	−19	07	30	170764	U	Sgr	11433	β966	112	248	115	245	120	240
18	32	01.9	−45	45	26	170523	δ²	Tel			145	215	157	203	nv	nv
18	32	21.2	−39	42	15	170642	—	CrA			137	223	145	215	168	192
18	32	34.3	+57	02	44	171635	45	Dra			14	346	cp	cp	cp	cp
18	33	23.0	−38	43	34	170867	κ²	CrA		DUN 222	135	225	143	217	163	197
18	33	23.2	−38	43	13	170868	κ¹	CrA			135	225	143	217	163	197
18	33	30.1	−42	18	45	170845	θ	CrA			141	219	151	209	nv	nv
18	35	02.3	−10	58	38	171391	—	Sct			107	253	110	250	114	246
18	35	12.3	−08	14	39	171443	α	Sct		1 Aql	95	265	95	265	96	264
18	36	56.2	+38	47	01	172167	α	Lyr	11510	3	45	315	37	323	17	343
18	38	20.9	+08	50	02	172171	X	Oph	11524	Hu 198	81	279	80	280	77	283
18	42	16.3	−09	03	09	172748	δ	Sct	11581	2 Aql	99	261	100	260	103	257
18	42	37.8	+55	32	22	173524	46	Dra			19	341	cp	cp	cp	cp
18	43	02.1	−71	25	42	171759	ζ	Pav		h5048	nv	nv	nv	nv	(cp)	(cp)
18	43	31.2	−08	16	31	173009	ε	Sct	11601	3 Aql	95	265	95	265	96	264
18	43	46.8	−38	19	25	172777	λ	CrA			135	225	143	217	163	197
18	44	19.3	−35	38	32	172910	—	Sgr			131	229	138	222	153	207
18	44	20.2	+39	40	15	173583	ε¹ᴮ	Lyr	11635B	4	43	317	35	325	12	348
18	44	20.3	+39	40	12	173582	ε¹ᴬ	Lyr	11635A	4, Σ2382	43	317	35	325	12	348
18	44	22.8	+39	36	46	173607	ε²ᶜ	Lyr	11635C	5, Σ2383	43	317	35	325	12	348
18	44	22.8	+39	36	46	173608	ε²ᴰ	Lyr	11635D	5	43	317	35	325	12	348
18	44	46.3	+37	36	18	173648	ζ¹	Lyr	11639A	6, β968	46	314	38	322	21	339
18	44	48.1	+37	35	40	173649	ζ²	Lyr	11639D	7	46	314	38	322	21	339
18	44	49.8	+02	03	36	173370	4	Aql			88	272	87	273	87	273
18	45	26.6	−64	52	17	172555	—	Pav			nv	nv	nv	nv	(cp)	(cp)
18	45	28.3	+05	29	59	173495	Σ2375	(Ser)	11640		84	276	83	277	82	278
18	45	39.3	−26	59	27	173300	φ	Sgr		27	120	240	125	235	133	227
18	45	39.6	+20	32	47	173667	110	Her	11658	h2839	67	293	63	297	58	302
18	46	04.4	+26	39	43	173780	—	Lyr			60	300	55	305	47	313

2000.0 R.A.			2000.0 Declin.			HD	Star	Const.	ADS	Also Known As	Rising and Setting Azimuths					
											R(30)	S(30)	R(40)	S(40)	R(50)	S(50)
18	47	01.2	+18	10	53	173880	111	Her			69	291	66	294	61	299
18	47	10.4	−04	44	53	173764	β	Sct		6 Aql	106	254	108	252	112	248
18	47	28.9	−05	42	18	173819	R	Sct			100	260	102	258	104	256
18	47	44.4	−40	24	22	173540	μ	CrA			138	222	147	213	179	181
18	48	50.4	−43	40	48	173715	η¹	CrA			142	218	153	207	nv	nv
18	49	40.0	−20	19	29	174116	29	Sgr	11713	See 362	113	247	117	243	122	238
18	49	52.8	+32	33	03	174602	ν²	Lyr	11737	9, Ho 440	52	308	46	314	34	326
18	50	04.7	+33	21	46	174638	β	Lyr	11745	10, Σ139	51	309	45	315	32	328
18	51	11.9	+59	23	18	175306	o	Dra	11779	47, Σ2420	8	352	cp	cp	cp	cp
18	52	12.9	−62	11	16	173948	λ	Pav		h5062	nv	nv	nv	nv	(cp)	(cp)
18	52	39.5	−52	06	27	174295	κ	Tel			155	205	nv	nv	nv	nv
18	53	13.5	+50	42	29	175535	—	Dra			28	332	cp	cp	cp	cp
18	53	43.5	+36	58	18	175426	δ¹	Lyr		11	47	313	40	320	24	336
18	54	10.1	−22	44	42	174974	ν¹	Sgr	11794	32, β1033	116	244	119	241	126	234
18	54	23.7	+71	17	50	176524	υ	Dra		52	cp	cp	cp	cp	cp	cp
18	54	30.1	+36	53	56	175588	δ²	Lyr	11825	12	47	313	40	320	24	336
18	54	43.0	−15	36	11	175156	—	Sct			90	270	90	270	90	270
18	54	44.3	−87	36	21	164461	χ	Oct			nv	nv	(cp)	(cp)	(cp)	(cp)
18	54	44.8	+22	38	43	175492	113	Her	11820	β646	64	296	61	299	54	306
18	55	07.0	−22	40	17	175190	ν²	Sgr		35	116	244	119	241	126	234
18	55	15.8	−26	17	48	175191	σ	Sgr		34	120	240	125	235	133	227
18	55	20.0	+43	56	46	175865	R	Lyr		13	38	322	27	333	cp	cp
18	56	13.1	+04	12	13	175638	θ¹ᴬ	Ser	11853	63, Σ2417	85	275	85	275	84	276
18	56	14.5	+04	12	07	175639	θ¹ᴮ	Ser	11853	63	85	275	85	275	84	276
18	56	57.0	−67	14	01	174694	κ	Pav			nv	nv	nv	nv	(cp)	(cp)
18	57	01.5	+32	54	05	176051	β648	(Lyr)	11871		52	308	46	314	34	326
18	57	03.6	−05	50	46	175751	η	Sct			96	264	97	263	98	262
18	57	20.4	−20	39	23	175687	ξ¹	Sgr			113	247	117	243	122	238
18	57	43.7	−21	06	24	175775	ξ²	Sgr		37	114	246	118	242	124	236
18	58	14.6	+17	21	39	176155	FF	Aql	11884	Ho 91	70	290	68	292	63	297
18	58	27.6	−52	56	18	175510	λ	Tel			155	205	nv	nv	nv	nv
18	58	36.3	−60	12	02	175329	ω	Pav			180	180	nv	nv	(cp)	(cp)
18	58	43.3	−37	06	26	175813	ε	CrA			134	226	142	218	159	201
18	58	56.5	+32	41	22	176437	γ	Lyr	11908	14	52	308	46	314	34	326
18	59	05.6	+13	37	21	176303	11	Aql	11902	Σ2424	75	285	73	287	70	290
18	59	23.6	−12	50	26	176162	Kui 89	(Sgr)			104	256	106	254	109	251
18	59	37.3	+15	04	06	176411	ε	Aql		13	73	287	70	290	66	294
19	00	00.8	+32	08	44	176670	λ	Lyr		15	52	308	46	314	34	326
19	01	26.3	+46	56	05	177196	16	Lyr	11964	h1362	34	326	20	340	cp	cp
19	01	40.7	−05	44	20	176678	12	Aql			96	264	97	263	98	262
19	02	36.6	−29	52	49	176687	ζ	Sgr	11950	38	124	236	129	231	139	221
19	03	06.7	−42	05	43	176638	ζ	CrA			141	219	151	209	nv	nv
19	04	40.9	−21	44	30	177241	o	Sgr	11996	39, See 369	114	246	118	242	124	236
19	05	24.5	+13	51	48	177724	ζ	Aql	12026	17, β287	75	285	73	287	70	290
19	06	14.8	−04	52	57	177756	λ	Aql		16	95	265	95	265	96	264
19	06	19.8	−52	20	27	177171	ρ	Tel			155	205	nv	nv	nv	nv
19	06	22.0	+08	13	48	177940	R	Aql		h4866	81	279	80	280	77	283
19	06	25.0	−37	03	48	177474	γ	CrA		h5084	134	226	142	218	159	201
19	06	56.3	−27	40	14	177716	τ	Sgr		40	122	238	126	234	135	225
19	06	58.5	+11	04	17	178125	18	Aql		Y	77	283	76	284	73	287

2000.0 R.A.			Declin.			HD	Star	Const.	ADS	Also Known As	Rising and Setting Azimuths					
											R(30)	S(30)	R(40)	S(40)	R(50)	S(50)
19	07	18.0	+36	06	01	178475	ι	Lyr		18	47	313	40	320	24	336
19	07	25.5	+32	30	06	178449	17	Lyr	12061	Σ2461	52	308	46	314	34	326
19	08	20.8	−40	29	48	177873	δ	CrA			138	222	147	213	179	181
19	08	45.1	+34	45	37	178849	Σ2470	(Lyr)	12093		50	310	43	317	30	330
19	08	59.8	+06	04	24	178596	19	Aql			83	277	82	278	81	279
19	09	04.3	+34	36	02	178911	Σ2474	(Lyr)	12101		50	310	43	317	30	330
19	09	09.7	+76	33	38	180777	59	Dra			cp	cp	cp	cp	cp	cp
19	09	28.2	−37	54	16	178253	α	CrA			134	226	142	218	159	201
19	09	45.7	−21	01	25	178524	π	Sgr		41	114	246	118	242	124	236
19	10	01.6	−39	20	27	178345	β	CrA			137	223	145	215	168	192
19	11	40.4	+56	51	33	180006	53	Dra			17	343	cp	cp	cp	cp
19	12	33.1	+67	39	42	180711	δ	Dra		57	cp	cp	cp	cp	cp	cp
19	13	42.6	+02	17	38	179761	21	Aql	12182	h879, V1288	88	272	87	273	87	273
19	13	45.4	+39	08	46	180163	η	Lyr	12197	20, Σ2487	43	317	35	325	12	348
19	13	55.1	+57	42	18	180610	54	Dra			14	346	cp	cp	cp	cp
19	15	32.3	−25	15	24	179950	ψ	Sgr	12214	42	119	241	123	237	131	229
19	15	32.8	+73	21	20	181984	τ	Dra		60	cp	cp	cp	cp	cp	cp
19	16	12.9	+21	23	26	180554	1	Vul	12243	h2862	66	294	62	298	56	304
19	16	22.0	+38	08	01	180809	θ	Lyr		21	45	315	37	323	17	343
19	16	32.6	−33	31	18	180093	RY	Sgr			129	231	135	225	148	212
19	16	41.6	−19	18	25	180275	R	Sgr			112	248	115	245	120	240
19	17	06.0	+53	22	07	181276	κ	Cyg		1	23	337	cp	cp	cp	cp
19	17	38.0	−18	57	11	180540	43	Sgr			111	249	114	246	119	241
19	17	48.9	+11	35	44	180868	ω¹	Aql		25	77	283	76	284	73	287
19	18	32.4	+01	05	07	180972	23	Aql	12289	Σ2492	89	271	89	271	88	272
19	18	48.4	+19	36	38	181182	U	Sge			68	292	65	295	60	300
19	20	32.8	−05	24	57	181391	26	Aql			96	264	97	263	98	262
19	20	40.0	+65	42	52	182564	π	Dra		58	cp	cp	cp	cp	cp	cp
19	21	40.3	−17	50	50	181577	ρ¹	Sgr		44	110	250	112	248	117	243
19	21	43.5	−15	57	18	181615	υ	Sgr		46	107	253	110	250	114	246
19	22	38.2	−44	27	32	181454	β¹	Sgr		DUN 226	143	217	155	205	nv	nv
19	22	50.8	+26	15	45	182255	3	Vul			60	300	55	305	47	313
19	22	51.0	−54	25	25	181296	η	Tel			159	201	nv	nv	nv	nv
19	23	13.1	−44	47	59	181623	β²	Sgr			143	217	155	205	nv	nv
19	23	53.0	−40	36	58	181869	α	Sgr			138	222	147	213	179	181
19	24	07.5	+29	37	17	182568	2	Cyg			56	304	51	309	41	319
19	24	58.1	+11	56	40	182572	31	Aql			77	283	76	284	73	287
19	25	16.4	−24	30	31	182369	χ¹	Sgr		47	118	242	122	238	129	231
19	25	27.7	+42	47	05	182989	RR	Lyr			39	321	29	331	cp	cp
19	25	28.5	+19	47	55	182762	4	Vul	12425	h2871	68	292	65	295	60	300
19	25	29.6	−23	57	44	182416	χ³	Sgr		49	117	243	121	239	127	233
19	25	29.8	+03	06	53	182640	δ	Aql		30	87	273	86	274	85	275
19	26	09.0	+36	19	04	183056	4	Cyg		V1741	47	313	40	320	24	336
19	26	31.0	+00	20	19	182835	ν	Aql		32	90	270	90	270	90	270
19	26	33.6	+27	19	20	183032	Σ2525	(Vul)	12447		58	302	54	306	45	315
19	28	42.2	+24	39	54	183439	α	Vul		6	62	298	58	302	51	309
19	29	42.2	+51	43	47	184006	ι²	Cyg		10	26	334	cp	cp	cp	cp
19	30	39.7	−02	47	20	183630	36	Aql			92	268	93	267	93	267
19	30	43.1	+27	57	35	183912	β¹	Cyg	12540	6	58	302	54	306	45	315
19	30	45.2	+27	57	55	183914	β²	Cyg	12540		58	302	54	306	45	315

2000.0 R.A.			2000.0 Declin.			HD	Star	Const.	ADS	Also Known As	R(30)	S(30)	R(40)	S(40)	R(50)	S(50)
19	31	46.2	+34	27	11	184171	8	Cyg			50	310	43	317	30	330
19	32	21.5	+69	39	40	185144	σ	Dra		61	cp	cp	cp	cp	cp	cp
19	34	05.3	+07	22	44	184406	μ	Aql	12607	38, β653	82	278	81	279	79	281
19	34	34.8	+19	46	24	184606	9	Vul	12622	β1130	68	292	65	295	60	300
19	35	07.2	−10	33	38	184492	37	Aql			102	258	103	257	106	254
19	35	12.8	−48	05	57	184127	ι	Tel			149	211	166	194	nv	nv
19	36	26.4	+50	13	16	185395	θ	Cyg	12695	13, β1131	28	332	cp	cp	cp	cp
19	36	37.8	+44	41	42	185351	—	Cyg			37	323	25	335	cp	cp
19	36	42.3	−24	53	01	184707	52	Sgr	12654	β654	118	242	122	238	129	231
19	36	43.2	−01	17	11	184930	41	Aql	12663		91	269	91	269	92	268
19	36	43.2	−01	17	11	184930	ι	Aql	12663	41	91	269	91	269	92	268
19	36	49.2	+50	11	59	185456	R	Cyg			28	332	cp	cp	cp	cp
19	36	53.4	−07	01	39	184915	κ	Aql		39	98	262	99	261	101	259
19	37	17.3	+16	27	46	185194	ε	Sge	12693	4	71	289	69	291	65	295
19	39	11.5	+05	23	52	185507	σ	Aql	12737	44, h2886	84	276	83	277	82	278
19	39	22.5	+30	09	12	185734	φ	Cyg			55	305	49	311	39	321
19	40	05.7	+18	00	50	185758	α	Sge	12766	5	69	291	66	294	61	299
19	40	43.3	−16	17	36	185644	54	Sgr	12767	h599	109	251	111	249	115	245
19	40	50.1	+45	31	29	186155	—	Cyg			35	325	23	337	cp	cp
19	41	02.9	+17	28	33	185958	β	Sge		6	70	290	68	292	63	297
19	42	31.0	−16	07	27	186005	55	Sgr			109	251	111	249	115	245
19	42	33.9	+11	49	36	186203	χ	Aql	12808	47, OΣ380	77	283	76	284	73	287
19	43	37.7	+48	46	42	186686	RT	Cyg			31	329	14	346	cp	cp
19	44	16.5	+37	21	16	186675	15	Cyg			46	314	38	322	21	339
19	44	58.4	+45	07	51	186882	δ	Cyg	12880	18, Σ2579	35	325	23	337	cp	cp
19	46	15.5	+10	36	48	186791	γ	Aql		50	78	282	77	283	74	286
19	46	21.6	−19	45	40	186648	56	Sgr			112	248	115	245	120	240
19	46	25.5	+33	43	40	187013	17	Cyg	12913	Σ2580	51	309	45	315	32	328
19	47	23.2	+18	32	02	187076	δ	Sge		7	69	291	66	294	61	299
19	48	01.1	−56	21	46	186543	ν	Tel			163	197	nv	nv	nv	nv
19	48	10.3	+70	16	04	188119	ε	Dra	13007	63, Σ2603	cp	cp	cp	cp	cp	cp
19	48	58.6	+19	08	31	187362	ζ	Sge	12973	8, Σ2585	68	292	65	295	60	300
19	50	33.8	+32	54	51	187796	χ	Cyg			52	308	46	314	34	326
19	50	33.9	+38	43	21	187849	19	Cyg	13014	h603, V1509	45	315	37	323	17	343
19	50	37.6	+52	59	17	188056	20	Cyg			25	335	cp	cp	cp	cp
19	50	46.9	+08	52	06	187642	α	Aql	13009	53	81	279	80	280	77	283
19	51	01.5	+10	24	56	187691	o	Aql	13012	54	78	282	77	283	74	286
19	51	04.0	+22	36	36	187811	12	Vul			64	296	61	299	54	306
19	52	28.3	+01	00	20	187929	η	Aql		55	89	271	89	271	88	272
19	53	17.3	+57	31	25	188665	23	Cyg			14	346	cp	cp	cp	cp
19	53	27.6	+24	04	47	188260	13	Vul			62	298	58	302	51	309
19	54	14.8	+08	27	41	188310	ξ	Aql		59	81	279	80	280	77	283
19	55	15.5	−41	52	06	188114	ι	Sgr			139	221	149	211	nv	nv
19	55	18.7	+06	24	24	188512	β	Aql	13110	60, OΣ532	83	277	82	278	81	279
19	55	37.7	+52	26	20	189037	ψ	Cyg	13148	24, Σ2605	25	335	cp	cp	cp	cp
19	55	50.3	−26	17	58	188376	ω	Sgr		58	120	240	125	235	133	227
19	55	51.6	+38	29	12	188892	22	Cyg			45	315	37	323	17	343
19	55	55.2	+58	50	46	189276	—	Cyg			12	348	cp	cp	cp	cp
19	56	14.1	+11	25	25	188728	φ	Aql		61	77	283	76	284	73	287
19	56	18.3	+35	05	00	188947	η	Cyg	13149	21, β980	49	311	42	318	27	333

R.A.	2000.0 Declin.	HD	Star	Const.	ADS	Also Known As	R(30)	S(30)	R(40)	S(40)	R(50)	S(50)
19 56 56.7	−27 10 12	188603	59	Sgr			122	238	126	234	135	225
19 57 56.9	−15 29 29	188899	61	Sgr			107	253	110	250	114	246
19 58 42.8	−41 51 04	188813	RU	Sgr			139	221	149	211	nv	nv
19 58 45.3	+19 29 32	189319	γ	Sge		12	68	292	65	295	60	300
19 58 57.1	−26 11 44	189005	60	Sgr			120	240	125	235	133	227
19 59 44.1	−35 16 35	189103	θ¹	Sgr			131	229	138	222	153	207
19 59 51.2	−34 41 53	189118	θ²	Sgr			130	230	137	223	150	210
19 59 55.1	+37 02 35	189687	V1746	Cyg			46	314	38	322	21	339
19 59 55.1	+37 02 35	189687	25	Cyg			46	314	38	322	21	339
20 00 35.4	−72 54 38	188228	ε	Pav			nv	nv	nv	nv	(cp)	(cp)
20 01 06.0	+27 45 13	189849	15	Vul		NT	58	302	54	306	45	315
20 01 21.5	+50 06 17	190147	26	Cyg	13278		28	332	cp	cp	cp	cp
20 01 44.5	−59 22 34	189124	ν	Pav			172	188	nv	nv	(cp)	(cp)
20 01 52.3	−66 56 39	188887	μ²	Pav			nv	nv	nv	nv	(cp)	(cp)
20 02 01.3	+24 56 17	190004	16	Vul	13277	OΣ395	62	298	58	302	51	309
20 02 39.4	−27 42 36	189763	62	Sgr		V3872	122	238	126	234	135	225
20 02 48.9	+67 52 25	190940	ρ	Dra		67	cp	cp	cp	cp	cp	cp
20 03 33.4	−37 56 27	189831	—	Sgr			134	226	142	218	159	201
20 04 19.5	−32 03 22	190056	—	Sgr			128	232	134	226	146	214
20 05 09.4	+19 59 28	190608	η	Sge		16	68	292	65	295	60	300
20 06 53.3	+23 36 52	190993	17	Vul			63	297	59	301	53	307
20 07 23.1	−52 52 51	190421	ξ	Tel			155	205	nv	nv	nv	nv
20 08 43.2	−66 10 56	190248	δ	Pav			nv	nv	nv	nv	(cp)	(cp)
20 08 53.2	+77 42 41	192907	κ	Cep	13524	1, Σ2675	cp	cp	cp	cp	cp	cp
20 09 25.5	+36 50 23	191610	28	Cyg		V1624	47	313	40	320	24	336
20 09 52.2	+20 53 48	191570	θ	Sge	13442	17, Σ2637	67	293	63	297	58	302
20 11 18.2	−00 49 17	191692	θ	Aql		65	90	270	90	270	90	270
20 13 17.9	+46 48 57	192514	30	Cyg	13554	h1495	34	326	20	340	cp	cp
20 13 23.8	+56 34 04	192696	33	Cyg			17	343	cp	cp	cp	cp
20 13 37.8	+46 44 29	192577	o¹	Cyg		31, V695	34	326	20	340	cp	cp
20 14 14.4	+28 41 41	192518	21	Vul		NU	57	303	52	308	43	317
20 14 16.5	+15 11 51	192425	ρ	Aql		67	73	287	70	290	66	294
20 14 31.9	+36 48 23	192640	29	Cyg			47	313	40	320	24	336
20 14 54.9	+09 05 20	192502	R	Del			80	280	78	282	76	284
20 15 15.8	+25 35 31	192685	β983	(Vul)	13589	QR	61	299	57	303	49	311
20 15 28.2	+47 42 52	192909	o²	Cyg		32, V1488	32	328	17	343	cp	cp
20 15 30.1	+23 30 31	192713	22	Vul			63	297	59	301	53	307
20 15 46.0	+27 48 51	192806	23	Vul			58	302	54	306	45	315
20 16 55.2	+40 21 54	193092	—	Cyg	13640	β661	42	318	33	327	cp	cp
20 17 38.8	−12 30 30	192876	α¹	Cap	13632	5, β295	104	256	106	254	109	251
20 17 47.0	+38 01 59	193237	P	Cyg			45	315	37	323	17	343
20 18 03.2	−12 32 42	192947	α²	Cap	13645	6, h608	104	256	106	254	109	251
20 18 39.0	+34 58 58	193370	35	Cyg			50	310	43	317	30	330
20 19 23.5	−19 07 07	193150	σ	Cap	13675	7	112	248	115	245	120	240
20 19 36.3	+47 53 42	193680	U	Cyg			32	328	17	343	cp	cp
20 20 39.7	−12 45 33	193432	ν	Cap	13714	8	104	256	106	254	109	251
20 21 00.5	−14 46 53	193495	β	Cap		9	106	254	108	252	112	248
20 22 13.6	+40 15 24	194093	γ	Cyg	13765	37, β665	42	318	33	327	1	359
20 23 51.5	+32 11 25	194317	39	Cyg			52	308	46	314	34	326
20 25 38.8	−56 44 07	193924	α	Pav		h5193	163	197	nv	nv	(cp)	(cp)

2000.0 R.A.	2000.0 Declin.	HD	Star	Const.	ADS	Also Known As	Rising and Setting Azimuths R(30)	S(30)	R(40)	S(40)	R(50)	S(50)
20 27 19.1	−18 12 42	194636	π	Cap	13860	10, β60	111	249	114	246	119	241
20 28 51.5	−17 48 49	194943	ρ	Cap	13887	11, β61	110	250	112	248	117	243
20 29 23.6	+30 22 07	195295	41	Cyg			55	305	49	311	39	321
20 29 34.8	+62 59 39	195725	θ	Cep		2	cp	cp	cp	cp	cp	cp
20 29 38.9	−02 53 08	195135	69	Aql			92	268	93	267	93	267
20 30 03.4	+48 57 06	195556	ω¹	Cyg		45, β699	31	329	14	346	cp	cp
20 31 30.3	+74 57 17	196502	73	Dra		AF	cp	cp	cp	cp	cp	cp
20 33 12.7	+11 18 12	195810	ε	Del		2	77	283	76	284	73	287
20 33 54.1	+35 15 03	196093	47	Cyg			49	311	42	318	27	333
20 33 55.0	−44 30 58	195569	ν	Mic			143	217	155	205	nv	nv
20 33 56.9	+13 01 38	195943	η	Del		3	75	285	73	287	70	290
20 35 18.4	+14 40 27	196180	ζ	Del		4	74	286	72	288	68	292
20 35 34.7	−60 34 54	195627	φ¹	Pav			180	180	nv	nv	(cp)	(cp)
20 36 43.5	−02 32 59	196321	70	Aql			92	268	93	267	93	267
20 37 32.9	+14 35 43	196524	β	Del	14073	6, β151	74	286	72	288	68	292
20 37 34.0	−47 17 29	196171	α	Ind		h5209	148	212	163	197	(cp)	(cp)
20 37 35.2	−61 31 48	195961	ρ	Pav			nv	nv	nv	nv	(cp)	(cp)
20 37 49.0	+11 22 40	196544	ι	Del		5	77	283	76	284	73	287
20 38 20.2	−01 06 19	196574	71	Aql	14081	β672	91	269	91	269	92	268
20 38 31.2	+21 12 04	196724	29	Vul			66	294	62	298	56	304
20 38 31.8	+24 06 58	196740	28	Vul			62	298	58	302	51	309
20 39 07.7	+10 05 10	196755	κ	Del	14101	7, OΣ533	78	282	77	283	74	286
20 39 16.3	−14 57 17	196662	τ	Cap	14099	14, Hu200	106	254	108	252	112	248
20 39 24.8	+00 29 11	196758	1	Aqr	14108	h2984	90	270	90	270	90	270
20 39 38.1	+15 54 43	196867	α	Del		9	73	287	70	290	66	294
20 40 02.4	−60 32 56	196378	φ²	Pav			180	180	nv	nv	(cp)	(cp)
20 40 02.9	−18 08 19	196777	υ	Cap		15	111	249	114	246	119	241
20 41 25.8	+45 16 49	197345	α	Cyg	14172	50	35	325	23	337	cp	cp
20 41 57.1	−66 45 39	196519	υ	Pav			nv	nv	nv	nv	(cp)	(cp)
20 43 04.8	+17 05 20	197420	S	Del			70	290	68	292	63	297
20 43 27.3	+15 04 28	197461	δ	Del		11	73	287	70	290	66	294
20 44 02.2	−51 55 16	197157	η	Ind			154	206	(cp)	(cp)	(cp)	(cp)
20 44 52.4	+25 16 15	197752	30	Vul			61	299	57	303	49	311
20 44 57.4	−66 12 11	197051	β	Pav			nv	nv	nv	nv	(cp)	(cp)
20 45 17.3	+61 50 20	198149	η	Cep	14276	3	cp	cp	cp	cp	cp	cp
20 45 21.0	+57 34 47	198084	—	Cep			14	346	cp	cp	cp	cp
20 45 39.6	+30 43 11	197912	52	Cyg	14259	Σ2726	55	305	49	311	39	321
20 46 05.6	−25 16 16	197692	ψ	Cap		16	119	241	123	237	131	229
20 46 12.6	+33 58 13	197989	ε	Cyg	14274	53, β676	51	309	45	315	32	328
20 46 38.6	+16 07 27	197963	γ¹	Del		12, Σ2727	71	289	69	291	65	295
20 46 39.3	+16 07 27	197964	γ²	Del		12	71	289	69	291	65	295
20 47 10.7	+34 22 27	198134	T	Cyg	14290	β677	50	310	43	317	30	330
20 47 24.4	+36 29 27	198183	λ	Cyg	14296	54, OΣ413	47	313	40	320	24	336
20 47 40.5	−09 29 45	198001	ε	Aqr		2	100	260	102	258	104	256
20 47 44.1	−05 01 40	198026	3	Aqr		EN	96	264	97	263	98	262
20 48 29.0	−43 59 19	197937	ι	Mic			142	218	153	207	nv	nv
20 48 56.2	+46 06 51	198478	55	Cyg	14337	h1581, V1661	34	326	20	340	cp	cp
20 49 18.0	−68 46 36	197635	σ	Pav			nv	nv	nv	nv	(cp)	(cp)
20 49 28.9	−46 13 37	198048	ζ	Ind			146	214	160	200	(cp)	(cp)
20 49 58.0	−33 46 48	198232	α	Mic		h5224	129	231	135	225	148	212

2000.0 R.A.	Declin.	HD	Star	Const.	ADS	Also Known As	R(30)	S(30)	R(40)	S(40)	R(50)	S(50)
20 50 04.8	+44 03 34	198639	56	Cyg			37	323	25	335	cp	cp
20 51 30.0	−51 36 30	198308	ι	Ind			154	206	(cp)	(cp)	(cp)	(cp)
20 51 49.2	−26 55 09	198542	ω	Cap		18	120	240	125	235	133	227
20 51 58.7	−33 10 38	198529	β	Mic			129	231	135	225	148	212
20 52 07.6	+27 05 49	198809	31	Vul			58	302	54	306	45	315
20 52 39.1	−08 59 00	198743	μ	Aqr			99	261	100	260	103	257
20 53 14.7	+44 23 14	199081	57	Cyg			37	323	25	335	cp	cp
20 54 33.5	+28 03 28	199169	32	Vul			57	303	52	308	43	317
20 54 48.5	−58 27 15	198700	β	Ind			168	192	(cp)	(cp)	(cp)	(cp)
20 55 36.6	+13 43 18	199253	17	Del			75	285	73	287	70	290
20 57 10.3	+41 10 02	199629	ν	Cyg		58	41	319	31	329	cp	cp
20 59 04.3	+04 17 37	199766	ε	Equ	14499	1, Σ2737	85	275	85	275	84	276
20 59 49.5	+47 31 16	200120	59	Cyg	14526	Σ2743, V832	32	328	17	343	cp	cp
21 01 10.8	+46 09 21	200310	60	Cyg	14549	OΣ426	34	326	20	340	cp	cp
21 01 17.4	−32 15 28	199951	γ	Mic		1 PsA	128	232	134	226	146	214
21 02 12.2	+07 10 47	200256	λ	Equ	14556	2, Σ2742	82	278	81	279	79	281
21 02 57.8	−38 37 54	200163	ζ	Mic			135	225	143	217	163	197
21 04 24.2	−19 51 18	200499	η	Cap		22	112	248	115	245	120	240
21 04 42.8	−77 01 26	199532	α	Oct			(cp)	(cp)	(cp)	(cp)	(cp)	(cp)
21 04 55.8	+43 55 40	200905	ξ	Cyg		62	38	322	27	333	cp	cp
21 05 14.1	−54 43 37	200365	μ	Ind			159	201	(cp)	(cp)	(cp)	(cp)
21 05 56.7	−17 13 58	200761	θ	Cap		23	110	250	112	248	117	243
21 06 24.6	−32 20 30	200763	—	Mic			128	232	134	226	146	214
21 06 36.0	+47 38 54	201251	63	Cyg	14649		32	328	17	343	cp	cp
21 06 53.7	+38 44 57	201091	61A	Cyg	14636	Σ2758, V1803	45	315	37	323	17	343
21 06 55.2	+38 44 30	201092	61B	Cyg	14636		45	315	37	323	17	343
21 07 07.6	−25 00 21	200914	24	Cap	14632	See 439	119	241	123	237	131	229
21 08 44.8	−88 57 24	177482	σ	Oct			nv	nv	(cp)	(cp)	(cp)	(cp)
21 09 31.8	+68 29 25	202012	T	Cep			cp	cp	cp	cp	cp	cp
21 09 35.5	−11 22 18	201381	ν	Aqr		13	103	257	104	256	107	253
21 10 20.5	+10 07 53	201601	γ	Equ	14702	5, β71	78	282	77	283	74	286
21 12 56.1	+30 13 37	202109	ζ	Cyg		64	55	305	49	311	39	321
21 13 20.4	−70 07 36	201371	o	Pav			nv	nv	nv	nv	(cp)	(cp)
21 14 28.8	+10 00 25	202275	δ	Equ	14773	7, OΣ535	78	282	77	283	74	286
21 14 47.4	+38 02 44	202444	τ	Cyg	14787	65	45	315	37	323	17	343
21 15 37.8	−20 39 06	202320	φ	Cap		28	113	247	117	243	122	238
21 15 49.3	+05 14 52	202447	α	Equ		8	84	276	83	277	82	278
21 17 24.9	+39 23 41	202850	σ	Cyg		67	43	317	35	325	12	348
21 17 55.0	+34 53 49	202904	υ	Cyg	14831	66, OΣ433	50	310	43	317	30	330
21 17 56.2	−32 10 21	202627	ε	Mic			128	232	134	226	146	214
21 18 27.0	+43 56 46	203064	68	Cyg		V1809	38	322	27	333	cp	cp
21 18 34.7	+62 35 08	203280	α	Cep	14858	5	cp	cp	cp	cp	cp	cp
21 19 22.1	+64 52 19	203467	6	Cep			cp	cp	cp	cp	cp	cp
21 19 51.9	−53 26 59	202730	θ	Ind		h5258	157	203	(cp)	(cp)	(cp)	(cp)
21 20 45.5	−40 48 35	203006	θ¹	Mic			138	222	147	213	179	181
21 22 05.1	+19 48 16	203504	1	Peg	14909		68	292	65	295	60	300
21 22 14.7	−16 50 05	203387	ι	Cap		32	109	251	111	249	115	245
21 22 53.5	+06 48 40	203562	β	Equ	14920	10, h3023	83	277	82	278	81	279
21 24 24.7	−41 00 24	203585	θ²	Mic		β766	139	221	149	211	nv	nv
21 26 26.7	−65 21 59	203608	γ	Pav			nv	nv	nv	nv	(cp)	(cp)

	2000.0						Also	Rising and Setting Azimuths					
R.A.		Declin.		HD	Star	Const.	ADS	Known As	R(30)	S(30)	R(40)	S(40)	R(50)	S(50)
21 26 39.9	−22 24 41			204075	ζ	Cap	14971	34, See 446	116	244	119	241	126	234
21 27 21.3	+37 07 01			204403	70	Cyg			46	314	38	322	21	339
21 28 39.5	+70 33 39			205021	β	Cep		8	cp	cp	cp	cp	cp	cp
21 28 43.3	−21 48 26			204381	36	Cap			114	246	118	242	124	236
21 29 26.9	+46 32 26			204771	71	Cyg			34	326	20	340	cp	cp
21 29 56.8	+23 38 20			204724	2	Peg	15027	β685	63	297	59	301	53	307
21 31 33.3	−05 34 16			204867	β	Aqr	15050	22, H936	96	264	97	263	98	262
21 32 05.7	−41 10 46			204783	ξ	Gru			139	221	149	211	nv	nv
21 33 58.8	+45 35 31			205435	ρ	Cyg		73	35	325	23	337	cp	cp
21 34 46.5	+38 32 03			205512	72	Cyg			45	315	37	323	17	343
21 35 12.6	+78 37 29			206362	S	Cep			cp	cp	cp	cp	cp	cp
21 36 56.9	+40 24 49			205835	74	Cyg			42	318	33	327	cp	cp
21 37 04.7	−19 27 58			205637	ε	Cap		39	112	248	115	245	120	240
21 37 45.0	−07 51 15			205767	ξ	Aqr			98	262	99	261	101	259
21 37 55.1	+62 04 55			206165	9	Cep		V337	cp	cp	cp	cp	cp	cp
21 40 05.4	−16 39 45			206088	γ	Cap		40	109	251	111	249	115	245
21 40 11.0	+43 16 26			206330	75	Cyg	15208		38	322	27	333	cp	cp
21 41 27.6	+10 49 53			214923	ζ	Peg	16182	42	78	282	77	283	74	286
21 41 28.6	−77 23 24			205478	ν	Oct			nv	nv	(cp)	(cp)	(cp)	(cp)
21 41 32.8	−14 02 51			206301	42	Cap			106	254	108	252	112	248
21 41 55.2	+71 18 42			206952	11	Cep			cp	cp	cp	cp	cp	cp
21 42 05.6	+51 11 23			206672	π¹	Cyg		78	26	334	cp	cp	cp	cp
21 42 39.4	−18 51 59			206453	κ	Cap		43	111	249	114	246	119	241
21 43 03.9	+72 19 13			207130	—	Cep			cp	cp	cp	cp	cp	cp
21 43 30.3	+58 46 48			206936	μ	Cep	15271	β690	12	348	cp	cp	cp	cp
21 44 08.2	+28 44 35			206827	μ²	Cyg		78	57	303	52	308	43	317
21 44 08.5	+28 44 34			206826	μ¹	Cyg	15270	78, Σ2822	57	303	52	308	43	317
21 44 11.0	+09 52 30			206778	ε	Peg	15268	8	80	280	78	282	76	284
21 44 30.6	+17 21 00			206859	9	Peg			70	290	68	292	63	297
21 44 38.5	+25 38 42			206901	κ	Peg	15281	10, Σ2824/β989	61	299	57	303	49	311
21 44 56.7	−33 01 33			206742	ι	PsA		9	129	231	135	225	148	212
21 45 00.2	−09 04 57			206834	46	Cap			100	260	102	258	104	256
21 45 26.8	+61 07 15			207260	ν	Cep		10	cp	cp	cp	cp	cp	cp
21 46 32.0	−11 21 58			207052	λ	Cap		48	103	257	104	256	107	253
21 46 47.5	+49 18 35			207330	π²	Cyg		81	29	331	10	350	cp	cp
21 47 02.3	−16 07 38			207098	δ	Cap		49	109	251	111	249	115	245
21 47 44.1	−30 53 54			207155	θ	PsA		10	125	235	131	229	141	219
21 49 50.6	+30 10 27			207650	14	Peg			55	305	49	311	39	321
21 50 54.2	−82 43 09			206240	λ	Oct		h5278	nv	nv	(cp)	(cp)	(cp)	(cp)
21 52 00.3	+55 47 32			208063	Σ2840B	(Cep)	15405		19	341	cp	cp	cp	cp
21 52 00.9	+55 47 49			208095	Σ2840A	(Cep)	15405		19	341	cp	cp	cp	cp
21 53 03.7	+25 55 31			208057	16	Peg			61	299	57	303	49	311
21 53 17.7	−13 33 07			207958	μ	Cap		51	105	255	107	253	110	250
21 53 55.6	−37 21 54			207971	γ	Gru			134	226	142	218	159	201
21 56 39.1	+63 37 33			208816	VV	Cep			cp	cp	cp	cp	cp	cp
21 57 55.0	−54 59 34			208450	δ	Ind			159	201	(cp)	(cp)	(cp)	(cp)
21 59 14.8	+73 10 48			209369	16	Cep			cp	cp	cp	cp	cp	cp
22 00 50.1	−28 27 13			209014	η	PsA	15536	12, β276	123	237	128	232	137	223
22 03 18.7	−02 09 19			209409	o	Aqr			92	268	93	267	93	267
22 03 21.3	−56 47 10			209100	ε	Ind			163	197	(cp)	(cp)	(cp)	(cp)

2000.0 R.A.	Declin.	HD	Star	Const.	ADS	Also Known As	R(30)	S(30)	R(40)	S(40)	R(50)	S(50)
22 03 47.3	+64 37 41	209790	ξ	Cep	15600	17, Σ2863	cp	cp	cp	cp	cp	cp
22 05 08.8	+62 16 48	209975	19	Cep	15624	β697	cp	cp	cp	cp	cp	cp
22 05 40.7	+05 03 31	209747	ν	Peg		22	84	276	83	277	82	278
22 05 46.9	−00 19 11	209750	α	Aqr		34	90	270	90	270	90	270
22 06 01.9	+45 00 52	209945	—	Lac			35	325	23	337	cp	cp
22 06 06.8	−39 32 36	209688	λ	Gru			137	223	145	215	168	192
22 06 26.1	−13 52 11	209819	ι	Aqr		33	105	255	107	253	110	250
22 07 00.6	+25 20 42	210027	ι	Peg		24	61	299	57	303	49	311
22 08 13.9	−46 57 40	209952	α	Gru			146	214	160	200	nv	nv
22 08 22.9	−32 59 19	210049	μ	PsA		14	128	232	134	226	146	214
22 08 25.9	−34 02 38	210066	υ	PsA			130	230	137	223	150	210
22 09 48.3	+72 20 29	210807	24	Cep			cp	cp	cp	cp	cp	cp
22 09 59.1	+33 10 42	210459	π²	Peg		29	51	309	45	315	32	328
22 10 08.7	−32 32 55	210302	τ	PsA		15	128	232	134	226	146	214
22 10 11.9	+06 11 52	210418	θ	Peg		26	83	277	82	278	81	279
22 10 38.8	+70 07 58	210884	Σ2883	(Cep)	15719		cp	cp	cp	cp	cp	cp
22 10 51.2	+58 12 05	210745	ζ	Cep		21	12	348	cp	cp	cp	cp
22 11 30.6	+59 24 53	210839	λ	Cep		22	8	352	cp	cp	cp	cp
22 11 48.5	+56 50 22	210855	—	Cep			17	343	cp	cp	cp	cp
22 13 52.6	+39 42 54	211073	—	Lac	15758	h1746	43	317	35	325	12	348
22 14 18.7	−27 46 01	210934	λ	PsA		16	122	238	126	234	135	225
22 15 01.9	+57 02 37	211336	ε	Cep		23	14	346	cp	cp	cp	cp
22 15 36.9	−41 20 48	211088	μ¹	Gru			139	221	149	211	nv	nv
22 15 58.1	+37 44 56	211388	1	Lac			46	314	38	322	21	339
22 16 26.5	−41 37 39	211202	μ²	Gru			139	221	149	211	nv	nv
22 16 49.9	−07 47 00	211391	θ	Aqr		43	98	262	99	261	101	259
22 18 30.1	−60 15 35	211416	α	Tuc			180	180	nv	nv	nv	nv
22 20 01.4	−80 26 23	210967	ε	Oct			nv	nv	(cp)	(cp)	(cp)	(cp)
22 20 11.8	−07 49 16	211838	ρ	Aqr		46	98	262	99	261	101	259
22 21 01.5	+46 32 12	212120	2	Lac	15862	h1755	34	326	20	340	cp	cp
22 21 19.2	+28 19 50	212097	32	Peg	15863	Ho 615	57	303	52	308	43	317
22 21 31.0	+12 12 19	212076	31	Peg		IN	76	284	74	286	71	289
22 21 39.3	−01 23 14	212061	γ	Aqr	15864	48, h3106	91	269	91	269	92	268
22 23 33.5	+52 13 45	212496	β	Lac			25	335	cp	cp	cp	cp
22 23 33.8	+45 21 00	212468	Σ2902	(Lac)	15900		35	325	23	337	cp	cp
22 24 30.9	+49 28 35	212593	4	Lac			29	331	10	350	cp	cp
22 24 36.7	−72 15 20	211998	ν	Ind			(cp)	(cp)	(cp)	(cp)	(cp)	(cp)
22 25 16.5	+01 22 39	212571	π	Aqr			89	271	89	271	88	272
22 27 20.0	−64 58 00	212581	δ	Tuc		h5334	nv	nv	(cp)	(cp)	(cp)	(cp)
22 27 51.5	+04 41 44	212943	35	Peg			85	275	85	275	84	276
22 28 04.0	+57 41 52	239960	Kr60A	(Cep)	15972		14	346	cp	cp	cp	cp
22 28 39.1	−39 07 55	212953	ν	Gru			137	223	145	215	168	192
22 28 49.6	−00 01 13	213051	ζ¹	Aqr	15971	55, Σ2909	90	270	90	270	90	270
22 28 50.0	−00 01 12	213052	ζ²	Aqr	15971		90	270	90	270	90	270
22 29 10.2	+58 24 55	213306	δ	Cep	15987	27, β702	12	348	cp	cp	cp	cp
22 29 16.1	−43 29 45	213009	δ¹	Gru			142	218	153	207	nv	nv
22 29 31.8	+47 42 25	213310	5	Lac			32	328	17	343	cp	cp
22 29 45.4	−43 44 58	213080	δ²	Gru		DUN 239	142	218	153	207	nv	nv
22 29 57.9	+04 25 54	213235	37	Peg	15988	Σ2912	85	275	85	275	84	276
22 30 29.1	+43 07 25	213420	6	Lac			38	322	27	333	cp	cp

2000.0 R.A.	Declin.	HD	Star	Const.	ADS	Also Known As	R(30)	S(30)	R(40)	S(40)	R(50)	S(50)
22 30 38.7	−10 40 41	213320	σ	Aqr			102	258	103	257	106	254
22 31 17.4	+50 16 57	213558	α	Lac	16021	7, β703	28	332	cp	cp	cp	cp
22 31 30.3	−32 20 46	213398	β	PsA		17, DUN 240	128	232	134	226	146	214
22 33 00.0	−61 58 57	213442	ν	Tuc			nv	nv	(cp)	(cp)	(cp)	(cp)
22 34 41.6	−20 42 30	213845	υ	Aqr			113	247	117	243	122	238
22 35 21.3	−00 07 03	213998	η	Aqr			90	270	90	270	90	270
22 35 46.0	+73 38 36	214470	31	Cep			cp	cp	cp	cp	cp	cp
22 35 51.9	+39 37 43	214167	8B	Lac			43	317	35	325	12	348
22 35 52.2	+39 38 04	214168	8A	Lac	16095	Σ2922	43	317	35	325	12	348
22 37 22.3	+51 32 43	214454	9	Lac			26	334	cp	cp	cp	cp
22 37 45.3	−04 13 41	214376	κ	Aqr			95	265	95	265	96	264
22 38 37.8	+56 47 45	214665	—	Lac	16140		17	343	cp	cp	cp	cp
22 38 38.9	+63 35 04	214734	30	Cep			cp	cp	cp	cp	cp	cp
22 39 15.6	+39 03 01	214680	10	Lac	16148	S 813	43	317	35	325	12	348
22 30 30.8	+44 16 35	214868	11	Lac			37	323	25	335	cp	cp
22 40 39.3	−27 02 37	214748	ε	PsA		18	122	238	126	234	135	225
22 41 28.5	+40 13 32	214993	12	Lac		DD	42	318	33	327	cp	cp
22 41 45.3	+29 18 27	214994	o	Peg		43	56	304	51	309	41	319
22 42 40.0	−46 53 05	214952	β	Gru			146	214	160	200	nv	nv
22 43 00.1	+30 13 17	215182	η	Peg	16211	44, β1144	55	305	49	311	39	321
22 43 30.0	−41 24 52	215104	ρ	Gru			139	221	149	211	nv	nv
22 43 35.2	−18 49 50	215167	66	Aqr			111	249	114	246	119	241
22 44 05.4	+41 49 09	215373	13	Lac	16227	OΣ479	41	319	31	329	cp	cp
22 45 37.8	−53 30 00	215369	η	Gru			157	203	nv	nv	nv	nv
22 46 03.3	−81 22 54	214846	β	Oct			nv	nv	(cp)	(cp)	(cp)	(cp)
22 46 31.8	+23 33 56	215665	λ	Peg		47	63	297	59	301	53	307
22 46 41.5	+12 10 22	215648	ξ	Peg	16261	46, h301	76	284	74	286	71	289
22 47 28.8	+83 09 14	216446	OΣ482	(Cep)	16294		cp	cp	cp	cp	cp	cp
22 48 33.2	−51 19 01	215789	ε	Gru			154	206	nv	nv	nv	nv
22 49 35.4	−13 35 33	216032	τ²	Aqr		71	105	255	107	253	110	250
22 49 40.7	+66 12 02	216228	ι	Cep		32	cp	cp	cp	cp	cp	cp
22 50 00.1	+24 36 06	216131	μ	Peg		48	62	298	58	302	51	309
22 50 22.9	−80 07 27	215573	ξ	Oct			nv	nv	(cp)	(cp)	(cp)	(cp)
22 51 49.3	+41 18 46	216369	h1823	(Lac)	16321		41	319	31	329	cp	cp
22 52 02.0	+43 18 45	216397	15	Lac	16325	β451	38	322	27	333	cp	cp
22 52 24.0	+09 50 09	216385	σ	Peg		49	80	280	78	282	76	284
22 52 31.5	−32 52 32	216336	γ	PsA		22, h5367	128	232	134	226	146	214
22 52 36.8	−07 34 47	216386	λ	Aqr		73	98	262	99	261	101	259
22 54 24.6	+84 20 47	217382	—	Cep			cp	cp	cp	cp	cp	cp
22 54 38.9	−15 49 15	216627	δ	Aqr		76	107	253	110	250	114	246
22 55 13.6	+08 48 58	216735	ρ	Peg		50	81	279	80	280	77	283
22 55 56.8	−32 32 23	216763	δ	PsA		23	128	232	134	226	146	214
22 56 25.9	+49 44 01	216946	—	Lac			29	331	10	350	cp	cp
22 57 39.0	−29 37 20	216956	α	PsA		24	124	236	129	231	139	221
23 00 05.0	+56 56 44	217476	V509	Cas			17	343	cp	cp	cp	cp
23 00 52.8	−52 45 15	217364	ζ	Gru			155	205	nv	nv	nv	nv
23 01 55.2	+42 19 34	217675	o	And		1	39	321	29	331	cp	cp
23 02 36.2	+42 45 28	217782	2	And	16467	β1147	39	321	29	331	cp	cp
23 03 29.7	−34 44 58	217792	π	PsA			130	230	137	223	150	210
23 03 32.8	+67 12 34	218029	—	Cep			cp	cp	cp	cp	cp	cp

2000.0 R.A.			2000.0 Declin.			HD	Star	Const.	ADS	Also Known As	Rising and Setting Azimuths R(30)	S(30)	R(40)	S(40)	R(50)	S(50)
23	03	46.4	+28	04	58	217906	β	Peg	16483	53, h1842	57	303	52	308	43	317
23	03	52.5	+03	49	12	217891	β	Psc		4	87	273	86	274	85	275
23	04	10.9	+50	03	08	218031	3	And			28	332	cp	cp	cp	cp
23	04	39.5	−53	57	55	217902	κ	Gru			157	203	nv	nv	nv	nv
23	04	45.6	+15	12	19	218045	α	Peg		54	73	287	70	290	66	294
23	05	32.2	−35	51	52	217987	Lacaille 9352	(PsA)			131	229	138	222	153	207
23	06	36.8	+59	25	12	218376	1	Cas			8	352	cp	cp	cp	cp
23	06	40.8	−23	44	35	218240	86	Aqr	16511		117	243	121	239	127	233
23	06	52.7	−43	31	14	218227	θ	Gru			142	218	153	207	nv	nv
23	07	00.2	+09	24	34	218329	55	Peg			80	280	78	282	76	284
23	07	06.6	+25	28	06	218356	56	Peg			61	299	57	303	49	311
23	07	53.8	+75	23	16	218658	π	Cep	16538	33, OΣ489	cp	cp	cp	cp	cp	cp
23	09	26.7	−21	10	21	218594	88	Aqr			114	246	118	242	124	236
23	09	31.4	+08	40	38	218634	57	Peg	16550	Σ2982, GZ	81	279	80	280	77	283
23	09	54.7	−22	27	27	218640	89	Aqr			116	244	119	241	126	234
23	10	21.5	−45	14	48	218670	ι	Gru			145	215	157	203	nv	nv
23	11	44.1	+08	43	12	218918	59	Peg			81	279	80	280	77	283
23	12	32.9	+49	24	23	219080	7	And			29	331	10	350	cp	cp
23	14	19.3	−06	02	56	219215	φ	Aqr		90	97	263	98	262	99	261
23	15	53.4	−09	05	16	219449	ψ¹	Aqr	16633	91, β1220	100	260	102	258	104	256
23	16	50.8	−07	43	36	219576	χ	Aqr		92	98	262	99	261	101	259
23	17	09.9	+03	16	56	219615	γ	Psc		6	87	273	86	274	85	275
23	17	25.7	−58	14	08	219571	γ	Tuc			168	192	nv	nv	nv	nv
23	17	44.6	+49	00	55	219734	8	And	16656	β717	29	331	10	350	cp	cp
23	17	54.1	−09	10	57	219688	ψ²	Aqr		93	100	260	102	258	104	256
23	18	37.4	+68	06	42	219916	o	Cep	16666	34, Σ3001	cp	cp	cp	cp	cp	cp
23	18	49.4	−32	31	55	219784	γ	Scl			128	232	134	226	146	214
23	18	57.6	−09	36	38	219832	ψ³	Aqr	16671	95	100	260	102	258	104	256
23	19	06.6	−13	27	32	219834	94	Aqr	16672		105	255	107	253	110	250
23	20	20.5	+05	22	53	220009	7	Psc			84	276	83	277	82	278
23	20	38.2	+23	44	25	220061	τ	Peg		62	63	297	59	301	53	307
23	22	39.1	−15	02	21	220278	97	Aqr	16708	Hu295	107	253	110	250	114	246
23	22	58.1	−20	06	02	220321	98	Aqr			113	247	117	243	122	238
23	23	04.5	+12	18	50	220363	66	Peg	16715	Ho 300	76	284	74	286	71	289
23	24	50.2	+62	16	59	220652	4	Cas			cp	cp	cp	cp	cp	cp
23	25	22.7	+23	24	15	220657	υ	Peg		68	63	297	59	301	53	307
23	26	02.7	−20	38	31	220704	99	Aqr			113	247	117	243	122	238
23	26	55.9	+01	15	20	220825	κ	Psc		8	89	271	89	271	88	272
23	27	58.0	+06	22	44	220954	θ	Psc		10	83	277	82	278	81	279
23	28	03.9	−87	28	57	219765	τ	Oct			nv	nv	(cp)	(cp)	(cp)	(cp)
23	29	09.2	+12	45	38	221115	70	Peg			76	284	74	286	71	289
23	30	01.9	+58	32	57	221253	AR	Cas	16795	OΣ496	12	348	cp	cp	cp	cp
23	31	17.3	+39	14	11	221345	14	And			43	317	35	325	12	348
23	32	58.2	−37	49	07	221507	β	Scl			134	226	142	218	159	201
23	33	16.5	−20	54	52	221565	101	Aqr			113	247	117	243	122	238
23	33	57.1	+31	19	32	221673	72	Peg	16836	β720	54	306	48	312	37	323
23	35	04.5	−42	36	55	221760	ι	Phe			141	219	151	209	nv	nv
23	37	33.8	+46	27	30	222107	λ	And		16	34	326	20	340	cp	cp
23	37	50.9	−45	29	33	222095	—	Phe			145	215	157	203	nv	nv
23	38	08.1	+43	16	05	222173	ι	And		17	38	322	27	333	cp	cp

	2000.0							Also	Rising and Setting Azimuths					
R.A.			Declin.		HD	Star	Const.	ADS	Known As	R(30)	S(30)	R(40)	S(40)	R(50)	S(50)
23 39 20.8	+77 37 57				222404	γ	Cep		35	cp	cp	cp	cp	cp	cp
23 39 47.0	−14 13 18				222345	ω¹	Aqr		102	106	254	108	252	112	248
23 39 57.0	+05 37 35				222368	ι	Psc		17	84	276	83	277	82	278
23 40 24.4	+44 20 02				224439	κ	And	16916	19, h1898	37	323	25	335	cp	cp
23 40 38.1	−32 04 24				222433	μ	Scl			128	232	134	226	146	214
23 41 45.7	−17 48 59				222574	104	Aqr			110	250	112	248	117	243
23 42 02.7	+01 46 48				222603	λ	Psc		18	89	271	89	271	88	272
23 42 43.2	−14 32 42				222661	ω²	Aqr	16944	105, β279	106	254	108	252	112	248
23 43 22.3	+10 19 54				222764	77	Peg			78	282	77	283	74	286
23 43 49.4	−15 17 04				222800	R	Aqr			107	253	110	250	114	246
23 43 59.4	+29 21 42				222842	78	Peg	16957	AGC 14	56	304	51	309	41	319
23 46 02.0	+46 25 13				223047	ψ	And		20	34	326	20	340	cp	cp
23 46 23.4	+03 29 13				223075	19	Psc		TX	87	273	86	274	85	275
23 46 32.9	−41 33 29				223065	SX	Phe			139	221	149	211	nv	nv
23 47 03.4	+58 39 07				223165	τ	Cas		5	12	348	cp	cp	cp	cp
23 47 15.9	−50 13 35				223145	σ	Phe			152	208	180	180	nv	nv
23 47 54.7	+67 48 25				223274	—	Cep			cp	cp	cp	cp	cp	cp
23 48 50.1	+62 12 53				223385	6	Cas	17022	OΣ508, V566	cp	cp	cp	cp	cp	cp
23 48 55.5	−28 07 49				223352	δ	Scl	17021	β1013/h3216	123	237	128	232	137	223
23 51 21.2	−18 54 33				223640	108	Aqr		ET	111	249	114	246	119	241
23 52 06.8	−82 01 08				223647	γ¹	Oct			nv	nv	(cp)	(cp)	(cp)	(cp)
23 52 29.2	+19 07 13				223768	φ	Peg		81	68	292	65	295	60	300
23 54 23.0	+57 29 58				224014	ρ	Cas		7	14	346	cp	cp	cp	cp
23 57 35.2	−64 17 55				224392	η	Tuc			nv	nv	(cp)	(cp)	(cp)	(cp)
23 57 45.5	+25 08 29				224427	ψ	Peg		84	61	299	57	303	49	311
23 58 24.7	+51 23 19				224490	R	Cas			26	334	cp	cp	cp	cp
23 58 40.3	−03 33 22				224533	27	Psc	17137	β730	93	267	94	266	95	265
23 58 55.7	−52 44 45				224554	π	Phe			155	205	nv	nv	nv	nv
23 59 00.4	+55 45 18				224572	σ	Cas	17140	8, Σ3049	19	341	cp	cp	cp	cp
23 59 18.6	+06 51 48				224617	ω	Psc		28	83	277	82	278	81	279
23 59 55.0	−65 34 38				224686	ε	Tuc			nv	nv	(cp)	(cp)	(cp)	(cp)

Star Names

Name	Desig.	Name	Desig.	Name	Desig.	Name	Desig.
Acamar	ϑ Eri	Alula Borealis	ν UMa	Denebola	β Leo	Markab	α Peg, κ Vel
Achernar	α Eri	Alya	ϑ Ser	Diadem	α Com	Matar	η Peg
Acrux	α Cru	Alzirr	ξ Gem	Diphda	β Cet	Mebsuta	ε Gem
Acubens	α Cnc	Ancha	ϑ Aqr	Dnoce	ι UMa	Megrez	δ UMa
Adhara	ε CMa	Antares	α Sco	Dschubba	δ Sco	Meissa	λ Ori
Al Anz	ε Aur	Arcturus	α Boo	Dubhe	α UMa	Mekbuda	ζ Gem
Albaldah	π Sgr	Arietis	α Ari	Ed Asich	ι Dra	Menkalinan	β Aur
Al Bali	ε Aqr	Arkab	η Sgr	Elacrab	β Sco	Menkar	α Cet
Albireo	β Cyg	Arkab Posterior	β² Sgr	Electra	17 Tau	Menkent	ϑ Cen
Al Chiba	α Crv	Arkab Prior	β¹ Sgr	El Nath	β Tau, α Ari	Menkib	ξ Per
Alcor	80 UMa	Arneb	α Lep	Eltanin	γ Dra	Merak	β UMa
Alcyone	η Tau	Ascella	ζ Sgr	Enif	ε Peg	Merope	23 Tau
Aldebaran	α Tau	Asellus Aust.	δ Cnc	Erakis	μ Cep	Mesarthim	γ Ari
Alderamin	α Cep	Asellus Bor.	γ Cnc	Er Rai	γ Cep	Metallah	α Tri
Aldhafera	ζ Leo	Asellus Primus	ϑ Boo	Fomalhaut	α PsA	Miaplacidus	β Car
Aldhibah	ζ Dra	Asellus Sec.	ι Boo	Gacrux	γ Cru	Mimosa	β Cru
Alfirk	β Cep	Asellus Tert.	κ Boo	Gemma	α CrB	Minkar	ε Crv
Algeiba, Algieba	γ Leo	Asmidiske	ξ Pup	Gienah	γ Crv, ε Cyg	Mintaka	δ Ori
Algenib	γ Peg, α Per	Asterope	21 Tau	Girtab	κ Sco	Mira	o Cet
Al Giedi	α¹ Cap	Atlas	27 Tau	Gomeisa	β CMi	Mirach	β And
Algol	β Per	Atria	α TrA	Graffias	β Sco	Mirfak	α Per
Algorab	δ Crv	Auva	δ Vir	Hadar	β Cen	Mizar	ζ UMa
Alhena	γ Gem	Avior	ε Car	Hoedus I	ζ Aur	Muliphein	γ CMa
Alioth	ε UMa	Baham	ϑ Peg	Hoedus II	η Aur	Muphrid	η Boo
Alkaid	η UMa	Becrux	β Cru	Hamal	α Ari	Murzim	β CMa
Alkalurops	μ Boo	Bellatrix	γ Ori	Han	ζ Oph	Muscida	o UMa
Al Kaprah	κ UMa	Benetnasch	η UMa	Haris	γ Boo	Nair al Saif	ι Ori
Alkes	α Crt	Betelgeuse	α Ori	Hassaleh	ι Aur	Naos	ζ Pup
Almach	γ And	Botein	δ Ari	Heze	ζ Vir	Nash	γ Sgr
Almaaz	ε Aur	Brachium	σ Lib	Homam	ζ Peg	Nekkar	β Boo
Al Nair	α Gru	Canopus	α Car	Izar	ε Boo	Nihal	β Lep
Al Nasl	γ Sgr	Capella	α Aur	Jabbah	ν Sco	Nodus I	ζ Dra
Alnilam	ε Ori	Caph	β Cas	Kaffeljidhmah	γ Cet	North Star	α UMi
Alnitak	ζ Ori	Caput Trianguli	α Tri	Kapteyn's Star	— Pic	Nunki	σ Sgr
Al Niyat	σ Sco	Castor	α Gem	Kaus Australis	ε Sgr	Nusakan	β CrB
Alphard	α Hya	Cebalrai	β Oph	Kaus Borealis	λ Sgr	Peacock	α Pav
Alphecca	α CrB	Celaeno	16 Tau	Kaus Meridion.	δ Sgr	Phad	γ UMa
Alpheratz	α And	Cheleb	β Oph	Keid	o² Eri	Phaet	α Col
Al Rami	α Sgr	Chort	ε Leo	Kochab	β UMi	Phecda	γ UMa
Al Rischa	α Psc	Cor Caroli	α² CVn	Kornephoros	β Her	Pherkad	γ UMi
Alshain	β Aql	Cursa	β Eri	Kraz	β Crv	Phurud	ζ CMa
Altair	α Aql	Dabih	β Cap	Kursa	β Eri	Plaskett's Star	— Mon
Altarf	β Cnc	Deneb	α Cyg	La Superba	Y CVn	Pleione	28 Tau
Althalimain	λ Aql	Deneb Algiedi	δ Cap	Lesath	υ Sco	Polaris	α UMi
Aludra	η CMa	Deneb el Okab	ε, ζ Aql	Lesuth	υ Sco	Pollux	β Gem
Alula Australis	ξ UMa	Deneb Kaitos	β Cet	Maia	20 Tau	Porrima	γ Vir

(Continued)

Procyon	α CMi	Sadachbia	γ Aqr	Sheliak	β Lyr	Tejat Prior	η Gem
Propus	η Gem	Sadal		Sheratan	β Ari	Thuban	α Dra
Proxima Cent.	α^c Cen	Melik	α Aqr	Sirius	α CMa	Unukalhai	α Ser
Ras Algethi	α Her	Sadal		Sirrah	α And	Vega	α Lyr
Ras Alhague	α Oph	Suud	β Aqr	Skat	δ Aqr	Vindemiatrix	ε Vir
Rasalmothallath	α Tri	Sadatoni	ζ Aur	Spica	α Vir	Wasat	δ Gem
Ras Elased Aust.	ε Leo	Sadr	γ Cyg	Sualocin	α Del	Wei	ε Sco
Rastaban	β Dra	Saiph	κ Ori	Suhail al		Wesen	δ CMa
Regulus	α Leo	Sargas	ϑ Sco	Muhlif	γ^2 Vel	Wezn	β Col
Rigel	β Ori	Sarin	δ Her	Sulafat	γ Lyr	Yed Posterior	ε Oph
Rigel Kentaurus	α Cen	Sartan	α Cnc	Talitha	ι UMa	Yed Prior	δ Oph
Rotanev	β Del	Scheat	β Peg	Tania Australis	μ UMa	Zaurak	γ Eri
Ruchbah	δ Cas	Schedar	α Cas	Tania Borealis	λ UMa	Zosma	δ Leo
Rukbat	α Sgr	Segin	ε Cas	Tarazed	γ Aql	Zubenalgubi	σ Lib
Rutilicus	β Her	Seginus	γ Boo	Taygeta	19 Tau	Zubenelakrab	γ Lib
Saak	η Boo	Shaula	λ Sco	Tegmine	ζ Cnc	Zubenelgenubi	α Lib
Sabik	η Oph	Shedir	α Cas	Tejat Posterior	μ Gem	Zubeneschamali	β Lib

NGC Objects Found in *StarList 2000*

Type: OC = open cluster   EN = emission nebula   SN = supernova
       GC = globular cluster   PN = planetary nebula   DN = dark nebula
        I = irregular   E/RN = comb. emission and reflection nebula

       G = galaxy (followed by description:)
       S = spiral (a = tight; b = medium; c = loose; SB = with bar)
       E = elliptical (0: round; 7: very elongated)
       S0 = lenticular (spiral, but with older stars, as in an elliptical galaxy)

Object	Const.	Note	Messier	R. A. (2000)	Decl.	Type	Mag.
I.2602	Car	e		10^h 43.2	−64° 24′	OC	1.9
I.2944	Cen	I		11 36.6	−63 02	DN	—
I.2948	Cen	I		11 38.8	−63 32	Nb	—
I.434	Ori	f		05 41.0	−02 24	Nb	—
I.4665	Oph	b		17 46.3	+05 43	OC	4.2
I.4725	Sgr	s	M25	18 31.6	−19 15	OC	4.6
I.4756	Ser	g		18 39.0	+05 27	OC	~5
I.5217	Lac	a		22 23.9	+50 58	PN	~13
55	Scl	c		00 14.9	−39 11	G-SB	8.0
104	Tuc	b		00 24.1	−72 05	GC	4.0
224	And	h	M31	00 42.7	+41 16	G-Sb	3.4
362	Tuc	b		01 03.2	−70 51	GC	6.6
404	And	b		01 09.4	+35 43	G-Sa	10.1
457	Cas	c		01 19.1	+58 20	OC	6.4
584	Cet	g		01 31.3	−06 52	G-E	10.4
598	Tri	a	M33	01 33.9	+30 39	G-Sc	5.7
615	Cet	g		01 35.1	−07 20	G-Sb	11.5
650	Per	m	M76	01 42.4	+51 34	PN	11.5
681	Cet	e		01 49.2	−10 26	G-Sab	11.8
701	Cet	e		01 51.1	−09 42	G-Sc	12.2
752	And	c		01 57.8	+37 41	OC	5.7
869	Per	g		02 19.0	+57 09	OC	~4
884	Per	g		02 22.4	+57 07	OC	~4
891	And	c		02 22.6	+42 21	G-Sb	10.0
1039	Per	h	M34	02 42.0	+42 47	OC	5.2
1055	Cet	d		02 41.8	+00 26	G-Sb	10.6
1068	Cet	d	M77	02 42.7	−00 01	G-Sb	8.8
1316	For	a		03 22.7	−37 12	G-S0	8.9
1513	Per	i		04 10.0	+49 31	OC	8.4

(Continued)

Object	Const.	Note	Messier	R. A.		Decl.		Type	Mag.
				(2000)					
1528	Per	i		04^h 15.4		+51° 14′		OC	6.4
1555	Tau	d		04 22.9		+19 32		N	—
1559	Ret	a		04 17.6		−62 47		G-SBc	10.5
1904	Lep	b, i	M79	05 24.5		−24 33		GC	8.0
1952	Tau	f	M1	05 34.5		+22 01		SNR	8.4
1976	Ori	h	M42	05 35.4		−05 27		EN	~4.0
1982	Ori	h	M43	05 35.6		−05 16		EN	~9.0
2017	Lep	a, j		05 39.4		−17 51		—	—
2068	Ori	f	M78	05 46.7		+00 03		RN	~8.0
2090	Col	a		05 47.0		−34 14		G-Sc	~12
2099	Aur	i	M37	05 52.4		+32 33		OC	5.6
2168	Gem	g	M35	06 08.9		+24 20		OC	5.1
2244	Mon	c, e		06 32.4		+04 52		OC	4.8
2261	Mon	d		06 39.2		+08 44		E/RN	var
2264	Mon	d		06 41.1		+09 53		C+N	3.9
2287	CMa	a	M41	06 47.0		−20 44		OC	4.5
2323	Mon	a	M50	07 03.2		−08 20		OC	5.9
2354	CMa	d		07 14.3		−25 44		OC	6.5
2362	CMa	l		07 18.8		−24 57		C+N	4.1
2392	Gem	d		07 29.2		+20 55		PN	8.3
2422	Pup	c	M47	07 36.6		−14 30		OC	4.4
2437	Pup	c	M46	07 41.8		−14 49		OC	6.1
2447	Pup	c	M93	07 44.6		−23 52		OC	6.2
2477	Pup	a		07 52.3		−38 33		OC	5.8
2516	Car	c		08 00.5		−60 52		OC	—
2547	Vel	a		08 10.9		−49 16		OC	5.5
2548	Hya	p	M48	08 13.8		−05 48		OC	5.8
2632	Cnc	c	M44	08 40.1		+19 59		OC	3.1
2660	Vel	g		08 42.2		−47 09		OC	8.8
2841	UMa	h		09 22.0		+50 58		G-Sb	9.3
2903	Leo	i		09 32.2		+21 30		G-Sb	8.9
3031	UMa	p	M81	09 55.6		+69 04		G-Sb	6.8
3034	UMa	p	M82	09 55.8		+69 41		G-I	8.4
3115	Sex	a		10 05.2		−07 43		G-E	9.2
3185	Leo	f		10 17.6		+21 41		G-SBa	12.2
3187	Leo	f		10 17.8		+21 52		G-S	13.1
3190	Leo	f		10 18.1		+21 50		G-Sa	11.0
3193	Leo	f		10 18.4		+21 54		G-E	10.9
3324	Car	d		10 37.3		−58 38		C+N	6.7
3351	Leo	a	M95	10 44.0		+11 42		G-SBb	9.7
3356	Uma	b		10 44.2		+06 45		G-Sb	~13
3368	Leo	a	M96	10 46.8		+11 49		G-Sbp	9.2
3372	Car	d		10 43.8		−59 52		Nb	—
3379	Leo	a	M105	10 47.8		+12 35		G-E1	9.3
3521	Leo	j		11 05.8		−00 02		G-Sb	8.7
3532	Car	d		11 06.4		−58 40		OC	3.0
3587	UMa	b	M97	11 14.8		+55 01		PN	11.2
3623	Leo	h	M65	11 18.9		+13 05		G-Sb	9.3

(Continued)

Object	Const.	Note	Messier	R. A. (2000)		Decl.		Type	Mag.
3627	Leo	h	M66	11^h	20.2	+12°	59'	G-Sb	9.0
3992	UMa	c	M109	11	57.6	+53	23	G-Sb	9.8
4038	Crv	c		12	01.9	−18	52	G-Sc	10.7
4064	Com	h		12	04.2	+18	27	G-SBb	11.5
4147	Com	h		12	10.1	+18	33	GC	10.3
4244	CVn	d		12	17.5	+37	49	G-S	10.2
4349	Cru	j		12	24.5	−61	54	OC	7.4
4361	Crv	h		12	24.5	−18	48	PN	10.3
4372	Mus	c		12	25.8	−72	40	GC	7.8
4565	Com	c		12	36.3	+25	59	G-Sb	9.6
4594	Vir	g	M104	12	40.0	−11	37	G-Sb	8.3
4755	Cru	c		12	53.6	−60	20	OC	4.2
4826	Com	e	M64	12	56.7	+21	41	G-Sb	8.5
4833	Mus	d		12	59.6	−70	53	GC	7.4
5024	Com	a	M53	13	12.9	+18	10	GC	7.7
5053	Com	a		13	16.4	+17	42	GC	9.8
5055	CVn	f	M63	13	15.8	+42	02	G-Sb	8.6
5102	Cen	k		13	22.0	−36	38	G-S0	9.7
5139	Cen	h		13	26.8	−47	29	GC	3.7
5194/5	CVn	g	M51	13	29.9	+47	12	G-Sc	8.1
5272	Com (CVn)	b	M3	13	42.2	+28	23	GC	6.4
5694	Hya	m		14	39.6	−26	32	GC	10.2
5904	Ser	e	M5	15	18.6	+02	05	GC	5.8
6025	TrA	b		16	03.7	−60	30	OC	5.1
6067	Nor	a		16	13.2	−54	13	OC	5.6
6087	Nor	c		16	18.9	−57	54	OC	5.4
6093	Sco	a	M80	16	17.0	−22	59	GC	7.2
6121	Sco	a	M4	16	23.6	−26	32	GC	5.9
6152	Nor	a		16	32.7	−52	37	OC	~8
6171	Oph	e	M107	16	32.5	−13	03	GC	8.1
6205	Her	f	M13	16	41.7	+36	28	GC	5.9
6218	Oph	i	M12	16	47.2	−01	57	GC	6.6
6231	Sco	t		16	54.0	−41	48	C+N	2.6
6254	Oph	i	M10	16	57.1	−04	06	GC	6.6
6266	Sco	a	M62	17	01.2	−30	07	GC	6.6
6273	Oph	k	M19	17	02.6	−26	16	GC	7.2
6333	Oph	j	M9	17	19.2	−18	31	GC	7.9
6334	Sco	k		17	20.5	−35	43	Nb	—
6341	Her	h	M92	17	17.1	+43	08	GC	6.5
6402	Oph	l	M14	17	37.6	−03	15	GC	7.6
6405	Sco	k	M6	17	40.1	−32	13	OC	4.2
6475	Sco	a, k	M7	17	53.9	−34	49	OC	3.3
6514	Sgr	i	M20	18	02.6	−23	02	E/RN	~8.5
6522	Sgr	d		18	03.6	−30	02	GC	8.6
6523	Sgr	i	M8	18	03.8	−24	23	EN	5.8
6584	Tel	a		18	18.6	−52	13	GC	9.2
6611	Ser	c	M16	18	18.8	−13	47	EN+OC	6.0

(Continued)

				(2000)			
Object	Const.	Note	Messier	R. A.	Decl.	Type	Mag.
6637	Sgr	f	M69	18^h 31.4	−32° 21′	GC	7.7
6656	Sgr	i	M22	18 36.4	−23 54	GC	5.1
6664	Sct	a		18 36.7	−08 13	OC	9.0
6681	Sgr	f	M70	18 43.2	−32 18	GC	8.1
6694	Sct	b	M26	18 45.2	−09 24	OC	8.0
6705	Sct	c	M11	18 51.1	−06 16	OC	5.8
6715	Sgr	g	M54	18 55.1	−30 29	GC	7.7
6720	Lyr	b	M57	18 53.6	+33 02	PN	9.0
6723	CrA (Sgr)	b		18 59.6	−36 38	GC	7.3
6726	CrA	a		19 01.7	−36 53	Nb	—
6727	CrA	a		19 01.8	−36 54	Nb	—
6729	CrA	a		19 01.9	−36 57	Nb	—
6752	Pav	a		19 10.9	−59 59	GC	5.4
6809	Sgr	g	M55	19 40.0	−30 58	GC	7.0
6818	Sgr	q		19 44.0	−14 09	PN	9.9
6822	Sgr	q		19 44.9	−14 48	G-I	~9
6826	Cyg	h		19 44.8	+50 31	PN	9.8
6838	Sge	a	M71	19 53.8	+18 47	GC	8.3
6853	Vul	b	M27	19 59.6	+22 42	PN	8.1
6992	Cyg	f, p		20 56.4	+31 43	Nb	—
6995	Cyg	f, p		20 57.1	+31 13	Nn	—
7000	Cyg	a		20 58.8	+44 20	EN	—
7009	Aqr	j		21 04.2	−11 22	PN	8.3
7078	Peg	d	M15	21 30.0	+12 10	GC	6.4
7089	Aqr	b	M2	21 33.5	−00 49	GC	6.5
7092	Cyg	k	M39	21 32.2	+48 26	OC	4.6
7099	Cap	e	M30	21 40.4	−23 11	GC	7.5
7209	Lac	c		22 05.2	+46 30	OC	6.7
7243	Lac	a		22 15.3	+49 53	OC	6.4
7293	Aqr	k		22 29.6	−20 48	PN	6.5
7331	Peg	f		22 37.1	+34 25	G-Sb	9.5
7479	Peg	a		23 04.9	+12 19	G-Sb	11.0
7662	And	g		23 25.9	+42 33	PN	9.2
7789	Cas	j		23 57.0	+56 44	OC	6.7

Additional Messier objects, not listed in *StarList 2000*

6618	Sgr		M17	18 20.8	−16 11	EN	~7.0
6613	Sgr		M18	18 19.9	−17 08	OC	6.9
6531	Sgr		M21	18 04.6	−22 30	OC	5.9
6494	Sgr		M23	17 56.8	−19 01	OC	5.5
—	Sgr		M24	18 16.9	−18 29	—	4.5
6626	Sgr		M28	18 24.5	−24 52	GC	6.9
6913	Cyg		M29	20 23.9	+38 32	OC	6.6
221	And		M32	00 42.7	+40 52	G-E2	8.2
1960	Aur		M36	05 36.1	+34 08	OC	6.0
1912	Aur		M38	05 28.7	+35 50	OC	6.4

(Continued)

Object	Const.	Note	Messier	R. A. (2000)	Decl.	Type	Mag.
—	UMa		M40	12^h 22.4	+58° 05′	—	8.0
—	Tau		M45	03 47.0	+24 07	OC	1.2
4472	Vir		M49	12 29.8	+08 00	G-E4	8.4
7654	Cas		M52	23 24.2	+61 35	OC	6.9
6779	Lyr		M56	19 16.6	+30 11	GC	8.2
4579	Vir		M58	12 37.7	+11 49	G-SB	9.8
4621	Vir		M59	12 42.0	+11 39	G-E3	9.8
4649	Vir		M60	12 43.7	+11 33	G-E1	8.8
4303	Vir		M61	12 21.9	+04 28	G-Sc	9.7
2682	Cnc		M67	08 50.4	+11 49	OC	6.9
4590	Hya		M68	12 39.5	−26 45	GC	8.2
6981	Aqr		M72	20 53.5	−12 32	GC	9.4
6994	Aqr		M73	20 58.9	−12 38	OC	—
628	Psc		M74	01 36.7	+15 47	G-Sc	9.2
6864	Sgr		M75	20 06.1	−21 55	GC	8.6
5236	Hya		M83	13 37.0	−29 52	G-Sc	10.1
4374	Vir		M84	12 25.1	+12 53	G-E1	9.3
4382	Com		M85	12 25.4	+18 11	G-Ep	9.3
4406	Vir		M86	12 26.2	+12 57	G-E3	9.2
4486	Vir		M87	12 30.8	+12 24	G-E1	8.6
4501	Com		M88	12 32.0	+14 25	G-Sb	9.5
4552	Vir		M89	12 35.7	+12 33	G-E0	9.8
4569	Vir		M90	12 36.8	+13 10	G-Sb	9.5
4548	Com		M91	12 35.4	+14 30	G-SBb	10.2
4736	CVn		M94	12 50.9	+41 07	G-Sbp	8.1
4192	Com		M98	12 13.8	+14 54	G-Sb	10.1
4254	Com		M99	12 18.8	+14 25	G-Sc	9.8
4321	Com		M100	12 22.9	+15 49	G-Sc	9.4
5457	UMa		M101	14 03.2	+54 21	G-Sc	7.7
5866	Dra		M102	15 06.5	+55 46	G-E6p	10.0
581	Cas		M103	01 33.2	+60 42	OC	7.4
4258	CVn		M106	12 19.0	+47 18	G-Sbp	8.3
3556	UMa		M108	11 11.5	+55 40	G-Sc	10.0
205	And		M110	00 40.4	+41 41	G-E6	8.0

Index of Stars by Constellation

(Continued)

For $\alpha\beta\gamma^1\gamma^2\delta\eta^2\eta^3\kappa\lambda^2\mu\nu\pi\varphi\omega$

Gem $\alpha\beta\gamma\delta\epsilon\zeta\eta\theta\iota\kappa\lambda\mu\nu\xi$**o**$\pi\rho\sigma\tau\upsilon\varphi\chi\omega$, 1, 26, 30, 38, 51, 56, 57, 63, 64, 65, 74, 81; R (unnamed: 2)

Gru $\alpha\beta\gamma\delta^1\delta^2\epsilon\zeta\eta\theta\iota\kappa\lambda\mu^1\mu^2\nu\xi\rho$

Her $\alpha^1\alpha^2\beta\gamma\delta\epsilon\zeta\eta\theta\iota\kappa^A\kappa^B\lambda\mu\nu\xi$**o**$\pi\rho^A\rho^B\sigma\tau\upsilon\varphi\chi\omega$, 5, 29, 30, 42, 43, 51, 52, 60, 68, 69, 70, 72, 87, 90, 93, 95^A, 95^B, 98, 99, 100^A, 100^B, 102, 104, 106, 107, 109, 110, 111, 113, Hu 1176, Σ2319; S, V656 (unnamed: 3)

Hor $\alpha\beta\delta\zeta\eta\iota\lambda\mu\nu$; R

Hya $\alpha\beta\gamma\delta\epsilon\zeta\eta\theta\iota\kappa\lambda\mu\nu\xi$**o**$\pi\rho\sigma\tau^1\tau^2\upsilon^1\upsilon^2\varphi^3\chi^1\chi^2\psi\omega$, 6, 9, 12, 23, 26, 27, 44, 47, 50, 51, 52, 54, 56, 58, β411, Σ1474, C, F, G, I, b^3; R, T, U, II (unnamed: 8)

Hyi $\alpha\beta\gamma\delta\epsilon\zeta\eta^1\eta^2\kappa\lambda\mu\nu\pi^1\pi^2$

Ind $\alpha\beta\delta\epsilon\zeta\eta\theta\iota\mu\nu$

Lac $\alpha\beta$, 1, 2, 4, 5, 6, 8^A, 8^B, 9, 10, 11, 12, 13, 15, Σ2902, h1823 (unnamed: 4)

Leo $\alpha\beta\gamma^1\gamma^2\delta\epsilon\zeta\eta\theta\iota\kappa\lambda\mu\nu\xi$**o**$\pi\rho\sigma\tau\varphi\chi\psi\omega$, 6, 10, 31, 40, 48, 54^A, 54^B, 58, 59, 60, 61, 72, 75, 87, 91, 93; R

LMi β, 8, 10, 19, 21, 30, 37, 41, 42, 46; R

Lep $\alpha\beta\gamma^A\gamma^B\delta\epsilon\zeta\eta\theta\iota\kappa\lambda\mu\nu$, 17, h3750, h3752, h3780; R (unnamed: 4)

Lib $\alpha^1\alpha^2\beta\gamma\delta\epsilon\zeta^4\eta\theta\iota^1\kappa\lambda\mu\nu\xi^2\rho\sigma\upsilon$, 11, 12, 16, 18, 36, 37, 42, 48, Σ1962^A, Σ1962^B; S (unnamed: 1)

Lup $\alpha\beta\gamma\delta\epsilon\zeta\eta\theta\iota\kappa^1\kappa^2\lambda\mu\nu^1\xi^1\xi^2$**o**$\pi^1\pi^2\rho\sigma\tau^1\tau^2\upsilon\varphi^1\varphi^2\chi\psi^1\psi^2\omega$, 1, 2, h (unnamed: 11)

Lyn α, 1, 2, 5, 12, 15, 16, 18, 19^A, 19^B, 21, 24, 27, 31, 35, 38; Kui 37, Σ1338; R, RR (unnamed: 5)

Lyr $\alpha\beta\gamma\delta^1\delta^2\epsilon^{1A}\epsilon^{1B}\epsilon^{2C}\epsilon^{2D}\zeta^1\zeta^2\eta\theta\iota\kappa\lambda\mu\nu^2$, 16, 17, β648, Σ2333, Σ2470, Σ2474; R, W, RR (unnamed: 1)

Men $\alpha\beta\gamma\delta\eta\theta\kappa$

Mic $\alpha\beta\gamma\epsilon\zeta\theta^1\theta^2\iota\nu$ (unnamed: 1)

Mon $\alpha\beta^A\beta^B\gamma\delta\epsilon^A\epsilon^B\zeta$, 2, 3, 10, 13, 15, 17, 18, 19, 20, 25, 27, 28, Plaskett's; U (unnamed: 7)

Mus $\alpha\beta\gamma\delta\epsilon\zeta^1\zeta^2\eta\theta\iota\lambda\mu$; GT (unnamed: 5)

Nor $\gamma^1\gamma^2\delta\epsilon\eta\theta\iota^1\kappa\lambda\mu$; R

Oct $\alpha\beta\gamma^1\gamma^3\delta\epsilon\zeta\theta\iota\lambda\nu\xi\pi^2\sigma\tau\varphi\chi$

Oph $\alpha\beta\gamma\delta\epsilon\zeta\eta\theta\iota\kappa\lambda\mu\nu\xi$**o**^{A}**o**$^B\rho\sigma\tau^A\tau^B\upsilon\varphi\chi\psi\omega$, 20, 30, 36, 41, 44, 45, 51, 58, 66, 67, 68, 70, 71, 72, 74, Σ2178, Σ2276, Barnard's; U, X, V2105 (unnamed: 3)

Ori $\alpha\beta\gamma\delta^A\delta^C\epsilon\zeta^A\zeta^B\eta\theta^{1A}\theta^{1B}\theta^{1C}\theta^{1D}\theta^{2A}\iota\kappa\lambda^A\lambda^B\mu\nu\xi$**o**$^1\pi^1\pi^2\pi^3\pi^4\pi^5\pi^6\rho\sigma^A\sigma^E\tau\upsilon\varphi^1\varphi^2\chi^1\chi^2\psi^1\psi^2\omega$; 6, 9, 11, 15, 22, 23, 27, 29, 31, 32, 42, 49, 51, 56, 60, 64, 69, 71, 74, 77, Σ747^A, Σ747^B; U (unnamed: 4)

Pav $\alpha\beta\gamma\delta\epsilon\zeta\eta\iota\kappa\lambda\mu^2\nu\xi$**o**$\pi\rho\sigma\upsilon\varphi^1\varphi^2\omega$; NU (unnamed: 1)

Peg $\alpha\beta\gamma\epsilon\zeta\eta\theta\iota\kappa\lambda\mu\nu\xi$**o**$\pi^2\rho\sigma\tau\upsilon\varphi\chi\psi$, 1, 2, 9, 14, 16, 31, 32, 35, 37, 55, 56, 57, 59, 66, 70, 72, 77, 78, 85

Per $\alpha\beta\gamma\delta\epsilon\zeta\eta\theta\iota\kappa\lambda\mu\nu\xi$**o**$\pi\rho\sigma\tau\varphi\psi\omega$, 4, 9, 12, 16, 17, 21, 24, 29, 31, 32, 34, 42, 48, 52, 53, 54, 58, Σ331^A, Σ331^B, Σ431, Σ552, b^1, k; R, S, X (unnamed: 3)

Phe $\alpha\beta\gamma\delta\epsilon\zeta\eta\iota\kappa\lambda^1\mu\nu\pi\rho\sigma\upsilon\varphi\chi\psi$; SX (unnamed: 2)

Pic $\alpha\beta\gamma\delta\zeta\eta^1\eta^2\lambda$, Kapteyn's (unnamed: 3)

Psc $\alpha^A\alpha^B\beta\gamma\delta\epsilon\zeta^A\zeta^B\eta\theta\iota\kappa\lambda\mu\nu\xi$**o**$\rho\sigma\tau\upsilon\varphi\chi\psi^1\upsilon^1\omega$, 7, 19, 27, 29, 30, 33, 47, 64, 65^A, 65^B, 82, 89, 91, 107

PsA $\alpha\beta\gamma\delta\epsilon\eta\theta\iota\lambda\mu\pi\tau\upsilon$, Lacaille 9352

Pup $\zeta\nu\xi$**o**$\pi\rho\sigma\tau$, 1, 3, 4, 6, 9, 11, 12, 16, 19, 20, a, b, c, f, h^2, k^1, k^2, p, q, t, v^1, y, A, H, I, J, L$_2$, N, O, P, Q; V, W, KQ, MX, NS, NV, NW, OS, OU, PU (unnamed: 22)

Pyx $\alpha\beta\gamma\delta\zeta\eta\theta\kappa\lambda$ (unnamed: 2)

Ret $\alpha\beta\gamma\delta\epsilon\zeta^1\zeta^2\eta\iota\kappa$

Sge $\alpha\beta\gamma\delta\epsilon\zeta\eta\theta$; U

Sgr $\alpha\beta^1\beta^2\gamma^1\gamma^2\delta\epsilon\zeta\eta\theta^1\theta^2\iota\lambda\mu\nu^1\nu^2\xi^1\xi^2$**o**$\pi\rho^1\sigma\tau\upsilon\varphi\chi^1\chi^3\psi\omega$, 4, 11, 21, 29, 43, 52, 54, 55, 56, 59, 60, 61, 62; Kui 89; R, U, X, Y, RU, RY (unnamed: 6)

Sco $\alpha\beta^1\beta^2\delta\epsilon\zeta^1\zeta^2\eta\theta\iota^1\iota^2\kappa\lambda\mu^1\mu^2\nu^{AB}\nu^C\xi^A\xi^B$**o**$\pi\rho\sigma\tau\upsilon\chi\psi\omega^1\omega^2$, 1, 2, 13, 22, G, H, N; Σ1999, B1833; RR, V973 (unnamed: 12)

Scl $\alpha\beta\gamma\delta\epsilon\zeta\eta\theta\iota\kappa^1\kappa^2\lambda^1\mu\pi\sigma\tau$; R, S

Sct $\alpha\beta\gamma\delta\epsilon\zeta\eta$; R (unnamed: 2)

Ser $\alpha\beta\gamma\delta^A\delta^B\epsilon\zeta\eta\theta^{1A}\theta^{1B}\iota\kappa\lambda\mu\nu\xi$**o**$\pi\rho\sigma\tau^1\tau^4\chi\omega$, 3, 5, 10, 36, 59, Σ2375; R

Sex $\alpha\beta\gamma\delta\epsilon$; SS

(Continued)

Tau $\alpha\beta\gamma\delta^1\delta^2\delta^3\epsilon\zeta\eta\theta^1\theta^2\iota\kappa^1\kappa^2\lambda\mu\nu\xi\mathbf{o}\pi\rho\sigma^1\sigma^2\tau\upsilon\phi\chi\psi\omega^1\omega^2$, 4, 5, 10, 16, 17, 19, 20, 21, 23, 27, 28, 30, 37, 41, 47, 66, 71, 75, 79, 80, 88, 90, 94, 104, 109, 111, 114, 119, 125, 126, 132, 134, 136, 139, Σ422, Σ572; R, RW (unnamed: 2)

Tel $\alpha\delta^1\delta^2\epsilon\zeta\eta\iota\kappa\lambda\nu\xi\rho$

Tri $\alpha\beta\gamma\delta\epsilon$, 6, 10, 14; R

TrA $\alpha\beta\gamma\delta\epsilon\zeta\theta\iota\kappa$; LP (unnamed: 2)

Tuc $\alpha\beta^1\beta^2\beta^3\gamma\delta\epsilon\zeta\eta\iota\kappa\lambda^1\lambda^2\nu\rho$

UMa $\alpha\beta\gamma\delta\epsilon\zeta^A\zeta^B\eta\theta\iota\kappa\lambda\mu\nu\xi^A\xi^B\mathbf{o}\pi^2\rho\sigma^1\sigma^2\tau\upsilon\phi\chi\psi\omega$, 15, 16, 18, 23, 24, 26, 27, 31, 36, 37, 38, 44, 46, 47, 49, 55, 56, 67, 78, 80, 83, Grb 1830, Σ1415; R, T, CS, Lalande 21185 (unnamed: 5)

UMi $\alpha\beta\gamma\delta\epsilon\zeta\eta\theta\lambda$, 4, 5, 11, 19; RR (unnamed: 3)

Vel $\gamma^1\gamma^2\delta\kappa\lambda\mu\mathbf{o}\phi\psi$, a, b, c, d, e, f, g, h, i, k^2, l, m, n, p, t, u, w, x, B, C, D, H, I, J, L, M, N; Y, FZ, GU, GX, GZ, HY, IS, LN (unnamed: 16)

Vir $\alpha\beta\gamma\delta\epsilon\zeta\eta\theta\iota\kappa\lambda\nu\xi\mathbf{o}\pi\rho\sigma\tau\upsilon\phi\chi\psi\omega$, 16, 32, 49, 53, 57, 59, 61, 69, 70, 74, 76, 78, 82, 84, 89, 90, 107, 109, Σ1719, Σ1833; R, S, CU, ET

Vol $\alpha\beta\gamma^1\gamma^2\delta\epsilon\zeta\eta\theta\iota\kappa^1\kappa^2$ (unnamed: 2)

Vul α, 1, 3, 4, 9, 12, 13, 15, 16, 17, 21, 22, 23, 28, 29, 30, 31, 32, β983, Σ2525